Financial Aid for Asian Americans 2017-2019

Gail Ann Schlachter
R. David Weber

A List of Scholarships, Fellowships, Grants, Awards, and
Other Sources of Free Money Available Primarily or
Exclusively to Asian Americans, Plus a Set of Six Indexes
(Program Title, Sponsoring Organization, Residency,
Tenability, Subject, and Deadline Date)

AdmitHub
Boston, Massachusetts

AdmitHub
Harvard Innovation Launch Lab
114 Western Ave.
Boston, MA 02134
   (617) 575-9369
      E-mail: rsp@admithub.com
Visit our web site: www.admithub.com

Manufactured in the United States of America

Contents

Foreword

About Dr. Gail Schlachter and Reference Service Press

Dr. Gail Ann Schlachter (1943-2015), original founder of Reference Service Press, was working as a librarian in the mid-1970s when she recognized that women applying for college faced significant obstacles finding information about financial aid resources designed to help them. This challenge inspired her to publish her ground-breaking book, Directory of Financial Aids for Women, in 1977. The book's success prompted additional financial aid directories for other underserved communities, including the present volume for Asian Americans.

By 1985, the business had become so successful that she left her job as a publishing company executive to run her company, Reference Service Press, full-time. Over the years, the company's offerings expanded to more than two dozen financial aid titles covering many different types of students, including the present volume for Asian Americans. The company's success was driven by its database of tens of thousands of financial aid programs, laboriously hand-built over the decades and kept current to exacting specifications. In 1995, Reference Service Press once again broke new ground by launching one of the first-ever searchable electronic databases of financial aid resources (initially through America Online). For more background about the founding and success of Reference Service Press, see Katina Strauch's 1997 "Against the Grain" interview with Dr. Schlachter, available at http://docs.lib.purdue.edu/cgi/viewcontent.cgi?article=2216&context=atg.

Dr. Schlachter was also a major figure in the library community for nearly five decades. She served: as reference book review editor for RQ (now Reference and User Services Quarterly) for 10 years; as president of the American Library Association's Reference and User Services Association; as editor of the Reference and User Services Association Quarterly; seven terms on the American Library Association's governing council; and as a member of the association's Executive Board at the time of her death. She was posthumously inducted into the California Library Association Hall of Fame. The University of Wisconsin School of Library and Information Studies named Dr. Schlachter an "Alumna of the Year," and she was recognized with both the Isadore Gilbert Mudge Citation and the Louis Shores/Oryx Press Award.

Dr. Schlachter will be remembered for how her financial aid directories helped thousands of students achieve their educational and professional dreams. She also will be remembered for her countless contributions to the library profession. And, as an American Library Association Executive Board resolution from June 2015 says, she will be remembered, "most importantly, for her mentorship, friendship, and infectious smile." Yet, despite her impressive lifetime of professional accomplishments, Dr. Schlachter always was most proud of her family, including her husband Stuart Hauser, her daughter Dr. Sandy Hirsh (and Jay Hirsh) and son Eric Goldman (and Lisa Goldman), and her grandchildren Hayley, Leah, Jacob, and Dina.

Introduction

WHY THIS DIRECTORY IS NEEDED

Despite our country's ongoing economic volatility and increased college costs, the financial aid picture for minorities has never looked brighter. Currently, billions of dollars are set aside each year specifically for Asian Americans, African Americans, Hispanic Americans, and Native Americans. This funding is open to minorities at any level (high school through postdoctoral and professional) for a variety of activities, including study, research, travel, training, career development, and creative projects.

While numerous print and online listings have been prepared to identify and describe general financial aid opportunities (those open to all segments of society), those resources have never covered more than a small portion of the programs designed primarily or exclusively for minorities. As a result, many advisors, librarians, scholars, researchers, and students often have been unaware of the extensive funding available to Asian Americans and other minorities. But, with the ongoing publication of *Financial Aid for Asian Americans,* that has all changed. Here, in just one place, Asian American students, professionals, and postdoctorates now have current and detailed information about the special resources set aside specifically for them.

Financial Aid for Asian Americans is prepared biennially as part of Reference Service Press' four-volume *Minority Funding Set* (the other volumes in the set cover funding for African Americans, Hispanic Americans, and Native Americans). Each of the volumes in this set is sold separately, or the complete set can be purchased at a discounted price.

No other source, in print or online, offers the extensive coverage of funding for minorities provided by these titles. That's why the Grantsmanship Center labeled the set "a must for every organization serving minorities," *Reference Sources for Small and Medium-Sized Libraries* called the titles "the absolute best guides for finding funding," and *Reference Books Bulletin* selected each of the volumes in the *Minority Funding Set* as their "Editor's Choice." *Financial Aid for Asian Americans,* itself, has also received rave reviews. *Al Jahdid* called the directory "an excellent resource," the Miami-Dade Public Library System included it in its list of "Essential Titles for the College Bound," and *Small Press* found it both "inclusive" and "valuable." Perhaps *Choice* sums up the critical reaction best: "a unique and valuable resource; highly recommended."

WHAT'S UPDATED?

The preparation of each new edition of *Financial Aid for Asian Americans* involves extensive updating and revision. To make sure that the information included here is both reliable and current, the editors at Reference Service Press 1) reviewed and updated all relevant programs covered in the previous edition of the directory, 2) collected information on all programs open to Asian Americans that were added to Reference Service Press' funding database since the last edition of the directory, and then 3) searched extensively for new program leads in a variety of sources, including printed directories, news reports, journals, newsletters, house organs, annual reports, and sites on the Internet. We only include program descriptions that are written directly from information supplied by the sponsoring organization in print or online (no information is ever taken from secondary sources). When that information could not be found, we sent up to four collection letters (followed by up to three telephone or e-mail inquiries, if necessary) to those sponsors. Despite our best efforts, however, some sponsoring organizations still failed to respond and, as a result, their programs are not included in this edition of the directory.

The 2017-2019 edition of *Financial Aid for Asian Americans* completely revises and updates the previous (eighth) edition. Programs that have ceased operations have been dropped from the directory. Similarly, programs that have broadened their scope and no longer focus on Asian Americans have also been removed from the listing. Profiles of continuing programs have been rewritten to reflect current requirements; nearly 75 percent of the continuing programs reported substantive changes in their locations, requirements (particularly application deadline), benefits, or eligibility requirements since the 2014-2016 edition. In addition, hundreds of new entries have been added to the program section of the directory. The resulting listing describes the nearly 1,150 biggest and best sources of free money available to Asian Americans, including scholarships, fellowships, grants, awards, and other funding opportunities.

WHAT MAKES THIS DIRECTORY UNIQUE?

The 2017-2019 edition of *Financial Aid for Asian Americans* will help Americans with origins from Asia or subcontinent Asia and Pacific island nations (e.g., Japan, China, the Philippines, Vietnam, Korea, Laos, Cambodia, Taiwan, Burma, Thailand, Malaysia, Indonesia, Singapore, Brunei, Macao, Hong Kong, India, Pakistan, Bangladesh, Tonga) tap into the billions of dollars available to them, as minorities, to support study, research, creative activities, past accomplishments, future projects, professional development, and many other activities. The listings cover every major subject area, are sponsored by more than 750 different private and public agencies and organizations, and are open to Asian Americans at any level, from college-bound high school students through professionals and postdoctorates.

Not only does *Financial Aid for Asian Americans* provide the most comprehensive coverage of available funding (1,147 entries), but it also displays the most informative program descriptions (on the average, more than twice the detail found in any other listing). In addition to this extensive and focused coverage, *Financial Aid for Asian Americans* also offers several other unique features. First of all, hundreds of funding opportunities listed here have never been covered in any other source. So, even if you have checked elsewhere, you will want to look at *Financial Aid for Asian Americans* for additional leads. And, here's another plus: all of the funding programs in this edition of the directory offer "free" money; not one of the programs will ever require you to pay anything back (provided, of course, that you meet the program requirements).

Further, unlike other funding directories, which generally follow a straight alphabetical arrangement, *Financial Aid for Asian Americans* groups entries by intended recipients (undergraduates, graduate students, or professionals/postdoctorates), to make it easy for you to search for appropriate programs. This same convenience is offered in the indexes, where title, sponsoring organization, geographic, subject, and deadline date entries are each subdivided by recipient group.

Finally, we have tried to anticipate all the ways you might wish to search for funding. The volume is organized so you can identify programs not only by intended recipient, but by subject focus, sponsoring organization, program title, residency requirements, where the money can be spent, and even deadline date. Plus, we've included all the information you'll need to decide if a program is right for you: purpose, eligibility requirements, financial data, duration, special features, limitations, number awarded, and application date. You even get fax numbers, toll-free numbers, e-mail addresses, and web sites (when available), along with complete contact information.

WHAT'S EXCLUDED?

While this book is intended to be the most comprehensive source of information on funding available to Asian Americans, there are some programs we've specifically excluded from the directory:

- *Programs that do not accept applications from U.S. citizens or residents.* If a program is open only to foreign nationals or excludes Americans from applying, it is not covered.

- *Programs that are open equally to all segments of the population.* Only funding opportunities set aside primarily or exclusively for Asian Americans are included here.

- *Money for study or research outside the United States.* Since there are comprehensive and up-to-date directories that describe the available funding for study, research, and other activities abroad, (see the list of Reference Service Press titles opposite the directory's title page), only programs that fund activities in the United States are covered here.

- *Very restrictive programs.* In general, programs are excluded if they are open only to a limited geographic area (less than a state) or offer limited financial support (less than $500). Note, however, that the vast majority of programs included here go way beyond that, paying up to full tuition or stipends that exceed $20,000 a year!

- *Programs administered by individual academic institutions solely for their own students.* The directory identifies "portable" programs—ones that can be used at any number of schools. Financial aid administered by individual schools specifically for their own students is not covered. Check directly with the schools you are considering to get information on their offerings.

- *Scholarships offered by individual law firms.* Many law firms attempt to promote diversity by offering scholarships to Asian American and other underrepresented students, but usually tie the stipend to employment at the firm.

- *Money that must be repaid.* Only "free money" is identified here. If a program requires repayment or charges interest, it's not listed. Now you can find out about billions of dollars in aid and know (if you meet the program requirements) that not one dollar of that will ever need to be repaid.

HOW THE DIRECTORY IS ORGANIZED

Financial Aid for Asian Americans is divided into two sections: 1) a detailed list of funding opportunities open to Asian Americans and 2) a set of six indexes to help you pinpoint appropriate funding programs.

Financial Aid Programs Open to Asian Americans. The first section of the directory describes nearly 1,150 sources of free money available to Asian Americans. The focus is on financial aid aimed at American citizens or residents to support study, research, or other activities in the United States. The programs listed here are sponsored by more than 750 different government agencies, professional organizations, corporations, sororities and fraternities, foundations, religious groups, educational associations, and military/veterans organizations. All areas of the sciences, social sciences, and humanities are covered.

To help you focus your search, the entries in this section are grouped into the following three chapters:

- **Undergraduates:** Included here are 516 scholarships, grants, awards, and other sources of free money that support undergraduate study, training, research, or creative activities. These programs are open to high school seniors, high school graduates, currently-enrolled college students, and students returning to college after an absence. Money is available to support these students in any type of public or private postsecondary institution, ranging from technical schools and community colleges to major universities in the United States.

- **Graduate Students:** Described here are nearly 486 fellowships, grants, awards, and other sources of free money that support post-baccalaureate study, training, research, and creative activities. These programs are open to students applying to, currently enrolled in, or returning to a master's, doctoral, professional, or specialist program in public or private graduate schools in the United States.

- **Professionals/Postdoctorates:** Included here are 145 funding programs for U.S. citizens or residents who 1) are in professional positions (e.g., artists, writers), whether or not they have an advanced degree; 2) are master's or professional degree recipients; 3) have earned a doctoral degree or its equivalent (e.g., Ph.D., Ed.D., M.D.); or 4) have recognized stature as established scientists, scholars, academicians, or researchers.

Within each of these three chapters, entries appear alphabetically by program title. Since some of the programs supply assistance to more than one specific group, those are listed in all relevant chapters. For example, the Asian American Architects and Engineers Foundation Scholarships support both undergraduate or graduate study, so the program is described in both the Undergraduates *and* Graduate Students chapters.

Each program entry has been designed to give you a concise profile that, as the sample on page 7 illustrates, includes information (when available) on organization address and telephone numbers (including toll-free and fax numbers), e-mail address and web site, purpose, eligibility, money awarded, duration, special features, limitations, number of awards, and application deadline.

The information reported for each of the programs in this section was gathered from research conducted through the middle of 2017. While the listing is intended to cover as comprehensively as possible the biggest and best sources of free money available to Asian Americans, some sponsoring organizations did not post information online or respond to our research inquiries and, consequently, are not included in this edition of the directory.

Indexes. To help you find the aid you need, we have constructed six indexes; these will let you access the listings by program title, sponsoring organization, residency, tenability, subject focus, and deadline date. These indexes use a word-by-word alphabetical arrangement. Note: numbers in the index refer to entry numbers, not to page numbers in the book.

Program Title Index. If you know the name of a particular funding program and want to find out where it is covered in the directory, use the Program Title Index. To assist you in your search, every program is listed by all its known names, former names, and abbreviations. Since one program can be included in more than one place (e.g., a program providing assistance to both undergraduate and graduate students is described in both the first and second chapter), each entry number in the index has been coded to indicate the intended recipient group (for example, "U" = Undergraduates; "G" = Graduate Students). By using this coding system, you can avoid duplicate entries and turn directly to the programs that match your eligibility characteristics.

Sponsoring Organization Index. This index makes it easy to identify agencies that offer funding primarily or exclusively to Asian Americans. More than 750 organizations are indexed here. As in the Program Title Index, we've used a code to help you determine which organizations sponsor programs that match your educational level.

Residency Index. Some programs listed in this book are restricted to Asian Americans in a particular state or region. Others are open to Asian Americans wherever they live. This index helps you identify programs available only to residents in your area as well as programs that have no residency requirements. Further, to assist you in your search, we've also indicated the recipient level for the funding offered to residents in each of the areas listed in the index.

Tenability Index. This index identifies the geographic locations where the funding described in *Financial Aid for Asian Americans* may be used. Index entries (city, county, state, region) are arranged alphabetically (word by word) and subdivided by recipient group. Use this index when you are looking for money to support your activities in a particular geographic area.

Subject Index. This index allows you to identify the subject focus of each of the financial aid opportunities described in *Financial Aid for Asian Americans*. More than 200 different subject terms are listed. Extensive "see" and "see also" references, as well as recipient group subdivisions, will help you locate appropriate funding opportunities.

Calendar Index. Since most financial aid programs have specific deadline dates, some may have closed by the time you begin to look for funding. You can use the Calendar Index to determine which programs are still open. This index is arranged by recipient group (Undergraduates, Graduate Students, and Professionals/Postdoctorates) and subdivided by the month during which the deadline falls. Filing dates can and quite often do vary from year to year; consequently, this index should be used only as a guide for deadlines beyond 2016.

HOW TO USE THE DIRECTORY

Here are some tips to help you get the most out of the funding opportunities listed in *Financial Aid for Asian Americans.*

To Locate Funding by Recipient Group.   To bring together programs with a similar educational focus, this directory is divided into three chapters: Undergraduates, Graduate Students, and Professionals/Postdoctorates. If you want to get an overall picture of the sources of free money available to Asian Americans in any of these categories, turn to the appropriate chapter and then review the entries there. Since each of these chapters functions as a self-contained entity, you can browse through any of them without having to first consulting an index.

To Find Information on a Particular Financial Aid Program.   If you know the name of a particular financial aid program, and the group eligible for that award, then go directly to the appropriate chapter in the directory (e.g., Undergraduates, Graduate Students), where you will find the program profiles arranged alphabetically by title. To save time, though, you should always check the Program Title Index first if you know the name of a specific award but are not sure in which chapter it has been listed. Plus, since we index each program by all its known names and abbreviations, you'll also be able to track down a program there when you only know the popular rather than official name.

To Locate Programs Sponsored by a Particular Organization.   The Sponsoring Organization Index makes it easy to identify agencies that provide financial assistance to Asian Americans or to identify specific financial aid programs offered by a particular organization. Each entry number in the index is coded to identify recipient group (Undergraduates, Graduate Students, Professionals/Postdoctorates), so that you can easily target appropriate entries.

To Browse Quickly Through the Listings.   Look at the listings in the chapter that relates to you (Undergraduates, Graduate Students, or Professionals/Postdoctorates) and read the "Summary" paragraph in each entry. In seconds, you'll know if this is an opportunity that you might want to pursue. If it is, be sure to read the rest of the information in the entry, to make sure you meet all of the program requirements before writing or going online for an application form. Please, save your time and energy. Don't apply if you don't qualify!

To Locate Funding Available to Asian Americans from or Tenable in a Particular City, County, or State.   The Residency Index identifies financial aid programs open to Asian Americans in a specific state, region, etc. The Tenability Index shows where the money can be spent. In both indexes, "see" and "see also" references are used liberally, and index entries for a particular geographic area are subdivided by recipient group (Undergraduates, Graduate Students, and Professionals/Postdoctorates) to help you identify the funding that's right for you. When using these indexes, always check the listings under the term "United States," since the programs indexed there have no geographic restrictions and can be used in any area.

To Locate Financial Aid Programs Open to Asian Americans in a Particular Subject Area.   Turn to the Subject Index first if you are interested in identifying funding programs for Asian Americans that are focused on a particular subject area. To make your search easier, the intended recipient groups (Undergraduates, Graduate Students, Professionals/Postdoctorates) are clearly labeled in the more than 200 subject listings. Extensive cross-references are also provided. Since a large number of programs are not restricted by subject, be sure to check the references listed under the "General programs" heading in the index, in addition to the specific terms that directly relate to your interest areas. The listings under "General programs" can be used to fund activities in any subject area (although the programs may be restricted in other ways).

To Locate Financial Aid Programs for Asian Americans by Deadline Date.   If you are working with specific time constraints and want to weed out the financial aid programs whose filing dates you won't be able to meet, turn first to the Calendar Index and check the program references listed under the appropriate recipient group and month. Note: not all sponsoring organizations supplied deadline information; those programs are listed under the "Deadline not specified" entries in the index. To identify every relevant financial aid program, regardless of filing date, go the appropriate chapter and read through all the entries there that match your educational level.

To Locate Financial Aid Programs Open to All Segments of the Population. Only programs available to Asian Americans are listed in this publication. However, there are thousands of other programs that are open equally to all segments of the population. To identify these programs, talk to your local librarian, check with your financial aid office on campus, look at the list of RSP print resources on the page opposite the title page in this directory, or see if your library subscribes to Reference Service Press' interactive online funding database: *RSP FundingFinder.* For more information on that award-winning resource, go online to: www.rspfunding.com/esubscriptions.html.

PLANS TO UPDATE THE DIRECTORY

This volume, covering 2017-2019, is the ninth edition of *Financial Aid for Asian Americans.* The next biennial edition will cover the years 2019-2021 and will be issued by the beginning of 2019.

ACKNOWLEDGEMENTS

A debt of gratitude is owed all the organizations that contributed information to the 2017-2019 edition of *Financial Aid for Asian Americans.* Their generous cooperation has helped to make this publication a current and comprehensive survey of awards.

SAMPLE ENTRY

(1) **[86]**

(2) **AT&T FOUNDATION APIASF SCHOLARSHIPS**

(3) Asian & Pacific Islander American Scholarship Fund
2025 M Street, N.W., Suite 610
Washington, DC 20036-3363
(202) 986-6892   Fax: (202) 530-0643
E-mail: info@apiasf.org
Web: www.apiasf.org/scholarship_apiasf_att.html

(4) **Summary** To provide financial assistance to Asian and Pacific Islander Americans who are entering college for the first time.

(5) **Eligibility** This program is open to U.S. citizens, nationals, permanent residents, and citizens of the Freely Associated States who are first-time incoming college students and of Asian or Pacific Islander heritage. Applicants must be enrolling full time at an accredited 2- or 4-year college or university in the United States. They must have a GPA of 2.7 or higher or the GED equivalent. In addition, they must complete the FAFSA and apply for federal financial aid.

(6) **Financial data** The stipend is $2,500.

(7) **Duration** 1 year; nonrenewable.

(8) **Additional information** This program is sponsored by the AT&T Foundation and administered by the Asian & Pacific Islander American Scholarship Fund (APIASF).

(9) **Number awarded** Varies each year; recently, 5 were awarded.

(10) **Deadline** January of each year.

DEFINITION

(1) **Entry number:** The consecutive number that is given to each entry and used to identify the entry in the index.

(2) **Program title:** Title of scholarship, fellowship, grant, award, or other source of free money described in the directory.

(3) **Sponsoring organization:** Name, address, and telephone number, toll-free number, fax number, e-mail address, and/or web site (when information was available) for organization sponsoring the program.

(4) **Summary:** Identifies the major program requirements; read the rest of the entry for additional detail.

(5) **Eligibility:** Qualifications required of applicants, plus information on application procedure and selection process.

(6) **Financial data:** Financial details of the program, including fixed sum, average amount, or range of funds offered, expenses for which funds may and may not be applied, and cash-related benefits supplied (e.g., room and board).

(7) **Duration:** Period for which support is provided; renewal prospects.

(8) **Additional information:** Any unusual (generally nonmonetary) benefits, features, restrictions, or limitations associated with the program.

(9) **Number awarded:** Total number of recipients each year or other specified period.

(10) **Deadline:** The month by which applications must be submitted.

ABOUT THE AUTHORS

Dr. Gail Ann Schlachter (1943-2015) worked for more than three decades as a library manager, a library educator, and an administrator of library-related publishing companies. Among the reference books to her credit are the biennially-issued *Directory of Financial Aids for Women* and two award-winning bibliographic guides: *Minorities and Women: A Guide to Reference Literature in the Social Sciences* (which was chosen as an "outstanding reference book of the year" by *Choice)* and *Reference Sources in Library and Information Services* (which won the first Knowledge Industry Publications "Award for Library Literature"). She was the reference book review editor for *RQ* (now *Reference and User Services Quarterly)* for 10 years, was a past president of the American Library Association's Reference and User Services Association, was the editor-in-chief of the *Reference and User Services Association Quarterly,* and was serving her sixth term on the American Library Association's governing council at the time of her death. In recognition of her outstanding contributions to reference service, Dr. Schlachter was named the University of Wisconsin School of Library and Information Studies "Alumna of the Year" and was awarded both the Isadore Gilbert Mudge Citation and the Louis Shores/Oryx Press Award.

Dr. R. David Weber taught history and economics at Los Angeles Harbor College (in Wilmington, California) for many years and continues to teach history there as an emeritus professor. During his years at Harbor College, and earlier at East Los Angeles College, he directed the Honors Program and was frequently chosen the "Teacher of the Year." He has written a number of critically-acclaimed reference works, including *Dissertations in Urban History* and the three-volume *Energy Information Guide.* With Gail Schlachter, he is the author of Reference Service Press' *Financial Aid for Persons with Disabilities and Their Families,* which was selected by *Library Journal* as one of the "best reference books of the year," and a number of other financial aid titles, including the *College Student's Guide to Merit and Other No-Need Funding,* which was chosen as one of the "outstanding reference books of the year" by *Choice.*

Financial Aid Programs Open to Asian Americans

Undergraduates ●

Graduate Students ●

Professionals/Postdoctorates ●

Undergraduates

Listed alphabetically by program title and described in detail here are 516 scholarships, grants, awards, and other sources of "free money" set aside for college-bound high school seniors and continuing or returning undergraduate students of Asian origins (including those of subcontinent Asian and Pacific Islander descent). This funding is available to support study, training, research, and/or creative activities in the United States.

[1]
100TH INFANTRY BATTALION LEGACY ORGANIZATION SCHOLARSHIP

100th Infantry Battalion Legacy Organization
Attn: Scholarship Committee
520 Kamoku Street
Honolulu, HI 96826-5120
(808) 637-5324   E-mail: info@100thlegacy.org
Web: www.100thlegacy.org

Summary To provide financial assistance to high school seniors in Hawaii who plan to attend college in any state.

Eligibility This program is open to seniors graduating from high schools in Hawaii and planning to attend an institution of higher in any state. Applicants must submit an essay about the medics of the 100th Infantry Battalion and the role they played during World War II in Italy and France, how they were considered unsung heroes, and the impact they had on the battalion. Selection is based on that essay (50%), academics (20%), community service (15%), and leadership (15%).

Financial data The stipend is $3,000.

Duration 1 year; nonrenewable.

Number awarded 1 each year.

Deadline March of each year.

[2]
100TH INFANTRY BATTALION MEMORIAL SCHOLARSHIP FUND

Hawai'i Community Foundation
Attn: Scholarship Department
827 Fort Street Mall
Honolulu, HI 96813
(808) 566-5570   Toll Free: (888) 731-3863
Fax: (808) 521-6286
E-mail: scholarships@hcf-hawaii.org
Web: hcf.scholarships.ngwebsolutions.com

Summary To provide financial assistance for college or graduate school to descendants of 100th Infantry Battalion World War II veterans.

Eligibility This program is open to entering and continuing full-time undergraduate and graduate students at 2- and 4-year colleges and universities. Applicants must be a direct descendant of a World War II veteran of the 100th Infantry Battalion (which was comprised of Americans of Japanese descent). They must be able to demonstrate academic achievement (GPA of 3.0 or higher), an active record of extra-curricular activities and community service (especially volunteer work connected with the activities of the 100th Infantry Battalion Veterans organization), and a willingness to promote the legacy of the 100th Infantry Battalion of World War II. Along with their application, they must submit a short statement indicating their reasons for attending college, their planned course of study, their career goals, and what community service means to them. They must also submit a separate essay on the historical significance of the 100th Infantry Battalion and what the stories of those soldiers have to teach all American citizens. Neither current residency in Hawaii nor financial need is required.

Financial data The amounts of the awards depend on the availability of funds and the need of the recipient. Recently, the average value of the scholarships awarded by the foundation was $2,800.

Duration 1 year.

Additional information This program began in 2006.

Number awarded Varies each year; recently, 2 were awarded.

Deadline February of each year.

[3]
100TH INFANTRY BATTALION VETERANS STANLEY IZUMIGAWA SCHOLARSHIP FUND

Hawai'i Community Foundation
Attn: Scholarship Department
827 Fort Street Mall
Honolulu, HI 96813
(808) 566-5570   Toll Free: (888) 731-3863
Fax: (808) 521-6286
E-mail: scholarships@hcf-hawaii.org
Web: hcf.scholarships.ngwebsolutions.com

Summary To provide financial assistance for college or graduate school to descendants of 100th Infantry Battalion World War II veterans.

Eligibility This program is open to entering and continuing full-time undergraduate and graduate students at 2- and 4-year colleges and universities. Applicants must be a direct descendant of a World War II veteran of the 100th Infantry Battalion (which was comprised of Americans of Japanese descent). They must be able to demonstrate academic achievement (GPA of 3.0 or higher), an active record of extra-curricular activities and community service, especially volunteer work connected with the activities of the 100th Infantry Battalion Veterans organization, including (but not limited to) educational programs, memorial services, and the anniversary banquet. Along with their application, they must submit a short statement indicating their reasons for attending college, their planned course of study, their career goals, and what community service means to them. They must also submit a separate essay on the historical significance of the 100th Infantry Battalion and what the stories of those soldiers have to teach all American citizens. Neither current residency in Hawaii nor financial need is required.

Financial data The amounts of the awards depend on the availability of funds and the need of the recipient. Recently, the average value of the scholarships awarded by the foundation was $2,800.

Duration 1 year.

Additional information This program began in 2014.

Number awarded 1 or more each year.

Deadline February of each year.

[4]
AAF-LOUISVILLE EDUCATION FOUNDATION DIVERSITY SCHOLARSHIP

American Advertising Federation-Louisville
Attn: AAF-Louisville Education Foundation
130 St. Matthews Avenue, Suite 302
Louisville, KY 40207
(502) 895-2500   Fax: (502) 895-2555
E-mail: mary@louisvilleadfed.org
Web: www.louisvilleadfed.org

Summary To provide financial assistance to Asian American and other residents of Kentucky and southeastern Indiana who come from a diverse ethnic background and are working on an undergraduate degree in a field related to advertising.

Eligibility This program is open to residents of Kentucky and the Indiana counties of Clark, Floyd, and Harrison who are U.S. citizens of Asian, African, Hispanic, Native American, Middle Eastern, or Pacific Island descent. Applicants must be 1) entering their junior or senior year at a 4-year college or university in any state; or 2) enrolled in their last year of an associate degree or technical certificate program. They must be enrolled full time and have a GPA of 3.0 or higher. Their major may involve any field related to advertising or marketing communications, including communications, mass communications, journalism, public relations, marketing, business communications, graphic arts, computer design, multi-media, or English. Along with their application, they must submit a 500-word essay on their understanding of and need for a more diverse and inclusive workforce for the benefit of the community and the Louisville advertising and communications industry.

Financial data The stipend is $2,500.

Duration 1 year.

Number awarded 1 each year.

Deadline April of each year.

[5]
AAFO SCHOLARSHIPS

Asian American Foundation of Oregon
P.O. Box 51117
Eugene, OR 97405
(541) 914-4235
Web: www.aaforegon.org

Summary To provide financial assistance to residents of Oregon who have been involved in Asian American cultural activities and are interested in attending college in any state.

Eligibility The program is open to residents of Oregon who have demonstrated interest and effort in Asian American cultural activities. Applicants must be graduating high school seniors or current undergraduate students at a college or university in any state. They must have a GPA of 2.5 or higher. Along with their application, they must submit a 250-word essay that describes their college plans, career interests, relationship to and interest in Asian culture, and/or future commitment to the Asian American community. U.S. citizenship is required.

Financial data The stipend is $1,000.

Duration 1 year.

Number awarded 2 each year.

Deadline February of each year.

[6]
AAJA/NBC SUMMER PARTNERSHIP PROGRAM

Asian American Journalists Association
Attn: Student Programs Coordinator
5 Third Street, Suite 1108
San Francisco, CA 94103
(415) 346-2051, ext. 102   Fax: (415) 346-6343
E-mail: programs@aaja.org
Web: www.aaja.org/apply-for-a-scholarship-now

Summary To provide an opportunity for student members of the Asian American Journalists Association (AAJA) to work as a summer intern at NBC News.

Eligibility This program is open to AAJA members who are at least sophomores and working on a bachelor's degree at a college or university in the United States. Applicants must have a serious interest in preparing for a career in broadcast journalism; production experience is not required but is preferred. They must be interested in working as an intern on NBC News daily programs or for CNBC. Along with their application, they must submit 1) a 150-word essay on why they want to prepare for a career in broadcast journalism and what they want to gain from the experience; and 2) a 50-word essay on how they would contribute to AAJA's mission.

Financial data The stipend is $500 per week.

Duration 10 weeks during the summer.

Number awarded 4 each year: 3 for daily programs and 1 for CNBC.

Deadline February of each year.

[7]
AAJA-MN BROADCAST INTERNSHIP

Asian American Journalists Association-Minnesota
  Chapter
c/o Nancy Yang, Internship Committee Chair
Minnesota Public Radio
480 Cedar Street
St. Paul, MN 55101
(651) 290-1500
Web: www.aajamn.com/awards.html

Summary To provide work experience at television stations in the Twin Cities area to undergraduate and graduate student members of the Minnesota Chapter of the Asian American Journalists Association (AAJA).

Eligibility This program is open to full time undergraduate and graduate student members of the AAJA Minnesota Chapter who are currently taking journalism classes and preparing for a career in broadcast journalism. Applicants must be interested in an internship at a television station in the Twin Cities area. Along with their application, they must submit a 500-word essay on their involvement or interest in the Asian American community and how, if they are awarded this scholarship, they would contribute to the field of journalism and/or media issues involving the Asian Pacific American and Pacific Islander community. Selection is based on academic achievement, commitment to journalism, sensitivity to Asian American and Pacific Islander issues as demonstrated by community involvement, and demonstrated journalistic ability.

Financial data The stipend is $1,000.

Duration 8 to 10 weeks in the summer, fall, or spring.

Number awarded 1 each year.

Deadline January of each year for summer, June of each year for fall, or October of each year for spring.

[8]
AAJA-MN/MN NEWSPAPER GUILD PRINT INTERNSHIP

Asian American Journalists Association-Minnesota
  Chapter
c/o Nancy Yang, Internship Committee Chair
Minnesota Public Radio
480 Cedar Street
St. Paul, MN 55101
(651) 290-1500
Web: www.aajamn.com/awards.html

Summary To provide work experience at newspapers in the Twin Cities area to undergraduate and graduate student members of the Minnesota Chapter of the Asian American Journalists Association (AAJA).

Eligibility This program is open to full time undergraduate and graduate student members of the AAJA Minnesota Chapter who are currently taking journalism classes and preparing for a career in print journalism. Applicants must be interested in an internship at a newspaper in the Twin Cities area. Along with their application, they must submit a 500-word essay on their involvement or interest in the Asian American community and how, if they are awarded this scholarship, they would contribute to the field of journalism and/or media issues involving the Asian Pacific American and Pacific Islander community. Selection is based on academic achievement, commitment to journalism, sensitivity to Asian American and Pacific Islander issues as demonstrated by community involvement, and demonstrated journalistic ability.

Financial data The stipend is $1,000.

Duration 7 to 8 weeks in the summer, fall, or spring.

Additional information This program is co-sponsored by the Minnesota Newspaper Guild.

Number awarded 1 each year.

Deadline January of each year for summer, June of each year for fall, or October of each year for spring.

[9]
AAPINA SCHOLARSHIP

Asian American/Pacific Islander Nurses Association
c/o Rei Serafica, Awards Committee Chair
University of Nevada at Las Vegas
School of Nursing
BHS 440
4505 South Maryland Parkway, Mail Code 3018
Las Vegas, NV 89154-3018
(702) 895-5746   Fax: (702) 895-4807
E-mail: reimund.serafica@unlv.edu
Web: www.aapina.org/aapina-scholarship

Summary To provide financial assistance to members of the Asian American/Pacific Islander Nurses Association (AAPINA) who are working on an undergraduate or graduate degree in nursing.

Eligibility This program is open to undergraduate and graduate (master's or doctoral) students who have been AAPINA members for at least 2 years. Applicants must have a GPA of 3.5 or higher. Along with their application, they must submit a 1- to 2-page essay on their previous and current leadership activities and potential for contributing to AAPINA. Selection is based on academic progress, extracurricular activities, leadership skills, and participation in AAPINA.

Financial data The stipend is $1,000.

Duration 1 year.

Number awarded 1 each year.

Deadline January of each year.

[10]
AAUW CAREER DEVELOPMENT GRANTS

American Association of University Women
Attn: AAUW Educational Foundation
1111 16th Street, N.W.
Washington, DC 20036-4873
(202) 785-7700   Toll Free: (800) 326-AAUW
Fax: (202) 872-1425   TDD: (202) 785-7777
E-mail: aauw@applyists.com
Web: www.aauw.org

Summary To provide financial assistance to Asian American and other women of color who are seeking career advancement, career change, or reentry into the workforce.

Eligibility This program is open to women who are U.S. citizens or permanent residents, have earned a bachelor's degree, received their most recent degree more than 4 years ago, and are making career changes, seeking to advance in current careers, or reentering the workforce. Applicants must be interested in working toward a master's degree, second bachelor's or associate degree, professional degree (e.g., M.D., J.D.), certification program, or technical school certificate. They must be planning to undertake course work at an accredited 2- or 4-year college or university (or a technical school that is licensed, accredited, or approved by the U.S. Department of Education). Primary consideration is given to women of color and women pursuing their first advanced degree or credentials in nontraditional fields. Support is not provided for prerequisite course work or for Ph.D. course work or dissertations. Selection is based on demonstrated commitment to education and equity for women and girls, reason for seeking higher education or technical training, degree to which study plan is consistent with career objectives, potential for success in chosen field, documentation of opportunities in chosen field, feasibility of study plans and proposed time schedule, validity of proposed budget and budget narrative (including sufficient outside support), and quality of written proposal.

Financial data Grants range from $2,000 to $12,000. Funds may be used for tuition, fees, books, supplies, local transportation, dependent child care, or purchase of a computer required for the study program.

Duration 1 year, beginning in July; nonrenewable.

Additional information The filing fee is $35.

Number awarded Varies each year; recently, 63 of these grants, with a value of $670,000, were awarded.

Deadline December of each year.

[11]
ABE AND ESTHER HAGIWARA STUDENT AID AWARD

Japanese American Citizens League
Attn: National Scholarship Awards
1765 Sutter Street
San Francisco, CA 94115
(415) 345-1075   Fax: (415) 345-1077
E-mail: pwada@jacl.org
Web: www.jacl.org/jacl-national-scholarship-program

Summary To provide financial assistance for college or graduate school to student members of the Japanese American Citizens League (JACL) who can demonstrate severe financial need.

Eligibility This program is open to JACL members who are enrolled or planning to enroll at a college, university, trade school, or business college. Applicants must be undergraduate or graduate students who are able to demonstrate that, without this aid, they will have to delay or terminate their education. They must submit information on their involvement in JACL and a 2-page essay on a topic that changes annually but relates to Japanese Americans. Selection is based on that essay, financial need, academic history, JACL involvement, school activities, work history, scholastic honors, and community involvement.

Financial data Stipends generally average more than $2,000.

Duration 1 year; nonrenewable.

Number awarded At least 1 each year.

Deadline March of each year.

[12]
ACCELERATOR APPLICATIONS DIVISION SCHOLARSHIP

American Nuclear Society
Attn: Scholarship Coordinator
555 North Kensington Avenue
La Grange Park, IL 60526-5535
(708) 352-6611   Toll Free: (800) 323-3044
Fax: (708) 352-0499   E-mail: outreach@ans.org
Web: www.ans.org/honors/scholarships/aad

Summary To provide financial assistance to Asian American and other underrepresented undergraduate students who are interested in preparing for a career dealing with accelerator applications aspects of nuclear science or nuclear engineering.

Eligibility This program is open to students entering their junior year in physics, engineering, or materials science at an accredited institution in the United States. Applicants must submit a description of their long- and short-term professional objectives, including their research interests related to accelerator aspects of nuclear science and engineering. Selection is based on that statement, faculty recommendations, and academic performance. Special consideration is given to members of underrepresented groups (women and minorities), students who can demonstrate financial need, and applicants who have a record of service to the American Nuclear Society (ANS).

Financial data The stipend is $1,000 per year.

Duration 1 year (the junior year); may be renewed for the senior year.

Additional information This program is offered by the Accelerator Applications Division (AAD) of the ANS.

Number awarded 1 each year.

Deadline January of each year.

[13]
ACCESS PATH TO PSYCHOLOGY AND LAW EXPERIENCE (APPLE) PROGRAM

American Psychological Association
Attn: Division 41 (American Psychology-Law Society)
c/o Jennifer Hunt, Minority Affairs Committee Chair
Buffalo State University of New York, Psychology
  Department
Classroom Building C308
1300 Elmwood Avenue
Buffalo, NY 14222
(716) 878-3421   E-mail: huntjs@buffalostate.edu
Web: www.apadivisions.org

Summary To provide an opportunity for undergraduate students from Asian American and other underrepresented groups to gain research and other experience to prepare them for graduate work in psychology and law.

Eligibility This program is open to undergraduate students who are members of underrepresented groups, including, but are not limited to, racial and ethnic minorities; first-generation college students; lesbian, gay, bisexual, and transgender students; and physically disabled students. Applicants must be interested in participating in a program in which they work on research for approximately 10 hours per week; participate in GRE classes and/or other development opportunities; attend a conference of the American Psychology-Law Society (AP-LS); submit a proposal to present their research at an AP-LS conference or in the Division 41 program of an American Psychological Association (APA) conference; submit a summary of their research experience to the AP-LS Minority Affairs Committee chair within 1 month of its completion; and correspond with a secondary mentor from the Minority Affairs Committee to participate in the ongoing assessment of this program. Selection is based on the quality of the proposed research and mentoring experience and the potential for the student to become a successful graduate student.

Financial data Grants range up to $3,000, including a stipend of $1,200 per semester or $800 per quarter or summer, $100 for research expenses, and up to $500 to attend the AP-LS conference.

Duration Up to 1 year.

Number awarded 6 each year.

Deadline November of each year.

[14]
ACCOUNTANCY BOARD OF OHIO EDUCATION ASSISTANCE PROGRAM

Accountancy Board of Ohio
Attn: Executive Director
77 South High Street, Suite 1802
Columbus, OH 43215-6128
(614) 466-4135   Fax: (614) 466-2628
E-mail: john.e.patterson@acc.ohio.gov
Web: www.acc.ohio.gov

Summary To provide financial assistance to Asian American and other minority or financially disadvantaged students enrolled in an accounting education program at Ohio academic institutions approved by the Accountancy Board of Ohio.

Eligibility This program is open to minority and financially disadvantaged Ohio residents who apply as full-time juniors or seniors in an accounting program at an accredited college or university in the state. Students who remain in good standing at their institutions and who enter a qualified fifth-year program are then eligible to receive these funds. Minority is defined as Asians, Blacks, Native Americans, and Hispanics. Financial disadvantage is defined according to information provided on the Free Application for Federal Student Aid (FAFSA). U.S. citizenship or permanent resident status is required.

Financial data The amount of the stipend is determined annually but does not exceed the in-state tuition at Ohio public universities (currently, $13,067).

Duration 1 year (the fifth year of an accounting program). Funds committed to students who apply as juniors must be used within 4 years and funds committed to students who apply as seniors must be used within 3 years. The award is nonrenewable and may only be used when the student enrolls in the fifth year of a program.

Number awarded Several each year.

Deadline Applications may be submitted at any time.

[15]
ACT SIX SCHOLARSHIPS

Act Six
c/o Degrees of Change
1109 A Street, Suite 101
P.O. Box 1573
Tacoma, WA 98401
(253) 642-6712   E-mail: tim.herron@actsix.org
Web: www.actsix.org

Summary To provide financial assistance to Asian American and other residents of Washington and Oregon who come from diverse backgrounds and are interested in attending designated private faith-based universities in those states.

Eligibility This program is open to high school seniors or recent graduates and planning to enter college as freshmen who come from diverse, multicultural backgrounds. Applicants must be residents of the following regions and interested in attending designated colleges for that region: Portland: George Fox University or Warner Pacific College; Spokane: Gonzaga University or Whitworth University; Tacoma-Seattle: Gonzaga University, Northwest University, Pacific Lutheran University, or Whitworth University; or Yakima Valley: Heritage University. Students are not required to make a faith commitment, but they must be willing to explore Christian spirituality as it relates to service and leadership. Ethnicity and family income are considered as factors in selecting an intentionally diverse group of scholars, but there are no income restrictions and students from all ethnic backgrounds are encouraged to apply.

Financial data The program makes up the difference between any other assistance the student receives and full tuition. For recipients who demonstrate financial need in excess of tuition, awards cover some or all of the cost of room and board, books, travel, and personal expenses.

Duration 1 year; may be renewed.

Number awarded Varies each year; recently, 56 were awarded.

Deadline November of each year.

[16]
ACXIOM DIVERSITY SCHOLARSHIP PROGRAM

Acxiom Corporation
601 East Third Street
P.O. Box 8190
Little Rock, AR 72203-8190
(501) 342-1000   Toll Free: (877) 314-2049
E-mail: Candice.Davis@acxiom.com
Web: www.acxiom.com/about-acxiom/careers

Summary To provide financial assistance and possible work experience to Asian American and other upper-division and graduate students who are members of a diverse population that historically has been underrepresented in the information technology work force.

Eligibility This program is open to juniors, seniors, and graduate students who are working full time on a degree in a field of information technology, including computer science, computer information systems, management information systems, information quality, information systems, engineering, mathematics, statistics, or related areas of study. Women, veterans, minorities, and individuals with disabilities are encouraged to apply. Applicants must have a GPA of 3.0 or higher. Along with their application, they must submit a 500-word essay describing how the scholarship will help them achieve their academic, professional, and personal goals. Selection is based on academic achievement, relationship of field of study to information technology, and relationship of areas of professional interest to the sponsor's business needs.

Financial data The stipend is $5,000 per year.

Duration 1 year; may be renewed 1 additional year, provided the recipient remains enrolled full time, maintains a GPA of 3.0 or higher, and (if offered an internship) continues to meet internship expectations.

Additional information Recipients may be offered an internship (fall, spring, summer, year-round) at 1 of the sponsor's offices in Austin (Texas), Conway (Arkansas), Downers Grove (Illinois), Little Rock (Arkansas), Nashville (Tennessee), New York (New York), or Redwood City (California).

Number awarded Up to 5 each year.

Deadline December of each year.

[17]
A.D. OSHERMAN SCHOLARSHIP FUND

Greater Houston Community Foundation
Attn: Scholarships Assistant
5120 Woodway Drive, Suite 6000
Houston, TX 77056
(713) 333-2236   Fax: (713) 333-2220
E-mail: jlauver@ghcf.org
Web: www.ghcfscholar.org

Summary To provide financial assistance to residents of Texas who are Asian Americans or members of other designated groups and are interested in attending college in any state.

Eligibility This program is open to Texas residents who are graduating high school seniors or full-time freshmen, sophomores, or juniors at an accredited public 2- or 4-year college or university in any state. Applicants must qualify as a member of a recognized minority group, the first in their family to attend college, or a veteran with active service, particularly service in Iraq or Afghanistan. They must have a GPA of 2.75 or higher and a history of community service. Financial need is considered in the selection process.

Financial data The stipend is $2,500 per year for students at 4-year universities or $1,500 per year for students at 2-year colleges.

Duration 1 year; recipients may reapply.

Number awarded 2 each year.

Deadline March of each year.

[18]
ADDIE B. MORRIS SCHOLARSHIP

American Association of Railroad Superintendents
P.O. Box 200
La Fox, IL 60147
(331) 643-3369   E-mail: aars@supt.org
Web: www.railroadsuperintendents.org/Scholarships

Summary To provide financial assistance to undergraduate and graduate students, especially Asian Americans or other minorities working on a degree in transportation.

Eligibility This program is open to full-time undergraduate and graduate students enrolled at accredited colleges and universities in Canada or the United States. Applicants must have completed enough credits to have standing as a sophomore and must have a GPA of 2.75 or higher. Preference is given to minority students enrolled in the transportation field who can demonstrate financial need.

Financial data The stipend is $1,000. Funds are sent directly to the recipient's institution.

Duration 1 year.

Number awarded 1 or more each year.

Deadline June of each year.

[19]
ADVISORS OF AMERICA SCHOLARSHIP

Hmong American Education Fund
P.O. Box 17468
St. Paul, MN 55117
(651) 592-1576   E-mail: scholarships@thehaef.org
Web: www.thehaef.org

Summary To provide financial assistance to Hmong students who demonstrate a commitment to academic excellence and are interested in attending college in any state.

Eligibility This program is open to residents of any state who identify themselves as a person of Hmong descent. Applicants must be high school seniors, GED recipients, or students currently enrolled full time at a 2- or 4-year college or university in any state. They must be U.S. citizens or permanent residents and have a GPA of 3.0 or higher. Along with their application, they must submit transcripts and a 1,500-word essay on their commitment to education, their financial need (annual household income between $30,000 and $92,000), how this scholarship can help them, and their community service. Selection is based on academic excellence, commitment to helping their community, and financial need.

Financial data The stipend is $500 per year.

Duration 1 year; may be renewed up to 3 additional years.

Number awarded 1 each year.

Deadline March of each year.

[20]
AFSCME UNION SCHOLARSHIPS OF THE THURGOOD MARSHALL COLLEGE FUND

Thurgood Marshall College Fund
Attn: Senior Manager of Scholarship Programs
901 F Street, N.W., Suite 300
Washington, DC 20004
(202) 507-4851   Fax: (202) 652-2934
E-mail: deshuandra.walker@tmcfund.org
Web: www.tmcf.org

Summary To provide financial assistance and work experience with the American Federation of State, County and Municipal Employees (AFSCME) to Asian Pacific Islander American and other students of color interested in preparing for a career in the labor union movement.

Eligibility This program is open to students of color (Asian Pacific Islander American, African American, American Indian/Alaskan Native, Latino American) who are currently enrolled as sophomores or juniors at a college or university in any state. Applicants must be interested in participating in a summer field placement in a union organizing campaign at 1 of several locations across the country followed by a year of academic study at their college or university. They must have a current GPA of 2.5 or higher and a demonstrated interest in working through the union labor movement. Along with their application, they must submit a personal statement on an assigned topic, a letter of recommendation, and their current academic transcript.

Financial data The program provides 1) a stipend of up to $4,000 (provided by AFSCME) and on-site housing for the summer field placement; and 2) an academic scholarship of up to $6,300 for the school year, based on successful completion of the summer program and financial need.

Duration 10 weeks for the summer field placement; students who enter the program as sophomores are eligible for a second placement at AFSCME headquarters in Washington, D.C.; 1 year for the academic scholarship.

Additional information This program is sponsored by AFSCME.

Number awarded Varies each year.

Deadline February of each year.

[21]
AFTERCOLLEGE STEM INCLUSION SCHOLARSHIP

AfterCollege, Inc.
98 Battery Street, Suite 601
San Francisco, CA 94111
(415) 263-1300   Toll Free: (877) 725-7721
Fax: (415) 263-1307
E-mail: scholarships@aftercollege.com
Web: www.aftercollege.com

Summary To provide financial assistance to registered members of AfterCollege.com from Asian American and other underrepresented groups who are majoring in a field of science, technology, engineering, or mathematics (STEM) at a college or university in any state.

Eligibility This program is open to AfterCollege.com member currently enrolled at a college or university and working on a degree in a field of STEM. Applicants must be from a group underrepresented in their field of study, based on their gender, race, ethnic background, disability, sexual orientation, age, socio-economic status, nationality, or other non-visible differences. They must have a GPA of 3.0 or higher. Along with their application, they must submit a 200-word statement on their goals and the value that they bring in an academic and/or professional context. Selection is based primarily on that statement; other factors considered include academic accomplishment, work experience, honors and awards, and skills and languages.

Financial data The stipend is $500.

Duration 1 year.

Number awarded 1 or more each year.

Deadline March of each year.

[22]
AGAINST THE GRAIN ARTISTIC SCHOLARSHIP

Against the Grain Productions
3523 McKinney Avenue, Suite 231
Dallas, TX 75204
E-mail: outreach@againstthegrainproductions.com
Web: www.againstthegrainproductions.com

Summary To provide financial assistance to Asian and Pacific Island students working on an undergraduate degree in fields of visual and performing arts or communications.

Eligibility This program is open to high school seniors and current full-time students at accredited 2- and 4-year colleges and universities and vocational schools. Applicants must be of at least 50% Asian and/or Pacific Islander ethnicity and U.S. citizens, nationals, or permanent residents. They must be majoring in a field of the performing and/or visual arts or communications (e.g., film, theater, fashion, photography, graphic design, dance, music, journalism, mass communications) and have a GPA of 3.0 or higher. Selection is based on an essay and artistic portfolio, academic performance, leadership and community service, letters of recommendation, and an interview.

Financial data The stipend is $1,000. Funds are disbursed directly to the educational institution.

Duration 1 year.

Number awarded Varies each year; recently, 7 were awarded.

Deadline May of each year.

[23]
AGAINST THE GRAIN GROUNDBREAKER LEADERSHIP SCHOLARSHIP

Against the Grain Productions
3523 McKinney Avenue, Suite 231
Dallas, TX 75204
E-mail: outreach@againstthegrainproductions.com
Web: www.againstthegrainproductions.com

Summary To provide financial assistance to Asian and Pacific Island college seniors and graduate students who have demonstrated outstanding leadership that sets an example for their community.

Eligibility This program is open to full-time college seniors and graduate students in any field at accredited 4-year colleges and universities who have a GPA of 3.5 or higher. Applicants must be of at least 50% Asian and/or Pacific Islander ethnicity and U.S. citizens, nationals, or permanent residents. They must have demonstrated "exemplary leadership, vision, and passion that is blazing a trail for others to follow and changing lives in the Asian American community." Along with their application, they must submit a video that showcases their work and qualifications. Selection is based on that video, an essay, academic performance, leadership and community service, and an interview.

Financial data The stipend is $1,500. Funds are disbursed directly to the educational institution.

Duration 1 year.

Number awarded 1 or more each year.

Deadline May of each year.

[24]
AHIMA FOUNDATION DIVERSITY SCHOLARSHIPS

American Health Information Management Association
Attn: AHIMA Foundation
233 North Michigan Avenue, 21st Floor
Chicago, IL 60601-5809
(312) 233-1137   Fax: (312) 233-1537
E-mail: info@ahimafoundation.org
Web: www.ahimafoundation.org

Summary To provide financial assistance to Asian American and other members of the American Health Information Management Association (AHIMA) who are interested in working on an undergraduate or graduate degree in health information management (HIM) or health information technology (HIT) and who will contribute to diversity in the profession.

Eligibility This program is open to AHIMA members who are enrolled at least half time in an accredited program. Applicants must be working on a degree in HIM or HIT at the associate, bachelor's, post-baccalaureate, master's, or doctoral level. They must have a GPA of 3.5 or higher and at least 6 credit hours remaining after the date of the award. To qualify for this support, applicants must demonstrate how they will contribute to diversity in the health information management profession; diversity is defined as differences in race, ethnicity, nationality, gender, sexual orientation, socioeconomic status, age, physical capabilities, or religious beliefs. Along with their application, they must submit essays on assigned topics related to their involvement in the HIM profession. Selection is based on the clarity and completeness of thought in the essays; cumulative GPA; volunteer, work, and/or leadership experience; honors, awards, or recognitions; commitment to the HIM profession; and references.

Financial data Stipends are $1,000 for associate degree students, $1,500 for bachelor's degree or post-baccalaureate certificate students, $2,000 for master's degree students, or $2,500 for doctoral degree students.

Duration 1 year.

Number awarded 1 or more each year.

Deadline September of each year.

[25]
AIA/F DIVERSITY ADVANCEMENT SCHOLARSHIP

American Institute of Architects
Attn: AIA Foundation
1799 New York Avenue, N.W.
Washington, DC 20006-5292
(202) 626-7511   Fax: (202) 626-7420
E-mail: divscholarship@aia.org
Web: www.aia.org/about/initiatives/AIAB101856

Summary To provide financial assistance to Asian American and other high school and college students from diverse backgrounds who are interested in studying architecture in college.

Eligibility This program is open to students from minority and/or financially disadvantaged backgrounds who are high school seniors, students in a community college or technical school transferring to an accredited architectural program, or college freshmen entering a professional degree program at an accredited program of architecture. Students who have completed 1 or more years of a 4-year college curriculum are not eligible. Applicants must submit 2 or 3 drawings, including 1 freehand sketch of any real life object (e.g., buildings, people, objects, self-portrait) and 1 or 2 additional images of drawings or drafted floor plans or drawings using computer-aided design (CAD). Selection is based on those drawings and financial need.

Financial data Stipends range from $3,000 to $4,000 per year, depending upon individual need. Students must apply for supplementary funds from other sources.

Duration 1 year; may be renewed for up to 4 additional years or until completion of a degree.

Additional information This program was established in 1970 as the AIA/AAF Minority Disadvantaged Scholarship Program.

Number awarded 2 each year.

Deadline April of each year.

[26]
AICPA ASCEND SCHOLARSHIP

Ascend: Pan-Asian Leaders
Attn: Director of Programs
247 West 30th Street
New York, NY 10001
(212) 248-4888   Fax: (212) 344-5636
E-mail: scholarships@ascendleadership.org
Web: www.ascendleadership.org

Summary To provide financial assistance to undergraduate and graduate minority accounting students who are members of Ascend: Pan-Asian Leaders and of the American Institute of Certified Public Accountants (AICPA).

Eligibility This program is open to members of minority groups underrepresented in the accounting profession. Applicants must have completed at least 30 hours of college course work, including at least 6 hours in accounting, at a 4-year college or university in the United States or its territories as a full-time undergraduate or graduate student in an accounting-related field. They must be members of Ascend and AICPA, have a GPA of 3.0 or higher, and be U.S. citizens or permanent residents. Along with their application, they must submit a 500-word personal essay on how they have demonstrated leadership and teamwork in their academic studies, professional career, and/or extracurricular activities and community volunteer work; why they believe those qualities are important to transforming themselves into a better leader; their career goals after graduation; and the role Ascend has played in the achievement of their academic and career goals. They must also be able to demonstrate some financial need.

Financial data The stipend is $5,000. The program also provides travel and lodging for the Ascend annual national convention.

Duration 1 year.

Additional information Ascend was formed in 2004 as the National Asian American Society of Accountants. This program is sponsored by AICPA.

Number awarded 1 each year.

Deadline April of each year.

[27]
AIET MINORITIES AND WOMEN EDUCATIONAL SCHOLARSHIP PROGRAM

Appraisal Institute
Attn: Appraisal Institute Education Trust
200 West Madison Street, Suite 1500
Chicago, IL 60606
(312) 335-4133   Fax: (312) 335-4134
E-mail: educationtrust@appraisalinstitute.org
Web: www.appraisalinstitute.org

Summary To provide financial assistance to Asian American and other underrepresented undergraduate students majoring in real estate or allied fields.

Eligibility This program is open to members of groups underrepresented in the real estate appraisal profession. Those groups include women, Asians and Pacific Islanders, American Indians, Alaska Natives, Blacks or African Americans, and Hispanics. Applicants must be full- or part-time students enrolled in real estate courses within a degree-granting college, university, or junior college. They must have a GPA of 2.5 or higher and be able to demonstrate financial need. U.S. citizenship is required.

Financial data The stipend is $1,000. Funds are paid directly to the recipient's institution to be used for tuition and fees.

Duration 1 year.

Number awarded At least 1 each year.

Deadline April of each year.

[28]
AIKO SUSANNA TASHIRO HIRATSUKA MEMORIAL SCHOLARSHIP

Japanese American Citizens League
Attn: National Scholarship Awards
1765 Sutter Street
San Francisco, CA 94115
(415) 345-1075   Fax: (415) 345-1077
E-mail: pwada@jacl.org
Web: www.jacl.org/jacl-national-scholarship-program

Summary To provide financial assistance for undergraduate education in the performing arts to student members of the Japanese American Citizens League (JACL).

Eligibility This program is open to JACL members who are enrolled in undergraduate study in the performing arts. Applicants should provide a recording of themselves performing, along with published critical reviews and/or evaluations by their instructor. Along with their application, they must submit information on their involvement in JACL and a 2-page essay on a topic that changes annually but relates to Japanese Americans. Selection is based on that essay, academic history, JACL involvement, school activities, work history, scholastic honors, and community involvement. Professional artists are not eligible.

Financial data Stipends generally average more than $2,000.

Duration 1 year; nonrenewable.

Number awarded 1 each year.

Deadline March of each year.

[29]
ALAN COMPTON AND BOB STANLEY MINORITY AND INTERNATIONAL SCHOLARSHIP

Baptist Communicators Association
Attn: Scholarship Committee
4519 Lashley Court
Marietta, GA 30068
(678) 641-4457 E-mail: margaretcolson@bellsouth.net
Web: www.baptistcommunicators.org/about/scholarship.cfm

Summary To provide financial assistance to Asian American or other minority or international students who are working on an undergraduate degree to prepare for a career in Baptist communications.

Eligibility This program is open to undergraduate students of minority or international origin. Applicants must be majoring in communications, English, journalism, or public relations and have a GPA of 2.5 or higher. Their vocational objective must be in Baptist communications. Along with their application, they must submit a statement explaining why they want to receive this scholarship.

Financial data The stipend is $1,000.

Duration 1 year; recipients may reapply.

Additional information This program began in 1996.

Number awarded 1 each year.

Deadline March of each year.

[30]
ALICE YURIKO ENDO MEMORIAL SCHOLARSHIP

Japanese American Citizens League
Attn: National Scholarship Awards
1765 Sutter Street
San Francisco, CA 94115
(415) 345-1075 Fax: (415) 345-1077
E-mail: pwada@jacl.org
Web: www.jacl.org/jacl-national-scholarship-program

Summary To provide financial assistance to student members of the Japanese American Citizens League (JACL) who are working on an undergraduate degree, particularly in public or social service.

Eligibility This program is open to JACL members who are currently enrolled at a college, university, trade school, business college, or other institution of higher learning. Applicants must submit information on their involvement in JACL and a

2-page essay on a topic that changes annually but relates to Japanese Americans. Selection is based on that essay, academic history, JACL involvement, school activities, work history, scholastic honors, and community involvement. Preference is given to students with an interest in public or social service and/or residing in the Eastern District Council area.

Financial data Stipends generally average more than $2,000.

Duration 1 year; nonrenewable.

Number awarded 1 each year.

Deadline March of each year.

[31]
ALMA EXLEY SCHOLARSHIP

Community Foundation of Greater New Britain
Attn: Scholarship Manager
74A Vine Street
New Britain, CT 06052-1431
(860) 229-6018, ext. 305 Fax: (860) 225-2666
E-mail: cfarmer@cfgnb.org
Web: www.cfgnb.org

Summary To provide financial assistance to Asian American and other minority college students in Connecticut who are interested in preparing for a teaching career.

Eligibility This program is open to students of color (Asian Americans, African Americans, Hispanic Americans, and Native Americans) enrolled in a teacher preparation program in Connecticut. Applicant must 1) have been admitted to a traditional teacher preparation program at an accredited 4-year college or university in the state; or 2) be participating in the Alternate Route to Certification (ARC) program sponsored by the Connecticut Department of Higher Education.

Financial data The stipend is $1,500 per year for students at a 4-year college or university or $500 for a student in the ARC program.

Duration 2 years for students at 4-year colleges or universities; 1 year for students in the ARC program.

Number awarded 2 each year: 1 to a 4-year student and 1 to an ARC student.

Deadline October of each year.

[32]
ALVAN T. AND VIOLA D. FULLER JUNIOR RESEARCH FELLOWSHIP

American Cancer Society-New England Division
30 Speen Street
Framingham, MA 01701
(508) 270-4645 Toll Free: (800) 952-7664, ext. 4645
Fax: (508) 393-8607 E-mail: maureen.morse@cancer.org
Web: www.cancer.org

Summary To provide funding for summer cancer research to undergraduate students, especially Asian Americans and other minorities, in New England.

Eligibility This program is open to residents of New England currently enrolled as juniors or seniors at a college or university in any state. Applicants must be interested in working on a summer research project at a teaching hospital, university, or medical school in New England. They must be interested in working under the supervision of an accomplished cancer investigator. Preference is given to student with advanced science course work, laboratory skills, and an interest in research. Minority students and those with American Cancer Society volunteer experience are especially encouraged to apply.

Financial data　The grant is $4,500.

Duration　10 weeks during the summer.

Number awarded　1 or more each year.

Deadline　January of each year.

[33]
AMAC MEMBER AWARD

Airport Minority Advisory Council
Attn: AMAC Foundation
2001 Jefferson Davis Highway, Suite 500
Arlington, VA 22202
(703) 414-2622　　　　　　　Fax: (703) 414-2686
E-mail: terrifrierson@palladiumholdingsco.com
Web: amac-org.com/amac-foundation/scholarships

Summary　To provide financial assistance to Asian American and other underrepresented high school seniors and undergraduates who are preparing for a career in the aviation industry and are connected to Airport Minority Advisory Council (AMAC).

Eligibility　This program is open to minority and female high school seniors and current undergraduates who have a GPA of 2.5 or higher and a record of involvement in community and extracurricular activities. Applicants must be interested in working on a bachelor's degree in accounting, architecture, aviation, business administration, engineering, or finance as preparation for a career in the aviation or airport industry. They must be AMAC members, family of members, or mentees of member. Along with their application, they must submit a 750-word essay on how they have overcome barriers in life to achieve their academic and/or career goals; their dedication to succeed in the aviation industry and how AMAC can help them achieve their goal; and the most important issues that the aviation industry is facing today and how they see themselves changing those. Financial need is not considered in the selection process. U.S. citizenship is required.

Financial data　The stipend is $2,000 per year.

Duration　1 year; recipients may reapply.

Number awarded　4 each year.

Deadline　May of each year.

[34]
AMBASSADOR MINERVA JEAN FALCON HAWAI'I SCHOLARSHIP

Hawai'i Community Foundation
Attn: Scholarship Department
827 Fort Street Mall
Honolulu, HI 96813
(808) 566-5570　　　　　　　Toll Free: (888) 731-3863
Fax: (808) 521-6286
E-mail: scholarships@hcf-hawaii.org
Web: hcf.scholarships.ngwebsolutions.com

Summary　To provide financial assistance to Hawaii residents of Filipino ancestry who are interested in attending college in the state.

Eligibility　This program is open to Hawaii residents of Filipino ancestry who are enrolled in or planning to enroll in an accredited 2- or 4-year college or university in the state.

Applicants must be full-time students at the undergraduate or graduate level and able to demonstrate academic achievement (GPA of 2.7 or higher), good moral character, and financial need. Along with their application, they must submit a short statement indicating their reasons for attending college, their planned course of study, their career goals, and what community service means to them. They must also submit a 2-page essay on how they plan to be involved in the community as a Filipino-American student.

Financial data　The amounts of the awards depend on the availability of funds and the need of the recipient. Recently, the average value of the scholarships awarded by the foundation was $2,800.

Duration　1 year.

Additional information　This scholarship was first offered in 2001.

Number awarded　Varies each year.

Deadline　February of each year.

[35]
AMELIA KEMP MEMORIAL SCHOLARSHIP

Women of the Evangelical Lutheran Church in America
Attn: Scholarships
8765 West Higgins Road
Chicago, IL 60631-4101
(773) 380-2741　　　　Toll Free: (800) 638-3522, ext. 2741
Fax: (773) 380-2419　　　　E-mail: valora.starr@elca.org
Web: www.womenoftheelca.org

Summary　To provide financial assistance to Asian American and other lay women of color who are members of Evangelical Lutheran Church of America (ELCA) congregations and who wish to study on the undergraduate, graduate, professional, or vocational school level.

Eligibility　This program is open to ELCA lay women of color who are at least 21 years of age and have experienced an interruption of at least 2 years in their education since high school. Applicants must have been admitted to an educational institution to prepare for a career in other than ordained ministry. U.S. citizenship is required.

Financial data　The maximum stipend is $1,000 per year.

Duration　1 year; recipients may reapply for 1 additional year.

Number awarded　1 or more each year.

Deadline　February of each year.

[36]
AMERICAN ASSOCIATION OF JAPANESE UNIVERSITY WOMEN SCHOLARSHIP PROGRAM

American Association of Japanese University Women
Attn: Scholarship Committee
3543 West Boulevard
Los Angeles, CA 90016
E-mail: aajuwcholar@gmail.com
Web: www.aajuw.org/new-page-3

Summary　To provide financial assistance to female students currently enrolled in upper-division or graduate classes in California.

Eligibility　This program is open to women enrolled at accredited colleges or universities in California as juniors, seniors, or graduate students. Applicants must be involved in U.S.-Japan relations, cultural exchanges, and leadership development in the areas of their designated field of study. Along with their application, they must submit a current resume, an official transcript of the past 2 years of college work, 2 letters of recommendation, and an essay (up to 2 pages in English or 1,200 characters in Japanese) on what they hope to accomplish in their field of study and how that will contribute to better U.S.-Japan relations.

Financial data The stipend is $2,000.

Duration 1 year.

Additional information The association was founded in 1970 to promote the education of women as well as to contribute to U.S.-Japan relations, cultural exchanges, and leadership development.

Number awarded 1 to 3 each year. Since this program was established, it has awarded nearly $100,000 worth of scholarships to 110 women.

Deadline September of each year.

[37]
AMERICAN ASSOCIATION OF PHYSICISTS IN MEDICINE DIVERSITY RECRUITMENT THROUGH EDUCATION AND MENTORING (DREAM) PROGRAM

American Association of Physicists in Medicine
Attn: AAPM Education and Research Fund
One Physics Ellipse
College Park, MD 20740
(301) 209-3350   Fax: (301) 209-0862
E-mail: jackie@aapm.org
Web: www.aapm.org/education/GrantsFellowships.asp

Summary To provide an opportunity for Asian American and other minority upper-division students to gain summer work experience performing research in a medical physics laboratory or assisting with clinical service at a clinical facility.

Eligibility This program is open to minority undergraduates who are entering their junior or senior year at an Historically Black College or University (HBCU), Minority Serving Institution (MSI), or non-Minority Serving Institution. Applicants must be interested in gaining experience in medical physics by performing research in a laboratory or assisting with clinical service at a clinical facility. Preference is given to those who have declared a major in physics, engineering, or other science that requires mathematics at least through differential equations and junior-level courses in modern physics or quantum mechanics and electricity and magnetism or equivalent courses in engineering sciences. They must be U.S. citizens, U.S. permanent residents, or Canadian citizens. Work must be conducted under the supervision of a mentor who is a member of the American Association of Physicists in Medicine (AAPM) employed by a university, hospital, clinical facility, or radiological industry within the United States.

Financial data The stipend is $5,000.

Duration 10 weeks during the summer.

Additional information This program was formerly known as the American Association of Physicists in Medicine Minority Undergraduate Experience Program.

Number awarded Varies each year; recently, 9 were awarded.

Deadline February of each year.

[38]
AMERICAN BUS ASSOCIATION DIVERSITY SCHOLARSHIPS

American Bus Association
Attn: ABA Foundation
111 K Street, N.E., Ninth Floor
Washington, DC 20002
(202) 842-1645   Toll Free: (800) 283-2877
Fax: (202) 842-0850   E-mail: abainfo@buses.org
Web: www.buses.org/aba-foundation/scholarships/diversity

Summary To provide financial assistance for college to Asian Americans and members of other traditionally underrepresented groups who are preparing for a career in the transportation, travel, hospitality, and tourism industry.

Eligibility This program is open to members of traditionally underrepresented groups who have completed at least 1 year of study at a 2- or 4-year college or university. Applicants must be working on a degree in a course of study related to the transportation, travel, hospitality, and tourism industry. They must have a GPA of 3.0 or higher. Along with their application, they must submit a 500-word essay on the role they hope to play in advancing the future of the transportation, travel, hospitality, and tourism industry. Selection is based on academic achievement, character, leadership, financial need, and commitment to advancing the transportation, travel, hospitality, and tourism industry. Additional consideration is given to applicants who are affiliated with a company that is a member of the American Bus Association (ABA).

Financial data The stipend is $2,500.

Duration 1 or more each year.

Deadline April of each year.

[39]
AMERICAN SOCIETY OF INDIAN ENGINEERS SCHOLARSHIP PROGRAM

American Society of Indian Engineers
Attn: Scholarship Program
P.O. Box 741007
Houston, TX 77274
E-mail: asiehouston@gmail.com
Web: www.asiehouston.org/?s=scholarship

Summary To provide financial assistance to residents of any state who are of Indian origin and are working on an undergraduate or graduate degree in engineering or architecture at a college in the Houston area of Texas.

Eligibility This program is open to residents of any state who are of Indian origin and currently enrolled at a college or university in the greater Houston metropolitan area. Applicants must be working full time on an associate, bachelor's, or graduate degree in engineering or architecture. Along with their application, they must submit an essay about themselves, their achievements, career goals, and activities. Selection is based on that essay (50%), GPA (25%), and financial need (25%). An interview may also be required.

Financial data The stipend is $1,000.

Duration 1 year.

Number awarded Up to 10 each year.

Deadline September of each year.

[40]
ANA MULTICULTURAL EXCELLENCE SCHOLARSHIP

American Association of Advertising Agencies
Attn: AAAA Foundation
1065 Avenue of the Americas, 16th Floor
New York, NY 10018
(212) 262-2500   E-mail: ameadows@aaaa.org
Web: www.aaaa.org

Summary   To provide financial assistance to Asian American and other multicultural students who are working on an undergraduate degree in advertising.

Eligibility   This program is open to undergraduate students who are U.S. citizens of proven multicultural heritage and have at least 1 grandparent of multicultural heritage. Applicants must be participating in the Multicultural Advertising Intern Program (MAIP). They must be entering their senior year at an accredited college or university in the United States and have a GPA of 3.0 or higher. Selection is based on academic ability.

Financial data   The stipend is $2,500.

Duration   1 year.

Additional information   This program was established by the Association of National Advertisers (ANA) in 2001. The American Association of Advertising Agencies (AAAA) assumed administration in 2003.

Number awarded   2 each year.

Deadline   Deadline not specified.

[41]
ANAC STUDENT DIVERSITY MENTORSHIP SCHOLARSHIP

Association of Nurses in AIDS Care
Attn: Awards Committee
3538 Ridgewood Road
Akron, OH 44333-3122
(330) 670-0101   Toll Free: (800) 260-6780
Fax: (330) 670-0109   E-mail: anac@anacnet.org
Web: www.nursesinaidscare.org

Summary   To provide financial assistance to Asian American and other student nurses from minority groups who are interested in HIV/AIDS nursing and in attending the national conference of the Association of Nurses in AIDS Care (ANAC).

Eligibility   This program is open to student nurses from a diverse racial or ethnic background, defined to include Asians/Pacific Islanders, African Americans, Hispanics/Latinos, and American Indians/Alaskan Natives. Candidates must have a genuine interest in HIV/AIDS nursing, be interested in attending the ANAC national conference, and desire to develop a mentorship relationship with a member of the ANAC Diversity Specialty Committee. They may be 1) pre-licensure students enrolled in an initial R.N. or L.P.N./L.V.N. program (i.e. L.P.N./L.V.N., A.D.N., diploma, B.S./B.S.N.); or 2) current licensed R.N. students with an associate or diploma degree who are enrolled in a bachelor's degree program. Nominees may be recommended by themselves, nursing faculty members, or ANAC members, but their nomination must be supported by an ANAC member. Along with their nomination form, they must submit a 2,000-character essay describing their interest or experience in HIV/AIDS care and why they want to attend the ANAC conference.

Financial data   Recipients are awarded a $1,000 scholarship (paid directly to the school), up to $599 in reimbursement of travel expenses to attend the ANAC annual conference, free conference registration, an award plaque, a free ticket to the awards ceremony at the conference, and a 2-year ANAC membership.

Duration   1 year.

Additional information   The mentor will be assigned at the conference and will maintain contact during the period of study.

Number awarded   1 each year.

Deadline   August of each year.

[42]
APAICS SUMMER INTERNSHIPS

Asian Pacific American Institute for Congressional
   Studies
Attn: Summer Internship Program
1001 Connecticut Avenue, N.W., Suite 320
Washington, DC 20036
(202) 296-9200   Fax: (202) 296-9236
E-mail: internship@apaics.org
Web: www.apaics.org/summer-interns

Summary   To provide an opportunity for undergraduate students and recent graduates with an interest in issues affecting the Asian Pacific Islander American communities to work in Washington, D.C. during the summer.

Eligibility   This program is open to Asian American and Pacific Islander students currently enrolled in an accredited undergraduate institution; recent (within 90 days) graduates are also eligible. Applicants must be able to demonstrate interest in the political process, public policy issues, and Asian American and Pacific Islander community affairs; leadership abilities; and oral and written communication skills. They must be 18 years of age or older; U.S. citizens or permanent residents; and interested in working in Congress, federal agencies, or institutions that further the mission of the Asian Pacific American Institute for Congressional Studies (APAICS). Preference is given to students who have not previously had an internship in Washington, D.C.

Financial data   The stipend is $2,000.

Duration   8 weeks, starting in June.

Additional information   This program is sponsored by Southwest Airlines.

Number awarded   Varies each year; recently, 20 interns were selected for this program.

Deadline   January of each year.

[43]
APCA SCHOLARSHIPS

Asian Pacific Islanders for Professional and Community
   Advancement
c/o Yakun Gao, Scholarship Committee
P.O. Box 2694
San Ramon, CA 94583
(425) 633-4935   E-mail: scholarship@apca-att.org
Web: www.apca-att.org/scholarshipfaq.html

Summary To provide financial assistance to high school seniors, especially Asian Americans, from selected states who are interested in attending college in any state.

Eligibility This program offers national scholarships to seniors graduating from high schools in California, Florida, Georgia, Hawaii, metropolitan Washington, D.C. (including Maryland and Virginia), the midwest states (Illinois, Indiana, Michigan, Ohio, and Wisconsin), Missouri, the mountain states (Arizona and Colorado), Nevada, New Jersey, Texas, and Washington. Applicants must be planning to continue their education at an accredited 2- or 4-year college or university or vocational school in any state. They must have a GPA of 3.4 or higher. Along with their application, they must submit a 750-word essay on making a difference in their community. Financial need is not considered in the selection process. Students of all ethnic backgrounds are eligible, but a goal of the sponsoring organization is to promote growth and influence on issues that impact Asian Pacific Islanders. Students who are not awarded a national scholarship are eligible for state scholarships. U.S. citizenship or permanent resident status is required.

Financial data National scholarships are $2,000; Georgia state scholarships are $2,000 and other state scholarships are $1,000.

Duration 1 year; nonrenewable.

Additional information This program was established by an organization named the Asian/Pacific American Association for Advancement at AT&T, which offered the 4A-AT&T National Scholarship Program. In 2006, that organization merged with Asians for Corporate and Community Action to form Asian Pacific Islanders for Professional and Community Advancement (APCA). Both the former and current organizations are comprised of Asian Pacific American employees of AT&T, Inc.

Number awarded Varies each year; recently, 28 national scholarships and 50 state scholarships (13 in California, 2 in Florida, 15 in Georgia, 2 in Hawaii, 1 in metropolitan Washington D.C., 2 in the midwest states, 1 in Missouri, 1 in the mountain states, 7 in New Jersey, 3 in Texas, and 3 in Washington) were awarded.

Deadline February of each year.

[44]
APIQWTC SCHOLARSHIP

Asian Pacific Islander Queer Women and Transgender
  Community
c/o Amy Sueyoshi
San Francisco State University
College of Ethnic Studies
1600 Holloway Avenue
San Francisco, CA 94132
(415) 405-0774   E-mail: sueyoshi@sfsu.edu
Web: www.apiqwtc.org/resources/apiqwtc-scholarship

Summary To provide financial assistance to Asian Pacific Islander (API) lesbian and bisexual women and transgender individuals who are high school seniors, undergraduates, or graduate students interested in working on a degree in any field at a college in any state.

Eligibility This program is open to API high school seniors and current undergraduate or graduate students in any field. Applicants must identify as a lesbian, bisexual, or queer woman or a transgender individual. Along with their applica-

tion, they must submit a 2-page personal statement that covers their community involvement and future goals; how their cultural heritage, sexual orientation, and/or gender identity has influenced their life; any activities in which they have been involved; any relevant experiences up to the present; and how they see themselves involved in the community in the future, either through their career or otherwise.

Financial data The stipend is $1,000.

Duration 1 year.

Additional information The Asian Pacific Islander Queer Women and Transgender Community (APIQWTC) is a community of more than 10 organizations in the San Francisco Bay area provide support and community for queer Asian and Pacific Islander individuals, but its scholarships are available to students from any state.

Number awarded 2 each year.

Deadline February of each year.

[45]
ARIZONA CHAPTER JAPANESE AMERICAN CITIZENS LEAGUE SCHOLARSHIPS

Japanese American Citizens League-Arizona Chapter
5414 West Glenn Drive
Glendale, AZ 85301-2628
E-mail: arizonajacl@gmail.com
Web: www.jaclaz.org/services.html

Summary To provide financial assistance to graduating high school seniors in Arizona who are of Japanese heritage.

Eligibility This program is open to graduating high school seniors in Arizona who have a GPA of 3.0 or higher. Applicants or their parents must have been members of 1 of the following organizations for at least the preceding 3 years: Arizona Chapter of the Japanese American Citizens League (JACLA), the Phoenix Japanese Free Methodist Church, the Arizona Buddhist Church, a youth group of JACLA, a youth group of the Phoenix Free Methodist Church, or a youth group of the Arizona Buddhist Church. Financial need is not considered in the selection process.

Financial data The stipend is $1,000.

Duration 1 year.

Additional information This program includes the Sara Hutchings Clardy Scholarship Awards, the Joe Allman Scholarship, the Herbert Jensen Scholarship, the Tatsuko and Hiroshi (Nick) Nakagawa Scholarship, and the Betty and George Kishiyama Scholarship.

Number awarded 7 each year.

Deadline February of each year.

[46]
ARKANSAS CONFERENCE ETHNIC AND LANGUAGE CONCERNS COMMITTEE SCHOLARSHIPS

United Methodist Church-Arkansas Conference
Attn: Committee on Ethnic and Language Concerns
800 Daisy Bates Drive
Little Rock, AR 72202
(501) 324-8045   Toll Free: (877) 646-1816
Fax: (501) 324-8018   E-mail: mallen@arumc.org
Web: www.arumc.org/docs-and-forms

Summary To provide financial assistance to Asian American and other ethnic minority Methodist students from Arkansas who are interested in attending college or graduate school in any state.

Eligibility This program is open to ethnic minority undergraduate and graduate students who are active members of local congregations affiliated with the Arkansas Conference of the United Methodist Church (UMC). Applicants must be currently enrolled in an accredited institution of higher education in any state. Along with their application, they must submit an essay explaining how this scholarship will make them a leader in the UMC. Preference is given to students attending a UMC-affiliated college or university.

Financial data The stipend is $500 per semester ($1,000 per year) for undergraduates or $1,000 per semester ($2,000 per year) for graduate students.

Duration 1 year; may be renewed.

Number awarded 5 each year: 1 in each UMC Arkansas district.

Deadline February or September of each year.

[47]
ARSENIO AND CO BIT SIY SCHOLARSHIP

OCA Asian Pacific American Advocates-Wisconsin
  Chapter
c/o Albert Chen, Scholarship Committee Chair
120 North 73rd Street
Milwaukee, WI 53213
(414) 258-2410   E-mail: albertchen@aol.com
Web: www.ocawi.org/www/scholarships.html

Summary To provide financial assistance to high school seniors who are children of members or business affiliates of the Wisconsin Chapter of OCA Asian Pacific American Advocates (OCA-WI) and interested in attending college in any state.

Eligibility This program is open to graduating high school seniors whose parent has been an OCA-WI member or business affiliate for at least 2 years and who are planning to enroll full time at an accredited college or university in any state. Applicants must have a GPA of 3.0 or higher or rank in the top 20% of their class. Along with their application, they must submit a personal statement that includes information on their future college and career plans; a list of scholastic awards, honors, extracurricular activities, and honor societies and offices; ACT/SAT scores; and a description of their community service to OCA-WI and their community. Financial need is not considered in the selection process.

Financial data A stipend is awarded (amount not specified).

Duration 1 year.

Additional information This program began in 1993. OCA Asian Pacific American Advocates was previously named the Organization of Chinese Americans. It changed its name in 2014 to reflect its concern for all Asian Americans.

Number awarded 1 each year.

Deadline March of each year.

[48]
ARTHUR H. GOODMAN MEMORIAL SCHOLARSHIP

San Diego Foundation
Attn: Community Scholarships
2508 Historic Decatur Road, Suite 200
San Diego, CA 92106
(619) 814-1343   Fax: (619) 239-1710
E-mail: scholarships@sdfoundation.org
Web: www.sdfoundation.org

Summary To provide financial assistance to Asian American and other minority community college students in California or Arizona planning to transfer to a 4-year school in any state to prepare for a career in economic development.

Eligibility This program is open to women and minorities currently enrolled at a community college in California or Arizona and planning to transfer as a full- or part-time student at a 4-year school in any state. Applicants must submit information on their long-term career goal, a list of volunteer and extracurricular activities, documentation of financial need, and a 3-page personal statement on their commitment to community involvement and desire to prepare for a career in the field of economic development.

Financial data Stipends range from $1,500 to $3,000.

Duration 1 year.

Additional information This program was established in 1998 by the CDC Small Business Finance Corporation.

Number awarded Varies each year; recently, 5 were awarded.

Deadline April of each year.

[49]
ARTTABLE MENTORED INTERNSHIPS FOR DIVERSITY IN THE VISUAL ARTS PROFESSIONS

ArtTable Inc.
1 East 53rd Street, Fifth Floor
New York, NY 10022
(212) 343-1735   Fax: (866) 363-4188
E-mail: info@arttable.org
Web: www.arttable.org/summermentoredinternship

Summary To provide an opportunity for women who are Asian American or from other diverse backgrounds to gain mentored work experience during the summer and to prepare for a career as an art professional.

Eligibility This program is open to women who are college seniors, recent graduates, or graduate students and interested in preparing for a career as a visual arts professional (including administrative director, art adviser, art appraiser, art critic, art dealer, art librarian, arts funder, arts lawyer, conservator, curator, editor, educator, fundraiser, management consultant, public relations consultant, writer). Applicants must be from a cultural or ethnic background that is underrepresented in the field. They must be interested in working during the summer with a mentor at an art museum or similar facility. U.S. citizenship or permanent resident status is required.

Financial data The stipend is $3,000. The hosting institution or mentor receives $500 for administrative and other costs.

Duration 8 weeks during the summer.

Additional information This program began in 2000. Support is provided by the Samuel H. Kress Foundation.

Number awarded Varies each year; recently, 5 of these internships were awarded.

Deadline February of each year.

[50]
ASCEND SCHOLARSHIP

Ascend: Pan-Asian Leaders
Attn: Director of Programs
247 West 30th Street
New York, NY 10001
(212) 248-4888   Fax: (212) 344-5636
E-mail: scholarships@ascendleadership.org
Web: www.ascendleadership.org

Summary To provide financial assistance to members of Ascend: Pan-Asian Leaders who are college undergraduates with a career interest in accounting or finance.

Eligibility This program is open to members of Ascend who are enrolled as freshmen, sophomores, or juniors (in 5-year programs) at colleges and universities in the United States. Applicants must have a GPA of 3.5 or higher and a major in accounting or finance. Along with their application, they must submit a 500-word personal essay on how they have demonstrated leadership and teamwork in their academic studies, professional career, and/or extracurricular activities and community volunteer work; why they believe those qualities are important to transforming themselves into a better leader; their career goals after graduation; and the role Ascend has played in the achievement of their academic and career goals. Financial need is not considered in the selection process.

Financial data The stipend is $1,000.

Duration 1 year.

Additional information Ascend was formed in 2004 as the National Asian American Society of Accountants.

Number awarded 1 each year.

Deadline April of each year.

[51]
ASCPA EDUCATIONAL FOUNDATION DIVERSITY SCHOLARSHIPS

Alabama Society of Certified Public Accountants
Attn: ASCPA Educational Foundation
1041 Longfield Court
P.O. Box 242987
Montgomery, AL 36124-2987
(334) 834-7650   Toll Free: (800) 227-1711 (within AL)
Fax: (334) 834-7603
Web: www.ascpa.org

Summary To provide financial assistance to Asian American and other minority accounting students at colleges and universities in Alabama.

Eligibility This program is open to minority (Asian, Black or African American, Hispanic or Latino, or Native American) residents of any state enrolled at least half time at colleges and universities in Alabama with at least 1 full year of school remaining. Applicants must have declared a major in accounting and have completed intermediate accounting courses. They must have a GPA of 3.0 or higher overall and in all accounting classes. Along with their application, they must

submit a 25-word essay on why the scholarship is important to them. Financial need is not considered in the selection process. Preference is given to students who have a strong interest in a career as a C.P.A. in Alabama. U.S. citizenship or permanent resident status is required.

Financial data The stipend is $2,500.

Duration 1 year.

Additional information This program began in 2012.

Number awarded 5 each year.

Deadline March of each year.

[52]
ASEI UNDERGRADUATE SCHOLARSHIPS

American Society of Engineers of Indian Origin
Attn: Scholarship Program
P.O. Box 18215
Irvine, CA 92623
E-mail: scholarships@aseiusa.org
Web: www.aseiusa.org

Summary To provide financial assistance to undergraduate students of Indian origin (from India) who are majoring in engineering, computer sciences, or related areas.

Eligibility This program is open to undergraduate students of Indian origin (by birth, ancestry, or relation). They must be enrolled full time at an ABET-accredited college or university in the United States and majoring in engineering, computer science, or allied science and have a GPA of 3.2 or higher. They must be members of the American Society of Engineers of Indian Origin (ASEI). Selection is based on demonstrated ability, academic achievement (including GPA, honors, and awards), career objectives, faculty recommendations, involvement in science fair and campus activities, financial hardship, industrial exposure (including part-time work and internships), and involvement in ASEI and other community activities.

Financial data Stipends range from $500 to $1,000.

Duration 1 year.

Number awarded Several each year.

Deadline August of each year.

[53]
ASIAN AMERICAN ARCHITECTS/ENGINEERS ASSOCIATION STUDENT SCHOLARSHIPS

Asian American Architects/Engineers Association
Attn: Foundation
645 West Ninth Street, Unit 110-175
Los Angeles, CA 90015
(213) 896-9270   Fax: (213) 985-7404
E-mail: info@aaaesc.org
Web: www.aaaesc.org/foundation_student_scholarship

Summary To provide financial assistance to members of the Asian American Architects/Engineers Association (AAa/e) who are interested in working on an undergraduate or graduate degree at a school in southern California.

Eligibility This program is open to student members of AAa/e who are U.S. citizens, permanent residents, or noncitizens enrolled or planning to enroll full time at a college or university in southern California. Applicants must be graduating seniors, community college students, undergraduates, or graduate students working on or planning to work on a degree in architecture, civil engineering (environmental, geotechnical, structural, transportation), electrical engineering, mechanical engineering, landscape architecture, planning and urban design, or construction and construction management. Along with their application, they must submit 1) a 1-page personal statement on their involvement and service to the Asian Pacific Islander community, their interest in their field, and what makes them unique; 2) letters of recommendation from 2 faculty members or employers; and 3) a sample of their work, which may be a design or research project, a completed project, or a proposed project, including an assignment from a class, a senior project, or an assignment from work. For high school seniors and community college students, selection is based on personal statements (50%), recommendations (30%), and the work sample (20%); for undergraduate and graduate students, selection is based on the work sample (65%), personal statements (20%), and recommendations (15%).

Financial data   Stipends range up to $5,000.

Duration   1 year.

Number awarded   Varies each year; recently, 4 were awarded.

Deadline   June of each year.

[54]
ASIAN AMERICAN COMMUNITY COLLEGE SCHOLARSHIP

Scholarship Administrative Services, Inc.
Attn: MEFUSA Program
13730 Loumont Street
Whittier, CA 90601

Summary   To provide financial assistance to Asian American high school seniors who are interested in attending a community college.

Eligibility   This program is open to Asian American seniors graduating from high schools anywhere in the United States. Applicants must be planning to attend a community college on a full-time basis. Along with their application, they must submit a 1,000-word essay on their educational and career goals, how a community college education will help them to achieve those goals, and how they plan to serve the Asian American community after completing their education. Selection is based on the essay, high school GPA (2.5 or higher), SAT or ACT scores, involvement in the Asian American community, and financial need.

Financial data   The stipend is $5,000 per year.

Duration   1 year; may be renewed 1 additional year if the recipient maintains full-time enrollment and a GPA of 2.5 or higher.

Additional information   This program is sponsored by the Minority Educational Foundation of the United States of America (MEFUSA) and administered by Scholarship Administrative Services, Inc. MEFUSA was established in 2001 to meet the needs of minority students who "show a determination to get a college degree," but who, for financial or other personal reasons, are not able to attend a 4-year college or university. Requests for applications should be accompanied by a self-addressed stamped envelope, the student's e-mail address, and the name of the source where they found the scholarship information.

Number awarded   Up to 100 each year.

Deadline   April of each year.

[55]
ASIAN AMERICAN ESSAY SCHOLARSHIP PROGRAM

OCA Asian Pacific American Advocates-New Jersey Chapter
22 West Grand Avenue
P.O. Box 268
Montvale, NJ 07645-0268
(973) 873-8315   E-mail: nj_oca@yahoo.com
Web: www.oca-nj.com

Summary   To recognize and reward, with college scholarships, high school seniors in New Jersey who are of Asian American descent and submit outstanding essays on Asian American topics.

Eligibility   This competition is open to seniors graduating from high schools in New Jersey who are of Asian American descent. Applicants must be planning to attend a college or university in any state. They must submit a 2-page essay on a topic that changes annually but relates to being an Asian American. They must also provide personal information and a list of extracurricular activities. Selection is based on the essay's theme and content (50%), organization and development (15%), grammar and mechanics (15%), and style (10%); and community service and extracurricular activities (10%).

Financial data   Awards range from $300 to $2,000.

Duration   The competition is held annually.

Additional information   Recently, this program included the Robert E. Wone Memorial Scholarship and the Linda Lee Memorial Scholarship. OCA Asian Pacific American Advocates was previously named the Organization of Chinese Americans. It changed its name in 2014 to reflect its concern for all Asian Americans. Recipients must attend the sponsor's Asian American Heritage Month luncheon in May to accept the award.

Number awarded   Approximately 15 each year.

Deadline   April of each year.

[56]
ASIAN AMERICAN GOVERNMENT EXECUTIVES NETWORK SCHOLARSHIP

Asian American Government Executives Network
1001 Connecticut Avenue, N.W., Suite 320
Washington, DC 20036
(202) 558-7499   Fax: (202) 296-9236
E-mail: programs@aagen.org
Web: www.aagen.org/ScholarshipProg

Summary   To provide financial assistance to Asian American and Pacific Islander high school seniors and undergraduate students who are preparing for a career in government service.

Eligibility   This program is open to high school seniors and current undergraduates who support the sponsor's principles of helping to promote, expand, and support Asian American and Pacific Islander leadership in government. Applicants must submit transcripts and information about courses they plan to take and how those will improve their ability to serve at the local, state, and/or federal level. Selection is based on the relationship of their courses or field of study to service at the local, state, and/or federal government levels; academic achievement and excellence (based on SAT or ACT scores and a GPA of 3.3 or higher); school, employment, or extracurricular activities that demonstrate a seriousness of purpose in serving at leadership principles in government; letters of nomination and recommendation; and essays on their interest in public service. U.S. citizenship or permanent resident status is required.

Financial data Stipends are $1,500 or $1,000.

Duration 1 year; nonrenewable.

Number awarded 4 each year: 2 at $1,500 and 2 at $1,000.

Deadline May of each year.

[57]
ASIAN CORPORATE & ENTREPRENEUR LEADERS SCHOLARSHIPS

Asian Corporate & Entrepreneur Leaders
Attn: Scholarship Committee
P.O. Box 25527
Tempe, AZ 85285-5527
(480) 907-4471   E-mail: info@naaapphoenix.org
Web: www.acelphoenix.org/programs/scholarship-program

Summary To provide financial assistance to Asian American residents of Arizona interested in attending college in the state.

Eligibility This program is open to graduating high school seniors and current college students who are of Asian American descent and Arizona residents. Applicants must be enrolled or planning to enroll full time at a 2- or 4-year public college or university in the state. They must be U.S. citizens or permanent residents. Along with their application, they must submit a 500-word essay about themselves, their intended or current field of study, and their interests, expectations, and goals. Financial need is not considered in the selection process. Preference is given to students majoring in fields other than those of science, technology, engineering, or mathematics (STEM).

Financial data The stipend is $1,000.

Duration 1 year; recipients may reapply.

Additional information Asian Corporate & Entrepreneur Leaders was formerly the Phoenix Chapter of the National Association of Asian American Professionals (NAAAP).

Number awarded 1 or more each year.

Deadline May of each year.

[58]
ASIAN PACIFIC ISLANDER AMERICAN PUBLIC AFFAIRS ASSOCIATION COLLEGE SCHOLARSHIPS

Asian Pacific Islander American Public Affairs Association
Attn: Community Education Foundation
4000 Truxel Road, Suite 3
Sacramento, CA 95834
(916) 928-9988   Fax: (916) 678-7555
E-mail: info@apapa.org
Web: www.apapa.org/programs/youth-leadership

Summary To provide financial assistance to residents of California, especially those of Asian or Pacific Islander ancestry, who are attending college or graduate school in any state.

Eligibility This program is open to residents of California who are currently enrolled as an undergraduate or graduate student at an accredited 2- or 4-year college or university in any state. All students are eligible, but applications are especially encouraged from those who have Asian or Pacific Islander ancestry. They must have a GPA of 2.75 or higher. Along with their application, they must submit a personal statement demonstrating their commitment to the Asian Pacific Islander community. Selection is based on academic achievement, abilities, career goals, civic activities, leadership skills, and demonstrated commitment to the Asian Pacific Islander community. U.S. citizenship or permanent resident status is required.

Financial data The stipend is $1,000. Funds are paid directly to the student's institution.

Duration 1 year; nonrenewable.

Number awarded Varies each year; recently, 14 were awarded.

Deadline February of each year.

[59]
ASIAN REPORTER FOUNDATION SCHOLARSHIPS

Asian Reporter
Attn: AR Foundation
922 North Killingsworth Street, Suite 2D
Portland, OR 97217-2220
(503) 283-0595   Fax: (503) 283-4445
E-mail: arfoundation@asianreporter.com
Web: www.arfoundation.net

Summary To provide financial assistance for college to residents of Oregon and Clark County, Washington who are of Asian descent.

Eligibility This program is open to 2 categories of students: 1) Oregon residents attending Oregon schools of higher education; and 2) residents of Oregon or Clark County, Washington attending schools of higher education in Oregon or Washington. Applicants must be of Asian descent, have a GPA of 3.25 or higher, be a graduating high school senior or current college student working on or planning to work on an undergraduate degree as a full-time student, have a record of involvement in community- or school-related activities, and be able to demonstrate financial need.

Financial data The stipend is $1,000.

Duration 1 year; nonrenewable.

Number awarded Varies each year; recently, 7 were awarded.

Deadline March of each year.

[60]
ASIAN STUDENTS INCREASING ACHIEVEMENT (ASIA) SCHOLARSHIP PROGRAM

Ronald McDonald House Charities
Attn: U.S. Scholarship Program
One Kroc Drive
Oak Brook, IL 60523
(630) 623-7048   Fax: (630) 623-7488
E-mail: info@rmhc.org
Web: www.rmhc.org/rmhc-us-scholarships

Summary To provide financial assistance for college to Asian Pacific high school seniors in specified geographic areas.

Eligibility This program is open to high school seniors in designated McDonald's market areas who are legal residents of the United States and have at least 1 parent of Asian Pacific heritage. Applicants must be planning to enroll full time at an accredited 2- or 4-year college, university, or vocational/technical school. They must have a GPA of 2.7 or higher. Along with their application, they must submit a personal statement, up to 2 pages in length, on their Asian Pacific background, career goals, and desire to contribute to their community; information about unique, personal, or financial circumstances may be added. Selection is based on that statement, high school transcripts, a letter of recommendation, and financial need.

Financial data Stipends are determined by participating McDonald's areas, but most are $1,000 per year. Funds are paid directly to the recipient's school.

Duration 1 year; nonrenewable.

Additional information This program is a component of the Ronald McDonald House Charities U.S. Scholarship Program, which began in 1985. It is administered by International Scholarship and Tuition Services, Inc. For a list of participating McDonald's market areas, contact Ronald McDonald House Charities (RMHC).

Number awarded Varies each year; since RMHC began this program, it has awarded more than $60 million in scholarships.

Deadline January of each year.

[61]
ASIAN WOMEN IN BUSINESS SCHOLARSHIP FUND

Asian Women in Business
42 Broadway, Suite 1748
New York, NY 10004
(212) 868-1368   Fax: (877) 686-6870
E-mail: info@awib.org
Web: www.awib.org

Summary To provide financial assistance for college to Asian women who have demonstrated community leadership or entrepreneurial achievement.

Eligibility This program is open to women who are of Asian or Pacific Island ancestry and are U.S. citizens or permanent residents. Applicants must be enrolled full time at an accredited 4-year undergraduate institution in the United States and have a GPA of 3.0 or higher. They must be able to demonstrate either 1) a leadership role in a community endeavor; and/or 2) a record of entrepreneurial achievement (e.g., founded their own business). Additional funding is available to applicants who can demonstrate financial need.

Financial data The stipend is $2,500. Funds are paid directly to the recipient.

Duration 1 year; nonrenewable.

Additional information This program began in 2006.

Number awarded 4 each year.

Deadline September of each year.

[62]
ASSE DIVERSITY COMMITTEE UNDERGRADUATE SCHOLARSHIP

American Society of Safety Engineers
Attn: ASSE Foundation
Scholarship Award Program
520 North Northwest Highway
Park Ridge, IL 60068-2538
(847) 699-2929   Fax: (847) 296-3769
E-mail: assefoundation@asse.org
Web: foundation.asse.org/scholarships-and-grants

Summary To provide financial assistance to upper-division students who are Asian Americans or members of other diverse groups and working on a degree related to occupational safety.

Eligibility This program is open to students who are working on an undergraduate degree in occupational safety, health, environment, industrial hygiene, occupational health nursing, or a closely-related field (e.g., industrial or environmental engineering). Applicants must be full-time students who have completed at least 60 semester hours and have a GPA of 3.0 or higher. A goal of this program is to support individuals regardless of race, ethnicity, gender, religion, personal beliefs, age, sexual orientation, physical challenges, geographic location, university, or specific area of study. U.S. citizenship is not required. Membership in the American Society of Safety Engineers (ASSE) is not required, but preference is given to members.

Financial data The stipend is $1,000 per year.

Duration 1 year; recipients may reapply.

Number awarded 1 each year.

Deadline November of each year.

[63]
ASSOCIATED CHINESE UNIVERSITY WOMEN SCHOLARSHIPS

Associated Chinese University Women, Inc.
Attn: Shyrlene Lee, Scholarship Committee Chair
46-236 Kalali Street
Kaneohe, HI 96764
E-mail: shylee1@yahoo.com
Web: www.acuwhawaii.org/scholarship

Summary To provide financial assistance to residents of Hawaii who are of Chinese ancestry and interested in majoring in any field at a college in any state.

Eligibility This program is open to residents of Hawaii who are of Chinese ancestry or interested in Chinese culture. Applicants must be enrolled or planning to enroll full time at an accredited 4-year U.S. college or university with the objective of earning a baccalaureate degree in any field. They must have a GPA of 3.8 or higher. Along with their application, they must submit a personal statement on why they should be awarded this scholarship, including their plans for serving their community after graduation. Selection is based on academic achievement (including GPA and SAT score), character, extracurricular activities, school and/or community service, and financial need. U.S. citizenship or permanent resident status is required.

Financial data The stipend is $2,500.

Duration 1 year.

Number awarded Several each year.

Deadline March of each year.

[64]
ASSOCIATED FOOD AND PETROLEUM DEALERS MINORITY SCHOLARSHIPS

Associated Food and Petroleum Dealers
Attn: AFPD Foundation
5779 West Maple Road
West Bloomfield, MI 48322
(248) 671-9600　　　　Toll Free: (800) 666-6233
Fax: (866) 601-9610　　　E-mail: info@afpdonline.org
Web: www.afpdonline.org/michigan-scholarship.php

Summary To provide financial assistance to Asian American and other minority high school seniors and current college students from Michigan who are enrolled or planning to enroll at a college in any state.

Eligibility This program is open to Michigan residents who are high school seniors or college freshmen, sophomores, or juniors. Applicants must be members of 1 of the following minority groups: Asian, African American, Hispanic, Native American, or Arab/Chaldean. They must be enrolled or planning to enroll full time at a college or university in any state. Preferential consideration is given to applicants with a membership affiliation in the Associated Food and Petroleum Dealers (AFPD), although membership is not required. Selection is based on academic performance, leadership, and participation in school and community activities; college grades are considered if the applicant is already enrolled in college.

Financial data The stipend is $1,500 per year.

Duration 1 year; may be renewed 1 additional year.

Additional information This program is administered by International Scholarship and Tuition Services, Inc. The AFPD was formed in 2006 by a merger of the Associated Food Dealers of Michigan and the Great Lakes Petroleum Retailers and Allied Trades Association.

Number awarded At least 10 each year, of which at least 3 must be awarded to member customers.

Deadline March of each year.

[65]
ASSOCIATION OF ASIAN INDIAN WOMEN IN OHIO SCHOLARSHIP

Cleveland Foundation
Attn: Scholarship Processing
1422 Euclid Avenue, Suite 1300
Cleveland, OH 44115-2001
(216) 861-3810　　　　　Fax: (216) 861-1729
E-mail: mbaker@clevefdn.org
Web: www.clevelandfoundation.org

Summary To provide financial assistance to Asian Indian high school seniors in Ohio who plan to attend college in any state.

Eligibility This program is open to graduating high school seniors in Ohio who are of Asian Indian descent. Applicants must be planning to enroll at a college or university in any state. They must have a GPA of 2.0 or higher and be able to demonstrate financial need. Along with their application, they must submit a transcript and a 150-word essay about their goals.

Financial data A stipend is awarded (amount not specified).

Duration 1 year; nonrenewable.

Additional information This program is sponsored by the Association of Asian Indian Women in Ohio.

Number awarded 1 or more each year.

Deadline May of each year.

[66]
ATKINS NORTH AMERICA ACHIEVEMENT COLLEGE SCHOLARSHIP

Conference of Minority Transportation Officials
Attn: National Scholarship Program
100 M Street, S.E., Suite 917
Washington, DC 20003
(202) 506-2917　　　　　E-mail: info@comto.org
Web: www.comto.org/page/scholarships

Summary To provide financial assistance to Asian American and other minority undergraduates interested in working on a degree in transportation or a related field.

Eligibility This program is open to minority students who have completed at least 12 semester hours as full-time undergraduates. Applicants must be studying transportation, engineering, planning, or a related discipline. Along with their application they must submit a cover letter on their transportation-related career goals and life aspirations. Financial need is not considered in the selection process.

Financial data The stipend is $2,000. Funds are paid directly to the recipient's college or university.

Duration 1 year.

Additional information This program is sponsored by Atkins North America.

Number awarded 1 each year.

Deadline April of each year.

[67]
ATKINS NORTH AMERICA ACHIEVEMENT HIGH SCHOOL SCHOLARSHIP

Conference of Minority Transportation Officials
Attn: National Scholarship Program
100 M Street, S.E., Suite 917
Washington, DC 20003
(202) 506-2917　　　　　E-mail: info@comto.org
Web: www.comto.org/page/scholarships

Summary To provide financial assistance to Asian American and other minority high school seniors interested in working on a degree in transportation or a related field.

Eligibility This program is open to minority seniors graduating from high school with a GPA of 3.0 or higher. Applicants must be planning to study aspects of transportation, including technology, engineering, planning, or management. Along with their application they must submit a cover letter on their transportation-related career goals and life aspirations. Financial need is not considered in the selection process.

Financial data The stipend is $2,000. Funds are paid directly to the recipient's college or university.

Duration 1 year.

Additional information This program is sponsored by Atkins North America.

Number awarded 1 each year.

Deadline April of each year.

[68]
ATKINS NORTH AMERICA LEADERSHIP SCHOLARSHIP

Conference of Minority Transportation Officials
Attn: National Scholarship Program
100 M Street, S.E., Suite 917
Washington, DC 20003
(202) 506-2917   E-mail: info@comto.org
Web: www.comto.org/page/scholarships

Summary To provide financial assistance to Asian American and other minority undergraduate and graduate students interested in working on a degree in transportation or a related field.

Eligibility This program is open to minority 1) undergraduates who have completed at least 12 semester hours of study; and 2) graduate students. Applicants must be studying transportation, engineering, planning, or a related discipline. Along with their application they must submit a cover letter on their transportation-related career goals and life aspirations. Financial need is not considered in the selection process.

Financial data The stipend is $3,000. Funds are paid directly to the recipient's college or university.

Duration 1 year.

Additional information This program is sponsored by Atkins North America.

Number awarded 1 each year.

Deadline April of each year.

[69]
ATSUHIKO TATEUCHI MEMORIAL SCHOLARSHIP

Seattle Foundation
Attn: Scholarship Administrator
1200 Fifth Avenue, Suite 1300
Seattle, WA 98101-3151
(206) 515-2119   Fax: (206) 622-7673
E-mail: scholarships@seattlefoundation.org
Web: www.washboard.org

Summary To provide financial assistance to residents of Pacific Rim states who are of Japanese or other Asian ancestry and interested in working on an undergraduate degree at a college in any state.

Eligibility This program is open to residents of Alaska, California, Hawaii, Oregon, and Washington who are graduating high school seniors or undergraduates. Applicants must be attending or planning to attend a public or private community college, 4-year college or university, or trade/vocational school in any state. They must have a GPA of 3.0 or higher, be able to demonstrate financial need, and be of Japanese or other Asian ancestry. Along with their application, they must submit a 500-word essay on the most interesting book they have read and how it influenced them.

Financial data The stipend is $5,000 per year.

Duration 1 year; may be renewed up to 3 additional years.

Number awarded 10 each year.

Deadline February of each year.

[70]
AT&T FOUNDATION APIASF SCHOLARSHIPS

Asian & Pacific Islander American Scholarship Fund
2025 M Street, N.W., Suite 610
Washington, DC 20036-3363
(202) 986-6892   Toll Free: (877) 808-7032
Fax: (202) 530-0643   E-mail: info@apiasf.org
Web: www.apiasf.org/scholarship_apiasf_att.html

Summary To provide financial assistance to Asian and Pacific Islander Americans who are entering college for the first time.

Eligibility This program is open to U.S. citizens, nationals, permanent residents, and citizens of the Freely Associated States who are first-time incoming college students and of Asian or Pacific Islander heritage. Applicants must be enrolling full time at an accredited 2- or 4-year college or university in the United States. They must have a GPA of 2.7 or higher or the GED equivalent. In addition, they must complete the FAFSA and apply for federal financial aid.

Financial data The stipend is $2,500.

Duration 1 year.

Additional information This program is sponsored by the AT&T Foundation and administered by the Asian & Pacific Islander American Scholarship Fund (APIASF).

Number awarded Varies each year; recently, 5 were awarded.

Deadline January of each year.

[71]
AVIATION AND PROFESSIONAL DEVELOPMENT SCHOLARSHIP

Airport Minority Advisory Council
Attn: AMAC Foundation
2001 Jefferson Davis Highway, Suite 500
Arlington, VA 22202
(703) 414-2622   Fax: (703) 414-2686
E-mail: terrifrierson@palladiumholdingsco.com
Web: amac-org.com/amac-foundation/scholarships

Summary To provide financial assistance to Asian American minority high school seniors and undergraduates who are preparing for a career in the aviation industry and interested in participating in activities of the Airport Minority Advisory Council (AMAC).

Eligibility This program is open to minority and female high school seniors and current undergraduates who have a GPA of 2.5 or higher and a record of involvement in community and extracurricular activities. Applicants must be interested in working on a bachelor's degree in accounting, architecture, aviation, business administration, engineering, or finance as preparation for a career in the aviation or airport industry. They must be interested in participating in the AMAC program, including becoming a member if they are awarded a scholarship, and communicating with AMAC once each semester during the term of the scholarship. Along with their application, they must submit a 750-word essay on how they have overcome barriers in life to achieve their academic and/or career goals; their dedication to succeed in the aviation industry and how AMAC can help them achieve their goal; and the most important issues that the aviation industry is facing today and how they see themselves changing those.

Financial need is not considered in the selection process. U.S. citizenship is required.

Financial data   The stipend is $2,000 per year.

Duration   1 year; recipients may reapply.

Number awarded   4 each year.

Deadline   May of each year.

[72]
AWS FOX VALLEY SECTION SCHOLARSHIP

American Welding Society-Fox Valley Section
c/o AWS Foundation, Inc.
8669 N.W. 36th Street, Suite 130
Doral, FL 33166-6672
(305) 443-9353   Toll Free: (800) 443-9353, ext. 250
Fax: (305) 443-7559   E-mail: nprado-pulido@aws.org
Web: www.awssection.org/foxvalley/scholarship

Summary   To provide financial assistance to residents of Wisconsin and the Upper Peninsula of Michigan, especially Asian Americans and members of other underrepresented groups, who are interested in working on a certificate or degree in a welding-related field at a school in any state.

Eligibility   This program is open to residents of Wisconsin and the Upper Peninsula of Michigan who are U.S. citizens and either high school seniors or current undergraduate students. Applicants must be working or planning to work full or part time (preferable full time) on a welding program certificate or college degree focused on welding at a school in any state. They must have a GPA of 2.5 or higher. Financial need is not considered in the selection process. Preference is given to members of groups underrepresented in the welding industry.

Financial data   The stipend is $1,500 per year; funds are paid directly to the educational institution.

Duration   1 year; may be renewed for 1 additional year.

Number awarded   1 each year.

Deadline   February of each year.

[73]
AWS TIDEWATER VIRGINIA SECTION SCHOLARSHIP

American Welding Society-Tidewater Section
c/o Jackie Phillips, Section Chair
Newport News Shipbuilding
4101 Washington Avenue
Newport News, VA 23607
(757) 688-4469 E-mail: jacqueline.a.phillips@hii-nns.com
Web: www.awssection.org/tidewater/scholarship

Summary   To provide financial assistance to residents of Virginia, especially Asian Americans and members of other underrepresented groups, who are interested in working on an undergraduate degree in designated fields related to welding.

Eligibility   This program is open to students working on an associated or bachelor's degree in welding engineering, materials joining engineering, welding engineering technology, or materials joining engineering technology. Priority is given in the following order: first to residents of the Tidewater region of Virginia; second to residents of Virginia; and third to students at LeTourneau University. High school seniors must have a GPA of 2.4 or higher; students already enrolled in college must have a GPA of at least 2.1 overall and 2.3 in their major. Preference is given to full-time students, but part-time students are encouraged to apply if they are also working at a job or have other circumstances that prevent them from enrolling full time. U.S. citizenship is required. Financial need is considered in the selection process. Special consideration is given to applicants who are enrolled in an ABET-accredited program, have a documented working history that includes hands-on welding experience, have successfully completed a high school welding curriculum, or are from a group underrepresented in the welding industry.

Financial data   The stipend is $1,000 per year.

Duration   1 year; may be renewed up to 2 additional years upon reapplication.

Number awarded   1 or more each year.

Deadline   April of each year.

[74]
BEAUTIFUL MINDS SCHOLARSHIP

RentDeals.com
Attn: Scholarships
14173 Northwest Freeway, Suite 190
Houston, TX 77040
Toll Free: (800) 644-5012
Web: www.rentdeals.com/scholarship.php

Summary   To provide financial assistance to Asian American and other minority high school seniors who submit outstanding essays on finding their purpose and plan to attend college.

Eligibility   This program is open to graduating high school seniors who are members of minority groups and have a GPA of 3.0 or higher. Applicants must be planning to enroll at an accredited postsecondary institution and major in any field. Selection is based primarily on an essay on the topic, "Finding My Purpose."

Financial data   The stipend is $1,000.

Duration   1 year.

Number awarded   1 each year.

Deadline   March of each year.

[75]
BERYLE M. CHRISTESEN MEMORIAL SCHOLARSHIP

Hmong American Education Fund
P.O. Box 17468
St. Paul, MN 55117
(651) 592-1576   E-mail: scholarships@thehaef.org
Web: www.thehaef.org

Summary   To provide financial assistance to Hmong undergraduate and graduate students from Minnesota who are working on a degree in education, especially art education.

Eligibility   This program is open to students of Hmong descent who are residents of Minnesota and currently enrolled as full-time undergraduate or graduate students at 2- or 4-year colleges or universities in any state. Applicants must be U.S. citizens or permanent residents and have a GPA of 2.7 or higher. They must be working on a degree in education; preference is given to students preparing for a career in K-12 art education. Along with their application, they must submit a 1,500-word essay on their commitment to education, why they chose to go into education, and their community service. Selection is based on academic achievement.

Financial data The stipend is $1,000.

Duration 1 year; nonrenewable.

Number awarded 1 each year.

Deadline March of each year.

[76]
BILL BERNBACH DIVERSITY SCHOLARSHIPS

American Association of Advertising Agencies
Attn: AAAA Foundation
1065 Avenue of the Americas, 16th Floor
New York, NY 10018
(212) 262-2500   E-mail: bbscholarship@ddb.com
Web: www.aaaa.org

Summary To provide financial assistance to Asian American and other multicultural students interested in working on an undergraduate or graduate degree in advertising at designated schools.

Eligibility This program is open to Asian Americans, African Americans, Hispanic Americans, and Native Americans (including American Indians, Alaska Natives, Native Hawaiians, and other Pacific Islanders) who are interested in studying the advertising creative arts at designated institutions as a full-time student. Applicants must be working on or have already received an undergraduate degree and be able to demonstrate creative talent and promise. They must be U.S. citizens, nationals, or permanent residents. Along with their application, they must submit 10 samples of creative work in their respective field of expertise.

Financial data The stipend is $5,000.

Duration 1 year.

Additional information This program, which began in 1998, is currently sponsored by DDB Worldwide. The participating schools are the Art Center College of Design (Pasadena, California), Creative Circus (Atlanta, Georgia), Miami Ad School (Miami Beach, Florida), University of Oklahoma (Norman, Oklahoma), University of Texas at Austin, VCU Brandcenter (Richmond, Virginia), Savannah College of Art and Design (Savannah, Georgia), University of Oregon (Eugene), City College of New York, School of Visual Arts (New York, New York), Fashion Institute of Technology (New York, New York), and Howard University (Washington, D.C.).

Number awarded 3 each year.

Deadline May of each year.

[77]
BILL DICKEY GOLF SCHOLARSHIPS

Bill Dickey Scholarship Association
Attn: Scholarship Committee
1241 East Washington Street, Suite 101
Phoenix, AZ 85034
(602) 258-7851   Fax: (602) 258-3412
E-mail: andrea@bdscholar.org
Web: www.nmjgsa.org/scholarships.php

Summary To provide financial assistance to Asian American and other minority high school seniors and undergraduate students who excel at golf.

Eligibility This program is open to graduating high school seniors and current undergraduate students who are members of minority groups (Asian/Pacific Islander, African American, Hispanic, or American Indian/Alaskan Native). Applicants must submit a 500-word essay on a topic that changes

annually but relates to minorities and golf. Selection is based on academic achievement, leadership, evidence of community service, golfing ability, and financial need.

Financial data Stipends range from 1-time awards of $1,000 to 4-year awards of $3,500 per year. Funds are paid directly to the recipient's college.

Duration 1 year or longer.

Additional information This sponsor was established in 1984 as the National Minority Junior Golf Association and given its current name in 2006. Support is provided by the Jackie Robinson Foundation, PGA of America, Anheuser-Busch, the Tiger Woods Foundation, and other cooperating organizations.

Number awarded Varies; generally 80 or more each year.

Deadline May of each year.

[78]
BLUECROSS BLUESHIELD OF TENNESSEE COMMUNITY TRUST DIVERSITY SCHOLARSHIP

National Association of Health Services Executives-
    Memphis Chapter
Attn: Selection Committee
P.O. Box 40051
Memphis, TN 38174-0051
E-mail: nahsememphis@gmail.com
Web: www.bcbst.com

Summary This program is open to Asian American and other minority students who are residents of Tennessee working on an undergraduate degree in a field of health care at a college in the state.

Eligibility This program is open to minority residents of Tennessee who are currently enrolled as full-time sophomores or juniors at an accredited college or university in the state. Applicants must be working on a degree in a field of health care and have a GPA of 2.5 or higher. They must be U.S. citizens between 18 and 23 years of age. Along with their application, they must submit a 500-word essay on their particular field of study, why they chose to prepare for a career in health care, and how they plan to use their skills or knowledge to help raise awareness of health issues in their community.

Financial data The stipend is $10,000. Funds are paid directly to the recipient's university.

Duration 1 year.

Additional information This program is sponsored by BlueCross BlueShield of Tennessee in collaboration with the Memphis Chapter of the National Association of Health Services Executives (NAHSE).

Number awarded 3 each year: 1 each for the west, middle, and east region of Tennessee.

Deadline March of each year.

[79]
BONG HAK HYUN MEMORIAL SCHOLARSHIPS

Philip Jaisohn Memorial Foundation
Attn: Scholarship Committee
6705 Old York Road
Philadelphia, PA 19126
(215) 224-2000, ext. 116   Fax: (215) 224-9164
E-mail: info@jaisohn.org
Web: www.jaisohn.com/scholarships

Summary To provide financial assistance to Korean American undergraduate and graduate students who are studying health care or medicine.

Eligibility This program is open to Korean American undergraduate and graduate students who are currently enrolled at a college or university in the United States and working on a degree in health care or a field of medicine. Applicants must be able to demonstrate excellence in community activities and financial need. Along with their application, they must submit an essay on either "Who is Dr. Jaisohn to Me," or "The Significance of Dr. Jaisohn's Ideal to Korean Americans." They must also submit a 100-word statement on how they can contribute to and be involved in the activities of the Philip Jaisohn Memorial Foundation. Selection is based on potential, passion, and leadership.

Financial data The stipend is $1,500.

Duration 1 year.

Number awarded 2 each year.

Deadline August of each year.

[80]
BREAKTHROUGH TO NURSING SCHOLARSHIPS

National Student Nurses' Association
Attn: Foundation
45 Main Street, Suite 606
Brooklyn, NY 11201
(718) 210-0705 Fax: (718) 210-0710
E-mail: nsna@nsna.org
Web: www.nsna.org

Summary To provide financial assistance to Asian American and other minority undergraduate and graduate students who wish to prepare for careers in nursing.

Eligibility This program is open to students currently enrolled in state-approved schools of nursing or pre-nursing associate degree, baccalaureate, diploma, generic master's, generic doctoral, R.N. to B.S.N., R.N. to M.S.N., or L.P.N./ L.V.N. to R.N. programs. Graduating high school seniors are not eligible. Support for graduate education is provided only for a first degree in nursing. Applicants must be members of a racial or ethnic minority underrepresented among registered nurses (Asian, American Indian or Alaska Native, Hispanic or Latino, Native Hawaiian or other Pacific Islander, or Black or African American). They must be committed to providing quality health care services to underserved populations. Along with their application, they must submit a 200-word description of their professional and educational goals and how this scholarship will help them achieve those goals. Selection is based on academic achievement, financial need, and involvement in student nursing organizations and community health activities. U.S. citizenship or permanent resident status is required.

Financial data Stipends range from $1,000 to $2,000.

Duration 1 year.

Additional information Applications must be accompanied by a $10 processing fee.

Number awarded Varies each year; recently, 13 were awarded: 10 sponsored by the American Association of Critical-Care Nurses and 3 sponsored by the Mayo Clinic.

Deadline January of each year.

[81]
BROADCAST NEWS INTERNSHIP GRANTS

Asian American Journalists Association
Attn: Student Programs Coordinator
5 Third Street, Suite 1108
San Francisco, CA 94103
(415) 346-2051, ext. 102 Fax: (415) 346-6343
E-mail: programs@aaja.org
Web: www.aaja.org/apply-for-a-scholarship-now

Summary To provide a supplemental grant to student and other members of the Asian American Journalists Association (AAJA) working as a summer intern at a radio or television broadcasting company.

Eligibility This program is open to AAJA members who are full-time college students or recent college graduates. Applicants must have secured a summer internship at a television or radio broadcasting company before they apply. Along with their application, they must submit a 200-word essay on why they want to prepare for a career in broadcast journalism, what they want to gain from the experience, and why AAJA's mission is important to them; a letter of recommendation; a resume; proof of age (at least 18 years); verification of an internship; and statement of financial need.

Financial data This program includes the Lloyd LaCuesta Scholarship Fund at $1,000 and the Sam Chu Lin Internship Grant at $500. Funds are to be used for living expenses or transportation.

Duration Summer months.

Number awarded 2 each year.

Deadline April of each year.

[82]
BRONSON T.J. TREMBLAY MEMORIAL SCHOLARSHIP

Colorado Nurses Foundation
Attn: Scholarships
P.O. Box 3406
Englewood, CO 80155
(303) 694-4728 Toll Free: (800) 205-6655
Fax: (303) 200-7099 E-mail: mail@cnfound.org
Web: www.coloradonursesfoundation.com/?page_id=1087

Summary To provide financial assistance to Asian American and other non-white male undergraduate and graduate nursing students in Colorado.

Eligibility This program is open to non-white male Colorado residents who have been accepted as a student in an approved nursing program in the state. Applicants may be 1) second-year students in an associate degree program; 2) junior or senior level B.S.N. undergraduate students; 3) R.N.s enrolled in a baccalaureate or higher degree program in a school of nursing; 4) R.N.s with a master's degree in nursing, currently practicing in Colorado and enrolled in a doctoral program; or 5) students in the second or third year of a Doctorate Nursing Practice (D.N.P.) or Ph.D. program. Undergraduates must have a GPA of 3.25 or higher and graduate students must have a GPA of 3.5 or higher. Selection is based on professional philosophy and goals, dedication to the improvement of patient care in Colorado, demonstrated commitment to nursing, potential for leadership, involvement in community and professional organizations, recommendations, GPA, and financial need.

Financial data The stipend is $1,000.
Duration 1 year.
Number awarded 1 each year.
Deadline October of each year.

[83]
BROWN AND CALDWELL MINORITY SCHOLARSHIP

Brown and Caldwell
Attn: HR/Scholarship Program
1527 Cole Boulevard, Suite 300
Lakewood, CO 80401
(303) 239-5400   Fax: (303) 239-5454
E-mail: scholarships@brwncald.com
Web: www.brownandcaldwell.com/Scholarships.asp?id=1

Summary To provide financial assistance to Asian American and other minority students working on an undergraduate or graduate degree in an environmental or engineering field.

Eligibility This program is open to members of minority groups (Asians, African Americans, Hispanics, Pacific Islanders, Native Americans, or Alaska Natives) who are full-time juniors, seniors, or graduate students at an accredited 4-year college or university. Applicants must have a GPA of 3.0 or higher and a declared major in civil, chemical, or environmental engineering or an environmental science (e.g., biology, ecology, geology, hydrogeology). They must be U.S. citizens or permanent residents. Along with their application, they must submit an essay (up to 250 words) on a topic that changes annually but relates to their personal development. Financial need is not considered in the selection process.

Financial data The stipend is $5,000.
Duration 1 year.
Number awarded 1 each year.
Deadline May of each year.

[84]
BUICK ACHIEVERS SCHOLARSHIP PROGRAM

Scholarship America
Attn: Scholarship Management Services
One Scholarship Way
P.O. Box 297
St. Peter, MN 56082
(507) 931-1682   Toll Free: (866) 243-4644
Fax: (507) 931-9168
E-mail: buickachievers@scholarshipamerica.org
Web: www.buickachievers.com

Summary To provide financial assistance to entering and continuing college students, especially Asian Americans and students from other underrepresented groups, who are planning to major in specified fields related to engineering, design, or business.

Eligibility This program is open to high school seniors and graduates who are enrolled or planning to enroll full time at an accredited 4-year college or university as first-time freshmen or continuing undergraduates. Applicants must be interested in majoring in fields of engineering (chemical, computer, controls, electrical, energy, environmental, industrial, manufacturing, materials, mechanical, plastic/polymers, or software); technology (automotive technology, computer information systems, computer science, engineering technology, information technology, mechatronics); design (automotive, fine arts, graphic, industrial, product, transportation); or business (accounting, business administration, economics, ergonomics, finance, human resources, industrial hygiene, international business, labor and industrial relations, management information systems, marketing, mathematics, occupational health and safety, production management, statistics, or supply chain/logistics). U.S. citizenship or permanent resident status is required. Selection is based on academic achievement, financial need, participation and leadership in community and school activities, work experience, and interest in preparing for a career in the automotive or related industry. Special consideration is given to first-generation college students, women, minorities, military veterans, and dependents of military personnel.

Financial data Stipends are $25,000 per year.
Duration 1 year; may be renewed up to 3 additional years (and 1 additional year for students in a 5-year engineering program), provided the recipient remains enrolled full time, maintains a GPA of 3.0 or higher, and continues to major in an eligible field.

Additional information This program, which began in 2011, is funded by the General Motors Foundation.

Number awarded 100 each year.
Deadline February of each year.

[85]
CAIES SCHOLARSHIPS

Chinese American Institute of Engineers and Scientists
Attn: Scholarship Committee
1230 Powell Street
San Francisco, CA 94133
E-mail: caiesscholarship@gmail.com
Web: www.caies.org

Summary To provide financial assistance to Chinese American undergraduates studying architecture, engineering, or science.

Eligibility This program is open to Chinese American undergraduates who have completed at least 60 semester units with a GPA above their school's average. Applicants must be majoring in a field of architecture, engineering, or science. They must be able to demonstrate participation in community service activities and school-related extracurricular activities. Along with their application, they must submit a 500-word essay on their achievements and their awareness of the aims and purposes of the Chinese American Institute of Engineers and Scientists (CAIES).

Financial data Stipends vary but recently were $2,000.
Duration 1 year.
Number awarded Varies each year; recently, 6 were awarded.
Deadline April of each year.

[86]
CALIFORNIA CAPITOL SUMMER INTERNSHIP PROGRAM

Asian Pacific Islander American Public Affairs Association
Attn: Community Education Foundation
4000 Truxel Road, Suite 3
Sacramento, CA 95834
(916) 928-9988   Fax: (916) 678-7555
E-mail: info@apapa.org
Web: www.apapa.org/programs/youth-leadership

Summary To provide summer work experience at an office of state government in Sacramento to undergraduate and graduate student residents of California who are of Asian or Pacific Islander background.

Eligibility This program is open to undergraduate and graduate students who are of Asian or Pacific Islander background and residents of California attending college in the state. Applicants must be interested in a summer internship in Sacramento at an office of state government. They must have a GPA of 2.75 or higher. Along with their application, they must submit a 2-page statement on their Asian or Pacific Islander background, community and public service involvement, academic and career goals, and future plans for public services and/or politics and government involvement. Selection is based on GPA, demonstrated leadership, interpersonal skills, written and verbal communication skills, and community service.

Financial data Interns receive a stipend of $1,000 upon successful completion of the program.

Duration 8 weeks, beginning in June.

Additional information Interns must also complete 40 community service hours for the sponsor's Sacramento chapter.

Number awarded Up to 20 each year.

Deadline February of each year.

[87]
CALIFORNIA PLANNING FOUNDATION DIVERSITY IN PLANNING SCHOLARSHIP

American Planning Association-California Chapter
Attn: California Planning Foundation
c/o Kelly Main
California Polytechnic State University at San Luis Obispo
City and Regional Planning Department
Office 21-116B
San Luis Obispo, CA 93407-0283
(805) 756-2285   Fax: (805) 756-1340
E-mail: cpfapplications@gmail.com
Web: www.californiaplanningfoundation.org

Summary To provide financial assistance to Asian American and other undergraduate and graduate students in accredited planning programs at California universities who will increase diversity in the profession.

Eligibility This program is open to students entering their final year for an undergraduate or master's degree in an accredited planning program at a university in California. Applicants must be students who will increase diversity in the planning profession. Along with their application, they must submit 1) a 500-word personal statement explaining why planning is important to them, their potential contribution to the profession of planning in California, and how this scholar-

ship would help them to complete their degree; 2) a 500-word description of their experience in planning (e.g., internships, volunteer experiences, employment); and 3) a 500-word essay on what they consider to be 1 of the greatest planning challenges in California today. Selection is based on academic performance, increasing diversity in the planning profession, commitment to serve the planning profession in California, and financial need.

Financial data The stipend is $3,000. The award includes a 1-year student membership in the American Planning Association (APA) and payment of registration for the APA California Conference.

Duration 1 year.

Additional information The accredited planning programs are at 3 campuses of the California State University system (California State Polytechnic University at Pomona, California Polytechnic State University at San Luis Obispo, and San Jose State University), 3 campuses of the University of California (Berkeley, Irvine, and Los Angeles), and the University of Southern California.

Number awarded 1 each year.

Deadline March of each year.

[88]
CAMBODIAN HEALTH PROFESSIONALS ASSOCIATION OF AMERICA SCHOLARSHIP

Cambodian Health Professionals Association of America
1025 Atlantic Avenue
Long Beach, CA 90813
(562) 491-9292   Fax: (562) 491-1878
E-mail: admin@chpaa.org
Web: www.chpaa.org/scholarship.html

Summary To provide financial assistance to Cambodian American college students who are preparing for a career in a field of health care.

Eligibility This program is open to Cambodian Americans who are currently enrolled at a college or university in any state. Applicants must be preparing for a career in a field related to health care.

Financial data A stipend is awarded (amount not specified).

Duration 1 year.

Number awarded Varies each year; recently, 4 were awarded.

Deadline Deadline not specified.

[89]
CAMBODIAN SCHOLARSHIP FOR EXCELLENCE

College Now Greater Cleveland, Inc.
Attn: Managed Scholarships
50 Public Square, Suite 1800
Cleveland, OH 44113-2203
(216) 241-5587   Fax: (216) 241-6184
E-mail: info@collegenowgc.org
Web: www.collegenowgc.org

Summary To provide financial assistance to residents of Indiana, Michigan, or Ohio who are of Cambodian heritage and interested in attending college in any state.

Eligibility This program is open to residents of Indiana, Michigan, or Ohio who either were born in Cambodia or who have at least 1 parent born in Cambodia. Applicants must be enrolled or planning to enroll at a college or university in any state. They must have a GPA of 3.0 or higher and be able to demonstrate financial need.

Financial data   The stipend is $1,000 per year.

Duration   1 year; may be renewed, provided the recipient maintains a GPA of 3.0 or higher.

Additional information   This program was established in 2014 with support from the Burton D. Morgan Foundation.

Number awarded   2 each year.

Deadline   June of each year.

[90]
CAMMER-HILL GRANT

Wisconsin Women of Color Network, Inc.
c/o P.E. Kiram
756 North 35th Street, Suite 101
Milwaukee, WI 53208
(414) 899-2329   E-mail: pekiram64@gmail.com

Summary   To provide financial assistance for vocation/technical school or community college to Asian American and other adult women of color from Wisconsin.

Eligibility   This program is open to residents of Wisconsin who are adult women of color planning to continue their education at a vocational/technical school or community college in any state. Applicants must be a member of 1 of the following groups: Asian, African American, American Indian, or Hispanic. They must be able to demonstrate financial need. Along with their application, they must submit a 1-page essay on how this scholarship will help them accomplish their educational goal. U.S. citizenship is required.

Financial data   A stipend is awarded (amount not specified).

Duration   1 year.

Additional information   This program began in 1994.

Number awarded   1 each year.

Deadline   May of each year.

[91]
CANFIT PROGRAM CULINARY ARTS SCHOLARSHIPS

Communities-Adolescents-Nutrition-Fitness
Attn: Scholarship Program
P.O. Box 3989
Berkeley, CA 94703
(510) 644-1533, ext. 112   Toll Free: (800) 200-3131
Fax: (510) 843-9705   E-mail: info@canfit.org
Web: www.canfit.org/scholarships

Summary   To provide financial assistance to Asian American and other minority culinary arts students in California.

Eligibility   This program is open to Asian Americans, American Indians, Alaska Natives, African Americans, Pacific Islanders, and Latinos/Hispanics from California who are enrolled at a culinary arts college in the state. Applicants are not required to have completed any college units. Along with their application, they must submit 1) documentation of financial need; 2) letters of recommendation from 2 individuals; 3) a 1-to 2-page letter describing their academic goals and involvement in community nutrition and/or physical education activities; and 4) an essay of 500 to 1,000 words on a topic related to healthy foods for youth from low-income communities of color.

Financial data   A stipend is awarded (amount not specified).

Number awarded   1 or more each year.

Deadline   March of each year.

[92]
CANFIT PROGRAM UNDERGRADUATE SCHOLARSHIPS

Communities-Adolescents-Nutrition-Fitness
Attn: Scholarship Program
P.O. Box 3989
Berkeley, CA 94703
(510) 644-1533, ext. 112   Toll Free: (800) 200-3131
Fax: (510) 843-9705   E-mail: info@canfit.org
Web: www.canfit.org/scholarships

Summary   To provide financial assistance to Asian American and other minority undergraduate students who are working on a degree in nutrition, culinary arts, or physical education in California.

Eligibility   This program is open to Asian Americans, American Indians, Alaska Natives, African Americans, Pacific Islanders, and Latinos/Hispanics from California who are enrolled in an approved bachelor's degree program in nutrition, culinary arts, or physical education in the state. Applicants must have completed at least 50 semester units and have a GPA of 2.5 or higher. Along with their application, they must submit 1) documentation of financial need; 2) letters of recommendation from 2 individuals; 3) a 1-to 2-page letter describing their academic goals and involvement in community nutrition and/or physical education activities; and 4) an essay of 500 to 1,000 words on a topic related to healthy foods for youth from low-income communities of color.

Financial data   A stipend is awarded (amount not specified).

Number awarded   1 or more each year.

Deadline   March of each year.

[93]
CAPAL FEDERAL INTERNSHIP PROGRAM

Conference on Asian Pacific American Leadership
Attn: Scholarship Committee
P.O. Box 65073
Washington, DC 20035-5073
(877) 892-5427   Fax: (877) 892-5427
E-mail: scholarships@capal.org
Web: www.capal.org

Summary   To provide funding for summer internships with designated federal agencies to Asian Pacific American undergraduate and graduate students.

Eligibility   This program is open to Asian Pacific American (APA) undergraduate and graduate students who are working on a degree in any field. Applicants must be interested in a summer internship at a federal agency; recently, those included the Office of Personnel Management (OPM) and several agencies within the U.S. Department of Agriculture (Rural Development, Forest Service, Agricultural Research Service, and Food Safety and Inspection Service). Along with their application, they must submit a 750-word essay on 2 of the following topics: 1) their long-term career goals and how the summer internship experience will advance those; 2) their previous educational, community work, and internship experiences and how those experiences have influenced their long-term career goals; or 3) how they will use the experiences and knowledge that they gain during their summer in Washington to better serve the APA community and their local community. Selection is based on demonstrated commitment to public service, including service to the APA community; potential to benefit from the internship; demonstrated leadership and potential for continued growth in leadership skills; relevance of the proposed internship to overall public sector goals; academic achievement; and financial need. U.S. citizenship or permanent resident status is required.

Financial data Interns receive $3,000 as a stipend and $500 to help pay travel expenses.

Duration At least 6 weeks during the summer.

Additional information Assignments are available in Washington, D.C. or at sites nationwide.

Number awarded Varies each year; recently, 15 were awarded.

Deadline March of each year.

[94]
CAPAL PUBLIC SERVICE SCHOLARSHIPS

Conference on Asian Pacific American Leadership
Attn: Scholarship Committee
P.O. Box 65073
Washington, DC 20035-5073
(877) 892-5427   Fax: (877) 892-5427
E-mail: scholarships@capal.org
Web: www.capal.org

Summary To provide funding for summer internships in Washington, D.C. to Asian Pacific American undergraduate and graduate students.

Eligibility This program is open to Asian Pacific American (APA) undergraduate and graduate students who have secured an unpaid public sector internship within the Washington, D.C. metropolitan area at a federal government agency, a Capitol Hill legislative office, or a nonprofit organization. Applicants must demonstrate a desire to build skills and develop their commitment to public service and the APA community. Along with their application, they must submit a 750-word essay on 2 of the following topics: 1) their long-term career goals and how the summer internship experience will advance those; 2) their previous educational, community work, and internship experiences and how those experiences have influenced their long-term career goals; or 3) how they will use the experiences and knowledge that they gain during their summer in Washington to better serve the APA community and their local community. Selection is based on demonstrated commitment to public service, including service to the APA community; potential to benefit from the internship; demonstrated leadership and potential for continued growth in leadership skills; relevance of the proposed internship to overall public sector goals; academic achievement; and financial need.

Financial data Awardees receive a stipend of $3,500 to help pay expenses during their internship.

Duration At least 6 weeks during the summer.

Additional information This program began in 1992. Recipients must agree to have a Community Action Plan (CAP) proposed, approved, and presented before their departure from Washington, D.C. at the end of the summer.

Number awarded Varies each year; recently, 7 were awarded.

Deadline March of each year.

[95]
CAPAL-MAASU PUBLIC SERVICE SCHOLARSHIPS

Conference on Asian Pacific American Leadership
Attn: Scholarship Committee
P.O. Box 65073
Washington, DC 20035-5073
(877) 892-5427   Fax: (877) 892-5427
E-mail: scholarships@capal.org
Web: www.capal.org

Summary To provide funding for summer internships in Washington, D.C. to Asian Pacific American undergraduate and graduate students who are attending schools that are members of the Midwest Asian American Students Union (MAASU).

Eligibility This program is open to Asian Pacific American (APA) undergraduate and graduate students who have secured an unpaid public sector internship within the Washington, D.C. metropolitan area at a federal government agency, a Capitol Hill legislative office, or a nonprofit organization. Applicants must demonstrate a desire to build skills and develop their commitment to public service and the APA community. They must be attending an MAASU college or university in Colorado, Illinois, Indiana, Iowa, Kansas, Michigan, Minnesota, Missouri, Nebraska, North Dakota, Ohio, Oklahoma, South Dakota, or Wisconsin. Along with their application, they must submit a 750-word essay on 2 of the following topics: 1) their long-term career goals and how the summer internship experience will advance those; 2) their previous educational, community work, and internship experiences and how those experiences have influenced their long-term career goals; or 3) how they will use the experiences and knowledge that they gain during their summer in Washington to better serve the APA community and their local community. Selection is based on demonstrated commitment to public service, including service to the APA community; potential to benefit from the internship; demonstrated leadership and potential for continued growth in leadership skills; relevance of the proposed internship to overall public sector goals; academic achievement; and financial need.

Financial data The awardee receives a stipend of $3,500 to help pay expenses during the internship.

Duration At least 6 weeks during the summer.

Additional information Recipients must agree to have a Community Action Plan (CAP) proposed, approved, and presented before their departure from Washington, D.C. at the end of the summer.

Number awarded 1 each year.

Deadline March of each year.

[96]
CAPSTONE CORPORATION SCHOLARSHIP AWARD

National Naval Officers Association-Washington, D.C. Chapter
c/o LCDR Stephen Williams
P.O. Box 30784
Alexandria, VA 22310
(703) 566-3840   Fax: (703) 566-3813
E-mail: Stephen.Williams@navy.mil
Web: dcnnoa.memberlodge.com/page-309002

Summary To provide financial assistance to Asian American and other minority high school seniors from the Washington, D.C. area who plan to attend college in any state.

Eligibility This program is open to minority seniors graduating from high schools in the Washington, D.C. metropolitan area who plan to enroll full time at an accredited 2- or 4-year college or university in any state. Applicants must have a GPA of 3.0 or higher and be U.S. citizens or permanent residents. Selection is based on academic achievement, community involvement, and financial need.

Financial data The stipend is $1,000.

Duration 1 year; nonrenewable.

Additional information Recipients are not required to join or affiliate with the military in any way. This program is supported by Capstone Corporation, a minority-owned business incorporated in 1986 by former active-duty Navy officers.

Number awarded 1 each year.

Deadline March of each year.

[97]
CARL A. SCOTT BOOK FELLOWSHIPS

Council on Social Work Education
Attn: Chair, Carl A. Scott Memorial Fund
1701 Duke Street, Suite 200
Alexandria, VA 22314-3457
(703) 683-8080   Fax: (703) 683-8099
E-mail: info@cswe.org
Web: www.cswe.org

Summary To provide financial assistance to Asian American and other ethnic minority social work students in their last year of study for a baccalaureate or master's degree.

Eligibility This program is open to students from ethnic groups of color (Asian American, African American/Black, Hispanic/Latino, Native Hawaiian or other Pacific Islander, or American Indian/Alaska Native) who are in the last year of study for a social work degree in an accredited baccalaureate or master's degree program. Applicants must have a cumulative GPA of 3.0 or higher and be enrolled full time. They must demonstrate a commitment to work for equity and social justice in social work.

Financial data The stipend is $500.

Duration This is a 1-time award.

Number awarded 2 each year.

Deadline May of each year.

[98]
CARMEN E. TURNER SCHOLARSHIPS

Conference of Minority Transportation Officials
Attn: National Scholarship Program
100 M Street, S.E., Suite 917
Washington, DC 20003
(202) 506-2917   E-mail: info@comto.org
Web: www.comto.org/page/scholarships

Summary To provide financial assistance for college or graduate school to members of the Conference of Minority Transportation Officials (COMTO) and their families.

Eligibility This program is open to undergraduate and graduate students who have been members or whose parents, guardians, or grandparents have been members of COMTO for at least 1 year. Applicants must be working on a degree in a field related to transportation and have a GPA of 2.5 or higher. Along with their application they must submit a cover letter on their transportation-related career goals and life aspirations. Financial need is not considered in the selection process.

Financial data The stipend is $3,500. Funds are paid directly to the recipient's college or university.

Duration 1 year.

Number awarded 1 each year.

Deadline April of each year.

[99]
CAROLE SIMPSON RTDNF SCHOLARSHIP

Radio Television Digital News Foundation
Attn: Membership and Programs Manager
529 14th Street, N.W., Suite 1240
Washington, DC 20045
(202) 536-8356   Fax: (202) 223-4007
E-mail: karenh@rtdna.org
Web: www.rtdna.org/content/carole_simpson_scholarship

Summary To provide financial assistance to Asian American and other minority undergraduate students who are interested in preparing for a career in electronic journalism.

Eligibility This program is open to sophomore or more advanced minority undergraduate students enrolled in an electronic journalism sequence at an accredited or nationally-recognized college or university. Applicants must submit a cover letter that discusses their current and past journalism experience, describes how they would use the funds if they were to receive the scholarship, discusses their reasons for preparing for a career in electronic journalism, and includes 3 to 5 links to their best and most relevant work samples.

Financial data The stipend is $2,000, paid in semiannual installments of $1,000 each.

Duration 1 year.

Additional information The Radio Television Digital News Foundation (RTDNF) also provides an all-expense paid trip to the Excellence in Journalism conference held that year. The RTDNF was formerly the Radio and Television News Directors Foundation (RTNDF).

Number awarded 1 each year.

Deadline May of each year.

[100]
CAUSE LEADERSHIP ACADEMY INTERNSHIPS

Center for Asian Americans United for Self Empowerment
Attn: California Asian American Student Internship
  Coalition
260 South Los Robles Avenue, Suite 115
Pasadena, CA 91101
(626) 356-9838   Fax: (626) 356-9878
E-mail: info@causeusa.org
Web: www.causeusa.org/programs/leadership-academy

Summary To provide leadership experience at sites in southern California to college students from any state interested in Asian Pacific Islander American affairs.

Eligibility This program is open to graduating high school seniors and college undergraduates who have a GPA of 3.2 or higher and an interest in Asian Pacific Islander American affairs. Applicants must be interested in participating in a leadership academy that includes an internship placement in the office of an elected official. They should be interested in exploring a career in public office, public service, or community advocacy. Along with their application, they must submit a 1,000-word essay on why they want to become a Center for Asian Americans United for Self Empowerment (CAUSE) intern, how the CAUSE Leadership Academy will help them achieve their goals, and what they would like to gain from the academy. Since all assignments are in southern California, applicants should be residents of the area or prepared to live there during the summer. Selection is based on personal, academic, and extracurricular backgrounds.

Financial data A stipend of $1,500 is paid after completion of the internship.

Duration 9 weeks during the summer.

Additional information This program began in 1991 as the California Asian American Student Internship Coalition (CASIC). Financial support is provided by Southern California Edison and Southwest Airlines.

Number awarded Varies each year.

Deadline January of each year.

[101]
CESDA DIVERSITY SCHOLARSHIPS

Colorado Educational Services and Development
  Association
P.O. Box 40214
Denver, CO 80204
(303) 492-2178   E-mail: Maria.Barajas@colorado.edu
Web: www.cesda.org/#!scholarships/crq5

Summary To provide financial assistance to high school seniors in Colorado who are planning to attend college in the state and are either first-generation college students or Asian American or members of other underrepresented ethnic or racial minorities.

Eligibility This program is open to seniors graduating from high schools in Colorado who are 1) the first member of their family to attend college; 2) a member of an underrepresented ethnic or racial minority (Asian/Pacific Islander, African American, American Indian, Hispanic/Chicano/Latino); and/or 3) able to demonstrate financial need. Applicants must have a GPA of 2.8 or higher and be planning to enroll at a 2- or 4-year college or university in Colorado. U.S. citizenship or permanent resident status is required. Selection is based on leadership and community service (particularly within minority communities), past academic performance, personal and professional accomplishments, personal attributes, special abilities, academic goals, and financial need.

Financial data The stipend is $1,000.

Duration 1 year; nonrenewable.

Number awarded Varies each year.

Deadline March of each year.

[102]
CH2M HILL INDUSTRY PARTNER SCHOLARSHIP

Conference of Minority Transportation Officials
Attn: National Scholarship Program
100 M Street, S.E., Suite 917
Washington, DC 20003
(202) 506-2917   E-mail: info@comto.org
Web: www.comto.org/page/scholarships

Summary To provide financial assistance to Asian American and other minority high school and college students interested in working on a degree in a field related to transportation.

Eligibility This program is open to minority high school seniors and current undergraduates who have a GPA of 3.0 or higher. Applicants must be working on or planning to work on a degree in engineering with a focus on the field of transportation. Along with their application they must submit a cover letter on their transportation-related career goals and life aspirations. Financial need is not considered in the selection process.

Financial data The stipend is $3,000. Funds are paid directly to the recipient's college or university.

Duration 1 year.

Additional information This program is sponsored by CH2M Hill.

Number awarded 1 each year.

Deadline April of each year.

[103]
CHEN-PAI LEE MEMORIAL SCHOLARSHIPS

Chen-Pai Lee Scholarship Fund
P.O. Box 142801
Irving, TX 75014
E-mail: chenpailee.memorialscholarship@gmail.com
Web: www.chen-paileememorialscholarship.com

Summary To provide financial assistance to Taiwanese American high school seniors who plan to attend college in any state and major in any field.

Eligibility This program is open to graduating high school seniors who are Taiwanese descendants or who have at least 1 parent who is a Taiwanese descendant. Applicants must be planning to enroll full time at a 2- or 4-year college or university in any state. Along with their application, they must submit information on their work experience, a list of extracurricular activities, information on their community or volunteer service, and a 3-page essay on 1 of the following topics: 1) how they can contribute to Taiwan's progress to help the country achieve greater freedom and democracy; or 2) how they, as a descendant of Taiwanese immigrants, can contribute to U.S. society and make it better for future generations.

Financial data The stipend is $500.

Duration 1 year.

Number awarded Varies each year; recently, 6 were awarded.

Deadline January of each year.

[104]
CHER YEE LEE AND MA VANG SCHOLARSHIP

Hmong American Education Fund
P.O. Box 17468
St. Paul, MN 55117
(651) 592-1576   E-mail: scholarships@thehaef.org
Web: www.thehaef.org

Summary To provide financial assistance to Hmong residents of Minnesota who come from a large family and are interested in attending college or graduate school in any state.

Eligibility This program is open to residents of Minnesota who identify themselves as a person of Hmong descent and come from a family of 5 or more siblings. Applicants must be high school seniors, GED recipients, or current undergraduate or graduate students enrolled or planning to enroll full time at a 2- or 4-year college or university in any state. They must be U.S. citizens or permanent residents. Along with their application, they must submit transcripts and a 1,500-word essay on their commitment to education; their family, their struggles, and their triumphs; and how coming from a large family influenced their educational goals and overall life.

Financial data The stipend is $1,000.

Duration 1 year; nonrenewable.

Number awarded 1 each year.

Deadline March of each year.

[105]
CHERZONG V. VANG SCIENCE AND ENGINEERING SCHOLARSHIP

Hmong American Education Fund
P.O. Box 17468
St. Paul, MN 55117
(651) 592-1576   E-mail: scholarships@thehaef.org
Web: www.thehaef.org

Summary To provide financial assistance to Hmong residents of Minnesota who are working on an undergraduate or graduate degree in science or engineering at a college in any state.

Eligibility This program is open to residents of Minnesota who identify themselves as a person of Hmong descent. Applicants must be enrolled as full-time undergraduate or graduate students at a 2- or 4-year college or university in any state and working on a degree in science or engineering. They must be U.S. citizens or permanent residents and have a GPA of 3.3 or higher. Along with their application, they must submit transcripts and a 1,500-word essay on their commitment to education, the sciences, and/or engineering; their knowledge of the Hmong people; and their community service. Selection is based on academic achievement.

Financial data The stipend is $500.

Duration 1 year; nonrenewable.

Number awarded 1 each year.

Deadline March of each year.

[106]
CHINESE ACACIA CLUB SCHOLARSHIPS

Chinese Acacia Club
Attn: Scholarship Fund
c/o Fred Lau
P.O. Box 19165
Oakland, CA 94619
(510) 418-1188   Fax: (510) 357-1177
E-mail: pwc3028@att.net

Summary To provide financial assistance to high school seniors in California who plan to attend college in any state.

Eligibility This program is open to seniors graduating from high schools in California who have been accepted at a college or university in any state. Applicants must have a GPA of 3.8 or higher. They must submit a personal statement that covers their academic achievements, community service, extracurricular activities, career goals, and financial need. Semifinalists are invited to an interview in person, by telephone, or via Skype.

Financial data The stipend is $1,000.

Duration 1 year; nonrenewable.

Additional information This sponsor was established in 1946 as a Chinese Masonic club of Free and Accepted Masons under the auspices of the Grand Lodge of California. It began its scholarship program in 1986.

Number awarded Up to 3 each year.

Deadline June of each year.

[107]
CHINESE AMERICAN ASSOCIATION OF MINNESOTA SCHOLARSHIPS

Chinese American Association of Minnesota
Attn: Scholarship Program
P.O. Box 582584
Minneapolis, MN 55458-2584
E-mail: info@caam.org
Web: www.caam.org/scholarships

Summary To provide financial assistance to Minnesota residents of Chinese descent who are interested in attending college or graduate school in any state.

Eligibility This program is open to Minnesota residents of Chinese descent who are enrolled or planning to enroll full time at a postsecondary school, college, or graduate school in any state. Applicants must submit an essay on the role their Chinese heritage has played in their work, study, and accomplishments. Selection is based on academic record, leadership qualities, and community service; financial need is also considered for some awards. Membership in the Chinese American Association of Minnesota (CAAM) is not required. Priority is given to applicants who have not previously received a CAAM scholarship.

Financial data The stipend is $1,000.

Duration 1 year.

Additional information Recipients who are not CAAM members are expected to become members for at least 2 years.

Number awarded 1 or more each year.

Deadline November of each year.

[108]
CHINESE AMERICAN CITIZENS ALLIANCE FOUNDATION ESSAY CONTEST

Chinese American Citizens Alliance
1044 Stockton Street
San Francisco, CA 94108
(415) 434-2222   E-mail: info@cacanational.org
Web: www.cacanational.org/htmlPages/education.html

Summary To recognize and reward high school students of Chinese descent who write outstanding essays on a topic related to Asian Americans.

Eligibility This competition is open to high school students of Chinese descent. Candidates apply through their local lodge of the Chinese American Citizens Alliance and meet at a site arranged by that lodge, usually on the first Saturday in March. They are given a topic and devote the next 2 hours to writing a 500-word essay, in English, on that topic. The topic is assigned at the time of the competition (always relates to the Chinese and Asian American communities). Selection is based on originality, clarity of thought, and expression.

Financial data Prizes are $1,000 for first place, $700 for second place, $500 for third place, and $100 for merit awards.

Duration The competition is held annually.

Number awarded Varies each year; recently, prizes included 1 first place, 1 second place, 1 third place, and 10 merit awards.

Deadline February of each year.

[109]
CHINESE AMERICAN CITIZENS ALLIANCE FOUNDATION SCHOLARSHIPS

Chinese American Citizens Alliance Foundation
Attn: Scholarships
763 Yale Street
Los Angeles, CA 90012
(213) 628-6368   E-mail: cacafoundation@gmail.com
Web: www.cacafoundation.org

Summary To provide financial assistance to Chinese American undergraduate students at colleges and universities in California.

Eligibility This program is open to students of Chinese descent from California who have completed the sophomore year at a college or university in the state. Applicants must provide information on their volunteer work, accomplishments and honors received in college, organizational membership and offices held, previous scholarship awards, career plans, and how they will benefit from the scholarship. Financial need is not considered. Applicants must be available for an in-person interview in Los Angeles.

Financial data The stipend is $1,000.

Duration 1 year.

Additional information This program, which began in 1971, currently includes the following named scholarships: the Yoke Quong Jung Memorial Scholarship, the Huan Lin Cheng Memorial Scholarship, the Y.C. Hong Memorial Scholarship, the Collin and Susan Lai Scholarship, the Julius and Eleanor Sue Scholarship, the Robert and Edith Jung Scholarship, the James Bok Wong and Betty KC Yeow Scholarship, the Stanley and Mary Mu Scholarship, the Tim and Annie Siu Scholarship, the Ming and Josephine Ng Scholarship, and the Edward Jung Lew and Mary Lew Scholarship.

Number awarded 11 each year.

Deadline June of each year.

[110]
CHINESE AMERICAN LIONS CLUB OF ATLANTA SCHOLARSHIP

Asian/Pacific American Council of Georgia, Inc.
3510 Shallowford Road, N.E.
Atlanta, GA 30341
(770) 722-8486   Fax: (678) 717-6502
E-mail: info@apacga.org
Web: www.apacga.org/en/?p=423

Summary To provide financial assistance to members of the Asian/Pacific American Council of Georgia (APAC) who plan to attend college in any state.

Eligibility This program is open to members of the APAC who are graduating high school seniors planning to attend a college or university in any state. Selection is based on overall academic achievement, leadership qualities, extracurricular involvement, and community service.

Financial data The stipend is $1,000.

Duration 1 year.

Number awarded 1 each year.

Deadline March of each year.

[111]
CHINESE AMERICAN MUSEUM NATIONAL ART CONTEST

Chinese American Museum
Attn: Art Competition
125 Paseo de la Plaza, Suite 300
Los Angeles, CA 90012
(213) 473-5306   E-mail: educator@camla.org
Web: www.camla.org/education

Summary To recognize and reward students in grades K-12 who submit outstanding works on art on subjects related to Chinese culture.

Eligibility This competition is open to students in 4 grade-level divisions: K-3, 4-6, 7-9, and 10-12. Applicants must submit original freehand drawings using oil, watercolors, acrylic, crayon, pencil, or other medium. The subject of their work must relate to an assigned topic that changes annually but related to the history, cultural legacy, and continuing contributions of Chinese American. A recent topic for art work was "Delectable Delights."

Financial data In each of the 4 divisions, first place is $300, second $200, and third $100. Grand awards chosen from all entries are $500.

Duration The competition is held annually.

Additional information This competition is jointly sponsored by the Chinese American Citizens Alliance (CACA) and the Chinese American Museum.

Number awarded 14 each year: first, second, and third prizes in each of the 4 divisions plus 2 grand awards.

Deadline April of each year.

[112]
CHIPS QUINN SCHOLARS PROGRAM

Newseum Institute
Attn: Chips Quinn Scholars Program
555 Pennsylvania Avenue, N.W.
Washington, DC 20001
(202) 292-6271　　　　　　　　　Fax: (202) 292-6275
E-mail: kcatone@freedomforum.org
Web: www.newseuminstitute.org

Summary　To provide work experience to Asian American and other minority college students and recent graduates who are majoring in journalism.

Eligibility　This program is open to students of color who are college juniors, seniors, graduate students, or recent graduates with journalism majors or career goals in newspapers. Candidates must be nominated or endorsed by journalism faculty, campus media advisers, editors of newspapers, or leaders of minority journalism associations. Along with their application, they must submit a resume, transcripts, 2 letters of recommendation, and an essay of 200 to 400 words on why they want to be a Chips Quinn Scholar. Reporters and copy editors must also submit 6 samples of published articles they have written; photographers must submit 15 to 25 photographs on a DVD; multimedia journalists and graphic designers should submit 6 to 10 samples of their work on a DVD. Applicants must have a car and be available to work as a full-time intern during the spring or summer. U.S. citizenship or permanent resident status is required. Campus newspaper experience is strongly encouraged.

Financial data　Students chosen for this program receive a travel stipend to attend a Multimedia training program in Nashville, Tennessee prior to reporting for their internship, a $500 housing allowance from the Freedom Forum, and a competitive salary during their internship.

Duration　Internships are for 10 to 12 weeks, in spring or summer.

Additional information　This program began in 1991 in memory of the late John D. Quinn Jr., managing editor of the *Poughkeepsie Journal*. Funding is provided by the Freedom Forum, formerly the Gannett Foundation. After graduating from college and obtaining employment with a newspaper, alumni of this program are eligible to apply for fellowship support to attend professional journalism development activities.

Number awarded　Approximately 70 each year. Since the program began, more than 1,300 scholars have been selected.

Deadline　September of each year.

[113]
CHRISTIAN COLLEGE LEADERS SCHOLARSHIPS

Foundation for College Christian Leaders
2658 Del Mar Heights Road
PMB 266
Del Mar, CA 92014
(858) 481-0848　　　　　　　E-mail: LMHays@aol.com
Web: www.collegechristianleader.com

Summary　To provide financial assistance for college to Christian students from California, Oregon, and Washington, especially Asian Americans and other minorities.

Eligibility　This program is open to entering or continuing undergraduate students who reside or attend college in California, Oregon, or Washington. Applicants must have a GPA of 3.0 or higher, be able to document financial need (parents must have a combined income of less than $75,000), and be able to demonstrate Christian testimony and Christian leadership. Selection is based on identified leadership history, academic achievement, financial need, and demonstrated academic, vocational, and ministry training to further the Kingdom of Jesus Christ. Special consideration is given to minority students.

Financial data　A stipend is awarded (amount not specified).

Duration　1 year; may be renewed.

Additional information　The foundation, formerly known as the Eckmann Foundation, was founded in 1988.

Number awarded　Varies each year.

Deadline　May of each year.

[114]
CHUNGHI HONG PARK SCHOLARSHIPS

Korean-American Scientists and Engineers Association
Attn: Scholarship Committee
1952 Gallows Drive, Suite 300
Vienna, VA 22182
(703) 748-1221　　　　　　　Fax: (703) 748-1331
E-mail: hq@ksea.org
Web: scholarship.ksea.org/InfoUndergraduate.aspx

Summary　To provide financial assistance to women who are undergraduate student members of the Korean-American Scientists and Engineers Association (KSEA).

Eligibility　This program is open to women who are Korean American undergraduate students, are KSEA members, have completed at least 2 semesters as a college student, and are majoring in science, engineering, or a related field. Along with their application, they must submit an essay of 600 to 800 words on a topic that changes annually but relates to science or engineering; recently, students were asked how this scholarship would make a difference in their studies in science and engineering. Selection is based on the essay (25%), KSEA activities and community service (25%), recommendation letters (20%), and academic performance (30%).

Financial data　The stipend is $1,000.

Duration　1 year.

Number awarded　2 each year.

Deadline　March of each year.

[115]
CIC/ANNA CHENNAULT SCHOLARSHIP

Asian American Journalists Association
Attn: Student Programs Coordinator
5 Third Street, Suite 1108
San Francisco, CA 94103
(415) 346-2051, ext. 102　　　　　Fax: (415) 346-6343
E-mail: programs@aaja.org
Web: www.aaja.org/apply-for-a-scholarship-now

Summary　To provide financial assistance to high school seniors and current college students who are studying journalism and demonstrate sensitivity to Asian American and Pacific Islander issues.

Eligibility This program is open to graduating high school seniors and current college students who can demonstrate academic achievement, journalistic ability, commitment to the field of journalism, and sensitivity to Asian American and Pacific Islander issues. Applicants are not required to be members of the Asian American Journalists Association (AAJA), but they must be committed to its mission and they must agree to become a member if they are awarded this scholarship.

Financial data The stipend is $5,000. The winner also receives funding to help cover travel, lodging, and registration costs for attendance at the AAJA national annual convention.

Duration 1 year.

Additional information This program is sponsored by the Council for International Cooperation (CIC). The recipient participates in the Voices student news project at the AAJA convention and is paired with a professional print, online, or broadcast mentor at the convention.

Number awarded 1 each year.

Deadline May of each year.

[116]
CIE/USA-SEATTLE APA SCIENCE, ENGINEERING AND TECHNOLOGY SCHOLARSHIP AWARD PROGRAM FOR COLLEGE STUDENTS

Chinese Institute of Engineers/USA-Seattle Chapter
c/o XiaoXi Wang, Scholarship Chair
Boeing Company
6110 Manor Place
Everett, WA 98203
(425) 404-1253   E-mail: ciescholarship@cie-sea.org
Web: www.cie-sea.org

Summary To recognize and reward Asian Pacific American college students in Washington who have contributed to the fields of science, engineering, and technology.

Eligibility This award is available to students currently enrolled full time at a college or university in Washington who come from a family with an ethnic Asian Pacific background. Self-nominations are accepted, but nominations by teachers and coaches are preferred. Nomination packets must include 1) a 2-page description of applicable science, engineering, or technology projects, accomplishments, or activities; and 2) an essay by the student that includes a description of past volunteer or community service activities, a statement on their Asian Pacific family background, and a paragraph on future plans. Selection is based on that essay (20%), academic achievement (30%), volunteer and community service (25%), and extracurricular activities and accomplishments (25%).

Financial data Awards are $600.

Duration The awards are presented annually.

Number awarded 2 each year.

Deadline June of each year.

[117]
CLAY FORD MINORITY SCHOLARSHIPS

Florida Board of Accountancy
Florida Department of Business and Professional
  Regulation
Attn: Division of Certified Public Accounting
240 N.W. 76th Drive, Suite A
Gainesville, FL 32607-6656
(352) 333-2505   Fax: (352) 333-2508
E-mail: CPA.Applications@dbpr.state.fl.us
Web: www.myfloridalicense.com

Summary To provide financial assistance to Asian American and other minority or female residents of Florida who are entering the fifth year of an accounting program.

Eligibility This program is open to Florida residents who have completed at least 120 credit hours at a college or university in the state and have a GPA of 2.5 or higher. Applicants must be planning to remain in school as a full-time student for the fifth year required to sit for the C.P.A. examination. They must be members of a minority group, defined to include Asian Americans, African Americans, Hispanic Americans, Native Americans, or women. Selection is based on scholastic ability and performance and financial need.

Financial data Stipends range from $3,000 to $6,000 per semester.

Duration 1 semester; may be renewed 1 additional semester.

Number awarded Varies each year; a total of $200,000 is available for this program annually.

Deadline May of each year.

[118]
COCA-COLA FOUNDATION APIASF SCHOLARSHIPS

Asian & Pacific Islander American Scholarship Fund
2025 M Street, N.W., Suite 610
Washington, DC 20036-3363
(202) 986-6892   Toll Free: (877) 808-7032
Fax: (202) 530-0643   E-mail: info@apiasf.org
Web: www.apiasf.org/scholarship_apiasf_cocacola.html

Summary To provide financial assistance to Asian and Pacific Islander Americans who are the first member of their family to attend college.

Eligibility This program is open to U.S. citizens, nationals, permanent residents, and citizens of the Freely Associated States who are of Asian or Pacific Islander heritage and the first member of their immediate family to attend college. Applicants must be enrolling full time at an accredited 2- or 4-year college or university in the United States. They must have a GPA of 2.7 or higher or the GED equivalent. In addition, they must complete the FAFSA and apply for federal financial aid.

Financial data The stipend is $2,500.

Duration 1 year; nonrenewable.

Additional information This program is sponsored by the Coca-Cola Foundation and administered by the Asian & Pacific Islander American Scholarship Fund (APIASF).

Number awarded Varies each year; recently, 51 were awarded.

Deadline January of each year.

[119]
COLGATE "BRIGHT SMILES, BRIGHT FUTURES" MINORITY SCHOLARSHIPS

American Dental Hygienists' Association
Attn: Institute for Oral Health
444 North Michigan Avenue, Suite 3400
Chicago, IL 60611-3980
(312) 440-8900, ext. 244   Fax: (312) 440-6726
E-mail: institute@adha.net
Web: www.adha.org/ioh-associate-certificate-scholarships

Summary   To provide financial assistance to Asian American and other minority students or males of any race who are members of the American Dental Hygienists' Association (ADHA) and enrolled in certificate programs in dental hygiene.

Eligibility   This program is open to members of groups currently underrepresented in the dental hygiene profession (Asians, Native Americans, African Americans, Hispanics, and males) who are student or active members of the ADHA. Applicants must have a GPA of 3.5 or higher and have completed at least 1 year of full-time enrollment in an accredited dental hygiene certificate or associate degree program in the United States.

Financial data   The stipend is $1,250.

Duration   1 year; nonrenewable.

Additional information   These scholarships are sponsored by the Colgate-Palmolive Company.

Number awarded   2 each year.

Deadline   January of each year.

[120]
COLORADO EDUCATION ASSOCIATION MINORITY STUDENT SCHOLARSHIPS

Colorado Education Association
Attn: Ethnic Minority Advisory Council
1500 Grant Street
Denver, CO 80203
(303) 837-1500   Toll Free: (800) 332-5939
Web: www.coloradoea.org

Summary   To provide financial assistance to Asian American and other minority high school seniors in Colorado who are children of members of the Colorado Education Association (CEA) and planning to attend college in any state.

Eligibility   This program is open to seniors graduating from high schools in Colorado who are members of a minority ethnic group, defined to include Asians, American Indians/Alaska Natives, Blacks, Hispanics, Native Hawaiians/Pacific Islanders, and multi-ethnic. Applicants must be the dependent child of an active, retired, or deceased CEA member. They must be planning to attend an accredited institution of higher education in any state. Along with their application, they must submit brief statements on 1) their need for this scholarship; and 2) why they plan to pursue a college education.

Financial data   The stipend is $1,000.

Duration   1 year; nonrenewable.

Number awarded   4 each year.

Deadline   April of each year.

[121]
COMMUNICATIONS INTERNSHIP AWARD FOR STUDENTS OF COLOR

College and University Public Relations and Allied
   Professionals
237 South Fraser Street
P.O. Box 10034
State College, PA 16805-0034
Fax: (814) 863-3428   E-mail: ehanson@cuprap.org
Web: www.cuprap.org/awards/communications-internships

Summary   To provide an opportunity for Asian Americans and other students of color at institutions that are members of the College and University Public Relations and Allied Professionals (CUPRAP) to complete an internship in communications.

Eligibility   This program is open to students of color (i.e., Asian/Pacific Islanders, African Americans, Hispanics/Latinos, and Native Americans) who have completed the first year of college and are enrolled as a degree candidate in the second year or higher. Applicants must obtain and complete a verifiable internship of at least 150 hours in a communications-related field (e.g., print media, radio, television, public relations, advertising, graphic/web design). They must be enrolled full time at an accredited 2- or 4-year college or university that is a member of CUPRAP. Selection is based on financial need, academic ability, communication skills, and creativity as demonstrated through work samples.

Financial data   The stipend is $2,000, paid upon confirmation of employment in an internship position.

Duration   The internship award is presented annually; recipients may reapply.

Additional information   This internship award was first presented in 1983.

Number awarded   1 each year.

Deadline   January of each year.

[122]
COMTO COLORADO SCHOLARSHIPS

Conference of Minority Transportation Officials-Colorado
   Chapter
Attn: Scholarship Committee
1114 West Seventh Avenue
P.O. Box 13582
Denver, CO 80201
E-mail: DrMaryDavis@aol.com
Web: www.comtocolorado.org/scholarship-program

Summary   To provide financial assistance to Asian American and other minority high school seniors in Colorado who are interested in studying a transportation-related field at a college or university in any state.

Eligibility   This program is open to minority seniors graduating from high schools in Colorado with a GPA of 2.5 or higher. Applicants must be planning to attend an accredited college, university, or trade school in any state. They must be planning to major in archaeology and/or cultural resources, architecture, aviation, engineering (chemical, civil, electrical, mechanical, or structural), computer aided design, computer science, construction engineering technology, construction and/or construction management, diesel mechanics, electrical, electronics, environmental science and related fields, geology and/or geotechnical engineering, heating and air conditioning, hydraulic and/or elevator mechanics, public information and outreach programs, security systems, urban planning, or vehicle design and maintenance. Along with their application, they must submit an essay of 500 to 700 words on why they chose their planned field of study, how they think their course work and life experiences have helped them prepare for their college studies and the future, and why they are an excellent candidate for this scholarship. Selection is based on that essay (20%), GPA (15%), participation in career-related activities (10%), letters of recommendation (15%), high school citizenship (15%), and an interview (25%).

Financial data A stipend is awarded (amount not specified). Funds may be used for tuition, books, and/or room and board expenses.

Duration 1 year.

Number awarded Up to 10 each year.

Deadline March of each year.

[123]
CONNECTICUT EDUCATION FOUNDATION SCHOLARSHIPS FOR MINORITY HIGH SCHOOL STUDENTS

Connecticut Education Association
Attn: Connecticut Education Foundation, Inc.
21 Oak Street, Suite 500
Hartford, CT 06106-8001
(860) 525-5641   Toll Free: (800) 842-4316
Fax: (860) 725-6323   E-mail: jeffl@cea.org
Web: www.cea.org/cef/ethnic-minority-scholarship-fund

Summary To provide financial assistance to Asian American and other minority high school seniors in Connecticut who are interested in attending college in the state to prepare for a teaching career.

Eligibility This program is open to minority seniors (Asian or Pacific Islanders, Blacks, Native Americans or Alaskan Natives, and Hispanics or Latinos) graduating from high schools in Connecticut. Applicants have been accepted at an accredited 2- or 4-year college or university in the state and be planning to enter the teaching profession. They must have a GPA of 2.75 or higher. Finalists may be interviewed. Financial need is considered in the selection process.

Financial data The stipend is $2,000 per year.

Duration 1 year; may be renewed.

Number awarded At least 1 each year.

Deadline April of each year.

[124]
CONNECTICUT MINORITY TEACHER INCENTIVE GRANTS

Connecticut Office of Higher Education
Attn: Minority Teacher Incentive Grant Program
61 Woodland Street
Hartford, CT 06105-2326
(860) 947-1855   Toll Free: (800) 842-0229 (within CT)
Fax: (860) 947-1313   E-mail: mtip@ctohe.org
Web: www.ctohe.org/sfa/sfa.shtml

Summary To provide financial assistance and loan repayment to Asian American and other minority upper-division college students in Connecticut who are interested in teaching at public schools in the state.

Eligibility This program is open to juniors and seniors enrolled full time in Connecticut college and university teacher preparation programs. Applicants must be members of a minority group, defined as Asian American, African American, Hispanic/Latino, or Native American. They must be nominated by the education dean at their institution.

Financial data The maximum stipend is $5,000 per year. In addition, if recipients complete a credential and begin teaching at a public school in Connecticut within 16 months of graduation, they may receive up to $2,500 per year, for up to 4 years, to help pay off college loans.

Duration Up to 2 years.

Number awarded Varies each year.

Deadline October of each year.

[125]
CONNECTICUT SOCIETY OF CERTIFIED PUBLIC ACCOUNTANTS DIVERSITY SCHOLARSHIPS

Connecticut Society of Certified Public Accountants
Attn: CTCPA Educational Trust Fund
716 Brook Street, Suite 100
Rocky Hill, CT 06067-3433
(860) 258-0239   Toll Free: (800) 232-2232 (within CT)
Fax: (860) 258-4859   E-mail: jillb@ctcpas.org
Web: www.ctcpas.org/Content/ETF/Apply.aspx

Summary To provide financial assistance to Asian Americans and members of other traditionally underrepresented groups who are upper-division students from Connecticut and majoring in accounting.

Eligibility This program is open to members of groups traditionally underrepresented in accounting. Applicants must be juniors or seniors who are residents of Connecticut and/or currently attending a college or university in that state that is recognized by the Connecticut State Board of Accountancy. They must have a GPA of 3.0 or higher and a major in accounting.

Financial data The stipend is $1,000.

Duration 1 year.

Number awarded 1 each year.

Deadline September of each year.

[126]
CONNTESOL SCHOLARSHIPS

Connecticut Teachers of English to Speakers of Other Languages
P.O. Box 4108
Hamden, CT 06514
E-mail: ConnTESOL@gmail.com
Web: www.conntesol.org

Summary To provide financial assistance to Connecticut residents whose native language is not English and who are attending or planning to attend college in any state.

Eligibility This program is open to residents of Connecticut whose first language is not English. Awards are presented in 4 categories: 1) high school seniors entering a 2-year college; 2) high school seniors entering a 4-year college or university; 3) high school seniors who are presently or were previously enrolled in English Language Learning (ELL) or bilingual education classes and entering a 2- or 4-year college or university (designated the CAPELL Scholarship for its sponsor, the Connecticut Administrators of Programs for English Language Learners); and 4) adult education students entering a college or university. Applicants must submit an essay of 250 to 500 words on how the education they are receiving in the United States is influencing their life.

Financial data   The stipend is $1,000.

Duration   1 year.

Number awarded   At least 4 each year (1 in each category).

Deadline   May of each year.

[127]
COY AND MAE DELL YOUNG SCHOLARSHIP

National Naval Officers Association-Washington, D.C.
   Chapter
c/o LCDR Stephen Williams
P.O. Box 30784
Alexandria, VA 22310
(703) 566-3840   Fax: (703) 566-3813
E-mail: Stephen.Williams@Navy.mil
Web: dcnnoa.memberlodge.com/page-309002

Summary   To provide financial assistance to Asian American and other minority high school seniors from the Washington, D.C. area who are interested in attending college in any state.

Eligibility   This program is open to minority seniors graduating from high schools in the Washington, D.C. metropolitan area who plan to enroll full time at an accredited 2- or 4-year college or university in any state. Applicants must have a GPA of 2.7 or higher and be U.S. citizens or permanent residents. Selection is based on academic achievement, community involvement, and financial need.

Financial data   The stipend is $1,000.

Duration   1 year; nonrenewable.

Additional information   Recipients are not required to join or affiliate with the military in any way.

Number awarded   1 each year.

Deadline   March of each year.

[128]
CUBA WADLINGTON, JR. AND MICHAEL P. JOHNSON SCHOLARSHIP

Tulsa Community Foundation
Attn: Scholarships
7030 South Yale Avenue, Suite 600
Tulsa, OK 74136
(918) 494-8823   Fax: (918) 494-9826
E-mail: scholarships@tulsacf.org
Web: www.tulsacf.org/whatwedo/education/scholarships

Summary   To provide financial assistance to upper-division students at colleges in any state who are Asian Americans or members of other underrepresented groups in the energy industry.

Eligibility   This program is open to students entering their junior or senior year at a college or university in any state and preparing for a career in the energy industry with a major in accounting, engineering, finance, or technology. Applicants must be members of a group underrepresented in the energy industry (women and ethnic minorities). They must have a GPA of 3.0 or higher. Along with their application, they must submit a 2-page personal essay that includes their future or academic career goals, any adversity or challenge they have

overcome or anticipate in pursuit of their educational goals, and the importance of diversity in the workplace and how dealing with diversity in their own life has shaped them. Financial need is not considered in the selection process.

Financial data   The stipend is $2,000. Funds are paid directly to the university.

Duration   1 year; nonrenewable.

Additional information   This program is supported by the Williams Companies of Tulsa, Oklahoma.

Number awarded   Varies each year.

Deadline   June of each year.

[129]
DAMON P. MOORE SCHOLARSHIP

Indiana State Teachers Association
Attn: Scholarships
150 West Market Street, Suite 900
Indianapolis, IN 46204-2875
(317) 263-3400   Toll Free: (800) 382-4037
Fax: (800) 777-6128   E-mail: mshoup@ista-in.org
Web: www.ista-in.org/damon-p-moore-scholarship

Summary   To provide financial assistance to Asian American and other ethnic minority high school seniors in Indiana who are interested in studying education at a college in any state.

Eligibility   This program is open to ethnic minority public high school seniors in Indiana who are interested in studying education in college. Selection is based on academic achievement, leadership ability as expressed through co-curricular activities and community involvement, recommendations, and a 300-word essay on their educational goals and how they plan to use this scholarship.

Financial data   The stipend is $1,000.

Duration   1 year; may be renewed for 3 additional years if the recipient maintains at least a "C+" average and continues to pursue a teaching credential.

Additional information   This program began in 1987.

Number awarded   1 each year.

Deadline   February of each year.

[130]
DARDEN RESTAURANTS FOUNDATION APIASF SCHOLARSHIPS

Asian & Pacific Islander American Scholarship Fund
2025 M Street, N.W., Suite 610
Washington, DC 20036-3363
(202) 986-6892   Toll Free: (877) 808-7032
Fax: (202) 530-0643   E-mail: info@apiasf.org
Web: www.apiasf.org/scholarship_apiasf_darden.html

Summary   To provide financial assistance to Asian and Pacific Islander Americans who are entering college for the first time, especially those planning to major in hospitality management or culinary arts.

Eligibility   This program is open to U.S. citizens, nationals, and permanent residents who live in designated metropolitan areas (Atlanta, Boston, Charlotte, Chicago, Cleveland, Dallas, Denver, Detroit, Houston, Jacksonville, Kansas City, Los Angeles, Miami/Fort Lauderdale, Nashville, New York, Orlando, Philadelphia, Phoenix, Pittsburgh, Salt Lake City, San Antonio, San Francisco, Seattle, Tampa, or Washington, D.C.). Applicants must be first-time incoming college students of Asian or Pacific Islander heritage who are enrolling full time at an accredited 2- or 4-year college or university in the United States. They must have a GPA of 3.0 or higher or the GED equivalent. In addition, they must complete the FAFSA and apply for federal financial aid. Special consideration is given to applicants planning to major in hospitality management or culinary arts.

Financial data   The stipend is $2,500 per year.

Duration   2 years.

Additional information   This program is sponsored by Darden Restaurants and administered by the Asian & Pacific Islander American Scholarship Fund (APIASF).

Number awarded   Varies each year; recently, 2 were awarded.

Deadline   January of each year.

[131]
DAVID IBATA PRINT SCHOLARSHIP

Asian American Journalists Association-Chicago Chapter
c/o Lorene Yue
Crain's Chicago Business
150 North Michigan Avenue, 16th Floor
Chicago, IL 60601
E-mail: chicagoaaja@gmail.com
Web: www.aajachicago.wordpress.com

Summary   To provide funding to members of the Asian American Journalists Association (AAJA) who are interested in a summer internship at a Chicago publication.

Eligibility   This program is open to AAJA members who are college sophomores, juniors, seniors, graduate students or recent graduates. Applicants must be interested in an internship at Crain's Chicago Business. Along with their application, they must submit a resume that includes their job experience in journalism and 5 clips.

Financial data   AAJA-Chicago awards a $2,500 stipend for the internship and Crain's Chicago Business matches that with a grant of $2,500.

Duration   10 to 12 weeks during the summer.

Number awarded   1 each year.

Deadline   December of each year.

[132]
DAVID SANKEY MINORITY SCHOLARSHIP IN METEOROLOGY

National Weather Association
Attn: Executive Director
3100 Monitor Avenue, Suite 123
Norman, OK 73072
(405) 701-5167   Fax: (405) 701-5227
E-mail: exdir@nwas.org
Web: www.nwas.org

Summary   To provide financial assistance to Asian Americans and members of other underrepresented groups working on an undergraduate or graduate degree in meteorology.

Eligibility   This program is open to members of underrepresented ethnic groups who are either entering their sophomore or higher year of undergraduate study or enrolled as graduate students. Applicants must be working on a degree in meteorology. Along with their application, they must submit a 1-page statement explaining why they are applying for this scholarship. Selection is based on that statement, academic achievement, and 2 letters of recommendation.

Financial data   The stipend is $1,000.

Duration   1 year.

Additional information   This program began in 2002.

Number awarded   1 each year.

Deadline   April of each year.

[133]
DBT JUDO DOJO SENSEI MEMORIAL SCHOLARSHIP

Japanese American Community Graduation Program
P.O. Box 13665
Denver, CO 80201-3665
(303) 288-6083
Web: www.jacgp.com

Summary   To provide financial assistance to high school seniors of Japanese descent in the Rocky Mountain region who have participated in judo or other martial art and plan to attend college in any state.

Eligibility   This program is open to graduating high school seniors 1) who are residing in the Rocky Mountain region and an American citizen of Japanese ancestry or an American citizen whose legal parents are of Japanese ancestry; or 2) who are of Japanese ancestry residing in the Rocky Mountain region and have permanent residence status (green card) in the United States; or 3) who have a parent who is an active member of: Mile High Chapter of Japanese American Citizens League (JACL), Japanese American Association of Colorado, Nisei Veterans' Heritage Foundation, Simpson United Method Church, Tri-State/Denver Buddhist Temple, Denver Nisei Bowling Association, Brighton Japanese American Association, Japan Firms Association of Colorado, Sakura Foundation, Longmont Buddhist Temple, or Fort Lupton JACL. Applicants must be planning to attend a college or university in any state. They must have been associated with a recognized martial arts program. Along with their application, they must submit a 1-page essay on how the philosophy taught in their martial art classes guides them in the way they intend to live their life. Selection is based on that essay; longevity of enrollment, participation, and volunteerism in a martial art; school records; and school and community activities and awards.

Financial data   Stipends up to $5,000 are available.

Duration   1 year.

Additional information   This program is sponsored by the Denver Buddhist Temple (DBT) in honor of the Senseis who have taught or promoted the sport of judo in the community and the Rocky Mountain region.

Number awarded   1 each year.

Deadline   April of each year.

[134]
DELAWARE ATHLETIC TRAINERS' ASSOCIATION ETHNIC DIVERSITY ADVISORY COMMITTEE SCHOLARSHIP

Delaware Athletic Trainers' Association
c/o Education Committee Chair
University of Delaware
159 Fred Rust Ice Arena
Newark, DE 19716
(302) 831-6402   E-mail: kaminski@udel.edu
Web: www.delata.org/scholarship-applications.html

Summary To provide financial assistance to Asian American and other ethnic minority members of the National Athletic Trainers' Association (NATA) from Delaware who are working on an undergraduate or graduate degree in the field.

Eligibility This program is open to NATA members who are members of ethnic diversity groups and residents of Delaware or attending college in that state. Applicants must be enrolled full time in an undergraduate athletic training education program or a graduate athletic training program and have a GPA of 2.5 or higher. They must intend to prepare for the profession of athletic training. Along with their application, they must submit an 800-word statement on their athletic training background, experience, philosophy, and goals. Selection is based equally on academic performance and athletic training clinical achievement.

Financial data A stipend is awarded (amount not specified).

Duration 1 year.

Number awarded 1 or more each year.

Deadline February of each year.

[135]
DIGITASLBI MULTICULTURAL SCHOLARSHIP

American Association of Advertising Agencies
Attn: AAAA Foundation
1065 Avenue of the Americas, 16th Floor
New York, NY 10018
(212) 262-2500   E-mail: ameadows@aaaa.org
Web: www.aaaa.org

Summary To provide financial assistance to Asian American and other multicultural students who are working on an undergraduate degree in advertising.

Eligibility This program is open to undergraduate students of proven multicultural heritage. Applicants must be participating in the Multicultural Advertising Intern Program (MAIP). They must be enrolled at an accredited college or university in the United States and be able to demonstrate financial need.

Financial data The stipend is $5,000.

Duration 1 year.

Additional information This program is funded by DigitasLBi.

Number awarded 1 each year.

Deadline July of each year.

[136]
DISTINGUISHED RAVEN FAC MEMORIAL SCHOLARSHIPS

Edgar Allan Poe Literary Society
Attn: Raven Scholarship
4320 Saddle Ridge Trail
Flower Mound, TX 75028
E-mail: spikemilam@verizon.net
Web: www.ravens.org/scholar/scholarship.htm

Summary To provide financial assistance to descendants of Lao or Hmong individuals who served alongside Forward Air Controllers (FACs) in Laos between 1960 and 1975 and are interested in attending college.

Eligibility This program is open to high school seniors and graduates who are enrolled or planning to enroll full time at an accredited college, university, or junior college and work on an associate or bachelor's degree in any field. Applicants must be descendants of Lao or Hmong individuals who lived in Laos between 1960 and 1975 and served alongside FACs who flew under the call sign "Raven" or its predecessor "Butterfly." Along with their application, they must submit transcripts (including SAT and/or ACT scores), information on their extracurricular activities (including Lao/Hmong cultural activities), and a 500-word essay describing their goals. Selection is based on that essay, academic achievement, character, and service beyond self.

Financial data Stipends range from $500 to $2,500 per year.

Duration 1 year.

Additional information This program includes the Charles E. Engle Memorial Scholarship, the Gomer D. Reese, III Memorial Scholarship, the Henry L. Allen Memorial Scholarship, the James E. Cross Memorial Scholarship, the John A. Davidson, II Memorial Scholarship, the Joseph L. Chestnut Memorial Scholarship, the Park G. Bunker Memorial Scholarship, the Paul E. Williams Memorial Scholarship, the Richard G. Elzinga Memorial Scholarship, and the W. Grant Uhls Memorial Scholarship.

Number awarded Varies each year; recently, 10 were awarded: 1 at $2,500, 1 at $1,500, 4 at $1,000, and 4 at $500.

Deadline February of each year.

[137]
DIVERSITY IN PSYCHOLOGY AND LAW RESEARCH AWARD

American Psychological Association
Attn: Division 41 (American Psychology-Law Society)
c/o Kathy Gaskey, Administrative Officer
P.O. Box 11488
Southport, NC 28461-3936
(910) 933-4018   Fax: (910) 933-4018
E-mail: apls@ec.rr.com
Web: www.apadivisions.org

Summary To provide funding to student members of the American Psychology-Law Society (AP-LS) who are interested in conducting a research project related to diversity.

Eligibility This program is open to undergraduate and graduate student members of AP-LS who are interested in conducting research on issues related to psychology, law, multiculturalism, and/or diversity (e.g., research pertaining to psycholegal issues on race, gender, culture, sexual orientation). Students from underrepresented groups are strongly encouraged to apply; underrepresented groups include, but are not limited to: racial and ethnic minorities; first-generation college students; lesbian, gay, bisexual, and transgender students; and students with physical disabilities. Applicants must submit a project description that includes a statement of the research problem, the project's likely impact on the field of psychology and law broadly, methodology, budget, and an overview of relevant literature. Selection is based on the impact of the project on diversity and multiculturalism and the expected completion within the allocated time.

Financial data   The grant is $1,000.

Duration   The project must be completed within 1 year.

Number awarded   Up to 5 each year.

Deadline   November of each year.

[138]
DIVERSITY SUMMER HEALTH-RELATED RESEARCH EDUCATION PROGRAM

Medical College of Wisconsin
Attn: Office of Student Diversity Affairs
8701 Watertown Plank Road
Milwaukee, WI 53226
(414) 955-8735   Fax: (414) 955-0129
E-mail: studentdiversity@mcw.edu
Web: www.mcw.edu/Diversity-Programs.htm

Summary   To provide an opportunity for undergraduate residents of any state who are Hmong or come from other diverse backgrounds to participate in a summer research training experience at the Medical College of Wisconsin.

Eligibility   This program is open to U.S. citizens and permanent residents who come from an ethnically, economically, and/or educationally disadvantaged backgrounds. The program targets Hmong, African Americans, Mexican-Americans, Native Americans (American Indians, Alaska Natives, and Native Hawaiians), Pacific Islanders, mainland Puerto Ricans, and individuals with disabilities. Applicants must be interested in participating in a summer research training program at the Medical College of Wisconsin. They must have completed at least 1 year of undergraduate study at an accredited college or university (or be a community college student enrolled in at least 3 courses per academic term) and have a GPA of 3.4 or higher.

Financial data   The stipend is $10 per hour for a 40-hour week. Housing is provided for students who live outside Milwaukee County and travel expenses are paid for those who live outside Wisconsin.

Duration   10 weeks during the summer.

Additional information   Students are "matched" with a full-time faculty investigator to participate in a research project addressing the causes, prevention, and treatment of cardiovascular, pulmonary, or hematological diseases. This program is funded by the National Heart, Lung, and Blood Institute (NHLBI) of the National Institutes of Health (NIH). Participants are required to prepare an abstract of their research and make a brief oral presentation of their project at the conclusion of the summer.

Number awarded   Approximately 12 each year.

Deadline   January of each year.

[139]
DIVISION OF PHYSICAL SCIENCES RESEARCH EXPERIENCE FOR UNDERGRADUATES

American Museum of Natural History
Attn: Division of Physical Sciences
Central Park West at 79th Street
New York, NY 10024-5192
(212) 769-5055   E-mail: Fellowships-rggs@amnh.org
Web: www.amnh.org

Summary   To provide an opportunity for Asian American and other undergraduate students to gain research experience in designated physical sciences during the summer at the American Museum of Natural History in New York City.

Eligibility   This program is open to U.S. citizens and permanent residents who are currently working on a bachelor's degree. Applicants must be interested in participating in a research project at the American Museum of Natural History in the fields of earth and planetary sciences or astrophysics. Applications are especially encouraged from students who attend minority-serving institutions.

Financial data   Participants receive a stipend of approximately $5,100, dormitory housing on a nearby university campus or an equivalent housing stipend, a subsistence allowance, and (depending on need) reimbursement of travel costs to and from New York.

Duration   Approximately 10 weeks during the summer.

Additional information   This program is sponsored by the National Science Foundation as part of its Research Experiences for Undergraduates (REU) program.

Number awarded   Approximately 8 each year.

Deadline   January of each year.

[140]
DOMINION DIVERSITY SCHOLARSHIP PROGRAM

Dominion Resources Inc.
Attn: Diversity Team
701 East Cary Street, 13th Floor
Richmond, VA 23219
(804) 819-2000   E-mail: diversity@dom.com
Web: www.dom.com

Summary   To provide financial assistance and work experience to Asian American and other high school seniors and college students who will contribute to the diversity of the sponsor.

Eligibility   This program is open to high school seniors and current college students who will not graduate for at least 2 years. Community college students must be enrolled in a program that will prepare them to transfer to a 4-year institution. Applicants must commit to a paid intern work session during the summer following their first year of scholarship support. Along with their application, they must submit an essay of 1,000 to 1,250 words that 1) describes the experiences or ideas they would bring to the diversity of the sponsor; 2) includes the new perspectives or new talents they will contribute to the sponsor; and 3) describes how this diversity scholarship program will help them achieve their career goals. The sponsor defines diversity to include minorities, women, protected veterans, and individuals with disabilities.

Financial data   The scholarship stipend is $5,000. A competitive salary is paid for the internship.

Duration 1 year for the scholarship; 10 to 12 weeks during the summer for the internship.

Additional information The sponsor operates electric distribution and transmission companies in North Carolina and Virginia and natural gas distribution companies in Ohio and West Virginia.

Number awarded 30 each year.

Deadline May of each year.

[141]
DON SAHLI–KATHY WOODALL MINORITY STUDENT SCHOLARSHIP

Tennessee Education Association
Attn: Sahli-Woodall Scholarship Fund
801 Second Avenue North
Nashville, TN 37201-1099
(615) 242-8392   Toll Free: (800) 342-8367
Fax: (615) 259-4581   E-mail: jdemain@tea.nea.org
Web: www.teateachers.org

Summary To provide financial assistance to Asian American and other minority high school seniors in Tennessee who are interested in majoring in education at a college or university in the state.

Eligibility This program is open to minority high school seniors in Tennessee who are planning to attend a college or university in the state and major in education. Application must be made either by a Future Teachers of America chapter affiliated with the Tennessee Education Association (TEA) or by the student with the recommendation of an active TEA member. Selection is based on academic record, leadership ability, financial need, and demonstrated interest in becoming a teacher.

Financial data The stipend is $1,000.

Duration 1 year.

Number awarded 1 each year.

Deadline February of each year.

[142]
DOUVAS MEMORIAL SCHOLARSHIP

Wyoming Department of Education
Attn: Standards and Accountability
2300 Capitol Avenue, Second Floor
Cheyenne, WY 82002-0050
(307) 777-3793   Fax: (307) 777-6234
E-mail: stephanie.brady@wyo.gov
Web: edu.wyoming.gov

Summary To provide financial assistance to high school seniors or students in Wyoming who are Asian Americans or other first-generation Americans.

Eligibility This program is open to first-generation youth in Wyoming who demonstrate need and are motivated to attend college. First-generation Americans are those born in the United States but whose parents were not born here. Applicants must be high school seniors or between the ages of 18 and 22. They must be Wyoming residents and be willing to use the scholarship at Wyoming's community colleges or the University of Wyoming.

Financial data The stipend is $500, payable in 2 equal installments. Funds are paid directly to the recipient's school.

Duration 1 year.

Additional information This program began in 1995.

Number awarded 2 each year.

Deadline May of each year.

[143]
DR. JO ANN OTA FUJIOKA SCHOLARSHIP

Phi Delta Kappa International
Attn: PDK Educational Foundation
320 West Eighth Street, Suite 216
P.O. Box 7888
Bloomington, IN 47407-7888
(812) 339-1156   Toll Free: (800) 766-1156
Fax: (812) 339-0018   E-mail: scholarships@pdkintl.org
Web: www.pdkintl.org

Summary To provide financial assistance to Asian American and other high school seniors and undergraduates of color who plan to study education at a college in any state and have a connection to Phi Delta Kappa (PDK).

Eligibility This program is open to high school seniors and undergraduates of color who are majoring or planning to major in education and can meet 1 of the following criteria: 1) is a member of Educators Rising (formerly the Future Educators Association); 2) is the child or grandchild of a PDK member; or 3) has a reference letter written by a PDK member. Also eligible are undergraduate members of PDK or Educators Rising who are enrolled in a college education program. Applicants must submit a 500-word essay on a topic related to education that changes annually. Selection is based on the essay, academic standing, letters of recommendation, service activities, educational activities, and leadership activities; financial need is not considered.

Financial data The stipend is $2,000.

Duration 1 year.

Additional information This program began in 2006.

Number awarded 1 each year.

Deadline March of each year.

[144]
DR. KOU BLIAXA AND SONG VANG ANY DISCIPLINE SCHOLARSHIP

Hmong American Education Fund
P.O. Box 17468
St. Paul, MN 55117
(651) 592-1576   E-mail: scholarships@thehaef.org
Web: www.thehaef.org

Summary To provide financial assistance to Hmong undergraduate and graduate students from Minnesota who are working on a degree in any field.

Eligibility This program is open to students of Hmong descent who are residents of Minnesota and currently enrolled as full-time undergraduate or graduate students at 2- or 4-year colleges or universities in any state. Applicants must be U.S. citizens or permanent residents and have a GPA of 3.0 or higher. They may be working on a degree in any field. Along with their application, they must submit a 1,500-word essay on their commitment to education, their financial need, how this scholarship can help them, and their community service.

Financial data The stipend is $500.

Duration 1 year; nonrenewable.

Number awarded 1 each year.

Deadline March of each year.

[145]
DR. MARTIN LUTHER KING, JR. SCHOLARSHIP

North Carolina Association of Educators, Inc.
Attn: Human and Civil Rights Commission
700 South Salisbury Street
P.O. Box 27347
Raleigh, NC 27611-7347
(919) 832-3000, ext. 203
Toll Free: (800) 662-7924, ext. 203
Fax: (919) 839-8229   E-mail: derevana.leach@ncae.org
Web: www.ncae.org/get-involved/awards

Summary To provide financial assistance to Asian American and other high school seniors in North Carolina who plan to attend college in any state.

Eligibility This program is open to seniors graduating from high schools in North Carolina who plan to attend a college or university in any state. They must have a GPA of 2.5 or higher. Along with their application, they must submit 1-page essays on 1) how the philosophies and ideals of Dr. Martin Luther King influenced their life; and 2) why they feel they deserve this scholarship and their need for financial assistance. Selection is based on those essays; academic record; a resume of accomplishments, extracurricular activities, scholarships, affiliations, and organizations; and 2 letters of recommendation.

Financial data A stipend is awarded (amount not specified).

Duration 1 year.

Additional information This program was established in 1992 by the Minority Affairs Commission of the North Carolina Association of Educators (NCAE). It currently operates in partnership with the North Carolina Foundation for Public School Children.

Number awarded 1 or more each year.

Deadline January of each year.

[146]
DWIGHT MOSLEY SCHOLARSHIPS

United States Tennis Association
Attn: USTA Foundation
70 West Red Oak Lane
White Plains, NY 10604
(914) 696-7223   Fax: (914) 697-2307
E-mail: foundation@usta.com
Web: www.ustafoundation.com

Summary To provide financial assistance to female and male high school seniors (judged separately) who are Asian Americans or members of other diverse ethnic groups, have participated in an organized community tennis program, and plan to attend college in any state.

Eligibility This program is open to high school seniors from diverse ethnic backgrounds who have excelled academically, demonstrated achievements in leadership, and participated extensively in an organized community tennis program. Applicants must be planning to enroll as a full-time undergraduate student at a 4-year college or university. They must have a GPA of 3.0 or higher and be able to demonstrate financial need and sportsmanship. Along with their application, they must submit an essay of 1 to 2 pages about how their participation in a tennis and education program has influenced their life, including examples of special mentors, volunteer service,

and future goals. Females and males are considered separately.

Financial data The stipend is $2,500 per year. Funds are paid directly to the recipient's college or university.

Duration 4 years.

Number awarded 2 each year: 1 female and 1 male.

Deadline February of each year.

[147]
EASTERN REGION KOREAN AMERICAN COLLEGE/GRADUATE SCHOLARSHIPS

Korean American Scholarship Foundation
Eastern Region
1952 Gallows Road, Suite 310
Vienna, VA 22182
(703) 748-5935   Fax: (703) 748-1874
E-mail: erc.scholarship@kasf.org
Web: www.kasf.org/eastern

Summary To provide financial assistance to Korean American students from any state who are working on an undergraduate or graduate degree in any field at a school in eastern states.

Eligibility This program is open to Korean Americans who are high school seniors or full-time undergraduate or graduate students currently enrolled or planning to enroll at a college or university in an eastern state. Applicants may reside anywhere in the United States, provided they attend school in the sponsor's eastern region: Delaware, District of Columbia, Indiana, Kentucky, Maryland, North Carolina, Pennsylvania, Virginia, and West Virginia. They must have a GPA of 3.0 or higher. Both U.S. citizens and foreign nationals are eligible. Selection is based on academic achievement (25%), extracurricular activities (10%), an essay (10%), recommendations (10%), financial need (40%), and extra credit for having extraordinary circumstances (5%).

Financial data Stipends range up to $5,000.

Duration 1 year; renewable.

Number awarded Varies each year; recently, 46 were awarded.

Deadline July of each year.

[148]
ED BRADLEY SCHOLARSHIP

Radio Television Digital News Foundation
Attn: Membership and Programs Manager
529 14th Street, N.W., Suite 1240
Washington, DC 20045
(202) 536-8356   Fax: (202) 223-4007
E-mail: karenh@rtdna.org
Web: www.rtdna.org/content/ed_bradley_scholarship

Summary To provide financial assistance to Asian American and other minority undergraduate students who are preparing for a career in electronic journalism.

Eligibility This program is open to sophomore or more advanced minority undergraduate students enrolled in an electronic journalism sequence at an accredited or nationally-recognized college or university. Applicants must submit a cover letter that discusses their current and past journalism experience, describes how they would use the funds if they were to receive the scholarship, discusses their reasons for preparing for a career in electronic journalism, and includes 3 to 5 links to their best and most relevant work samples.

Financial data   The stipend is $10,000, paid in semiannual installments of $5,000 each.

Duration   1 year.

Additional information   The Radio Television Digital News Foundation (RTDNF) was formerly the Radio and Television News Directors Foundation (RTNDF).

Number awarded   1 each year.

Deadline   May of each year.

[149]
ED SHULL DIVERSITY SCHOLARSHIP

Tennessee Grocers & Convenience Store Association
Attn: Tennessee Grocers Education Foundation
1838 Elm Hill Pike, Suite 136
Nashville, TN 37210-3726
(615) 889-0136   Toll Free: (800) 238-8742
Fax: (615) 889-2877   E-mail: jkemp@tngrocer.org
Web: www.tngrocer.org/TGEF/availablescholarships

Summary   To provide financial assistance to part-time employees and children and spouses of full-time employees of companies that belong to the Tennessee Grocers & Convenience Store Association (TGCSA) who are Asian Americans or other ethnic minorities and interested in attending college in any state.

Eligibility   This program is open to ethnic minorities who are 1) part-time employees of companies that belong to TGCSA and have been employed for at least 6 months; and 2) children and spouses of full-time employees of those companies and who have been employed for at least 2 years. Applicants may be high school seniors or college freshmen, sophomores, or juniors enrolled or planning to enroll at a college or university in any state. Selection is based on academic record, test scores, participation in extracurricular activities, student employment, and recommendations.

Financial data   The stipend is $700.

Duration   1 year.

Additional information   This program is supported by the Quaker Oats Company.

Number awarded   1 each year.

Deadline   March of each year.

[150]
EDSA MINORITY SCHOLARSHIP

Landscape Architecture Foundation
Attn: Leadership in Landscape Scholarship Program
1129 20th Street, N.W., Suite 202
Washington, DC 20036
(202) 331-7070   Fax: (202) 331-7079
E-mail: scholarships@lafoundation.org
Web: www.lafoundation.org

Summary   To provide financial assistance to Asian American and other minority college students who are interested in studying landscape architecture.

Eligibility   This program is open to Asian American, African American, Hispanic, Native American, and minority college students of other cultural and ethnic backgrounds. Applicants must be entering their final 2 years of undergraduate study in landscape architecture or working on a graduate degree in that field. Along with their application, they must submit a

500-word essay on a design or research effort they plan to pursue (explaining how it will contribute to the advancement of the profession and to their ethnic heritage), 3 work samples, and 2 letters of recommendation. Selection is based on professional experience, community involvement, extracurricular activities, and financial need.

Financial data   The stipend is $5,000.

Additional information   This scholarship was formerly designated the Edward D. Stone, Jr. and Associates Minority Scholarship.

Number awarded   1 each year.

Deadline   February of each year.

[151]
EDUCATIONAL FOUNDATION OF THE COLORADO SOCIETY OF CERTIFIED PUBLIC ACCOUNTANTS MINORITY SCHOLARSHIPS

Colorado Society of Certified Public Accountants
Attn: Educational Foundation
7887 East Belleview Avenue, Suite 200
Englewood, CO 80111
(303) 773-2877   Toll Free: (800) 523-9082 (within CO)
Fax: (303) 773-6344
Web: www.cocpa.org

Summary   To provide financial assistance to Asian American and other minority upper-division and graduate students in Colorado who are majoring in accounting.

Eligibility   This program is open to Colorado minority residents (Asian American, Black or African American, Hispanic or Latino, Native American) who are upper-division or graduate students at colleges and universities in the state and have completed at least 6 semester hours of accounting courses. Applicants must have a GPA of at least 3.0 overall and 3.25 in accounting classes. They must be U.S. citizens or noncitizens legally living and studying in Colorado with a valid visa that enables them to become employed. Financial need is not considered in the selection process.

Financial data   The stipend is $2,500. Funds are paid directly to the recipient's school to be used for books, C.P.A. review materials, tuition, fees, and dormitory room and board.

Duration   1 year; recipients may reapply.

Number awarded   1 or more each year.

Deadline   May of each year for fall semester or quarter; November of each year for winter quarter or spring semester.

[152]
EDWARD S. ROTH SCHOLARSHIP

Society of Manufacturing Engineers
Attn: SME Education Foundation
One SME Drive
P.O. Box 930
Dearborn, MI 48121-0930
(313) 425-3300   Toll Free: (866) 547-6333
Fax: (313) 425-3411   E-mail: foundation@sme.org
Web: www.smeef.org

Summary   To provide financial assistance to Asian American and other students enrolled or planning to work on a bachelor's or master's degree in manufacturing engineering at selected universities.

Eligibility   This program is open to U.S. citizens who are graduating high school seniors or currently-enrolled undergraduate or graduate students. Applicants must be enrolled or planning to enroll as a full-time student at 1 of 13 selected 4-year universities to work on a bachelor's or master's degree in manufacturing engineering. They must have a GPA of 3.0 or higher. Preference is given to 1) students demonstrating financial need; 2) minority students; and 3) students participating in a co-op program. Along with their application, they must submit a brief statement about why they chose their major, their career and educational objectives, and how this scholarship will help them attain those objectives.

Financial data Stipends range from $1,000 to $6,000 and recently averaged approximately $2,000.

Duration 1 year; may be renewed.

Additional information The eligible institutions are California Polytechnic State University at San Luis Obispo, California State Polytechnic State University at Pomona, University of Miami (Florida), Bradley University (Illinois), Central State University (Ohio), Miami University (Ohio), Boston University, Worcester Polytechnic Institute (Massachusetts), University of Massachusetts, St. Cloud State University (Minnesota), University of Texas at Rio Grande Valley, Brigham Young University (Utah), and Utah State University.

Number awarded 2 each year.

Deadline January of each year.

[153]
ELAINE REIKO AKAGI SCHOLARSHIP

Japanese American Citizens League-Seattle Chapter
P.O. Box 18558
Seattle, WA 98118
(253) 256-2204   E-mail: bcaldwell44@yahoo.com
Web: www.jaclseattle.org

Summary To provide financial assistance to Japanese Americans and other people of color who are working on a degree in special education at a school in any state.

Eligibility This program is open to people of color who are enrolled at a college or university in any state. Applicants must have a declared major in special education and a GPA of 2.5 or higher. Along with their application, they must submit a list of extracurricular and community activities, 2 letters of recommendation, a list of awards or recognitions they have earned, and a 500-word essay on the importance of increasing the number of teachers of color in special education classrooms. In the selection process, consideration is given to how the applicants plan to give back to the education community, the reasons they wish to prepare for the field of education, their experiences in working with children with disabilities, their experience working with children of color, and the teaching field in which they are specializing; financial need is not considered.

Financial data The stipend is $3,000.

Duration 1 year.

Additional information This program began in 2011.

Number awarded 1 each year.

Deadline March of each year.

[154]
ELLIS INJURY LAW DIVERSITY SCHOLARSHIPS

Ellis Law Corporation
Attn: Scholarship
883 North Douglas Street
El Segundo, CA 90245
Toll Free: (888) 559-7672
E-mail: scholarships@alelaw.com
Web: www.ellisinjurylaw.com/scholarships

Summary To provide financial assistance to pre-law and law students who either are Asian Americans or members of another ethnic minority group or have been involved in diversity issues.

Eligibility This program is open to students accepted or enrolled at 1) a 4-year college or university with the intention of working on a law degree; and 2) an ABA-accredited law school. Applicants must be either members of an ethnic/racial minority or individuals who have made a demonstrative commitment to diversity within their school and/or community. They must have a GPA of 3.0 or higher. Along with their application, they must submit an essay of 1,500 to 2,000 words answering 3 questions about recent Supreme Court decisions regarding affirmative action. Selection is based on that essay and transcripts.

Financial data The stipend is $1,000.

Duration 1 year.

Additional information This program began in 2014.

Number awarded 3 each year.

Deadline December of each year.

[155]
EMERGING ARCHIVAL SCHOLARS PROGRAM

Archival Education and Research Institute
Center for Information as Evidence
c/o UCLA Graduate School of Education and Information
  Studies
Office of External Relations
2043 Moore Hall
Los Angeles, CA 90095-1521
(310) 206-0375   Fax: (310) 794-5324
Web: aeri.gseis.ucla.edu/fellowships.htm

Summary To provide an opportunity for Asian American and other minority undergraduate and graduate students to learn more about the field of archival studies and to be exposed to research in the field.

Eligibility This program is open to undergraduates who have completed their junior year and to students who have completed the first year of a master's degree program. Applicants must be Asian/Pacific Islander, African American, Hispanic/Latino, Native American, Puerto Rican, or any other person who will add diversity to the field of archival studies. They must have a GPA of 3.0 or higher, but they may be working on a degree in any field and are not required to have prior knowledge of or experience in archival studies. U.S. citizenship or permanent resident status is required. Applicants must be interested in attending the week-long Archival Education and Research Institute (AERI), held at a different university each summer, where they are assigned both a faculty research mentor and a Ph.D. student mentor who introduce them to doctoral research and careers in archival studies.

Financial data Grants provide payment of round-trip travel, accommodation, and most meals.

Duration These grants are offered annually.

Additional information This program, first offered in 2009, is supported by the Institute of Museum and Library Services. Scholars who indicate an interest in continuing on to a doctoral program in archival studies after completing the AERI may be invited to participate in a supervised research project that will last up to 1 year and to present results of their research in a poster session at the AERI of the following year.

Number awarded Up to 7 each year.

Deadline April of each year.

[156]
EMMA L. BOWEN FOUNDATION INTERNSHIPS

Emma L. Bowen Foundation
Attn: Senior Vice President, Eastern Region and National
  Recruitment
30 Rockefeller Plaza
(Campus 1221 Avenue of the Americas #28A41)
New York, NY 10112
(212) 975-2545   E-mail: sdrice@cbs.com
Web: www.emmabowenfoundation.com

Summary To provide financial assistance and work experience to Asian American and other minority students interested in preparing for a career in the media industry.

Eligibility This program is open to minority students who are rising high school seniors, graduating high school seniors, or college freshmen. Applicants must be interested in working at a media company during the summer and school breaks until they graduate from college. They must have a GPA of 3.0 or higher, plans to attend an accredited 4-year college or university, and an interest in the media industry as a career. Along with their application, they must submit an essay of 500 to 1,000 words on how the media industry helps to create the images that influence our decisions and perceptions on a daily basis. U.S. citizenship or permanent resident status is required.

Financial data Interns receive a stipend of $2,500 to $3,000 and matching compensation of $2,500 to $3,000 to help pay for college tuition and other expenses.

Duration 1 summer for the internship; 1 academic year for the educational support; may be renewed until the intern graduates from college if he or she maintains a GPA of 3.0 or higher.

Additional information This program began in 1989. The sponsoring companies have included Broadcast Music Inc., CBS Incorporated, Charter Communications, Comcast NBC Universal, C-SPAN, Cox Communications, Fox Television Stations, Inc., Gannett Television, National Association of Broadcasters Educational Foundation, Turner Entertainment Networks.

Number awarded Approximately 60 to 70 new interns are selected each year.

Deadline Applications may be submitted at any time.

[157]
EMPIRE STATE DIVERSITY HONORS SCHOLARSHIP PROGRAM

State University of New York
Attn: Office of Diversity, Equity and Inclusion
State University Plaza, T1000A
353 Broadway
Albany, NY 12246
(518) 320-1189   E-mail: carlos.medina@suny.edu
Web: system.suny.edu/odei/diversity-programs

Summary To provide financial assistance to residents of New York who are attending campuses of the State University of New York (SUNY) and contribute to the diversity of the student body.

Eligibility This program is open to U.S. citizens and permanent residents who are New York residents and enrolled as undergraduate students at any of the participating SUNY colleges. Applicants must be able to demonstrate 1) how they will contribute to the diversity of the student body, primarily by having overcome a disadvantage or other impediment to success in higher education; and 2) high academic achievement. Economic disadvantage, although not a requirement, may be the basis for eligibility. Membership in a racial or ethnic group that is underrepresented at the applicant's school or program may serve as a plus factor in making awards, but may not form the sole basis of selection.

Financial data The maximum stipend provided by the SUNY system is half the student's cost of attendance or $3,000, whichever is less. The individual campus must match the SUNY award in an equal amount.

Duration 1 year; renewable.

Number awarded Varies each year; recently, 929 students at 41 SUNY institutions received support from this program.

Deadline Deadline not specified.

[158]
ENCOURAGE MINORITY PARTICIPATION IN OCCUPATIONS WITH EMPHASIS ON REHABILITATION

Allina Health System
Courage Kenny Rehabilitation Institute-Volunteer
  Services
Attn: EMPOWER Scholarship Committee
3915 Golden Valley Road
Minneapolis, MN 55422
(612) 775-2728   E-mail: ckriempower@allina.com
Web: www.allinahealth.org

Summary To provide financial assistance to Asian Americans and other students of color from Minnesota and western Wisconsin interested in attending college in any state to prepare for a career in the medical rehabilitation field.

Eligibility This program is open to ethnically diverse students accepted at or enrolled in an institution of higher learning in any state. Applicants must be residents of Minnesota or western Wisconsin (Burnett, Pierce, Polk, and St. Croix counties). They must be able to demonstrate a career interest in the medical rehabilitation field by a record of volunteer involvement related to health care and must have a GPA of 2.0 or higher. Along with their application, they must submit a 1-page essay that covers their medical/rehabilitation career-related volunteer service, including detailed information about patients or clients with whom they worked, what they did, what they think they accomplished and gained from their experience and how it will assist them in your future endeavors. Financial need is considered in the selection process.

Financial data The stipend is $1,500.

Duration 1 year.

Additional information This program, established in 1995 by the Courage Center, is also identified by its acronym as the EMPOWER Scholarship Award. The Courage Kenny Rehabilitation Institute was established in 2013 when Courage Center merged with the Sister Kenny Rehabilitation Institute and became part of Allina Health.

Number awarded 2 each year.

Deadline May of each year.

[159]
ERIC LU SCHOLARSHIP AWARD

Asian/Pacific American Council of Georgia, Inc.
3510 Shallowford Road, N.E.
Atlanta, GA 30341
(770) 722-8486   Fax: (678) 717-6502
E-mail: info@apacga.org
Web: www.apacga.org/en/?p=423

Summary To provide financial assistance to members of the Asian/Pacific American Council of Georgia (APAC) who plan to attend college in any state.

Eligibility This program is open to members of the APAC who are graduating high school seniors planning to attend a college or university in any state. Selection is based on overall academic achievement, leadership qualities, extracurricular involvement, and community service.

Financial data The stipend is $1,000.

Duration 1 year.

Number awarded 1 each year.

Deadline March of each year.

[160]
ERNST & YOUNG ASCEND SCHOLARSHIPS

Ascend: Pan-Asian Leaders
Attn: Director of Programs
247 West 30th Street
New York, NY 10001
(212) 248-4888   Fax: (212) 344-5636
E-mail: scholarships@ascendleadership.org
Web: www.ascendleadership.org

Summary To provide financial assistance to members of Ascend: Pan-Asian Leaders who are undergraduates working on a degree in accounting or finance.

Eligibility This program is open to members of Ascend who are enrolled as full-time rising sophomores or juniors at colleges and universities in the United States. Applicants must have a GPA of 3.3 or higher and a major in accounting or finance. Along with their application, they must submit a 500-word personal essay on how they have demonstrated leadership and teamwork in their academic studies, professional career, and/or extracurricular activities and community volunteer work; why they believe those qualities are important to transforming themselves into a better leader; their career goals after graduation; and the role Ascend has played in the achievement of their academic and career goals. They must

also answer questions about their leadership experience. Financial need is not considered in the selection process.

Financial data The stipend is $5,000.

Duration 1 year.

Additional information Ascend was formed in 2004 as the National Asian American Society of Accountants. This program is sponsored by Ernst & Young LLP.

Number awarded 5 each year.

Deadline April of each year.

[161]
ESA FOUNDATION SCHOLARSHIP PROGRAM

Entertainment Software Association
Attn: ESA Foundation
317 Madison Avenue, 22nd Floor
New York, NY 10017
(917) 522-3250
Web: www.esafoundation.org/scholarship.asp

Summary To provide financial assistance to Asian American and members of other minority groups who are interested in attending college to prepare for a career in computer and video game arts.

Eligibility This program is open to women and members of minority groups who are high school seniors or undergraduates currently enrolled full time at an accredited 4-year college or university. Applicants must be interested in working on a degree leading to a career in computer and video game arts. They must be U.S. citizens and have a GPA of 2.75 or higher.

Financial data The stipend is $3,000.

Duration 1 year; nonrenewable.

Additional information This program began in 2007.

Number awarded Up to 30 each year: 15 to graduating high school seniors and 15 to current undergraduates.

Deadline March of each year.

[162]
FAACPA EDUCATIONAL FUND SCHOLARSHIPS

Filipino-American Association of Certified Public
    Accountants
Attn: FAACPA Educational Fund
P.O. Box 2035
Seattle, WA 98111
Web: www.faacpa.com

Summary To provide financial assistance to Filipino American and other residents of any state studying accounting at colleges and universities in Washington.

Eligibility This program is open to residents of any state who have completed at least 2 quarters of study of accounting at a 2- or 4-year college or university in Washington. Applicants must submit a personal statement that includes their career goals and interests, what sparked their interest in accounting, and why they should be awarded this scholarship. They must be U.S. citizens or have applied for citizenship. Selection is based on their personal statement, academic achievement (GPA of 3.0 or higher), campus and/or community activities, work history, and financial need.

Financial data A stipend is awarded (amount not specified).

Duration 1 year; may be renewed up to 2 additional years.

Additional information This program is sponsored by the Educational Fund of the Filipino-American Association of Certified Public Accountants (FAACPA), an organization established by a group of Filipino Americans who were Certified Public Accountants. Its goal remains to serve the Filipino American community of Seattle and the state of Washington.

Number awarded 1 or more each year.

Deadline July of each year.

[163]
FACC PRESIDENT'S YOUTH AWARD

Filipino-American Community of Colorado
Attn: Scholarship Director
1900 Harlan Street
Edgewater, CO 80214
(303) 921-9692   E-mail: FACCScholarships@gmail.com
Web: www.coloradofilipinos.org

Summary To provide financial assistance to members of the Filipino-American Community of Colorado (FACC) who are high school seniors and planning to attend college in any state.

Eligibility This program is open to graduating high school seniors who have been junior members of FACC and active in its youth and cultural activities for at least 3 years. Applicants must be planning to attend a college or university in any state. They must be nominated by at least 3 officers of the FACC. Along with their application, they must submit an essay on their educational plans as those relate to their career objectives and future goals.

Financial data The stipend is $500.

Duration 1 year.

Additional information This program began in 1991.

Number awarded Up to 3 each year.

Deadline April of each year.

[164]
FACC SCHOLASTIC ACHIEVEMENT AWARD

Filipino-American Community of Colorado
Attn: Scholarship Director
1900 Harlan Street
Edgewater, CO 80214
(303) 921-9692   E-mail: FACCScholarships@gmail.com
Web: www.coloradofilipinos.org

Summary To provide financial assistance to Filipino Americans who are high school seniors in Colorado or attending college in that state.

Eligibility This program is open to Filipino Americans who are either 1) seniors graduating from high schools in Colorado and planning to attend a college or university in any state; or 2) residents of any state entering the final year of full-time undergraduate study at a college or university in Colorado. Applicants must have a GPA of 3.1 or higher. Along with their application, they must submit a description of their educational plans as those relate to their career objectives and future goals.

Financial data The stipend is $750.

Duration 1 year.

Additional information This program began in 1981.

Number awarded Up to 3 each year.

Deadline April of each year.

[165]
FACES SCHOLARSHIP

Filipino-American Communications Employees of AT&T
Doris Moore
AT&T Services, Inc.
430 East Main Street
Barrington, IL 60010-3219
(847) 248-6326   E-mail: dm4762@att.com

Summary To provide financial assistance to high school seniors who have ties to the Filipino American community and plan to attend college in any state.

Eligibility This program is open to graduating high school seniors who plan to enroll at a 2- or 4-year college or university in the United States. Applicants must reside in an area served by AT&T in North America and have ties to the Filipino American community. They must be U.S. citizens or permanent residents. Along with their application, they must submit transcripts; copies of their SAT, PSAT, or ACT scores; a resume; and a 1,000-word essay on a topic that changes annually. Merit scholarships require a GPA of 3.0 or higher; opportunity scholarships require a GPA of 2.75 or higher.

Financial data Stipends for merit scholarships are $6,000, $4,000, and $2,600; stipends for opportunity scholarships are $1,500.

Duration 1 year.

Number awarded 3 merit scholarships (1 at $6,000, 1 at $4,000, and 1 at $2,600) and 6 opportunity scholarships (all at $1,500) are awarded each year.

Deadline April of each year.

[166]
FALLEN HEROES SCHOLARSHIPS

Vietnamese American Armed Forces Association
Attn: Scholarship Selection Committee
6200 Rolling Road
P.O. Box 2382
Springfield, VA 22152
(714) 386-9896   E-mail: vaafa.org@gmail.com
Web: www.vaafa.org/programs/fallen-heroes-scholarship

Summary To provide financial assistance to Vietnamese Americans who are involved in community service and are interested in attending college to major in any field.

Eligibility This program is open to students who are enrolled full time or accepted for enrollment as an undergraduate at an accredited college or university. Applicants must be of Vietnamese American or Vietnamese Amerasian descent. They must have a GPA of 3.0 or higher, be able to demonstrate financial need, and have a record of active involvement in a community service organization.

Financial data The stipend is $1,000.

Duration 1 year.

Additional information This program was established to honor Vietnamese Americans who served in the U.S. armed forces and lost their lives on active duty. Recipients of these scholarships are encouraged to learn about those Fallen Heroes and to work to promote the recognition and memory of them within their community.

Number awarded 12 each year.

Deadline May of each year.

[167]
FAPAC DISTINGUISHED PUBLIC SERVICE SCHOLARSHIP

Federal Asian Pacific American Council
Attn: FAPAC Endowment Fund
P.O. Box 23184
Washington, DC 20026-3184
(202) 366-0626   E-mail: scholarships@fapac.org
Web: www.fapac.org/scholarship

Summary   To provide financial assistance for college to Asian Pacific Americans.

Eligibility   This program is open to Asian Pacific Americans who are U.S. citizens. Applicants must be high school seniors or current college students and have a GPA of 3.0 or higher. Along with their application, they must submit a 2-page essay on a topic that changes annually but relates to Asians and public service. Selection is based on 1) demonstrated commitment to public service, including services to the Asian American and Pacific Islander communities (50%); and 2) demonstrated leadership and potential for continued growth in leadership skills and academic achievement (50%).

Financial data   The stipend is $5,000.

Duration   1 year.

Additional information   The sponsor is an organization of Asian Pacific Americans employed by the federal government and the District of Columbia. Beginning in 2013, the scholarship is named, on a rotational basis, after Secretary Norman Y. Mineta (in 2017, 2020, etc.), Secretary Elaine L. Chao (2018, 2021, etc.), and Congressman Dalip Singh Saund (in 2019, 2022, etc.).

Number awarded   1 each year.

Deadline   February of each year.

[168]
FARM CREDIT EAST SCHOLARSHIPS

Farm Credit East
Attn: Scholarship Program
240 South Road
Enfield, CT 06082
(860) 741-4380   Toll Free: (800) 562-2235
Fax: (860) 741-4389
E-mail: specialoffers@famcrediteast.com
Web: www.farmcrediteast.com

Summary   To provide financial assistance to residents of designated northeastern states, especially Asian Americans and other minorities, who plan to attend school in any state to work on an undergraduate or graduate degree in a field related to agriculture, forestry, or fishing.

Eligibility   This program is open to residents of Connecticut, Maine, Massachusetts, New Jersey, Rhode Island, and portions of New York and New Hampshire. Applicants must be working on or planning to work on an associate, bachelor's, or graduate degree in production agriculture, agribusiness, the forest products industry, or commercial fishing at a college or university in any state. They must submit a 200-word essay on why they wish to prepare for a career in agriculture, forestry, or fishing. Selection is based on the essay, extracurricular activities (especially farm work experience and activities indicative of an interest in preparing for a career in agriculture or agribusiness), and interest in agriculture. The program includes diversity scholarships reserved for members of minority groups (Asian, Black or African American, American Indian or Alaska Native, Native Hawaiian or other Pacific Islander, or Hispanic or Latino).

Financial data   The stipend is $1,500. Funds are paid directly to the student to be used for tuition, room and board, books, and other academic charges.

Duration   1 year; nonrenewable.

Additional information   Recipients are given priority for an internship with the sponsor in the summer following their junior year. Farm Credit East was formerly named First Pioneer Farm Credit.

Number awarded   Varies each year; recently, 32, including several diversity scholarships, were awarded.

Deadline   April of each year.

[169]
FEDEX APIASF SCHOLARSHIPS

Asian & Pacific Islander American Scholarship Fund
2025 M Street, N.W., Suite 610
Washington, DC 20036-3363
(202) 986-6892   Toll Free: (877) 808-7032
Fax: (202) 530-0643   E-mail: info@apiasf.org
Web: www.apiasf.org/scholarship_apiasf_fedex.html

Summary   To provide financial assistance to Asian and Pacific Islander Americans who are entering college for the first time.

Eligibility   This program is open to U.S. citizens, nationals, permanent residents, and citizens of the Freely Associated States who are first-time incoming college students and of Asian or Pacific Islander heritage. Applicants must be enrolling full time at an accredited 2- or 4-year college or university in the United States. They must have a GPA of 3.0 or higher or the GED equivalent. In addition, they must complete the FAFSA and apply for federal financial aid.

Financial data   The stipend is $2,500 per year.

Duration   4 years.

Additional information   This program is sponsored by FedEx and administered by the Asian & Pacific Islander American Scholarship Fund (APIASF).

Number awarded   Varies each year; recently, 6 were awarded.

Deadline   January of each year.

[170]
FILIPINO AMERICAN LEAGUE OF ENGINEERS AND ARCHITECTS SCHOLARSHIP PROGRAM

Filipino American League of Engineers and Architects
Attn: FALEA Foundation
P.O. Box 4135
Honolulu, HI 96812-4135
(808) 448-2807   E-mail: ftcruzata@aol.com
Web: www.falea.org/scholarship.html

Summary   To provide financial assistance to Hawaii residents who are of Filipino descent and are interested in attending college in any state to prepare for a career in engineering, architecture, or a related field.

Eligibility   This program is open to high school seniors and currently-enrolled college students who are Hawaii residents and of Filipino descent. Applicants must be enrolled or planning to enroll full time at a college or university in any state to work on a degree in engineering, architecture, surveying, or a related field. They must have a GPA of 3.0 or higher. Along with their application, they must submit an essay on why they are seeking the scholarship, the extracurricular activities in which they have been involved, the positions they have held in organizations or clubs, their community service, and other information they feel might be helpful.

Financial data The stipend is $1,000.

Duration 1 year.

Additional information This program began in 1994.

Number awarded Varies each year; recently, 5 were awarded.

Deadline November of each year.

[171]
FILIPINO CHAMBER OF COMMERCE OF HAWAII SCHOLARSHIPS

Filipino Chamber of Commerce of Hawaii
Attn: Foundation Scholarship Committee
1523 Lehia Street
P.O. Box 1572
Honolulu, HI 96806-1572
(808) 728-1700   E-mail: filipinochamberhi@gmail.com
Web: www.filipinochamber.org

Summary To provide financial assistance to high school seniors in Hawaii who have an interest in business and are planning to attend college in any state.

Eligibility This program is open to seniors graduating from high schools in Hawaii who have a GPA of 3.5 or higher and have been accepted at a 4-year college or university in any state. Applicants must submit a 1-page essay describing how they expect to promote Hawaii's business community, broaden opportunities for Filipino entrepreneurs and other businesses, strengthen business links between Hawaii and the Philippines, and support the well-being of the community. Selection is based on that essay, academic record (including SAT and/or ACT scores), awards and honors, and activities.

Financial data Stipends are $5,000 or $3,000.

Duration 1 year.

Additional information The highest-ranked applicant receives the Renato and Maria A.F. Etrata Foundation/Filipino Chamber Foundation Scholarship.

Number awarded Varies each year; recently, 5 were awarded: 1 at $5,000 and 4 at $3,000.

Deadline March of each year.

[172]
FILIPINO NURSES' ORGANIZATION OF HAWAI'I SCHOLARSHIP

Hawai'i Community Foundation
Attn: Scholarship Department
827 Fort Street Mall
Honolulu, HI 96813
(808) 566-5570   Toll Free: (888) 731-3863
Fax: (808) 521-6286
E-mail: scholarships@hcf-hawaii.org
Web: hcf.scholarships.ngwebsolutions.com

Summary To provide financial assistance to Hawaii residents of Filipino ancestry who are interested in attending college in any state to prepare for a career as a nurse.

Eligibility This program is open to Hawaii residents of Filipino ancestry who are enrolled or planning to enroll full time

at a college or university in any state and work on an undergraduate or graduate degree in nursing. Applicants must be able to demonstrate academic achievement (GPA of 2.7 or higher), good moral character, and financial need. Along with their application, they must submit a short statement indicating their reasons for attending college, their planned course of study, their career goals, and what community service means to them.

Financial data The amounts of the awards depend on the availability of funds and the need of the recipient. Recently, the average value of the scholarships awarded by the foundation was $2,800.

Duration 1 year.

Number awarded Varies each year; recently, 2 were awarded.

Deadline February of each year.

[173]
FILIPINO WOMEN'S LEAGUE COMMUNITY COLLEGE SCHOLARSHIP PROGRAM

Filipino Women's League
Attn: Community Scholarship Committee
P.O. Box 419
Pearl City, HI 96782
Web: www.filipinowomensleague.org/scholarships

Summary To provide financial assistance to Hawaii high school seniors who are of Filipino descent and are interested in attending a community college in the state.

Eligibility This program is open to Hawaii residents who are graduating high school seniors, of Filipino ancestry, and enrolling full time at a community college in the state. Applicants must have a high school GPA of 3.5 or higher. Selection is based primarily on financial need; other selection criteria include scholastic achievement (measured by transcripts and SAT or ACT scores), educational goals, and extracurricular interests.

Financial data The award provides for full or partial payment of tuition (to a maximum of $1,500 per year). Payment is made directly to the financial aid office of the recipient's college.

Duration 1 year.

Number awarded 1 or more each year.

Deadline March of each year.

[174]
FILIPINO WOMEN'S LEAGUE UNIVERSITY SCHOLARSHIP PROGRAM

Filipino Women's League
Attn: Community Scholarship Committee
P.O. Box 419
Pearl City, HI 96782
Web: www.filipinowomensleague.org/scholarships

Summary To provide financial assistance to Hawaii high school seniors who are of Filipino descent and are interested in attending a university in the state.

Eligibility This program is open to Hawaii residents who are graduating high school seniors, of Filipino ancestry, and enrolling full time at a 4-year college or university in the state. Applicants must have a high school GPA of 3.5 or higher. Selection is based primarily on financial need; other selection criteria include scholastic achievement (measured by transcripts and SAT or ACT scores), educational goals, and extracurricular interests.

Financial data Stipends provide full or partial payment of tuition (to a maximum of $1,500 per year). Funds are paid directly to the financial aid office of the recipient's university.

Duration 1 year; nonrenewable.

Number awarded 1 or more each year.

Deadline March of each year.

[175]
FIRST TRANSIT SCHOLARSHIP

Conference of Minority Transportation Officials
Attn: National Scholarship Program
100 M Street, S.E., Suite 917
Washington, DC 20003
(202) 506-2917 E-mail: info@comto.org
Web: www.comto.org/page/scholarships

Summary To provide financial assistance to Asian American and other minority upper-division and graduate students in engineering or other field related to transportation.

Eligibility This program is open to minority juniors, seniors, and graduate students in transporation, planning, engineering or other technical transportation-related disciplines. Applicants must submit a cover letter on their transportation-related career goals and life aspirations. Financial need is not considered in the selection process.

Financial data The stipend is $6,000. Funds are paid directly to the recipient's college or university.

Duration 1 year.

Additional information This program is sponsored by First Transit Inc.

Number awarded 1 each year.

Deadline April of each year.

[176]
FORUM FOR CONCERNS OF MINORITIES SCHOLARSHIPS

American Society for Clinical Laboratory Science
Attn: Forum for Concerns of Minorities
1861 International Drive, Suite 200
McLean, VA 22102
(571) 748-3770 E-mail: ascls@ascls.org
Web: www.ascls.org/forum-for-concerns-of-minorities

Summary To provide financial assistance to Asian American and other minority students in clinical laboratory scientist and clinical laboratory technician programs.

Eligibility This program is open to minority students who are enrolled in a program in clinical laboratory science, including clinical laboratory science/medical technology (CLS/MT) and clinical laboratory technician/medical laboratory technician (CLT/MLT). Applicants must be able to demonstrate financial need. Membership in the American Society for Clinical Laboratory Science is encouraged but not required.

Financial data Stipends depend on the need of the recipients and the availability of funds.

Duration 1 year.

Number awarded 2 each year: 1 to a CLS/MT student and 1 to a CLT/MLT student.

Deadline March of each year.

[177]
FRANCES SONN NAM MEMORIAL SCHOLARSHIP

Asian & Pacific Islander American Scholarship Fund
2025 M Street, N.W., Suite 610
Washington, DC 20036-3363
(202) 986-6892 Toll Free: (877) 808-7032
Fax: (202) 530-0643 E-mail: info@apiasf.org
Web: www.apiasf.org

Summary To provide financial assistance to Asian and Pacific Islander Americans who are entering their junior year of college and majoring in specified fields.

Eligibility This program is open to U.S. citizens, nationals, permanent residents, or citizens of the Freely Associated States who are of Asian or Pacific Islander heritage. Applicants must be entering their junior year of full-time study at an accredited 4-year college or university in the United States and preparing for a career in law, public service, or government affairs. They must have a GPA of 3.0 or higher. In addition, they must complete the FAFSA and apply for federal financial aid.

Financial data The stipend is $4,000 per year.

Duration 2 years.

Additional information This scholarship is sponsored by Sodexo.

Number awarded 2 each year.

Deadline January of each year.

[178]
FRANCIS M. KEVILLE MEMORIAL SCHOLARSHIP

Construction Management Association of America
Attn: CMAA Foundation
7926 Jones Branch Drive, Suite 800
McLean, VA 22101-3303
(703) 677-3361 E-mail: foundation@cmaanet.org
Web: www.cmaafoundation.org

Summary To provide financial assistance to Asian American and other minority undergraduate and graduate students working on a degree in construction management.

Eligibility This program is open to women and members of minority groups who are enrolled as full-time undergraduate or graduate students. Applicants must have completed at least 1 year of study and have at least 1 full year remaining for a bachelor's or master's degree in construction management or a related field. Along with their application, they must submit essays on why they are interested in a career in construction management and why they should be awarded this scholarship. Selection is based on that essay (20%), academic performance (40%), recommendation of the faculty adviser (15%), and extracurricular activities (25%); a bonus of 5% is given to student members of the Construction Management Association of America (CMAA).

Financial data The stipend is $5,000. Funds are disbursed directly to the student's university.

Duration 1 year.

Number awarded 1 each year.

Deadline April of each year.

[179]
FRANK GILBERT MEMORIAL SCHOLARSHIP

South Carolina Professional Association for Access and
  Equity
Attn: Financial Secretary
P.O. Box 71297
North Charleston, SC 29415
(843) 670-4890   E-mail: anderson4569@bellsouth.net
Web: www.scpaae.org/#!scholarships/c11tv

Summary To provide financial assistance to undergraduate students at colleges and universities in South Carolina who are recognized as underrepresented minorities on their campus and have been involved in public service.

Eligibility This program is open to residents of any state who have completed at least 12 semester hours at a college or university in South Carolina. Applicants must be recognized as an underrepresented ethnic minority on their campus. They must have a GPA of 3.5 or higher. Along with their application, they must submit 1) a personal letter on their public service, academic and career goals, honors and awards, leadership skills and organization participation, community service, and a statement of why they would like to receive this scholarship; and 2) a paragraph defining access and equity and describing how they can assist in achieving access and equity within South Carolina. Financial need is not considered in the selection process.

Financial data The stipend is $1,500.

Duration 1 year.

Number awarded 1 or more each year.

Deadline February of each year.

[180]
FRED G. LEE MEMORIAL SCHOLARSHIPS

Chinese American Citizens Alliance-Portland Lodge
Attn: Scholarship Committee
2309 S.W. First, Number 142
Portland, OR 97201
(503) 221-8773   E-mail: scholarship@cacaportland.org
Web: www.cacaportland.org/scholarships.html

Summary To provide financial assistance to high school seniors of Chinese descent in Oregon or in Clark County, Washington who plan to attend college in any state.

Eligibility This program is open to seniors graduating from high schools in Oregon or in Clark County, Washington and planning to attend an accredited 2- or 4-year college or university in any state (although 1 scholarship is reserved for a student planning to attend college in Oregon or Washington). Applicants must be a U.S. citizen or permanent resident, have at least 1 parent who is a member of the Portland Lodge of the Chinese American Citizens Alliance, be active in school and community affairs, and have a GPA of 3.5 or higher. Along with their application, they must submit 2 essays of approximately 250 words: the relationship of their educational plans or goals to their Chinese heritage or knowledge of Chinese culture, and their personal philosophy and how their Chinese heritage or knowledge of Chinese culture has affected their perspective. Selection is based on scholarship, leadership in school, community activities, and financial need.

Financial data The stipend is $1,000 per year.

Duration Either 4 years or 1 year.

Number awarded 3 each year: 1 for 4 years and 2 for 1 year.

Deadline April of each year.

[181]
GAPA FOUNDATION SCHOLARSHIP

Gay Asian Pacific Alliance
Attn: GAPA Foundation
P.O. Box 22482
San Francisco, CA 94122
(415) 857-GAPA
E-mail: scholarship@gapafoundation.org
Web: www.gapafoundation.org/scholarships

Summary To provide financial assistance to lesbian, gay, bisexual, and transgender (LGBT) Asian and Pacific Islanders who are interested in attending college in any state.

Eligibility This program is open to high school seniors, college students, graduate school students, and vocational school students who identify both as Asian/Pacific Islander (API) and LGBT. Applicants must have a GPA of 2.5 or higher and a history of activism within either the API and/or the LGBT communities. They are not required to be members of either community, although preference is given to those who are members of both. Along with their application, they must submit 1) a brief statement about a significant challenge in their life that has helped shape them into the person they are today; 2) a brief statement about how they are currently active in the API and/or LGBTQ community; and 3) a 500-word essay describing a significant challenge facing the API/LGBT community today and what they would do to help solve this issue if they had the resources. Interviews may be scheduled (in person for applicants who live in the San Francisco Bay area, by phone for those who live elsewhere).

Financial data The stipend is $1,000.

Duration 1 year.

Additional information This program began in 1997 as the George Choy Memorial Scholarship.

Number awarded Up to 4 each year.

Deadline July of each year.

[182]
GARRETT A. MORGAN TRANSPORTATION ACHIEVEMENT SCHOLARSHIP

Conference of Minority Transportation Officials-Michigan
  Chapter
Attn: President
P.O. Box 32439
Detroit, MI 48232
(269) 491-7279   E-mail: averyk@michigan.gov
Web: www.comtomichigan.org/scholarships.html

Summary To provide financial assistance to Asian American and other minority high school seniors in Michigan who plan to attend college in any state to major in a transportation-related field.

Eligibility This program is open to seniors graduating from high schools in Michigan who are members of minority groups. Applicants must be planning to attend an accredited college, university, or vocational/technical institute and major in the field of transportation or a transportation-related discipline. They must have a GPA of 2.5 or higher. U.S. citizenship or legal resident status is required.

Financial data The stipend ranges from $500 to $3,000. Funds are paid directly to the student.

Duration 1 year.

Number awarded 1 or more each year.

Deadline April of each year.

[183]
GATES MILLENNIUM SCHOLARS PROGRAM

Bill and Melinda Gates Foundation
P.O. Box 10500
Fairfax, VA 22031-8044
Toll Free: (877) 690-GMSP   Fax: (703) 205-2079
Web: www.gmsp.org

Summary To provide financial assistance to outstanding low-income Asian American and other minority students, particularly those interested in majoring in specific fields in college.

Eligibility This program is open to Asian Pacific Islander Americans, African Americans, Alaska Natives, American Indians, and Hispanic Americans who are graduating high school seniors with a GPA of 3.3 or higher. Principals, teachers, guidance counselors, tribal higher education representatives, and other professional educators are invited to nominate students with outstanding academic qualifications, particularly those likely to succeed in the fields of computer science, education, engineering, library science, mathematics, public health, or science. Nominees should have significant financial need and have demonstrated leadership abilities through participation in community service, extracurricular, or other activities. U.S. citizenship, nationality, or permanent resident status is required. Nominees must be planning to enter an accredited college or university as a full-time, degree-seeking freshman in the following fall.

Financial data The program covers the cost of tuition, fees, books, and living expenses not paid for by grants and scholarships already committed as part of the recipient's financial aid package.

Duration 4 years or the completion of the undergraduate degree, if the recipient maintains at least a 3.0 GPA.

Additional information This program, established in 1999, is funded by the Bill and Melinda Gates Foundation and administered by the United Negro College Fund with support from the American Indian Graduate Center, the Hispanic Scholarship Fund, and the Asian & Pacific Islander American Scholarship Fund.

Number awarded 1,000 new scholarships are awarded each year.

Deadline January of each year.

[184]
GEETA RASTOGI MEMORIAL SCHOLARSHIP

Upakar: Indian American Scholarship Foundation
9101 Friars Road
Bethesda, MD 20817
E-mail: upakarfoundation@hotmail.com
Web: www.upakarfoundation.org

Summary To provide financial assistance to Asian Indian high school seniors who plan to attend a 4-year college and major in a field of the performing arts.

Eligibility This program is open to graduating high school seniors who either were born or have at least 1 parent who was born in India. Applicants must be planning to enroll at a 4-year college or university and major in the performing arts. They must be U.S. citizens or permanent residents and have a GPA of 3.6 or higher. Their family income must be less than $75,000 per year.

Financial data The stipend is $2,000 per year.

Duration Up to 4 years, provided the recipient maintains a GPA of 3.3 or higher.

Additional information This program began in 2011.

Number awarded 1 every 4 years.

Deadline April of each year.

[185]
GENERAL MILLS FOUNDATION APIASF SCHOLARSHIP

Asian & Pacific Islander American Scholarship Fund
2025 M Street, N.W., Suite 610
Washington, DC 20036-3363
(202) 986-6892   Toll Free: (877) 808-7032
Fax: (202) 530-0643   E-mail: info@apiasf.org
Web: www.apiasf.org

Summary To provide financial assistance to Asian and Pacific Islander Americans from Minnesota who are entering college for the first time.

Eligibility This program is open to U.S. citizens, nationals, and permanent residents who are of Asian or Pacific Islander heritage and live in Minnesota; preference is given to residents of the Minneapolis-St. Paul Twin Cities. Applicants must be enrolling full time at an accredited 2- or 4-year college or university in the United States as a first-year student. They must have a GPA of 2.7 or higher or the GED equivalent. In addition, they must complete the FAFSA and apply for federal financial aid.

Financial data The stipend is $2,500 per year.

Duration 2 years.

Additional information This scholarship is sponsored by the General Mills Foundation and administered by the Asian & Pacific Islander American Scholarship Fund (APIASF).

Number awarded Varies each year; recently, 2 were awarded.

Deadline January of each year.

[186]
GENERAL VANG PAO SCHOLARSHIP

Hmong American Education Fund
P.O. Box 17468
St. Paul, MN 55117
(651) 592-1576   E-mail: scholarships@thehaef.org
Web: www.thehaef.org

Summary To provide financial assistance to Hmong undergraduate and graduate students who demonstrate leadership.

Eligibility This program is open to students of Hmong descent who are currently enrolled as full-time undergraduate or graduate students at 2- or 4-year colleges or universities in any state. Applicants must be U.S. citizens or permanent residents and have a GPA of 3.0 or higher. Along with their application, they must submit a 1,500-word essay on their commitment to education, their leadership qualities, their financial need, how this scholarship can help them, and their community service. Selection is based on academic excellence, leadership qualities, commitment to helping their community, and financial need.

Financial data   The stipend is $2,500.

Duration   1 year; nonrenewable.

Number awarded   1 each year.

Deadline   March of each year.

[187]
GENERATION GOOGLE SCHOLARSHIPS FOR CURRENT UNIVERSITY STUDENTS

Google Inc.
Attn: Scholarships
1600 Amphitheatre Parkway
Mountain View, CA 94043-8303
(650) 253-0000   Fax: (650) 253-0001
E-mail: generationgoogle@google.com
Web: www.google.com

Summary   To provide financial assistance to members of underrepresented groups, including Filipinos, enrolled as undergraduate or graduate students in a computer-related field.

Eligibility   This program is open to students enrolled as full-time undergraduate or graduate students at a college or university in the United States or Canada. Applicants must be members of a group underrepresented in computer science: Filipinos/Native Hawaiians/Pacific Islanders, African Americans, Hispanics, or American Indians. They must be working on a degree in computer science, computer engineering, or a closely-related field. Selection is based on academic achievement, leadership, and passion for computer science and technology.

Financial data   The stipend is $10,000 per year for U.S. students or $C5,000 for Canadian students.

Duration   1 year; may be renewed.

Additional information   Recipients are also invited to attend Google's Computer Science Summer Institute at Mountain View, California, Seattle, Washington, or Cambridge, Massachusetts in the summer.

Number awarded   Varies each year.

Deadline   February of each year.

[188]
GENERATION GOOGLE SCHOLARSHIPS FOR HIGH SCHOOL SENIORS

Google Inc.
Attn: Scholarships
1600 Amphitheatre Parkway
Mountain View, CA 94043-8303
(650) 253-0000   Fax: (650) 253-0001
E-mail: generationgoogle@google.com
Web: www.google.com

Summary   To provide financial assistance to members of underrepresented groups, including Filipinos, planning to work on a bachelor's degree in a computer-related field.

Eligibility   This program is open to high school seniors planning to enroll full time at a college or university in the United States or Canada. Applicants must be members of a group underrepresented in computer science: Filipinos/Native Hawaiians/Pacific Islanders, African Americans, Hispanics, American Indians, women, or people with a disability. They must be interested in working on a bachelor's degree in computer science, computer engineering, or a closely-related field. Selection is based on academic achievement, leadership, and passion for computer science and technology.

Financial data   The stipend is $10,000 per year for U.S. students or $C5,000 for Canadian students.

Duration   1 year; may be renewed for up to 3 additional years or until graduation, whichever comes first.

Additional information   Recipients are required to attend Google's Computer Science Summer Institute at Mountain View, California, Seattle, Washington, or Cambridge, Massachusetts in the summer.

Number awarded   Varies each year.

Deadline   February of each year.

[189]
GEOLOGICAL SOCIETY OF AMERICA MINORITY STUDENT SCHOLARSHIP PROGRAM

Geological Society of America
Attn: Program Officer-Grants, Awards and Recognition
3300 Penrose Place
P.O. Box 9140
Boulder, CO 80301-9140
(303) 357-1060   Toll Free: (888) 443-4472, ext. 1060
Fax: (303) 357-1070   E-mail: awards@geosociety.org
Web: www.geosociety.org

Summary   To provide financial assistance to Asian American and other minority undergraduate student members of the Geological Society of America (GSA) working on a degree in geoscience.

Eligibility   This program is open to GSA members who are U.S. citizens and members of a minority group working on an undergraduate degree. Applicants must have taken at least 2 introductory geoscience courses and be enrolled in additional geoscience courses for the upcoming academic year. Selection is based on the scientific merits of the proposal, the capability of the investigator, and the reasonableness of the budget.

Financial data   The stipend is $1,500. Funds may be used to pay college fees, purchase text books, or attend GSA field courses or conferences. Winners also receive meeting registration for the GSA annual meeting where the awards are presented and a complimentary GSA membership for the following year.

Duration   1 year.

Additional information   This program is sponsored by ExxonMobil.

Number awarded   6 each year: 1 in each GSA geographic section.

Deadline   January of each year.

[190]
GO RED MULTICULTURAL SCHOLARSHIP FUND

American Heart Association
Attn: Go Red for Women
7272 Greenville Avenue
Dallas, TX 75231-4596
Toll Free: (800) AHA-USA1
E-mail: GoRedScholarship@heart.org
Web: www.goredforwomen.org

Summary To provide financial assistance to Asian American and other women from multicultural backgrounds who are preparing for a career in a field of health care.

Eligibility This program is open to women who are currently enrolled at an accredited college, university, health care institution, or program and have a GPA of 3.0 or higher. Applicants must be U.S. citizens or permanent residents of Asian/Pacific Islander, Hispanic, African American, or other minority origin. They must be working on an undergraduate or graduate degree as preparation for a career as a nurse, physician, or allied health care worker. Selection is based on community involvement, a personal essay, transcripts, and 2 letters of recommendation.

Financial data The stipend is $2,500.

Duration 1 year.

Additional information This program, which began in 2012, is supported by Macy's.

Number awarded 16 each year.

Deadline December of each year.

[191]
GOLDEN APPLE SCHOLARS OF ILLINOIS

Golden Apple Foundation
Attn: Scholars Program
8 South Michigan Avenue, Suite 700
Chicago, IL 60603-3463
(312) 407-0006   Fax: (312) 407-0344
E-mail: info@goldenapple.org
Web: www.goldenapple.org/becoming-a-scholar

Summary To provide forgivable loans to residents of Illinois, especially Asian Americans and other minorities, who wish to study education at an Illinois college and teach in the state.

Eligibility This program is open to 1) seniors graduating from high schools in Illinois and planning to attend any of 52 designated colleges and universities in the state; 2) sophomores at any of those 52 institutions; and 3) community college students planning to transfer to any of those 52 4-year institutions. Applicants must be committed to teaching as a profession. The program strongly encourages nomination of prospective teachers for which there is currently a shortage, especially minority and bilingual teachers. Selection is based on 3 or 4 essays included on the application, ACT scores and transcripts, letters of reference, and an interview.

Financial data Scholars receive a scholarship/loan of $2,500 per year for their freshman and sophomore year and $5,000 per year for their junior and senior year. They also receive a stipend of $2,000 per year for participating in a summer teaching internship. If they complete a bachelor's degree and teach for 5 years in an Illinois school of need, the loan is forgiven. Schools of need are defined as those either having Chapter I status by the U.S. Department of Education or having mediocre to poor PSAE or ISAT scores.

Duration 4 years, provided the recipient maintains a GPA of 2.0 or higher during the freshman year and 2.5 or higher in subsequent years. Students who enter the program after their sophomore year receive 2 years of support.

Additional information During the annual summer institutes, scholars participate in teaching internships and seminars on the art and craft of teaching. This program was established in 1988.

Number awarded Varies each year; recently, 175 were awarded.

Deadline November of each year for high school seniors; April of each year for college sophomores.

[192]
GOLDEN DOOR SCHOLARS PROGRAM

Golden Door Scholars
c/o Red Ventures
1101 521 Corporate Center Drive
Fort Mill, SC 29707
E-mail: info@goldendoorscholars.org
Web: www.goldendoorscholars.org/apply-now.html

Summary To provide financial assistance for college to undocumented students, especially those from designated states.

Eligibility This program is open to undocumented students who are high school seniors or high school graduates who have not yet entered a 4-year college (including students currently attending a community college). Applicants must be planning to work on a 4-year degree. They must be eligible for Deferred Action for Childhood Arrivals (DACA). Along with their application, they must submit brief statements on their intended field of concentration, why they are choosing it, and why they should be selected as a recipient of this scholarship. Strong preference is given to applicants from Georgia, North Carolina, South Carolina, and Tennessee.

Financial data The program provides funding to cover tuition (less other scholarships), room, and board. The program cooperates with participating colleges and universities in the preferred states that have agreed to provide recipients with substantial scholarship support or reduced tuition.

Duration Until completion of a 4-year degree.

Additional information This program began in 2012.

Number awarded Varies each year, recently, 13 were awarded.

Deadline October of each year.

[193]
GORDON STAFFORD SCHOLARSHIP IN ARCHITECTURE

Stafford King Wiese Architects
Attn: Scholarship Selection Committee
622 20th Street
Sacramento, CA 95811
(916) 930-5900   Fax: (916) 290-0100
E-mail: info@skwaia.com
Web: www.skwarchitects.com/about/scholarship

Summary To provide financial assistance to Asian Americans and members of other minority groups from California interested in studying architecture at a college in any state.

Eligibility This program is open to California residents currently enrolled at accredited schools of architecture in any state as first-year new or first-year transfer students and working on a bachelor's or 5-year master's degree. Applicants must be able to demonstrate minority status (defined as Pacific Asian, Asian Indian, Black, Hispanic, or Native American). They must submit a 500-word statement expressing their desire to prepare for a career in architecture. Finalists are interviewed and must travel to Sacramento, California at their own expense for the interview.

Financial data The stipend is $3,000 per year. That includes $1,500 deposited in the recipient's school account and $1,500 paid to the recipient directly.

Duration 1 year; may be renewed up to 4 additional years.

Additional information This program began in 1995.

Number awarded Up to 5 each year.

Deadline June of each year.

[194]
GRANT THORNTON ASCEND SCHOLARSHIP

Ascend: Pan-Asian Leaders
Attn: Director of Programs
247 West 30th Street
New York, NY 10001
(212) 248-4888   Fax: (212) 344-5636
E-mail: scholarships@ascendleadership.org
Web: www.ascendleadership.org

Summary To provide financial assistance to members of Ascend: Pan-Asian Leaders who are college undergraduates with a career interest in accounting or finance.

Eligibility This program is open to members of Ascend who are enrolled as freshmen, sophomores, or juniors (in 5-year programs) at colleges and universities in the United States. Applicants must have a GPA of 3.5 or higher and a major in accounting or finance. Along with their application, they must submit a 500-word personal essay on how they have demonstrated leadership and teamwork in their academic studies, professional career, and/or extracurricular activities and community volunteer work; why they believe those qualities are important to transforming themselves into a better leader; their career goals after graduation; and the role Ascend has played in the achievement of their academic and career goals. Financial need is not considered in the selection process.

Financial data The stipend is $2,000.

Duration 1 year.

Additional information Ascend was formed in 2004 as the National Asian American Society of Accountants. This program is sponsored by Grant Thornton.

Number awarded 2 each year.

Deadline April of each year.

[195]
GREAT LAKES SECTION IFT DIVERSITY SCHOLARSHIP

Institute of Food Technologists-Great Lakes Section
c/o Andrea Kirk, Scholarship Chair
Post Foods, LLC
275 Cliff Street
Battle Creek, MI 49014
E-mail: greatlakesift@gmail.com
Web: www.greatlakesift.org/student-scholarships

Summary To provide financial assistance to Asian Americans and other minority members of the Great Lakes Section of the Institute of Food Technologists (IFT) from any state who are working on an undergraduate or graduate degree related to food technology at a college in Michigan.

Eligibility This program is open to minority residents of any state who are members of the IFT Great Lakes Section (GLS) and working full time on an undergraduate or graduate degree in food science, nutrition, food engineering, food packaging, or related fields at a college or university in Michigan. Applicants must have a GPA of 3.0 or higher and plans for a career in the food industry. Along with their application, they must submit a 1-page personal statement that covers their academic program, future plans and career goals, extracurricular activities (including involvement in community, university, GLS, or national IFT activities), and work experience. Financial need is not considered in the selection process.

Financial data The stipend is $1,000.

Duration 1 year; nonrenewable.

Number awarded 1 each year.

Deadline February of each year.

[196]
HAEF SCHOLARSHIPS

Hmong American Education Fund
P.O. Box 17468
St. Paul, MN 55117
(651) 592-1576   E-mail: scholarships@thehaef.org
Web: www.thehaef.org

Summary To provide financial assistance to Hmong residents of Minnesota who are planning to attend college in any state.

Eligibility This program is open to residents of Minnesota who identify themselves as a person of Hmong descent. Applicants must be high school seniors or GED recipients planning to enroll full time at a 2- or 4-year college or university in any state. They must be U.S. citizens or permanent residents and have a GPA of 3.0 or higher. Along with their application, they must submit transcripts and a 1,500-word essay on their goals, why they deserve this scholarship, their financial need, how this scholarship can help them, and their community service. Men and women are considered separately.

Financial data The stipend is $1,000.

Duration 1 year; nonrenewable.

Number awarded 2 each year: 1 to a man and 1 to a woman.

Deadline March of each year.

[197]
HANA SCHOLARSHIPS

United Methodist Church
Attn: General Board of Higher Education and Ministry
Office of Loans and Scholarships
1001 19th Avenue South
P.O. Box 340007
Nashville, TN 37203-0007
(615) 340-7342   Fax: (615) 340-7367
E-mail: umscholar@gbhem.org
Web: www.gbhem.org

Summary To provide financial assistance to upper-division and graduate Methodist students who are of Hispanic, Asian, Native American, or Pacific Islander ancestry.

Eligibility This program is open to full-time juniors, seniors, and graduate students at accredited colleges and universities in the United States who have been active, full members of a United Methodist Church (UMC) for at least 3 years prior to applying. Applicants must have at least 1 parent who is Asian, Hispanic, or Native American. They must be able to demonstrate involvement in their Hispanic, Asian, or Native American (HANA) community in the UMC. Selection is based on that involvement, academic ability (GPA of at least 2.85), and financial need. U.S. citizenship or permanent resident status is required.

Financial data Stipends range from $1,000 to $3,000.

Duration 1 year; recipients may reapply.

Number awarded 50 each year.

Deadline February of each year.

[198]
HANAYAGI ROKUMIE MEMORIAL JAPANESE CULTURAL SCHOLARSHIP

Japanese American Citizens League
Attn: National Scholarship Awards
1765 Sutter Street
San Francisco, CA 94115
(415) 345-1075 Fax: (415) 345-1077
E-mail: pwada@jacl.org
Web: www.jacl.org/jacl-national-scholarship-program

Summary To provide financial assistance for college to student members of the Japanese American Citizens League (JACL) who are high school seniors and excel in Japanese cultural activity.

Eligibility This program is open to JACL members who are high school seniors interested in attending a college, university, trade school, business college, or other institution of higher learning. Applicants must excel in Japanese cultural activity, including nihon buyo (classical dance); ikebana (flower arrangement); classical instruments (e.g., shamisen, koto, shakuhachi, taiko); martial arts (e.g., aikido, karate, judo kendo); or chado (tea ceremony). They may study any field in college. Along with their application, they must submit information on their involvement in JACL and a 2-page essay on a topic that changes annually but relates to Japanese Americans. Selection is based on that essay, academic history, JACL involvement, school activities, work history, scholastic honors, and community involvement.

Financial data Stipends generally average more than $2,000.

Duration 1 year; nonrenewable.

Additional information This program began in 2006.

Number awarded 1 each year.

Deadline February of each year.

[199]
HANNAH GRISWOLD GRANT

Delta Kappa Gamma Society International-Alpha Kappa
 State Organization
c/o Carol Kraus, Professional Affairs Committee Chair
151 Atwoodville Road
Mansfield Center, CT 06250
E-mail: yveskraus@earthlink.net
Web: www.deltakappagamma.org/CT/grants.php

Summary To provide financial assistance to Asian American and other minority high school seniors in Connecticut who are interested in working on a degree in education at a school in the state.

Eligibility This program is open to minority seniors graduating from high schools in Connecticut who plan to enroll at a college or university in the state to work on a degree in education. Applicants must be able to demonstrate qualities consistent with the promise of leadership in education, including scholarship and community service. Along with their application, they must submit an essay of at least 200 words on their career plans in education, including their experiences with children. Financial need is not considered in the selection process.

Financial data The stipend is $750.

Duration 1 semester.

Number awarded 1 each year.

Deadline March of each year.

[200]
HATTIE J. HILLIARD SCHOLARSHIP

Wisconsin Women of Color Network, Inc.
c/o P.E. Kiram
756 North 35th Street, Suite 101
Milwaukee, WI 53208
(414) 899-2329 E-mail: pekiram64@gmail.com

Summary To provide financial assistance to Asian American and othr women of color from Wisconsin who are interested in studying art at a school in any state.

Eligibility This program is open to residents of Wisconsin who are women of color enrolled or planning to enroll at a college, university, or vocational/technical school in any state. Applicants must be a member of 1 of the following groups: Asian, African American, American Indian, or Hispanic. Their field of study must be art, graphic art, commercial art, or a related area. They must be able to demonstrate financial need. Along with their application, they must submit a 1-page essay on how this scholarship will help them accomplish their educational goal. U.S. citizenship is required.

Financial data A stipend is awarded (amount not specified).

Duration 1 year.

Additional information This program began in 1995.

Number awarded 1 each year.

Deadline May of each year.

[201]
HAWAII KOREAN CHAMBER OF COMMERCE SCHOLARSHIPS

Hawaii Korean Chamber of Commerce
Attn: Scholarship Committee
P.O. Box 2296
Honolulu, HI 96804
(808) 599-5959 Fax: (808) 599-8622
Web: www.hkccweb.org/en/scholarships.html

Summary To provide financial assistance to Hawaii residents who are of Korean ancestry and interested in attending college in any state.

Eligibility This program is open to residents of Hawaii who are of at least 50% Korean ancestry. Applicants must be graduating high school seniors or current undergraduates who are enrolled or planning to enroll full time at an accredited 4-year college or university in any state. Along with their application, they must submit an essay of 250 to 500 words that covers why they feel they are qualified to receive this scholarship, how they will participate in and contribute to their community after completing their program of study, whether or not their goal includes service to the Korean American community, and how their education will enable them to contribute to the Korean American community. Financial need is also considered in the selection process.

Financial data   The stipend is $2,000.

Duration   1 year.

Number awarded   3 each year.

Deadline   May of each year.

[202]
HEALTH RESEARCH AND EDUCATIONAL TRUST SCHOLARSHIPS

New Jersey Hospital Association
Attn: Health Research and Educational Trust
760 Alexander Road
P.O. Box 1
Princeton, NJ 08543-0001
(609) 275-4224   Fax: (609) 452-8097
E-mail: jhritz@njha.com
Web: www.njha.com/education/scholarships

Summary   To provide financial assistance to New Jersey residents, especially Asian Americans and other minorities, who are working on an undergraduate or graduate degree in a field related to health care administration at a school in any state.

Eligibility   This program is open to residents of New Jersey enrolled in an upper-division or graduate program in hospital or health care administration, public administration, nursing, or other allied health profession at a school in any state. Graduate students working on an advanced degree to prepare to teach nursing are also eligible. Applicants must have a GPA of 3.0 or higher and be able to demonstrate financial need. Along with their application, they must submit a 2-page essay (on which 50% of the selection is based) describing their academic plans for the future. Minorities and women are especially encouraged to apply.

Financial data   The stipend is $2,000.

Duration   1 year.

Additional information   This program began in 1983.

Number awarded   Varies each year; recently, 3 were awarded.

Deadline   June of each year.

[203]
HELEN LEE SCHOLARSHIP

Philip Jaisohn Memorial Foundation
Attn: Scholarship Committee
6705 Old York Road
Philadelphia, PA 19126
(215) 224-2000, ext. 116   Fax: (215) 224-9164
E-mail: info@jaisohn.org
Web: www.jaisohn.com/scholarships

Summary   To provide financial assistance to Korean American undergraduate and graduate students who demonstrate significant financial need.

Eligibility   This program is open to Korean American undergraduate and graduate students who are currently enrolled at a college or university in the United States. Applicants must be able to demonstrate academic excellence, leadership and service to their school and community, and financial need. Along with their application, they must submit a 100-word essay on either "Who is Dr. Jaisohn to Me," or "The Significance of Dr. Jaisohn's Ideal to Korean Ameri-

cans." They must also submit a brief statement on how they can contribute to and be involved in the activities of the Philip Jaisohn Memorial Foundation. Selection is based primarily on financial need.

Financial data   The stipend is $2,000.

Duration   1 year.

Number awarded   2 each year.

Deadline   August of each year.

[204]
HENRY AND CHIYO KUWAHARA CREATIVE ARTS AWARD

Japanese American Citizens League
Attn: National Scholarship Awards
1765 Sutter Street
San Francisco, CA 94115
(415) 345-1075   Fax: (415) 345-1077
E-mail: pwada@jacl.org
Web: www.jacl.org/jacl-national-scholarship-program

Summary   To provide financial assistance to undergraduate and graduate student members of the Japanese American Citizens League (JACL) interested in completing a project in the creative arts.

Eligibility   This program is open to JACL members who are working on an undergraduate or graduate degree in the creative arts. Professional artists are not eligible. Applicants must submit a detailed proposal for a project they wish to create, including a time plan, anticipated date of completion, and itemized budget. They must also submit information on their involvement in JACL and a 2-page essay on a topic that changes annually but relates to Japanese Americans. Selection is based on that essay, academic history, JACL involvement, school activities, work history, scholastic honors, and community involvement. Preference is given to students who are interested in creative projects that reflect the Japanese American experience and culture.

Financial data   Stipends generally average more than $2,000.

Duration   1 year; nonrenewable.

Number awarded   At least 1 each year.

Deadline   March of each year.

[205]
HENRY AND CHIYO KUWAHARA MEMORIAL SCHOLARSHIPS

Japanese American Citizens League
Attn: National Scholarship Awards
1765 Sutter Street
San Francisco, CA 94115
(415) 345-1075   Fax: (415) 345-1077
E-mail: pwada@jacl.org
Web: www.jacl.org/jacl-national-scholarship-program

Summary   To provide financial assistance for undergraduate or graduate study to members of the Japanese American Citizens League (JACL).

Eligibility   This program is open to JACL members who are high school seniors, undergraduates, or graduate students. Applicants must be attending or planning to attend a college, university, trade school, or business college. They must submit information on their involvement in JACL and a 2-page essay on a topic that changes annually but relates to Japanese Americans. Selection is based on that essay, academic history, JACL involvement, school activities, work history, scholastic honors, and community involvement.

Financial data Stipends generally average more than $2,000.

Duration 1 year; nonrenewable.

Number awarded 6 each year: 2 each to entering freshmen, continuing undergraduates, and entering or currently-enrolled graduate students.

Deadline February of each year for graduating high school seniors; March of each year for current undergraduate or graduate students.

[206]
HIDEKO AND ZENZO MATSUYAMA SCHOLARSHIPS

Hawai'i Community Foundation
Attn: Scholarship Department
827 Fort Street Mall
Honolulu, HI 96813
(808) 566-5570   Toll Free: (888) 731-3863
Fax: (808) 521-6286
E-mail: scholarships@hcf-hawaii.org
Web: hcf.scholarships.ngwebsolutions.com

Summary To provide financial assistance to Hawaii residents of Japanese ancestry who are interested in attending college in any state.

Eligibility This program is open to graduates of high schools or recipients of GED certificates in Hawaii who were born in the state and are of Japanese ancestry. Applicants must be enrolled or planning to enroll full time at an accredited 2- or 4-year college or university in any state as an undergraduate student. They must be able to demonstrate academic achievement (GPA of 3.0 or higher), good moral character, and financial need. Along with their application, they must submit a short statement indicating their reasons for attending college, their planned course of study, their career goals, and what community service means to them.

Financial data The amounts of the awards depend on the availability of funds and the need of the recipient. Recently, the average value of the scholarships awarded by the foundation was $2,800.

Duration 1 year.

Additional information This program began in 2006.

Number awarded Varies each year; recently, 13 were awarded.

Deadline February of each year.

[207]
HIGH SCHOOL AND COLLEGE STUDENT ESSAY, POETRY AND VIDEO CONTEST

Go For Broke National Education Center
355 East First Street, Suite 200
Los Angeles, CA 90012
(310) 222-5711   Fax: (310) 222-5700
E-mail: chris@goforbroke.org
Web: www.goforbroke.org

Summary To recognize and reward college and high school students who submit outstanding essays, poetry, or videos relating to the World War II experience of Japanese American soldiers.

Eligibility This contest is open to high school (grades 9-12) and college (undergraduate and graduate) students. Applicants must submit an essay or poem of 250 to 500 words or a video 3 to 5 minutes in length. The topic of the entries may be 1) the Japanese American World War II soldier experience and its relevance to our lives today; 2) a specific Japanese American World War II soldier and elements of his experience that are most meaningful to the student; or 3) what the Japanese American World War II experience can teach us about the Constitution, rights, and responsibilities.

Financial data Awards are $1,000 for winners and $250 for other finalists.

Duration The contest is held annually.

Additional information This contest began in 2013.

Number awarded Awards are presented to 6 winners and 10 other finalists.

Deadline June of each year.

[208]
HIGH SCHOOL SENIOR SCHOLARSHIPS OF THE JAPANESE AMERICAN CITIZENS LEAGUE

Japanese American Citizens League
Attn: National Scholarship Awards
1765 Sutter Street
San Francisco, CA 94115
(415) 345-1075   Fax: (415) 345-1077
E-mail: pwada@jacl.org
Web: www.jacl.org/jacl-national-scholarship-program

Summary To provide financial assistance for college to student members of the Japanese American Citizens League (JACL) who are high school seniors.

Eligibility This program is open to JACL members who are high school seniors interested in attending a college, university, trade school, business college, or other institution of higher learning. Applicants must submit information on their involvement in JACL and a 2-page essay on a topic that changes annually but relates to Japanese Americans. Selection is based on that essay, academic history, JACL involvement, school activities, work history, scholastic honors, and community involvement.

Financial data Stipends generally average more than $2,000.

Duration 1 year; nonrenewable.

Additional information This program includes the following named awards: the Deni and June Uejima Memorial Scholarship, the Kenji Kasai Memorial Scholarship, the Mitsugi Murakami Kasai (Ret.) Memorial Scholarship, the Mush and Haru Kuroiwa Scholarship, the Mr. and Mrs. Takashi Moriuchi Scholarship, the Patricia and Gail Ishimoto Memorial Scholarship, the Sam and Florence Kuwahara Memorial Scholarship, and the Shigeki "Shake" Ushio Memorial Leadership Scholarship.

Number awarded Up to 10 each year.

Deadline February of each year.

[209]
HILO CHINESE SCHOOL SCHOLARSHIP

Hawai'i Community Foundation
Attn: Scholarship Department
827 Fort Street Mall
Honolulu, HI 96813
(808) 566-5570   Toll Free: (888) 731-3863
Fax: (808) 521-6286
E-mail: scholarships@hcf-hawaii.org
Web: hcf.scholarships.ngwebsolutions.com

Summary To provide financial assistance to residents of Hawaii of Chinese ancestry who are working on an undergraduate or graduate degree in any field at a college in any state.

Eligibility This program is open to residents of Hawaii who are currently enrolled full time at an accredited 2- or 4-year college or university in any state. First preference is given to descendants of Hilo Chinese School alumni; second preference is given to students of Chinese ancestry. Applicants must be working on an undergraduate or graduate degree in any field. They must have a GPA of 2.5 or higher be able to demonstrate financial need. Along with their application, they must submit a short statement indicating their reasons for attending college, their planned course of study, their career goals, and what community service means to them.

Financial data The amounts of the awards depend on the availability of funds and the need of the recipient. Recently, the average value of the scholarships awarded by the foundation was $2,800.

Duration 1 year.

Additional information The Hilo Chinese School opened in 1930 to teach Chinese language. When the school closed, a trust was established to support this program.

Number awarded 1 or more each year.

Deadline February of each year.

[210]
HMONG HOME HEALTH CARE SCHOLARSHIPS

Hmong American Education Fund
P.O. Box 17468
St. Paul, MN 55117
(651) 592-1576   E-mail: scholarships@thehaef.org
Web: www.thehaef.org

Summary To provide financial assistance to Hmong residents of Minnesota who are interested in attending college or graduate school in any state to study health care or social services.

Eligibility This program is open to residents of Minnesota who identify themselves as a person of Hmong descent. Applicants must be high school seniors, GED recipients, or current undergraduate or graduate students enrolled or planning to enroll full time at a 2- or 4-year college or university in any state. They must be U.S. citizens or permanent residents and have a GPA of 3.2 or higher. Their field of study must be health care, social services, or a related field. Along with their application, they must submit transcripts and a 1,500-word essay on their educational accomplishments, community service, financial need, and how this scholarship can help them.

Financial data The stipend is $750.

Duration 1 year; nonrenewable.

Additional information Support for this program is provided by Hmong Home Health Care, Inc.

Number awarded 2 each year.

Deadline March of each year.

[211]
HNTB SCHOLARSHIP

Conference of Minority Transportation Officials
Attn: National Scholarship Program
100 M Street, S.E., Suite 917
Washington, DC 20003
(202) 506-2917   E-mail: info@comto.org
Web: www.comto.org/page/scholarships

Summary To provide financial assistance to Asian American and other minority high school seniors interested in working on a degree in transportation or a related field.

Eligibility This program is open to minority seniors graduating from high school with a GPA of 3.0 or higher. Applicants must have been accepted at an accredited university or technical college with the intent to study transportation or a transportation-related discipline. They must be able to demonstrate leadership skills and activities. Along with their application they must submit a cover letter on their transportation-related career goals and life aspirations. Financial need is not considered in the selection process.

Financial data The stipend is $5,000. Funds are paid directly to the recipient's college or university.

Duration 1 year.

Additional information This program is sponsored by HNTB Corporation.

Number awarded 1 each year.

Deadline April of each year.

[212]
HORACE AND SUSIE REVELS CAYTON SCHOLARSHIP

Public Relations Society of America-Puget Sound
  Chapter
Attn: Diane Bevins
1006 Industry Drive
P.O. Box 58530
Seattle, WA 98138-1530
(206) 623-8632   Fax: (206) 575-9255
E-mail: prsascholarship@asi-seattle.net
Web: www.prsapugetsound.org/Page.aspx?nid=73

Summary To provide financial assistance to Asian American and other minority upperclassmen from Washington who are interested in preparing for a career in public relations.

Eligibility This program is open to U.S. citizens who are members of minority groups, defined as Asian Americans, African Americans, Hispanic/Latino Americans, Native Americans, and Pacific Islanders. Applicants must be full-time juniors or seniors attending a college in Washington or Washington students (who graduated from a Washington high school or whose parents live in the state year-round) attending college elsewhere. They must have overcome barriers in pursuit of personal or academic goals. Selection is based on academic achievement, financial need, and demonstrated aptitude in public relations and related courses, activities, and/or internships.

Financial data The stipend is $3,500.

Duration 1 year.

Additional information This program began in 1992.

Number awarded 1 each year.

Deadline May of each year.

[213]
H.R. CHUNG LEADERSHIP SCHOLARSHIP

Philip Jaisohn Memorial Foundation
Attn: Scholarship Committee
6705 Old York Road
Philadelphia, PA 19126
(215) 224-2000, ext. 116   Fax: (215) 224-9164
E-mail: info@jaisohn.org
Web: www.jaisohn.com/scholarships

Summary To provide financial assistance to Korean American undergraduate and graduate students who demonstrate involvement in extracurricular, athletic, and community activities.

Eligibility This program is open to Korean American undergraduate and graduate students who are currently enrolled at a college or university in the United States. Applicants must be able to demonstrate academic excellence, leadership and service to their school and community, and financial need. Along with their application, they must submit a 100-word essay on either "Who is Dr. Jaisohn to Me," or "The Significance of Dr. Jaisohn's Ideal to Korean Americans." They must also submit a brief statement on how they can contribute to and be involved in the activities of the Philip Jaisohn Memorial Foundation. Selection is based primarily on leadership in extracurricular activities, varsity sports, or community involvement.

Financial data The stipend is $1,500.

Duration 1 year.

Number awarded 1 each year.

Deadline August of each year.

[214]
HYATT HOTELS FUND FOR MINORITY LODGING MANAGEMENT STUDENTS

American Hotel & Lodging Educational Foundation
Attn: Manager of Foundation Programs
1250 I Street, N.W., Suite 1100
Washington, DC 20005-5904
(202) 289-3180   Fax: (202) 289-3199
E-mail: foundation@ahlef.org
Web: www.ahlef.org

Summary To provide financial assistance to Asian American and other minority college students working on a degree in hotel management.

Eligibility This program is open to students majoring in hospitality management at a 4-year college or university as at least a junior. Applicants must be members of a minority group (Asian, African American, Hispanic, American Indian, Alaskan Native, or Pacific Islander). They must be enrolled full time. Along with their application, they must submit a 500-word essay on their personal background, including when they became interested in the hospitality field, the traits they possess or will need to succeed in the industry, and their plans as related to their educational and career objectives and future goals. Selection is based on industry-related work experience; financial need; academic record and educational

qualifications; professional, community, and extracurricular activities; personal attributes, including career goals; the essay; and neatness and completeness of the application. U.S. citizenship or permanent resident status is required.

Financial data The stipend is $2,000.

Duration 1 year.

Additional information Funding for this program, established in 1988, is provided by Hyatt Hotels & Resorts.

Number awarded Varies each year; recently, 18 were awarded. Since this program was established, it has awarded scholarships worth $702,000 to 351 minority students.

Deadline April of each year.

[215]
IDAHO STATE BROADCASTERS ASSOCIATION SCHOLARSHIPS

Idaho State Broadcasters Association
1674 Hill Road, Suite 3
Boise, ID 83702
(208) 345-3072   Fax: (208) 343-8046
E-mail: isba@qwestoffice.net
Web: www.idahobroadcasters.org/index.php/scholarships

Summary To provide financial assistance to students, especially Asian Americans and members of other diverse groups, at Idaho colleges and universities who are preparing for a career in the broadcasting field.

Eligibility This program is open to full-time students at Idaho schools who are preparing for a career in broadcasting, including business administration, sales, journalism, or engineering. Applicants must have a GPA of at least 2.0 for the first 2 years of school or 2.5 for the last 2 years. Along with their application, they must submit a letter of recommendation from the general manager of a broadcasting station that is a member of the Idaho State Broadcasters Association and a 1-page essay describing their career plans and why they want the scholarship. Applications are encouraged from a broad and diverse student population. Financial need is not considered in the selection process.

Financial data The stipend is $1,000.

Duration 1 year.

Number awarded At least 2 each year.

Deadline March of each year.

[216]
ILLINOIS BROADCASTERS ASSOCIATION MULTICULTURAL INTERNSHIPS

Illinois Broadcasters Association
Attn: MIP Coordinator
200 Missouri Avenue
Carterville, IL 62918
(618) 985-5555   Fax: (618) 985-6070
E-mail: iba@ilba.org
Web: www.ilba.org/careers/internship-program

Summary To provide funding to Asian American and other minority college students in Illinois who are majoring in broadcasting and interested in interning at a radio or television station in the state.

Eligibility This program is open to currently-enrolled minority students majoring in broadcasting at a college or university in Illinois. Applicants must be interested in a fall, spring, or summer internship at a radio or television station that is a member of the Illinois Broadcasters Association. Along with their application, they must submit 1) a 250-word essay on how they expect to benefit from a grant through this program; and 2) at least 2 letters of recommendation from a broadcasting faculty member or professional familiar with their career potential and 1 other letter. The internship coordinator of the sponsoring organization selects those students nominated by their schools who have the best opportunity to make it in the world of broadcasting and matches them with internship opportunities that would otherwise be unpaid.

Financial data This program provides a grant to pay the living expenses for the interns in the Illinois communities where they are assigned. The amount of the grant depends on the length of the internship.

Duration 16 weeks in the fall and spring terms or 12 weeks in the summer.

Number awarded 12 each year: 4 in each of the 3 terms.

Deadline Deadline not specified.

[217]
ILLINOIS DREAM FUND SCHOLARSHIPS

Illinois Dream Fund
c/o Chicago Community Trust
225 North Michigan Avenue, Suite 2200
Chicago, IL 60601
(312) 616-8000   Fax: (312) 616-7955
E-mail: info@illinoisdreamfund.org
Web: www.illinoisdreamfund.org

Summary To provide financial assistance to undocumented residents of Illinois who are interested in attending college in any state.

Eligibility This program is open to undocumented immigrants who are incoming freshmen, current undergraduates, or transfer students. Applicants must have resided with their parents or guardians while attending high school in Illinois and have graduated (or be graduating) from a high school or received a GED in Illinois after attending an Illinois high school for at least 3 years. They must have a GPA of 2.5 or higher and be attending or planning to attend a college or university in any state. Financial need is considered in the selection process.

Financial data The stipend is $6,000 for students at 4-year institutions or $2,000 for students at 2-year colleges. Funds are paid directly to the recipient's school.

Duration 1 year.

Number awarded Varies each year.

Deadline March of each year.

[218]
ILLINOIS MINORITY REAL ESTATE SCHOLARSHIP

Illinois Association of Realtors
Attn: Illinois Real Estate Educational Foundation
522 South Fifth Street
P.O. Box 2607
Springfield, IL 62708
Toll Free: (866) 854-REEF   Fax: (217) 529-5893
E-mail: lclayton@iar.org
Web: www.ilreef.org

Summary To provide financial assistance to Illinois residents who are Asian Americans or members of other minority groups and preparing for a career in real estate.

Eligibility This program is open to residents of Illinois who are Asian, African American, Hispanic or Latino, or Native American. Applicants must be interested in preparing for a career in real estate by pursuing: 1) courses to meet Illinois broker license requirements; 2) course work to meet Illinois broker license requirement; 3) course work required for Illinois appraisal licensing/certification; 4) professional development unrelated to obtaining license/certification; or 5) an undergraduate or graduate program of study. Along with their application, they must submit information on their employment history, transcripts, evidence of financial need, and an essay that describes their career goals and explains why they believe they should receive scholarship assistance through this program.

Financial data The maximum stipend is $500.

Duration Funds must be used within 24 months of the award date.

Number awarded 1 or more each year.

Deadline Applications may be submitted at any time, but they must be received at least 12 weeks prior to the beginning of the school term for which financial assistance is requested.

[219]
ILLINOIS NURSES FOUNDATION CENTENNIAL SCHOLARSHIP

Illinois Nurses Association
Attn: Illinois Nurses Foundation
P.O. Box 636
Manteno, IL 60950
(815) 468-8804   Fax: (773) 304-1419
E-mail: info@ana-illinois.org
Web: www.ana-illinois.org

Summary To provide financial assistance to nursing undergraduate and graduate students who are Asian Americans or members of other underrepresented groups.

Eligibility This program is open to students working on an associate, bachelor's, or master's degree at an accredited NLNAC or CCNE school of nursing. Applicants must be members of a group underrepresented in nursing (Asians, African Americans, Hispanics, American Indians, or males). Undergraduates must have earned a passing grade in all nursing courses taken to date and have a GPA of 2.85 or higher. Graduate students must have completed at least 12 semester hours of graduate work and have a GPA of 3.0 or higher. All applicants must be willing to 1) act as a spokesperson to other student groups on the value of the scholarship to continuing their nursing education; and 2) be profiled in any media or marketing materials developed by the Illinois Nurses Foundation. Along with their application, they must submit a narrative of 250 to 500 words on how they, as nurses, plan to affect policy at either the state or national level that impacts on nursing or health care generally, or how they believe they will impact the nursing profession in general.

Financial data A stipend is awarded (amount not specified).

Duration 1 year.

Number awarded 1 or more each year.

Deadline March of each year.

[220]
INDIAN AMERICAN SCHOLARSHIP FUND FINANCIAL AID SCHOLARSHIPS

India American Cultural Association
Attn: Indian American Scholarship Fund
2407 Waterford Cove
Decatur, GA 30033
E-mail: rajeshmkurup@gmail.com
Web: www.iasf.org/Scholarships.html

Summary To provide need-based financial assistance to high school seniors in Georgia who are of Indian descent and plan to attend college in any state.

Eligibility This program is open to seniors graduating from high schools in Georgia who are of Indian descent (at least 1 grandparent was born in India). Applicants must be planning to attend a 4-year college or university in any state as a full-time student. Along with their application, they must submit an official school transcript, resume, SAT or ACT score report, the best essay they submitted to a college to which they applied, and documentation of financial need. Selection is based primarily on financial need.

Financial data Stipends range from $1,000 to $2,500 per year.

Duration 1 year; may be renewed up to 3 additional years.

Additional information This program was established in 1993.

Number awarded The sponsor normally awards 4 4-year scholarships, 1 2-year scholarship, and 8 to 12 1-year scholarships.

Deadline May of each year.

[221]
INDIAN AMERICAN SCHOLARSHIP FUND MERIT-BASED SCHOLARSHIPS

India American Cultural Association
Attn: Indian American Scholarship Fund
2407 Waterford Cove
Decatur, GA 30033
E-mail: rajeshmkurup@gmail.com
Web: www.iasf.org/Scholarships.html

Summary To provide merit-based financial assistance to high school seniors in Georgia who are of Indian descent and plan to attend college in any state.

Eligibility This program is open to seniors graduating from high schools in Georgia who are of Indian descent (at least 1 grandparent was born in India). Applicants must be planning to attend a 4-year college or university in any state as a full-time student. Along with their application, they must submit an official school transcript, resume, and SAT or ACT score report. Financial need is not considered in the selection process.

Financial data Stipends range from $500 to $1,000 per year.

Duration 1 year; some scholarships may be renewed.

Additional information This program was established in 1993.

Number awarded The sponsor normally awards 4 4-year scholarships, 1 2-year scholarship, and 8 to 12 1-year scholarships.

Deadline April of each year.

[222]
INDIANA INDUSTRY LIAISON GROUP SCHOLARSHIP

Indiana Industry Liaison Group
c/o Candee Chambers, Vice Chair
DirectEmployers Association
9002 North Purdue Road, Suite 100
Indianapolis, IN 46268
(317) 874-9000   Toll Free: (866) 268-6202
E-mail: vchair@indianailg.org
Web: www.indianailg.org

Summary To provide financial assistance to students from any state enrolled at colleges and universities in Indiana who have been involved in activities to promote diversity.

Eligibility This program is open to residents of any state currently enrolled at an accredited college or university in Indiana. Applicants must either 1) be enrolled in programs or classes related to diversity/Affirmative Action (AA)/Equal Employment Opportunity (EEO); or 2) have work or volunteer experience with diversity/AA/EEO organizations. Along with their application, they must submit an essay of 400 to 500 words on 1 of the following topics: 1) their personal commitment to diversity/AA/EEO within their community or business; 2) a time or situation in which they were able to establish and/or sustain a commitment to diversity; 3) a time when they have taken a position in favor of affirmative action and/or diversity; or 4) activities in which they have participated within their community that demonstrate their personal commitment to moving the community's diversity agenda forward. Financial need is not considered in the selection process.

Financial data The stipend is $1,000.

Duration 1 year.

Number awarded 1 each year.

Deadline January of each year.

[223]
INFRASTRUCTURE ENGINEERING SCHOLARSHIP

Conference of Minority Transportation Officials
Attn: National Scholarship Program
100 M Street, S.E., Suite 917
Washington, DC 20003
(202) 506-2917   E-mail: info@comto.org
Web: www.comto.org/page/scholarships

Summary To provide financial assistance to Asian American and other minority upper-division and graduate students interested in working on a degree in transportation or a related field.

Eligibility This program is open to minority juniors, seniors, and graduate student at an accredited college, university, or vocational/technical school. Applicants must be studying transportation, engineering, planning, or a related discipline. They must have a GPA of 2.5 or higher. Along with their application they must submit a cover letter on their transportation-related career goals and life aspirations. Financial need is not considered in the selection process. Membership in the Conference of Minority Transportation Officials is considered a plus but is not required.

Financial data The stipend is $2,500. Funds are paid directly to the recipient's college or university.

Duration 1 year.

Additional information This program is sponsored by Infrastructure Engineering Inc.

Number awarded 1 each year.

Deadline April of each year.

[224]
INTERMOUNTAIN SECTION AWWA DIVERSITY SCHOLARSHIP

American Water Works Association-Intermountain
  Section
Attn: Member Services Coordinator
3430 East Danish Road
Sandy, UT 84093
(801) 712-1619, ext. 2   Fax: (801) 487-6699
E-mail: nicoleb@ims-awwa.org
Web: ims-awwa.site-ym.com/group/StudentPO

Summary To provide financial assistance to Asian American and other minority undergraduate and graduate students working on a degree in the field of water quality, supply, and treatment at a university in the Intermountain West.

Eligibility This program is open to 1) women; and 2) students who identify as Asian, Hispanic or Latino, Black or African American, Native Hawaiian or other Pacific Islander, or American Indian or Alaska Native. Applicants must be entering or enrolled in an undergraduate or graduate program at a college or university in the Intermountain West (defined to include all or portions of Arizona, Colorado, Idaho, Montana, Nevada, New Mexico, Utah, or Wyoming) that relates to water quality, supply, or treatment. Along with their application, they must submit a 2-page essay on their academic interests and career goals and how those relate to water quality, supply, or treatment. Selection is based on that essay, letters of recommendation, and potential to contribute to the field of water quality, supply, and treatment in the Intermountain West.

Financial data The stipend is $1,000. The winner also receives a 1-year student membership in the Intermountain Section of the American Water Works Association (AWWA).

Duration 1 year; nonrenewable.

Number awarded 1 each year.

Deadline November of each year.

[225]
INTERNATIONAL COMMUNICATIONS INDUSTRIES FOUNDATION SCHOLARSHIPS

InfoComm International
International Communications Industries Foundation
11242 Waples Mill Road, Suite 200
Fairfax, VA 22030
(703) 273-7200   Toll Free: (800) 659-7469
Fax: (703) 278-8082   E-mail: jhardwick@infocomm.org
Web: www.infocomm.org

Summary To provide financial assistance to undergraduate and graduate students who are interested in preparing for a career in the audiovisual (AV) industry, especially Asian Americans and other minorities.

Eligibility This program is open to second-year students at 2-year colleges, juniors and seniors at 4-year institutions, and graduate students. Applicants must have a GPA of 2.75 or higher and be majoring or planning to major in audiovisual subjects or related fields, including audio, video, audiovisual, radio/television/film, or other field related to a career in the audiovisual industry. Students in other programs, such as journalism, may be eligible if they can demonstrate a relationship to career goals in the AV industry. Minority and women candidates are especially encouraged to apply. Selection is based on essays about their career interests, presentation of the application, GPA, AV-related experience, work experience, and letters of recommendation.

Financial data The stipend is $4,000. Funds are sent directly to the school.

Duration 1 year.

Additional information InfoComm International, formerly the International Communications Industries Association, established the International Communications Industries Foundation (ICIF) to manage its charitable and educational activities.

Number awarded Varies each year.

Deadline April of each year.

[226]
INTERPUBLIC GROUP SCHOLARSHIP AND INTERNSHIP

New York Women in Communications, Inc.
Attn: NYWICI Foundation
355 Lexington Avenue, 15th Floor
New York, NY 10017-6603
(212) 297-2133   Fax: (212) 370-9047
E-mail: nywicipr@nywici.org
Web: www.nywici.org/foundation/scholarships

Summary To provide financial assistance and work experience to Asian American women and those from other ethnically diverse groups who are residents of designated eastern states and enrolled as juniors at a college in any state to prepare for a career in advertising or public relations.

Eligibility This program is open to female residents of New York, New Jersey, Connecticut, or Pennsylvania who are from ethnically diverse groups and currently enrolled as juniors at a college or university in any state. Also eligible are women who reside outside the 4 states but are currently enrolled at a college or university within 1 of the 5 boroughs of New York City. Applicants must be preparing for a career in advertising or public relations and have a GPA of 3.2 or higher. They must be available for a summer internship with Interpublic Group (IPG) in New York City. Along with their application, they must submit a 2-page resume; a personal essay of 300 words on an assigned topic that changes annually; 2 letters of recommendation; and an official transcript. Selection is based on academic record, need, demonstrated leadership, participation in school and community activities, honors and other awards or recognition, work experience, goals and aspirations, and unusual personal and/or family circumstances. U.S. citizenship or permanent status is required.

Financial data The scholarship stipend ranges up to $10,000; the internship is salaried (amount not specified).

Duration 1 year.

Additional information This program is sponsored by IPG, a holding company for a large number of firms in the advertising industry.

Number awarded 2 each year.

Deadline January of each year.

[227]
IRTS SUMMER FELLOWSHIP PROGRAM

International Radio and Television Society Foundation
Attn: Director, Special Projects
420 Lexington Avenue, Suite 1601
New York, NY 10170-0101
(212) 867-6650   Toll Free: (888) 627-1266
Fax: (212) 867-6653   E-mail: apply@irts.org
Web: irtsfoundation.org/summer-fellowship-program

Summary   To provide summer work experience to upper-division and graduate students, especially Asian Americans and other minorities, who are interested in working during the summer in broadcasting and related fields in the New York City area.

Eligibility   This program is open to juniors, seniors, and graduate students at 4-year colleges and universities. Applicants must either be a communications major or have demonstrated a strong interest in the field through extracurricular activities or other practical experience. Minority (Asian/Pacific Islander, African American, Hispanic/Latino, American Indian/Alaskan Native) students are especially encouraged to apply.

Financial data   Travel, housing, and a living allowance are provided.

Duration   9 weeks during the summer.

Additional information   The first week consists of a comprehensive orientation to broadcasting, cable, advertising, and new media. Then, the participants are assigned an 8-week fellowship. This full-time "real world" experience in a New York-based corporation allows them to reinforce or redefine specific career goals before settling into a permanent job. Fellows have worked at all 4 major networks, at local New York City radio and television stations, and at national rep firms, advertising agencies, and cable operations. This program includes fellowships reserved for students at designated universities (University of Pennsylvania, Brooklyn College, City College of New York, College of the Holy Cross) and the following named awards: the Thomas S. Murphy Fellowship (sponsored by ABC National Television Sales), the Helen Karas Memorial Fellowship, the Mel Karmazin Fellowship, the Neil Postman Memorial Summer Fellowship, the Ari Bluman Memorial Summer Fellowship (sponsored by Group M), the Thom Casadonte Memorial Fellowship (sponsored by Bloomberg), the Joanne Mercado Memorial Fellowship (sponsored by Nielsen), the Donald V. West Fellowship (sponsored by the Library of American Broadcasting Foundation), the Leslie Moonves Fellowship (sponsored by CBS Television Station Sales, and the Sumner M. Redstone Fellowship (sponsored by CBS Television Station Sales). Other sponsors include the National Academy of Television Arts & Sciences, Fox Networks, NBCUniversal, and Unilever.

Number awarded   Varies; recently, 30 were awarded.

Deadline   November of each year.

[228]
JACOBS ENGINEERING SCHOLARSHIP

Conference of Minority Transportation Officials
Attn: National Scholarship Program
100 M Street, S.E., Suite 917
Washington, DC 20003
(202) 506-2917   E-mail: info@comto.org
Web: www.comto.org/page/scholarships

Summary   To provide financial assistance to Asian American and other minority upper-division and graduate student members of the Conference of Minority Transportation Officials (COMTO) working on a degree in transportation or a related field.

Eligibility   This program is open to minority juniors, seniors, and graduate student who are COMTO members. Applicants must be studying transportation, engineering (civil, construction, or environmental), safety, urban planning, or a related discipline. They must have a GPA of 3.0 or higher. Along with their application they must submit a cover letter on their transportation-related career goals and life aspirations. Financial need is not considered in the selection process. Membership in the Conference of Minority Transportation Officials is considered a plus but is not required.

Financial data   The stipend is $2,500. Funds are paid directly to the recipient's college or university.

Duration   1 year.

Additional information   This program is sponsored by Jacobs Engineering Group.

Number awarded   1 or more each year.

Deadline   April of each year.

[229]
JACOBS ENGINEERING TRANSPORTATION SCHOLARSHIP

Conference of Minority Transportation Officials
Attn: National Scholarship Program
100 M Street, S.E., Suite 917
Washington, DC 20003
(202) 506-2917   E-mail: info@comto.org
Web: www.comto.org/page/scholarships

Summary   To provide financial assistance to Asian American and other minority upper-division and graduate student members of the Conference of Minority Transportation Officials (COMTO) and family of members working on a degree in transportation or a related field.

Eligibility   This program is open to minority juniors, seniors, and graduate student who are COMTO members or whose parents, guardians, or grandparents are members. Applicants must be studying transportation, engineering (civil, construction, or environmental), safety, urban planning, or a related discipline. They must have a GPA of 3.0 or higher. Along with their application they must submit a cover letter on their transportation-related career goals and life aspirations. Financial need is not considered in the selection process.

Financial data   The stipend is $2,500. Funds are paid directly to the recipient's college or university.

Duration   1 year.

Additional information   This program is sponsored by Jacobs Engineering Group.

Number awarded   1 or more each year.

Deadline   April of each year.

[230]
JAISOHN JOURNALISM SCHOLARSHIP

Philip Jaisohn Memorial Foundation
Attn: Scholarship Committee
6705 Old York Road
Philadelphia, PA 19126
(215) 224-2000, ext. 116   Fax: (215) 224-9164
E-mail: info@jaisohn.org
Web: www.jaisohn.com/scholarships

Summary   To provide financial assistance to Korean American undergraduate and graduate students who are working on a degree in journalism.

Eligibility   This program is open to Korean American undergraduate and graduate students who are currently enrolled at a college or university in the United States. Applicants must be working on a degree in journalism. They must be able to demonstrate academic excellence, leadership and service to their school and community, and financial need. Along with their application, they must submit a 100-word essay on either "Who is Dr. Jaisohn to Me," or "The Significance of Dr. Jaisohn's Ideal to Korean Americans." They must also submit a brief statement on how they can contribute to and be involved in the activities of the Philip Jaisohn Memorial Foundation.

Financial data   The stipend is $1,000.

Duration   1 year.

Number awarded   1 each year.

Deadline   August of each year.

[231]
JAMES B. MORRIS SCHOLARSHIPS

James B. Morris Scholarship Fund
Attn: Scholarship Selection Committee
P.O. Box 12145
Des Moines, IA 50312
(515) 864-0922
Web: www.morrisscholarship.org

Summary   To provide financial assistance to Asian American and other minority undergraduate, graduate, and law students from Iowa.

Eligibility   This program is open to minority students (Asian/Pacific Islanders, African Americans, Hispanics, or Native Americans) who are interested in working on an undergraduate or graduate degree. Applicants must be either Iowa residents attending a college or university anywhere in the United States or non-Iowa residents who are attending a college or university in Iowa. Along with their application, they must submit an essay of 250 to 500 words on why they are applying for this scholarship, activities or organizations in which they are involved, and their future plans. Selection is based on the essay, academic achievement (GPA of 2.5 or higher), community service, and financial need. U.S. citizenship is required.

Financial data   The stipend ranges from $1,000 to $2,500 per year.

Duration   1 year; may be renewed.

Additional information   This fund was established in 1978 in honor of the J.B. Morris family, who founded the Iowa branch of the National Association for the Advancement of Colored People and published the *Iowa Bystander* newspaper. The program includes the Ann Chapman Scholarships, the Vincent Chapman, Sr. Scholarships, the Catherine Williams Scholarships, and the Brittany Hall Memorial Scholarships. Support for additional scholarships is provided by EMC Insurance Group and Wells Fargo Bank.

Number awarded   Varies each year; recently, 22 were awarded.

Deadline   February of each year.

[232]
JAMES CARLSON MEMORIAL SCHOLARSHIP

Oregon Office of Student Access and Completion
Attn: Scholarship Processing Coordinator
1500 Valley River Drive, Suite 100
Eugene, OR 97401-2146
(541) 687-7422   Toll Free: (800) 452-8807, ext. 7422
Fax: (541) 687-7414   TDD: (800) 735-2900
E-mail: cheryl.a.connolly@state.or.us
Web: app.oregonstudentaid.gov/Catalog/Default.aspx

Summary   To provide financial assistance to Oregon residents, especially Asian Americans and members of other diverse groups, who are majoring in education on the undergraduate or graduate school level at a school in any state.

Eligibility   This program is open to residents of Oregon who are U.S. citizens or permanent residents and enrolled at a college or university in any state. Applicants must be either 1) college seniors or fifth-year students majoring in elementary or secondary education; or 2) graduate students working on an elementary or secondary certificate. Full-time enrollment and financial need are required. Priority is given to 1) students who come from diverse environments and submit an essay of 250 to 350 words on their experience living or working in diverse environments; 2) dependents of members of the Oregon Education Association; and 3) applicants committed to teaching autistic children.

Financial data   Stipends for scholarships offered by the Oregon Office of Student Access and Completion (OSAC) range from $1,000 to $10,000 but recently averaged $4,368.

Duration   1 year; nonrenewable.

Additional information   This program is administered by the OSAC with funds provided by the Oregon Community Foundation.

Number awarded   Varies each year; recently, 3 were awarded.

Deadline   February of each year.

[233]
JAMES E. WEBB INTERNSHIPS

Smithsonian Institution
Attn: Office of Fellowships and Internships
470 L'Enfant Plaza, Suite 7102
P.O. Box 37012, MRC 902
Washington, DC 20013-7012
(202) 633-7070   Fax: (202) 633-7069
E-mail: siofi@si.edu
Web: www.smithsonianofi.com

Summary   To provide internship opportunities throughout the Smithsonian Institution to Asian American and other minority upper-division and graduate students in business or public administration.

Eligibility   This program is open to minorities who are juniors, seniors, or graduate students majoring in areas of business or public administration (finance, human resource management, accounting, or general business administration). Applicants must have a GPA of 3.0 or higher. They must seek placement in offices, museums, and research institutes within the Smithsonian Institution.

Financial data Interns receive a stipend of $600 per week and a travel allowance.

Duration 10 weeks during the summer, fall, or spring.

Number awarded Varies each year; recently, 8 of these internships were awarded.

Deadline January of each year for summer or fall; September of each year for spring.

[234]
JAMES ECHOLS SCHOLARSHIP

California Association for Health, Physical Education, Recreation and Dance
Attn: Chair, Scholarship Committee
1501 El Camino Avenue, Suite 3
Sacramento, CA 95815-2748
(916) 922-3596   Toll Free: (800) 499-3596 (within CA)
Fax: (916) 922-0133   E-mail: reception@cahperd.org
Web: www.cahperd.org

Summary To provide financial assistance to Asian American and other minority student members of the California Association for Health, Physical Education, Recreation and Dance.

Eligibility This program is open to California residents who have been members of the association for at least 60 days and are attending a 2- or 4-year college or university in the state. Applicants must be undergraduate or graduate students working on a degree in health education, physical education, recreation, or dance and have completed at least 60 semester hours of college work. Selection is based on scholastic proficiency (a GPA of 3.0 or higher); leadership ability in school, community, and professional activities; and personal qualities of enthusiasm, cooperativeness, responsibility, initiative, and ability to work with others. This scholarship is awarded to the highest-ranked minority (Asian, African American, Latino, or Native American) applicant.

Financial data The stipend is $1,000.

Duration 1 year.

Number awarded 1 each year.

Deadline November of each year.

[235]
JAMES J. WYCHOR SCHOLARSHIPS

Minnesota Broadcasters Association
Attn: Scholarship Program
3033 Excelsior Boulevard, Suite 440
Minneapolis, MN 55416
(612) 926-8123   Toll Free: (800) 245-5838
Fax: (612) 926-9761
E-mail: llasere@minnesotabroadcasters.com
Web: www.minnesotabroadcasters.com/career-prep

Summary To provide financial assistance to Minnesota residents, especially Asian Americans and other minorities, who are interested in studying broadcasting at a college in any state.

Eligibility This program is open to residents of Minnesota who are accepted or enrolled at an accredited postsecondary institution in any state offering a broadcast-related curriculum. Applicants must have a high school or college GPA of 2.5 or higher and must submit a 500-word essay on why they wish to prepare for a career in broadcasting or electronic media. Employment in the broadcasting industry is not required, but students who are employed must include a letter from their general manager describing the duties they have performed as a radio or television station employee and evaluating their potential for success in the industry. Financial need is not considered in the selection process. Some of the scholarships are awarded only to minority or women candidates.

Financial data The stipend is $1,500.

Duration 1 year; recipients who are college seniors may reapply for an additional 1-year renewal as a graduate student.

Number awarded 10 each year, distributed as follows: 3 within the 7-county metro area, 5 allocated geographically throughout the state (northeast, northwest, central, southeast, southwest), and 2 reserved specifically for women and minority applicants.

Deadline June of each year.

[236]
JANE C. WALDBAUM ARCHAEOLOGICAL FIELD SCHOOL SCHOLARSHIP

Archaeological Institute of America
c/o Boston University
656 Beacon Street, Sixth Floor
Boston, MA 02215-2006
(617) 358-4184   Fax: (617) 353-6550
E-mail: fellowships@aia.bu.edu
Web: www.archaeological.org/grants/708

Summary To provide funding to upper-division and graduate students, especially Asian Americans and other minorities, who are interested in participating in an archaeological field project in the United States or any other country.

Eligibility This program is open to junior and senior undergraduates and first-year graduate students who are currently enrolled at a college or university in the United States or Canada. Minority and disadvantaged students are encouraged to apply. Applicants must be interested in participating in an archaeological excavation or survey project in any country. They may not have previously participated in an archaeological excavation. Students majoring in archaeology or related disciplines are especially encouraged to apply.

Financial data The grant is $1,000.

Duration At least 1 month during the summer.

Additional information These scholarships were first awarded in 2007.

Number awarded Varies each year; recently, 15 were awarded.

Deadline February of each year.

[237]
JANE SONG MEMORIAL SCHOLARSHIPS

Philip Jaisohn Memorial Foundation
Attn: Scholarship Committee
6705 Old York Road
Philadelphia, PA 19126
(215) 224-2000, ext. 116   Fax: (215) 224-9164
E-mail: info@jaisohn.org
Web: www.jaisohn.com/scholarships

Summary   To provide financial assistance to Korean American undergraduate and graduate students who are studying nursing.

Eligibility   This program is open to Korean American undergraduate and graduate students who are currently enrolled at a college or university in the United States and working on a degree in nursing or other field of patient care. Applicants must be able to demonstrate excellence in community activities and financial need. Along with their application, they must submit an essay on either "Who is Dr. Jaisohn to Me," or "The Significance of Dr. Jaisohn's Ideal to Korean Americans." They must also submit a 100-word statement on how they can contribute to and be involved in the activities of the Philip Jaisohn Memorial Foundation. Selection is based on potential, passion, and leadership.

Financial data   The stipend is $1,500.

Duration   1 year.

Number awarded   2 each year.

Deadline   August of each year.

[238]
JAPANESE AMERICAN ASSOCIATION OF NEW YORK GENERAL SCHOLARSHIPS

Japanese American Association of New York, Inc.
Attn: Scholarship Committee
49 West 45th Street, 11th Floor
New York, NY 10036
(212) 840-6942   Fax: (212) 840-0616
E-mail: info@jaany.org
Web: www.jaany.org/general_scholarship.html

Summary   To provide financial assistance to high school seniors in the New York tri-state area who are of Japanese descent and plan to attend college in any state.

Eligibility   This program is open to seniors of Japanese descent graduating from high schools in the New York tri-state area who plan to attend a college or university in any state. Applicants must submit their latest transcript with a copy of SAT or ACT scores, a letter of recommendation from their school counselor or teacher, and information on any special financial circumstances. Selection is based on that information as well as a 500-word essay on a topic that changes annually but relates to Japan and/or Japanese Americans.

Financial data   Stipends range from $1,000 to $10,000. Airline tickets to Japan may also be presented to some recipients.

Duration   1 year.

Number awarded   Varies each year; recently, 11 were awarded.

Deadline   May of each year.

[239]
JAPANESE AMERICAN ASSOCIATION OF NEW YORK MUSIC SCHOLARSHIP AWARDS

Japanese American Association of New York, Inc.
Attn: Scholarship Committee
49 West 45th Street, 11th Floor
New York, NY 10036
(212) 840-6942   Fax: (212) 840-0616
E-mail: info@jaany.org
Web: www.jaany.org/music_scholarship.html

Summary   To recognize and reward Japanese and Japanese American students who participate in a music competition.

Eligibility   This music competition is open to students who are Japanese or Americans of Japanese descent. Recently, the competition was limited to ensembles from trio to quintet; applicants performed 1 piece from the Classical era and another from the Romantic era or the 20th century at the recital in New York.

Financial data   Awards range from $2,000 to $5,000.

Duration   The competition is held annually.

Number awarded   2 each year.

Deadline   September of each year.

[240]
JAPANESE AMERICAN CITIZENS LEAGUE UNDERGRADUATE SCHOLARSHIPS

Japanese American Citizens League
Attn: National Scholarship Awards
1765 Sutter Street
San Francisco, CA 94115
(415) 345-1075   Fax: (415) 931-4671
E-mail: ncwnp@jacl.org
Web: www.jacl.org/edu/scholar.htm

Summary   To provide financial assistance for college to student members of the Japanese American Citizens League (JACL).

Eligibility   This program is open to JACL members who are currently enrolled at a college, university, trade school, business college, or other institution of higher learning. Applicants must submit information on their involvement in JACL and a 2-page essay on a topic that changes annually but relates to Japanese Americans. Selection is based on that essay, academic history, JACL involvement, school activities, work history, scholastic honors, and community involvement.

Financial data   Stipends generally average more than $2,000.

Duration   1 year; nonrenewable.

Additional information   This program includes the following named awards that impose no specialized requirements: the Dr. Thomas T. Yatabe Memorial Scholarship, the Kenji Kajiwara Memorial Scholarship, the Saburo Kido Memorial Scholarship, and the Shigeru "Shig" Nakahira Memorial Scholarship.

Number awarded   Up to 6 each year.

Deadline   March of each year.

[241]
JAPANESE AMERICAN VETERANS ASSOCIATION MEMORIAL SCHOLARSHIPS

Japanese American Veterans Association
c/o Terry Shima, Outreach and Education Committee
  Chair
415 Russell Avenue, Number 1005
Gaithersburg, MD 20877
(301) 987-6746   E-mail: ttshima@comcast.net
Web: www.javadc.org

Summary To provide financial assistance for college or graduate school to relatives of Japanese American veterans and military personnel.

Eligibility This program is open to graduating high school seniors and students currently working on an undergraduate or graduate degree at a college, university, or school of specialized study. Applicants must be related, by blood or marriage, to 1) a person who served with the 442nd Regimental Combat Team, the 100th Infantry Battalion, or other unit associated with those; 2) a person who served in the U.S. Military Intelligence Service during or after World War II; 3) a person of Japanese ancestry who is serving or has served in the U.S. armed forces and been honorable discharged; or 4) a member of the Japanese American Veterans Association (JAVA) whose membership extends back at least 1 year.

Financial data The stipend is $1,500.

Duration 1 year; recipients may reapply.

Additional information These scholarships, first awarded in 2008, include the following named awards: the Orville C. Shirey Memorial Scholarship, the Joseph Ichiuji Memorial Scholarship, the Phil and Douglas Ishio Scholarship, the Kiyoko Tsuboi Taubkin Scholarship, the Ranger Grant Hirabayashi Memorial Scholarship, the Victor and Teru Matsui Scholarship, the Betty Shima Scholarship, the Mitsugi Kasai Scholarship, and the U.S. Senator Daniel K. Inouye Scholarship.

Number awarded 10 each year.

Deadline April of each year.

[242]
JAY LEE SOCIAL SERVICE SCHOLARSHIP

Philip Jaisohn Memorial Foundation
Attn: Scholarship Committee
6705 Old York Road
Philadelphia, PA 19126
(215) 224-2000, ext. 116   Fax: (215) 224-9164
E-mail: info@jaisohn.org
Web: www.jaisohn.com/scholarships

Summary To provide financial assistance to Korean American undergraduate and graduate students who have participated in social service activities.

Eligibility This program is open to Korean American undergraduate and graduate students who are currently enrolled at a college or university in the United States. Applicants must be able to demonstrate excellence in community service activities and financial need. Along with their application, they must submit a 100-word essay on either "Who is Dr. Jaisohn to Me," or "The Significance of Dr. Jaisohn's Ideal to Korean Americans." They must also submit a brief statement on how they can contribute to and be involved in the activities of the Philip Jaisohn Memorial Foundation. Selection is based on community service and future potential.

Financial data The stipend is $1,000.

Duration 1 year.

Number awarded 1 each year.

Deadline August of each year.

[243]
JIMMY A. YOUNG MEMORIAL EDUCATION RECOGNITION AWARD

American Association for Respiratory Care
Attn: American Respiratory Care Foundation
9425 North MacArthur Boulevard, Suite 100
Irving, TX 75063-4706
(972) 243-2272   Fax: (972) 484-2720
E-mail: info@arcfoundation.org
Web: www.arcfoundation.org

Summary To provide financial assistance to college students, especially Asian Americans and other minorities, who are interested in becoming respiratory therapists.

Eligibility Candidates must be enrolled in an accredited respiratory therapy program, have completed at least 1 semester/quarter of the program, and have a GPA of 3.0 or higher. Preference is given to nominees of minority origin. Applications must include 6 copies of an original referenced paper on some aspect of respiratory care and letters of recommendation. The foundation prefers that the candidates be nominated by a school or program, but any student may initiate a request for sponsorship by a school (in order that a deserving candidate is not denied the opportunity to compete simply because the school does not initiate the application).

Financial data The stipend is $1,000. The award also provides airfare, 1 night's lodging, and registration for the association's international congress.

Duration 1 year.

Number awarded 1 each year.

Deadline June of each year.

[244]
JOANN JETER MEMORIAL DIVERSITY SCHOLARSHIP

Associates Foundation
Attn: Claudia Perot, Scholarship Committee Chair
JCD 6
P.O. Box 3621
Portland, OR 97208-3621
(503) 230-3754
Web: www.theassociatesonline.org

Summary To provide financial assistance to Asian American and other students who reflect elements of diversity and are interested in working on an undergraduate or graduate degree in any field.

Eligibility This program is open to students who are enrolled or planning to enroll as a full-time undergraduate or graduate student at an accredited 4-year college or university or a full-time student at a 2-year college enrolled in a program leading to an academic degree. Applicants must be from a diverse background, including first-generation college student, cultural and/or ethnic minority background, low-income, or other clearly articulated aspects of diversity as presented in an essay.

Financial data The stipend ranges from $500 to $1,000.
Duration 1 year.
Number awarded Varies each year; recently, 3 were awarded.
Deadline April of each year.

[245]
JOHN AND MURIEL LANDIS SCHOLARSHIPS
American Nuclear Society
Attn: Scholarship Coordinator
555 North Kensington Avenue
La Grange Park, IL 60526-5535
(708) 352-6611   Toll Free: (800) 323-3044
Fax: (708) 352-0499   E-mail: outreach@ans.org
Web: committees.ans.org/need/apply.html

Summary To provide financial assistance to undergraduate or graduate students, especially Asian Americans and other minorities, who are interested in preparing for a career in nuclear-related fields and can demonstrate financial need.

Eligibility This program is open to undergraduate and graduate students at colleges or universities located in the United States who are preparing for, or planning to prepare for, a career in nuclear science, nuclear engineering, or a nuclear-related field. Qualified high school seniors are also eligible. Applicants must have greater than average financial need and have experienced circumstances that render them disadvantaged. Along with their application, they must submit an essay on their academic and professional goals, experiences that have affected those goals, etc. Selection is based on that essay, academic achievement, letters of recommendation, and financial need. Women and members of minority groups are especially urged to apply. U.S. citizenship is not required.

Financial data The stipend is $5,000, to be used to cover tuition, books, fees, room, and board.
Duration 1 year; nonrenewable.
Number awarded Up to 9 each year.
Deadline January of each year.

[246]
JOHN DEERE SCHOLARSHIP FOR FEMALE AND MINORITY STUDENTS
American Welding Society
Attn: AWS Foundation, Inc.
8669 N.W. 36th Street, Suite 130
Doral, FL 33166-6672
(305) 443-9353   Toll Free: (800) 443-9353, ext. 250
Fax: (305) 443-7559   E-mail: nprado-pulido@aws.org
Web: www.aws.org/foundation/page/john-deere-scholarship

Summary To provide financial assistance to Asian American and other minority undergraduate students, especially those from designated states, who are working on a degree in welding engineering or welding engineering technology at a university in any state.

Eligibility This award is available to U.S. citizens who are women or members of minority groups. Preference is given to residents of Illinois, Iowa, Kansas Minnesota, Missouri, Nebraska, North Dakota, South Dakota, or Wisconsin. Applicants must have completed at least 1 semester of full-time study in a 4-year undergraduate program of welding engineering, welding engineering technology, or mechanical or manufacturing engineering with a welding emphasis. They must have a GPA of 3.0 or higher. Along with their application, they must submit a statement of unmet financial need (although financial need is not required to apply), transcripts, 2 letters of recommendation, and a personal statement that provides their personal objectives and values, their career objectives with a statement of why they want to prepare for a career in welding, participation and leadership in campus and outside organizations, participation in American Welding Society (AWS) student and section activities, and general background information.

Financial data The stipend is $2,500.
Duration 1 year; nonrenewable.
Additional information This program is sponsored by John Deere.
Number awarded 1 each year.
Deadline February of each year.

[247]
JONATHAN T.Y. YEH MEMORIAL STUDENT PRIZE
American Folklore Society
Attn: Timothy Lloyd, Executive Director
Indiana University
Eigenmann Hall
1900 East Tenth Street
Bloomington, IN 47406
(812) 856-2379   Fax: (812) 856-2483
E-mail: timlloyd@indiana.edu
Web: www.afsnet.org/?page=YehAward

Summary To recognize and reward outstanding student papers on a subject dealing with Asian and/or Asian American folklore.

Eligibility This competition is open to full-time undergraduate and graduate students under 30 years of age. Applicants must submit a 10- to 12-page research paper dealing with Asian and/or Asian American folklore studies. They must be able to demonstrate prospects for publication of their scholarly work and a dedication to research and/or teaching folklore studies.

Financial data The prize is $500.
Duration The prize is awarded annually.
Additional information This prize is awarded by the Transnational Asia/Pacific Section of the American Folklore Society (AFS).
Number awarded 1 each year.
Deadline May of each year.

[248]
JUSTINE E. GRANNER MEMORIAL SCHOLARSHIP
Iowa United Methodist Foundation
2301 Rittenhouse Street
Des Moines, IA 50321
(515) 974-8927
Web: www.iumf.org/scholarships/general

Summary To provide financial assistance to members of United Methodist churches in Iowa who are Asian Americans or other ethnic minorities and interested in majoring in a health-related field.

Eligibility This program is open to ethnic minority students who are members of United Methodist churches and preparing for a career in nursing, public health, or a related field at a college or school of nursing in Iowa. Preference is given to graduates of Iowa high schools. Applicants must have a GPA of 3.0 or higher. They must submit transcripts, 3 letters of recommendation, ACT and/or SAT scores, and documentation of financial need.

Financial data The stipend is $1,000.

Duration 1 year.

Number awarded 1 each year.

Deadline February of each year.

[249]
KAISER PERMANENTE COLORADO DIVERSITY SCHOLARSHIP PROGRAM

Kaiser Permanente
Attn: Diversity Development Department
10065 East Harvard Avenue, Suite 400
Denver, CO 80231
Toll Free: (877) 457-4772
E-mail: co-diversitydevelopment@kp.org

Summary To provide financial assistance to Colorado residents who are Asian Pacific Americans or members of other diverse groups and interested in working on an undergraduate or graduate degree in a health care field at a public college in the state.

Eligibility This program is open to all residents of Colorado, including those who identify as 1 or more of the following: Asian Pacific, African American, Latino, lesbian, gay, bisexual, transgender, intersex, Native American, U.S. veteran, and/or a person with a disability. Applicants must be enrolled or planning to enroll full time at a publicly-funded college, university, or technical school in Colorado as 1) a graduating high school senior with a GPA of 2.7 or higher; 2) a GED recipient with a GED score of 520 or higher; 3) an undergraduate student; or 4) a graduate or doctoral student. They must be preparing for a career in health care (e.g., athletic training, audiology, cardiovascular perfusion technology, clinical medical assisting, cytotechnology, dental assisting, dental hygiene, diagnostic medicine, dietetics, emergency medical technology, medicine, nursing, occupational therapy, pharmacy, phlebotomy, physical therapy, physician assistant, radiology, respiratory therapy, social work, sports medicine, surgical technology). Selection is based on academic achievement, character qualities, community outreach and volunteering, and financial need.

Financial data Stipends range from $1,400 to $2,600 per year.

Duration 1 year; may be renewed.

Number awarded Varies each year; recently, 17 were awarded.

Deadline March of each year.

[250]
KAISER PERMANENTE NORTHWEST HEALTH CARE CAREER SCHOLARSHIPS

Kaiser Permanente Northwest
Attn: Community Health Careers Coordinator
500 N.E. Multnomah Street, Suite 100
Portland, OR 97232
(503) 813-4478   E-mail: kpnwscholarship@gmail.com
Web: www.kpnwscholarship.scholarsapply.org/Awards

Summary To provide financial assistance to Asian American and other underrepresented seniors at designated high schools in Oregon and southwestern Washington who plan to attend college in any state to prepare for a career as a health care professional.

Eligibility This program is open to seniors graduating from 106 approved high schools in Oregon and 26 in southwestern Washington. Applicants must be planning to enroll full time at a college or university in any state to prepare for a career as a medical or dental health care professional. They must have a GPA of 2.5 or higher. Proof of U.S. citizenship or permanent resident status is not required; undocumented students and those with Deferred Action for Childhood Arrival (DACA) status are eligible. Preference is given to students who 1) can demonstrate financial need; 2) are the first member of their family to attend college; 3) speak English plus a second language fluently; 4) are a member of a diverse population, including an ethnic or racial group underrepresented in the health professions (Asian or Pacific Islander, Black or African American, Hispanic or Latino, Native American), LGBTQ, and those with a disability; 5) engage in organized health and wellness activities at school and/or school-based health center activities; or 6) regularly volunteer or work in a public health setting such as a free clinic or health education organization.

Financial data Most stipends are $2,000 per year. Some awards are for $10,000 or $5,000 ($5,000 or $2,500 per year).

Duration 1 year (the freshman year of college) for the $2,000 awards or 2 years (the freshmen and sophomore years) for the $10,000 and $5,000 students; recipients may apply for 1 additional year (the junior year of college) of funding at $2,000.

Additional information This program began in 2008.

Number awarded At least 1 at each of the 132 approved high schools plus 24 to former recipients entering their junior year of college.

Deadline January of each year.

[251]
KANSAS ETHNIC MINORITY SCHOLARSHIP PROGRAM

Kansas Board of Regents
Attn: Student Financial Assistance
1000 S.W. Jackson Street, Suite 520
Topeka, KS 66612-1368
(785) 296-3518   Fax: (785) 296-0983
E-mail: loldhamburns@ksbor.org
Web: www.kansasregents.org/scholarships_and_grants

Summary To provide financial assistance to Asian American and other minority students in Kansas who are interested in attending college in the state.

Eligibility Eligible to apply are Kansas residents who fall into 1 of these minority groups: Asian, Pacific Islander, American Indian, Alaskan Native, African American, or Hispanic. Applicants may be current college students (enrolled in community colleges, colleges, or universities in Kansas), but high school seniors graduating in the current year receive priority consideration. Minimum academic requirements include 1 of the following: 1) ACT score of 21 or higher or combined mathematics and critical reading SAT score of 990 or higher; 2) cumulative GPA of 3.0 or higher; 3) high school rank in upper 33%; 4) completion of the Kansas Scholars Curriculum (4 years of English, 4 years of mathematics, 3 years of science, 3 years of social studies, and 2 years of foreign language); 5) selection by the National Merit Corporation in any category; or 6) selection by the College Board as a Hispanic Scholar. Selection is based primarily on financial need.

Financial data A stipend of up to $1,850 is provided, depending on financial need and availability of state funds.

Duration 1 year; may be renewed for up to 3 additional years (4 additional years for designated 5-year programs), provided the recipient maintains a 2.0 cumulative GPA and has financial need.

Number awarded Approximately 200 each year.

Deadline April of each year.

[252]
KANSAS SPJ MINORITY STUDENT SCHOLARSHIP

Society of Professional Journalists-Kansas Professional Chapter
c/o Denise Neil, Scholarship Committee
Wichita Eagle
825 East Douglas Avenue
P.O. Box 820
Wichita, KS 67201-0820
(316) 268-6327   E-mail: dneil@wichitaeagle.com

Summary To provide financial assistance to residents of any state enrolled at colleges and universities in Kansas who are Asian Americans or members of other racial or ethnic minority group and interested in a career in journalism.

Eligibility This program is open to residents of any state who are members of a racial or ethnic minority group and entering their junior or senior year at colleges and universities in Kansas. Applicants must be seriously considering a career in journalism. They must be enrolled at least half time and have a GPA of 2.5 or higher. Along with their application, they must submit a professional resume, 4 to 6 examples of their best work (clips or stories, copies of photographs, tapes or transcripts of broadcasts, printouts of web pages) and a 1-page cover letter about themselves, how they came to be interested in journalism, their professional goals, and (if appropriate) their financial need for this scholarship.

Financial data The stipend is $1,000.

Duration 1 year.

Number awarded 1 each year.

Deadline March of each year.

[253]
KATHY MANN MEMORIAL SCHOLARSHIP

Wisconsin Education Association Council
Attn: Scholarship Committee
33 Nob Hill Drive
P.O. Box 8003
Madison, WI 53708-8003
(608) 276-7711   Toll Free: (800) 362-8034, ext. 278
Fax: (608) 276-8203   E-mail: BrisackM@weac.org
Web: www.weac.org

Summary To provide financial assistance to Asian American and other minority high school seniors whose parent is a member of the Wisconsin Education Association Council (WEAC) and who plan to study education at a college in any state.

Eligibility This program is open to high school seniors whose parent is an active WEAC member, an active retired member, or a person who died while holding a WEAC membership. Applicants must be members of a minority group (Asian or Pacific Islander, American Indian, Eskimo or Aleut, Hispanic, or Black). They must rank in the top 25% of their graduating class or have a GPA of 3.0 or higher, plan to major or minor in education at a college in any state, and intend to teach in Wisconsin. Selection is based on an essay on why they want to enter the education profession and what they hope to accomplish, GPA, letters of recommendation, school and community activities, and financial need.

Financial data The stipend is $1,450 per year.

Duration 4 years, provided the recipient maintains a GPA of 3.0 or higher.

Number awarded 1 each year.

Deadline February of each year.

[254]
KAY LONGCOPE SCHOLARSHIP AWARD

National Lesbian & Gay Journalists Association
2120 L Street, N.W., Suite 850
Washington, DC 20037
(202) 588-9888   Fax: (202) 588-1818
E-mail: info@nlgfa.org
Web: www.nlgja.org/resources/longcope

Summary To provide financial assistance to Asian American and other lesbian, gay, bisexual, and transgender (LGBT) undergraduate and graduate students of color who are interested in preparing for a career in journalism.

Eligibility This program is open to LGBT students of color who are current or incoming undergraduate or graduate students at a college, university, or community college. Applicants must be planning a career in journalism and be committed to furthering the sponsoring organization's mission of fair and accurate coverage of the LGBT community. They must demonstrate an awareness of the issues facing the LGBT community and the importance of fair and accurate news coverage. For undergraduates, a declared major in journalism and/or communications is desirable but not required; non-journalism majors may demonstrate their commitment to a journalism career through work samples, internships, and work on a school news publication, online news service, or broadcast affiliate. Graduate students must be enrolled in a journalism program. Along with their application, they must submit a 1-page resume, 5 work samples, official transcripts, 3 letters of recommendation, and a 750-word news story on a designated subject involving the LGBT community. U.S. citizenship or permanent resident status is required. Selection is based on journalistic and scholastic ability.

Financial data   The stipend is $3,000.

Duration   1 year.

Additional information   This program began in 2008.

Number awarded   1 each year.

Deadline   May of each year.

[255]
KENTUCKY LIBRARY ASSOCIATION SCHOLARSHIP FOR MINORITY STUDENTS

Kentucky Library Association
c/o Executive Director
5932 Timber Ridge Drive, Suite 101
Prospect, KY 40059
(502) 223-5322   Fax: (502) 223-4937
E-mail: info@kylibasn.org
Web: www.klaonline.org/scholarships965.cfm

Summary   To provide financial assistance to Asian Americans or members of othr minority groups who are residents of Kentucky or attending school there and are working on an undergraduate or graduate degree in library science.

Eligibility   This program is open to members of minority groups (defined as American Indian, Alaskan Native, Black, Hispanic, Pacific Islander, or other ethnic group) who are entering or continuing at a graduate library school accredited by the American Library Association (ALA) or an undergraduate library program accredited by the National Council for Teacher Education (NCATE). Applicants must be residents of Kentucky or a student in a library program in the state. Along with their application, they must submit a statement of their career objectives, why they have chosen librarianship as a career, and their reasons for applying for this scholarship. Selection is based on that statement, cumulative undergraduate and graduate GPA (if applicable), academic merit and potential, and letters of recommendation. U.S. citizenship or permanent resident status is required.

Financial data   The stipend is $1,000.

Duration   1 year; nonrenewable.

Number awarded   1 or more each year.

Deadline   June of each year.

[256]
KENTUCKY MINORITY EDUCATOR RECRUITMENT AND RETENTION SCHOLARSHIPS

Kentucky Department of Education
Attn: Office of Next-Generation Learners
500 Mero Street, 19th Floor
Frankfort, KY 40601
(502) 564-1479   Fax: (502) 564-4007
TDD: (502) 564-4970
E-mail: jennifer.baker@education.ky.gov
Web: www.education.ky.gov

Summary   To provide forgivable loans to Asian Americans and other minority undergraduate and graduate students enrolled in Kentucky public institutions who want to become teachers.

Eligibility   This program is open to residents of Kentucky who are undergraduate or graduate students pursuing initial teacher certification at a public university or community college in the state. Applicants must have a GPA of 2.75 or higher and either maintain full-time enrollment or be a part-time student within 18 semester hours of receiving a teacher education degree. They must be U.S. citizens and meet the Kentucky definition of a minority student.

Financial data   Stipends are $5,000 per year at the 8 state universities in Kentucky or $2,000 per year at community and technical colleges. This is a scholarship/loan program. Recipients are required to teach 1 semester in Kentucky for each semester or summer term the scholarship is received. If they fail to fulfill that requirement, the scholarship converts to a loan payable at 6% annually.

Duration   1 year; may be renewed up to 3 additional years.

Additional information   The Kentucky General Assembly established this program in 1992.

Number awarded   Varies each year.

Deadline   Each state college of teacher education sets its own deadline.

[257]
KOREAN HONOR SCHOLARSHIP

Embassy of the Republic of Korea in the USA
2320 Massachusetts Avenue, N.W.
Washington, DC 20008
(202) 939-5679   Fax: (202) 342-1597
Web: usa.mofa.go.kr

Summary   To provide financial assistance to undergraduate and graduate students of Korean or Korean American heritage.

Eligibility   This program is open to students of Korean or Korean American heritage. Applicants must be entering or enrolled full time in an undergraduate or graduate degree program at a college or university in the United States or Canada. They must have a GPA of 3.5 or higher (3.0 or higher for students in music or art). Along with their application, they must submit a 600-word essay (in English) on a topic that changes annually but relates to their Korean heritage. Selection is based on that essay, academic achievement, awards, honors, performances, extracurricular activities, and a letter of recommendation. Students with disabilities are especially encouraged to apply.

Financial data   The stipend is $3,000 or $1,000.

Duration   1 year; nonrenewable.

Additional information   This program began in 1981 when the government of the Republic of Korea donated $1 million to commemorate the 100th anniversary of the establishment of diplomatic relations between Korea and the United States. Subsequent donations have added to the fund.

Number awarded   1 at $3,000 and approximately 35 each year at $1,000 (including 2 or 3 for students in music or art and 1 or 2 for students with disabilities). Since the program began, it has awarded more than 3,000 of these scholarships.

Deadline   June of each year.

[258]
KOREAN NURSES ASSOCIATION OF SOUTHERN CALIFORNIA REGISTERED NURSE EDUCATION SCHOLARSHIPS

Korean Nurses Association of Southern California
1254 West Sixth Street, Suite 809
Los Angeles, CA 90017
(213) 434-1019   E-mail: kanascrn@gmail.com
Web: www.koamrn.org

Summary   To provide financial assistance to Korean nurses in California who wish to attend college in southern California to work on a bachelor's or graduate degree.

Eligibility   This program is open to Korean registered nurses who are enrolled or entering a baccalaureate or higher degree nursing program in southern California. Applicants must be citizens or permanent residents of the United States. Along with their application, they must submit a 1-page essay on their reasons for selecting nursing as a career, including their professional goals and objectives. Selection is based on that essay, work experience in nursing and related fields, community service and volunteer work experience, cumulative GPA, and letters of recommendation. Priority consideration is given to members of the Korean Nurses Association of Southern California and their immediate family members.

Financial data   A stipend is awarded (amount not specified).

Duration   1 year; may be renewed 1 additional year.

Number awarded   1 or more each year.

Deadline   November of each year.

[259]
KOREAN UNIVERSITY CLUB SCHOLARSHIP

Hawai'i Community Foundation
Attn: Scholarship Department
827 Fort Street Mall
Honolulu, HI 96813
(808) 566-5570   Toll Free: (888) 731-3863
Fax: (808) 521-6286
E-mail: scholarships@hcf-hawaii.org
Web: hcf.scholarships.ngwebsolutions.com

Summary   To provide financial assistance to residents of Hawaii who are of Korean ancestry and interested in attending college in any state.

Eligibility   This program is open to residents of Hawaii who are enrolled or planning to enroll full time at a 2- or 4-year college or university in any state. Applicants must be of Korean ancestry. They must be able to demonstrate academic achievement (GPA of 2.7 or higher), good moral character, and financial need. Along with their application, they must submit a short statement indicating their reasons for attending college, their planned course of study, their career goals, and what community service means to them.

Financial data   The amounts of the awards depend on the availability of funds and the need of the recipient. Recently, the average value of the scholarships awarded by the foundation was $2,800.

Duration   1 year.

Additional information   The Korean University Club of Hawaii was established in 1936 and began awarding scholarships to students of Korean ancestry in 1950.

Number awarded   1 or more each year.

Deadline   February of each year.

[260]
KOREAN-AMERICAN ADVENTIST SCHOLARSHIP FOUNDATION

Korean-American Adventist Scholarships
c/o Korean Adventist Press
619 South New Hampshire Avenue
Los Angeles, CA 90005
(213) 388-6100   E-mail: sdascholarship@gmail.com
Web: www.sdascholarship.org/?page_id=15

Summary   To provide financial assistance to Korean-American Adventists who are interested in working on an undergraduate or graduate degree in any field.

Eligibility   This program is open to Korean-American Adventists who are high school seniors or students currently enrolled in college or graduate school. Applicants must have a GPA of 3.0 or higher. Along with their application, they must submit a 1- to 2-page personal essay that describes their personal history, life passions, long-term goals, and financial situation. Their pastor must provide an evaluation of their spiritual dedication, motivation, citizenship, church activities, academic achievement, and financial need.

Financial data   The stipend is $1,000.

Duration   1 year.

Additional information   This program began in 2004.

Number awarded   20 each year.

Deadline   May of each year.

[261]
KSEA UNDERGRADUATE SCHOLARSHIPS

Korean-American Scientists and Engineers Association
Attn: Scholarship Committee
1952 Gallows Drive, Suite 300
Vienna, VA 22182
(703) 748-1221   Fax: (703) 748-1331
E-mail: hq@ksea.org
Web: scholarship.ksea.org/InfoUndergraduate.aspx

Summary   To provide financial assistance to undergraduate student members of the Korean-American Scientists and Engineers Association (KSEA).

Eligibility   This program is open to Korean American undergraduate students who are KSEA members, have completed at least 2 semesters as a college student, and are majoring in science, engineering, or a related field. Along with their application, they must submit an essay of 600 to 800 words on a topic that changes annually but relates to science or engineering; recently, students were asked how this scholarship would make a difference in their studies in science and engineering. Selection is based on the essay (25%), KSEA activities and community service (25%), recommendation letters (20%), and academic performance (30%).

Financial data   The stipend is $1,000.

Duration   1 year.

Additional information   This program includes the following named scholarships: the Inyong Ham Scholarship, the Wan-Kyoo Cho Scholarship, the Shoon Kyung Kim Scholarship, the Nam Sook and Je Hyun Kim Scholarship, the SeAh-Haiam Scholarship, the Yohan and Rumie Cho Scholarship, the Changkiu Riew and Hyunsoo Kim Scholarship, the Woojin

Scholarship, the Jae S. and Kyuho Lim Scholarship, and the Hyundai Scholarship.

Number awarded Approximately 20 each year.

Deadline March of each year.

[262]
KYUTARO AND YASUO ABIKO MEMORIAL SCHOLARSHIP

Japanese American Citizens League
Attn: National Scholarship Awards
1765 Sutter Street
San Francisco, CA 94115
(415) 345-1075   Fax: (415) 345-1077
E-mail: pwada@jacl.org
Web: www.jacl.org/jacl-national-scholarship-program

Summary To provide financial assistance for college to student members of the Japanese American Citizens League (JACL), especially those majoring in journalism or agriculture.

Eligibility This program is open to JACL members who are currently enrolled at a college, university, trade school, business college, or other institution of higher learning. Applicants must submit information on their involvement in JACL and a 2-page essay on a topic that changes annually but relates to Japanese Americans. Selection is based on that essay, academic history, JACL involvement, school activities, work history, scholastic honors, and community involvement. Preference is given to students majoring in journalism or agriculture.

Financial data Stipends generally average more than $2,000.

Duration 1 year; nonrenewable.

Number awarded At least 1 each year.

Deadline March of each year.

[263]
LAGRANT FOUNDATION UNDERGRADUATE SCHOLARSHIPS

Lagrant Foundation
Attn: Senior Talent Acquisition and Fundraising Manager
633 West Fifth Street, 48th Floor
Los Angeles, CA 90071
(323) 469-8680, ext. 223   Fax: (323) 469-8683
E-mail: erickainiguez@lagrant.com
Web: www.lagrantfoundation.org/Scholarship%20Program

Summary To provide financial assistance to Asian American and other minority college students who are interested in majoring in advertising, public relations, or marketing.

Eligibility This program is open to Asian Americans/Pacific Islanders, African Americans, Hispanics/Latinos, and Native Americans/American Indians who are full-time students at a 4-year accredited institution. Applicants must have a GPA of 2.75 or higher and be either majoring in advertising, marketing, or public relations or minoring in communications with plans to prepare for a career in advertising, marketing, or public relations. Along with their application, they must submit 1) a 1- to 2-page essay outlining their career goals; what steps they will take to increase ethnic representation in the fields of advertising, marketing, and public relations; and the role of an advertising, marketing, or public relations practitioner; 2) a paragraph describing the college and/or community activities in which they are involved; 3) a brief paragraph

describing any honors and awards they have received; 4) a letter of reference; 5) a resume; and 6) an official transcript. U.S. citizenship or permanent resident status is required.

Financial data The stipend is $2,500.

Duration 1 year.

Number awarded Varies each year; recently, 22 were awarded.

Deadline February of each year.

[264]
LAO AMERICAN NEW GENERATION SCHOLARSHIP FOR LAO STUDENTS

Lao American New Generation, Inc.
Attn: Scholarship Committee
21 Acorn Drive
Windsor Locks, CT 06096
E-mail: LANGscholarship@gmail.com
Web: www.laoamericanct.org/?p=274

Summary To provide financial assistance to Lao American high school seniors from Connecticut who are interested in attending college in any state.

Eligibility This program is open to seniors graduating from high schools in Connecticut who are of Laotian ancestry. Applicants must be attending or planning to attend college in any state. They must be members of Lao American New Generation (LANG), Inc. Along with their application, they must submit 300-word essays on 1) how their Lao identity has contributed to their success; 2) what they have learned during their time volunteering; and 3) what a college degree means for them. Selection is based on those essays, academic success, and service to the community, especially the Lao community.

Financial data The stipend is $500.

Duration 1 year.

Additional information This program began in 2014.

Number awarded 2 each year.

Deadline April of each year.

[265]
LAO AMERICAN WOMEN ASSOCIATION OF WASHINGTON D.C. METROPOLITAN AREA COLLEGE SCHOLARSHIP FUND

Lao American Women Association
Attn: Scholarship Committee
3908 Carroll Court
Chantilly, VA 20151
(703) 283-8698   E-mail: info@lawadc.org
Web: www.lawadc.org/em-schol.htm

Summary To provide financial assistance to high school seniors of Lao ancestry in the Washington, D.C. area who plan to attend college in any state.

Eligibility This program is open to seniors graduating from high schools in the Washington, D.C. metropolitan area who are of Lao parentage. Applicants must have a GPA of 3.0 or higher and be planning to attend college in any state in the following fall. Along with their application, they must submit a 150-word personal statement on their purpose or motivations for going to college. Financial need is considered in the selection process (must have family income less than $75,000 per year). U.S. citizenship or permanent resident status is required.

Financial data   The stipend is $1,000.

Duration   1 year.

Additional information   This program began in 2004.

Number awarded   1 or more each year.

Deadline   April of each year.

[266]
LAO AMERICAN WOMEN ASSOCIATION OF WASHINGTON D.C. METROPOLITAN AREA VOCATIONAL TRAINING/GED SCHOLARSHIP FUND

Lao American Women Association
Attn: Scholarship Committee
3908 Carroll Court
Chantilly, VA 20151
(703) 283-8698   E-mail: info@lawadc.org
Web: www.lawadc.org/em-schol.htm

Summary   To provide financial assistance to women of Lao ancestry in the Washington, D.C. area who need additional training to find a job.

Eligibility   This program is open to women in the Washington, D.C. metropolitan area who are of Lao parentage. Applicants must be in need of additional training to find a job, to obtain work at a higher level, or to complete a GED certificate. They must provide information on their personal situation, proposed training program, work experience, family and community activities, and financial situation. They must also submit a 150-word personal statement on their family and community activities. Financial need is considered in the selection process (must have family income less than $75,000 per year).

Financial data   The stipend is $1,000 for vocational training or $500 for GED completion.

Duration   1 year.

Number awarded   Either 1 scholarship for vocational training or 2 for GED completion are awarded each year.

Deadline   April of each year.

[267]
LAPIZ FAMILY SCHOLARSHIP

Asian Pacific Fund
Attn: Scholarship Coordinator
465 California Street, Suite 809
San Francisco, CA 94104
(415) 395-9985 E-mail: scholarship@asianpacificfund.org
Web: www.asianpacificfund.org

Summary   To provide financial assistance to students enrolled at campuses of the University of California (UC) who are children of farm workers.

Eligibility   This program is open to residents of California who will be enrolled as a full time undergraduate at a UC campus in the following fall. Preference is given to students at UC Davis and UC Santa Cruz. Applicants may be of any ethnic or racial background but they must be a farm worker or the child of farm or migrant workers. They must have a GPA of 3.0 or higher and be able to demonstrate financial need. Along with their application, they must submit essays of 250 to 500 words each on 1) their experience as a farm worker or child of a farm worker and how that experience relates to their educational and career goals; 2) a project, experience, or person related to their academic and career goals that inspired them;

and 3) their academic and career goals, hopes, and dreams for the future. U.S. citizenship or permanent resident status is required. Selection is based on personal strengths (responsibility, maturity, motivation, ability to overcome hardships); potential to succeed, including time management skills and realistic goals; and academic achievement.

Financial data   The stipend is $2,000 per year.

Duration   1 year; may be renewed 1 additional year.

Number awarded   1 each year.

Deadline   February of each year.

[268]
LAURENCE R. FOSTER MEMORIAL SCHOLARSHIPS

Oregon Office of Student Access and Completion
Attn: Scholarship Processing Coordinator
1500 Valley River Drive, Suite 100
Eugene, OR 97401-2146
(541) 687-7422   Toll Free: (800) 452-8807, ext. 7422
Fax: (541) 687-7414   TDD: (800) 735-2900
E-mail: cheryl.a.connolly@state.or.us
Web: app.oregonstudentaid.gov/Catalog/Default.aspx

Summary   To provide financial assistance to residents of Oregon, especially Asian Americans and others from diverse backgrounds, who are enrolled at a college or graduate school in any state to prepare for a public health career.

Eligibility   This program is open to residents of Oregon who are enrolled at least half time at a 4-year college or university in any state to prepare for a career in public health (not private practice). Preference is given first to applicants from diverse environments; second to persons employed in, or graduate students working on a degree in, public health; and third to juniors and seniors majoring in a health program (e.g., nursing, medical technology, physician assistant). Applicants must be able to demonstrate financial need. Along with their application, they must submit essays of 250 to 350 words on 1) what public health means to them; 2) the public health aspect they intend to practice and the health and population issues impacted by that aspect; and 3) their experience living or working in diverse environments.

Financial data   Stipends for scholarships offered by the Oregon Office of Student Access and Completion (OSAC) range from $1,000 to $10,000 but recently averaged $4,368.

Duration   1 year.

Additional information   This program is administered by the OSAC with funds provided by the Oregon Community Foundation.

Number awarded   Varies each year; recently, 6 were awarded.

Deadline   February of each year.

[269]
LCDR JANET COCHRAN AND CDR CONNIE GREENE SCHOLARSHIP

National Naval Officers Association-Washington, D.C.
  Chapter
c/o LCDR Stephen Williams
P.O. Box 30784
Alexandria, VA 22310
(703) 566-3840   Fax: (703) 566-3813
E-mail: Stephen.Williams@Navy.mil
Web: dcnnoa.memberlodge.com/page-309002

Summary   To provide financial assistance to Asian American and other female minority high school seniors from the Washington, D.C. area who are interested in attending college in any state.

Eligibility   This program is open to female minority seniors graduating from high schools in the Washington, D.C. metropolitan area who plan to enroll full time at an accredited 2- or 4-year college or university in any state. Applicants must have a GPA of 2.5 or higher and be U.S. citizens or permanent residents. Selection is based on academic achievement, community involvement, and financial need.

Financial data   The stipend is $1,500.

Duration   1 year; nonrenewable.

Additional information   Recipients are not required to join or affiliate with the military in any way.

Number awarded   1 each year.

Deadline   March of each year.

[270]
LE HOANG NGUYEN COLLEGE SCHOLARSHIP

Vietnamese American Scholarship Foundation
P.O. Box 429
Stafford, TX 77497
E-mail: scholarships@vietscholarships.org
Web: www.vietscholarships.org/lhn.html

Summary   To provide financial assistance to high school seniors of Vietnamese descent in Texas who plan to attend college in any state.

Eligibility   This program is open to seniors graduating from high schools in Texas who are of Vietnamese descent. Applicants must be planning to enroll at an accredited college or university in any state. They must have a GPA of 3.0 or higher and a rank in their class in the top 10%. Along with their application, they must submit a 750-word essay on either 1) accomplishments that illustrate their aptitude for leadership; or 2) where they see themselves in 5 years. An interview may be required. Financial need is not considered in the selection process.

Financial data   The stipend is $500.

Duration   1 year; nonrenewable.

Number awarded   1 each year.

Deadline   May of each year.

[271]
LEADERSHIP FOR DIVERSITY SCHOLARSHIP

California School Library Association
Attn: CSL Foundation
6444 East Spring Street, Number 237
Long Beach, CA 90815-1553
Toll Free: (888) 655-8480   Fax: (888) 655-8480
E-mail: info@csla.net
Web: www.csla.net/awards-2/scholarships

Summary   To provide financial assistance to students who reflect the diversity of California's population and are interested in earning a credential as a library media teacher in the state.

Eligibility   This program is open to students who are Asian Americans or members of other traditionally underrepresented groups enrolled in a college or university library media teacher credential program in California. Applicants must intend to work as a library media teacher in a California school library media center for a minimum of 3 years. Along with their application, they must submit a 250-word statement on what they can contribute to the profession, their commitment to serving the needs of multicultural and multilingual students, and their financial need.

Financial data   The stipend is $1,500.

Duration   1 year.

Number awarded   1 each year.

Deadline   September of each year.

[272]
LEDGENT DIVERSITY UNDERGRADUATE SCHOLARSHIPS

Accounting and Financial Women's Alliance
Attn: Educational Foundation
2365 Harrodsburg Road, A325
Lexington, KY 40504
(859) 219-3532   Toll Free: (800) 326-2163
Fax: (859) 219-3577   E-mail: foundation@afwa.org
Web: www.afwa.org/foundation/scholarships

Summary   To provide financial assistance to Asian American and other minority undergraduates interested in preparing for a career in accounting or finance.

Eligibility   This program is open to members of minority groups (Asian Americans, African Americans, Hispanic Americans, or Native Americans) who are entering their third, fourth, or fifth year of undergraduate study at a college, university, or professional school of accounting. Applicants must have completed at least 60 semester hours with a declared major in accounting or finance and a GPA of 3.0 or higher. Along with their application, they must submit an essay of 150 to 250 words on their career goals and objectives, the impact they want to have on the accounting world, community involvement, and leadership examples. Selection is based on leadership, character, communication skills, scholastic average, and financial need. Membership in the Accounting and Financial Women's Alliance (AFWA) is not required. Applications must be submitted to a local ASWA chapter.

Financial data   A stipend is awarded (amount not specified).

Duration   1 year; recipients may reapply.

Additional information   This program is sponsored by Ledgent.

Number awarded   1 each year.

Deadline   Local chapters must submit their candidates to the national office by September of each year.

[273]
LEON BRADLEY SCHOLARSHIPS

American Association of School Personnel Administrators
Attn: Scholarship Program
11863 West 112th Street, Suite 100
Overland Park, KS 66210
(913) 327-1222   Fax: (913) 327-1223
E-mail: aaspa@aaspa.org
Web: www.aaspa.org/leon-bradley-scholarship

Summary   To provide financial assistance to Asian American and other minority undergraduates, paraprofessionals, and graduate students preparing for a career in teaching and school leadership at colleges in designated southeastern states.

Eligibility   This program is open to members of minority groups (Asian, American Indian, Alaskan Native, Pacific Islander, Black, Hispanic, Middle Easterner) currently enrolled full time at a college or university in Alabama, Florida, Georgia, Kentucky, North Carolina, South Carolina, Tennessee, or Virginia. Applicants must be 1) undergraduates in their final year (including student teaching) of an initial teaching certification program; 2) paraprofessional career-changers in their final year (including student teaching) of an initial teaching certification program; or 3) graduate students who have served as a licensed teacher and are working on a school administrator credential. They must have an overall GPA of 3.0 or higher. Priority is given to applicants who 1) can demonstrate work experience that has been applied to college expenses; 2) have received other scholarship or financial aid support; or 3) are seeking initial certification and/or endorsement in a state-identified critical area.

Financial data   Stipends are $2,500 for undergraduates in their final year, $1,500 for paraprofessionals in their final year, and $1,500 for graduate students.

Duration   1 year.

Number awarded   4 each year: 1 undergraduate, 1 paraprofessional, and 2 graduate students.

Deadline   May of each year.

[274]
LEONARD M. PERRYMAN COMMUNICATIONS SCHOLARSHIP FOR ETHNIC MINORITY STUDENTS

United Methodist Communications
Attn: Communications Ministry Team
810 12th Avenue South
P.O. Box 320
Nashville, TN 37202-0320
(615) 742-5481   Toll Free: (888) CRT-4UMC
Fax: (615) 742-5485   E-mail: scholarships@umcom.org
Web: www.umcom.org

Summary   To provide financial assistance to Asian American and other minority United Methodist college students who are interested in careers in religious communications.

Eligibility   This program is open to United Methodist ethnic minority students enrolled in accredited institutions of higher education as juniors or seniors. Applicants must be interested

in preparing for a career in religious communications. For the purposes of this program, "communications" is meant to cover audiovisual, electronic, and print journalism. Selection is based on Christian commitment and involvement in the life of the United Methodist church, academic achievement, journalistic experience, clarity of purpose, and professional potential as a religion communicator.

Financial data   The stipend is $2,500 per year.

Duration   1 year.

Additional information   The scholarship may be used at any accredited institution of higher education.

Number awarded   1 each year.

Deadline   March of each year.

[275]
LIBRARY OF CONGRESS JUNIOR FELLOWS PROGRAM

Library of Congress
Library Services
Attn: Junior Fellows Program Coordinator
101 Independence Avenue, S.E., Room LM-642
Washington, DC 20540-4600
(202) 707-6610   Fax: (202) 707-6269
E-mail: jrfell@loc.gov
Web: www.loc.gov/hr/jrfellows/index.html

Summary   To provide summer work experience at the Library of Congress (LC) to upper-division and graduate students and to recent graduates, especially Asian Americans and members of other underrepresented groups.

Eligibility   This program is open to U.S. citizens with subject expertise in the following areas: collections preservation; geography and maps; humanities, art, and culture; information technology; library sciences; or chemistry and science. Applicants must 1) be juniors or seniors at an accredited college or university; 2) be graduate students; or 3) have completed their degree in the past year. Women, minorities, and persons with disabilities are strongly encouraged to apply. Selection is based on academic achievement, letters of recommendation, and an interview.

Financial data   Fellows are paid a taxable stipend of $3,000.

Duration   10 weeks, beginning in either May or June. Fellows work a 40-hour week.

Additional information   Fellows work with primary source materials and assist selected divisions at LC in the organization and documentation of archival collections, production of finding aids and bibliographic records, preparation of materials for preservation and service, completion of bibliographical research, and digitization of LC's historical collections.

Number awarded   Varies each year; recently, 38 were awarded.

Deadline   January of each year.

[276]
LILY PABILONA EMERGING ENTREPRENEUR SCHOLARSHIP

Against the Grain Productions
3523 McKinney Avenue, Suite 231
Dallas, TX 75204
E-mail: outreach@againstthegrainproductions.com
Web: www.againstthegrainproductions.com

Summary To provide financial assistance to Asian and Pacific Island students working on an undergraduate or graduate degree in entrepreneurship.

Eligibility This program is open to high school seniors and current full-time students at accredited 2- and 4-year colleges and universities and vocational schools. Applicants must be of at least 50% Asian and/or Pacific Islander ethnicity and U.S. citizens, nationals, or permanent residents. They must be working on a degree in entrepreneurship and have a GPA of 3.0 or higher. Selection is based on an essay, academic performance, leadership and community service, letters of recommendation, and an interview.

Financial data The stipend is $5,000. Funds are disbursed directly to the educational institution.

Duration 1 year.

Additional information This program began in 2016.

Number awarded 2 each year.

Deadline May of each year.

[277]
LINDA YU BROADCAST SCHOLARSHIP

Asian American Journalists Association-Chicago Chapter
c/o Susanna Song
CBS 2 Broadcast Center
22 West Washington Street
Chicago, IL 60602
E-mail: ssong@cbs.com
Web: www.aajachicago.wordpress.com

Summary To provide funding to members of the Asian American Journalists Association (AAJA) who are interested in a summer internship at a Chicago television station.

Eligibility This program is open to AAJA members who are college juniors, seniors, or graduate students. Applicants must be interested in a broadcast news internship at a Chicago television station. Along with their application, they must submit a resume that includes their job experience in journalism and 5 writing samples.

Financial data The stipend is $2,500.

Duration 10 to 12 weeks during the summer.

Number awarded 1 each year.

Deadline December of each year.

[278]
#LIVELIKELYLY MEMORIAL SCHOLARSHIP

Against the Grain Productions
3523 McKinney Avenue, Suite 231
Dallas, TX 75204
E-mail: outreach@againstthegrainproductions.com
Web: www.againstthegrainproductions.com

Summary To provide financial assistance to Asian and Pacific Island students working on an undergraduate degree in fashion and/or graphic design.

Eligibility This program is open to high school seniors and current full-time students at accredited 2- and 4-year colleges and universities and vocational schools. Applicants must be of at least 50% Asian and/or Pacific Islander ethnicity and U.S. citizens, nationals, or permanent residents. They must be majoring in graphic and/or fashion design and have a GPA of 3.0 or higher. Selection is based on an essay and artistic portfolio, academic performance, leadership and community service, letters of recommendation, and an interview.

Financial data The stipend is $1,000. Funds are disbursed directly to the educational institution.

Duration 1 year.

Additional information This program began in 2015.

Number awarded Varies each year; recently, 2 were awarded.

Deadline May of each year.

[279]
LOS ANGELES CHAPTER OF AAJA SCHOLARSHIPS

Asian American Journalists Association-Los Angeles Chapter
Attn: Frank Buckley, Scholarship Chair
KTLA-TV
5800 Sunset Boulevard
Los Angeles, CA 90028
E-mail: aajalaawards@gmail.com
Web: www.aaja-la.org/category/programs/scholarships

Summary To provide financial assistance to Asian/Pacific Islander students in the Los Angeles area who are interested in careers in journalism.

Eligibility This program is open to Asian/Pacific Islander full-time students who are planning a career in radio, photography, print, news design, television, or multimedia journalism. Applicants must be attending a college or university in the Los Angeles area (Los Angeles, Orange, Riverside, San Bernardino, or Ventura counties). Membership in the Asian American Journalists Association (AAJA) is encouraged for applicants and required for recipients. Selection is based on academic achievement, commitment to the field of journalism, journalistic ability, sensitivity to Asian American and Pacific Islander issues, and financial need.

Financial data The stipend is $2,500.

Duration 1 year; may be renewed.

Number awarded Several each year.

Deadline January of each year.

[280]
LOUIS B. RUSSELL, JR. MEMORIAL SCHOLARSHIP

Indiana State Teachers Association
Attn: Scholarships
150 West Market Street, Suite 900
Indianapolis, IN 46204-2875
(317) 263-3369   Toll Free: (800) 382-4037
Fax: (800) 777-6128   E-mail: mshoup@ista-in.org
Web: www.ista-in.org/louis-b-russell-scholarship

Summary To provide financial assistance to Asian American and other ethnic minority high school seniors in Indiana who are interested in attending vocational school in any state.

Eligibility This program is open to ethnic minority high school seniors in Indiana who are interested in continuing their education in the area of industrial arts, vocational education, or technical preparation at an accredited postsecondary institution in any state. Selection is based on academic achievement, leadership ability as expressed through co-curricular activities and community involvement, recommendations, and a 300-word essay on their educational goals and how they plan to achieve those goals.

Financial data The stipend is $1,000.

Duration 1 year; may be renewed for 1 additional year, provided the recipient maintains a GPA of "C+" or higher.

Number awarded 1 each year.

Deadline February of each year.

[281]
LOUISE MORITZ MOLITORIS LEADERSHIP AWARD

Women's Transportation Seminar
Attn: WTS Foundation
1701 K Street, N.W., Suite 800
Washington, DC 20006
(202) 955-5085   Fax: (202) 955-5088
E-mail: wts@wtsinternational.org
Web: www.wtsinternational.org/education/scholarships

Summary To provide financial assistance to undergraduate women, especially Asian Americans and other minorities, interested in a career in transportation.

Eligibility This program is open to women who are working on an undergraduate degree in transportation or a transportation-related field (e.g., transportation engineering, planning, finance, or logistics). Applicants must have a GPA of 3.0 or higher. Along with their application, they must submit a 500-word statement about their career goals after graduation and why they think they should receive the scholarship award; their statement should specifically address the issue of leadership. Applications must be submitted first to a local chapter; the chapters forward selected applications for consideration on the national level. Minority women are especially encouraged to apply. Selection is based on transportation involvement and goals, job skills, academic record, and leadership potential; financial need is not considered.

Financial data The stipend is $5,000.

Duration 1 year.

Additional information Local chapters may also award additional funding to winners for their area.

Number awarded 1 each year.

Deadline Applications must be submitted by November to a local WTS chapter.

[282]
LOVE SCHOLARSHIP FOR DIVERSITY

International Council of Shopping Centers
Attn: ICSC Foundation
1221 Avenue of the Americas, 41st Floor
New York, NY 10020-1099
(646) 728-3628   Fax: (732) 694-1690
E-mail: foundation@icsc.org
Web: www.icsc.org

Summary To provide financial assistance to Asian American and other minority undergraduate students who are preparing for a career as a retail real estate professional.

Eligibility This program is open to U.S. citizens who are full-time juniors or seniors working on a degree related to the retail real estate profession. Applicants must be a member of an underrepresented ethnic minority group (Asian or Pacific Islander, American Indian or Alaskan Native, African American, Hispanic, Caribbean). They must have a GPA of 3.0 or higher.

Financial data The stipend is $1,000.

Duration 1 year.

Number awarded 1 or more each year.

Deadline January of each year.

[283]
LTK ENGINEERING SCHOLARSHIP

Conference of Minority Transportation Officials
Attn: National Scholarship Program
100 M Street, S.E., Suite 917
Washington, DC 20003
(202) 506-2917   E-mail: info@comto.org
Web: www.comto.org/page/scholarships

Summary To provide financial assistance to Asian American and other minority upper-division and graduate students in engineering or other field related to transportation.

Eligibility This program is open to full-time minority juniors, seniors, and graduate students in engineering or other technical transportation-related disciplines. Applicants must have a GPA of 3.0 or higher. Along with their application they must submit a cover letter on their transportation-related career goals and life aspirations. Financial need is not considered in the selection process.

Financial data The stipend is $6,000. Funds are paid directly to the recipient's college or university.

Duration 1 year.

Additional information This program is sponsored by LTK Engineering Services.

Number awarded 1 each year.

Deadline April of each year.

[284]
LTK ENGINEERING TRANSPORTATION PLANNING SCHOLARSHIP

Conference of Minority Transportation Officials
Attn: National Scholarship Program
100 M Street, S.E., Suite 917
Washington, DC 20003
(202) 506-2917   E-mail: info@comto.org
Web: www.comto.org/page/scholarships

Summary To provide financial assistance to Asian American and other minority upper-division and graduate students in planning or other field related to transportation.

Eligibility This program is open to full-time minority juniors, seniors, and graduate students in planning of other technical transportation-related disciplines. Applicants must have a GPA of 3.0 or higher. Along with their application they must submit a cover letter on their transportation-related career goals and life aspirations. Financial need is not considered in the selection process.

Financial data The stipend is $5,000. Funds are paid directly to the recipient's college or university.

Duration 1 year.

Additional information This program is sponsored by LTK Engineering Services.

Number awarded 1 each year.

Deadline April of each year.

[285]
MABEL SMITH MEMORIAL SCHOLARSHIP

Wisconsin Women of Color Network, Inc.
c/o P.E. Kiram
756 North 35th Street, Suite 101
Milwaukee, WI 53208
(414) 899-2329　　　　E-mail: pekiram64@gmail.com

Summary To provide financial assistance for vocation/technical school or community college to Asian Americans and other minority residents of Wisconsin.

Eligibility This program is open to residents of Wisconsin who are high school or GED-equivalent graduating seniors planning to continue their education at a vocational/technical school or community college in any state. Applicants must be a member of 1 of the following groups: African American, Asian, American Indian, Latina, or biracial. They must have a GPA of 2.0 or higher and be able to demonstrate financial need. Along with their application, they must submit a 1-page essay on how this scholarship will help them accomplish their educational goal. U.S. citizenship is required.

Financial data A stipend is awarded (amount not specified).

Duration 1 year.

Additional information This program began in 1990.

Number awarded 1 each year.

Deadline May of each year.

[286]
MAINE SECTION ASCE HIGH SCHOOL SCHOLARSHIP

American Society of Civil Engineers-Maine Section
c/o Leslie L. Corrow, Scholarship Chair
Kleinschmidt Associates
141 Main Street
P.O. Box 650
Pittsfield, ME 04967
(207) 487-3328　　　　　　Fax: (207) 487-3124
E-mail: scholarships@maineasce.org
Web: www.facebook.com/maineasce

Summary To provide financial assistance to high school seniors in Maine, especially Asian Americans and other minorities, who are interested in studying civil engineering in college.

Eligibility This program is open to graduating high school seniors who are Maine residents and who intend to study civil engineering in college. Women and minorities are especially encouraged to apply. Applicants must submit a 200-word statement describing why they have chosen civil engineering as a career and what they hope to accomplish by being a civil engineer. Selection is based on the statement, academic performance, extracurricular activities, and letters of recommendation.

Financial data A total of $4,000 is available for this program each year.

Duration 1 year; nonrenewable.

Number awarded Several each year.

Deadline January of each year.

[287]
MARCIA SILVERMAN MINORITY STUDENT AWARD

Public Relations Student Society of America
Attn: Vice President of Member Services
33 Maiden Lane, 11th Floor
New York, NY 10038-5150
(212) 460-1474　　　　　　Fax: (212) 995-0757
E-mail: prssa@prsa.org
Web: www.prssa.prsa.org

Summary To provide financial assistance to Asian American and other minority college seniors who are interested in preparing for a career in public relations.

Eligibility This program is open to minority (Asian, African American/Black, Hispanic/Latino, Native American, Alaskan Native, or Pacific Islander) students who are entering their senior year at an accredited 4-year college or university. Applicants must have a GPA of 3.0 or higher and be working on a degree in public relations, journalism, or other field to prepare for a career in public relations. Along with their application, they must submit an essay on their view of the public relations profession and their public relations career goals. Selection is based on academic achievement, demonstrated leadership, practical experience, commitment to public relations, writing skills, and letters of recommendation.

Financial data The stipend is $5,000.

Duration 1 year.

Additional information This program began in 2010.

Number awarded 1 each year.

Deadline June of each year.

[288]
MARJORIE BOWENS-WHEATLEY SCHOLARSHIPS

Unitarian Universalist Association
Attn: UU Women's Federation
258 Harvard Street
Brookline, MA 02446
(617) 838-6989　　　　　　E-mail: uuwf@uua.org
Web: www.uuwf.org

Summary To provide financial assistance to Asian American and other women of color who are working on an undergraduate or graduate degree to prepare for Unitarian Universalist ministry or service.

Eligibility This program is open to women of color who are either 1) aspirants or candidates for the Unitarian Universalist ministry; or 2) candidates in the Unitarian Universalist Association's professional religious education or music leadership credentialing programs. Applicants must submit a 1- to 2-page narrative that covers their call to UU ministry, religious education, or music leadership; their passions; how their racial/ethnic/cultural background influences their goals for their calling; and how the work of the program's namesake relates to their dreams and plans for their UU service.

Financial data The stipend is $1,500.

Duration 1 year.

Additional information This program began in 2009.

Number awarded Varies each year; recently, 2 were awarded.

Deadline March of each year.

[289]
MARK ANDO AND ITO FAMILY SCHOLARSHIP

Far West Athletic Trainers' Association
c/o Ned Bergert, Scholarship Chair
4942 Casa Oro Drive
Yorba Linda, CA 92886
(714) 501-3858   E-mail: nhbergert@gmail.com
Web: www.fwatad8.org/committees/scholarships-committee

Summary To provide financial assistance to members of the National Athletic Trainers Association (NATA) from any state who are of Asian descent and working on an undergraduate or graduate degree in its District 8.

Eligibility This program is open to students of Asian descent from any state who are enrolled as undergraduate or graduate students at colleges and universities in California, Guam, Hawaii, or Nevada and preparing for a career as an athletic trainer. Applicants must be student members of NATA and a District 8 member of NATA working on a bachelor's, master's, or doctoral degree in athletic training. They must have a GPA of 3.2 or higher and a record of distinction in their athletic training program, academic major, institution, intercollegiate athletics, and higher education. Along with their application, they must submit a statement on their athletic training background, experience, philosophy, and goals. Financial need is not considered in the selection process.

Financial data The stipend is $1,500.

Duration 1 year.

Additional information FWATA serves as District 8 of NATA.

Number awarded 1 each year.

Deadline February of each year.

[290]
MARTIN LUTHER KING, JR. MEMORIAL SCHOLARSHIP FUND

California Teachers Association
Attn: CTA Foundation for Teaching and Learning
1705 Murchison Drive
P.O. Box 921
Burlingame, CA 94011-0921
(650) 697-1400   E-mail: scholarships@cta.org
Web: www.cta.org

Summary To provide financial assistance for college or graduate school to Asian Pacific Americans and other racial and ethnic minorities who are members of the California Teachers Association (CTA), children of members, or members of the Student CTA.

Eligibility This program is open to members of racial or ethnic minority groups (Asians/Pacific Islanders, African Americans, American Indians/Alaska Natives, and Hispanics) who are 1) active CTA members; 2) dependent children of active, retired, or deceased CTA members; or 3) members of Student CTA. Applicants must be interested in preparing for a teaching career in public education or already engaged in such a career.

Financial data Stipends vary each year; recently, they ranged up to $6,000.

Duration 1 year.

Number awarded Varies each year; recently, 24 were awarded: 1 to a CTA member, 10 to children of CTA members, and 13 to Student CTA members.

Deadline February of each year.

[291]
MARTIN LUTHER KING JR. SCHOLARSHIP AWARDS

American Correctional Association
Attn: Scholarship Award Committee
206 North Washington Street, Suite 200
Alexandria, VA 22314
(703) 224-0000   Toll Free: (800) ACA-JOIN
Fax: (703) 224-0179   E-mail: execoffice@aca.org
Web: www.aca.org

Summary To provide financial assistance for undergraduate or graduate study to Asian Americans and other minorities interested in a career in the criminal justice field.

Eligibility Members of the American Correctional Association (ACA) may nominate a minority person for these awards. Nominees do not need to be ACA members, but they must have been accepted to or be enrolled in an undergraduate or graduate program in criminal justice at a 4-year college or university. Along with the nomination package, they must submit a 250-word essay describing their reflections on the ideals and philosophies of Dr. Martin Luther King and how they have attempted to emulate those qualities in their lives. They must provide documentation of financial need, academic achievement, and commitment to the principles of Dr. King.

Financial data A stipend is awarded (amount not specified). Funds are paid directly to the recipient's college or university.

Duration 1 year.

Number awarded 1 each year.

Deadline May of each year.

[292]
MARY E. BORDER SCHOLARSHIP

Kansas 4-H
c/o K-State Research and Extension
201 Umberger Hall
Manhattan, KS 66506-3404
(785) 532-5800   Fax: (785) 532-5981
Web: www.kansas4-h.org/p.aspx?tabid=479

Summary To provide financial assistance to members of Kansas 4-H who are Asian Pacific Americans or other minority or economically-disadvantaged high school seniors or returning adults planning to enroll at a college in any state and major in any field.

Eligibility This program is open to residents of Kansas who have completed at least 1 year of 4-H work and are planning to enrolled at a college in any state and major in any field. Applicants may be 1) economically-disadvantaged high school seniors; 2) high school seniors who are members of minority groups (Asian/Pacific Islander, African American, American Indian/Alaska Native, Hispanic/Latino); or 3) adults returning to college. Along with their application, they must submit a 1-page summary of 4-H leadership, community service, participation, and recognition; a 1-page essay on how 4-H has impacted them; and a 1-page summary of non-4-H leadership, community service, participation, and recognition in school and community. Selection is based on 4-H leadership (40%), 4-H citizenship and community service (30%), 4-H participation and recognition (20%), and non-4-H leadership, citizenship, and recognition (10%).

Financial data The stipend is $1,500.

Duration 1 year.

Number awarded 1 each year.

Deadline January of each year.

[293]
MARY MOY QUON ING MEMORIAL SCHOLARSHIP

Asian American Journalists Association
Attn: Student Programs Coordinator
5 Third Street, Suite 1108
San Francisco, CA 94103
(415) 346-2051, ext. 102   Fax: (415) 346-6343
E-mail: programs@aaja.org
Web: www.aaja.org/apply-for-a-scholarship-now

Summary To provide financial assistance to student members of the Asian American Journalists Association (AAJA) entering their sophomore year of college and interested in majoring in journalism.

Eligibility This program is open to AAJA members planning to enroll full time as college sophomores and study journalism. Applicants must submit a 500-word essay on their involvement or interest in the Asian American community and how, if they are awarded this scholarship, they would contribute to the field of journalism and/or media issues involving the Asian Pacific American and Pacific Islander community. Print applicants must submit up to 4 photocopied or printed articles; broadcast applicants must submit up to 3 stories (total length less than 10 minutes) copied onto CDs; photojournalism applicants must submit a portfolio with no more than 10 entries. Selection is based on academic achievement, commitment to journalism, sensitivity to Asian American and Pacific Islander issues, demonstrated journalistic ability, and financial need.

Financial data The stipend is $2,000.

Duration 1 year.

Number awarded 1 each year.

Deadline May of each year.

[294]
MARY WOLFSKILL TRUST FUND INTERNSHIP

Library of Congress
Library Services
Attn: Junior Fellows Program Coordinator
101 Independence Avenue, S.E., Room LM-642
Washington, DC 20540-4600
(202) 707-9929   Fax: (202) 707-6269
E-mail: jfla@loc.gov
Web: www.loc.gov

Summary To provide summer work experience in the Manuscript Division of the Library of Congress (LC) to upper-division and graduate students, especially Asian Americans and other minorities.

Eligibility This program is open to undergraduate and graduate students who have expertise in library science or collections conservation and preservation. Applicants must be interested in gaining an introductory knowledge of the principles, concepts, and techniques of archival management through a summer internship in the LC Manuscript Division. They should be able to demonstrate an ability to communicate effectively in writing and have knowledge of integrated library systems, basic library applications, and other information technologies. Knowledge of American history is beneficial. Applications from minorities and students at smaller and lesser-known schools are particularly encouraged. U.S. citizenship is required.

Financial data The stipend is $3,000.

Duration 10 weeks during the summer. Fellows work a 40-hour week.

Number awarded 1 each year.

Deadline January of each year.

[295]
MASSMUTUAL SCHOLARS PROGRAM

Massachusetts Mutual Life Insurance Company
1295 State Street
Springfield, MA 01111-0001
Toll Free: (800) 542-6767
Web: www.massmutual.scholarsapply.org

Summary To provide financial assistance to undergraduates who are Asian Americans or others who reflect the diversity of the country and are preparing for a career in the insurance and financial services industry.

Eligibility This program is open to full-time students from diverse backgrounds who are entering their sophomore, junior, senior, or fifth-year senior year at an accredited college or university in the United States, Puerto Rico, U.S. Virgin Islands, or Guam. Applicants must be U.S. citizens or permanent residents and have a GPA of 3.0 or higher. They may be majoring in any field, but preference is given to students who demonstrate 1) an interest in preparing for a career in the insurance and financial services industry; and 2) leadership and participation in extracurricular activities. Financial need is considered in the selection process.

Financial data The stipend is $2,500 for students at 2-year colleges or $5,000 for students at 4-year institutions.

Duration 1 year.

Number awarded 30 each year.

Deadline March of each year.

[296]
MATT FONG ASIAN AMERICANS IN PUBLIC FINANCE SCHOLARSHIPS

Asian Pacific Fund
Attn: Scholarship Coordinator
465 California Street, Suite 809
San Francisco, CA 94104
(415) 395-9985 E-mail: scholarship@asianpacificfund.org
Web: www.asianpacificfund.org

Summary To provide financial assistance to Asian residents of any state working on a degree related to public finance at a college in California.

Eligibility This program is open to residents of any state who are at least 50% Asian. Applicants must be entering their sophomore, junior, or senior year at a 4-year college or university in California with a major in accounting, business administration, political science, public policy, or a related field. They must have a GPA of 3.0 or higher and be able to demonstrate financial need. Preference is given to students who can demonstrate a record of community service or volunteer work.

Financial data   The stipend is $1,500.

Duration   1 year; nonrenewable.

Number awarded   2 each year.

Deadline   February of each year.

[297]
MCGUIREWOODS/NLF INTERNSHIP PROGRAM

National Asian Pacific American Bar Association
Attn: NAPABA Law Foundation
1612 K Street, N.W., Suite 510
Washington, DC 20006
(202) 775-9555   Fax: (202) 775-9333
E-mail: aasaria@napaba.org
Web: www.napaba.org/?page=NLF_FI

Summary   To provide funding to undergraduate and law students interested in a summer internship at the National Asian Pacific American Bar Association (NAPABA) and its Law Foundation (NLF).

Eligibility   This program is open to 1) undergraduates interested in working on issues that affect Asian Pacific Americans; and 2) law students interested in working as a clerk. Assignments for undergraduates require working 50% of their time on NAPABA projects and 50% on NLF projects. Assignments for law students require full-time work for NAPABA. Tasks involve promoting justice, equity, and opportunity for Asian Pacific Americans; fostering professional development, legal scholarship, advocacy, and community involvement; and developing and supporting programs to educate the legal profession and Asian Pacific American communities about legal issues affecting those communities.

Financial data   The stipend for the law clerk is $4,50. The stipend for the fundraising and policy intern is $3,000.

Duration   10 weeks during the summer.

Additional information   These internships were first awarded in 2010 with support from McGuireWoods LLP.

Number awarded   2 each year: 1 law clerk and 1 fundraising and policy intern.

Deadline   March of each year.

[298]
MCKINNEY FAMILY FUND SCHOLARSHIP

Cleveland Foundation
Attn: Scholarship Processing
1422 Euclid Avenue, Suite 1300
Cleveland, OH 44115-2001
(216) 861-3810   Fax: (216) 861-1729
E-mail: mbaker@clevefdn.org
Web: www.clevelandfoundation.org

Summary   To provide financial assistance to residents of Ohio, especially Asian Americans or members of other minority groups, who are interested in attending college or graduate school in any state.

Eligibility   This program is open to U.S. citizens who have been residents of Ohio for at least 2 years. Applicants must be high school seniors or graduate students and interested in working full or part time on an associate, bachelor's, master's, or doctoral degree at an accredited college or university in any state. They must have a GPA of 2.5 or higher. Preference

is given to applicants of minority descent. Selection is based on evidence of sincerity toward obtaining an academic credential. Financial need may be used as a tiebreaker.

Financial data   The stipend is $2,000 per year. Funds are paid directly to the school and must be applied to tuition, fees, books, supplies, and equipment required for course work.

Duration   1 year; may be renewed up to 3 additional.

Number awarded   1 or more each year.

Deadline   March of each year.

[299]
MEDIA GENERAL MINORITY SCHOLARSHIP AND TRAINING PROGRAM

Media General
Attn: Angie Cartwright, Human Resources
9101 Burnet Road
Austin, TX 78758
(512) 380-4400
Web: www.mediageneral.com/careers/scholarship.html

Summary   To provide scholarship/loans to Asian Americans and other minority undergraduates interested in earning a degree in a field related to broadcast journalism and working at a station owned by LIN Television Corporation.

Eligibility   This program is open to U.S. citizens and permanent residents of non-white origin who are enrolled as a sophomore or junior at a college or university. Applicants must have a declared major in broadcast journalism, digital multimedia, mass/speech/digital communication, television production, or marketing and a GPA of 3.0 or higher. Along with their application, they must submit a list of organizations and activities in which they have held leadership positions, 3 references, a 50-word description of their career goals, a list of personal achievements and honors, and a 500-word essay about themselves. Financial need is not considered in the selection process.

Financial data   The program pays for tuition and fees, books, and room and board, to a maximum of $10,000 per year. Recipients must sign an employment agreement that guarantees them part-time employment as an intern during school and a 2-year regular position at a television station owned by Media General following graduation. If they fail to honor the employment agreement, they must repay all scholarship funds received.

Duration   2 years.

Additional information   This program began in 1998 under LIN Television Corporation, which was acquired by Media General in 2014. Media General owns 71 television stations in 48 media markets in the United States. Recipients of these scholarships must work at a station selected by Media General management.

Number awarded   2 each year: 1 for a student in broadcast television and 1 for a student in digital media.

Deadline   January of each year.

[300]
MELLON UNDERGRADUATE CURATORIAL FELLOWSHIP PROGRAM

Art Institute of Chicago
Attn: Coordinator, Andrew W. Mellon Academic Programs
111 South Michigan Avenue
Chicago, IL 60603
(312) 443-3581   E-mail: fmings@artic.edu
Web: www.artic.edu/mellon

Summary To provide an opportunity for undergraduates who are Asian Americans or members of other groups historically underrepresented in the curatorial field to gain academic training and work experience to prepare for a career as an art curator.

Eligibility This program is open to undergraduates (typically freshmen or sophomores) who can commit 2 years to a program of preparation for a career as an art curator. Applicants must be studying art history, art, or the museum field at a college or university in the vicinity of 5 designated art museums. They must be members of groups historically underrepresented in the curatorial field and interested in continuing on to graduate school for advanced study in a relevant academic discipline. They must also be available to work with a mentor at the museum during the academic year to gain experience with curators and staff on exhibitions, collections, and programs and to participate in a summer internship. Interested students first apply to participate in a Summer Academy at the museum in their area. Selection for the Academy is based on academic record, extracurricular activities, background or other experiences, and expected contribution to the program. Based on performance during the Academy and personal interviews, Curatorial Fellows are selected at each of the 5 museums.

Financial data Students selected for the Summer Academies receive a per diem allowance. Students selected as fellows receive an academic stipend of $4,000 per year and a grant of $6,000 for the summer internship.

Duration The Summer Academy lasts 1 week. The fellowship is 2 years, including 10-week summer internships.

Additional information The Andrew W. Mellon Foundation established this program in 2013. In addition to the Art Institute of Chicago, it also operates at the High Museum of Art in Atlanta, the Los Angeles County Museum of Art, the Museum of Fine Arts, Houston, and the Nelson-Atkins Museum of Art in Kansas City. Students who attend college in the vicinity of those museums should contact them about this program.

Number awarded 15 students at each of the 5 museums are selected each year to participate in the Summer Academy. Of those, 2 are selected at each museum to receive the Curatorial Fellowship.

Deadline February of each year.

[301]
MICHAEL BAKER SCHOLARSHIP FOR DIVERSITY IN ENGINEERING

Association of Independent Colleges and Universities of Pennsylvania
101 North Front Street
Harrisburg, PA 17101-1404
(717) 232-8649   Fax: (717) 233-8574
E-mail: info@aicup.org
Web: www.aicup.org/Foundation-Scholarships

Summary To provide financial assistance to Asian American and other minority students from any state enrolled at member institutions of the Association of Independent Colleges and Universities of Pennsylvania (AICUP) who are majoring in designated fields of engineering.

Eligibility This program is open to full-time undergraduate students from any state enrolled at designated AICUP colleges and universities who are women and/or members of the following minority groups: Asians, American Indians, Alaska Natives, Blacks/African Americans, Hispanics/Latinos, Native Hawaiians, or Pacific Islanders. Applicants must be juniors majoring in architectural, civil, or environmental engineering with a GPA of 3.0 or higher. Along with their application, they must submit a 2-page essay on what they believe will be the greatest challenge facing the engineering profession over the next decade, and why.

Financial data The stipend is $2,500 per year.

Duration 1 year; may be renewed 1 additional year if the recipient maintains appropriate academic standards.

Additional information This program, sponsored by the Michael Baker Corporation, is available at the 88 private colleges and universities in Pennsylvania that comprise the AICUP.

Number awarded 1 each year.

Deadline April of each year.

[302]
MICHIGAN ACCOUNTANCY FOUNDATION FIFTH/ GRADUATE YEAR SCHOLARSHIP PROGRAM

Michigan Association of Certified Public Accountants
Attn: Michigan Accountancy Foundation
5480 Corporate Drive, Suite 200
P.O. Box 5068
Troy, MI 48007-5068
(248) 267-3680   Toll Free: (888) 877-4CPE (within MI)
Fax: (248) 267-3737   E-mail: MAF@micpa.org
Web: www.mafonline.org/?page_id=35

Summary To provide financial assistance to students at Michigan colleges and universities, especially Asian Americans and members of other underrepresented groups, who are working on a degree in accounting.

Eligibility This program is open to students enrolled full time at accredited Michigan colleges and universities with a declared concentration in accounting. Applicants must be seniors planning to enter the fifth or graduate year of their school's program. They must intend to or have successfully passed the Michigan C.P.A. examination and intend to practice public accounting in the state. Along with their application, they must submit 500-word statements about 1) examples of their leadership roles and extracurricular activities, community involvement and volunteerism, how they are financing their education, and the accomplishments of which they are most proud; and 2) their professional goals for the next 5 years and any special circumstances they wish to have considered. Special consideration is given to applicants who are single parents, physically challenged, minority, or self-supporting. U.S. citizenship or eligibility for permanent employment in the United States is required.

Financial data The stipend is $3,000; funds are disbursed directly to the recipient's college or university.

Duration 1 year.

Additional information This program includes the William E. Balhoff Leadership Scholarship, the Jeff Bergeron Leadership Scholarship, the Robert A. Bogan Scholarship (limited to a student from the metropolitan Detroit area), the Kenneth Bouyer Leadership Scholarship, the Peggy A. Dzierzawski Leadership Scholarship, the George Johnson Leadership Scholarship, the Thomas McTavish Leadership Scholarship, the Randy Paschke Leadership Scholarship, and the Governor Rick Snyder Leadership Scholarship.

Number awarded 15 to 20 each year.

Deadline January of each year.

[303]
MICHIGAN CHAPTER COMTO SCHOLARSHIPS

Conference of Minority Transportation Officials-Michigan
  Chapter
Attn: President
P.O. Box 32439
Detroit, MI 48232
(269) 491-7279   E-mail: averyk@michigan.gov
Web: www.comtomichigan.org/scholarships.html

Summary To provide financial assistance to Asian American and other minority undergraduate and graduate students in Michigan who are working on a degree in a transportation-related field.

Eligibility This program is open to members of minority groups enrolled full time as sophomores, juniors, seniors, or graduate students at colleges or universities in Michigan. Applicants must be working on a degree in engineering, planning, or other transportation-related discipline. Graduate students must be members of the Conference of Minority Transportation Officials (COMTO); if undergraduates are not already members, they must become a member within 30 days of the scholarship award. U.S. citizenship or legal resident status is required.

Financial data The stipend ranges from $500 to $3,000. Funds are paid directly to the student.

Duration 1 year.

Number awarded Varies each year; recently, 7 were awarded: 1 at $3,000, 1 at $2,000, 2 at $1,000, and 3 at $500.

Deadline April of each year.

[304]
MIDWESTERN REGION KOREAN AMERICAN SCHOLARSHIPS

Korean American Scholarship Foundation
Midwestern Region
c/o Augie Lee, Scholarship Committee Chair
379 Hollow Hill Drive
Wauconda, IL 60010
(847) 721-9930   E-mail: mwrc.scholarship@kasf.org
Web: www.kasf.org/midwestern

Summary To provide financial assistance to Korean American students from any state who are working on or planning to work on an undergraduate or graduate degree in any field at a school in the Midwest.

Eligibility This program is open to Korean American students who are currently enrolled or planning to enroll at a college or university in the midwestern states as full-time undergraduate or graduate students. Applicants may reside anywhere in the United States as long as they attend school in the midwestern region: Illinois, Iowa, Kansas, Michigan, Minnesota, Missouri, Nebraska, North Dakota, South Dakota, and Wisconsin. They must have a GPA of 3.0 or higher. Both U.S. citizens and foreign nationals are eligible. Selection is based on academic achievement (25%), extracurricular activities (10%), an essay (10%), recommendations (10%), financial need (40%), and extra credit for having extraordinary circumstances (5%).

Financial data Stipends range from $1,000 to $2,000.

Duration 1 year; renewable.

Number awarded Varies each year; recently, 14 were awarded.

Deadline July of each year.

[305]
MIDWIVES OF COLOR-WATSON MIDWIFERY STUDENT SCHOLARSHIP

American College of Nurse-Midwives
Attn: ACNM Foundation, Inc.
8403 Colesville Road, Suite 1550
Silver Spring, MD 20910-6374
(240) 485-1850   Fax: (240) 485-1818
E-mail: foundation@acnmf.org
Web: www.midwife.org

Summary To provide financial assistance for midwifery education to Asian Americans and other students of color who belong to the American College of Nurse-Midwives (ACNM).

Eligibility This program is open to ACNM members of color who are currently enrolled in an accredited basic midwife education program and have successfully completed 1 academic or clinical semester/quarter or clinical module. Applicants must submit they must submit a 150-word essay on their 5-year midwifery career plans; a 150-word essay on their intended future participation in the local, regional, and/or national activities of the ACNM; a 150-word essay on their need for financial assistance; and a 100-word statement on how they would use the funds if they receive the scholarship. Selection is based on academic excellence, leadership potential, and financial need.

Financial data The stipend is $3,000.

Duration 1 year.

Number awarded Varies each year; recently, 3 were awarded.

Deadline February of each year.

[306]
MINNESOTA ASSOCIATION FOR KOREAN AMERICANS SCHOLARSHIPS

Minnesota Association for Korean Americans
Attn: Scholarship Committee
P.O. Box 390553
Edina, MN 55439-0553
E-mail: homg0083@umn.edu
Web: www.makaweb.org

Summary To provide financial assistance to Korean American high school seniors in Minnesota who are planning to attend college in any state.

Eligibility This program is open to seniors graduating from high schools in Minnesota who are of Korean origin or heritage. Applicants must be planning to attend college in any state. They must be U.S. citizens or permanent residents and have a GPA of 3.0 or higher. Along with their application, they must submit grade transcripts, SAT and/or ACT scores, 2 letters of recommendation, and a 2- or 3-page essay on a topic that changes annually; recently, students were asked to identify a person who has had a significant influence on them and explain the impact. Selection is based on the essay, academic achievement, honors, extracurricular activities, and letters of recommendation.

Financial data Stipends range from $1,000 to $1,500.

Duration 1 year; nonrenewable.

Number awarded Approximately 15 to 20 each year.

Deadline September of each year.

[307]
MINNESOTA SOCIAL SERVICE ASSOCIATION DIVERSITY SCHOLARSHIP

Minnesota Social Service Association
Attn: Membership and Diversity Committee
125 Charles Avenue
St. Paul, MN 55103
(651) 644-0556   Fax: (651) 224-6540
E-mail: ajorgensen@mnssa.org
Web: www.mnssa.org

Summary To provide financial assistance to Asian American and other students from a diverse background who are enrolled in an undergraduate program in the health and human services field at a college in the upper Midwest.

Eligibility This program is open to residents of any state entering their junior or senior year at a college or university in Iowa, Minnesota, North Dakota, South Dakota, or Wisconsin. Applicants must be working full time on a degree in the health and human services field and have a GPA of 3.0 or higher. They must be from a diverse background, which may be along the dimensions of race, ethnicity, gender, sexual orientation, socioeconomic status, age, physical ability, religion, or other ideology. Financial need is considered in the selection process.

Financial data The stipend is $1,000.

Duration 1 year.

Number awarded 1 each year.

Deadline May of each year.

[308]
MINNESOTA TAIWANESE AMERICAN COMMUNITY SCHOLARSHIP AWARDS

Taiwanese Association of America-Minnesota Chapter
c/o John Ko
11030 Stonemill Farms Curve
Woodbury, MN 55129-5222
Web: taiwaneseamericanhistory.org

Summary To provide financial assistance to undergraduate and graduate students who identify with the Taiwanese American community and are attending college in Minnesota.

Eligibility This program is open to undergraduate and graduate students currently enrolled at a college or university in Minnesota. Applicants must be able to identify with the Taiwanese American community. Financial need is not considered in the selection process.

Financial data The stipend is $1,500.

Duration 1 year.

Additional information This program includes the Suji Lee Scholarship Award and the Li-Huey Lai Memorial Scholarship Award.

Number awarded At least 2 each year.

Deadline September of each year.

[309]
MINORITIES IN GOVERNMENT FINANCE SCHOLARSHIP

Government Finance Officers Association
Attn: Scholarship Committee
203 North LaSalle Street, Suite 2700
Chicago, IL 60601-1210
(312) 977-9700   Fax: (312) 977-4806
Web: www.gfoa.org

Summary To provide financial assistance to Asian American and other minority upper-division and graduate students who are preparing for a career in state and local government finance.

Eligibility This program is open to upper-division and graduate students who are preparing for a career in public finance by working on a degree in public administration, accounting, finance, political science, economics, or business administration (with a specific focus on government or nonprofit management). Applicants must be members of a minority group, citizens or permanent residents of the United States or Canada, and able to provide a letter of recommendation from a representative of their school. Selection is based on career plans, academic record, plan of study, letters of recommendation, and GPA. Financial need is not considered.

Financial data The stipend is $6,000.

Duration 1 year.

Additional information This program defines minorities as Blacks or African Americans, American Indians or Alaskan Natives, Hispanics or Latinos, Native Hawaiians or other Pacific Islanders, or Asians.

Number awarded 1 each year.

Deadline February of each year.

[310]
MINORITY SCHOLARSHIP AWARD FOR ACADEMIC EXCELLENCE IN PHYSICAL THERAPY

American Physical Therapy Association
Attn: Honors and Awards Program
1111 North Fairfax Street
Alexandria, VA 22314-1488
(703) 684-APTA   Toll Free: (800) 999-APTA, ext. 8082
Fax: (703) 684-7343   TDD: (703) 683-6748
E-mail: honorsandawards@apta.org
Web: www.apta.org

Summary To provide financial assistance to Asian American and other minority students who are interested in becoming a physical therapist or physical therapy assistant.

Eligibility This program is open to U.S. citizens and permanent residents who are members of the following minority groups: Asian, African American or Black, Native Hawaiian or other Pacific Islander, American Indian or Alaska Native, or Hispanic/Latino. Applicants must be in the final year of a professional physical therapy or physical therapy assistant education program. They must submit a personal essay outlining their professional goals and minority service. U.S. citizenship or permanent resident status is required. Selection is based on 1) demonstrated evidence of contributions in the area of minority affairs and services with an emphasis on contributions made while enrolled in a physical therapy program; 2) potential to contribute to the profession of physical therapy; and 3) scholastic achievement. Preference is given to members of the American Physical Therapy Association (APTA).

Financial data The stipend varies; recently, stipends were $5,000 for physical therapy professional education students or $2,000 for physical therapy assistant students.

Duration 1 year.

Number awarded Varies each year; recently, 7 professional education students and 1 physical therapy assistant student received awards.

Deadline November of each year.

[311]
MINORITY SCHOLARSHIP IN CLASSICS AND CLASSICAL ARCHAEOLOGY

Society for Classical Studies
Attn: Executive Director
New York University
20 Cooper Square
New York, NY 10003
(212) 992-7828   Fax: (212) 995-3531
E-mail: xd@classicalstudies.org
Web: www.classicalstudies.org

Summary To provide Asian American and other minority undergraduates with summer training as preparation for advanced work in the classics or classical archaeology.

Eligibility Eligible to apply are minority (Asian American, African American, Hispanic American, and Native American) undergraduate students who wish to engage in summer study as preparation for graduate work in the classics or classical archaeology. Applicants may propose participation in summer programs in Italy, Greece, Egypt, or other classical centers; language training at institutions in the United States, Canada, or Europe; or other relevant courses of study. Selection is based on academic qualifications, especially in clas-

sics; demonstrated ability in at least 1 classical language; quality of the proposal for study with respect to preparation for a career in classics; and financial need.

Financial data The maximum award is $4,500.

Duration 1 summer.

Additional information This program includes 1 scholarship supported by the Gladys Krieble Delmas Foundation.

Number awarded 2 each year.

Deadline December of each year.

[312]
MINORITY TEACHER EDUCATION SCHOLARSHIPS

Florida Fund for Minority Teachers, Inc.
Attn: Executive Director
G415 Norman Hall
618 S.W. 12th Street
P.O. Box 117045
Gainesville, FL 32611-7045
(352) 392-9196   Fax: (352) 846-3011
E-mail: info@ffmt.org
Web: www.ffmt.org/mtes-application-active

Summary To provide scholarship/loans to Florida residents who are Asian Americans or members of other minority groups preparing for a career as a teacher.

Eligibility This program is open to Florida residents who are Asian American/Pacific Islander, African American/Black, Hispanic/Latino, or American Indian/Alaskan Native. Applicants must be entering their junior year in a teacher education program at a participating college or university in Florida. Along with their application, they must submit an essay of 100 to 300 words on how their life experiences have impacted them to go into the field of education. Special consideration is given to community college graduates. Selection is based on writing ability, communication skills, overall academic performance, and evidence of commitment to the youth of America (preferably demonstrated through volunteer activities).

Financial data The stipend is $4,000 per year. Recipients are required to teach 1 year in a Florida public school for each year they receive the scholarship. If they fail to teach in a public school, they are required to repay the total amount of support received at an annual interest rate of 8%.

Duration Up to 2 consecutive years, provided the recipient remains enrolled full time with a GPA of 2.5 or higher.

Additional information For a list of the 22 participating public institutions and the 16 participating private institutions, contact the Florida Fund for Minority Teachers (FFMT). Recipients are also required to attend the annual (FFMT) recruitment and retention conference.

Number awarded Varies each year.

Deadline June of each year for fall semester; October of each year for spring semester.

[313]
MINORITY TEACHERS OF ILLINOIS SCHOLARSHIP PROGRAM

Illinois Student Assistance Commission
Attn: Scholarship and Grant Services
1755 Lake Cook Road
Deerfield, IL 60015-5209
(847) 948-8550   Toll Free: (800) 899-ISAC
Fax: (847) 831-8549   TDD: (800) 526-0844
E-mail: isac.studentservices@isac.illinois.gov
Web: www.isac.org

Summary To provide scholarship/loans to Asian American and other minority students in Illinois who plan to become teachers at the preschool, elementary, or secondary level.

Eligibility Applicants must be Illinois residents, U.S. citizens or eligible noncitizens, members of a minority group (Asian American, African American/Black, Hispanic American, or Native American), and high school graduates or holders of a General Educational Development (GED) certificate. They must be enrolled at least half time as an undergraduate or graduate student, have a GPA of 2.5 or higher, not be in default on any student loan, and be enrolled or accepted for enrollment in a teacher education program.

Financial data Grants up to $5,000 per year are awarded. This is a scholarship/loan program. Recipients must agree to teach full time 1 year for each year of support received. The teaching agreement may be fulfilled at a public, private, or parochial preschool, elementary school, or secondary school in Illinois; at least 30% of the student body at those schools must be minority. It must be fulfilled within the 5-year period following the completion of the undergraduate program for which the scholarship was awarded. The time period may be extended if the recipient serves in the U.S. armed forces, enrolls full time in a graduate program related to teaching, becomes temporarily disabled, is unable to find employment as a teacher at a qualifying school, or takes additional courses on at least a half-time basis to obtain certification as a teacher in Illinois. Recipients who fail to honor this work obligation must repay the award with 5% interest.

Duration 1 year; may be renewed for a total of 8 semesters or 12 quarters.

Number awarded Varies each year.

Deadline Priority consideration is given to applications received by February of each year.

[314]
MIRIAM WEINSTEIN PEACE AND JUSTICE EDUCATION AWARD

Philanthrofund Foundation
Attn: Scholarship Committee
1409 Willow Street, Suite 109
Minneapolis, MN 55403-2241
(612) 870-1806   Toll Free: (800) 435-1402
Fax: (612) 871-6587   E-mail: info@PfundOnline.org
Web: www.pfundonline.org/scholarships.html

Summary To provide financial assistance to Asian American and other minority students from Minnesota who have supported gay, lesbian, bisexual, and transgender (GLBT) activities and are interested in working on a degree in education.

Eligibility This program is open to residents of Minnesota and students attending a Minnesota educational institution who are members of a religious, racial, or ethnic minority. Applicants must be self-identified as GLBT or from a GLBT family and have demonstrated a commitment to peace and justice issues. They may be attending or planning to attend trade school, technical college, college, or university (as an undergraduate or graduate student). Preference is given to students who have completed at least 2 years of college and are working on a degree in education. Selection is based on the applicant's 1) affirmation of GLBT or allied identity; 2) evidence of experience and skills in service and leadership; and 3) evidence of service, leading, and working for change in GLBT communities, including serving as a role model, mentor, and/or adviser.

Financial data The stipend is $3,000. Funds must be used for tuition, books, fees, or dissertation expenses.

Duration 1 year.

Number awarded 1 each year.

Deadline January of each year.

[315]
MISSOURI MINORITY TEACHING SCHOLARSHIP PROGRAM

Missouri Department of Higher Education
Attn: Student Financial Assistance
205 Jefferson Street
P.O. Box 1469
Jefferson City, MO 65102-1469
(573) 751-2361   Toll Free: (800) 473-6757
Fax: (573) 751-6635   E-mail: info@dhe.mo.gov
Web: www.dhe.mo.gov/ppc/grants/minorityteaching.php

Summary To provide scholarships and forgivable loans to Asian American and other minority high school seniors, high school graduates, and college students in Missouri who are interested in preparing for a teaching career in mathematics or science.

Eligibility This program is open to Missouri residents who are Asian American, African American, Hispanic American, or Native American. Applicants must be 1) high school seniors, college students, or returning adults (without a degree) who rank in the top 25% of their high school class and have scores in the top 25% of the ACT or SAT examination (recently, that meant a composite score of 24 or higher on the ACT or 1360 or higher on the composite critical reading and mathematics SAT); or 2) baccalaureate degree-holders who are returning to an approved mathematics or science teacher education program. They must be a U.S. citizen or permanent resident or otherwise lawfully present in the United States. All applicants must be enrolled full time in an approved teacher education program at a community college, 4-year college, or university in Missouri. Selection is based on high school class rank, ACT or SAT scores, school and community activities, career interest in teaching, leadership skills, employment experience, and recommendations.

Financial data The stipend is $3,000 per year, of which $2,000 is provided by the state as a forgivable loan and $1,000 is provided by the school as a scholarship. Recipients must commit to teaching in a Missouri public elementary or secondary school for 5 years following graduation. If they fail to fulfill that obligation, they must repay the state portion of the scholarship with interest at 9.5%.

Duration Up to 4 years.

Number awarded   Up to 100 each year.
Deadline   May of each year.

[316]
MNACC STUDENT OF COLOR SCHOLARSHIP

Minnesota Association of Counselors of Color
c/o Cristina Montañez, Scholarship Committee
University of Minnesota at Morris
600 East Fourth Street
Morris, MN 56267
E-mail: scholarships@mnacc.org
Web: www.mnacc.org

Summary   To provide financial assistance to Asian Americans and other high school seniors of color in Minnesota who plan to attend college in the area.

Eligibility   This program is open to seniors graduating from public and private high schools in Minnesota who are students of color. Applicants must be planning to enroll full time at a 4-year college or university, a 2-year college, or a trade or technical college that is a member of the Minnesota Association of Counselors of Color (MnACC). Along with their application, they must submit an essay, up to 500 words in length, on their choice of assigned topics.

Financial data   Stipends are $1,000 or $500.

Duration   1 year; nonrenewable.

Additional information   These scholarships may be used at approximately 67 MnACC member institutions, including colleges, universities, and technical schools in Minnesota as well as selected schools in Iowa, Michigan, North Dakota, South Dakota, and Wisconsin.

Number awarded   Varies each year; recently, 26 were awarded.

Deadline   March of each year.

[317]
MONTGOMERY SUMMER RESEARCH DIVERSITY FELLOWSHIPS

American Bar Foundation
Attn: Summer Research Diversity Fellowship
750 North Lake Shore Drive
Chicago, IL 60611-4403
(312) 988-6515   Fax: (312) 988-6579
E-mail: fellowships@abfn.org
Web: www.americanbarfoundation.org

Summary   To provide an opportunity for undergraduate students who are Asian Americans or members of other diverse groups to work on a summer research project in the field of law and social science.

Eligibility   This program is open to U.S. citizens and permanent residents who are African Americans, Hispanic/Latinos, Asians, Puerto Ricans, Native Americans, or other individuals who will add diversity to the field of law and social science such as persons with disabilities and LGBTQ individuals. Applicants must be sophomores or juniors in college, have a GPA of 3.0 or higher, be majoring in the social sciences or humanities, and be willing to consider an academic or research career. Along with their application, they must submit a 200-word essay on their future plans and why this fellowship would contribute to them, another essay on an assigned topic, official transcripts, and a letter of recommendation from a faculty member familiar with their work.

Financial data   Participants receive a stipend of $3,600.

Duration   35 hours per week for 8 weeks during the summer.

Additional information   Students are assigned to an American Bar Foundation Research Professor who involves the student in the design and conduct of the professor's research project and who acts as mentor during the student's tenure.

Number awarded   4 each year.

Deadline   February of each year.

[318]
MOSS ADAMS DIVERSITY SCHOLARSHIPS

Moss Adams LLP
Attn: Moss Adams Foundation
999 Third Avenue, Suite 3300
Seattle, WA 98104
(206) 302-6800   Toll Free: (800) 243-4936
Fax: (206) 652-2098   E-mail: careers@mossadams.com
Web: www.mossadams.com/about/careers/home

Summary   To provide financial assistance to Asian Americans or other students who will promote diversity in the accounting profession.

Eligibility   This program is open to sophomores working on a bachelor's degree in accounting. Applicants should be able to promote diversity, defined to include students from diverse racial and ethnic backgrounds, women, LGBT individuals, military veterans, and people with disabilities. They must have a GPA of 3.0 or higher. Selection is based on academic achievement, demonstrated leadership skills, extracurricular activities (particularly those in leadership roles in diversity organizations), and communication skills.

Financial data   The stipend is $2,500.

Duration   1 year.

Number awarded   Up to 12 each year.

Deadline   March of each year.

[319]
MOSS ADAMS FOUNDATION DIVERSITY SCHOLARSHIPS

Moss Adams LLP
Attn: Moss Adams Foundation
999 Third Avenue, Suite 3300
Seattle, WA 98104
(206) 302-6800   Toll Free: (800) 243-4936
Fax: (206) 652-2098   E-mail: careers@mossadams.com
Web: www.mossadams.com/about/careers/home

Summary   To provide financial assistance to students who are working on a bachelor's degree in accounting and are Asian Americans or will promote diversity in the profession in other ways.

Eligibility   This program is open to students entering their junior year of a bachelor's degree program in accounting who have a GPA of 3.0 or higher. Applicants must be members of diverse racial and ethnic backgrounds, women, LGBT individuals, military veterans, or people with disabilities. Selection is based on academic achievement, demonstrated leadership skills, extracurricular activities (particularly those in leadership roles in diversity organizations), and effective communication skills.

Financial data   The stipend is $2,500.

Duration   1 year.

Number awarded   Approximately 7 each year.

Deadline   March of each year.

[320]
MOSS ADAMS FOUNDATION SCHOLARSHIP

Educational Foundation for Women in Accounting
Attn: Foundation Administrator
136 South Keowee Street
Dayton, OH 45402
(937) 424-3391   Fax: (937) 222-5749
E-mail: info@efwa.org
Web: www.efwa.org/scholarships_graduate.php

Summary   To provide financial support to women, including Asian American and other minority women, who are working on an accounting degree.

Eligibility   This program is open to women who are enrolled in an accounting degree program at an accredited college or university. Applicants must meet 1 of the following criteria: 1) women pursuing a fifth-year requirement either through general studies or within a graduate program; 2) women returning to school as current or reentry juniors or seniors; or 3) minority women. Selection is based on aptitude for accounting and business, commitment to the goal of working on a degree in accounting (including evidence of continued commitment after receiving this award), clear evidence that the candidate has established goals and a plan for achieving those goals (both personal and professional), financial need, and a demonstration of how the scholarship will impact her life. U.S. citizenship is required.

Financial data   The stipend is $1,000.

Duration   1 year.

Additional information   This program was established by Rowling, Dold & Associates LLP, a woman-owned C.P.A. firm based in San Diego. It was renamed when that firm merged with Moss Adams LLP.

Number awarded   2 each year: 1 to an undergraduate and 1 to a graduate student.

Deadline   April of each year.

[321]
MQ BUDDHIST YOUTH ASSOCIATION SCHOLARSHIP

MQ Buddhist Youth Association
c/o Ngoc Son Buddhist Temple
8318 S.E. Harney Street
Portland, OR 97266
(503) 432-9363   E-mail: contact@minh-quang.com
Web: www.minh-quang.com/resources.html

Summary   To provide financial assistance to high school seniors of Vietnamese descent in Oregon who plan to attend college in any state.

Eligibility   This program is open to seniors graduating from high school in Oregon who are of Vietnamese descent. Applicants must be planning to enroll at a college or university in any state. They must have a GPA of 2.75 or higher. Along with their application, they must submit transcripts, a letter of recommendation describing their community involvement, and an essay of 750 to 1,000 words on what the motto of the Vietnamese Buddhist Youth Association (Compassion-Wisdom-Courage) means to them. Selection is based on that essay

(75%, plus up to 10% extra if the essay is written in Vietnamese) and a letter of recommendation (25%).

Financial data   The stipend is $500.

Duration   1 year.

Number awarded   1 each year.

Deadline   May of each year.

[322]
MSCPA MINORITY SCHOLARSHIPS

Missouri Society of Certified Public Accountants
Attn: MSCPA Educational Foundation
540 Maryville Centre Drive, Suite 200
P.O. Box 958868
St. Louis, MO 63195-8868
(314) 997-7966   Toll Free: (800) 264-7966 (within MO)
Fax: (314) 997-2592   E-mail: dhull@mocpa.org
Web: www.mocpa.org/students/scholarships

Summary   To provide financial assistance to Asian American and other minority residents of Missouri who are working on an undergraduate or graduate degree in accounting at a university in the state.

Eligibility   This program is open to members of minority groups underrepresented in the accounting profession (Black/African American, Hispanic/Latino, Native American, Asian American) who are currently working full time on an undergraduate or graduate degree in accounting at a college or university in Missouri. Applicants must either be residents of Missouri or the children of members of the Missouri Society of Certified Public Accountants (MSCPA). They must be U.S. citizens, have completed at least 30 semester hours of college work, have a GPA of 3.3 or higher, and be student members of the MSCPA. Selection is based on the GPA, involvement in MSCPA, educator recommendations, and leadership potential. Financial need is not considered.

Financial data   The stipend is $1,250 per year.

Duration   1 year; may be renewed.

Number awarded   Varies each year; recently, 3 were awarded.

Deadline   February of each year.

[323]
MSIPP INTERNSHIPS

Department of Energy
Office of Environmental Management
Savannah River National Laboratory
Attn: MSIPP Program Manager
Building 773-41A, 232
Aiken, SC 29808
(803) 725-9032   E-mail: connie.yung@srnl.doe.gov
Web: srnl.doe.gov/msipp/internships.htm

Summary   To provide an opportunity for undergraduate and graduate students at Minority Serving Institutions (MSIs) to work on a summer research project at designated National Laboratories of the U.S. Department of Energy (DOE).

Eligibility   This program is open to full-time undergraduate and graduate students enrolled at an accredited MSI. Applicants must be interested in working during the summer on a research project at a participating DOE National Laboratory. They must be working on a degree in a field of science, technology, engineering, or mathematics (STEM); the specific field depends on the particular project on which they wish to work. Their GPA must be 3.0 or higher. U.S. citizenship is required.

Financial data   The stipend depends on the cost of living at the location of the host laboratory.

Duration   10 weeks during the summer.

Additional information   This program is administered at the Savannah River National Laboratory (SRNL) in Aiken, South Carolina, which serves as the National Laboratory for the DOE Office of Environmental Management. The other participating National Laboratories are Argonne National Laboratory (ANL) in Argonne, Illinois, Idaho National Laboratory (INL) in Idaho Falls, Idaho, Los Alamos National Laboratory (LANL) in Los Alamos, New Mexico, Oak Ridge National Laboratory (ORNL) in Oak Ridge, Tennessee, and Pacific Northwest National Laboratory (PNNL) in Richland, Washington. The program began in 2016.

Number awarded   Varies each year. Recently, the program offered 11 research projects at SRNL, 12 at ANL, 1 at INL, 7 at LANL, 4 at ORNL, and 7 at PNNL.

Deadline   March of each year.

[324]
MULTICULTURAL AUDIENCE DEVELOPMENT INITIATIVE INTERNSHIPS

Metropolitan Museum of Art
Attn: Internship Programs
1000 Fifth Avenue
New York, NY 10028-0198
(212) 570-3710   Fax: (212) 570-3782
E-mail: mmainterns@metmuseum.org
Web: www.metmuseum.org

Summary   To provide summer work experience at the Metropolitan Museum of Art to college undergraduates, graduate students, and recent graduates who are Asian Americans or from other diverse backgrounds.

Eligibility   This program is open to members of diverse groups who are undergraduate juniors and seniors, students currently working on a master's degree, or individuals who completed a bachelor's or master's degree within the past year. Ph.D. students may be eligible to apply during the first 12 months of their program, provided they have not yet achieved candidacy. Students from various academic backgrounds are encouraged to apply, but they must be interested in preparing for a career in the arts and museum fields. Freshmen and sophomores are not eligible.

Financial data   The stipend is $3,750.

Duration   10 weeks, beginning in June.

Additional information   Interns are assigned to departmental projects (curatorial, administration, or education) at the Metropolitan Museum of Art; other assignments may include giving gallery talks and working at the Visitor Information Center. The assignment is for 35 hours a week. The internships are funded by the Multicultural Audience Initiative at the museum.

Number awarded   1 or more each year.

Deadline   January of each year.

[325]
MULTICULTURAL UNDERGRADUATE INTERNSHIPS AT THE GETTY CENTER

Getty Foundation
Attn: Multicultural Undergraduate Internships
1200 Getty Center Drive, Suite 800
Los Angeles, CA 90049-1685
(310) 440-7320   Fax: (310) 440-7703
E-mail: summerinterns@getty.edu
Web: www.getty.edu

Summary   To provide summer work experience at facilities of the Getty Center to Asian American and other minority undergraduates with ties to Los Angeles County, California.

Eligibility   This program is open to currently-enrolled undergraduates who either reside or attend college in Los Angeles County, California. Applicants must be members of groups currently underrepresented in museum professions and fields related to the visual arts and humanities: individuals of Asian, African American, Latino/Hispanic, Native American, or Pacific Islander descent. They may be majoring in any field, including the sciences and technology, and are not required to have demonstrated a previous commitment to the visual arts. Along with their application, they must submit a personal statement of up to 500 words on why they are interested in this internship, including what they hope to gain from the program, their interest or involvement in issues of multiculturalism, aspects of their past experience that they feel are most relevant to the application, and any specific career or educational avenues they are interested in exploring. U.S. citizenship or permanent resident status is required.

Financial data   The stipend is $5,000.

Duration   10 weeks during the summer.

Additional information   Internships are available at the Getty Center in Los Angeles, the Getty Villa in Malibu, and approximately 65 arts and museum organizations in Los Angeles County.

Number awarded   15 to 20 each year.

Deadline   January of each year.

[326]
MUTUAL OF OMAHA ACTUARIAL SCHOLARSHIP FOR MINORITY STUDENTS

Mutual of Omaha
Attn: Strategic Staffing-Actuarial Recruitment
3300 Mutual of Omaha Plaza
Omaha, NE 68175
Toll Free: (800) 365-1405
E-mail: diversity@mutualofomaha.com
Web: www.mutualofomaha.com

Summary   To provide financial assistance and work experience to Asian American and other minority undergraduate students who are preparing for an actuarial career.

Eligibility   This program is open to members of minority groups (Asian or Pacific Islander, African American, Hispanic, Native American, or Alaskan Eskimo) who have completed at least 24 semester hours of full-time study. Applicants must be working on an actuarial or mathematics-related degree with the goal of preparing for an actuarial career. They must have a GPA of 3.4 or higher and have passed at least 1 actuarial examination. Prior to accepting the award, they must be available to complete a summer internship at the sponsor's home office in Omaha, Nebraska. Along with their application, they must submit a 1-page personal statement on why they are interested in becoming an actuary and how they are preparing themselves for an actuarial career. Status as a U.S. citizen, permanent resident, asylee, or refugee must be established.

Financial data The scholarship stipend is $5,000 per year. Funds are paid directly to the student. For the internship, students receive an hourly rate of pay, subsidized housing, and financial incentives for successful examination results received during the internship period.

Duration 1 year. Recipients may reapply if they maintain a cumulative GPA of 3.4 or higher.

Number awarded Varies each year.

Deadline October of each year.

[327]
MV TRANSIT COLLEGE SCHOLARSHIP

Conference of Minority Transportation Officials
Attn: National Scholarship Program
100 M Street, S.E., Suite 917
Washington, DC 20003
(202) 506-2917   E-mail: info@comto.org
Web: www.comto.org/page/scholarships

Summary To provide financial assistance to Asian American and other minority college student members of the Conference of Minority Transportation Officials (COMTO) and family of members working on a degree in transportation or a related field.

Eligibility This program is open to minority undergraduate students who have been COMTO members or whose parents, guardians, or grandparents have been members for at least 1 year. Applicants must be majoring in transportation, engineering, planning, or a related discipline. They must have a GPA of 2.0 or higher. Along with their application they must submit a cover letter on their transportation-related career goals and life aspirations. Financial need is not considered in the selection process.

Financial data The stipend is $4,000. Funds are paid directly to the recipient's college or university.

Duration 1 year.

Additional information This program is sponsored by MV Transportation, Inc.

Number awarded 1 or more each year.

Deadline April of each year.

[328]
MV TRANSIT HIGH SCHOOL SENIOR SCHOLARSHIP

Conference of Minority Transportation Officials
Attn: National Scholarship Program
100 M Street, S.E., Suite 917
Washington, DC 20003
(202) 506-2917   E-mail: info@comto.org
Web: www.comto.org/page/scholarships

Summary To provide financial assistance to Asian American and other minority high school seniors who are members of the Conference of Minority Transportation Officials (COMTO) or family of members and interested in working on a degree in transportation or a related field.

Eligibility This program is open to minority high school seniors who have been COMTO members or whose parents, guardians, or grandparents have been members for at least 1 year. Applicants must be planning to enroll at an accredited college, university, or vocational/technical institute and major in a transportation-related field. They must have a GPA of 2.0 or higher. Along with their application they must submit a cover letter on their transportation-related career goals and life aspirations. Financial need is not considered in the selection process.

Financial data The stipend is $3,500. Funds are paid directly to the recipient's college or university.

Duration 1 year.

Additional information This program is sponsored by MV Transportation, Inc.

Number awarded 1 or more each year.

Deadline April of each year.

[329]
NAAAP BOSTON FUTURE LEADERSHIP AWARDS

National Association of Asian American Professionals-
  Boston Chapter
Attn: Scholarship Committee
P.O. Box 51922
Boston, MA 02205
(617) 506-3641   E-mail: naaap@naaapboston.org
Web: www.naaapboston.org

Summary To provide financial assistance to Asian American high school seniors from Massachusetts who plan to attend college in any state.

Eligibility This program is open to seniors of Asian heritage graduating from high schools in Massachusetts and planning to enroll full time at a 4-year college or university in any state. Applicants must submit official high school transcripts that include SAT and/or ACT scores and 2 letters of recommendation. They must also submit 2 essays of 500 words each on topics that change annually but relate to their involvement in the Asian American community. Selection is based on the essays, academic achievement, community service, extracurricular activities, leadership, and financial need. Personal interviews are conducted. U.S. citizenship or permanent resident status is required.

Financial data The stipend is $5,000.

Duration 1 year.

Additional information Recently, sponsors of this program included Liberty Mutual, MassMutual, and the Richard T.N. Lee Scholarship Fund.

Number awarded Varies each year; recently, 3 were awarded.

Deadline February of each year.

[330]
NASA APIASF SCHOLARSHIPS

Asian & Pacific Islander American Scholarship Fund
2025 M Street, N.W., Suite 610
Washington, DC 20036-3363
(202) 986-6892   Toll Free: (877) 808-7032
Fax: (202) 530-0643   E-mail: info@apiasf.org
Web: www.apiasf.org/scholarship_apiasf_nasa.html

Summary To provide financial assistance to Asian and Pacific Islander Americans who are entering college for the first time and planning to major in designated fields of engineering.

Eligibility This program is open to U.S. citizens, nationals, permanent residents, and citizens of the Freely Associated States who are first-time incoming college students and of Asian or Pacific Islander heritage. Applicants must be enrolling full time at an accredited 2- or 4-year college or university in the United States and majoring in computer science or engineering (aerospace, biomedical, computer, electrical or mechanical). They must have a GPA of 2.8 or higher or the GED equivalent. In addition, they must complete the FAFSA and apply for federal financial aid.

Financial data The stipend is $2,500.

Duration 1 year; nonrenewable.

Additional information This program is sponsored by the U.S. National Aeronautics and Space Administration (NASA) and administered by the Asian & Pacific Islander American Scholarship Fund (APIASF).

Number awarded Varies each year.

Deadline January of each year.

[331]
NASA SCHOLARSHIP AND RESEARCH OPPORTUNITIES (SRO) MINORITY UNIVERSITY RESEARCH AND EDUCATION PROJECT (MUREP) SCHOLARSHIPS

National Aeronautics and Space Administration
Attn: National Scholarship Deputy Program Manager
Office of Education and Public Outreach
Ames Research Center
Moffett Field, CA 94035
(650) 604-6958   E-mail: elizabeth.a.cartier@nasa.gov
Web: intern.nasa.gov

Summary To provide financial assistance and summer research experience at National Aeronautics and Space Administration (NASA) facilities to undergraduate students majoring in designated fields of science, technology, engineering, or mathematics (STEM) at a Minority Serving Institution (MSI).

Eligibility This program is open to U.S. citizens and nationals who are working on an undergraduate degree at an MSI and have a GPA of 3.0 or higher with at least 2 years of full-time study remaining. Applicants must be majoring in chemistry, computer and information science and engineering, engineering (aeronautical and aerospace, biomedical, chemical, civil, computer, electrical and electronic, environmental, industrial and operations research, materials, mechanical, nuclear, ocean, optical, polymer, or systems) geosciences (including geophysics, hydrology, physical and dynamic meteorology, physical oceanography, planetary science), life sciences (including biochemistry, cell biology, developmental biology, evolutionary biology, genetics, physiology), materials research, mathematical sciences, or physics and astronomy. They must be available for an internship at a NASA center performing aeronautical research during the summer between their junior and senior years. Along with their application, they must submit a 1,000-word essay on 1) their professional goals and what attracted them to their intended STEM field of study; 2) the events and individuals that have been critical in influencing their academic and career deci-

sions; and 3) how receiving the MUREP scholarship would help them accomplish their professional goals. Financial need is not considered in the selection process.

Financial data Students receive 75% of their tuition and education-related costs, up to $9,000 per academic year. The stipend for the summer internship is $6,000.

Duration 2 years.

Number awarded Up to 20 each year.

Deadline March of each year.

[332]
NATIONAL ASSOCIATION OF GEOSCIENCE TEACHERS SCHOLARSHIPS FOR FIELD STUDY

National Association of Geoscience Teachers
Attn: Executive Director
Carleton College W-SERC
One North College Street
Northfield, MN 55057
(507) 222-7096   Fax: (507) 222-5175
E-mail: cmanduca@carlton.edu
Web: www.nagt.org/nagt/programs/field_scholarships.html

Summary To provide funding to advanced undergraduate students, especially Asian Americans or other minorities, interested in participating in field-based courses in geoscience.

Eligibility This program is open to upper-division students who are interested in attending a field course in an aspect of geoscience (including geophysics, soil science, and hydrology) that focuses on their practicing skills of field observation, data collection, analysis, and synthesis. Applicants must have a GPA of 3.0 or higher. Along with their application, they must submit a 250-word essay on how the field camp experience fits into their long-term academic and career goals. Selection is based on the importance of the field experience in meeting educational and career goals, quality of the field aspects of the course, and the importance of the financial award in allowing them to participate in the program. The program includes awards designed for minority students, and the Association for Women Geoscientists supports 2 awards designated for women.

Financial data The stipend ranges up to $750.

Duration This program was previously limited to students attending a traditional summer field camp, but now supports students attending field-based courses any time of year.

Number awarded Varies each year; recently, 17 were awarded.

Deadline February of each year.

[333]
NATIONAL CO-OP SCHOLARSHIP PROGRAM

World Association for Cooperative Education (WACE)
600 Suffolk Street, Suite 125
Lowell, MA 01854
(978) 934-1870   E-mail: Marty_ford@uml.edu
Web: www.waceinc.org/scholarship/index.html

Summary To provide financial assistance to students, especially Asian Americans and other minorities, who are participating or planning to participate in cooperative education projects at designated colleges and universities.

Eligibility This program is open to high school seniors and community college transfer students entering 1 of the 11 partner colleges and universities. Applicants must be planning to participate in college cooperative education. They must have a GPA of 3.5 or higher. Along with their application, they must submit a 1-page essay describing why they have chosen to enter a college cooperative education program. Applications are especially encouraged from minorities, women, and students interested in science, mathematics, engineering, and technology. Selection is based on merit; financial need is not considered.

Financial data The stipend is $6,000 per year.

Duration 1 year; may be renewed up to 3 additional years or (for some programs) up to 4 additional years.

Additional information The schools recently participating in this program were Clarkson University (Potsdam, New York), Drexel University (Philadelphia, Pennsylvania), Johnson & Wales University (Providence, Rhode Island; Charleston, South Carolina; Norfolk, Virginia; North Miami, Florida; Denver, Colorado; and Charlotte, North Carolina), Kettering University (Flint, Michigan), Rochester Institute of Technology (Rochester, New York), State University of New York at Oswego (Oswego, New York), University of Cincinnati (Cincinnati, Ohio), University of Massachusetts at Lowell, University of Toledo (Toledo, Ohio), Merrimack College (North Andover, Massachusetts), and Wentworth Institute of Technology (Boston, Massachusetts). Applications must be sent directly to the college or university.

Number awarded Varies each year; recently, 195 were awarded: 10 at Clarkson, 30 at Drexel, 15 at Johnson & Wales, 20 at Kettering, 15 at Rochester Tech, 15 at SUNY Oswego, 15 at Cincinnati, 15 at UM Lowell, 15 at Toledo, 15 at Merrimack, and 30 at Wentworth Tech.

Deadline February of each year.

[334]
NATIONAL PRESS CLUB SCHOLARSHIP FOR JOURNALISM DIVERSITY

National Press Club
Attn: Executive Director's Office
529 14th Street, N.W., 13th Floor
Washington, DC 20045
(202) 662-7599
Web: www.press.org/about/scholarships/diversity

Summary To provide funding to high school seniors who are planning to major in journalism in college and who are Asian Americans or will bring diversity to the field in other ways.

Eligibility This program is open to high school seniors who have been accepted to college and plan to prepare for a career in journalism. Applicants must submit 1) a 500-word essay explaining how they would add diversity to U.S. journalism; 2) up to 5 work samples demonstrating an ongoing interest in journalism through work on a high school newspaper or other media; 3) letters of recommendation from 3 people; 4) a copy of their high school transcript; 5) documentation of financial need; 6) a letter of acceptance from the college or university of their choice; and 7) a brief description of how they have pursued journalism in high school.

Financial data The stipend is $2,000 for the first year and $2,500 for each subsequent year. The program also provides an additional $500 book stipend, designated the Ellen Masin Persina Scholarship, for the first year.

Duration 4 years.

Additional information The program began in 1990.

Number awarded 1 each year.

Deadline February of each year.

[335]
NATWA SINGLE-MOTHER-STUDENT SCHOLARSHIPS

North American Taiwanese Women's Association
Attn: Scholarship Committee
25267 Sullivan Lane
Novi, MI 48375
E-mail: sw32048@gmail.com
Web: www.natwa.com/page/scholarship.html

Summary To provide financial assistance to single mothers who identify with the North American Taiwanese community and are attending college.

Eligibility This program is open to single mothers of any age or race currently enrolled full time at a 2- or 4-year college or university in the United States or Canada. Applicants must be able to demonstrate financial need and achievement in school, community, or work activities. They must have a GPA of 2.5 or higher (or 62.5% in Canada). Along with their application, they must submit essays of 500 to 1,000 words on 1) their future planning; and 2) what they know about Taiwan.

Financial data The stipend is $1,000.

Duration 1 year.

Additional information This program began in 2000.

Number awarded 2 each year.

Deadline March of each year.

[336]
NAVAL RESEARCH LABORATORY SUMMER RESEARCH PROGRAM FOR HBCU/MI UNDERGRADUATES AND GRADUATES

Naval Research Laboratory
Attn: Personnel Operations Branch
4555 Overlook Avenue, S.W.
Washington, DC 20375-5320
(202) 767-8313
Web: www.nrl.navy.mil/hbcu/description

Summary To provide research experience at the Naval Research Laboratory (NRL) to undergraduate and graduate students in fields of science, technology, engineering, and mathematics (STEM) at minority institutions.

Eligibility This program is open to undergraduate and graduate students who have completed at least 1 year of study at an Historically Black College or University (HBCU), Minority Institution (MI), or Tribal College or University (TCU). Applicants must be working on a degree in a field of STEM and have a cumulative GPA of 3.0 or higher. They must be interested in participating in a research program at NRL under the mentorship of a senior staff scientist. U.S. citizenship or permanent resident status is required.

Financial data The stipend is $810 per week for undergraduates or $1,050 per week for graduate students. Subsidized housing is provided at a motel in the area.

Duration 10 weeks during the summer.

Additional information This program is conducted in accordance with a planned schedule and a working agreement between NRL, the educational institution, and the student.

Number awarded   Varies each year.

Deadline   February of each year.

[337]
NAVY/MARINE CORPS JROTC SCHOLARSHIP

National Naval Officers Association-Washington, D.C.
  Chapter
c/o LCDR Stephen Williams
P.O. Box 30784
Alexandria, VA 22310
(703) 566-3840   Fax: (703) 566-3813
E-mail: Stephen.Williams@navy.mil
Web: dcnnoa.memberlodge.com/page-309002

Summary   To provide financial assistance to Asian American and other minority high school seniors from the Washington, D.C. area who have participated in Navy or Marine Corps Junior Reserve Officers Training Corps (JROTC) and are planning to attend college in any state.

Eligibility   This program is open to minority seniors graduating from high schools in the Washington, D.C. metropolitan area who have participated in Navy or Marine Corps JROTC. Applicants must be planning to enroll full time at an accredited 2- or 4-year college or university in any state. They must have a GPA of 2.5 or higher. Selection is based on academic achievement, community involvement, and financial need. U.S. citizenship or permanent resident status is required.

Financial data   The stipend is $1,000.

Duration   1 year; nonrenewable.

Additional information   Recipients are not required to join or affiliate with the military in any way after college.

Number awarded   1 each year.

Deadline   March of each year.

[338]
NBCUNIVERSAL APIASF SCHOLARSHIPS

Asian & Pacific Islander American Scholarship Fund
2025 M Street, N.W., Suite 610
Washington, DC 20036-3363
(202) 986-6892   Toll Free: (877) 808-7032
Fax: (202) 530-0643   E-mail: info@apiasf.org
Web: www.apiasf.org

Summary   To provide financial assistance to Asian and Pacific Islander Americans who are upper-division students working on a degree in journalism or communications.

Eligibility   This program is open to U.S. citizens, nationals, permanent residents, and citizens of the Freely Associated States who are upper-division college students and of Asian or Pacific Islander heritage. Applicants must be enrolled full time at an accredited college or university in the United States and working on a degree in journalism or communications. They must have a GPA of 2.7 or higher or the GED equivalent. In addition, they must complete the FAFSA and apply for federal aid.

Financial data   The stipend is $2,500.

Duration   1 year; nonrenewable.

Additional information   This program is sponsored by NBCUniversal and administered by the Asian & Pacific Islander American Scholarship Fund (APIASF).

Number awarded   Varies each year; recently, 17 were awarded.

Deadline   January of each year.

[339]
NCPACA UNDERGRADUATE SCHOLARSHIPS

National Council of Philippine American Canadian
  Accountants
c/o Ed Ortiz, Scholarship Chair
333 South Des Plaines Street, Suite 2-N
Chicago, IL 60661
(312) 876-1900   Fax: (312) 876-1911
E-mail: ecortiz@ecortiz.com
Web: www.ncpacafoundation.com/shout-out.html

Summary   To provide financial assistance to undergraduate accounting students who are connected to the National Council of Philippine American Canadian Accountants (NCPACA).

Eligibility   This program is open to full-time undergraduate students who have completed at least 60 semester hours (including at least 12 semester hours in accounting) at a 4-year college or university in the United States or Canada. Applicants must submit a 500-word essay on 1) why they want to become a CPA and how attaining that licensure will contribute to their goals; and 2) how they could reach other college and/or high school students to promote the CPA profession. They must have a GPA of 3.0 or higher both cumulatively and in accounting. Selection is based primarily on academic achievement; financial need is evaluated as a secondary consideration.

Financial data   The stipend is $5,000. Payments are sent directly to the recipient's school.

Duration   1 year.

Additional information   Recipients must attend the annual conference of the NCPACA.

Number awarded   1 or more each year.

Deadline   July of each year.

[340]
NELLIE STONE JOHNSON SCHOLARSHIP

Nellie Stone Johnson Scholarship Program
P.O. Box 40309
St. Paul, MN 55104
(651) 738-1404   Toll Free: (866) 738-5238
E-mail: info@nelliestone.org
Web: www.nelliestone.org/scholarship-program

Summary   To provide financial assistance to Asian American and other racial minority union members and their families who are interested in working on an undergraduate or graduate degree in any field at a Minnesota state college or university.

Eligibility   This program is open to students in undergraduate and graduate programs at a 2- or 4-year institution that is a component of Minnesota State Colleges and Universities (MnSCU). Applicants must be a minority (Asian, American Indian, Alaska Native, Black/African American, Chicano(a) or Latino(a), Native Hawaiian, or Pacific Islander) and a union member or the child, grandchild, or spouse of a minority union member. They must submit a 2-page essay about their background, educational goals, career goals, and commitment to the causes of human or civil rights. Undergraduates must have a GPA of 2.0 or higher; graduate students must have a GPA of 3.0 or higher. Preference is given to Minnesota residents. Selection is based on the essay, commitment to human or civil rights, extracurricular activities, volunteer activities, community involvement, academic standing, and union verification.

Financial data Stipends are $1,200 per year for full-time students or $500 per year for part-time students.

Duration 1 year; may be renewed up to 3 additional years for students working on a bachelor's degree, 1 additional year for students working on a master's degree, or 1 additional year for students in a community or technical college program.

Number awarded Varies each year; recently, 18 were awarded.

Deadline May of each year.

[341]
NEW ENGLAND COUNSELORS OF COLOR BRIDGING ACCESS TO COLLEGE BOOK SCHOLARSHIPS

New England Counselors of Color Bridging Access to College
c/o Renee Gadsden, President
Boston College
Undergraduate Admissions
140 Commonwealth Avenue
Chestnut Hill, MA 02467
(617) 552-3100   E-mail: renee.gadsden@bc.edu
Web: www.necbac.org/students

Summary To provide funding for purchase of books to high school seniors of color in New England who plan to enroll at an institution belonging to the New England Counselors of Color Bridging Access to College (NECBAC).

Eligibility This program is open to students of color who are graduating seniors at high schools in New England and planning to enroll full time at a NECBAC institution. Applicants must submit high school transcripts and a 500-word essay on a topic of their choice.

Financial data The stipend is $500.

Duration These are 1-time awards.

Additional information NECBAC institutions are 4-year private colleges and universities located in New England.

Number awarded Varies each year; recently, 5 were awarded.

Deadline May of each year.

[342]
NEW LEADER SCHOLARSHIPS

10,000 Degrees
Attn: Manager, Scholarship Programs
1650 Los Gamos Drive, Suite 110
San Rafael, CA 94903
(415) 451-4002   Fax: (415) 459-0527
E-mail: jchoi@10000degrees.org
Web: www.10000degrees.org

Summary To provide financial assistance to Asian American and other upper-division students of color from any state who are preparing for careers in specified fields at public universities in the San Francisco Bay area.

Eligibility This program is open to full-time upper-division students at public universities in the San Francisco Bay area who have a GPA of 3.5 or higher (consideration may be given to students with a GPA of 3.2 to 3.49 under special circumstances). Preference is given to students who come from financially and educationally disadvantaged backgrounds, including recent immigrants, undocumented students, and students of color. Applicants must be preparing for a career in the social sciences, human services, public interest law, health-related fields, or public service. Financial need is considered in the selection process. Finalists are interviewed.

Financial data The stipend is $8,000 per year.

Duration 1 year; may be renewed for the senior year and/or for graduate study at a public university in California.

Additional information This program began in 2000 through the Marin Community Foundation, which continues to select the recipients. Administrative support is provided by 10,000 Degrees (formerly named the Marin Education Fund). The eligible universities are California State University, East Bay; San Francisco State University; San Jose State University; Sonoma State University; and the University of California at Berkeley.

Number awarded Several each year.

Deadline March of each year.

[343]
NEW LIFE CHURCH ANNUAL SCHOLARSHIPS

New Life Church of Chicago
Attn: Scholarship Committee
1200 West Northwest Highway
Palatine, IL 60067
(847) 359-5200   Fax: (847) 359-8409
E-mail: scholarship@NLChicago.org
Web: www.newlife-chicago.org/zbxe/main_banner/56490

Summary To provide financial assistance for college, graduate school, or seminary to Korean Americans who are either the child of a pastor or studying theology.

Eligibility This program is open to Korean Americans who are either 1) the child of a pastor or missionary and currently enrolled in college or graduate school; or 2) currently studying theology at a seminary or graduate school. Applicants must have completed at least 15 credit hours of undergraduate study or 8 credit hours as a graduate student and have a GPA of 3.0 or higher. Selection is based on transcripts, 2 letters of recommendation, a 500-word personal testimony and vision statement, and financial need.

Financial data The stipend is $1,500.

Duration 1 year.

Additional information This program began in 2002.

Number awarded 12 each year.

Deadline October of each year.

[344]
NEW YORK EXCEPTIONAL UNDERGRADUATE/ GRADUATE STUDENT SCHOLARSHIP

Conference of Minority Transportation Officials
Attn: National Scholarship Program
100 M Street, S.E., Suite 917
Washington, DC 20003
(202) 506-2917   E-mail: info@comto.org
Web: www.comto.org/page/scholarships

Summary To provide financial assistance to Asian American or other minority students who are members or relatives of members of the Conference of Minority Transportation Officials (COMTO) in New York and working on an undergraduate or graduate degree in transportation.
Eligibility This program is open to minorities who have been members or relatives of members of COMTO in New York for at least 1 year. Applicants must be enrolled full time at an accredited college, university, or vocational/technical institute and working on an undergraduate or graduate degree in a transportation-related discipline. They must have a GPA of 3.5 or higher. Along with their application they must submit a cover letter on their transportation-related career goals and life aspirations. Financial need is not considered in the selection process.
Financial data The stipend is $5,000. Funds are paid directly to the recipient's college or university.
Duration 1 year.
Number awarded 1 each year.
Deadline April of each year.

[345]
NISEI VETERANS COMMITTEE/WOMEN'S AUXILIARY CLUB SCHOLARSHIP

Nisei Veterans Committee
Attn: NVC Foundation
1212 South King Street
Seattle, WA 98144-2025
(206) 322-1122   E-mail: scholarship@nvcfoundation.org
Web: www.seattlenvc.org/education/scholarship

Summary To provide financial assistance for college to high school seniors who are related to a member of the Nisei Veterans Committee or the NVC Foundation.
Eligibility This program is open to high school seniors who are relatives of members of the Nisei Veterans Committee (an organization of Japanese American veterans) or of the NVC Foundation. Applicants must be planning to attend a college or university. Along with their application, they must submit essays on 1) what the Nisei veterans' legacy means to them; and 2) their future aspirations and life plans. Special consideration is given to students who have helped support the NVC organization. Financial need is considered in the selection process.
Financial data The stipend is $2,500.
Duration 1 year.
Number awarded 1 each year.
Deadline January of each year.

[346]
NJUA EXCELLENCE IN DIVERSITY SCHOLARSHIP

New Jersey Utilities Association
50 West State Street, Suite 1117
Trenton, NJ 08608
(609) 392-1000   Fax: (609) 396-4231
E-mail: info@njua.com
Web: www.njua.com/excellence_in_diversity_scholarship

Summary To provide financial assistance to Asian American or other minority, female, or disabled high school seniors in New Jersey interested in attending college in any state.
Eligibility This program is open to seniors graduating from high schools in New Jersey who are women, minorities (Asian, Black or African American, Hispanic or Latino, American Indian or Alaska Native, Native Hawaiian or Pacific Islander, or 2 or more races), and persons with disabilities. Applicants must be planning to work on a bachelor's degree at a college or university in any state. Along with their application, they must submit a 500-word essay explaining their career ambition and why they have chosen that career. Children of employees of any New Jersey Utilities Association-member company are ineligible. Selection is based on overall academic excellence and demonstrated financial need. U.S. citizenship or permanent resident status is required.
Financial data The stipend is $1,500 per year. Funds are paid to the recipient's college or university.
Duration 4 years.
Number awarded 1 each year.
Deadline April of each year.

[347]
NONG KHAI JUNIOR VANG SCHOLARSHIP

Hmong American Education Fund
P.O. Box 17468
St. Paul, MN 55117
(651) 592-1576   E-mail: scholarships@thehaef.org
Web: www.thehaef.org

Summary To provide financial assistance to Hmong undergraduate and graduate students who demonstrate academic achievement.
Eligibility This program is open to students of Hmong descent who are currently enrolled as full-time undergraduate or graduate students at 2- or 4-year colleges or universities in any state. Applicants must be U.S. citizens or permanent residents and have a GPA of 3.0 or higher. Along with their application, they must submit a 1,500-word essay on their commitment to education, their financial need, how this scholarship can help them, and their community service. Selection is based on commitment to academic achievement, drive to achieve their goals, commitment to helping their community, and financial need.
Financial data The stipend is $500.
Duration 1 year; nonrenewable.
Number awarded 1 each year.
Deadline March of each year.

[348]
NORA STONE SMITH SCHOLARSHIP

Seattle Foundation
Attn: Scholarship Administrator
1200 Fifth Avenue, Suite 1300
Seattle, WA 98101-3151
(206) 515-2119   Fax: (206) 622-7673
E-mail: scholarships@seattlefoundation.org
Web: www.washboard.org

Summary To provide financial assistance for college to high school seniors who have been enrolled in English as a Second Language/English Language Learners (ESL/ELL) programs.
Eligibility This program is open to seniors graduating from high schools who are current or former ESL/ELL students, regardless of their citizenship status. Applicants must be

planning to enroll full time at a 2- or 4-year college, university, or vocational/trade school. Along with their application, they must submit a 250-word essay about themselves, where they are from, how they came to be here, their educational achievements, and their future goals. Financial need is considered in the selection process.

Financial data   The maximum stipend is $2,000 per year.

Duration   1 year; may be renewed up to 3 additional years.

Number awarded   10 each year.

Deadline   March of each year.

[349]
NORMA KORNEGAY CLARKE SCHOLARSHIP

Northeast Human Resources Association
Attn: Director of Professional Development
490 Virginia Road, Suite 32
Concord, MA 01742-2747
(781) 239-8718   Fax: (781) 237-8745
E-mail: nreiser@nehra.com
Web: www.nehra.com/?page=DIScholarshipApp

Summary   To provide financial assistance for college to high school seniors from the New England states who are Asian American or have promoted diversity in other ways.

Eligibility   This program is open to seniors who are graduating from high schools in New England and planning to attend a college or university. Applicants should have demonstrated academic responsibility, performed community service, offered a helping hand to fellow students, and promoted harmony among diverse groups. They must have a GPA of 3.0 or higher and be able to demonstrate financial need. Along with their application, they must submit a 750-word personal statement explaining what diversity means to them, how they promote diversity in their community or school, and how they propose to promote diversity in the future.

Financial data   The stipend is $5,000.

Duration   1 year.

Additional information   The sponsor is an affiliate of the Society for Human Resource Management (SHRM). Its Diversity and Inclusion Committee focuses on veterans, the GLBT community, people with disabilities, gender equity, and race/ethnicity. The Back Bay Staffing Group established this program in 1998.

Number awarded   1 each year.

Deadline   February of each year.

[350]
NORTH AMERICAN TAIWANESE WOMEN'S ASSOCIATION COMMUNITY SCHOLARSHIPS

North American Taiwanese Women's Association
Attn: Scholarship Committee
25267 Sullivan Lane
Novi, MI 48375
E-mail: sw32048@gmail.com
Web: www.natwa.com/page/scholarship.html

Summary   To provide financial assistance to high school seniors and college students who identify with the North American Taiwanese community.

Eligibility   This program is open to high school seniors and college students enrolled or planning to enroll full time at a 2- or 4-year college or university in the United States or Canada. Applicants must be able to demonstrate financial need and

achievement in school, community, or work activities. They must have a GPA of 3.0 or higher. Along with their application, they must submit an essay describing an outstanding achievement they have accomplished in a non-academic activity or project. Students submit applications to their local chapter of the North American Taiwanese Women's Association (NATWA). Each chapter determines the specific details of its selection process, but gives primary consideration to the applicant's demonstrated achievement in a non-academic area.

Financial data   Stipends are determined by each chapter but range from $500 to $1,000. Funds are paid directly to the school.

Duration   1 year.

Additional information   For the name and address of your local scholarship chair, contact NATWA.

Number awarded   Varies each year.

Deadline   Each chapter sets its own deadline.

[351]
NORTH CAROLINA CPA FOUNDATION OUTSTANDING MINORITY ACCOUNTING STUDENT SCHOLARSHIPS

North Carolina Association of Certified Public
    Accountants
Attn: North Carolina CPA Foundation, Inc.
P.O. Box 80188
Raleigh, NC 27623-0188
(919) 469-1040, ext. 130   Toll Free: (800) 722-2836
Fax: (919) 378-2000   E-mail: nccpafound@ncacpa.org
Web: www.ncacpa.org/scholarship-recipients

Summary   To provide financial assistance to Asian American and other minority undergraduate students working on a degree in accounting at colleges and universities in North Carolina.

Eligibility   This program is open to North Carolina residents who are members of a minority group, defined as Asian or Pacific Islander, Black, Native American/Alaskan Native, Middle-Eastern, or Hispanic, and enrolled full time in an accounting program at a college or university in the state. Applicants must have completed at least 36 semester hours, including at least 1 college or university-level accounting course, and have a GPA of 3.0 or higher. They must be sponsored by an accounting faculty member. Selection is based on the content of an essay on a topic related to the public accounting profession (35%), essay grammar (35%), and extracurricular activities (30%).

Financial data   Stipends are $2,000 or $1,000.

Duration   1 year; may be renewed up to 2 additional years.

Number awarded   2 each year: 1 at $2,000 and 1 at $1,000.

Deadline   February of each year.

[352]
NORTH DAKOTA DEPARTMENT OF TRANSPORTATION EDUCATIONAL GRANT PROGRAM

North Dakota Department of Transportation
608 East Boulevard Avenue
Bismarck, ND 58505-0700
(701) 328-2550   Toll Free: (855) ND-ROADS
Fax: (701) 328-0319   TDD: (800) 366-6888
E-mail: dot@nd.gov
Web: www.dot.nd.gov/dotnet2/view/careers.aspx

Summary To provide forgivable loans to undergraduates in North Dakota colleges and universities, especially Asian Americans and other minorities, who are majoring in fields related to the needs and missions of the North Dakota Department of Transportation.

Eligibility This program is open to students who are attending an institution of higher learning in North Dakota, have completed 1 year of study, and are majoring in civil engineering, construction engineering, diesel technology, engineering technology, or other field that meets the needs and missions of the department. Current department employees are also eligible for aid if they have completed 1 year of study or have worked for the department as a classified employee for at least 2 years. All applicants must be attending a college or university in North Dakota. Priority is given to students who are available for summer employment with the department. Women and minorities are particularly encouraged to apply. Selection is based on: potential to contribute to the department's program, financial need, academic achievement, and relevant experience.

Financial data The maximum stipend is $2,000 per year. These are forgivable loans. Recipients who fail to honor their work obligation must repay the grant on a prorated basis at 6% interest. Funds must be used only for educational expenses, including tuition, required fees, books, materials, and necessary personal expenses while attending college.

Duration 1 year; may be renewed up to 2 additional years.

Additional information Upon graduation, recipients must agree to work for the department for a period of time at least equal to the grant study period.

Number awarded Varies each year; recently, 14 of these grants were awarded.

Deadline Deadline not specified.

[353]
NORTH DAKOTA UNITED FOUNDATION ETHNIC MINORITY SCHOLARSHIPS

North Dakota Education Association
Attn: North Dakota United Foundation
301 North Fourth Street
Bismarck, ND 58501-4020
(701) 223-0450   Toll Free: (800) 369-NDEA
Fax: (701) 224-8535   E-mail: foundation@ndunited.org
Web: www.ndunited.org

Summary To provide financial assistance to Asian American and other minority undergraduates working on a degree in teacher preparation at a college or university in North Dakota.

Eligibility This program is open to minority undergraduates from any state attending institutions of higher education

in North Dakota. Applicants must be enrolled in a teacher preparation program. They must be members of the North Dakota United Foundation of the North Dakota Education Association (NDEA) or other state affiliate of the National Education Association (NEA) of American Federation of Teachers (AFT). Along with their application, they must submit an essay of 300 to 500 words on their personal goals, strengths, weaknesses, and philosophy of education. Special consideration is given to students attending tribal colleges.

Financial data The stipend is $750.

Duration 1 year.

Additional information This program began in 1988.

Number awarded At least 2 each year.

Deadline March of each year.

[354]
NORTH TEXAS EXCEPTIONAL HIGH SCHOOL STUDENT SCHOLARSHIP

Conference of Minority Transportation Officials
Attn: National Scholarship Program
100 M Street, S.E., Suite 917
Washington, DC 20003
(202) 506-2917   E-mail: info@comto.org
Web: www.comto.org/page/scholarships

Summary To provide financial assistance to Asian American and other minority high school seniors who are members or family of members of the Conference of Minority Transportation Officials (COMTO) in New York and planning to work on a degree in transportation.

Eligibility This program is open to minority residents of Texas who have been members or whose parents, guardians, or grandparents have been members of COMTO for at least 1 year. Applicants must be high school seniors who have been accepted at an accredited college, university, or vocational/technical institute and planning to work on a degree in a transportation-related discipline. They must have a GPA of 2.0 or higher. Along with their application they must submit a cover letter on their transportation-related career goals and life aspirations. Financial need is not considered in the selection process.

Financial data The stipend is $3,000. Funds are paid directly to the recipient's college or university.

Duration 1 year.

Number awarded 1 each year.

Deadline April of each year.

[355]
NORTH TEXAS EXCEPTIONAL UNDERGRADUATE/GRADUATE STUDENT SCHOLARSHIP

Conference of Minority Transportation Officials
Attn: National Scholarship Program
100 M Street, S.E., Suite 917
Washington, DC 20003
(202) 506-2917   E-mail: info@comto.org
Web: www.comto.org/page/scholarships

Summary To provide financial assistance to Asian American and other minority residents of Texas who are working on an undergraduate or graduate degree in transportation.

Eligibility This program is open to minorities who are residents of Texas enrolled at an accredited college, university, or vocational/technical institute and working on an undergraduate or graduate degree in a transportation-related discipline. Applicants must have a GPA of 2.5 or higher. Along with their application they must submit a cover letter on their transportation-related career goals and life aspirations. Financial need is not considered in the selection process. Membership in the Conference of Minority Transportation Officials (COMTO) is considered a plus but is not required.

Financial data The stipend is $4,500. Funds are paid directly to the recipient's college or university.

Duration 1 year.

Number awarded 1 each year.

Deadline April of each year.

[356]
NORTHEASTERN REGION KOREAN AMERICAN SCHOLARSHIPS

Korean American Scholarship Foundation
Northeastern Region
Attn: Scholarship Committee Chair
1411 Broadway, Fourth Floor
New York, NY 10018
E-mail: nerc.scholarship@kasf.org
Web: www.kasf.org/northeastern

Summary To provide financial assistance to Korean American students from any state who are working on an undergraduate or graduate degree in any field at a school in northeastern states.

Eligibility This program is open to residents of any state who are 1) U.S. citizens of Korean heritage; 2) Korean citizens who have a valid visa to study in the United States; and 3) citizens of any other country who are of Korean heritage and have a valid visa to study in the United States. Applicants must be enrolled or planning to enroll as a full-time undergraduate or graduate student at a college or university in Connecticut, Maine, Massachusetts, New Hampshire, New Jersey, New York, Ohio, Rhode Island, or Vermont. Selection is based on academic achievement, school and community activities, letters of recommendation, a personal essay, and financial need.

Financial data Stipends range from $1,000 to $2,000.

Duration 1 year; renewable.

Number awarded Varies each year; recently, 67 were awarded.

Deadline July of each year.

[357]
NORTHWEST FARM CREDIT SERVICES MINORITY SCHOLARSHIPS

Northwest Farm Credit Services
Attn: Public Relations and Events Manager
P.O. Box 2515
Spokane, WA 99220-2515
(509) 340-5467   Toll Free: (800) 743-2125
Fax: (800) 255-1789
E-mail: heidi.whitman@northwestfcs.com
Web: www.northwestfcs.com

Summary To provide financial assistance to Asian American and other minority students who are majoring in a field related to agricultural business at universities in designated northwestern states.

Eligibility This program is open to members of minority ethnic groups (African American or Black, American Indian or Alaska Native, Asian, Latino/Hispanic, or Pacific Islander) currently enrolled as full-time sophomores or higher at 4-year universities in Alaska, Idaho, Montana, Oregon, Utah, or Washington. Applicants must be studying accounting, business, finance, agricultural business, or economics. They must have a GPA of 3.0 or higher and be U.S. citizens or legal residents. Along with their application, they must submit a 1-page essay on how they will use their education and degree to make a positive impact. Selection is based on that essay (20%), academic achievement (20%), leadership (25%), participation in extracurricular activities (25%), and letters of recommendation (10%).

Financial data The stipend is $2,000.

Duration 1 year; nonrenewable.

Number awarded 4 each year.

Deadline February of each year.

[358]
NORTHWEST JOURNALISTS OF COLOR SCHOLARSHIP AWARDS

Northwest Journalists of Color
c/o Anika Anand
The Evergrey
P.O. Box 30854
Seattle, WA 98113
E-mail: anikaanand00@gmail.com
Web: www.aajaseattle.org/scholarships

Summary To provide financial assistance to students from Washington state who demonstrate a commitment to the importance of diverse cultural backgrounds and are interested in careers in journalism.

Eligibility This program is open to students who are 1) current high school juniors or seniors in Washington; 2) residents of any state attending a 2- or 4-year college, university, or vocational school in Washington; or 3) seniors graduating from Washington high schools and planning to attend a 2- or 4-year college, university, or vocational school in any state. Applicants must be preparing for a career in broadcast, photo, or print journalism. They do not need to identify as a student of color, but strong preference is given to applicants who demonstrate an understanding of and commitment to the importance of diverse cultural backgrounds and experiences in newsrooms. Along with their application, they must submit 1) a 500-word essay about their interest in a career as a journalist; 2) link to a resume; 3) up to 3 work samples; and 4) a 250-word statement of financial need.

Financial data Stipends range up to $2,500 per year.

Duration 1 year; may be renewed.

Additional information This program, established in 1986, is sponsored by local chapters of the Asian American Journalists Association, the Native American Journalists Association, the Black Journalists Association of Seattle, and the National Association of Hispanic Journalists.

Number awarded Varies each year.

Deadline April of each year.

[359]
NOVAL-DC LEADERSHIP SCHOLARSHIP

National Organization for Vietnamese American
　Leadership
P.O. Box 34437
Washington, DC 20043
(202) 670-5370　　　　　　E-mail: info@vietfest.com
Web: www.vietfest.com/noval-dc-scholarship

Summary　To provide financial assistance to Vietnamese American college students who have ties to the Washington, D.C. metropolitan area and are committed to serving the Vietnamese American community in that region.

Eligibility　This program is open to Vietnamese American undergraduates who reside or attend college in the Virginia, Maryland, and Washington metropolitan area. Applicants must be able to demonstrate a commitment to serving the Vietnamese American community in that region. Along with their application, they must submit a 1,000-word essay, in English or Vietnamese, on a topic that changes annually but relates to the Vietnamese community. Selection is based on that essay, academic performance, and community service.

Financial data　The stipend is $1,000.

Duration　1 year.

Number awarded　1 each year.

Deadline　July of each year.

[360]
NSCA MINORITY SCHOLARSHIPS

National Strength and Conditioning Association
Attn: NSCA Foundation
1885 Bob Johnson Drive
Colorado Springs, CO 80906-4000
(719) 632-6722, ext. 152　　　Toll Free: (800) 815-6826
Fax: (719) 632-6367　　　E-mail: foundation@nsca.org
Web: www.nsca.com/foundation/nsca-scholarships

Summary　To provide financial assistance to Asian American and other minorities who are interested in working on an undergraduate or graduate degree in strength training and conditioning.

Eligibility　This program is open to Asian Americans, Blacks, Hispanics, and Native Americans who are 17 years of age and older. Applicants must have been accepted into an accredited postsecondary institution to work on an undergraduate or graduate degree in the strength and conditioning field. Along with their application, they must submit a 500-word essay on their personal and professional goals and how receiving this scholarship will assist them in achieving those goals. Selection is based on that essay, academic achievement, strength and conditioning experience, honors and awards, community involvement, letters of recommendation, and involvement in the National Strength and Conditioning Association (NSCA).

Financial data　The stipend is $1,500.

Duration　1 year.

Additional information　The NSCA is a nonprofit organization of strength and conditioning professionals, including coaches, athletic trainers, physical therapists, educators, researchers, and physicians. This program was first offered in 2003.

Number awarded　Varies each year; recently, 5 were awarded.

Deadline　March of each year.

[361]
NSRCF SCHOLARSHIPS

Nisei Student Relocation Commemorative Fund, Inc.
19 Scenic Drive
Portland, CT 06480
E-mail: info@nsrcfund.org
Web: www.nsrcfund.org/scholarships.overview.php

Summary　To provide financial assistance for college to high school seniors in specified geographic areas who are of southeast Asian descent.

Eligibility　Each year, this program operates in a different city or state (recently, Rhode Island and eastern Massachusetts). Within the selected area, graduating high school seniors and recent GED recipients are eligible to apply if they are first- or second-generation students from Cambodia, Laos, or Vietnam. Applicants must be planning to attend an accredited 2- or 4-year college or university or a vocational program in any state. Selection is based on academic achievement; educational and career goals; extracurricular activities and/or work experience; financial need; and a personal essay on educational, career, and personal goals. Finalists may be interviewed.

Financial data　Stipends for named scholarships are $2,000; other stipends range up to $1,500.

Duration　1 year.

Additional information　This program began in 1983. The 19 named scholarships currently available include the American Friends Service Committee Scholarship, the Hiroko Fujita and Paul Fukami Scholarship, the Michihiko and Bernice Hayashida Scholarship, the Nobu (Kumekawa) and Yosh Hibino Scholarship, the Shim and Chiyo Hiraoka Scholarship, the Tama (Yoshimura) and Jiro Ishihara Scholarship, the Yutaka and Maureen Kobayashi Scholarship, the Ryozo Glenn Kumekawa Scholarship, the Colonel Joseph Y. Kurata Scholarship, the Audrey Logan Scholarship, the Alice Abe Matsumoto Scholarship, the Hisaye Hamaoka Mochizuki Scholarship, the Koh, Mitsu, and Dr. Kotaro Murai Scholarship, the Dr. Kenji Murase Scholarship, the Kaizo and Shizue Naka Scholarship, the Lafayette and Mayme Noda Scholarship, the Gladys Ishida Stone Scholarship, the Michi Nishiura Weglyn Scholarship, and the Kay Yamashita Scholarship.

Number awarded　Varies each year; recently, 15 of the named scholarships (at $2,000 each) and 26 other scholarships (4 at $1,500, 10 at $1,500, 1 at $750, and 10 at $500) were awarded. Since the program was established, it has awarded nearly $758,000 to 775 students.

Deadline　March of each year.

[362]
OCA GEORGIA SCHOLARSHIPS

OCA Asian Pacific American Advocates-Georgia Chapter
Attn: Vice President of Education
P.O. Box 767278
Roswell, GA 30076
E-mail: victor.eng@oca-georgia.org
Web: www.oca-georgia.org/scholarship

Summary To provide financial assistance to Asian Pacific American high school seniors in Georgia who are interested in attending college in any state.

Eligibility This program is open to seniors graduating from high schools in Georgia who are of Asian Pacific American descent. Applicants must be planning to attend a college or university in any state. Selection is based on academic achievement, community and cultural service, and athletics. Special emphasis is placed on student show extraordinary ability and accomplishments and whose potential to attend college may be at risk because of financial constraints.

Financial data The stipend is $1,000.

Duration 1 year.

Additional information OCA Asian Pacific American Advocates was previously named the Organization of Chinese Americans. It changed its name in 2014 to reflect its concern for all Asian Americans.

Number awarded 2 each year.

Deadline December of each year.

[363]
OCA-AXA ACHIEVEMENT SCHOLARSHIPS

OCA Asian Pacific American Advocates
1322 18th Street, N.W.
Washington, DC 20036-1803
(202) 223-5500   Fax: (202) 296-0540
E-mail: oca@ocanational.org
Web: www.ocanational.org/?page=Programs_Scholarship

Summary To provide financial assistance for college to Asian Pacific Americans who are entering their first year of college and can demonstrate academic merit.

Eligibility This program is open to graduating high school seniors of Asian and/or Pacific Islander ethnicity who are entering their first year at a college, university, or community college in the following fall. Applicants must be able to demonstrate academic achievement, leadership ability, and community service. They must have a cumulative GPA of 3.0 or higher and be a U.S. citizen, national, or permanent resident. Financial need is considered in the selection process.

Financial data The stipend is $2,000.

Duration 1 year.

Additional information This program, was established in 2004 with funding provided by the AXA Foundation and administration by the Organization of Chinese Americans (OCA). That organization changed its name to OCA Asian Pacific American Advocates in 2014 to reflect its concern for all Asian Americans.

Number awarded 10 each year.

Deadline April of each year.

[364]
OCA-UPS GOLD MOUNTAIN SCHOLARSHIP

OCA Asian Pacific American Advocates
1322 18th Street, N.W.
Washington, DC 20036-1803
(202) 223-5500   Fax: (202) 296-0540
E-mail: oca@ocanational.org
Web: www.ocanational.org/?page=Programs_Scholarship

Summary To provide financial assistance for college to Asian Pacific Americans who are the first person in their family to attend an institution of higher education.

Eligibility This program is open to graduating high school seniors of Asian and/or Pacific Islander ethnicity who are entering their first year at a college, university, or community college in the following fall. Applicants must be the first person in their immediate family to attend college, have a cumulative GPA of 3.0 or higher, be able to demonstrate financial need, and be a U.S. citizen, national, or permanent resident.

Financial data The stipend is $2,000.

Duration 1 year.

Additional information This program, established in 1999, is funded by the UPS Foundation and administered by the Organization of Chinese Americans (OCA). That organization changed its name to OCA Asian Pacific American Advocates in 2014 to reflect its concern for all Asian Americans.

Number awarded 15 each year.

Deadline April of each year.

[365]
OCA-WI GENERAL SCHOLARSHIPS

OCA Asian Pacific American Advocates-Wisconsin
   Chapter
c/o Albert Chen, Scholarship Committee Chair
120 North 73rd Street
Milwaukee, WI 53213
(414) 258-2410   E-mail: albertchen@aol.com
Web: www.ocawi.org/www/scholarships.html

Summary To provide financial assistance to high school seniors who are children of members or business affiliates of the Wisconsin Chapter of OCA Asian Pacific American Advocates (OCA-WI) and interested in attending college in any state.

Eligibility This program is open to graduating high school seniors whose parent has been an OCA-WI member or business affiliate for at least 2 years and who are planning to enroll full time at an accredited college or university in any state. Applicants must have a GPA of 3.0 or higher or rank in the top 20% of their class. Along with their application, they must submit a personal statement that includes information on their future college and career plans; a list of scholastic awards, honors, extracurricular activities, and honor societies and offices; SAT/ACT scores; and a description of their community service to OCA-WI and their community. Financial need is not considered in the selection process.

Financial data A stipend is awarded (amount not specified).

Duration 1 year.

Additional information This program began in 1988. It includes the following named scholarships (awarded on a rotating basis): the Professor Kwang Yu Memorial Scholarship, the Dr. Benjamin P.C. Ho and Mrs. Lien-Haw (T'ao) Ho Memorial Scholarship, the Benjamin Tsong-Wei Wu Memorial Scholarship, the Professor Shien-Ming (Samuel) Wu Memorial Scholarship, the Yulin and King Ying Hsi Memorial Scholarship, the Maryanne Yu Tsao Memorial Scholarship, the Lulin Walter Memorial Scholarship, and the Dr. Shao-Lin Chen Scholarship.

Number awarded Varies each year; recently, 4 were awarded.

Deadline March of each year.

[366]
OHIO HIGH SCHOOL ATHLETIC ASSOCIATION MINORITY SCHOLAR ATHLETE SCHOLARSHIPS

Ohio High School Athletic Association
Attn: Foundation
4080 Roselea Place
Columbus, OH 43214
(614) 267-2502   Fax: (614) 267-1677
Web: www.ohsaa.org/School-Resources

Summary   To provide financial assistance to Asian American and other minority high school seniors in Ohio who have participated in athletics and plan to attend college in any state.

Eligibility   This program is open to minority seniors graduating from high schools in Ohio that are members of the Ohio High School Athletic Association (OHSAA). Applicants must have received at least 3 varsity letters in 1 sport or 4 letters in 2 sports and have a GPA of 3.25 or higher. They must be planning to attend a college or university in any state. Along with their application, they must submit a 1-page essay on the role that interscholastic athletics has played in their life and how such participation will benefit them in the future. Selection is based on that essay, GPA, ACT and SAT scores, varsity letters earned, and athletic honors.

Financial data   The stipend is $1,000.

Duration   1 year.

Number awarded   6 each year: 1 in each OHSSA District.

Deadline   April of each year.

[367]
OHIO NEWSPAPERS FOUNDATION MINORITY SCHOLARSHIPS

Ohio Newspaper Association
Attn: Foundation
1335 Dublin Road, Suite 216-B
Columbus, OH 43215-7038
(614) 486-6677, ext. 1010   Fax: (614) 486-6373
E-mail: ariggs@ohionews.org
Web: www.ohionews.org/aws/ONA/pt/sp/scholarships

Summary   To provide financial assistance to Asian American and other minority high school seniors in Ohio planning to attend college in any state to prepare for a career in the newspaper industry.

Eligibility   This program is open to high school seniors in Ohio who are members of minority groups (Asian American, African American, Hispanic, or American Indian) and planning to prepare for a career in the newspaper industry, especially advertising, communications, journalism, or marketing. Applicants must have a high school GPA of 2.5 or higher and demonstrate writing ability in an autobiography of 750 to 1,000 words that describes their academic and career interests, awards, extracurricular activities, and journalism-related activities. They must be planning to attend a college or university in Ohio.

Financial data   The stipend is $1,500.

Duration   1 year; nonrenewable.

Additional information   This program began in 1990.

Number awarded   1 each year.

Deadline   March of each year.

[368]
OHIO NURSES FOUNDATION MINORITY STUDENT SCHOLARSHIP

Ohio Nurses Association
Attn: Ohio Nurses Foundation
4000 East Main Street
Columbus, OH 43213-2983
(614) 237-5414   Fax: (614) 237-6081
E-mail: info@ohionursesfoundation.org
Web: www.ohionursesfoundation.org

Summary   To provide financial assistance to Asian American and other minority residents of Ohio who are interested in working on a degree in nursing at a school in any state.

Eligibility   This program is open to residents of Ohio who are members of a minority group and interested in attending college in any state to prepare for a career as a nurse. Applicants must be attending or have attended a high school in the state. If still in high school, they must have a cumulative GPA of 3.5 or higher at the end of their junior year. If out of high school, they may not have had a break of more than 2 years between high school and enrollment in a nursing program. Selection is based on a personal statement, high school or college academic records, school activities, and community services.

Financial data   The stipend is $1,000.

Duration   1 year; recipients may reapply for 1 additional year if they remain enrolled full time and maintain a cumulative GPA of 2.5 or higher.

Number awarded   1 or more each year.

Deadline   January of each year.

[369]
OHIO SOCIETY OF CPAS COLLEGE SCHOLARSHIP PROGRAM

Ohio Society of CPAs
Attn: Ohio CPA Foundation
535 Metro Place South
P.O. Box 1810
Dublin, OH 43017-7810
(614) 764-2727, ext. 344
Toll Free: (800) 686-2727, ext. 344
Fax: (614) 764-5880   E-mail: oscpa@ohio-cpa.com
Web: www.ohiocpa.com

Summary   To provide financial assistance to undergraduate and graduate student members of the Ohio Society of CPAs, especially Asian Americans and members of other underrepresented groups, who are working on a degree in accounting at colleges and universities in the state.

Eligibility   This program is open to U.S. citizens who are Ohio residents working on undergraduate or graduate degrees in accounting at colleges and universities in the state in order to complete the 150 hours required for the C.P.A. examination. Applicants must have completed at least 30 hours of college credit and have a GPA of 3.0 or higher. Awards are available to 3 categories of students: 1) 2-year awards, for students at community colleges or other 2-year institutions; 2) 4-year awards, for students at 4-year colleges and universities; and 3) diversity awards, for students from underrepresented ethnic, racial, or cultural groups.

Financial data   The stipend is $2,000.

Duration   1 year; nonrenewable.

Number awarded Varies each year; recently, 20 were awarded.

Deadline November of each year.

[370]
OKLAHOMA CAREERTECH FOUNDATION TEACHER RECRUITMENT/RETENTION SCHOLARSHIP FOR STUDENTS

Oklahoma CareerTech Foundation
Attn: Administrator
1500 West Seventh Avenue
Stillwater, OK 74074-4364
(405) 743-5453 Fax: (405) 743-5541
E-mail: leden@careertech.ok.gov
Web: www.okcareertech.org

Summary To provide financial assistance to residents of Oklahoma who are Asian Americans or other students reflecting the diversity of the state and attending a college or university in the state to prepare for a career in the Oklahoma CareerTech system.

Eligibility This program is open to residents of Oklahoma who are juniors or seniors at an institution of higher education in the state. Applicants must be working on a bachelor's degree and teacher certification in Oklahoma's CareerTech system. They must reflect the ethnic diversity of the state. Along with their application, they must submit brief statements on their interest and commitment to the CareerTech teaching profession and their financial need.

Financial data The stipend ranges from $500 per semester to $1,500 per year.

Duration 1 semester; may be renewed, provided the recipient maintains a GPA of 2.5 or higher.

Number awarded 1 or more each year.

Deadline May of each year.

[371]
OLFIELD DUKES MULTICULTURAL STUDENT AWARD

Public Relations Student Society of America
Attn: Vice President of Member Services
33 Maiden Lane, 11th Floor
New York, NY 10038-5150
(212) 460-1474 Fax: (212) 995-0757
E-mail: DukesScholarship@prsa.org
Web: www.prssa.prsa.org

Summary To provide financial assistance to Asian American and other multicultural college seniors who are interested in preparing for a career in public relations.

Eligibility This program is open to multicultural (Asian, African American/Black, Hispanic/Latino, Native American, Alaskan Native, or Pacific Islander) students who are entering their junior year at an accredited 4-year college or university. Applicants must have a GPA of 3.0 or higher and be working on a degree in public relations, journalism, or other field to prepare for a career in public relations. Selection is based on academic achievement, specific examples of commitment to service and social responsibility, awards and honors received for academic or extracurricular achievements, writing skills, and letters of recommendation.

Financial data The stipend is $1,000.

Duration 1 year.

Additional information This program began in 2013 with support from Prudential Financial and Weber Shandwick.

Number awarded 1 each year.

Deadline June of each year.

[372]
OPERATION JUMP START III SCHOLARSHIPS

American Association of Advertising Agencies
Attn: AAAA Foundation
1065 Avenue of the Americas, 16th Floor
New York, NY 10018
(212) 262-2500 E-mail: ameadows@aaaa.org
Web: www.aaaa.org

Summary To provide financial assistance to Asian American and other multicultural art directors and copywriters interested in working on an undergraduate or graduate degree in advertising.

Eligibility This program is open to Asian Americans, African Americans, Hispanic Americans, and Native Americans who are U.S. citizens or permanent residents. Applicants must be incoming graduate students at 1 of 6 designated portfolio schools or full-time juniors at 1 of 2 designated colleges. They must be able to demonstrate extreme financial need, creative talent, and promise. Along with their application, they must submit 10 samples of creative work in their respective field of expertise.

Financial data The stipend is $5,000 per year.

Duration Most awards are for 2 years.

Additional information Operation Jump Start began in 1997 and was followed by Operation Jump Start II in 2002. The current program began in 2006. The 6 designated portfolio schools are the AdCenter at Virginia Commonwealth University, the Creative Circus in Atlanta, the Portfolio Center in Atlanta, the Miami Ad School, the University of Texas at Austin, and Pratt Institute. The 2 designated colleges are the Minneapolis College of Art and Design and the Art Center College of Design at Pasadena, California.

Number awarded 20 each year.

Deadline Deadline not specified.

[373]
OREGON CHINESE CONSOLIDATED BENEVOLENT ASSOCIATION SCHOLARSHIPS

Oregon Chinese Consolidated Benevolent Association
315 N.W. Davis Street
Portland, OR 97209
(503) 223-9070
Web: www.ccbaportland.org/scholarships

Summary To provide financial assistance to Chinese high school seniors in Oregon who plan to attend college in any state.

Eligibility This program is open to seniors graduating from high schools in Oregon who are at least half Chinese ethnicity. Applicants must be planning to attend an accredited college or university in any state. They must be U.S. citizens or permanent residents and have a GPA of 2.75 or higher. Along with their application, they must submit transcripts that include SAT and/or ACT scores; a list of Chinese community organization and Chinese church or temple service activities; a list of Chinese cultural and Chinese educational activities; a list of other school, community, church, temple, and service activities; information on participation in high school athletic and team sports; information on participation in personal athletics, club sports, or non-high school sports; and a 300-word essay on their long-term educational, career, and personal goals and how and why they would participate in the Chinese community. They may also submit documentation of financial need if they wish that to be considered. Selection is based on any or a combination of the following: academic performance, community service and leadership activities, athletic achievement, and/or financial need and work ethics.

Financial data Stipends range from $500 to $1,500.

Duration 1 year.

Additional information Selection of recipients is made by the Oregon Chinese Consolidated Benevolent Association.

Number awarded Varies each year; the program includes 18 named scholarships.

Deadline May of each year.

[374]
OREGON-IDAHO CONFERENCE UMC ETHNIC MINORITY LEADERSHIP AWARDS

United Methodist Church-Oregon-Idaho Conference
Attn: Scholarship Coordinator
1505 S.W. 18th Avenue
Portland, OR 97201-2524
(503) 226-7031   Toll Free: (800) J-WESLEY
E-mail: linda@umoi.org
Web: www.umoi.org/scholarships

Summary To provide financial assistance to Asian American and other ethnic minority Methodists from Oregon and Idaho who are interested in attending a college or graduate school in any state.

Eligibility This program is open to members of ethnic minority groups (Asian, African American, Native American, Pacific Islander, or Hispanic) who have belonged to a congregation affiliated with the Oregon-Idaho Conference of the United Methodist Church (UMC) for at least 1 year. Applicants must be enrolled or planning to enroll full time as an undergraduate or graduate student at a 2- or 4-year college or university in any state. Along with their application, they must submit personal statements on 1) their faith development; and 2) where they sense God is calling the church in the present and future. Selection is based primarily on demonstrated leadership excellence and/or the potential for leadership excellence in the UMC and in community projects or activities, but other factors, including financial need, are also considered.

Financial data The stipend is $750.

Duration 1 year.

Number awarded 1 each year.

Deadline April of each year.

[375]
PA STUDENT SCHOLARSHIPS

American Academy of Physician Assistants
Attn: Physician Assistant Foundation
2318 Mill Road, Suite 1300
Alexandria, VA 22314-6868
(703) 836-2272   Fax: (703) 684-1924
E-mail: pafoundation@aapa.org
Web: www.pa-foundation.org

Summary To provide financial assistance to student members of the American Academy of Physician Assistants (AAPA) who are Asian Americans or other underrepresented minorities or economically and/or educationally disadvantaged.

Eligibility This program is open to AAPA student members attending a physician assistant program accredited by the Commission on Accreditation of Allied Health Education Programs. Applicants must qualify as 1) an underrepresented minority (Asian other than Chinese, Filipino, Japanese, Korean, Asian Indian, or Thai, American Indian, Alaska Native, Black or African American, Hispanic or Latino, Native Hawaiian or other Pacific Islander); 2) economically disadvantaged (with income below a specified level); or 3) educationally disadvantaged (from a high school with low SAT scores, from a school district in which less than half of graduates go on to college, has a diagnosed physical or mental impairment, English is not their primary language, the first member of their family to attend college). They must have completed at least 1 semester of PA studies.

Financial data Stipends are $2,500, $2,000, or $1,000.

Duration 1 year; nonrenewable.

Additional information This program includes the AAPA Past Presidents Scholarship, the Bristol-Myers Squibb Endowed Scholarship, the National Commission on Certification of Physician Assistants Endowed Scholarships, the Procter & Gamble Endowed Scholarship, and the PA Foundation Scholarships.

Number awarded Varies each year; recently, 32 were awarded: 3 at $2,500, 27 at $2,000, and 2 at $1,000.

Deadline January of each year.

[376]
PACCO REGULAR COLLEGE SCHOLARSHIP PROGRAM

Philippine American Chamber of Commerce of Oregon
5424 North Michigan Avenue
Portland, OR 97217
(503) 285-1994   E-mail: mason.jan.pbx@gmail.com
Web: www.pacco.org/apply.html

Summary To provide financial assistance to Filipino residents of Oregon and southwestern Washington who are interested in attending college in the area, especially to study areas of science, technology, engineering, arts/architecture, or mathematics (STEAM).

Eligibility This program is open to residents of Oregon and southwestern Washington who are of Filipino descent and either high schools seniors or current college students. Applicants must be enrolled or planning to enroll full time at 2- or 4-year colleges, universities, or vocational/technical schools in the area. Along with their application, they must submit a 500-word essay on the importance of a college education. Preference is given to students majoring in a field of STEAM.

Financial data The stipend is $500.

Duration 1 year.

Number awarded Up to 4 each year.

Deadline March of each year.

[377]
PAGE EDUCATION FOUNDATION GRANTS

Page Education Foundation
901 North Third Street, Suite 355
P.O. Box 581254
Minneapolis, MN 55458-1254
(612) 332-0406   Fax: (612) 332-0403
E-mail: info@page-ed.org
Web: www.page-ed.org

Summary To provide funding to Asian American or other high school seniors of color in Minnesota who plan to attend college in the state.

Eligibility This program is open to students of color who are graduating from high schools in Minnesota and planning to enroll full time at a postsecondary school in the state. Applicants must submit a 500-word essay that deals with why they believe education is important, their plans for the future, and the service-to-children project they would like to complete in the coming school year. Selection is based on the essay, 3 letters of recommendation, and financial need.

Financial data Stipends range from $1,000 to $2,500 per year.

Duration 1 year; may be renewed up to 3 additional years.

Additional information This program was founded in 1988 by Alan Page, a former football player for the Minnesota Vikings. While attending college, the Page Scholars fulfill a 50-hour service-to-children contract that brings them into contact with K-8 students of color.

Number awarded Varies each year; recently, 503 Page Scholars (210 new recipients and 293 renewals) were enrolled, of whom 260 were African American, 141 Asian American, 70 Chicano/Latino, 13 American Indian, and 19 biracial or multiracial.

Deadline April of each year.

[378]
PANYHA FOUNDATION STUDENT SCHOLARSHIP PROGRAM

Panyha Foundation
Attn: Student Scholarships
4994 Park Boulevard North
Pinellas Park, FL 33781
(727) 289-7293   Fax: (727) 289-7293
E-mail: info@panyhafoundation.org
Web: www.panyhafoundation.org/education.html

Summary To provide financial assistance to Asian Americans who are interested in attending college in any state.

Eligibility This program is open to incoming freshmen of Asian descent at accredited 4-year colleges and universities in any state, current full-time undergraduates at such institutions, and full-time students at community colleges planning to transfer to a 4-year college or university in the state. Applicants must be U.S. citizens or permanent residents and have a GPA of 3.0 or higher. Along with their application, they must submit a resume, transcripts, a copy of their SAT and/or ACT scores (high school seniors only), a 1,000-word personal statement on their future educational and career goals, and a 250-word essay on what they value most about being Asian American and what "Panyha" means to them.

Financial data Stipends range up to $2,500 per year.

Duration Up to 4 years, provided the recipient remains enrolled full time, maintains a GPA of 3.0 or higher, and provides documentation of community service.

Additional information When this program began, it provided support to Lao-Americans attending college in Florida. Its scholarships are now available to all students of Asian descent in all states.

Number awarded Varies each year.

Deadline May of each year.

[379]
PAUL STEPHEN LIM ASIAN-AMERICAN PLAYWRITING AWARDS

John F. Kennedy Center for the Performing Arts
Education Department
Attn: Kennedy Center American College Theater Festival
2700 F Street, N.W.
Washington, DC 20566
(202) 416-8864   Fax: (202) 416-8860
E-mail: ghenry@kennedy-center.org
Web: web.kennedy-center.org

Summary To recognize and reward outstanding Asian America student playwrights.

Eligibility Students at any accredited junior or senior college in the United States are eligible to compete, provided their college agrees to participate in the Kennedy Center American College Theater Festival (KCACTF). Undergraduate students must be carrying at least 6 semester hours, graduate students must be enrolled in at least 3 semester hours, and continuing part-time students must be enrolled in a regular degree or certificate program. This award is presented to the author of the best play on any subject who is of Asian heritage.

Financial data The winning playwright receives a cash award of $1,000 for a full-length play or $500 for a 1-act play. Other benefits include appropriate membership in the Dramatists Guild and an all-expense paid professional development opportunity.

Duration The awards are presented annually.

Additional information This program, which began in 2011, is part of the Michael Kanin Playwriting Awards Program. The sponsoring college or university must pay a registration fee of $275 for each production.

Number awarded 2 each year.

Deadline November of each year.

[380]
PCMA EDUCATION FOUNDATION DIVERSITY SCHOLARSHIP

Professional Convention Management Association
Attn: PCMA Education Foundation
35 East Wacker Drive, Suite 500
Chicago, IL 60601
(312) 423-7262   Toll Free: (877) 827-7262
Fax: (312) 423-7222   E-mail: foundation@pcma.org
Web: www.pcma.org

Summary To provide financial assistance to student members of the Professional Convention Management Association (PCMA) who are Asian Americans or members of other underrepresented groups and are majoring in a field related to the meetings or hospitality industry.

Eligibility This program is open to PCMA members who are currently enrolled in at least 6 credit hours with a major directly related to the meetings or hospitality industry. Applicants must be students traditionally underrepresented in the industry, including (but not limited to) those identifying by a certain race, sex, color, religion, creed, sexual orientation, gender identity or expression, or disability, as well as those with a history of overcoming adversity. They must have a GPA of 2.75 or higher. Along with their application, they must submit a 750-word essay that details how they became interested in the meetings and events industry and a short paragraph describing the potential impact receiving this scholarship would have for them. Selection is based on that essay, academic record, meetings industry experience, and a letter of recommendation.

Financial data The stipend is $2,500.

Duration 1 year.

Number awarded 1 each year.

Deadline March of each year.

[381]
PDEF MICKEY WILLIAMS MINORITY SCHOLARSHIPS

Society of Nuclear Medicine and Molecular Imaging
Attn: Grants and Awards
1850 Samuel Morse Drive
Reston, VA 20190-5316
(703) 708-9000, ext. 1255   Fax: (703) 708-9015
E-mail: grantinfo@snm.org
Web: www.snmmi.org

Summary To provide financial support to Asian American and other minority students working on an associate or bachelor's degree in nuclear medicine technology.

Eligibility This program is open to members of the Technologist Section of the Society of Nuclear Medicine and Molecular Imaging (SNMMI-TS) who are accepted or enrolled in a baccalaureate or associate degree program in nuclear medicine technology. Applicants must be members of a minority group: Asian American, African American, Native American (including American Indian, Eskimo, Hawaiian, and Samoan), Hispanic American, or Pacific Islander. They must have a cumulative GPA of 2.5 or higher and be able to demonstrate financial need. Along with their application, they must submit an essay on their reasons for entering the nuclear medicine technology field, their career goals, and their financial need. U.S. citizenship or permanent resident status is required.

Financial data The stipend is $2,500.

Duration 1 year; may be renewed for 1 additional year.

Additional information This program is supported by corporate sponsors of the Professional Development and Education Fund (PDEF) of the SNMMI-TS.

Number awarded Varies each year; recently, 2 were awarded.

Deadline December of each year.

[382]
PEGGY PETERMAN SCHOLARSHIP

Tampa Bay Times
Attn: Director of Corporate Giving
490 First Avenue South
St. Petersburg, FL 33701
(727) 893-8780   Toll Free: (800) 333-7505, ext. 8780
Fax: (727) 892-2257   E-mail: waclawek@tampabay.com
Web: www.tampabay.com

Summary To provide financial assistance to Asian American and other minority undergraduate and graduate students who are interested in preparing for a career in the newspaper industry and who accept an internship at the *Tampa Bay Times*.

Eligibility This program is open to minority college sophomores, juniors, seniors, and graduate students from any state who are interested in preparing for a career in the newspaper industry. Applicants must be interested in an internship at the *Tampa Bay Times* and must apply for that at the same time as they apply for this scholarship. They should have experience working on a college publication and at least 1 professional internship.

Financial data The stipend is $5,000.

Duration Internships are for 12 weeks during the summer. Scholarships are for 1 year.

Number awarded 1 each year.

Deadline October of each year.

[383]
PENNSYLVANIA ACADEMY OF NUTRITION AND DIETETICS FOUNDATION DIVERSITY SCHOLARSHIP

Pennsylvania Academy of Nutrition and Dietetics
Attn: Foundation
96 Northwoods Boulevard, Suite B2
Columbus, OH 43235
(614) 436-6136   Fax: (614) 436-6181
E-mail: padafoundation@eatrightpa.org
Web: www.eatrightpa.org/scholarshipapp.cfm

Summary To provide financial assistance to members of the Pennsylvania Academy of Nutrition and Dietetics who are Asian Americans or members of other minority groups and working on an associate or bachelor's degree in dietetics.

Eligibility This program is open to academy members who are Asian or Pacific Islander, Black, Hispanic, or Native American (Alaskan Native, American Indian, or Hawaiian Native). Applicants must be 1) enrolled in the first year of study in an accredited dietetic technology program; or 2) enrolled in the third year of study in an accredited undergraduate or coordinated program in dietetics. They must have a GPA of 2.5 or higher. Along with their application, they must submit a letter indicating their intent and the reason they are applying for the scholarship, including a description of their personal financial situation. Selection is based on academic achievement (20%), commitment to the dietetic profession (30%), leadership ability (30%), and financial need (20%).

Financial data The stipend is $1,000.

Duration 1 year.

Additional information The Pennsylvania Academy of Nutrition and Dietetics is the Pennsylvania affiliate of the Academy of Nutrition and Dietetics.

Number awarded 1 or more each year.

Deadline April of each year.

[384]
PFATS-NFL CHARITIES MINORITY SCHOLARSHIPS

Professional Football Athletic Trainers Society
c/o Britt Brown, ATC, Associate Athletic Trainer
Dallas Cowboys
One Cowboys Parkway
Irving, TX 75063
(972) 497-4992   E-mail: bbrown@dallascowboys.net
Web: www.pfats.com/about/scholarships

Summary To provide financial assistance to Asian American and other ethnic minority undergraduate and graduate students working on a degree in athletic training.

Eligibility This program is open to ethnic minority students who are working on an undergraduate or graduate degree in athletic training. Applicants must have a GPA of 2.5 or higher. Along with their application, they must submit a cover letter, a curriculum vitae, and a letter of recommendation from their supervising athletic trainer. Female athletic training students are encouraged to apply.

Financial data A stipend is awarded (amount not specified).

Duration 1 year.

Additional information Recipients also have an opportunity to work at summer training camp of a National Football League (NFL) team. Support for this program, which began in 1993, is provided by NFL Charities.

Number awarded 1 or more each year.

Deadline March of each year.

[385]
PGA OF AMERICA DIVERSITY SCHOLARSHIP PROGRAM

Professional Golfers' Association of America
Attn: PGA Foundation
100 Avenue of the Champions
Palm Beach Gardens, FL 33418
Toll Free: (888) 532-6662   E-mail: sjubb@pgahq.com
Web: www.pgafoundation.com

Summary To provide financial assistance to Asian Americans and other minorities interested in attending a designated college or university to prepare for a career as a golf professional.

Eligibility This program is open to women and minorities interested in becoming a licensed PGA Professional. Applicants must be interested in attending 1 of 20 colleges and universities that offer the Professional Golf Management (PGM) curriculum sanctioned by the PGA.

Financial data The stipend is $3,000 per year.

Duration 1 year; may be renewed.

Additional information This program began in 1993. Programs are offered at the following universities: Arizona State University (Tempe), Campbell University (Buies Creek, North Carolina), Clemson University (Clemson, South Carolina), Coastal Carolina University (Conway, South Carolina), Eastern Kentucky University (Richmond), Ferris State University (Big Rapids, Michigan), Florida State University (Tallahassee), Florida Gulf Coast University (Fort Myers), Methodist University (Fayetteville, North Carolina), Mississippi State University (Mississippi State), New Mexico State University (Las Cruces), North Carolina State University (Raleigh), Pennsylvania State University (University Park), Sam Houston State University (Huntsville), University of Central Oklahoma (Edmond), University of Colorado at Colorado Springs, University of Idaho (Moscow), University of Maryland Eastern Shore (Princess Anne), University of Nebraska at Lincoln, and University of Nevada at Las Vegas.

Number awarded Varies each year; recently, 20 were awarded.

Deadline Deadline not specified.

[386]
PHI TAU PHI EAST AMERICA CHAPTER UNDERGRADUATE SCHOLARSHIP AWARDS

Phi Tau Phi Scholastic Honor Society-East America Chapter
c/o Dr. Heng-Chun Li, Scholarship Selection Committee
39 Kennedy Circle
Closter, NJ 07624
(201) 767-9325   E-mail: hengshun.li@gmail.com
Web: ptp1921.weebly.com/scholarship.html

Summary To provide financial assistance to college juniors and seniors of Chinese heritage at colleges and universities in eastern states.

Eligibility This program is open to juniors and seniors enrolled at an accredited institution of higher education east of a line along Ohio, Kentucky, and Alabama. Applicants must be of Chinese heritage or interested in and committed to Chinese heritage and culture, have a GPA of 3.5 or higher, and be sponsored by a member of Phi Tau Phi. Along with their application, they must submit a 1-page essay on their professional goals, achievements, financial need, and Chinese cultural interests.

Financial data The stipend is $1,000.

Duration 1 year.

Additional information Phi Tau Phi, first organized in 1921 in China and reestablished in 1964 in the United States, is a relatively small honor society of scholars, mainly of Chinese heritage, in various disciplines of science, technology, art, and humanities. Students who have difficulty in locating a sponsor should contact the Scholarship Selection Committee.

Number awarded 1 or 2 each year.

Deadline September of each year.

[387]
PHI TAU PHI MID-AMERICA CHAPTER SCHOLARSHIPS

Phi Tau Phi Scholastic Honor Society-Mid-America Chapter
c/o Arthur Yuan, Scholarship Committee Chair
John Marshall Law School
315 South Plymouth Court
Chicago, IL 60604
E-mail: ayuan@jmls.edu
Web: www.phitauphima.org/awards.html

Summary To provide financial assistance to undergraduate and graduate students of Chinese heritage at colleges and universities in selected midwestern states.

Eligibility This program is open to undergraduate and graduate students enrolled at colleges and universities in Illinois, Indiana, Iowa, Kansas, Michigan, Minnesota, Ohio, Texas, and Wisconsin who have a GPA of 3.5 or higher. Applicants must be of Chinese descent and interested in and committed to Chinese heritage and culture. They must be entering their junior or senior year of undergraduate study or their second year or higher of graduate work. Along with their application, they must submit a 500-word essay on their professional goals and achievements.

Financial data The stipend is $1,000.

Duration 1 year.

Additional information Phi Tau Phi, first organized in 1921 in China and reestablished in 1964 in the United States, is a relatively small honor society of scholars, mainly of Chinese heritage, in various disciplines of science, technology, art, and the humanities.

Number awarded 4 each year.

Deadline July of each year.

[388]
PHI TAU PHI WEST AMERICA CHAPTER SCHOLARSHIP AWARDS

Phi Tau Phi Scholastic Honor Society-West America
  Chapter
c/o Jason Cong, President
University of California at Los Angeles
Computer Science
4711 BH
P.O. Box 951596
Los Angeles, CA 90095-1596
(310) 206-2775   E-mail: cong@cs.ucla.edu
Web: ptp.cms.caltech.edu/scholarship.html

Summary To provide financial assistance to upper-division and graduate students of Chinese heritage from any state at colleges and universities in southern California.

Eligibility This program is open to juniors, seniors, and graduate students from any state enrolled at accredited institutions of higher education in southern California. Applicants must be of Chinese heritage or have a demonstrated interest in Chinese and culture. They must have a GPA of 3.4 or higher. Along with their application, they must submit a 1-page essay on their professional goals, achievements, and interest in Chinese culture. Financial need is not considered in the selection process.

Financial data The stipend is $1,000.

Duration 1 year.

Additional information Phi Tau Phi, first organized in 1921 in China and reestablished in 1964 in the United States, is a relatively small honor society of scholars, mainly of Chinese heritage, in various disciplines of science, technology, art, and the humanities.

Number awarded Varies each year; recently, 4 were awarded: 2 to undergraduates and 2 to graduate students.

Deadline August of each year.

[389]
PHILIPPINE NURSES ASSOCIATION HAWAII FOUNDATION SCHOLARSHIP FUND

Hawai'i Community Foundation
Attn: Scholarship Department
827 Fort Street Mall
Honolulu, HI 96813
(808) 566-5570   Toll Free: (888) 731-3863
Fax: (808) 521-6286
E-mail: scholarships@hcf-hawaii.org
Web: hcf.scholarships.ngwebsolutions.com

Summary To provide financial assistance to residents of Hawaii who are of Filipino ancestry and interested in working on an undergraduate or graduate degree in nursing at a college in any state.

Eligibility This program is open to residents of Hawaii who are of Filipino ancestry and enrolled or planning to enroll full time at a 2- or 4-year college or university in any state. Applicants must be interested in working on an undergraduate or graduate degree in nursing. They must be able to demonstrate academic achievement (GPA of 3.5 or higher), good moral character, and financial need. Along with their application, they must submit a short statement indicating their reasons for attending college, their planned course of study, their career goals, and what community service means to them.

Financial data The amounts of the awards depend on the availability of funds and the need of the recipient. Recently, the average value of the scholarships awarded by the foundation was $2,800.

Duration 1 year.

Additional information The Philippine Nurses Association Hawaii Foundation established this program in 2005.

Number awarded Varies each year.

Deadline February of each year.

[390]
PHILIPPINE NURSES ASSOCIATION OF NORTHERN CALIFORNIA UNDERGRADUATE NURSING STUDENT SCHOLARSHIP

Philippine Nurses Association of Northern California, Inc.
c/o Tess Estrin, Scholarship Committee Chair
11 Duval Drive
South San Francisco, CA 94080
E-mail: tessestrin@gmail.com
Web: www.pnanorthcal.org

Summary To provide financial assistance to Filipino Americans from any state enrolled in an undergraduate nursing program at a school in northern California.

Eligibility This program is open to Filipino American residents of any state who are currently enrolled in at least the third year of an accredited undergraduate nursing program in northern California. Applicants must have a GPA of 3.0 or higher and a record of participation in extracurricular or community activities. They must have demonstrated leadership ability or potential both within and outside the clinical setting. Along with their application, they must submit brief statements on their strengths and opportunities for improvement, their career goals, why they need a scholarship, how they can contribute to the goals of the Philippine Nurses Association of Northern California (PNANC), and an accomplishment or activity as a nursing student that has impacted their life or the life of another person.

Financial data The stipend is $1,000.

Duration 1 year.

Additional information The recipient must commit to participate in at least 4 PNANC activities during the following 2 years.

Number awarded 1 each year.

Deadline October of each year.

[391]
PHYLLIS G. MEEKINS SCHOLARSHIP

Ladies Professional Golf Association
Attn: LPGA Foundation
100 International Golf Drive
Daytona Beach, FL 32124-1082
(386) 274-6200   Fax: (386) 274-1099
E-mail: foundation.scholarships@lpga.com
Web: www.lpga.com

Summary To provide financial assistance to Asian American and other minority female graduating high school seniors who played golf in high school and plan to continue to play in college.

Eligibility This program is open to female high school seniors who are members of a recognized minority group. Applicants must have a GPA of 3.0 or higher and a background in golf. They must be planning to enroll full time at a college or university in the United States and play competitive golf. Along with their application, they must submit a letter that describes how golf has been an integral part of their lives and includes their personal, academic, and professional goals; their chosen discipline of study; and how this scholarship will be of assistance. Financial need is considered in the selection process. U.S. citizenship or legal resident status is required.

Financial data The stipend is $1,250.

Duration 1 year.

Additional information This program began in 2006.

Number awarded 1 each year.

Deadline May of each year.

[392]
PNAGA ANNUAL SCHOLARSHIP FOR UNDERGRADUATE NURSING STUDIES

Philippine Nurses Association of Georgia
c/o Merlyn Walker, Treasurer
3216 Christian Springs Drive
Lithonia, GA 30038
(404) 910-3764   E-mail: thepnaga@gmail.com
Web: sites.google.com/site/thepnaga/scholarships

Summary To provide financial assistance to members of the Philippine Nurses Association of Georgia (PNAGA) and their families who are working on an undergraduate degree in nursing at a school in any state.

Eligibility This program is open to residents of Georgia who are of Filipino descent and enrolled at an accredited nursing school in any state. Applicants must be affiliate members of PNAGA or the spouse of child of an active PNAGA member. Along with their application, they must submit a resume or curriculum vitae, a letter of recommendation, and a 150-word essay on their professional career goals.

Financial data The stipend is $500.

Duration 1 year.

Number awarded 1 or more each year.

Deadline April of each year.

[393]
PRAXAIR LIMITED SCHOLARSHIPS

American Welding Society
Attn: AWS Foundation, Inc.
8669 N.W. 36th Street, Suite 130
Doral, FL 33166-6672
(305) 443-9353   Toll Free: (800) 443-9353, ext. 212
Fax: (305) 443-7559   E-mail: vpinsky@aws.org
Web: app.aws.org/foundation/scholarships/praxair.html

Summary To provide financial assistance to students, especially Asian Americans and members of other underrepresented groups, who are interested in working on a degree or certificate in welding at college within designated sections of the American Welding Society.

Eligibility This program is open to high school seniors who are planning to enroll full or part time (full time is preferred) in a degree or certificate welding program at a 2- or 4-year college or university. Applicants must be entering an academic institution located within 1 of 13 AWS sections and be residents of the state in which the section is located. They must be U.S. citizens and have a GPA of 2.5 or higher. Along with their application, they must submit a personal statement that covers their demonstrated timeliness and completion of assignments; creativity in solving problems; demonstrated responsibility on own initiative; ability to work well with others; organizational skills; participation in class, and outside organizations; participation in student and section activities; general background; and career objectives. Preference is given to applicants from groups underrepresented in the welding industry. Financial need is not required.

Financial data The stipend is $2,000 per year; funds are paid directly to the educational institution.

Duration 1 year; may be renewed for 1 additional year.

Additional information This program is supported by Praxair, Inc. The participating sections are Chicago, Cleveland, Dallas (for North Texas), Detroit, Fox Valley (for Wisconsin and the Upper Peninsula of Michigan), Houston, Kansas City (for 18 counties of eastern Kansas or 41 counties of western Missouri), Los Angeles, North Dakota, Portland, Utah, Tulsa, and North Carolina (divided between Charlotte and Research Triangle Park).

Number awarded 26 each year: 2 in each of the participating sections.

Deadline March of each year.

[394]
PRIMARY CARE RESOURCE INITIATIVE FOR MISSOURI

Missouri Department of Health and Senior Services
Attn: Primary Care and Rural Health
P.O. Box 570
Jefferson City, MO 65102-0570
(573) 751-6219   Toll Free: (800) 891-7415
Fax: (573) 522-8146   E-mail: info@health.mo.gov
Web: health.mo.gov/living/families/primarycare/primo

Summary To provide scholarship/loans to residents of Missouri, especially Asian Americans and other minorities, who are interested in working as a health care professional in an underserved area of the state following graduation.

Eligibility This program is open to residents of Missouri who have lived for 1 or more years in the state for purposes other than attending an educational institution. Applicants must have been accepted by or currently be attending a Missouri school offering a course of study leading to a degree in 1) primary care medicine; 2) dentistry; 3) dental hygiene; 4) psychiatry; 5) psychology; 6) licensed clinical social work; or 7) licensed professional counseling. Physicians and dentists in primary care residency programs are also eligible. Priority is given to residents of medically underserved areas in Missouri, minority group members, and previous recipients.

Financial data Loans range from $5,000 to $20,000 per year. This is a scholarship/loan program. Loans of 5 years or more are forgiven at the rate of 20% per year for qualifying employment in an area of defined need (a geographic area or a population that is experiencing a shortage of primary health care providers in Missouri). Loans for less than 5 years are forgiven on a year-for-year basis. If the loan is not forgiven by service, it must be repaid within 60 months at 9.5% interest.

Duration Full-time undergraduate students may receive up to 4 loans. Part-time medical students may receive loans for up to 4 or 6 years, depending on the length of their program. Physicians and dentists in primary care residency programs may receive up to 3 years of loans.

Additional information This program is also known as the PRIMO Loan Program.

Number awarded Varies each year; recently, a total of 32 of these loans were granted.

Deadline April of each year.

[395]
PRINT AND ONLINE NEWS INTERNSHIP GRANT

Asian American Journalists Association
Attn: Student Programs Coordinator
5 Third Street, Suite 1108
San Francisco, CA 94103
(415) 346-2051, ext. 102   Fax: (415) 346-6343
E-mail: programs@aaja.org
Web: www.aaja.org/apply-for-a-scholarship-now

Summary To provide a supplemental grant to members of the Asian American Journalists Association (AAJA) working as a summer intern at a print or online journalism company.

Eligibility This program is open to AAJA members who are full-time college students or recent college graduates. Applicants must have secured a summer internship at a print or online news outlet before they apply. Along with their application, they must submit a 200-word essay on why they want to prepare for a career in print or online journalism, what they want to gain from the experience, and why AAJA's mission is important to them; a letter of recommendation; a resume; proof of age (at least 18 years); verification of an internship; and statement of financial need.

Financial data The grant is $1,000. Funds are to be used for living expenses or transportation.

Duration Summer months.

Additional information This program began in 2006 as the William Woo Internship Fund.

Number awarded 1 each year.
Deadline April of each year.

[396]
PROFESSIONAL STAFFING GROUP SCHOLARSHIP

Northeast Human Resources Association
Attn: Director of Professional Development
490 Virginia Road, Suite 32
Concord, MA 01742-2747
(781) 239-8718   Fax: (781) 237-8745
E-mail: nreiser@nehra.com
Web: www.nehra.com/?page=DIScholarshipApp

Summary To provide financial assistance for college to high school seniors from the New England states who are Asian Americans or have promoted diversity in other ways.

Eligibility This program is open to seniors who are graduating from high schools in New England and planning to attend a college or university. Applicants should have exemplified living an inclusive life and promoting diversity through education. They must have a GPA of 3.0 or higher and be able to demonstrate financial need. Along with their application, they must submit a 750-word personal statement explaining what diversity means to them, how they promote diversity in their community or school, and how they propose to promote diversity in the future.

Financial data The stipend is $5,000.

Duration 1 year.

Additional information The sponsor is an affiliate of the Society for Human Resource Management (SHRM). Its Diversity and Inclusion Committee focuses on veterans, the GLBT community, people with disabilities, gender equity, and race/ethnicity. The Professional Staffing Group established this program in 2004.

Number awarded 1 each year.

Deadline February of each year.

[397]
PROFESSOR CHEN WEN-CHEN SCHOLARSHIPS

Professor Chen Wen-Chen Memorial Foundation
Attn: Scholarship Committee
P.O. Box 136
Kingston, NJ 08528
(609) 936-1352   E-mail: cwcmfusa@gmail.com
Web: www.cwcmf.net/html/cwcmf_about.html

Summary To provide financial assistance to students at North American colleges and universities who have been involved in the Taiwanese community.

Eligibility This program is open to students who have participated in Taiwanese social-political movements or have made significant contributions to the Taiwanese community in North America. Applicants must be currently enrolled at a college or university in North America. Along with their application, they must submit a 2-page essay on what they, as a younger generation Taiwanese or Taiwanese American, can do to promote the sovereignty and democracy of Taiwan. Selection is based on character, academic ability, financial need, and participation in Taiwanese American community affairs.

Financial data The stipend ranges from $1,000 to $1,500.
Duration 1 year.

Number awarded 4 to 6 each year.

Deadline May of each year.

[398]
PRSA DIVERSITY MULTICULTURAL SCHOLARSHIPS

Public Relations Student Society of America
Attn: Vice President of Member Services
33 Maiden Lane, 11th Floor
New York, NY 10038-5150
(212) 460-1474 Fax: (212) 995-0757
E-mail: prssa@prsa.org
Web: www.prssa.prsa.org

Summary To provide financial assistance to Asian American or other minority college students who are interested in preparing for a career in public relations.

Eligibility This program is open to minority (Asian, African American/Black, Hispanic/Latino, Native American, Alaskan Native, or Pacific Islander) students who are at least juniors at an accredited 4-year college or university. Applicants must be enrolled full time, be able to demonstrate financial need, and have a GPA of 3.0 or higher. Membership in the Public Relations Student Society of America is preferred but not required. A major or minor in public relations is preferred; students who attend a school that does not offer a public relations degree or program must be enrolled in a communications degree program (e.g., journalism, mass communications).

Financial data The stipend is $1,500.

Duration 1 year.

Additional information This program began in 1989.

Number awarded 2 each year.

Deadline May of each year.

[399]
PSI CHI DIVERSITY ARTICLE AWARDS

Psi Chi
825 Vine Street
P.O. Box 709
Chattanooga, TN 37401-0709
(423) 756-2044 Fax: (877) 774-2443
E-mail: awards@psichi.org
Web: www.psichi.org/?page=diversityinfo

Summary To recognize and reward undergraduate and graduate student members of Psi Chi (an honor society in psychology) who submit outstanding articles on issues of diversity for publication in society journals.

Eligibility This program is open to undergraduate and graduate students who have either 1) had an article published in the *Psi Chi Journal of Psychological Research* ; or 2) submitted an article for publication in *Eye on Psi Chi*. The article must relate to issues of diversity, defined to include ethnic minorities, LGBTQ, gender, economic factors, mental disability, physical disability, or nontraditional students. Selection is based on content-originality and impact, research or practitioner, results or outcomes, scholarship content, and relevance (50%); focus-diversity goals and objectives are strongly developed, order of ideas is explicitly and consistently clear, logical, and effective, and conclusions are well-formulated and supported by the results or outcomes (35%); and language-style and mechanics (15%).

Financial data The awards are $600.

Duration The awards are presented annually.

Number awarded 2 each year: 1 for an article published in the *Psi Chi Journal of Psychological Research* and 1 for an article submitted to *Eye on Psi Chi*.

Deadline October of each year.

[400]
PUGET SOUND CHAPTER SHARON D. BANKS MEMORIAL UNDERGRADUATE SCHOLARSHIP

Women's Transportation Seminar-Puget Sound Chapter
c/o Laurie Thomsen, Scholarship Co-Chair
Osborn Consulting, Inc.
1800 112th Avenue N.E.
Bellevue, WA 98004
(425) 451-4009 Fax: (888) 391-8517
E-mail: laurie@osbornconsulting.com
Web: www.wtsinternational.org

Summary To provide financial assistance to women undergraduate students from Washington, especially Asian Americans and other minorities, who are working on a degree related to transportation.

Eligibility This program is open to women who are residents of Washington, studying at a college in the state, or working as an intern in the state. Applicants must be currently enrolled in an undergraduate degree program in a transportation-related field, such as engineering, planning, finance, or logistics. They must have a GPA of 3.0 or higher and plans to prepare for a career in a transportation-related field. Minority women are especially encouraged to apply. Along with their application, they must submit a 500-word statement about their career goals after graduation and why they think they should receive this scholarship award. Selection is based on that statement, academic record, and transportation-related activities or job skills. Financial need is not considered.

Financial data The stipend is $4,000.

Duration 1 year.

Additional information The winner is also nominated for scholarships offered by the national organization of the Women's Transportation Seminar.

Number awarded 1 each year.

Deadline November of each year.

[401]
PWC ASCEND SCHOLARSHIPS

Ascend: Pan-Asian Leaders
Attn: Director of Programs
247 West 30th Street
New York, NY 10001
(212) 248-4888 Fax: (212) 344-5636
E-mail: scholarships@ascendleadership.org
Web: www.ascendleadership.org

Summary To provide financial assistance to members of Ascend: Pan-Asian Leaders who are college undergraduates with a career interest in accounting or finance.

Eligibility This program is open to members of Ascend who are enrolled as freshmen, sophomores, or juniors (in 5-year programs) at colleges and universities in the United States. Applicants must have a GPA of 3.5 or higher and a major in accounting or finance. Along with their application, they must submit a 500-word personal essay on how they have demonstrated leadership and teamwork in their academic studies, professional career, and/or extracurricular activities and community volunteer work; why they believe those qualities are important to transforming themselves into a better leader; their career goals after graduation; and the role Ascend has played in the achievement of their academic and career goals. They must also answer questions on whether they are authorized to work in the United States without employer sponsorship, if they are willing to be interviewed for an internship with PricewaterhouseCoopers (PwC), if they have worked for other Big 4 accounting firms, and if they completed a PwC talent profile at the firm's web site. Financial need is not considered in the selection process.

Financial data The stipend is $1,000.

Duration 1 year.

Additional information Ascend was formed in 2004 as the National Asian American Society of Accountants. This program, sponsored by PricewaterhouseCoopers (PwC), began in 2008.

Number awarded 2 each year.

Deadline April of each year.

[402]
RACE RELATIONS MULTIRACIAL STUDENT SCHOLARSHIP

Christian Reformed Church
Attn: Office of Race Relations
1700 28th Street, S.E.
Grand Rapids, MI 49508
(616) 224-5883   Toll Free: (877) 864-3977
Fax: (616) 224-0834   E-mail: elugo@crcna.org
Web: www.crcna.org/race/scholarships

Summary To provide financial assistance to Asian American and other minority undergraduate and graduate students interested in attending colleges related to the Christian Reformed Church in North America (CRCNA).

Eligibility This program is open to students of color in the United States and Canada. Normally, applicants are expected to be members of CRCNA congregations who plan to pursue their educational goals at Calvin Theological Seminary or any of the colleges affiliated with the CRCNA. They must be interested in training for the ministry of racial reconciliation in church and/or in society. Along with their application, they must submit paragraphs about their personal history and family, Christian faith, and Christian leadership goals. Students who have no prior history with the CRCNA must attend a CRCNA-related college or seminary for a full academic year before they are eligible to apply for this program. Students entering their sophomore year must have earned a GPA of 2.0 or higher as freshmen; students entering their junior year must have earned a GPA of 2.3 or higher as sophomores; students entering their senior year must have earned a GPA of 2.6 or higher as juniors.

Financial data First-year students receive $500 per semester. Other levels of students may receive up to $2,000 per academic year.

Duration 1 year.

Additional information This program was first established in 1971 and revised in 1991. Recipients are expected to train to engage actively in the ministry of racial reconciliation in church and in society. They must be able to work in the United States or Canada upon graduating and must consider working for 1 of the agencies of the CRCNA.

Number awarded Varies each year; recently, 31 students received a total of $21,000 in support.

Deadline March of each year.

[403]
RAMA SCHOLARSHIP FOR THE AMERICAN DREAM

American Hotel & Lodging Educational Foundation
Attn: Manager of Foundation Programs
1250 I Street, N.W., Suite 1100
Washington, DC 20005-5904
(202) 289-3180   Fax: (202) 289-3199
E-mail: foundation@ahlef.org
Web: www.ahlef.org

Summary To provide financial assistance to Asian American and other minority undergraduate and graduate students working on a degree in hotel management at designated schools.

Eligibility This program is open to U.S. citizens and permanent residents enrolled as full- or part-time undergraduate or graduate students with a GPA of 2.5 or higher. Applicants must be attending 1 of 13 designated hospitality management schools, which select the recipients. Preference is given to students of Asian-Indian descent and other minority groups and to JHM Hotel employees and their dependents.

Financial data The stipend varies at each of the participating schools, but ranges from $1,000 to $3,000.

Duration 1 year.

Additional information This program was established by JHM Hotels, Inc. in 1998. The participating institutions are Bethune-Cookman University, California State Polytechnic University at Pomona, Cornell University, Florida International University, Georgia State University, Greenville Technical College, Howard University, Johnson & Wales University (Charlotte, North Carolina), New York University, University of Central Florida, University of Houston, University of South Carolina, and Virginia Polytechnic Institute and State University.

Number awarded Varies each year; recently, 20 were awarded. Since the program was established, it has awarded more than $726,000 to 446 recipients.

Deadline April of each year.

[404]
RDW GROUP, INC. MINORITY SCHOLARSHIP FOR COMMUNICATIONS

Rhode Island Foundation
Attn: Donor Services Administrator
One Union Station
Providence, RI 02903
(401) 427-4011   Fax: (401) 331-8085
E-mail: rbogert@rifoundation.org
Web: www.rifoundation.org

Summary To provide financial assistance to Rhode Island Asian American and other undergraduate and graduate students of color interested in preparing for a career in communications at a school in any state.

Eligibility This program is open to undergraduate and graduate students at colleges and universities in any state who are Rhode Island residents of color. Applicants must intend to work on a degree in communications (including computer graphics, art, cinematography, or other fields that would prepare them for a career in advertising). They must be able to demonstrate financial need and a commitment to a career in communications. Along with their application, they must submit an essay (up to 300 words) on the impact they would like to have on the communications field.

Financial data The stipend is approximately $2,000 per year.

Duration 1 year; recipients may reapply.

Additional information This program is sponsored by the RDW Group, Inc.

Number awarded 1 each year.

Deadline April of each year.

[405]
RENAE WASHINGTON-LORINE DUBOSE MEMORIAL SCHOLARSHIPS

Oklahoma CareerTech Foundation
Attn: Oklahoma Association of Minorities in Career and
  Technology Education
c/o Patti Pouncil, Scholarship Committee Chair
3 CT Circle
Drumright, OK 74030
918) 352-2551, ext. 285
Web: www.okcareertech.org

Summary To provide financial assistance to Asian American and other minority students enrolled at Oklahoma Career and Technology Education (CTE) centers.

Eligibility This program is open to residents of Oklahoma who are members of an ethnic minority group (Asian, American Indian/Alaskan, African American, Hispanic, Native Hawaiian/Pacific Islander). Applicants must be enrolled full time at a CTE center in the state. Along with their application, they must submit a 100-word essay on why they have applied for this scholarship. Financial need is considered in the selection process.

Financial data The stipend is $1,000.

Duration 1 year.

Number awarded 2 each year.

Deadline May of each year.

[406]
RESOURCES FOR THE FUTURE SUMMER INTERNSHIPS

Resources for the Future
Attn: Internship Coordinator
1616 P Street, N.W., Suite 600
Washington, DC 20036-1400
(202) 328-5020   Fax: (202) 939-3460
E-mail: IC@rff.org
Web: www.rff.org

Summary To provide internships to undergraduate and graduate students, especially Asian Americans and other minorities, who are interested in working on research projects in public policy during the summer.

Eligibility This program is open to undergraduate and graduate students (with priority to graduate students) interested in an internship at Resources for the Future (RFF). Applicants must be working on a degree in the social and nat-

ural sciences and have training in economics and quantitative methods or an interest in public policy. They should display strong writing skills and a desire to analyze complex environmental policy problems amenable to interdisciplinary methods. The ability to work without supervision in a careful and conscientious manner is essential. Women and minority candidates are strongly encouraged to apply. Both U.S. and non-U.S. citizens are eligible, if the latter have proper work and residency documentation.

Financial data The stipend is $375 per week for graduate students or $350 per week for undergraduates. Housing assistance is not provided.

Duration 10 weeks during the summer; beginning and ending dates can be adjusted to meet particular student needs.

Number awarded Varies each year.

Deadline March of each year.

[407]
RHODE ISLAND ASSOCIATION OF CHINESE AMERICANS SCHOLARSHIPS

Rhode Island Association of Chinese Americans
48 Blackstone Avenue
Pawtucket, RI 02860
(401) 722-   E-mail: scholarship@riaca.us
Web: www.riaca.us/RIACA_Scholarship.html

Summary To provide financial assistance to high school seniors who are members of the Rhode Island Association of Chinese Americans (RIACA) and interested in attending college in any state.

Eligibility This program is open to ethnic Chinese seniors graduating from high schools in Rhode Island or southern Massachusetts who are members of RIACA and planning to attend college in any state. Applicants must be U.S. citizens or permanent residents. Along with their application, they must submit transcripts, SAT/ACT scores, an endorsement from a member of RIACA, and an essay (in English or Chinese) on why they deserve this scholarship. Selection is based on that essay; academic excellence; extracurricular activities and leadership skills; community service; participation in RIACA social activities; participation in Chinese language school, Chinese culture club, or similar activities; special talents, awards, or recognitions; and an interview.

Financial data The stipend is $3,000.

Duration 1 year.

Number awarded 5 to 6 each year.

Deadline November of each year.

[408]
RICHARD GILDER GRADUATE SCHOOL REU BIOLOGY PROGRAM

American Museum of Natural History
Attn: Richard Gilder Graduate School
Central Park West at 79th Street
New York, NY 10024-5192
(212) 769-5055   E-mail: Fellowships-rggs@amnh.org
Web: www.amnh.org

Summary To provide an opportunity for undergraduate students, especially Asian Americans and other students at minority-serving institutions, to gain research experience in biology during the summer at the American Museum of Natural History in New York City.

Eligibility This program is open to U.S. citizens, nationals, and permanent residents who are currently working on an associate or bachelor's degree. Applicants must be interested in participating in a research project at the American Museum of Natural History under the mentorship of its curators, faculty, and postdoctoral fellows. Research projects involve diverse fields of comparative biology, including paleontology, genomics, population biology, conservation biology, phylogenetics, and taxonomy. Applications are especially encouraged from students who attend community colleges, undergraduate-only institutions, and minority-serving institutions.

Financial data Participants receive a stipend of $5,000, per diem costs for housing and meals, relocation expenses, and transportation subsidies.

Duration 10 weeks during the summer.

Additional information This program is sponsored by the National Science Foundation as part of its Research Experiences for Undergraduates (REU) program.

Number awarded Approximately 8 each year.

Deadline February of each year.

[409]
RICHARD LOUIE MEMORIAL INTERNSHIP FOR HIGH SCHOOL STUDENTS

Freer and Sackler Galleries
Attn: Education Department
1050 Independence Avenue, S.W.
P.O. Box 37012, MRC 707
Washington, DC 20013-7012
(202) 633-0466   TDD: (202) 786-2374
E-mail: asiainternship@si.edu
Web: www.asia.si.edu/research/richardlouie.asp

Summary To enable Asian American high school students in the Washington, D.C. area to gain practical experience in a museum setting.

Eligibility This program is students at high schools in the Washington, D.C. area who are 16 years of age or older and of Asian descent. High school graduates are also eligible for the term immediately following their graduation. Applicants must be seeking an internship at the Smithsonian's Freer and Sackler Galleries, with their renowned collection of Asian art. They need not be planning a career in museum work or Asian studies, but they should be interested in learning about museum work and Asian art. Preference is given to students who are fluent in an Asian language and/or have demonstrated a serious interest in Asian art and culture.

Financial data The stipend is $1,500. No housing or transportation is provided.

Duration Interns who complete 200 internship hours within the span of 1 year receive the stipend.

Number awarded Varies each year.

Deadline October of each year for spring terms; March of each year for summer term; July of each year for fall term.

[410]
RICHARD S. SMITH SCHOLARSHIP

United Methodist Church
Attn: General Board of Discipleship
Young People's Ministries
P.O. Box 340003
Nashville, TN 37203-0003
(615) 340-7184   Toll Free: (877) 899-2780, ext. 7184
Fax: (615) 340-7063
E-mail: youngpeople@umcdiscipleship.org
Web: www.umcyoungpeople.org/grants-scholarships

Summary To provide financial assistance to Asian American and other minority high school seniors who wish to prepare for a Methodist church-related career.

Eligibility This program is open to graduating high school seniors who are members of racial/ethnic minority groups and have been active members of a United Methodist Church for at least 1 year. Applicants must have been admitted to an accredited college or university to prepare for a church-related career. They must have maintained at least a "C" average throughout high school and be able to demonstrate financial need. Along with their application, they must submit brief essays on their participation in church projects and activities, a leadership experience, the role their faith plays in their life, the church-related vocation to which God is calling them, and their extracurricular interests and activities. U.S. citizenship or permanent resident status is required.

Financial data The stipend is $1,000.

Duration 1 year; nonrenewable.

Additional information This program began in 1997. Recipients must enroll full time in their first year of undergraduate study.

Number awarded 2 each year.

Deadline May of each year.

[411]
ROBERT HALF INTERNATIONAL ASCEND SCHOLARSHIPS

Ascend: Pan-Asian Leaders
Attn: Director of Programs
247 West 30th Street
New York, NY 10001
(212) 248-4888   Fax: (212) 344-5636
E-mail: scholarships@ascendleadership.org
Web: www.ascendleadership.org

Summary To provide financial assistance to members of Ascend: Pan-Asian Leaders who are upper-division students working on a degree in accounting or finance.

Eligibility This program is open to members of Ascend who are enrolled as juniors or seniors at colleges and universities in the United States. Applicants must have a GPA of 3.5 or higher and a major in accounting or finance. Along with their application, they must submit a 500-word personal essay on how they have demonstrated leadership and teamwork in their academic studies, professional career, and/or extracurricular activities and community volunteer work; why they believe those qualities are important to transforming themselves into a better leader; their career goals after graduation; and the role Ascend has played in the achievement of their academic and career goals. Financial need is not considered in the selection process.

Financial data The stipend is $2,500.

Duration 1 year.

Additional information Ascend was formed in 2004 as the National Asian American Society of Accountants. This program is sponsored by Robert Half International Inc.

Number awarded 2 each year.

Deadline April of each year.

[412]
ROSA L. PARKS COLLEGE SCHOLARSHIP

Conference of Minority Transportation Officials
Attn: National Scholarship Program
100 M Street, S.E., Suite 917
Washington, DC 20003
(202) 506-2917   E-mail: info@comto.org
Web: www.comto.org/page/scholarships

Summary To provide financial assistance to Asian American and other students who have a tie to the Conference of Minority Transportation Officials (COMTO) and are interested in working on an undergraduate or master's degree in transportation.

Eligibility This program is open to 1) undergraduates who have completed at least 60 semester credit hours in a transportation discipline; and 2) students working on a master's degree in transportation who have completed at least 15 credits. Applicants must be or have a parent, guardian, or grandparent who has been a COMTO member for at least 1 year. They must have a GPA of 3.0 or higher. Along with their application they must submit a cover letter on their transportation-related career goals and life aspirations. Financial need is not considered in the selection process.

Financial data The stipend is $4,500. Funds are paid directly to the recipient's college or university.

Duration 1 year.

Number awarded 1 each year.

Deadline April of each year.

[413]
ROSA L. PARKS HIGH SCHOOL SCHOLARSHIP

Conference of Minority Transportation Officials
Attn: National Scholarship Program
100 M Street, S.E., Suite 917
Washington, DC 20003
(202) 506-2917   E-mail: info@comto.org
Web: www.comto.org/page/scholarships

Summary To provide financial assistance for college to children and grandchildren of members of the Conference of Minority Transportation Officials (COMTO) who are interested in studying any field.

Eligibility This program is open to high school seniors who are members or whose parent, guardian, or grandparent has been a COMTO member for at least 1 year and who have been accepted at an accredited college, university, or vocational/technical institution. Applicants must have a GPA of 3.0 or higher. Along with their application they must submit a cover letter on their transportation-related career goals and life aspirations. Financial need is not considered in the selection process.

Financial data The stipend is $4,500. Funds are paid directly to the recipient's college or university.

Duration 1 year.

Number awarded 1 each year.

Deadline April of each year.

[414]
ROSALIND P. WALTER COLLEGE SCHOLARSHIPS

United States Tennis Association
Attn: USTA Foundation
70 West Red Oak Lane
White Plains, NY 10604
(914) 696-7223   Fax: (914) 697-2307
E-mail: foundation@usta.com
Web: www.ustafoundation.com

Summary To provide financial assistance to female and male high school seniors (judged separately) who are Asian Americans or members or other diverse groups and have contributed to their community, have participated in an organized community tennis program, and plan to attend college in any state.

Eligibility This program is open to high school seniors from diverse ethnic backgrounds who have excelled academically, demonstrated commitment to their community, and participated extensively in an organized community tennis program. Applicants must be planning to enroll as a full-time undergraduate student at a 4-year college or university. They must have a GPA of 3.0 or higher and be able to demonstrate financial need and sportsmanship. Along with their application, they must submit an essay of 1 to 2 pages about how their participation in a tennis and education program has influenced their life, including examples of special mentors, volunteer service, and future goals. Females and males are considered separately.

Financial data The stipend is $2,500 per year. Funds are paid directly to the recipient's college or university.

Duration 4 years.

Number awarded 2 each year: 1 female and 1 male.

Deadline February of each year.

[415]
ROYCE OSBORN MINORITY STUDENT SCHOLARSHIPS

American Society of Radiologic Technologists
Attn: ASRT Foundation
15000 Central Avenue, S.E.
Albuquerque, NM 87123-3909
(505) 298-4500, ext. 1392
Toll Free: (800) 444-2778, ext. 1392
Fax: (505) 298-5063   E-mail: foundation@asrt.org
Web: foundation.asrt.org/what-we-do/scholarships

Summary To provide financial assistance to Asian American and other minority students enrolled in entry-level radiologic sciences programs.

Eligibility This program is open to Asians, Blacks or African Americans, American Indians or Alaska Natives, Hispanics or Latinos, and Native Hawaiians or other Pacific Islanders who are enrolled in an accredited entry-level program in radiography, sonography, magnetic resonance, or nuclear medicine. Applicants must be able to finish their degree or certificate in the year for which they are applying. They must be U.S. citizens, nationals, or permanent residents have a GPA of 3.0 or higher. Along with their application, they must submit

9 essays of 200 words each on assigned topics related to their personal situation and interest in a career in radiologic science. Selection is based on those essays, academic and professional achievements, recommendations, and financial need.

Financial data The stipend is $4,000. Funds are paid directly to the recipient's institution.

Duration 1 year.

Number awarded 5 each year.

Deadline January of each year.

[416]
RUTH WEBB MINORITY SCHOLARSHIP

California Academy of Physician Assistants
2318 South Fairview Street
Santa Ana, CA 92704-4938
(714) 427-0321   Fax: (714) 427-0324
E-mail: capa@capanet.org
Web: www.capanet.org

Summary To provide financial assistance to Asian American or other minority student members of the California Academy of Physician Assistants (CAPA) enrolled in physician assistant programs in California.

Eligibility This program is open to student members of CAPA enrolled in primary care physician assistant programs in California. Applicants must be members of a minority group (Asian/Pacific Islander, African American, Hispanic, or Native American/Alaskan Native). They must have maintained good academic standing and conducted activities to promote the physician assistant profession. Along with their application, they must submit an essay describing the activities they have performed to promote the physician assistant profession, the importance of representing minorities in their community, and why they should be awarded this scholarship. Financial need is considered in the selection process.

Financial data The stipend is $2,000.

Duration 1 year.

Number awarded 1 each year.

Deadline December of each year.

[417]
RYU FAMILY FOUNDATION SCHOLARSHIP GRANTS

Ryu Family Foundation, Inc.
Attn: Jenny Kang
186 Parish Drive
Wayne, NJ 07470
(646) 250-0317   E-mail: RyuFoundation@gmail.com
Web: www.ryufoundation.org

Summary To provide financial assistance to Korean and Korean American students in the Northeast who are working on an undergraduate or graduate degree in any field.

Eligibility This program is open to Korean Americans (U.S. citizens) and Koreans (with or without permanent resident status). Applicants must be enrolled full time and working on an undergraduate or graduate degree; have a GPA of 3.5 or higher; be able to document financial need; and be either residing or attending college in 1 of the following 10 northeastern states: Connecticut, Delaware, Maine, Massachusetts, New Hampshire, New Jersey, New York, Pennsylvania, Rhode Island, or Vermont. Along with their application, they must submit a 500-word essay on a subject that changes annually; recently, students were asked to write on 1 of the following: 1) what they would you like to do to change the world for the better; 2) something they have done in the past that has made a difference in their family; or 3) a book or article they have read that has inspired them.

Financial data A stipend is awarded (amount not specified). Checks are made out jointly to the recipient and the recipient's school.

Duration 1 year; may be renewed.

Number awarded Approximately 18 each year.

Deadline November of each year.

[418]
SAJA SCHOLARSHIPS

South Asian Journalists Association
Attn: Zainab Imam, Secretary
c/o Columbia Journalism School
Pulitzer Hall
2950 Broadway
New York, NY 10027
E-mail: secretary@saja.org
Web: www.saja.org/scholarships

Summary To provide financial assistance for undergraduate and graduate study to journalism students of south Asian descent.

Eligibility This program is open to students of south Asian descent (including Bangladesh, Bhutan, India, Maldives, Nepal, Pakistan, and Sri Lanka; Indo-Caribbeans are also eligible). Applicants must be serious about preparing for a journalism career and must provide evidence they plan to do so through courses, internships, or freelancing. They may be 1) high school seniors about to enroll in an accredited college or university; 2) current students in an accredited college or university in the United States or Canada; or 3) students enrolled or about to enter a graduate program in the United States or Canada. Applicants with financial hardship are given special consideration. Selection is based on interest in journalism, writing skills, participation in the sponsoring organization, reasons for entering journalism, and financial need.

Financial data The stipends are $2,000 for high school seniors, $3,000 for undergraduates, or $5,000 for graduate students.

Duration 1 year.

Additional information Recipients are expected to give back to the South Asian Journalists Association (SAJA) by volunteering at the annual convention or at other events during the year.

Number awarded Varies each year; recently, 11 were awarded: a to a high school senior, 6 to undergraduates, and 4 to graduate students.

Deadline March of each year.

[419]
SAM CHU LIN SCHOLARSHIP

Asian American Journalists Association-Los Angeles
 Chapter
Attn: Frank Buckley, Scholarship Chair
KTLA-TV
5800 Sunset Boulevard
Los Angeles, CA 90028
E-mail: aajalaawards@gmail.com
Web: www.aaja-la.org/category/programs/scholarships

Summary To provide financial assistance to Asian/Pacific Islander students in the Los Angeles area who are interested in careers in broadcast journalism.

Eligibility This program is open to Asian/Pacific Islander full-time students who are planning a career in broadcast journalism. Applicants must be attending a college or university in the Los Angeles area (Los Angeles, Orange, Riverside, San Bernardino, or Ventura counties). Membership in the Asian American Journalists Association (AAJA) is encouraged for applicants and required for recipients. Selection is based on academic achievement, commitment to the field of journalism, journalistic ability, sensitivity to Asian American and Pacific Islander issues, and financial need.

Financial data The stipend is $2,500.

Duration 1 year; may be renewed.

Number awarded 1 each year.

Deadline January of each year.

[420]
SAPA SCHOLARSHIP AND EXCELLENCE IN EDUCATION PROGRAM

Sino-American Pharmaceutical Professionals Association
Attn: Scholarship Office
P.O. Box 292
Nanuet, NY 10954
E-mail: sapa_scholarship@yahoo.com
Web: www.sapaweb.org/new/index.htm

Summary To provide financial assistance to high school seniors who plan to major in life sciences in college.

Eligibility This program is open to graduating high school seniors who have a GPA of 3.3 or higher and an SAT score of at least 2000 or an ACT score of at least 30. Applicants must be planning to enroll full time at a college or university in any state and major in a life science. Eligible fields include applied science, biochemistry, biology, botany, chemical engineering, chemistry, computer science, entomology, environmental engineering, environmental science, mathematics, mechanical engineering, microbiology, molecular genetics, pharmacy/pharmacology, physics, physiology, zoology. They must be U.S. citizens or permanent residents. Along with their application, they must submit a 600-word essay on why they want to prepare for a life science-related career. Selection is based on academic performance and demonstrated potential for and commitment to a career in life science.

Financial data The stipend is $1,000.

Duration 1 year.

Additional information The sponsor, the Sino-American Pharmaceutical Professionals Association (SAPA), was established in 1999 and began offering scholarships in 2003. It is 1 of the most active and well-recognized Chinese-heritage enduring professional organizations in the United States.

Number awarded 2 or more each year.

Deadline May of each year.

[421]
SCHOLARSHIPS FOR MINORITY ACCOUNTING STUDENTS

American Institute of Certified Public Accountants
Attn: Academic and Career Development Division
220 Leigh Farm Road
Durham, NC 27707-8110
(919) 402-4931   Fax: (919) 419-4705
E-mail: scholarships@aicpa.org
Web: www.aicpa.org

Summary To provide financial assistance to Asian Americans and other minorities interested in studying accounting at the undergraduate or graduate school level.

Eligibility This program is open to minority undergraduate and graduate students, enrolled full time, who have a GPA of 3.3 or higher (both cumulatively and in their major) and intend to pursue a C.P.A. credential. The program defines minority students as those whose heritage is Asian American, Black or African American, Hispanic or Latino, or Native American. Undergraduates must have completed at least 30 semester hours, including at least 6 semester hours of a major in accounting. Graduate students must be working on a master's degree in accounting, finance, taxation, or a related program. Applicants must be U.S. citizens or permanent residents and student affiliate members of the American Institute of Certified Public Accountants (AICPA). Along with their application, they must submit 500-word essays on 1) why they want to become a C.P.A. and how attaining that licensure will contribute to their goals; and 2) how they would spread the message about accounting and the C.P.A. profession in their community and school. In the selection process, some consideration is given to financial need.

Financial data Stipends range up to $5,000 per year. Funds are disbursed directly to the recipient's school.

Duration 1 year; may be renewed up to 3 additional years or until completion of a bachelor's or master's degree, whichever is earlier.

Additional information This program began in 1969. Additional support is provided by the Accounting Education Foundation of the Texas Society of Certified Public Accountants, the New Jersey Society of Certified Public Accountants, Robert Half International, and the Virgin Islands Society of Certified Public Accountants.

Number awarded Varies each year; recently, 97 students received funding through this program.

Deadline March of each year.

[422]
SCHOLARSHIPS FOR RACIAL JUSTICE

Higher Education Consortium for Urban Affairs
Attn: Student Services
2233 University Avenue West, Suite 210
St. Paul, MN 55114-1698
(651) 287-3300   Toll Free: (800) 554-1089
Fax: (651) 659-9421   E-mail: hecua@hecua.org
Web: www.hecua.org

Summary To provide financial assistance to Asian Americans and other students of color who are enrolled in programs of the Higher Education Consortium for Urban Affairs (HECUA) at participating colleges and universities and are committed to undoing institutionalized racism.

Eligibility This program is open to students at member colleges and universities who are participating in HECUA programs. Applicants must be a student of color who can demonstrate a commitment to undoing institutionalized racism. Along with their application, they must submit a reflective essay of 550 to 1,700 words on the personal, social, or political influences in their lifetime that have motivated them to work on racial justice issues.

Financial data The stipend is $4,000.

Duration 1 semester.

Additional information This program began in 2012. Consortium members include Augsburg College (Minneapolis, Minnesota), Augustana College (Sioux Falls, South Dakota), Carleton College (Northfield, Minnesota), College of Saint Scholastica (Duluth, Minnesota), Colorado College (Colorado Springs, Colorado), Denison University (Granville, Ohio), Gustavus Adolphus College (St. Peter, Minnesota), Hamline University (St. Paul, Minnesota), Macalester College (St. Paul, Minnesota), Northland College (Ashland, Wisconsin), Saint Mary's University (Winona, Minnesota), Saint Catherine University (St. Paul, Minnesota), Saint Olaf College (Northfield, Minnesota), Swarthmore College (Swarthmore, Pennsylvania), University of Minnesota (Twin Cities, Duluth, Morris, Crookston, Rochester), and University of Saint Thomas (St. Paul, Minnesota).

Number awarded Several each year.

Deadline April of each year for summer and fall programs; November of each year for January and spring programs.

[423]
SCHOLARSHIPS FOR SOCIAL JUSTICE

Higher Education Consortium for Urban Affairs
Attn: Student Services
2233 University Avenue West, Suite 210
St. Paul, MN 55114-1698
(651) 287-3300   Toll Free: (800) 554-1089
Fax: (651) 659-9421   E-mail: hecua@hecua.org
Web: www.hecua.org

Summary To provide financial assistance to Asian Americans and students from other targeted groups who are enrolled in programs of the Higher Education Consortium for Urban Affairs (HECUA) at participating colleges and universities.

Eligibility This program is open to students at member colleges and universities who are participating in HECUA programs. Applicants must be a first-generation college student, from a low-income family, and/or a student of color. Along with their application, they must submit a reflective essay of 500 to 1,700 words, drawing on their life experiences and their personal and academic goals, on what they believe they can contribute to the mission of HECUA to equip students with the knowledge, experiences, tools, and passion to address issues of social justice and social change. The essay should also explain how the HECUA program will benefit them and the people, issues, and communities they care about.

Financial data The stipend is $1,500. Funds are applied as a credit to the student's HECUA program fees for the semester.

Duration 1 semester.

Additional information This program began in 2006. Consortium members include Augsburg College (Minneapolis, Minnesota), Augustana College (Sioux Falls, South Dakota), Carleton College (Northfield, Minnesota), College of Saint Scholastica (Duluth, Minnesota), Colorado College (Colorado Springs, Colorado), Denison University (Granville, Ohio), Gustavus Adolphus College (St. Peter, Minnesota), Hamline University (St. Paul, Minnesota), Macalester College (St. Paul, Minnesota), Northland College (Ashland, Wisconsin), Saint Mary's University (Winona, Minnesota), Saint Catherine University (St. Paul, Minnesota), Saint Olaf College (Northfield, Minnesota), Swarthmore College (Swarthmore, Pennsylvania), University of Minnesota (Twin Cities, Duluth, Morris, Crookston, Rochester), and University of Saint Thomas (St. Paul, Minnesota).

Number awarded Several each year.

Deadline April of each year for summer and fall programs; November of each year for January and spring programs.

[424]
SC-PAAE SCHOLARSHIPS

South Carolina Professional Association for Access and
   Equity
Attn: Financial Secretary
P.O. Box 71297
North Charleston, SC 29415
(843) 670-4890   E-mail: anderson4569@bellsouth.net
Web: www.scpaae.org/#!scholarships/c11tv

Summary To provide financial assistance to undergraduate students at colleges and universities in South Carolina who are recognized as underrepresented minorities on their campus.

Eligibility This program is open to residents of any state who have completed at least 12 semester hours at a college or university in South Carolina. Applicants must be recognized as an underrepresented ethnic minority on their campus. They must have a GPA of 2.75 or higher. Along with their application, they must submit 1) a personal letter on their academic and career goals, honors and awards, leadership skills and organization participation, community service, and a statement of why they would like to receive this scholarship; and 2) a paragraph defining access and equity and describing how they can assist in achieving access and equity within South Carolina. Financial need is not considered in the selection process.

Financial data Stipends are $750 for students at 2-year institutions or $1,000 for students at 4-year institutions.

Duration 1 year.

Number awarded Varies each year.

Deadline February of each year.

[425]
SEED SCHOLARSHIPS

The SEED Foundation
Attn: Scholarship Director
1325 Lance Lane
Carol Stream, IL 60188
E-mail: info@seedfoundation.org
Web: www.seedfoundation.org/scholarship.html

Summary To provide financial assistance to high school seniors who are of Asian-Indian heritage and interested in attending college and majoring in any field.

Eligibility This program is open to graduating high school seniors who are of Asian Indian heritage with at least 1 parent of Indian ancestry. Applicants must be planning to enroll full time at a college or university in the United States. They must have a GPA of 3.0 or higher and be U.S. citizens or permanent residents.

Financial data Stipends range up to $10,000.

Duration 1 year.

Additional information This program began in 1998.

Number awarded Varies each year; recently, 3 were awarded. Since the program began, it has awarded $243,000 in scholarships to 41 students.

Deadline April of each year.

[426]
SEO UNDERGRADUATE CAREER PROGRAM

Sponsors for Educational Opportunity
Attn: Career Program
55 Exchange Place
New York, NY 10005
(212) 979-2040   Toll Free: (800) 462-2332
Fax: (646) 706-7113
E-mail: careerprogram@seo-usa.org
Web: www.seocareer.org

Summary To provide Asian American and other undergraduate students of color with an opportunity to gain summer work experience in selected fields.

Eligibility This program is open to students of color at colleges and universities in the United States. Applicants must be interested in a summer internship in 1 of the following fields: asset management, consulting, engineering, finance and accounting, human resources, investment banking, investment research, marketing and sales, nonprofit sector, private equity, sales and trading, technology with banks, technology with global companies, or transaction services. Freshmen are not eligible. Sophomores are eligible for asset management, finance and accounting, investment banking, sales and trading, technology with banks, and transaction services. Juniors are eligible for all fields. Seniors and current graduate students are not eligible. All applicants must have a cumulative GPA of 3.0 or higher. Personal interviews are required.

Financial data Interns receive a competitive stipend of up to $1,300 per week.

Duration 10 weeks during the summer.

Additional information This program began in 1980. Corporate leadership internships are in the New York metro area, New Jersey, Connecticut, Iowa, Massachusetts, North Carolina, Ohio, California, and other areas; banking and private equity internships are in New York City with limited opportunities in New Jersey, Connecticut and possibly Miami or Houston; nonprofit internships are in New York City.

Number awarded Approximately 300 to 400 each year.

Deadline December of each year for sales and trading; January of each year for asset management, consulting, investment banking, investment research, nonprofit sector, private equity, and transaction services; February of each year for engineering, finance and accounting, human resources, marketing and sales, and technology.

[427]
SHARON D. BANKS MEMORIAL UNDERGRADUATE SCHOLARSHIP

Women's Transportation Seminar
Attn: WTS Foundation
1701 K Street, N.W., Suite 800
Washington, DC 20006
(202) 955-5085   Fax: (202) 955-5088
E-mail: wts@wtsinternational.org
Web: www.wtsinternational.org/education/scholarships

Summary To provide financial assistance to undergraduate women, especially Asian Americans and other minorities, who are interested in a career in transportation.

Eligibility This program is open to women who are working on an undergraduate degree in transportation or a transportation-related field (e.g., transportation engineering, planning, finance, or logistics). Applicants must have a GPA of 3.0 or higher and be interested in a career in transportation. Along with their application, they must submit a 500-word statement about their career goals after graduation and why they think they should receive the scholarship award. Applications must be submitted first to a local chapter; the chapters forward selected applications for consideration on the national level. Minority women are especially encouraged to apply. Selection is based on transportation involvement and goals, job skills, and academic record; financial need is not considered.

Financial data The stipend is $5,000.

Duration 1 year.

Additional information This program began in 1992. Local chapters may also award additional funding to winners in their area.

Number awarded 1 each year.

Deadline Applications must be submitted by November to a local WTS chapter.

[428]
SHIRO KASHINO MEMORIAL SCHOLARSHIPS

Nisei Veterans Committee
Attn: NVC Foundation
1212 South King Street
Seattle, WA 98144-2025
(206) 322-1122   E-mail: scholarship@nvcfoundation.org
Web: www.seattlenvc.org/education/scholarship

Summary To provide financial assistance to high school seniors and current college students who are related to a member of the Nisei Veterans Committee or the NVC Foundation.

Eligibility This program is open to college-bound high school seniors and students who are already enrolled in college and are relatives of members of the Nisei Veterans Committee (an organization of Japanese American veterans) or of the NVC Foundation. Applicants must submit essays on 1) what the Nisei veterans' legacy means to them; and 2) their future aspirations and life plans. Special consideration is given to students who have helped support the NVC organization. Financial need is considered in the selection process.

Financial data   The stipend is $2,500.

Duration   1 year.

Number awarded   3 each year.

Deadline   January of each year.

[429]
SHUI KUEN AND ALLEN CHIN SCHOLARSHIP

Asian Pacific Fund
Attn: Scholarship Coordinator
465 California Street, Suite 809
San Francisco, CA 94104
(415) 395-9985 E-mail: scholarship@asianpacificfund.org
Web: www.asianpacificfund.org

Summary   To provide financial assistance for college to students who have worked or whose parent has worked in an Asian restaurant.

Eligibility   This program is open to students who are entering or currently enrolled full time in an undergraduate degree program at an accredited college or university in any state. Applicants or their parents must have worked at an Asian restaurant (Asian-owned or Asian cuisine). They must have a GPA of 3.0 or higher and be able to demonstrate financial need. Along with their application, they must submit essays of 250 to 500 words each on 1) their academic and career goals, hopes, and dreams for the future; 2) their experience as a restaurant worker or child of a restaurant worker, what they learned from that experience, and how that experience has affected their values; 3) any community service or school projects that have shaped their ideas about the Asian American community; and 4) any unusual family or personal circumstances that have affected their achievement in school, work, or extracurricular activities. Preference is given to students who have been involved in community advocacy and social justice work on behalf of Asian American, immigrant, gay and lesbian, or other progressive causes. U.S. citizenship or permanent resident status is required.

Financial data   The stipend is $1,000 per year.

Duration   1 year; recipients may reapply.

Additional information   This program began in 2007.

Number awarded   Up to 2 each year.

Deadline   February of each year.

[430]
SIA YANG SCHOLARSHIP

Hmong American Education Fund
P.O. Box 17468
St. Paul, MN 55117
(651) 592-1576   E-mail: scholarships@thehaef.org
Web: www.thehaef.org

Summary   To provide financial assistance to Hmong and southeast Asian refugees from of any state who have lost a parent through death and are interested in working on an undergraduate or graduate degree in any field.

Eligibility   This program is open to students of Hmong or other southeast Asian refugee descent who are high school seniors, GED recipients, or current full-time undergraduate or graduate students at 2- or 4-year colleges or universities in any state. Applicants must be U.S. citizens or permanent residents. They must have lost at least 1 parent through death. Along with their application, they must submit a 1,500-word essay on their commitment to education, how losing a parent or both parents has impacted them, and their community service. Selection is based on academic achievement.

Financial data   The stipend is $1,000.

Duration   1 year; nonrenewable.

Number awarded   1 each year.

Deadline   March of each year.

[431]
SMITHSONIAN MINORITY AWARDS PROGRAM

Smithsonian Institution
Attn: Office of Fellowships and Internships
470 L'Enfant Plaza, Suite 7102
P.O. Box 37012, MRC 902
Washington, DC 20013-7012
(202) 633-7070   Fax: (202) 633-7069
E-mail: siofi@si.edu
Web: www.smithsonianofi.com

Summary   To provide funding to Asian American and other minority undergraduate and graduate students interested in conducting research at the Smithsonian Institution.

Eligibility   This program is open to members of U.S. minority groups underrepresented in the Smithsonian's scholarly programs. Applicants must be undergraduates or beginning graduate students interested in conducting research in the Institution's disciplines and in the museum field. They must be U.S. citizens or permanent residents and have a GPA of 3.0 or higher.

Financial data   Students receive a grant of $600 per week.

Duration   Up to 10 weeks.

Additional information   Recipients must carry out independent research projects in association with the Smithsonian's research staff. Eligible fields of study currently include animal behavior, ecology, and environmental science (including an emphasis on the tropics); anthropology (including archaeology); astrophysics and astronomy; earth sciences and paleobiology; evolutionary and systematic biology; history of science and technology; history of art (especially American, contemporary, African, Asian, and 20th-century art); American crafts and decorative arts; social and cultural history of the United States; and folklife. Students are required to be in residence at the Smithsonian for the duration of the fellowship.

Number awarded   Varies each year; recently, 25 were granted: 2 for fall, 19 for summer, and 4 for spring.

Deadline   January of each year for summer and fall residency; September of each year for spring residency.

[432]
SMITHSONIAN MINORITY STUDENT INTERNSHIP

Smithsonian Institution
Attn: Office of Fellowships and Internships
470 L'Enfant, Suite 7102
P.O. Box 37012, MRC 902
Washington, DC 20013-7012
(202) 633-7070　　　　　　Fax: (202) 633-7069
E-mail: siofi@si.edu
Web: www.smithsonianofi.com/minority-internship-program

Summary To provide Asian American and other minority undergraduate or graduate students with the opportunity to work on research or museum procedure projects in specific areas of history, art, or science at the Smithsonian Institution.

Eligibility Internships are offered to minority students who are actively engaged in undergraduate or graduate study or have graduated within the past 4 months. Applicants must be U.S. citizens or permanent residents who have an overall GPA of 3.0 or higher. Applicants must be interested in conducting research in any of the following fields of interest to the Smithsonian: animal behavior, ecology, and environmental science (including an emphasis on the tropics); anthropology (including archaeology); astrophysics and astronomy; earth sciences and paleobiology; evolutionary and systematic biology; history of science and technology; history of art (especially American, contemporary, African, Asian, and 20th-century art); American crafts and decorative arts; social and cultural history of the United States; and folklife.

Financial data The program provides a stipend of $600 per week; travel allowances may also be offered.

Duration 10 weeks during the summer or academic year.

Number awarded Varies each year.

Deadline January of each year for summer or fall; September of each year for spring.

[433]
SOO YUEN BENEVOLENT ASSOCIATION SCHOLARSHIPS

Soo Yuen Benevolent Association
806 Clay Street
San Francisco, CA 94108
(415) 421-0602　　　　　　Fax: (415) 421-0606
Web: www.sooyuen.org/?q=node/1434

Summary To provide financial assistance for college to children of members of the Soo Yuen Benevolent Association.

Eligibility This program is open to high school seniors whose parents have been members of the association for at least 1 year. Membership in the association is limited to members of the following clans: Louie (including Loui, Lui, Lei), Fong (including Fang), and Kwong (including Kwang, Kuang, and Kong). Applicants must have a GPA of 3.0 or higher and be planning to attend college in any state. As part of the selection process, a personal interview may be required.

Financial data A stipend is awarded (amount not specified).

Duration 1 year.

Number awarded 1 or more each year.

Deadline January of each year.

[434]
SOUTHERN REGION KOREAN AMERICAN SCHOLARSHIPS

Korean American Scholarship Foundation
Southern Region
Attn: Scholarship Committee Chair
6065 Sweet Creek Road
Johns Creek, GA 30097
E-mail: src.scholarship@kasf.org
Web: www.kasf.org/southern

Summary To provide financial assistance to Korean American students from any state who are working on or planning to work on an undergraduate or graduate degree in any field at a school in southern states.

Eligibility This program is open to Korean American students who are enrolled or planning to enroll at a college or university in the southern states as full-time undergraduate or graduate students. Applicants may reside anywhere in the United States, but they must attend school in the southern region: Alabama, Florida, Georgia, South Carolina, and Tennessee. Both U.S. citizens and foreign nationals are eligible. Selection is based on academic achievement (GPA of 3.0 or higher), school activities, community service, and financial need.

Financial data Stipends are $1,000 for undergraduate, graduate, or professional students or $500 for high school students.

Duration 1 year; renewable.

Number awarded Varies each year; recently, 26 college and graduate scholarships and 6 high school scholarships were awarded.

Deadline July of each year.

[435]
SOUTHWESTERN REGION KOREAN AMERICAN SCHOLARSHIPS

Korean American Scholarship Foundation
Southern Region
Attn: Scholarship Committee Chair
P.O. Box 420242
Houston, TX 77242
E-mail: swrc.scholarship@kasf.org
Web: www.kasf.org/southwestern

Summary To provide financial assistance to Korean American students from any state who are working on or planning to work on an undergraduate or graduate degree in any field at a school in southwestern states.

Eligibility This program is open to residents of any state who are 1) U.S. citizens of Korean heritage; 2) Korean citizens who have a valid visa to study in the United States; and 3) citizens of any other country who are of Korean heritage and have a valid visa to study in the United States. Applicants must be enrolled or planning to enroll as a full-time undergraduate or graduate student at a college or university in Arkansas, Louisiana, Mississippi, Oklahoma, or Texas. Selection is based on academic performance, extracurricular activities, community service, letters of recommendation, an essay, character and integrity, and financial need.

Financial data Stipends range from $1,000 to $2,000.

Duration 1 year; nonrenewable.

Number awarded Varies each year; recently, 27 were awarded.

Deadline July of each year.

[436]
SPORTS JOURNALISM INSTITUTE INTERNSHIPS/SCHOLARSHIPS

Sports Journalism Institute
c/o Gregory Lee, Executive Sports Editor
South Florida Sun Sentinel
500 East Broward Boulevard
Fort Lauderdale, FL 33394
(617) 929-2840   E-mail: gleejr@gmail.com
Web: sportsjournalisminstitute.org/blog/application

Summary To provide student journalists (especially Asian Americans and other students of color) with an opportunity to learn more about sports journalism during the summer.

Eligibility This program is open to college juniors and sophomores, especially members of ethnic and racial minority groups. Applicants must be interested in participating in a summer program that includes class sessions in sports journalism followed by an internship in the sports department of a daily newspaper. They must submit a current college transcript, 2 letters of recommendation, up to 7 writing samples or clips, and an essay of up to 500 words stating why they should be chosen to participate in the program. Selection is based on academic achievement, demonstrated interest in sports journalism as a career, and the essay. Eligibility is not limited to journalism majors.

Financial data All expenses are paid during the class sessions. A salary is paid during the internship portion. At the conclusion of the program, participants receive a $500 scholarship for the following year of college.

Duration The class sessions last 1 week; the internship lasts 8 weeks (June through mid-August); the college scholarship is for 1 year.

Additional information This program began in 1993. The class sessions take place at the University of Missouri. Funding is provided by the Chicago Tribune Foundation, Hearst Newspapers/Houston Chronicle, and Associated Press Sports Editors. The institute works with the National Association of Black Journalists (NABJ), the Asian American Journalists Association (AAJA), and the National Association of Hispanic Journalists (NAHJ).

Number awarded 12 each year.

Deadline November of each year.

[437]
STANFORD CHEN INTERNSHIP GRANTS

Asian American Journalists Association
Attn: Student Programs Coordinator
5 Third Street, Suite 1108
San Francisco, CA 94103
(415) 346-2051, ext. 102   Fax: (415) 346-6343
E-mail: programs@aaja.org
Web: www.aaja.org/apply-for-a-scholarship-now

Summary To provide supplemental grants to student members of the Asian American Journalists Association (AAJA) working as interns at small or medium-size news organizations.

Eligibility This program is open to AAJA members who are college juniors, seniors, or graduate students with a serious intent to prepare for a career in journalism (print, online, broadcast, or photography). Applicants must have already secured an internship with a print company (daily circulation less than 100,000) or broadcast company (market smaller than the top 50). Along with their application, they must submit a 200-word essay on the kind of experience they expect as an intern at a small to medium-size media company, their career goals, and why AAJA's mission is important to them; a resume; verification of the internship; a letter of recommendation; and a statement of financial need.

Financial data The grant is $1,750. Funds are to be used for living expenses or transportation.

Duration Summer months.

Additional information This program began in 1998.

Number awarded Varies each year; recently, 4 were awarded.

Deadline April of each year.

[438]
STATE COUNCIL ON ADAPTED PHYSICAL EDUCATION CULTURAL DIVERSITY STUDENT SCHOLARSHIP

California Association for Health, Physical Education, Recreation and Dance
Attn: State Council on Adapted Physical Education
1501 El Camino Avenue, Suite 3
Sacramento, CA 95815-2748
(916) 922-3596   Toll Free: (800) 499-3596 (within CA)
Fax: (916) 922-0133
E-mail: califstatecouncilape@gmail.com
Web: www.califstatecouncilape.org

Summary To provide financial assistance to Asian American and other culturally diverse members of the California Association for Health, Physical Education, Recreation and Dance (CAHPERD) who are preparing to become a student teacher in the field of adapted physical education.

Eligibility This program is open to CAHPERD members who are attending a California college or university and specializing in the field of adapted physical education. Applicants must be members of an ethnic or cultural minority group (e.g., Asian American, Filipino, African American, American Indian/ Native American, Mexican American, other Latino, Pacific Islander). They must be planning to become a student teacher during the following academic year. Along with their application, they must submit a 300-word statement of their professional goals and philosophy of physical education for individuals with disabilities. Selection is based on academic proficiency; leadership ability; personal qualities; school, community, and professional activities; and experience and interest in working with individuals with disabilities.

Financial data The stipend is $1,000.

Duration 1 year.

Number awarded 1 each year.

Deadline January of each year.

[439]
STOKES EDUCATIONAL SCHOLARSHIP PROGRAM

National Security Agency
Attn: MB3, Stokes Program
9800 Savage Road, Suite 6779
Fort Meade, MD 20755-6779
(410) 854-4725   Toll Free: (866) NSA-HIRE
Web: www.nsa.gov

Summary To provide high school seniors, especially Asian American and other minorities, with scholarship/loans and work experience at the National Security Agency (NSA).

Eligibility This program is open to graduating high school seniors, particularly minorities, who are planning a college major in electrical or computer engineering or computer science. Applicants must have minimum scores of 1600 on the SAT (1100 on critical reading and mathematics, 500 in writing) or 25 on the ACT. They must have a GPA of 3.0 or higher and be able to demonstrate leadership abilities. U.S. citizenship and eligibility to obtain a high-level security clearance are required.

Financial data The stipend covers payment of tuition and mandatory fees, to a maximum of $30,000 per year. Other benefits include a year-round salary, a housing allowance and travel reimbursement during summer employment if the distance between the agency and school exceeds 75 miles health and life insurance, and participation in federal retirement plans. Following graduation, participants must work for the agency for 1 and a half times their length of study, usually 5 years. Students who leave agency employment earlier must repay the tuition cost.

Duration Up to 4 years, followed by employment at the agency for 5 years.

Additional information Participants must attend classes full time and work at the agency during the summer in jobs tailored to their course of study. They must maintain at least a 3.0 GPA. This program, established in 1986, was formerly known as the National Security Agency Undergraduate Training Program.

Number awarded Varies each year.

Deadline November of each year.

[440]
STUDENT OPPORTUNITY SCHOLARSHIPS OF THE PRESBYTERIAN CHURCH (USA)

Presbyterian Church (USA)
Attn: Office of Financial Aid for Service
100 Witherspoon Street
Louisville, KY 40202-1396
(502) 569-5224   Toll Free: (888) 728-7228; ext. 5224
Fax: (502) 569-8766   TDD: (800) 833-5955
E-mail: finaid@pcusa.org
Web: www.presbyterianmission.org

Summary To provide financial assistance to Presbyterian college students, especially Asian Americans and others of racial/ethnic minority heritage.

Eligibility This program is open to active members of the Presbyterian Church (USA) who are entering their sophomore, junior, or senior year of college as full-time students in a bachelor's degree program. Preference is given to applicants who are members of racial/ethnic minority groups (Asian American, African American, Hispanic American, Native American, Alaska Native). Applicants must have a GPA of 2.5 or higher and be able to demonstrate financial need.

Financial data Stipends range up to $2,000 per year, depending upon the financial need of the recipient.

Duration 1 year; may be renewed if the recipient continues to need financial assistance and demonstrates satisfactory academic progress.

Number awarded Approximately 80 each year.

Deadline May of each year.

[441]
SUMMER AFFIRMATIVE ACTION INTERNSHIP PROGRAM

Wisconsin Office of State Employment Relations
Attn: Division of Affirmative Action Workforce Planning
101 East Wilson Street, Fourth Floor
P.O. Box 7855
Madison, WI 53707-7855
(608) 266-6475   Fax: (608) 267-1020
E-mail: OSERDAA@wi.gov
Web: oser.state.wi.us/category.asp?linkcatid=342

Summary To provide an opportunity for Asian Americans and members of other underrepresented groups to gain summer work experience with agencies of the state of Wisconsin.

Eligibility This program is open to women, ethnic/racial minorities (Asian, Black or African American, Native Hawaiian or other Pacific Islander, American Indian or Alaska Native, or Hispanic or Latino), and persons with disabilities. Applicants must be sophomores, juniors, seniors, or graduate students at an accredited 4-year college or university or second-year students in the second year of a 2-year technical or vocational school program. They must be 1) Wisconsin residents enrolled full time at a school in Wisconsin or any other state; or 2) residents of other states who are enrolled full time at a school in Wisconsin.

Financial data Most internships provide a competitive stipend.

Duration Summer months.

Additional information This program began in 1974. Internships are available in criminal justice, engineering, finance/accounting, human resources, information technology, legal research, library science, public administration, recreational leadership, research analyst, social work, vocational/rehabilitation therapy, and various other government jobs.

Number awarded Varies each year. Since the program was established, it has placed more than 3,100 students with more than 30 different agencies and universities throughout the state.

Deadline February of each year.

[442]
SUMMER RESEARCH OPPORTUNITIES PROGRAM (SROP)

Committee on Institutional Cooperation
Attn: Academic and International Programs
1819 South Neil Street, Suite D
Champaign, IL 61820-7271
(217) 333-8475   Fax: (217) 244-7127
E-mail: cic@staff.cic.net
Web: www.cic.net/students/srop/introduction

Summary To provide an opportunity for undergraduates, especially Asian Americans and other students from diverse backgrounds, to gain research experience at member institutions of the Committee on Institutional Cooperation (CIC) during the summer.

Eligibility This program is open to students currently enrolled in a degree-granting program at a college or university who have a GPA of 3.0 or higher and an interest in continuing on to graduate school. Applicants must be interested in conducting a summer research project under the supervision of a faculty mentor at a CIC member institution. The program is designed to increase educational access for students from diverse backgrounds; members of racial and ethnic minority groups and low-income first-generation students are especially encouraged to apply. U.S. citizenship or permanent resident status is required.

Financial data Participants are paid a stipend that depends on the participating CIC member institution, but ranges from $3,000 to $6,000. Faculty mentors receive a $500 research allowance for the cost of materials.

Duration 8 to 10 weeks during the summer.

Additional information Participants work directly with faculty mentors at the institution of their choice and engage in other enrichment activities, such as workshops and social gatherings. In July, all participants come together at 1 of the CIC campuses for the annual SROP conference. The participating CIC member institutions are University of Illinois at Urbana-Champaign, University of Iowa, University of Michigan, University of Minnesota, University of Nebraska at Lincoln, University of Wisconsin at Madison, Michigan State University, Northwestern University, Ohio State University, Pennsylvania State University, Purdue University, and Rutgers University. Students are required to write a paper and an abstract describing their projects and to present the results of their work at a campus symposium.

Number awarded Varies each year.

Deadline February of each year.

[443]
SUMMER RESEARCH PROGRAM IN ECOLOGY

Harvard University
Harvard Forest
324 North Main Street
Petersham, MA 01366
(978) 724-3302   Fax: (978) 724-3595
E-mail: hfapps@fas.harvard.edu
Web: harvardforest.fas.harvard.edu/other-tags/reu

Summary To provide an opportunity for undergraduate students and recent graduates, especially Asian Americans and members of other diverse groups, to participate in a summer ecological research project at Harvard Forest in Petersham, Massachusetts.

Eligibility This program is open to undergraduate students and recent graduates interested in participating in a mentored research project at the Forest. The research may relate to the effects of natural and human disturbances on forest ecosystems, including global climate change, hurricanes, forest harvest, changing wildlife dynamics, or invasive species. Investigators come from many disciplines, and specific projects center on population and community ecology, paleoecology, land use history, aquatic ecology, biochemistry, soil science, ecophysiology, and atmosphere-biosphere exchanges. Students from diverse backgrounds are strongly encouraged to apply.

Financial data The stipend is $5,775. Free housing, meals, and travel reimbursement for 1 round trip are also provided.

Duration 11 weeks during the summer.

Additional information Funding for this program is provided by the National Science Foundation (as part of its Research Experience for Undergraduates program).

Number awarded Up to 25 each year.

Deadline February of each year.

[444]
SUMMER TRANSPORTATION INTERNSHIP PROGRAM FOR DIVERSE GROUPS

Department of Transportation
Attn: Summer Transportation Internship Program for Diverse Groups
Eighth Floor E81-105
1200 New Jersey Avenue, S.E.
Washington, DC 20590
(202) 366-2907   E-mail: Crystal.Taylor@dot.gov
Web: www.fhwa.dot.gov/education/stipdg.cfm

Summary To enable Asian American and other diverse undergraduate, graduate, and law students to gain work experience during the summer at facilities of the U.S. Department of Transportation (DOT).

Eligibility This program is open to all qualified applicants, but it is designed to provide women, persons with disabilities, and members of diverse social and ethnic groups with summer opportunities in transportation. Applicants must be U.S. citizens currently enrolled in a degree-granting program of study at an accredited institution of higher learning at the undergraduate (community or junior college, university, college, or Tribal College or University) or graduate level. Undergraduates must be entering their junior or senior year; students attending a Tribal or community college must have completed their first year of school; law students must be entering their second or third year of school. Students who will graduate during the spring or summer are not eligible unless they have been accepted for enrollment in graduate school. The program accepts applications from students in all majors who are interested in working on transportation-related topics and issues. Preference is given to students with a GPA of 3.0 or higher. Undergraduates must submit a 1-page essay on their transportation interests and how participation in this program will enhance their educational and career plans and goals. Graduate students must submit a writing sample representing their educational and career plans and goals. Law students must submit a legal writing sample.

Financial data The stipend is $4,000 for undergraduates or $5,000 for graduate and law students. The program also provides housing and reimbursement of travel expenses from interns' homes to their assignment location.

Duration 10 weeks during the summer.

Additional information Assignments are at the DOT headquarters in Washington, D.C., a selected modal administration, or selected field offices around the country.

Number awarded 80 to 100 each year.

Deadline January of each year.

[445]
SUMMER UNDERGRADUATE RESEARCH FELLOWSHIPS IN ORGANIC CHEMISTRY

American Chemical Society
Division of Organic Chemistry
1155 16th Street, N.W.
Washington, DC 20036
(202) 872-4401   Toll Free: (800) 227-5558, ext. 4401
E-mail: division@acs.org
Web: www.organicdivision.org/?nd=p_surf_program

Summary To provide an opportunity for college juniors, especially Asian Americans and other minorities, to work on a research project in organic chemistry during the summer.

Eligibility This program is open to students who are currently enrolled as juniors at a college or university in the United States and are nominated by their school. Nominees must be interested in conducting a research project in organic chemistry at their home institution during the following summer. The project must be mentored by a member of the Organic Division of the American Chemical Society. Along with their application, students must submit brief statements on the project they propose to undertake, their background that has prepared them to do this work, their proposed methodology, and how a summer research project fits into their long-range plans. U.S. citizenship or permanent resident status is required. Selection is based on demonstrated interest and talent in organic chemistry, merit and feasibility of the research project, commitment of a faculty mentor to support the student, academic record (particularly in organic chemistry and related sciences), and importance of the award in facilitating the personal and career plans of the student. Applications from minorities are especially encouraged.

Financial data Grants range up to $5,000. The program also covers the costs of a trip by all participants to an industrial campus in the fall for a dinner, award session, scientific talks, a tour of the campus, and a poster session where the results of the summer research investigations are presented.

Duration Summer months.

Additional information Current corporate sponsors of this program include Pfizer and Cubist Pharmaceuticals.

Number awarded Up to 12 each year.

Deadline January of each year.

[446]
SURETY AND FIDELITY INDUSTRY SCHOLARSHIP PROGRAM

The Surety Foundation
Attn: Scholarship Program for Minority Students
1101 Connecticut Avenue, N.W., Suite 800
Washington, DC 20036
(202) 463-0600, ext. 638   Fax: (202) 463-0606
E-mail: scarradine@surety.org
Web: www.thesuretyfoundation.org

Summary To provide financial assistance to Asian Pacific American and other minority undergraduates working on a degree in a field related to insurance.

Eligibility This program is open to full-time undergraduates who are U.S. citizens and members of a minority group (Asian/Pacific Islander, Black, Native American/Alaskan Native, Hispanic). Applicants must have completed at least 30 semester hours of study at an accredited 4-year college or university and have a declared major in insurance/risk management, accounting, business, or finance. They must have a GPA of 3.0 or higher and be able to demonstrate financial need.

Financial data The stipend is $5,000 per year.

Duration 1 year; recipients may reapply.

Additional information This program, established in 2003 by The Surety & Fidelity Association of America, includes the Adrienne Alexander Scholarship and the George W. McClellan Scholarship.

Number awarded Varies each year; recently, 3 were awarded.

Deadline January of each year.

[447]
SUSHI TANGO SCHOLARSHIPS

Hmong American Education Fund
P.O. Box 17468
St. Paul, MN 55117
(651) 592-1576   E-mail: scholarships@thehaef.org
Web: www.thehaef.org

Summary To provide financial assistance to Hmong residents of Minnesota who are planning to attend college in any state.

Eligibility This program is open to residents of Minnesota who identify themselves as a person of Hmong descent. Applicants must be high school seniors or GED recipients planning to enroll full time at a 2- or 4-year college or university in any state. They must be U.S. citizens or permanent residents and have a GPA of 3.0 or higher. Along with their application, they must submit transcripts and a 1,500-word essay on their commitment to education, their financial need, how this scholarship can help them, and their community service.

Financial data The stipend is $500.

Duration 1 year; nonrenewable.

Additional information This program is supported by Mr. and Mrs. Pao Thao, owners of Sushi Tango restaurant.

Number awarded 2 each year.

Deadline March of each year.

[448]
SYNOD OF LAKES AND PRAIRIES RACIAL ETHNIC SCHOLARSHIPS

Synod of Lakes and Prairies
Attn: Committee on Racial Ethnic Ministry
2115 Cliff Drive
Eagen, MN 55122-3327
(651) 357-1140   Toll Free: (800) 328-1880, ext. 202
Fax: (651) 357-1141 E-mail: mkes@lakesandprairies.org
Web: www.lakesandprairies.org

Summary To provide financial assistance to Asian American and other minority residents of the Presbyterian Church (USA) Synod of Lakes and Prairies who are working on an undergraduate or graduate degree at a college or seminary in any state as preparation for service to the church.

Eligibility This program is open to members of Presbyterian churches who reside within the Synod of Lakes and Prairies (Iowa, Minnesota, Nebraska, North Dakota, South Dakota, and Wisconsin). Applicants must be members of ethnic minority groups studying at least half time for service in the Presbyterian Church (USA) as a teaching elder, ordained minister, commissioned ruling elder, lay professional, or volunteer. They must be in good academic standing, making progress toward an undergraduate or graduate degree, and able to demonstrate financial need. Along with their application, they must submit essays of 200 to 500 words on 1) what the church needs to do to be faithful to its mission in the world today; and 2) the people, practices, or events that influence their commitment to Christ in ways that renew their fair and strengthen their service.

Financial data Stipends range from $850 to $3,500.

Duration 1 year.

Number awarded Varies each year; recently, 9 were awarded.

Deadline September of each year.

[449]
SYNOD OF THE COVENANT RACIAL ETHNIC SCHOLARSHIPS

Synod of the Covenant
Attn: Ministries in Higher Education Committee
6450 Weatherfield Court, Unit 1A
Maumee, OH 43537
(419) 754-4050
Toll Free: (800) 848-1030 (within MI and OH)
Fax: (419) 754-4051
E-mail: SOC@synodofthecovenant.org
Web: www.synodofthecovenant.org/filing-cabinet

Summary To provide financial assistance to Asian American and other ethnic students working on an undergraduate degree (with priority given to Presbyterian applicants from Ohio and Michigan).

Eligibility This program is open to ethnic minority students working full or part time on a baccalaureate degree or certification at a college, university, or vocational school in any state. Applicants must have a GPA of 3.0 or higher and be able to demonstrate participation in a Presbyterian church. Priority is given to Presbyterian applicants from the states of Michigan and Ohio. Financial need is considered in the selection process.

Financial data The maximum amount allowed within a calendar year is $600 (for full-time students in their first year), $800 (for renewals to full-time students), or $400 (for part-time students). Funds are made payable to the session for distribution.

Duration Students are eligible to receive scholarships 1 time per year, up to a maximum of 5 years. Renewals are granted, provided 1) the completed application is received before the deadline date; 2) the recipient earned at least a 2.0 GPA last year; and 3) the application contains evidence of Presbyterian church participation and continued spiritual development.

Number awarded Varies each year; recently, 51 of these scholarships, with a total value of $40,000, were awarded.

Deadline August of each year for fall; January of each year for spring.

[450]
TAIWANESE AMERICAN COMMUNITY SCHOLARSHIP AWARD

Taiwan Culture Center
Attn: Taiwanese American Community Scholarship Award
P.O. Box 1838
Bethesda, MD 20817
E-mail: tacsa@TaiwanCultureCtr.org
Web: www.taiwanculturectr.org/new/scholarship

Summary To provide financial assistance to high school seniors in the Washington, D.C. metropolitan area, especially Taiwanese Americans, who plan to attend college in any state.

Eligibility This program is open to seniors graduating from high schools in the Washington, D.C. metropolitan area, defined to include the District of Columbia; the Maryland counties of Frederick, Howard, Montgomery, and Prince George's; the Virginia city of Alexandria; and the Virginia counties of Arlington, Fairfax, Loudoun, and Prince William. All qualified students from all ethnic groups are eligible if they are U.S. citizens or permanent residents, but a Taiwanese American Community Category is reserved for students who originated from Taiwan and whose parents, grandparents, or themselves have participated in Taiwanese American community activities. Applicants must submit a 250-word autobiography, a copy of their SAT/ACT score, their resume, transcripts, and a 500-word essay on their most rewarding experience from participation in community services. Selection is based on that essay (10%), academic achievement (30%), leadership (30%), community activities and services (20%), and extracurricular activities (10%).

Financial data The stipend is $500.

Duration 1 year.

Number awarded Varies each year; recently, 10 (4 from Maryland, 4 from Virginia, and 2 from Washington, D.C.) were awarded.

Deadline April of each year.

[451]
TAIWANESE AMERICAN FOUNDATION OF BOSTON COLLEGE AND UNIVERSITY SCHOLARSHIP PROGRAM

Taiwanese American Foundation of Boston
c/o C.Y. Wang
15 Crescent Road
Lexington, MA 02421
E-mail: info@taf-boston.org
Web: www.taf-boston.org/program.htm

Summary To provide funding to college juniors interested in conducting research or other projects related to Taiwanese studies.

Eligibility This program is open to current college juniors who are concentrating on Taiwanese studies or enrolled in a broader course in Asian studies. To apply, they must submit a resume or personal experience statement, a detailed proposal of the thesis to be written or project to be undertaken (up to 5 pages), and 2 letters of recommendation.

Financial data The maximum grant is $3,000.

Duration 1 year.

Additional information Recipients must submit a final report on their study or research, including an explanation of how grant funds were spent.

Number awarded 1 or more each year.

Deadline January or August of each year.

[452]
TAIWANESE AMERICAN SCHOLARSHIP FUND

Asian Pacific Community Fund
Attn: Taiwanese American Scholarship Fund
1145 Wilshire Boulevard, First Floor
Los Angeles, CA 90017
(213) 624-6400, ext. 6   Fax: (213) 624-6406
E-mail: scholarships@apcf.org
Web: www.tascholarshipfund.org

Summary To provide financial assistance to high school seniors and college freshmen who are of Taiwanese descent.

Eligibility This program is open to high school seniors and current first-year college students who reside in the United States. Applicants must be U.S. citizens and direct blood descendants of Taiwanese citizens who are enrolled or planning to enroll at a college or university in the United States. They must have a GPA of 3.0 or higher and a family income at or below the low level. All majors are eligible.

Financial data The stipend is $2,500.

Duration 1 year.

Additional information This program began in 2014.

Number awarded 14 each year.

Deadline March of each year.

[453]
TARGET APIASF SCHOLARSHIPS

Asian & Pacific Islander American Scholarship Fund
2025 M Street, N.W., Suite 610
Washington, DC 20036-3363
(202) 986-6892   Toll Free: (877) 808-7032
Fax: (202) 530-0643   E-mail: info@apiasf.org
Web: www.apiasf.org/scholarship_apiasf_target.html

Summary To provide financial assistance to Asian and Pacific Islander Americans who are upper-division students, especially those preparing for a career in pharmacy.

Eligibility This program is open to U.S. citizens, nationals, permanent residents, and citizens of the Freely Associated States who are upper-division college students and of Asian or Pacific Islander heritage. Applicants must be enrolled full time at an accredited college or university in the United States. They must have a GPA of 2.7 or higher or the GED equivalent. In addition, they must complete the FAFSA and apply for federal financial aid. Preference is given to applicants who are preparing for a career in pharmacy.

Financial data The stipend is $2,500.

Duration 1 year; nonrenewable.

Additional information This program is sponsored by Target Stores and administered by the Asian & Pacific Islander American Scholarship Fund (APIASF).

Number awarded Varies each year; recently, 8 were awarded.

Deadline January of each year.

[454]
TENNESSEE MINORITY TEACHING FELLOWS PROGRAM

Tennessee Student Assistance Corporation
Parkway Towers
404 James Robertson Parkway, Suite 1510
Nashville, TN 37243-0820
(615) 741-1346   Toll Free: (800) 342-1663
Fax: (615) 741-6101   E-mail: TSAC.Aidinfo@tn.gov
Web: www.tn.gov

Summary To provide scholarship/loans to Asian American and other minority residents of Tennessee who wish to attend college in the state to prepare for a career in the teaching field.

Eligibility This program is open to minority residents of Tennessee who are either high school seniors planning to enroll full time at a college or university in the state or continuing college students at a Tennessee college or university. High school seniors must have a GPA of 2.75 or higher and an ACT score of at least 18 or a combined mathematics and critical reading SAT score of at least 860. Continuing college students must have a college GPA of 2.5 or higher. All applicants must agree to teach at the K-12 level in a Tennessee public school following graduation from college. Along with their application, they must submit a 250-word essay on why they chose teaching as a profession. U.S. citizenship is required.

Financial data The scholarship/loan is $5,000 per year. Recipients incur an obligation to teach at the preK-12 level in a Tennessee public school 1 year for each year the award is received.

Duration 1 year; may be renewed for up to 3 additional years, provided the recipient maintains full-time enrollment and a cumulative GPA of 2.5 or higher.

Additional information This program began in 1989.

Number awarded 20 new awards are granted each year.

Deadline April of each year.

[455]
TEXAS CHAPTER AAJA SCHOLARSHIPS

Asian American Journalists Association-Texas Chapter
c/o Alanna Quillen, President
KTBS 3 News
312 East Kings Highway
Shreveport, LA 71104
(318) 861-5800   E-mail: alanna.quillen@gmail.com
Web: www.aajatexas.org/programs/student-programs

Summary   To provide financial assistance to students from designated southwestern states who are working on an undergraduate or graduate degree in journalism and can demonstrate an awareness of Asian American issues.

Eligibility   This program is open to graduating high school seniors, undergraduates, and graduate students who are either 1) residents of Arkansas, Louisiana, New Mexico, Oklahoma, or Texas; or 2) attending or planning to attend an accredited college or university in those states. Applicants are not required to be members of the Asian American Journalists Association (AAJA). Along with their application, they must submit a 250-word autobiography that explains why they are interested in a career in journalism, a 500-word essay on the role of ethnic diversity in news coverage (both for the subjects of the news events and the journalists involved), their most recent official transcript, 2 letters of recommendation, and a resume. Work samples to be submitted are 3 legible clips from print journalism students; 3 to 5 prints or slides with captions or descriptions from print photojournalism students; 3 to 5 samples of work from design journalism students; 2 taped VHS or DVD excerpts with corresponding scripts from television broadcast students; 2 edited VHS or DVD excepts from television photojournalism students; 3 taped cassette excerpts with corresponding scripts from radio broadcast students; or 3 legible online articles from web journalism students. Selection is based on commitment to journalism, awareness of Asian American issues, journalistic ability, and scholastic ability.

Financial data   The stipend is $1,000.

Duration   1 year.

Additional information   Scholarship winners are also given a 1-year free membership in the AAJA Texas chapter.

Number awarded   2 each year.

Deadline   May of each year.

[456]
THAI-AMERICAN ASSOCIATION OF ILLINOIS SCHOLARSHIP FUND

Thai-American Association of Illinois
c/o Dr. Ninnart Sathissarat
7059 West 75th Street
Chicago, IL 60638
(815) 254-0976   E-mail: drsat87@hotmail.com

Summary   To provide financial assistance to high school seniors in Illinois who are of Thai descent and planning to attend college in any state.

Eligibility   This program is open to seniors graduating from high schools in Illinois who are of Thai descent. Applicants must be planning to enroll at a college or university in any state. They must have a GPA of 2.75 or higher and be able to demonstrate financial need. Along with their application, they must submit an essay of 1 to 2 pages about their family and their goals in life.

Financial data   The stipend is $500.

Duration   1 year.

Additional information   This program began in 2011.

Number awarded   3 each year.

Deadline   September of each year.

[457]
THE ANHELO PROJECT DREAM SCHOLARSHIP

The Anhelo Project
c/o Joanna Maravilla-Cano
P.O. Box 08290
Chicago, IL 60608
(773) 609-4252
E-mail: dreamscholarshipchicago@gmail.com
Web: theanheloproject.org/dream-scholarship

Summary   To provide financial assistance to undocumented residents of Illinois who are attending college in Chicago.

Eligibility   This program is open to undocumented students who are residents of Illinois. Applicants must be enrolled full time at an accredited college or university in Chicago and have completed at least 12 credit hours with a cumulative GPA of 2.75 or higher. They must be able to demonstrate leadership through community involvement (on and/or off campus) and financial need. Holders of F-1 student visas and international students are not eligible.

Financial data   A stipend is awarded (amount not specified).

Duration   1 year.

Additional information   Recipients must commit 20 hours of volunteer time to The Anhelo Project events during the following academic year.

Number awarded   Varies each year.

Deadline   March of each year.

[458]
THE CLOISTERS SUMMER INTERNSHIP FOR COLLEGE STUDENTS

Metropolitan Museum of Art
Attn: The Cloisters
Fort Tryon Park
New York, NY 10040
(212) 650-2280 E-mail: cloistersinterns@metmuseum.org
Web: www.metmuseum.org

Summary   To provide art museum work experience during the summer at The Cloisters of the Metropolitan Museum of Art to college students, especially Asian Americans or members of other diverse groups, who are majoring in art or museum studies.

Eligibility   This program is open to undergraduate students, especially freshmen and sophomores, who are interested in art and museum careers. They must enjoy working with children, have an interest in medieval art, and be willing to intern at the Metropolitan Museum of Art. Applicants of diverse backgrounds are particularly encouraged to apply.

Financial data   The internship stipend is $3,150.

Duration   9 weeks, beginning in June.

Additional information Interns are assigned to the education department of The Cloisters, the branch museum of the Metropolitan Museum of Art devoted to the art of medieval Europe. They conduct gallery workshops for New York City day campers. This program is funded in part by the Norman and Rosita Winston Foundation, Inc.

Number awarded 8 each year.

Deadline January of each year.

[459]
THE HIGH-REACHING, UNDERPRIVILEGED STUDENTS TO SECURE ASSISTANCE FOR INTELLECTUAL NEEDS (HUSSAIN) SCHOLARSHIP

Philadelphia Foundation
1234 Market Street, Suite 1800
Philadelphia, PA 19107-3794
(215) 563-6417 Fax: (215) 563-6882
E-mail: scholarships@philafound.org
Web: www.philafound.org

Summary To provide financial assistance to residents of any state who are of South Asian ancestry and attending college in the Philadelphia region.

Eligibility This program is open to students from any state whose descent is from a member country of the South Asian Association for Regional Cooperation (SAARC): Afghanistan, Bangladesh, Bhutan, Indian, Maldives, Nepal, Pakistan, and Sri Lanka. Applicants must be enrolled at a college or university in the Philadelphia region. They must have a GPA of 3.0 or higher and be able to demonstrate the potential to succeed despite adversity. Along with their application, they must submit an essay the covers the details of the adversity they are overcoming or have overcome, the accomplishments they have achieved despite their adversity, and their current/future educational goals and the ways (if any) in which their adversity has influenced those goals.

Financial data The stipend is $1,000.

Duration 1 year; nonrenewable.

Additional information This program was established by Dr. Fahmida Hussain to honor her father.

Number awarded 1 each year.

Deadline May of each year.

[460]
THE REV. J.K. FUKUSHIMA SCHOLARSHIP

Montebello Plymouth Congregational Church
144 South Greenwood Avenue
Montebello, CA 90640
(323) 721-5568 Fax: (323) 721-7955
E-mail: mpccucc@gmail.com
Web: www.montebelloucc.org

Summary To provide financial assistance to undergraduate and graduate students who are preparing for a career in Christian ministry and can demonstrate a commitment to the Asian American community.

Eligibility This program is open to 1) third- or fourth-year college students; and 2) graduate and professional students who have not completed a bachelor's or master's degree in theological studies. Applicants must be enrolled or have been accepted at an accredited school of theology. They must be working on a degree that will provide them with the skills and understanding necessary to further the development of Christian ministries. Along with their application, they must submit an essay on their commitment to the Asian American community.

Financial data The stipend is $500.

Duration 1 year.

Number awarded 1 or more each year.

Deadline May of each year.

[461]
THEDREAM.US SCHOLARSHIPS

TheDream.US
c/o International Scholarship and Tuition Services, Inc.
1321 Murfreesboro Road, Suite 800
Nashville, TN 37217
Toll Free: (855) 670-ISTS
E-mail: contactus@applyists.com
Web: www.thedream.us/scholars

Summary To provide financial assistance to students from any state who qualify for Deferred Action for Childhood Arrivals (DACA) or Temporary Protected Status (TPS) and wish to attend designated partner colleges in designated states.

Eligibility This program is open to students who came to the United States prior to their 16th birthday, are DACA or TPS eligible, and have applied for or received DACA or TPS approval. Applicants may reside in any state but they must be interested in working full time on an associate or bachelor's degree at an approved partner college in Arizona, California, Florida, Illinois, New York, Texas, Virginia, or Washington, D.C. and be eligible for in-state tuition (if applicable). They may be 1) first-time college students who are graduating from high school, earning a GED diploma, or have already graduated or earned a GED diploma; have an unweighted high school GPA of 2.5 or higher; and demonstrate significant unmet financial need; or 2) community college graduates who are earning an associate degree or have earned an associate degree; have not yet enrolled in a bachelor's degree program; have a college GPA of 3.0 or higher; and demonstrate significant unmet financial need. Along with their application, they must submit 200-word essays on 1) their educational and career goals; and 2) a challenging family or personal circumstance that affected their achievement or participation in school, work, or community activities and how they overcame it.

Financial data Support is provided up to a total of $12,500 for an associate degree or $25,000 for a bachelor's degree.

Duration 1 year; may be renewed until completion of an associate or bachelor's degree, provided the recipient maintains a GPA of 3.0 or higher, remains enrolled full time, continues to qualify for DACA or TPS, and remains current on all their college accounts and charged.

Additional information For a list of partner colleges, contact TheDream.US. Scholarship America is the fiscal sponsor for this program. International Scholarship and Tuition Services administers it.

Number awarded Varies each year.

Deadline March of each year.

[462]
THOMAS DARGAN MINORITY SCHOLARSHIP

KATU-TV
Attn: Human Resources
2153 N.E. Sandy Boulevard
P.O. Box 2
Portland, OR 97207-0002
(503) 231-4222
Web: www.katu.com

Summary To provide financial assistance to Asian American and other minority students from Oregon and Washington who are studying broadcasting or communications in college.

Eligibility This program is open to minority (Asian, Black/African American, Hispanic or Latino, Native Hawaiian or Pacific Islander, American Indian or Alaska Native) U.S. citizens, currently enrolled as a sophomore or higher at a 4-year college or university or an accredited community college in Oregon or Washington. Residents of Oregon or Washington enrolled at a school in any state are also eligible. Applicants must be majoring in broadcasting or communications and have a GPA of 3.0 or higher. Community college students must be enrolled in a broadcast curriculum that is transferable to a 4-year accredited university. Finalists are interviewed. Selection is based on financial need, academic achievement, and an essay on personal and professional goals.

Financial data The stipend is $6,000. Funds are sent directly to the recipient's school.

Duration 1 year; recipients may reapply if they have maintained a GPA of 3.0 or higher.

Additional information Winners are also eligible for a paid internship in selected departments at Fisher Broadcasting/KATU in Portland, Oregon.

Number awarded 1 each year.

Deadline April of each year.

[463]
THOMAS G. NEUSOM SCHOLARSHIPS

Conference of Minority Transportation Officials
Attn: National Scholarship Program
100 M Street, S.E., Suite 917
Washington, DC 20003
(202) 506-2917   E-mail: info@comto.org
Web: www.comto.org/page/scholarships

Summary To provide financial assistance for college or graduate school to Asian American and other minority members of the Conference of Minority Transportation Officials (COMTO) and their families.

Eligibility This program is open to undergraduate and graduate students who have been members of COMTO or whose parents, guardians, or grandparents have been members for at least 1 year. Applicants must be working (either full or part time) on a degree in a field related to transportation and have a GPA of 2.5 or higher. Along with their application they must submit a cover letter on their transportation-related career goals and life aspirations. Financial need is not considered in the selection process.

Financial data The stipend is $5,500. Funds are paid directly to the recipient's college or university.

Duration 1 year.

Number awarded 1 each year.

Deadline April of each year.

[464]
THOMAS R. PICKERING FOREIGN AFFAIRS FELLOWSHIPS

The Washington Center for Internships
Attn: Foreign Affairs Fellowship Program
1333 16th Street, N.W.
Washington, DC 20036-2205
(202) 238-7900   Fax: (202) 238-7700
E-mail: info@twc.org
Web: www.twc.edu

Summary To provide forgivable loans to undergraduate and graduate students, especially Asian Americans or members of other underrepresented groups, who are interested in preparing for a career with the Department of State's Foreign Service.

Eligibility This program is open to U.S. citizens who are entering their senior year of undergraduate study or their first year of graduate study. Applicants must be planning to work on a 2-year full-time master's degree program relevant to the work of the U.S. Foreign Service, including public policy, international affairs, public administration, business, economics, political science, sociology, or foreign languages. They must be preparing for a career in the Foreign Service. Applications are especially encouraged from women, members of minority groups historically underrepresented in the Foreign Service, and students with financial need.

Financial data The program pays for tuition, room, board, books, mandatory fees, and 1 round-trip ticket from the fellow's residence to academic institution, to a maximum of $37,500 per academic year.

Duration 2 years: the senior year of undergraduate study and the first year of graduate study for college seniors; the first 2 years of graduate school for entering graduate students.

Additional information This program is funded by the State Department and administered by The Washington Center for Internships. Fellows must commit to a minimum of 5 years of service in an appointment as a Foreign Service Officer following graduation and successful completion of the Foreign Service examination. If they fail to fulfill that commitment, they must refund all money received.

Number awarded Approximately 40 each year: 20 college seniors and 20 entering graduate students.

Deadline January of each year.

[465]
THZ FO FARM SCHOLARSHIP

Hawai'i Community Foundation
Attn: Scholarship Department
827 Fort Street Mall
Honolulu, HI 96813
(808) 566-5570   Toll Free: (888) 731-3863
Fax: (808) 521-6286
E-mail: scholarships@hcf-hawaii.org
Web: hcf.scholarships.ngwebsolutions.com

Summary To provide financial assistance to Hawaii residents of Chinese descent who are interested in working on an undergraduate or graduate degree in any field at a school in any state.

Eligibility This program is open to residents of Hawaii who are of Chinese ancestry and interested in studying any field as full-time undergraduate or graduate students at an accredited 2- or 4-year college or university in any state. Applicants must be able to demonstrate academic achievement (GPA of 2.7 or higher), good moral character, and financial need. Along with their application, they must submit a short statement indicating their reasons for attending college, their planned course of study, their career goals, and what community service means to them.

Financial data The amounts of the awards depend on the availability of funds and the need of the recipient. Recently, the average value of the scholarships awarded by the foundation was $2,800.

Duration 1 year.

Number awarded Varies each year; recently, 6 were awarded.

Deadline February of each year.

[466]
TONGAN CULTURAL SOCIETY SCHOLARSHIPS

Hawai'i Community Foundation
Attn: Scholarship Department
827 Fort Street Mall
Honolulu, HI 96813
(808) 566-5570   Toll Free: (888) 731-3863
Fax: (808) 521-6286
E-mail: scholarships@hcf-hawaii.org
Web: hcf.scholarships.ngwebsolutions.com

Summary To provide financial assistance to Hawaii residents of Tongan ancestry who are interested in attending college or graduate school in the state.

Eligibility This program is open to Hawaii residents of Tongan ancestry who are enrolled or planning to enroll at an accredited 4-year college or university in Hawaii. Applicants must be full-time undergraduate or graduate students and able to demonstrate academic achievement (GPA of 2.7 or higher), good moral character, and financial need. Along with their application, they must submit a short statement indicating their reasons for attending college, their planned course of study, their career goals, and what community service means to them.

Financial data The amounts of the awards depend on the availability of funds and the need of the recipient. Recently, the average value of the scholarships awarded by the foundation was $2,800.

Duration 1 year.

Number awarded Varies each year; recently, 3 were awarded.

Deadline February of each year.

[467]
TOUBY LYFOUNG MEMORIAL SCHOLARSHIP

Hmong American Education Fund
P.O. Box 17468
St. Paul, MN 55117
(651) 592-1576   E-mail: scholarships@thehaef.org
Web: www.thehaef.org

Summary To provide financial assistance to Hmong residents of any state who come from a lower middle class family and are interested in working on an undergraduate or graduate degree in any field.

Eligibility This program is open to students of Hmong descent who are high school seniors, GED recipients, or current full-time undergraduate or graduate students at 2- or 4-year colleges or universities in any state. Applicants must be U.S. citizens or permanent residents and have a GPA of 3.4 or higher. They must come from a lower middle class family. Along with their application, they must submit a 1,500-word essay on their commitment to education, their leadership qualities, their financial need, how this scholarship can help them, and their community service. Selection is based on academic excellence, leadership qualities, commitment to helping their community, and financial need or need based on hardship.

Financial data The stipend is $1,000.

Duration 1 year; nonrenewable.

Number awarded 1 each year.

Deadline March of each year.

[468]
TRAILBLAZER SCHOLARSHIP

Conference of Minority Transportation Officials
Attn: National Scholarship Program
100 M Street, S.E., Suite 917
Washington, DC 20003
(202) 506-2917   E-mail: info@comto.org
Web: www.comto.org/page/scholarships

Summary To provide financial assistance for college or graduate school to Asian American and other minority members of the Conference of Minority Transportation Officials (COMTO) and their families.

Eligibility This program is open to undergraduate and graduate students who have been members of COMTO or whose parents, guardians, or grandparents have been members for at least 1 year. Applicants must be working (either full or part time) on a degree in a field related to transportation and have a GPA of 2.5 or higher. Along with their application they must submit a cover letter on their transportation-related career goals and life aspirations. Financial need is not considered in the selection process.

Financial data The stipend is $2,500. Funds are paid directly to the recipient's college or university.

Duration 1 year.

Number awarded 1 each year.

Deadline April of each year.

[469]
TRANSPORTATION INDUSTRY COLLEGE SCHOLARSHIP

Conference of Minority Transportation Officials-Fort
  Lauderdale Chapter
Attn: Scholarship Committee
Victor Garcia, South Florida Regional Transportation
  Authority
801 N.W. 33rd Street
Pompano Beach, FL 33064
(954) 788-7925   Toll Free: (800) GO-SFRTA
Fax: (854) 788-7961   TDD: (800) 273-7545
E-mail: victorgarcia@comtoftlauderdale.org
Web: www.comtoftlauderdale.org/scholarship-program

Summary   To provide financial assistance to Asian American and other minority students working on a transportation-related undergraduate degree at a college in Florida.

Eligibility   This program is open to minority students currently enrolled at accredited colleges and universities in Florida. Applicants must be majoring in a transportation-related field and have a GPA of 2.5 or higher. They must be U.S. citizens or permanent residents. Along with their application, they must submit an essay of 500 to 750 words on their transportation-related career goals and life aspirations. Financial need is not considered in the selection process.

Financial data   The stipend is $1,500.

Duration   1 year; nonrenewable.

Additional information   This program began in 2015.

Number awarded   1 each year.

Deadline   April of each year.

[470]
TYLER J. VINEY MEMORIAL SCHOLARSHIP

Texas Society of Architects
Attn: Texas Architectural Foundation
500 Chicon Street
Austin, TX 78702
(512) 478-7386   Fax: (512) 478-0528
E-mail: foundation@texasarchitect.org
Web: www.texasarchitects.org/v/scholarships

Summary   To provide financial assistance to residents of any state, especially Asian Americans and other minorities, who are entering their fourth or fifth year of study at a school of architecture in Texas.

Eligibility   This program is open to residents of any state who are entering their fourth or fifth year of study at 1 of the 8 schools of architecture in Texas. Applicants must submit their application to the office of the dean of their school. Along with their application, they must submit essays on 1) the principal architectural areas or practice categories in which they are most interested, excel, or desire to develop their proficiency; and 2) career plans, short/long-range goals, vision, or other topic about which they are passionate. Selection is based on potential architectural talent, demonstrated interest in photography, and financial need. Priority is given to female and minority students.

Financial data   The stipend ranges up to $2,000.

Duration   1 year.

Number awarded   1 each year.

Deadline   February of each year.

[471]
UNITED HEALTH FOUNDATION APIASF SCHOLARSHIP

Asian & Pacific Islander American Scholarship Fund
2025 M Street, N.W., Suite 610
Washington, DC 20036-3363
(202) 986-6892   Toll Free: (877) 808-7032
Fax: (202) 530-0643   E-mail: info@apiasf.org
Web: www.apiasf.org/scholarship_apiasf_uhf.html

Summary   To provide financial assistance to Asian and Pacific Islander Americans from designated states who are entering the second year of college to prepare for a career in the health field.

Eligibility   This program is open to U.S. citizens, nationals, permanent residents, or citizens of the Freely Associated States who are of Asian or Pacific Islander heritage and reside in Arizona, California, Colorado, Florida, Georgia, Hawaii, Kansas, Minnesota, Nevada, New Mexico, New York, North Carolina, Tennessee, Texas, Washington, or Wisconsin. Applicants must be enrolling full time at an accredited 2- or 4-year college or university in the United States as a second-year student. They must have a GPA of 2.7 or higher or the GED equivalent and be preparing for a career in the health field (e.g., general practitioner, internist, family practitioner, ON/GYN, dentist, public health professional, mental health professional, nurse, physician assistant, pharmacist). In addition, they must complete the FAFSA and apply for federal financial aid. Preference is given to students who demonstrate the intent to work in an underserved community.

Financial data   The stipend is $5,000 per year.

Duration   3 years.

Additional information   This scholarship is sponsored by the United Health Foundation and administered by the Asian & Pacific Islander American Scholarship Fund (APIASF).

Number awarded   Varies each year; recently, 12 were awarded.

Deadline   January of each year.

[472]
UNITED METHODIST ETHNIC SCHOLARSHIPS

United Methodist Church
Attn: General Board of Higher Education and Ministry
Office of Loans and Scholarships
1001 19th Avenue South
P.O. Box 340007
Nashville, TN 37203-0007
(615) 340-7344   Fax: (615) 340-7367
E-mail: umscholar@gbhem.org
Web: www.gbhem.org

Summary   To provide financial assistance to undergraduate Methodist students who are Asian Americans of other ethnic minority ancestry.

Eligibility   This program is open to full-time undergraduate students at accredited colleges and universities in the United States who have been active, full members of a United Methodist Church for at least 1 year prior to applying. Applicants must have at least 1 parent who is Asian, African American, Hispanic, Native American, or Pacific Islander. They must have a GPA of 2.5 or higher and be able to demonstrate financial need. U.S. citizenship, permanent resident status, or membership in a central conference of the United Methodist

Church is required. Selection is based on church membership, involvement in church and community activities, GPA, and financial need.

Financial data Stipends range from $500 to $900.

Duration 1 year; recipients may reapply.

Number awarded Varies each year.

Deadline February of each year.

[473]
UNITED METHODIST FOUNDATION COLLEGE AND UNIVERSITY MERIT SCHOLARS PROGRAM

United Methodist Higher Education Foundation
Attn: Scholarships Administrator
60 Music Square East, Suite 350
P.O. Box 340005
Nashville, TN 37203-0005
(615) 649-3974   Toll Free: (800) 811-8110
Fax: (615) 649-3980
E-mail: umhefscholarships@umhef.org
Web: www.umhef.org

Summary To provide financial assistance to undergraduate students, especially Asian Americans and other minorities, who are attending colleges and universities affiliated with the United Methodist Church.

Eligibility This program is open to freshmen, sophomores, juniors, and seniors at United Methodist-related 4-year colleges and universities and to freshmen and sophomores at 2-year colleges. Nominees must have been active members of the United Methodist Church for at least 1 year prior to application. They must be planning to enroll full time and have a GPA of 3.0 or higher. Preference is given to ethnic minority and first generation college students. Financial need is considered in the selection process. U.S. citizenship or permanent resident status is required.

Financial data The stipend is $2,000.

Duration 1 year; nonrenewable.

Additional information Students may obtain applications from their school.

Number awarded 420 each year: 1 to a member of each class at each school.

Deadline Nominations from schools must be received by September of each year.

[474]
UNITED PARCEL SERVICE SCHOLARSHIP FOR MINORITY STUDENTS

Institute of Industrial and Systems Engineers
Attn: Scholarship Coordinator
3577 Parkway Lane, Suite 200
Norcross, GA 30092
(770) 449-0461, ext. 105   Toll Free: (800) 494-0460
Fax: (770) 441-3295   E-mail: bcameron@iisenet.org
Web: www.iienet2.org/Details.aspx?id=857

Summary To provide financial assistance to Asian American and other minority undergraduates who are studying industrial engineering at a school in the United States, Canada, or Mexico.

Eligibility Eligible to be nominated are minority undergraduate students enrolled at any school in the United States or its territories, Canada, or Mexico, provided the school's engineering program is accredited by an agency recognized by the Institute of Industrial and Systems Engineers (IISE) and the student is pursuing a full-time course of study in industrial engineering with a GPA of at least 3.4. Nominees must have at least 5 full quarters or 3 full semesters remaining until graduation. Students may not apply directly for these awards; they must be nominated by the head of their industrial engineering department. Nominees must be IISE members. Selection is based on scholastic ability, character, leadership, and potential service to the industrial engineering profession.

Financial data The stipend is $4,000.

Duration 1 year.

Additional information Funding for this program is provided by the UPS Foundation.

Number awarded 1 each year.

Deadline Schools must submit nominations by November of each year.

[475]
UPAKAR COMMUNITY COLLEGE SCHOLARSHIPS

Upakar: Indian American Scholarship Foundation
9101 Friars Road
Bethesda, MD 20817
E-mail: upakarfoundation@hotmail.com
Web: www.upakarfoundation.org

Summary To provide financial assistance to Asian Indian high school seniors who plan to attend a community college and major in any field.

Eligibility This program is open to graduating high school seniors who either were born or have at least 1 parent who was born in India. Applicants must be planning to enroll at a community college and then transfer to a 4-year institution. They must be U.S. citizens or permanent residents and have a GPA of 3.6 or higher. Their family income must be less than $75,000 per year.

Financial data The stipend is $500 per year for the first 2 years and $2,000 per year for the remaining 2 years.

Duration Up to 4 years, provided the recipient maintains a GPA of 3.3 or higher.

Additional information This program began in 2013.

Number awarded 1 or more each year.

Deadline April of each year.

[476]
UPAKAR SCHOLARSHIPS

Upakar: Indian American Scholarship Foundation
9101 Friars Road
Bethesda, MD 20817
E-mail: upakarfoundation@hotmail.com
Web: www.upakarfoundation.org

Summary To provide financial assistance to Asian Indian high school seniors who plan to attend a 4-year college and major in any field.

Eligibility This program is open to graduating high school seniors who either were born or have at least 1 parent who was born in India. Applicants must be planning to enroll at a 4-year college or university and major in any field. They must be U.S. citizens or permanent residents and have a GPA of 3.6 or higher. Their family income must be less than $75,000 per year.

Financial data The stipend is $2,000 per year.

Duration Up to 4 years, provided the recipient maintains a GPA of 3.3 or higher.

Number awarded Varies each year; recently, 6 were awarded.

Deadline April of each year.

[477]
UPS/CIC FOUNDATION SCHOLARSHIPS

Wisconsin Association of Independent Colleges and
Universities
Attn: Senior Vice President for Educational Services
122 West Washington Avenue, Suite 700
Madison, WI 53703-2723
(608) 256-7761, ext. 223   Fax: (608) 256-7065
E-mail: carole.trone@waicu.org
Web: www.waicu.org

Summary To provide financial assistance to students at member institution of the Wisconsin Association of Independent Colleges and Universities (WAICU) who are Asian Americans or members of other designated target populations.

Eligibility This program is open to students enrolled full time at WAICU member colleges or universities. The background of applicants must reflect 1 or more of the components of the target population for the UPS Foundation and the First Opportunity Program of the Council of Independent Colleges (CIC): first generation, low-income, minority, or new American students.

Financial data The stipend is $2,600.

Duration 1 year.

Additional information The WAICU member schools are Alverno College, Bellin College, Beloit College, Cardinal Stritch University, Carroll College, Carthage College, Columbia College of Nursing, Concordia University of Wisconsin, Edgewood College, Lakeland College, Lawrence University, Marian College, Marquette University, Medical College of Wisconsin, Milwaukee Institute of Art & Design, Milwaukee School of Engineering, Mount Mary College, Nashotah House Theological Seminary, Northland College, Ripon College, St. Norbert College, Silver Lake College of the Holy Family, Viterbo University, and Wisconsin Lutheran College. This program is supported by the UPS Foundation and administered nationally through CIC.

Number awarded Up to 24 each year: 1 at each of the member schools.

Deadline Each participating college sets its own deadline.

[478]
UPS DIVERSITY SCHOLARSHIPS OF THE AMERICAN SOCIETY OF SAFETY ENGINEERS

American Society of Safety Engineers
Attn: ASSE Foundation
Scholarship Award Program
520 North Northwest Highway
Park Ridge, IL 60068-2538
(847) 699-2929   Fax: (847) 296-3769
E-mail: assefoundation@asse.org
Web: foundation.asse.org/scholarships-and-grants

Summary To provide financial assistance to Asian American and other minority upper-division students working on a degree related to occupational safety.

Eligibility This program is open to students who are U.S. citizens and members of minority ethnic or racial groups. Applicants must be majoring in occupational safety, health, environment, industrial hygiene, occupational health nursing, or a closely-related field (e.g., industrial or environmental engineering). They must be full-time students who have completed at least 60 semester hours and have a GPA of 3.0 or higher. Membership in the American Society of Safety Engineers (ASSE) is not required, but preference is given to members.

Financial data The stipend is $5,250 per year.

Duration 1 year; recipients may reapply.

Additional information Funding for this program is provided by the UPS Foundation. Recipients may also be provided with the opportunity to attend a professional development conference related to safety.

Number awarded 3 each year.

Deadline November of each year.

[479]
US PAN ASIAN AMERICAN CHAMBER OF COMMERCE/DENNY'S HUNGRY FOR EDUCATION SCHOLARSHIP

US Pan Asian American Chamber of Commerce
Attn: Scholarship Coordinator
1329 18th Street, N.W.
Washington, DC 20036
(202) 296-5221   Toll Free: (800) 696-7818
Fax: (202) 296-5225   E-mail: info@uspaacc.com
Web: www.uspaacc.com/programs/college-scholarships

Summary To provide financial assistance for college to Asian Pacific American high school seniors who submit outstanding essays on childhood hunger.

Eligibility This program is open to high school seniors of Asian or Pacific Islander heritage who are U.S. citizens or permanent residents. Applicants must have a GPA of 3.3 or higher. Along with their application, they must submit a 300-word essay on how Denny's can impact childhood hunger in their community.

Financial data The stipend is $3,000. Funds are paid directly to the recipient's college or university.

Duration 1 year.

Additional information This program is sponsored by Denny's as 1 of its Hungry for Education scholarship activities.

Number awarded 1 or more each year.

Deadline March of each year.

[480]
US PAN ASIAN AMERICAN CHAMBER OF COMMERCE SCHOLARSHIPS

US Pan Asian American Chamber of Commerce
Attn: Scholarship Coordinator
1329 18th Street, N.W.
Washington, DC 20036
(202) 296-5221   Toll Free: (800) 696-7818
Fax: (202) 296-5225   E-mail: info@uspaacc.com
Web: www.celebrasianconference.com/scholarships

Summary To provide financial assistance for college to Asian Pacific American high school seniors who demonstrate financial need.

Eligibility This program is open to high school seniors of Asian or Pacific Islander heritage who are U.S. citizens or permanent residents. Applicants must be planning to enroll full time at an accredited postsecondary educational institution in the United States. Along with their application, they must submit a 500-word essay on their background, achievements, and personal goals. Selection is based on academic excellence (GPA of 3.3 or higher), leadership in extracurricular activities, community service involvement, and financial need.

Financial data Stipends range from $2,500 to $5,000. Funds are paid directly to the recipient's college or university.

Duration 1 year.

Additional information This program includes awards named after sponsoring corporations; recently, those included Ampcus, Chen Foundation, CVS Caremark, Enterprise Holdings, Ingersoll Rand, National Capitol Contracting, PepsiCo, Sai Systems International, and UPS Foundation. Funding is not provided for correspondence courses, Internet courses, or study in a country other than the United States.

Number awarded Varies each year; recently, 19, worth $77,000, were awarded.

Deadline March of each year.

[481]
UTAH ASIAN CHARITABLE FOUNDATION SCHOLARSHIP

Utah Asian Charitable Foundation
c/o Utah Asian Chamber of Commerce
P.O. Box 3178
Salt Lake City, UT 84110-3178
(801) 915-6333   E-mail: info@utahasianchamber.com

Summary To provide financial assistance to Asian students enrolled at colleges in Utah.

Eligibility This program is open to Asian students in Utah who either 1) can demonstrate financial need; or 2) have demonstrated strong scholarship, leadership, and community service. Applicants must be enrolled as undergraduates at a college, university, or other institution of higher learning within the state. Along with their application, they must submit a brief personal history that includes 1) academic, professional, and personal goals; 2) reasons why they feel they are a viable candidate for this scholarship; 3) scholarly or vocational accomplishments, honors, special awards, or recognition they have received; 4) community and school involvement; and 5) personal barriers or hardships they have had to overcome to achieve their educational goals.

Financial data The stipend ranges from $500 to $1,500 per year.

Duration 1 year; may be renewed up to 2 additional years.

Number awarded 5 or 6 each year.

Deadline April of each year.

[482]
VALLEY DENTAL ARTS SCHOLARSHIP

Hmong American Education Fund
P.O. Box 17468
St. Paul, MN 55117
(651) 592-1576   E-mail: scholarships@thehaef.org
Web: www.thehaef.org

Summary To provide financial assistance to Hmong residents of Minnesota who are interested in attending college in any state to study science or engineering.

Eligibility This program is open to residents of Minnesota who identify themselves as a person of Hmong descent. Applicants must be high school seniors, GED recipients, or current undergraduate students enrolled or planning to enroll full time at a 2- or 4-year college or university in any state. They must be U.S. citizens or permanent residents and have a GPA of 3.0 or higher. Their field of study must be science, engineering, or a related field. Along with their application, they must submit transcripts and a 1,500-word essay on their commitment to education, commitment to community service, and financial need, difficulties, or hardships.

Financial data The stipend is $500.

Duration 1 year; nonrenewable.

Additional information Support for this program is provided by Valley Dental Arts.

Number awarded 1 each year.

Deadline March of each year.

[483]
VASF ELEVATE SCHOLARSHIP

Vietnamese American Scholarship Foundation
P.O. Box 429
Stafford, TX 77497
E-mail: scholarships@vietscholarships.org
Web: www.vietscholarships.org/elevate.html

Summary To provide financial assistance to residents of any state who are of Vietnamese descent and interested in attending college.

Eligibility This program is open to residents of any state who are of Vietnamese descent and either seniors graduating from high school or students already enrolled at an accredited 4-year college or university. Applicants must have a GPA of 3.5 or higher and be able to demonstrate financial need. Along with their application, they must submit a 1,000-word essay on a project, experience, or person related to their academic and/or career goals that inspired them. They must have a record of academic excellence, community service, and leadership.

Financial data The stipend is $2,000.

Duration 1 year; nonrenewable.

Number awarded 1 each year.

Deadline May of each year.

[484]
VIETNAMESE AMERICAN DREAMS SCHOLARSHIP

New England Intercollegiate Vietnamese Student
  Association
c/o Tamm Bui, Scholarship Chair
34 Buswell Street
Box 5
Boston, MA 02215
(617) 646-9090   E-mail: newenglandivsa@gmail.com
Web: neivsa.weebly.com/dreams-scholarship.html

Summary To provide financial assistance to New England high school seniors of Vietnamese descent who plan to attend college in any state.

Eligibility This program is open to seniors graduating from high schools in New England who are of Vietnamese descent. Applicants must be planning to enroll at a college or university in any state. Along with their application, they must submit 500-word essays on their choice of 2 assigned topics that relate to their Vietnamese heritage and their work as an entering college student. Selection is based on academics, community involvement, and character. Finalists are contacted for interviews.

Financial data The stipend is $1,000.

Duration 1 year.

Additional information This program began in 2001.

Number awarded At least 1 each year.

Deadline March of each year.

[485]
VINCENT CHIN MEMORIAL SCHOLARSHIP

Asian American Journalists Association
Attn: Student Programs Coordinator
5 Third Street, Suite 1108
San Francisco, CA 94103
(415) 346-2051, ext. 102   Fax: (415) 346-6343
E-mail: programs@aaja.org
Web: www.aaja.org/apply-for-a-scholarship-now

Summary To provide financial assistance to student members of the Asian American Journalists Association (AAJA) who are high school seniors, undergraduates, or graduate students and interested in preparing for a career in journalism.

Eligibility This program is open to AAJA members who are working or planning to work full time on an undergraduate or graduate degree in journalism. Applicants must submit a brief essay on their choice of 4 topics: 1) could the attack that killed Vincent Chin happen again; 2) how Asian Americans are a single people; 3) should Asian Americans protest or conform in the face of incidents such as the murder of Vincent Chin; or 4) who was Lily Chin. Selection is based on academic achievement, commitment to journalism, sensitivity to Asian American and Pacific Islander issues, demonstrated journalistic ability, and financial need.

Financial data The stipend is $500.

Duration 1 year.

Number awarded 1 each year.

Deadline May of each year.

[486]
VIRGINIA ASIAN FOUNDATION STUDENT SCHOLARSHIPS

Virginia Asian Chamber of Commerce
Attn: Virginia Asian Foundation
Student Scholarship Selection Committee
P.O. Box 2640
Glen Allen, VA 23058
(804) 344-1540   E-mail: aabac@aabac.org
Web: www.aabac.org

Summary To provide financial assistance to Asian American students from Virginia interested in working on an undergraduate degree in any field.

Eligibility This program is open to seniors graduating from high schools in Virginia and students currently enrolled as undergraduates at a college or university in the state. Appli-

cants must be interested in fulfilling the sponsor's goal of promoting the Asian American entrepreneurial spirit in Virginia. They must have a GPA of 3.0 or higher and be working on a degree in a business-related or any other academic area. Along with their application, they must submit a statement of their interest in a business, entrepreneurship, or related field. Selection is based on academic performance, extracurricular activities, leadership, character, and record of giving back to the community.

Financial data Stipends are $1,500, $1,000 or $750.

Duration 1 year.

Number awarded Varies each year; recently, 3 were awarded: 1 each at $1,500, $1,000, and $750.

Deadline November of each year.

[487]
VIRGINIA NURSE PRACTITIONER/NURSE MIDWIFE SCHOLARSHIP PROGRAM

Virginia Department of Health
Attn: Office of Minority Health and Public Health Policy
Workforce Incentive Programs
109 Governor Street, Suite 714 West
Richmond, VA 23219
(804) 864-7435   Fax: (804) 864-7440
E-mail: IncentivePrograms@vdh.virginia.gov
Web: www.vdh.virginia.gov

Summary To provide forgivable loans to nursing students, especially Asian Americans and other minorities, in Virginia who are willing to work as nurse practitioners and/or midwives in the state following graduation.

Eligibility This program is open to U.S. citizens, nationals, immigrants, and political refugees who are enrolled or accepted for enrollment full or part time at a nurse practitioner program or a nurse midwifery program in Virginia. Applicants must have been residents of Virginia for at least 1 year. They must have a cumulative GPA of at least 2.5 in undergraduate and/or graduate courses. Along with their application, they must submit a narrative that includes the significance of this scholarship for their educational goals, any school or community activities, and any skill-set that is pertinent to the nursing profession. Preference is given to 1) residents of designated medically underserved areas of Virginia; 2) students enrolled in family practice, obstetrics and gynecology, pediatric, adult health, and geriatric nurse practitioner programs; and 3) minority students.

Financial data The stipend is $5,000 per year. Recipients must agree to serve in a designated medically underserved area of Virginia for a period of years equal to the number of years of scholarship support received. The required service must begin within 2 years of the recipient's graduation and must be in a facility that provides services to persons who are unable to pay for the service and that participates in all government-sponsored insurance programs designed to assure full access to medical care service for covered persons. If the recipient fails to complete the course of study, or pass the licensing examination, or provide the required service, all scholarship funds received must be repaid with interest and a penalty.

Duration 1 year; may be renewed for 1 additional year.

Number awarded Up to 5 each year.

Deadline June of each year.

[488]
VIRGINIA TEACHING SCHOLARSHIP LOAN PROGRAM

Virginia Department of Education
Division of Teacher Education and Licensure
Attn: Director of Teacher Education
P.O. Box 2120
Richmond, VA 23218-2120
(804) 371-2475   Toll Free: (800) 292-3820
Fax: (804) 786-6759
E-mail: JoAnne.Carver@doe.virginia.gov
Web: www.doe.virginia.gov

Summary To provide scholarship/loans to undergraduate and graduate students, especially Asian Americans and other minorities, in Virginia who are interested in a career in teaching.

Eligibility This program is open to Virginia residents who are enrolled full or part time as a sophomore, junior, senior, or graduate student in a state-approved teacher preparation program in Virginia, who were in the top 10% of their high school class, and have a GPA of 2.7 or higher. Applicants must meet 1 or more of the following criteria: 1) are enrolled in a program leading to endorsement in a critical shortage area; 2) are a male in an elementary or middle school education program; 3) are a minority teaching candidate in any endorsement area; or 4) are a student in an approved teacher education program leading to an endorsement in career and technical education. They must agree to engage in full-time teaching following graduation in 1) designated teacher shortage areas within Virginia; 2) a school with a high concentration of students eligible for free or reduced lunch; 3) within a school division with a shortage of teachers; or 4) in a rural or urban region of the state with a teacher shortage.

Financial data The maximum scholarship/loan is $10,000 per year for full-time students or a prorated amount for part-time students. Loans are forgiven by qualified teaching of 1 year for each year of support received. If the recipient fails to fulfill the teaching service requirement, the loan must be repaid with interest.

Duration 1 year; may be renewed.

Additional information Critical shortage teaching areas in Virginia are currently identified as special education, career and technical education (including technology education, trade and industrial education, business education, and family and consumer sciences), mathematics (6-12), foreign language (preK-12), English, middle school (6-8), elementary education (preK-6), history and social sciences, health and physical education (preK-12), and school counselor (preK-12).

Number awarded Varies each year.

Deadline Deadline not specified.

[489]
VSCPA MINORITY ACCOUNTING SCHOLARSHIPS

Virginia Society of Certified Public Accountants
Attn: Educational Foundation
4309 Cox Road
Glen Allen, VA 23060
(804) 612-9427   Toll Free: (800) 733-8272
Fax: (804) 273-1741   E-mail: foundation@vscpa.com
Web: www.vscpa.com

Summary To provide financial assistance to Asian American and other minority students enrolled in an undergraduate accounting program in Virginia.

Eligibility Applicants must be minority students (Asian, African American or Black, Hispanic or Latino, American Indian or Native Alaskan, Native Hawaiian or other Pacific Islander) currently enrolled in a Virginia college or university undergraduate accounting program. They must be U.S. citizens, be majoring in accounting, have completed at least 3 hours of accounting, be currently registered for 3 more credit hours of accounting, and have a GPA of 3.0 or higher. Selection is based on an essay, transcripts, a current resume, a faculty letter of recommendation, and financial need.

Financial data The stipend is $1,000.

Duration 1 year.

Number awarded Approximately 3 each year.

Deadline March of each year.

[490]
WARNER NORCROSS & JUDD PARALEGAL AND LEGAL SECRETARIAL SCHOLARSHIP

Grand Rapids Community Foundation
Attn: Education Program Officer
185 Oakes Street S.W.
Grand Rapids, MI 49503-4008
(616) 454-1751, ext. 103   Fax: (616) 454-6455
E-mail: rbishop@grfoundation.org
Web: www.grfoundation.org/scholarshipslist

Summary To provide financial assistance to Asian Americans and other minority residents of Michigan who are interested in working on a paralegal or legal secretarial studies degree at an institution in the state.

Eligibility This program is open to residents of Michigan who are students of color attending or planning to attend an accredited public or private 2- or 4-year college or university in the state. Applicants must have a declared major in paralegal or legal secretarial studies. They must be U.S. citizens or permanent residents and have a GPA of 2.5 or higher. Financial need is considered in the selection process.

Financial data The stipend is $2,000. Funds are paid directly to the recipient's institution.

Duration 1 year.

Additional information Funding for this program is provided by the law firm Warner Norcross & Judd LLP.

Number awarded 1 each year.

Deadline March of each year.

[491]
WARREN G. MAGNUSON EDUCATIONAL SUPPORT PERSONNEL SCHOLARSHIP GRANT

Washington Education Association
32032 Weyerhaeuser Way South
P.O. Box 9100
Federal Way, WA 98063-9100
(253) 765-7056   Toll Free: (800) 622-3393, ext. 7056
E-mail: Janna.Connor@Washingtonea.org
Web: www.washingtonea.org

Summary To provide funding to Educational Support Personnel (ESP) members of the Washington Education Association (WEA), especially Asian Americans and other minorities, who are interested in taking classes to obtain an initial teaching certificate.

Eligibility This program is open to WEA/ESP members who are engaged in course work related to obtaining an initial teaching certificate. Applicants must submit a plan for obtaining an initial certificate, a letter describing their passion to become a teacher, evidence of activities and/or leadership in the association, and 3 to 5 letters of reference. Minority members of the association are especially encouraged to apply; 1 of the scholarships is reserved for them.

Financial data The stipend is $1,500.

Duration These are 1-time grants.

Number awarded 3 each year, including 1 reserved for a minority member.

Deadline June of each year.

[492] WASHINGTON ADMIRAL'S FUND SCHOLARSHIP

National Naval Officers Association-Washington, D.C.
  Chapter
c/o LCDR Stephen Williams
P.O. Box 30784
Alexandria, VA 22310
(703) 566-3840   Fax: (703) 566-3813
E-mail: Stephen.Williams@navy.mil
Web: dcnnoa.memberlodge.com/page-309002

Summary To provide financial assistance to Asian American and other minority high school seniors from the Washington, D.C. area who are interested in attending a college or university in any state and enrolling in the Navy Reserve Officers Training Corps (NROTC) program.

Eligibility This program is open to minority seniors graduating from high schools in the Washington, D.C. metropolitan area who plan to enroll full time at an accredited 2- or 4-year college or university in any state. Applicants must be planning to enroll in the NROTC program. They must have a GPA of 2.5 or higher and be U.S. citizens or permanent residents. Selection is based on academic achievement, community involvement, and financial need.

Financial data The stipend is $1,000.

Duration 1 year; nonrenewable.

Additional information If the recipient fails to enroll in the NROTC unit, all scholarship funds must be returned.

Number awarded 1 each year.

Deadline March of each year.

[493] WASHINGTON DC AREA SUPPLY OFFICERS SCHOLARSHIP

National Naval Officers Association-Washington, D.C.
  Chapter
c/o LCDR Stephen Williams
P.O. Box 30784
Alexandria, VA 22310
(703) 566-3840   Fax: (703) 566-3813
E-mail: Stephen.Williams@navy.mil
Web: dcnnoa.memberlodge.com/page-309002

Summary To provide financial assistance to Asian American and other minority high school seniors from the Washington, D.C. area who are interested in attending college in any state.

Eligibility This program is open to minority seniors graduating from high schools in the Washington, D.C. metropolitan area who plan to enroll full time at an accredited 2- or 4-year college or university in any state. Applicants must have a GPA of 3.0 or higher and be U.S. citizens or permanent residents. Selection is based on academic achievement, community involvement, and financial need.

Financial data The stipend is $3,000.

Duration 1 year; nonrenewable.

Number awarded 1 each year.

Deadline March of each year.

[494] WASHINGTON, D.C. CHAPTER NNOA SCHOLARSHIPS FOR MINORITY STUDENTS

National Naval Officers Association-Washington, D.C.
  Chapter
c/o LCDR Stephen Williams
P.O. Box 30784
Alexandria, VA 22310
(703) 566-3840   Fax: (703) 566-3813
E-mail: Stephen.Williams@navy.mil
Web: dcnnoa.memberlodge.com/page-309002

Summary To provide financial assistance to Asian American and other minority high school seniors from the Washington, D.C. area who are interested in attending college in any state.

Eligibility This program is open to minority seniors graduating from high schools in the Washington, D.C. metropolitan area who plan to enroll full time at an accredited 2- or 4-year college or university in any state. Applicants must have a GPA of 2.5 or higher and be U.S. citizens or permanent residents. Selection is based on academic achievement, community involvement, and financial need.

Financial data The stipend is $2,000 or $1,000.

Duration 1 year; nonrenewable.

Additional information Recipients are not required to join or affiliate with the military in any way. In addition to a number of scholarships with additional requirements, this program includes the following named general scholarships: the Ester Boone Memorial Scholarships, the Mr. Charlie Tompkins Scholarship, and the Navy Federal Credit Union Scholarship.

Number awarded Varies each year; recently, 3 were awarded: 1 at $2,000 and 2 at $1,000.

Deadline March of each year.

[495] WASHINGTON SCIENCE TEACHERS ASSOCIATION SCIENCE LEADERSHIP SCHOLARSHIPS

Washington Science Teachers Association
Attn: Andy Boyd, President
2911 88th Street S.E.
Everett, WA 98109
(425) 337-5552   E-mail: boydscience@gmail.com
Web: www.wsta.net/WSTALeadershipScholarship

Summary To provide financial assistance to upper-division students and teachers in Washington, especially Asian Pacific Americans and other minorities, who are interested in training in science education.

Eligibility This program is open to juniors and seniors at colleges and universities in Washington who are working on certification in science education or in elementary education with an emphasis on science. Preference is given to Asian and Pacific Islanders, African Americans, Hispanics, Native Americans, and women.

Financial data The stipend is $2,000.

Duration 1 year; nonrenewable.

Additional information This program began in 2003 as the Peggy Vatter Memorial Scholarships.

Number awarded 1 or more each year.

Deadline June of each year.

[496]
WAYNE D. CORNILS SCHOLARSHIP

Idaho State Broadcasters Association
1674 Hill Road, Suite 3
Boise, ID 83702
(208) 345-3072   Fax: (208) 343-8046
E-mail: isba@qwestoffice.net
Web: www.idahobroadcasters.org/index.php/scholarships

Summary To provide financial assistance to Asian American and other less advantaged students at Idaho colleges and universities who are preparing for a career in the broadcasting field.

Eligibility This program is open to full-time students at Idaho schools who are preparing for a career in broadcasting, including business administration, sales, journalism, or engineering. Applicants must have a GPA of at least 2.0 for the first 2 years of school or 2.5 for the last 2 years. Along with their application, they must submit a letter of recommendation from the general manager of a broadcasting station that is a member of the Idaho State Broadcasters Association and a 1-page essay describing their career plans and why they want the scholarship. Applications are encouraged from a broad and diverse student population. This scholarship is reserved for a less advantaged applicant.

Financial data The stipend depends on the need of the recipient.

Duration 1 year.

Number awarded 1 each year.

Deadline March of each year.

[497]
WELLS FARGO APIASF SCHOLARSHIPS

Asian & Pacific Islander American Scholarship Fund
2025 M Street, N.W., Suite 610
Washington, DC 20036-3363
(202) 986-6892   Toll Free: (877) 808-7032
Fax: (202) 530-0643   E-mail: info@apiasf.org
Web: www.apiasf.org/scholarship_apiasf_wellsfargo.html

Summary To provide financial assistance to Asian and Pacific Islander Americans who are entering college for the first time.

Eligibility This program is open to U.S. citizens, nationals, permanent residents, and citizens of the Freely Associated States who are first-time incoming college students and of Asian or Pacific Islander heritage. Applicants must be enrolling full time at an accredited 2- or 4-year college or university in the United States. They must have a GPA of 2.7 or higher

or the GED equivalent. In addition, they must complete the FAFSA and apply for federal financial aid.

Financial data The stipend is $2,500.

Duration 1 year; nonrenewable.

Additional information This program is sponsored by Wells Fargo Bank and administered by the Asian & Pacific Islander American Scholarship Fund (APIASF).

Number awarded Approximately 200 each year.

Deadline January of each year.

[498]
WESTERN REGION KOREAN AMERICAN SCHOLARSHIPS

Korean American Scholarship Foundation
Western Region
Attn: Scholarship Committee
3540 Wilshire Boulevard, Suite 920
Los Angeles, CA 90010
(213) 380-KASF   Fax: (631) 380-5274
E-mail: wrc.scholarship@kasf.org
Web: www.kasf.org/westerrn

Summary To provide financial assistance to Korean American students from any state who are working on or planning to work on an undergraduate or graduate degree in any field at a school in western states.

Eligibility This program is open to residents of any state who are 1) U.S. citizens of Korean heritage; 2) Korean citizens who have a valid visa to study in the United States; and 3) citizens of any other country who are of Korean heritage and have a valid visa to study in the United States. Applicants must be enrolled or planning to enroll as a full-time undergraduate or graduate student at a college or university in Alaska, Arizona, California, Colorado, Hawaii, Idaho, Montana, Nevada, New Mexico, Oregon, Utah, Washington, or Wyoming. They must have a GPA of 3.0 or higher. Selection is based on academic achievement (25%), extracurricular activities (10%), an essay (10%), recommendations (10%), financial need (40%), and extra credit for having extraordinary circumstances (5%).

Financial data Stipends are at least $2,000.

Duration 1 year; renewable.

Number awarded Varies each year; recently, 50 were awarded.

Deadline July of each year.

[499]
WESTERN UNION FOUNDATION FAMILY SCHOLARSHIP PROGRAM

Western Union Foundation
c/o Institute of International Education
1400 K Street, N.W., Suite 700
Washington, DC 20005
(202) 686-8652   E-mail: wufoundaton@iie.org
Web: foundation.westernunion.com

Summary To provide financial assistance to pairs of students from the same family of immigrants, both of whom wish to attend college in any state.

Eligibility Applications to this program must be submitted jointly by 2 students who are members of the same family (parent and child, siblings). Both applicants must be 18 years of age or older, have been born outside of the United States, have been in this country for 7 years or less, and be planning to attend an accredited institution of higher education or non-profit training institute in any state. Funding is available for college or university tuition, language acquisition classes, technical or skill training, and/or financial literacy; graduate study is not supported.

Financial data Stipends range from $1,000 to $5,000 per family. Funds are paid directly to the educational institution.

Duration 1 year.

Additional information This program began in 2009.

Number awarded Varies each year.

Deadline May of each year.

[500]
WHAN SOON CHUNG SCHOLARSHIP

Philip Jaisohn Memorial Foundation
Attn: Scholarship Committee
6705 Old York Road
Philadelphia, PA 19126
(215) 224-2000, ext. 116   Fax: (215) 224-9164
E-mail: info@jaisohn.org
Web: www.jaisohn.com/scholarships

Summary To provide financial assistance to Korean American undergraduate and graduate students who are studying health care or medicine.

Eligibility This program is open to Korean American undergraduate and graduate students who are currently enrolled at a college or university in the United States and working on a degree in health care or a field of medicine. Applicants must be able to demonstrate excellence in community activities and financial need. Along with their application, they must submit an essay on either "Who is Dr. Jaisohn to Me," or "The Significance of Dr. Jaisohn's Ideal to Korean Americans." They must also submit a 100-word statement on how they can contribute to and be involved in the activities of the Philip Jaisohn Memorial Foundation. Selection is based on the applicant's desire to take Dr. Jaisohn as a role model to learn and spread his legacy.

Financial data The stipend is $1,500.

Duration 1 year.

Number awarded 1 each year.

Deadline August of each year.

[501]
WILLIAM K. SCHUBERT M.D. MINORITY NURSING SCHOLARSHIP

Cincinnati Children's Hospital Medical Center
Attn: Office of Diversity and Inclusion, MLC 9008
3333 Burnet Avenue
Cincinnati, OH 45229-3026
(513) 803-6416   Toll Free: (800) 344-2462
Fax: (513) 636-5643   TDD: (513) 636-4900
E-mail: diversity@cchmc.org
Web: www.cincinnatichildrens.org

Summary To provide financial assistance to Asian Americans and members of other underrepresented groups interested in working on a bachelor's or master's degree in nursing to prepare for licensure in Ohio.

Eligibility This program is open to members of groups underrepresented in the nursing profession (males, Asians, American Indians or Alaska Natives, Blacks or African Amer-

icans, Hawaiian Natives or other Pacific Islanders, or Hispanics or Latinos). Applicants must be enrolled or accepted in a professional bachelor's or master's registered nurse program at an accredited school of nursing to prepare for initial licensure in Ohio. They must have a GPA of 2.75 or higher. Along with their application, they must submit a 750-word essay that covers 1) their long-range personal, educational, and professional goals; 2) why they chose nursing as a profession; 3) how their experience as a member of an underrepresented group has influenced a major professional and/or personal decision in their life; 4) any unique qualifications, experiences, or special talents that demonstrate their creativity; and 5) how their work experience has contributed to their personal development.

Financial data The stipend is $2,750 per year.

Duration 1 year. May be renewed up to 3 additional years for students working on a bachelor's degree or 1 additional year for students working on a master's degree; renewal requires that students maintain a GPA of 2.75 or higher.

Number awarded 1 or more each year.

Deadline April of each year.

[502]
WILLIAM ORR DINGWALL FOUNDATION KOREAN ANCESTRY GRANTS

William Orr Dingwall Foundation
Attn: Scholarship Coordinator
P.O. Box 57088
Washington, DC 20037
E-mail: kag@dingwallfoundation.org
Web: www.dingwallfoundation.org/grants

Summary To provide financial assistance to undergraduates of Asian (preferably Korean) ancestry.

Eligibility This program is open to graduating high school seniors and undergraduates currently enrolled at a college or university in the United States. Applicants must be of Asian ancestry with at least 1 Asian grandparent; preference is given to students of Korean heritage. They must have a GPA of 3.5 or higher but may be majoring in any field. Selection is based on academic record, written statements, and letters of recommendation.

Financial data The stipend is $10,000 per year.

Duration 1 year; may be renewed up to 3 additional years, provided the recipient maintains a GPA of 3.5 or higher.

Number awarded Varies each year; recently, 34 were awarded.

Deadline March of each year.

[503]
WILLIAM RUCKER GREENWOOD SCHOLARSHIP

Association for Women Geoscientists-Potomac Chapter
Attn: Scholarships
P.O. Box 6644
Arlington, VA 22206-0644
E-mail: awgpotomacschol@hotmail.com
Web: www.awg.org/members/po_scholarships.htm

Summary To provide financial assistance to Asian American and other minority women from any state working on an undergraduate or graduate degree in the geosciences at a college in the Potomac Bay region.

Eligibility This program is open to minority women who are residents of any state and currently enrolled as full-time undergraduate or graduate geoscience majors at an accredited, degree-granting college or university in Delaware, the District of Columbia, Maryland, Virginia, or West Virginia. Selection is based on the applicant's 1) participation in geoscience or earth science educational activities; and 2) potential for leadership as a future geoscience professional.

Financial data The stipend is $1,000. The recipient also is granted a 1-year membership in the Association for Women Geoscientists (AWG).

Duration 1 year.

Number awarded 1 each year.

Deadline April of each year.

[504]
WILLIE BRADSHAW MEMORIAL ENDOWED SCHOLARSHIPS

North Carolina High School Athletic Association
Attn: Director of Grants and Fundraising
222 Finley Golf Course Road
P.O. Box 3216
Chapel Hill, NC 27515-3216
(919) 240-7371   Fax: (919) 240-7399
E-mail: mary@nchsaa.org
Web: www.nchsaa.org

Summary To provide financial assistance to Asian Pacific American and other minority seniors (males and females considered separately) at high schools in North Carolina who have participated in lacrosse and plan to attend college in any state.

Eligibility This program is open to Asian Pacific Islander American, Alaska Native/American Indian, African American, and Hispanic American seniors graduating from high schools that are members of the North Carolina High School Athletic Association (NCHSAA). Applicants must be U.S. citizens, nationals, or permanent residents planning to attend college in any state. They must have participated in a sanctioned varsity sport, demonstrate leadership abilities through participation in community service and extracurricular or other activities, have clean school and athletic disciplinary records, and have adjusted gross family income between $30,000 and $75,000 per year. Males and females are considered separately.

Financial data The stipend is $750 for regional winners; state winners receive an additional $1,000.

Duration 1 year; nonrenewable.

Number awarded 16 regional winners (1 male and 1 female in each of 8 regions) are selected each year; from those winners, 1 male and 1 female are selected as state winners.

Deadline February of each year.

[505]
WISCONSIN MINORITY TEACHER LOANS

Wisconsin Higher Educational Aids Board
131 West Wilson Street, Suite 902
P.O. Box 7885
Madison, WI 53707-7885
(608) 267-2212   Fax: (608) 267-2808
E-mail: deanna.schulz@wi.gov
Web: www.heab.state.wi.us/programs.html

Summary To provide forgivable loans to southeast Asians and other minorities in Wisconsin who are interested in teaching at schools in high demand areas of Milwaukee.

Eligibility This program is open to residents of Wisconsin who are African Americans, Hispanic Americans, American Indians, or southeast Asians (students who were admitted to the United States after December 31, 1975 and who are a former citizen of Laos, Vietnam, or Cambodia or whose ancestor was a citizen of 1 of those countries). Applicants must be enrolled at least half time as sophomores, juniors, or seniors at an independent or public institution in the state in a program leading to teaching licensure in a discipline identified as a teacher shortage area and have a GPA of 3.0 or higher. They must agree to teach at a public or private elementary or secondary school in the city of Milwaukee in a high-demand area related to their discipline. Financial need is not considered in the selection process.

Financial data Loans are provided up to $10,000 per year, or a maximum of $30,000. For each year the student teaches in an eligible school and receives a rating of proficient or distinguished on the educator effectiveness system, 25% of the loan is forgiven; if the student does not teach at an eligible school, the loan must be repaid at an interest rate of 5%.

Duration 1 year; may be renewed 2 additional years.

Additional information Eligible students should apply through their school's financial aid office.

Number awarded Varies each year.

Deadline Deadline dates vary by institution; check with your school's financial aid office.

[506]
WISCONSIN MINORITY UNDERGRADUATE RETENTION GRANTS

Wisconsin Higher Educational Aids Board
131 West Wilson Street, Suite 902
P.O. Box 7885
Madison, WI 53707-7885
(608) 267-2212   Fax: (608) 267-2808
E-mail: deanna.schulz@wi.gov
Web: www.heab.state.wi.us/programs.html

Summary To provide financial assistance to southeast Asian and other minorities in Wisconsin who are currently enrolled at a college in the state.

Eligibility This program is open to residents of Wisconsin who are African Americans, Hispanic Americans, American Indians, or southeast Asians (students who were admitted to the United States after December 31, 1975 and who are a former citizen of Laos, Vietnam, or Cambodia or whose ancestor was a citizen of 1 of those countries). Applicants must be enrolled at least half time as sophomores, juniors, seniors, or fifth-year undergraduates at a Wisconsin technical college, tribal college, or independent college or university in the state. They must be nominated by their institution and be able to demonstrate financial need.

Financial data Stipends range from $250 to $2,500 per year, depending on the need of the recipient.

Duration Up to 4 years.

Additional information The Wisconsin Higher Educational Aids Board administers this program for students at private nonprofit institutions, technical colleges, and tribal colleges. The University of Wisconsin has a similar program for students attending any of the branches of that system. Eligible students should apply through their school's financial aid office.

Number awarded Varies each year.

Deadline Deadline dates vary by institution; check with your school's financial aid office.

[507]
WISCONSIN UNITED METHODIST FOUNDATION HMONG SCHOLARSHIP

Wisconsin United Methodist Foundation
750 Windsor Street, Suite 305
Sun Prairie, WI 53590
(608) 837-9582   Toll Free: (888) 903-9863
Fax: (608) 837-2492   E-mail: wumf@wumf.org
Web: www.wumf.org/grantsScholars.html

Summary To provide financial assistance to Methodists from Wisconsin who are of Hmong heritage and interested in attending college in any state.

Eligibility This program is open to Hmong members of United Methodist Churches affiliated with the Wisconsin Conference who are enrolled or planning to enroll at a college or vocational school in any state. Applicants must submit an essay that describes their personal situation and vocational goals, church-related activities and involvement, school and community involvement, and financial plan for funding their education, including any special financial needs.

Financial data Stipends range from $500 to $1,000.

Duration 1 year.

Number awarded 1 or more each year.

Deadline March of each year.

[508]
WOMAN WHO MOVES THE NATION SCHOLARSHIP

Conference of Minority Transportation Officials
Attn: National Scholarship Program
100 M Street, S.E., Suite 917
Washington, DC 20003
(202) 506-2917   E-mail: info@comto.org
Web: www.comto.org/page/scholarships

Summary To provide financial assistance to Asian American and other minority women who are working on an undergraduate or graduate degree in specified fields to prepare for a management career in a transportation-related organization.

Eligibility This program is open to minority women who are working on an undergraduate or graduate degree with intent to lead in some capacity as a supervisor, manager, director, or other position in transit or a transportation-related organization. Applicants may be studying business, entrepreneurship, political science, or other specialized area. They must

have a GPA of 3.0 or higher. Along with their application they must submit a cover letter on their transportation-related career goals and life aspirations. Financial need is not considered in the selection process.

Financial data The stipend is $5,000. Funds are paid directly to the recipient's college or university.

Duration 1 year.

Number awarded 1 each year.

Deadline April of each year.

[509]
WOMEN'S TRANSPORTATION SEMINAR JUNIOR COLLEGE SCHOLARSHIP

Women's Transportation Seminar
Attn: WTS Foundation
1701 K Street, N.W., Suite 800
Washington, DC 20006
(202) 955-5085   Fax: (202) 955-5088
E-mail: wts@wtsinternational.org
Web: www.wtsinternational.org/education/scholarships

Summary To provide financial assistance to women, especially Asian Americans and other minorities, enrolled at a community college or trade school to prepare for a career in transportation.

Eligibility This program is open to women who are working on an associate or technical degree in transportation or a transportation-related field (e.g., transportation engineering, planning, finance, or logistics). Applicants must have a GPA of 3.0 or higher. Along with their application, they must submit a 500-word statement about their career goals after graduation and why they think they should receive the scholarship award. Applications must be submitted first to a local chapter; the chapters forward selected applications for consideration on the national level. Minority women are especially encouraged to apply. Selection is based on transportation involvement and goals, job skills, academic record, and leadership potential; financial need is not considered.

Financial data The stipend is $1,000.

Duration 1 year.

Additional information Local chapters may also award additional funding to winners for their area.

Number awarded 1 each year.

Deadline Applications must be submitted by November to a local WTS chapter.

[510]
WOODS HOLE OCEANOGRAPHIC INSTITUTION MINORITY FELLOWSHIPS

Woods Hole Oceanographic Institution
Attn: Academic Programs Office
Clark Laboratory 223, MS 31
360 Woods Hole Road
Woods Hole, MA 02543-1541
(508) 289-2219   Fax: (508) 457-2188
E-mail: education@whoi.edu
Web: www.whoi.edu/page.do?pid=9377

Summary To provide work experience to Asian Americans and other minority group members who are interested in preparing for careers in the marine sciences, oceanographic engineering, or marine policy.

Eligibility This program is open to ethnic minority undergraduates enrolled in U.S. colleges or universities who have completed at least 1 year of study and who are interested in the physical or natural sciences, mathematics, engineering, or marine policy. Applicants must be U.S. citizens or permanent residents and African American or Black; Asian American; Chicano, Mexican American, Puerto Rican or other Hispanic; or Native American, Alaska Native, or Native Hawaiian. They must be interested in participating in a program of study and research at Woods Hole Oceanographic Institution. Selection is based on previous academic and scientific achievements and promise as future ocean scientists or ocean engineers.

Financial data The stipend is $500 per week; trainees also receive free housing and additional support for travel to Woods Hole.

Duration 10 to 12 weeks during the summer or 1 semester during the academic year; renewable.

Additional information Trainees are assigned advisers who supervise their research programs and supplementary study activities. Some traineeships involve field work or research cruises. This program is conducted as part of the Research Experiences for Undergraduates (REU) Program of the National Science Foundation.

Number awarded 4 to 5 each year.

Deadline February of each year.

[511]
WORLD JOURNAL AWARD FOR CHINESE-AMERICAN STUDENTS

Scholarship America
Attn: Scholarship Management Services
One Scholarship Way
P.O. Box 297
St. Peter, MN 56082
(507) 931-1682
E-mail: dreamaward@scholarshipamerica.org
Web: www.scholarshipamerica.org/dream_award.php

Summary To provide financial assistance to Chinese-American college students who are working on a degree in any field and demonstrate financial need.

Eligibility This program is open to Chinese-American students currently enrolled full time in at least the first year at an accredited 2- or 4-year college, university, or vocational/technical school in any state. Applicants must have a GPA of 3.0 or higher and be able to demonstrate financial need. They must be U.S. citizens or permanent residents or have been granted deferred action status under the Deferred Action for Childhood Arrivals (DACA) Program. Community service, volunteerism, and overcoming barriers to school success are also considered in the selection process.

Financial data Stipends range from $5,000 to $15,000 for the first year, increasing by $1,000 per year in each subsequent year.

Duration 1 year; may be renewed until graduation (including the fifth year of a 5-year program).

Additional information This program began in 2013.

Number awarded Varies each year; recently, a total of 12 Dream Awards were presented.

Deadline December of each year.

[512]
WSP/PARSONS BRINCKERHOFF ENGINEERING SCHOLARSHIP

Conference of Minority Transportation Officials
Attn: National Scholarship Program
100 M Street, S.E., Suite 917
Washington, DC 20003
(202) 506-2917   E-mail: info@comto.org
Web: www.comto.org/page/scholarships

Summary To provide financial assistance to Asian American and other members of the Conference of Minority Transportation Officials (COMTO) and their families who are working on an undergraduate degree in engineering.

Eligibility This program is open to undergraduate students who are members and their parents, guardians, or grandparents who have been members of COMTO for at least 1 year. Applicants must be working on a degree in engineering and have a GPA of 3.0 or higher. Along with their application they must submit a cover letter on their transportation-related career goals and life aspirations. Financial need is not considered in the selection process.

Financial data The stipend is $2,500. Funds are paid directly to the recipient's college or university.

Duration 1 year.

Additional information This program is sponsored by WSP USA, formerly Parsons Brinckerhoff, Inc.

Number awarded 2 each year.

Deadline April of each year.

[513]
WSP/PARSONS BRINCKERHOFF GOLDEN APPLE SCHOLARSHIP

Conference of Minority Transportation Officials
Attn: National Scholarship Program
100 M Street, S.E., Suite 917
Washington, DC 20003
(202) 506-2917   E-mail: info@comto.org
Web: www.comto.org/page/scholarships

Summary To provide financial assistance to Asian American and other members of the Conference of Minority Transportation Officials (COMTO) and their children who are high school seniors planning to attend college to prepare for a career in transportation.

Eligibility This program is open to graduating high school seniors who are members of COMTO or whose parents are members. Applicants must be planning to attend an accredited college, university, or vocational/technical institution to prepare for a career in transportation. They must have a GPA of 2.0 or higher. Along with their application they must submit a cover letter on their transportation-related career goals and life aspirations. Financial need is not considered in the selection process.

Financial data The stipend is $2,500. Funds are paid directly to the recipient's college or university.

Duration 1 year.

Additional information This program is sponsored by WSP USA, formerly Parsons Brinckerhoff, Inc.

Number awarded 2 each year.

Deadline April of each year.

[514]
WTS TRANSPORTATION YOU HIGH SCHOOL SCHOLARSHIP

Women's Transportation Seminar
Attn: WTS Foundation
1701 K Street, N.W., Suite 800
Washington, DC 20006
(202) 955-5085　　　　　　　　Fax: (202) 955-5088
E-mail: wts@wtsinternational.org
Web: www.wtsinternational.org/education/scholarships

Summary　To provide financial assistance to female high school seniors, especially Asian Americans and other minorities, who are studying fields of science, technology, engineering, or mathematics (STEM) and planning to attend college to prepare for a career in transportation.

Eligibility　This program is open to women who are high school seniors with a GPA of 3.0 or higher. Applicants must be studying STEM fields in high school and be planning to attend college to prepare for a career in transportation (e.g., civil engineering, city planning, logistics, automotive engineering, truck repair). Along with their application, they must submit a 500-word statement about their career goals after graduation and why they think they should receive the scholarship. Applications must be submitted first to a local chapter; the chapters forward selected applications for consideration on the national level. Minority women are especially encouraged to apply. Selection is based on transportation involvement and goals, job skills, academic record, and leadership potential; financial need is not considered.

Financial data　The stipend is $1,000.

Duration　1 year.

Additional information　Local chapters may also award additional funding to winners for their area.

Number awarded　1 each year.

Deadline　Applications must be submitted by November to a local WTS chapter.

[515]
XEROX TECHNICAL MINORITY SCHOLARSHIP PROGRAM

Xerox Corporation
Attn: Technical Minority Scholarship Program
150 State Street, Fourth Floor
Rochester, NY 14614
Toll Free: (877) 747-3625　E-mail: xtmsp@rballiance.com
Web: www.xerox.com/jobs/minority-scholarships/enus.html

Summary　To provide financial assistance to Asian Americans and other minorities interested in undergraduate or graduate education in the sciences and/or engineering.

Eligibility　This program is open to minorities (people of Asian, African American, Pacific Islander, Native American, Native Alaskan, or Hispanic descent) working full time on a bachelor's, master's, or doctoral degree in chemistry, computing and software systems, engineering (chemical, computer, electrical, imaging, manufacturing, mechanical, optical, or software), information management, laser optics, materials science, physics, or printing management science. Applicants must be U.S. citizens or permanent residents with a GPA of 3.0 or higher and attending a 4-year college or university.

Financial data　Stipends range from $1,000 to $10,000.

Duration　1 year.

Number awarded　Varies each year, recently, 128 were awarded.

Deadline　September of each year.

[516]
XIA THAO SCHOLARSHIP

Hmong American Education Fund
P.O. Box 17468
St. Paul, MN 55117
(651) 592-1576　　　　　E-mail: scholarships@thehaef.org
Web: www.thehaef.org

Summary　To provide financial assistance to Hmong undergraduate and graduate students from Minnesota who demonstrate leadership.

Eligibility　This program is open to students of Hmong descent who are residents of Minnesota and currently enrolled as full-time undergraduate or graduate students at 2- or 4-year colleges or universities in any state. Applicants must be U.S. citizens or permanent residents and have a GPA of 3.0 or higher. Along with their application, they must submit a 1,500-word essay on their commitment to education, their leadership qualities, their financial need, how this scholarship can help them, and their community service. Selection is based on academic excellence, leadership qualities, commitment to helping their community, and financial need.

Financial data　The stipend is $500.

Duration　1 year; nonrenewable.

Number awarded　1 each year.

Deadline　March of each year.

Graduate Students

Listed alphabetically by program title and described in detail here are 486 fellowships, grants, awards, and other sources of "free money" set aside for incoming, continuing, or returning graduate students of Asian origins (including those of subcontinent Asian and Pacific Islander descent) who are working on a master's, doctoral, or professional degree. This funding is available to support study, training, research, and/or creative activities in the United States.

[517]
100TH INFANTRY BATTALION MEMORIAL SCHOLARSHIP FUND

Hawai'i Community Foundation
Attn: Scholarship Department
827 Fort Street Mall
Honolulu, HI 96813
(808) 566-5570   Toll Free: (888) 731-3863
Fax: (808) 521-6286
E-mail: scholarships@hcf-hawaii.org
Web: hcf.scholarships.ngwebsolutions.com

Summary To provide financial assistance for college or graduate school to descendants of 100th Infantry Battalion World War II veterans.

Eligibility This program is open to entering and continuing full-time undergraduate and graduate students at 2- and 4-year colleges and universities. Applicants must be a direct descendant of a World War II veteran of the 100th Infantry Battalion (which was comprised of Americans of Japanese descent). They must be able to demonstrate academic achievement (GPA of 3.0 or higher), an active record of extra-curricular activities and community service (especially volunteer work connected with the activities of the 100th Infantry Battalion Veterans organization), and a willingness to promote the legacy of the 100th Infantry Battalion of World War II. Along with their application, they must submit a short statement indicating their reasons for attending college, their planned course of study, their career goals, and what community service means to them. They must also submit a separate essay on the historical significance of the 100th Infantry Battalion and what the stories of those soldiers have to teach all American citizens. Neither current residency in Hawaii nor financial need is required.

Financial data The amounts of the awards depend on the availability of funds and the need of the recipient. Recently, the average value of the scholarships awarded by the foundation was $2,800.

Duration 1 year.

Additional information This program began in 2006.

Number awarded Varies each year; recently, 2 were awarded.

Deadline February of each year.

[518]
100TH INFANTRY BATTALION VETERANS STANLEY IZUMIGAWA SCHOLARSHIP FUND

Hawai'i Community Foundation
Attn: Scholarship Department
827 Fort Street Mall
Honolulu, HI 96813
(808) 566-5570   Toll Free: (888) 731-3863
Fax: (808) 521-6286
E-mail: scholarships@hcf-hawaii.org
Web: hcf.scholarships.ngwebsolutions.com

Summary To provide financial assistance for college or graduate school to descendants of 100th Infantry Battalion World War II veterans.

Eligibility This program is open to entering and continuing full-time undergraduate and graduate students at 2- and 4-year colleges and universities. Applicants must be a direct descendant of a World War II veteran of the 100th Infantry Battalion (which was comprised of Americans of Japanese descent). They must be able to demonstrate academic achievement (GPA of 3.0 or higher), an active record of extra-curricular activities and community service, especially volunteer work connected with the activities of the 100th Infantry Battalion Veterans organization, including (but not limited to) educational programs, memorial services, and the anniversary banquet. Along with their application, they must submit a short statement indicating their reasons for attending college, their planned course of study, their career goals, and what community service means to them. They must also submit a separate essay on the historical significance of the 100th Infantry Battalion and what the stories of those soldiers have to teach all American citizens. Neither current residency in Hawaii nor financial need is required.

Financial data The amounts of the awards depend on the availability of funds and the need of the recipient. Recently, the average value of the scholarships awarded by the foundation was $2,800.

Duration 1 year.

Additional information This program began in 2014.

Number awarded 1 or more each year.

Deadline February of each year.

[519]
AAJA-MN BROADCAST INTERNSHIP

Asian American Journalists Association-Minnesota
   Chapter
c/o Nancy Yang, Internship Committee Chair
Minnesota Public Radio
480 Cedar Street
St. Paul, MN 55101
(651) 290-1500
Web: www.aajamn.com/awards.html

Summary To provide work experience at television stations in the Twin Cities area to undergraduate and graduate student members of the Minnesota Chapter of the Asian American Journalists Association (AAJA).

Eligibility This program is open to full time undergraduate and graduate student members of the AAJA Minnesota Chapter who are currently taking journalism classes and preparing for a career in broadcast journalism. Applicants must be interested in an internship at a television station in the Twin Cities area. Along with their application, they must submit a 500-word essay on their involvement or interest in the Asian American community and how, if they are awarded this scholarship, they would contribute to the field of journalism and/or media issues involving the Asian Pacific American and Pacific Islander community. Selection is based on academic achievement, commitment to journalism, sensitivity to Asian American and Pacific Islander issues as demonstrated by community involvement, and demonstrated journalistic ability.

Financial data The stipend is $1,000.

Duration 8 to 10 weeks in the summer, fall, or spring.

Number awarded 1 each year.

Deadline January of each year for summer, June of each year for fall, or October of each year for spring.

[520]
AAJA-MN/MN NEWSPAPER GUILD PRINT INTERNSHIP

Asian American Journalists Association-Minnesota
    Chapter
c/o Nancy Yang, Internship Committee Chair
Minnesota Public Radio
480 Cedar Street
St. Paul, MN 55101
(651) 290-1500
Web: www.aajamn.com/awards.html

Summary   To provide work experience at newspapers in the Twin Cities area to undergraduate and graduate student members of the Minnesota Chapter of the Asian American Journalists Association (AAJA).

Eligibility   This program is open to full time undergraduate and graduate student members of the AAJA Minnesota Chapter who are currently taking journalism classes and preparing for a career in print journalism. Applicants must be interested in an internship at a newspaper in the Twin Cities area. Along with their application, they must submit a 500-word essay on their involvement or interest in the Asian American community and how, if they are awarded this scholarship, they would contribute to the field of journalism and/or media issues involving the Asian Pacific American and Pacific Islander community. Selection is based on academic achievement, commitment to journalism, sensitivity to Asian American and Pacific Islander issues as demonstrated by community involvement, and demonstrated journalistic ability.

Financial data   The stipend is $1,000.

Duration   7 to 8 weeks in the summer, fall, or spring.

Additional information   This program is co-sponsored by the Minnesota Newspaper Guild.

Number awarded   1 each year.

Deadline   January of each year for summer, June of each year for fall, or October of each year for spring.

[521]
AALFNY COMMUNITY SERVICE SCHOLARSHIPS

Asian American Bar Association of New York
Attn: Asian American Law Fund of New York, Inc.
c/o Sylvia Fung Chin
White & Case LLP
1155 Avenue of the Americas
New York, NY 10036-2787
(212) 819-8200   Fax: (212) 354-8113
E-mail: schin@whitecase.com
Web: www.aabany.org/?page=A5

Summary   To provide an opportunity for law students from any state to conduct a service project that will benefit the Asian American community of New York.

Eligibility   This program is open to students enrolled at least half time at ABA- or AALS-accredited law schools in the United States. Applicants must be interested in conducting a community service project as a volunteer for a nonprofit organization that serves the Asian American community of New York. The project should involve legal work and have a supervising attorney. Along with their application, they must submit a 750-word essay that covers 1) the most significant experiences in their background that have shaped and demonstrated their commitment to serving the needs of Asian Pacific Americans; 2) what they hope to learn, accomplish, or change through their project; 3) how they will use the experience that they will gain from their project; and 4) how they will serve the needs of the Asian American community in their future legal career. Selection is based on commitment to and interest in pro bono and/or public interest legal work with the Asian American community, leadership potential, maturity and responsibility, and financial need. U.S. citizenship or permanent resident status is required.

Financial data   The grant is $5,000. Funds are to be used to assist the students with their tuition while encouraging them to use their legal knowledge and training to benefit the Asian American community in New York.

Duration   Recipients are expected to volunteer for at least 6 weeks during the summer.

Additional information   This program began in 1993.

Number awarded   Up to 3 each year.

Deadline   March of each year.

[522]
AAPINA ETHNIC MINORITY NURSING AWARD

Asian American/Pacific Islander Nurses Association
c/o Rei Serafica, Awards Committee Chair
University of Nevada at Las Vegas
School of Nursing
BHS 440
4505 South Maryland Parkway, Mail Code 3018
Las Vegas, NV 89154-3018
(702) 895-5746   Fax: (702) 895-4807
E-mail: reimund.serafica@unlv.edu
Web: www.aapina.org/ethnic-minority-nursing-award

Summary   To provide funding to members of the Asian American/Pacific Islander Nurses Association (AAPINA) who are interested in conducting a pilot study on improving the health of Asian Americans or Pacific Islanders.

Eligibility   This program is open to graduate students who have been AAPINA members for at least 2 years. Applicants must be interested in conducting a pilot study that addresses issues to improve the health of Asian Americans or Pacific Islanders. Selection is based on significance of the study, investigators' experience and background, innovation, approach, environment.

Financial data   The grant is $800.

Duration   1 year.

Number awarded   1 each year.

Deadline   February of each year.

[523]
AAPINA SCHOLARSHIP

Asian American/Pacific Islander Nurses Association
c/o Rei Serafica, Awards Committee Chair
University of Nevada at Las Vegas
School of Nursing
BHS 440
4505 South Maryland Parkway, Mail Code 3018
Las Vegas, NV 89154-3018
(702) 895-5746   Fax: (702) 895-4807
E-mail: reimund.serafica@unlv.edu
Web: www.aapina.org/aapina-scholarship

Summary   To provide financial assistance to members of the Asian American/Pacific Islander Nurses Association

(AAPINA) who are working on an undergraduate or graduate degree in nursing.

Eligibility This program is open to undergraduate and graduate (master's or doctoral) students who have been AAPINA members for at least 2 years. Applicants must have a GPA of 3.5 or higher. Along with their application, they must submit a 1- to 2-page essay on their previous and current leadership activities and potential for contributing to AAPINA. Selection is based on academic progress, extracurricular activities, leadership skills, and participation in AAPINA.

Financial data The stipend is $1,000.

Duration 1 year.

Number awarded 1 each year.

Deadline January of each year.

[524]
AAUW CAREER DEVELOPMENT GRANTS

American Association of University Women
Attn: AAUW Educational Foundation
1111 16th Street, N.W.
Washington, DC 20036-4873
(202) 785-7700   Toll Free: (800) 326-AAUW
Fax: (202) 872-1425   TDD: (202) 785-7777
E-mail: aauw@applyists.com
Web: www.aauw.org

Summary To provide financial assistance to Asian American and other women of color who are seeking career advancement, career change, or reentry into the workforce.

Eligibility This program is open to women who are U.S. citizens or permanent residents, have earned a bachelor's degree, received their most recent degree more than 4 years ago, and are making career changes, seeking to advance in current careers, or reentering the workforce. Applicants must be interested in working toward a master's degree, second bachelor's or associate degree, professional degree (e.g., M.D., J.D.), certification program, or technical school certificate. They must be planning to undertake course work at an accredited 2- or 4-year college or university (or a technical school that is licensed, accredited, or approved by the U.S. Department of Education). Primary consideration is given to women of color and women pursuing their first advanced degree or credentials in nontraditional fields. Support is not provided for prerequisite course work or for Ph.D. course work or dissertations. Selection is based on demonstrated commitment to education and equity for women and girls, reason for seeking higher education or technical training, degree to which study plan is consistent with career objectives, potential for success in chosen field, documentation of opportunities in chosen field, feasibility of study plans and proposed time schedule, validity of proposed budget and budget narrative (including sufficient outside support), and quality of written proposal.

Financial data Grants range from $2,000 to $12,000. Funds may be used for tuition, fees, books, supplies, local transportation, dependent child care, or purchase of a computer required for the study program.

Duration 1 year, beginning in July; nonrenewable.

Additional information The filing fee is $35.

Number awarded Varies each year; recently, 63 of these grants, with a value of $670,000, were awarded.

Deadline December of each year.

[525]
ABE AND ESTHER HAGIWARA STUDENT AID AWARD

Japanese American Citizens League
Attn: National Scholarship Awards
1765 Sutter Street
San Francisco, CA 94115
(415) 345-1075   Fax: (415) 345-1077
E-mail: pwada@jacl.org
Web: www.jacl.org/jacl-national-scholarship-program

Summary To provide financial assistance for college or graduate school to student members of the Japanese American Citizens League (JACL) who can demonstrate severe financial need.

Eligibility This program is open to JACL members who are enrolled or planning to enroll at a college, university, trade school, or business college. Applicants must be undergraduate or graduate students who are able to demonstrate that, without this aid, they will have to delay or terminate their education. They must submit information on their involvement in JACL and a 2-page essay on a topic that changes annually but relates to Japanese Americans. Selection is based on that essay, financial need, academic history, JACL involvement, school activities, work history, scholastic honors, and community involvement.

Financial data Stipends generally average more than $2,000.

Duration 1 year; nonrenewable.

Number awarded At least 1 each year.

Deadline March of each year.

[526]
ACADEMIC LIBRARY ASSOCIATION OF OHIO DIVERSITY SCHOLARSHIP

Academic Library Association of Ohio
c/o Eileen Theodore-Shusta, Diversity Committee Chair
Ohio University
Library Administrative Services
422 Alden
30 Park Place
Athens, OH 45701
(740) 593-2989   E-mail: theodore@ohio.edu
Web: www.alaoweb.org/procmanual/policies.html#diversity

Summary To provide financial assistance to Asian American and other residents of Ohio who are working on a master's degree in library science at a school in any state and will contribute to diversity in the profession.

Eligibility This program is open to residents of Ohio who are enrolled or entering an ALA-accredited program for a master's degree in library science, either on campus or via distance education. Applicants must be able to demonstrate how they will contribute to diversity in the profession, including (but not limited to) race or ethnicity, sexual orientation, life experience, physical ability, and a sense of commitment to those and other diversity issues. Along with their application, they must submit 1) a list of participation in honor societies or professional organizations, awards, scholarships, prizes, honors, or class offices; 2) a list of their community, civic, organizational, or volunteer experiences; and 3) an essay on their understanding of and commitment to diversity in libraries, including how they, as library school students and future professionals, might address the issue.

Financial data The stipend is $1,500.
Duration 1 year.
Number awarded 2 each year.
Deadline March of each year.

[527]
ACC GREATER PHILADELPHIA DIVERSITY CORPORATE SUMMER INTERNSHIP

Association of Corporate Counsel-Greater Philadelphia
  Chapter
c/o Anne Bancroft, Diversity Committee Co-Chair
Exelon Business Services Company
2301 Market Street, Suite 23
Philadelphia, PA 19103
Toll Free: (800) 494-4000
E-mail: anne.bancroft@exeloncorp.com
Web: www.acc.com

Summary To provide an opportunity for Asian American and other law students from diverse backgrounds to gain summer work experience in corporate law at firms in the Philadelphia area.

Eligibility This program is open to students who are members of minority groups traditionally underrepresented in the legal profession (Asian/Pacific Islander, African American, Hispanic, American Indian/Alaska Native). Applications are solicited from law schools in the Philadelphia area, but students at all other law schools may be eligible if they are interested in a summer internship in corporate law at a firm in that area. Interested students must submit information about their financial status, a list of extracurricular activities, any relevant legal experience, a legal writing sample, and an essay of 250 to 500 words explaining why they qualify for this internship and what they hope to gain from the experience.

Financial data The stipend is $7,500.
Duration Summer months.
Number awarded Approximately 15 each year.
Deadline January of each year.

[528]
ACC NATIONAL CAPITAL REGION CORPORATE SCHOLARS PROGRAM

Association of Corporate Counsel-National Capital
  Region
Attn: Executive Director
P.O. Box 2147
Rockville, MD 20847-2147
(301) 881-3018   E-mail: Ilene.Reid-NCR@accglobal.com
Web: m.acc.com/chapters/ncr/scholars.cfm

Summary To provide an opportunity for summer work experience in the metropolitan Washington, D.C. area to Asian American and other minority students at law schools in the area who will contribute to the diversity of the profession.

Eligibility This program is open to students entering their second or third year of part- or full-time study at law schools in the Washington, D.C. metropolitan area (including suburban Maryland and all of Virginia). Applicants must be able to demonstrate how they contribute to diversity in the legal profession, based not only on ideas about gender, race, and ethnicity, but also concepts of socioeconomic background and their individual educational and career path. They must be interested in working during the summer at a sponsoring private corporation and nonprofit organizations in the Washington, D.C. area. Along with their application, they must submit a personal statement of 250 to 500 words explaining why they qualify for this program, a writing sample, their law school transcript, and a resume.

Financial data The stipend is at least $9,000.
Duration 10 weeks during the summer.
Additional information The sponsor is the local chapter of the Association of Corporate Counsel (ACC). It established this program in 2004 with support from the Minority Corporate Counsel Association (MCCA).
Number awarded Varies each year; recently, 13 of these internships were awarded.
Deadline January of each year.

[529]
ACCESS TO JUSTICE FELLOWSHIPS OF THE OREGON STATE BAR

Oregon State Bar
Attn: Diversity and Inclusion Department
16037 S.W. Upper Boones Ferry Road
P.O. Box 231935
Tigard, OR 97281-1935
(503) 620-0222
Toll Free: (800) 452-8260, ext. 338 (within OR)
Fax: (503) 684-1366   TDD: (503) 684-7416
E-mail: cling@osbar.org
Web: www.osbar.org/diversity/programs.html#access

Summary To provide summer work experience to Asian American and other law students in Oregon who have encountered barriers and will help the Oregon State Bar achieve its diversity and inclusion objectives.

Eligibility This program is open to students at law schools in Oregon who have experienced economic, social, or other barriers; who have a demonstrated commitment to increasing access to justice; who have personally experienced discrimination or oppression; and who will contribute to the Oregon State Bar's diversity and inclusion program, defined to include age, culture, disability, ethnicity, gender and gender identity or expression, geographic location, national origin, race, religion, sex, sexual orientation, and socio-economic status. They must be interested in working for a public employer or nonprofit organization in Oregon during the summer. Preference is given to students who indicate an intention to practice in Oregon. Along with their application, they must submit a 500-word personal statement on either 1) how their status as a person of diversity has influenced their decision to become a lawyer and how will it influence them throughout their legal professional career; or 2) a challenge they have faced, how they met the challenge, and how that experience will affect the decisions they will make as a legal professional. They must also submit a sample of their legal writing. Selection is based on the personal statement (35%), legal writing ability (25%), academic achievement (15%), work experience and honors (10%), and financial need (15%).

Financial data Fellows receive a stipend of $5,000.
Duration 3 months during the summer.
Number awarded 2 each year.
Deadline January of each year.

[530]
ACM/IEEE-CS GEORGE MICHAEL MEMORIAL HPC FELLOWSHIPS

Association for Computing Machinery
Attn: Awards Committee Liaison
2 Penn Plaza, Suite 701
New York, NY 10121-0701
(212) 626-0561   Toll Free: (800) 342-6626
Fax: (212) 944-1318   E-mail: acm-awards@acm.org
Web: awards.acm.org/hpcfell/nominations.cfm

Summary To provide financial assistance to doctoral students, especially Asian Americans and other minorities, who are working on a degree in high performance computing (HPC) and will contribute to diversity in the field.

Eligibility This program is open to students from any country who have completed at least 1 year full-time study in a Ph.D. program in HPC and have at least 1 year remaining before graduating. Applications from women, minorities, international students, and all who contribute to diversity are especially encouraged. Selection is based on overall potential for research excellence, degree to which technical interests align with those of the HPC community, demonstration of current and planned future use of HPC resources, evidence of a plan of student to enhance HPC-related skills, evidence of academic progress to date (including presentations and publications), and recommendation by faculty adviser.

Financial data The stipend is $5,000. Fellows also receive reimbursement of travel expenses to attend the conference of the Association for Computing Machinery (ACM).

Duration 1 year.

Additional information This program, which began in 2007, is sponsored by the IEEE Computer Society.

Number awarded Up to 6 each year.

Deadline April of each year.

[531]
ACXIOM DIVERSITY SCHOLARSHIP PROGRAM

Acxiom Corporation
601 East Third Street
P.O. Box 8190
Little Rock, AR 72203-8190
(501) 342-1000   Toll Free: (877) 314-2049
E-mail: Candice.Davis@acxiom.com
Web: www.acxiom.com/about-acxiom/careers

Summary To provide financial assistance and possible work experience to Asian American and other upper-division and graduate students who are members of a diverse population that historically has been underrepresented in the information technology work force.

Eligibility This program is open to juniors, seniors, and graduate students who are working full time on a degree in a field of information technology, including computer science, computer information systems, management information systems, information quality, information systems, engineering, mathematics, statistics, or related areas of study. Women, veterans, minorities, and individuals with disabilities are encouraged to apply. Applicants must have a GPA of 3.0 or higher. Along with their application, they must submit a 500-word essay describing how the scholarship will help them achieve their academic, professional, and personal goals. Selection is based on academic achievement, relationship of field of study to information technology, and relationship of areas of professional interest to the sponsor's business needs.

Financial data The stipend is $5,000 per year.

Duration 1 year; may be renewed 1 additional year, provided the recipient remains enrolled full time, maintains a GPA of 3.0 or higher, and (if offered an internship) continues to meet internship expectations.

Additional information Recipients may be offered an internship (fall, spring, summer, year-round) at 1 of the sponsor's offices in Austin (Texas), Conway (Arkansas), Downers Grove (Illinois), Little Rock (Arkansas), Nashville (Tennessee), New York (New York), or Redwood City (California).

Number awarded Up to 5 each year.

Deadline December of each year.

[532]
ADDIE B. MORRIS SCHOLARSHIP

American Association of Railroad Superintendents
P.O. Box 200
La Fox, IL 60147
(331) 643-3369   E-mail: aars@supt.org
Web: www.railroadsuperintendents.org/Scholarships

Summary To provide financial assistance to undergraduate and graduate students, especially Asian Americans or other minorities working on a degree in transportation.

Eligibility This program is open to full-time undergraduate and graduate students enrolled at accredited colleges and universities in Canada or the United States. Applicants must have completed enough credits to have standing as a sophomore and must have a GPA of 2.75 or higher. Preference is given to minority students enrolled in the transportation field who can demonstrate financial need.

Financial data The stipend is $1,000. Funds are sent directly to the recipient's institution.

Duration 1 year.

Number awarded 1 or more each year.

Deadline June of each year.

[533]
ADRIENNE M. AND CHARLES SHELBY ROOKS FELLOWSHIP FOR RACIAL AND ETHNIC THEOLOGICAL STUDENTS

United Church of Christ
Attn: Associate Director, Grant and Scholarship
  Administration
700 Prospect Avenue East
Cleveland, OH 44115-1100
(216) 736-2166   Toll Free: (866) 822-8224, ext. 2166
Fax: (216) 736-3783   E-mail: scholarships@ucc.org
Web: www.ucc.org/ministry_education_scholarships

Summary To provide financial assistance to Asian Americans and other minority students who are either enrolled at an accredited seminary preparing for a career of service in the United Church of Christ (UCC) or working on a doctoral degree in the field of religion.

Eligibility This program is open to members of underrepresented ethnic groups (Asian American, African American, Hispanic American, Native American Indian, or Pacific Islander) who have been a member of a UCC congregation for at least 1 year. Applicants must be either 1) enrolled in an accredited school of theology in the United States or Canada and working on an M.Div. degree with the intent of becoming a pastor or teacher within the UCC; or 2) doctoral (Ph.D., Th.D., or Ed.D.) students preparing for a scholarly teaching vocation in the field of religion. Seminary students must have a GPA in all postsecondary work of 3.0 or higher and must have begun the in-care process; preference is given to students who have demonstrated leadership (through a history of service to the church) and scholarship (through exceptional academic performance). For doctoral students, preference is given to applicants who have demonstrated academic excellence, teaching effectiveness, and commitment to the UCC and who intend to become professors in colleges, seminaries, or graduate schools.

Financial data   Grants range from $500 to $5,000 per year.

Duration   1 year; may be renewed.

Number awarded   Varies each year; recently, 12 of these scholarships, including 8 for M.Div. students and 4 for doctoral students, were awarded.

Deadline   February of each year.

[534]
AEF FELLOWSHIPS

Asian Pacific American Bar Association Educational Fund
P.O. Box 2209
Washington, DC 20013-2209
Fax: (202) 598-1233   E-mail: aefboard@gmail.com
Web: www.aefdc.com/fellowships

Summary   To provide funding to law students from any state who are interested in interning during the summer with a public interest organization that benefits either the Asian Pacific American community or the metropolitan Washington, D.C. community at large.

Eligibility   This program is open to law students who have obtained an unpaid internship with a public interest organization (e.g., government organizations and other nonprofits serving the public interest). The organization must serve either the greater Washington, D.C. area or the Asian Pacific American community. Applicants must submit an essay, up to 500 words, on the internship, how it will benefit the Asian Pacific American community or the metropolitan Washington, D.C. area, and how their past and/or present activities show commitment to the public interest and/or the Asian Pacific American community. Preference is given to applicants interning at direct service organizations. Selection is based primarily on the essay, but the applicant's maturity and responsibility are also considered.

Financial data   The stipend is $3,500.

Duration   At least 10 weeks or a total of 400 hours during the summer.

Number awarded   Varies each year; recently, 2 were funded.

Deadline   April of each year.

[535]
AEF LEGAL SERVICES AND ADVOCACY FELLOWSHIP

Asian Pacific American Bar Association Educational Fund
P.O. Box 2209
Washington, DC 20013-2209
Fax: (202) 598-1233   E-mail: aefboard@gmail.com
Web: www.aefdc.com/fellowships

Summary   To provide funding to law students from any state who are interested in interning during the summer with a public interest organization that benefits the Asian Pacific American community in the metropolitan Washington, D.C.

Eligibility   This program is open to law students who have secured an internship with a public interest organization that serves the greater Washington, D.C. area Asian Pacific American community. Applicants should have excellent written and oral communication skills, experience working with interpreters, and proficiency in at least 1 Asian language. Along with their application, they must submit an essay, up to 500 words, on their commitment to the Asian American and Pacific Islander issues and what they hope to gain from a mentorship relationship. Selection is based primarily on the essay, but the applicant's maturity and responsibility are also considered.

Financial data   The stipend is $5,000.

Duration   At least 10 weeks or a total of 400 hours during the summer.

Additional information   Recently, this program was available to students who had secured an internship with the Asian Pacific American Legal Resource Center (APALRC) in Washington, D.C.

Number awarded   1 each year.

Deadline   April of each year.

[536]
AGAINST THE GRAIN GROUNDBREAKER LEADERSHIP SCHOLARSHIP

Against the Grain Productions
3523 McKinney Avenue, Suite 231
Dallas, TX 75204
E-mail: outreach@againstthegrainproductions.com
Web: www.againstthegrainproductions.com

Summary   To provide financial assistance to Asian and Pacific Island college seniors and graduate students who have demonstrated outstanding leadership that sets an example for their community.

Eligibility   This program is open to full-time college seniors and graduate students in any field at accredited 4-year colleges and universities who have a GPA of 3.5 or higher. Applicants must be of at least 50% Asian and/or Pacific Islander ethnicity and U.S. citizens, nationals, or permanent residents. They must have demonstrated "exemplary leadership, vision, and passion that is blazing a trail for others to follow and changing lives in the Asian American community." Along with their application, they must submit a video that showcases their work and qualifications. Selection is based on that video, an essay, academic performance, leadership and community service, and an interview.

Financial data   The stipend is $1,500. Funds are disbursed directly to the educational institution.

Duration   1 year.

Number awarded 1 or more each year.

Deadline May of each year.

[537]
AHIMA FOUNDATION DIVERSITY SCHOLARSHIPS

American Health Information Management Association
Attn: AHIMA Foundation
233 North Michigan Avenue, 21st Floor
Chicago, IL 60601-5809
(312) 233-1137   Fax: (312) 233-1537
E-mail: info@ahimafoundation.org
Web: www.ahimafoundation.org

Summary To provide financial assistance to Asian American and other members of the American Health Information Management Association (AHIMA) who are interested in working on an undergraduate or graduate degree in health information management (HIM) or health information technology (HIT) and who will contribute to diversity in the profession.

Eligibility This program is open to AHIMA members who are enrolled at least half time in an accredited program. Applicants must be working on a degree in HIM or HIT at the associate, bachelor's, post-baccalaureate, master's, or doctoral level. They must have a GPA of 3.5 or higher and at least 6 credit hours remaining after the date of the award. To qualify for this support, applicants must demonstrate how they will contribute to diversity in the health information management profession; diversity is defined as differences in race, ethnicity, nationality, gender, sexual orientation, socioeconomic status, age, physical capabilities, or religious beliefs. Along with their application, they must submit essays on assigned topics related to their involvement in the HIM profession. Selection is based on the clarity and completeness of thought in the essays; cumulative GPA; volunteer, work, and/or leadership experience; honors, awards, or recognitions; commitment to the HIM profession; and references.

Financial data Stipends are $1,000 for associate degree students, $1,500 for bachelor's degree or post-baccalaureate certificate students, $2,000 for master's degree students, or $2,500 for doctoral degree students.

Duration 1 year.

Number awarded 1 or more each year.

Deadline September of each year.

[538]
AICPA ASCEND SCHOLARSHIP

Ascend: Pan-Asian Leaders
Attn: Director of Programs
247 West 30th Street
New York, NY 10001
(212) 248-4888   Fax: (212) 344-5636
E-mail: scholarships@ascendleadership.org
Web: www.ascendleadership.org

Summary To provide financial assistance to undergraduate and graduate minority accounting students who are members of Ascend: Pan-Asian Leaders and of the American Institute of Certified Public Accountants (AICPA).

Eligibility This program is open to members of minority groups underrepresented in the accounting profession. Applicants must have completed at least 30 hours of college course work, including at least 6 hours in accounting, at a 4-year college or university in the United States or its territories as a full-time undergraduate or graduate student in an accounting-related field. They must be members of Ascend and AICPA, have a GPA of 3.0 or higher, and be U.S. citizens or permanent residents. Along with their application, they must submit a 500-word personal essay on how they have demonstrated leadership and teamwork in their academic studies, professional career, and/or extracurricular activities and community volunteer work; why they believe those qualities are important to transforming themselves into a better leader; their career goals after graduation; and the role Ascend has played in the achievement of their academic and career goals. They must also be able to demonstrate some financial need.

Financial data The stipend is $5,000. The program also provides travel and lodging for the Ascend annual national convention.

Duration 1 year.

Additional information Ascend was formed in 2004 as the National Asian American Society of Accountants. This program is sponsored by AICPA.

Number awarded 1 each year.

Deadline April of each year.

[539]
ALBERT W. DENT STUDENT SCHOLARSHIP

American College of Healthcare Executives
Attn: Scholarship Committee
One North Franklin Street, Suite 1700
Chicago, IL 60606-3529
(312) 424-2800   Fax: (312) 424-0023
E-mail: contact@ache.org
Web: www.ache.org

Summary To provide financial assistance to Asian American and other minority graduate student members of the American College of Healthcare Executives (ACHE).

Eligibility This program is open to ACHE student associates entering their final year of classroom work in a health care management master's degree program. Applicants must be minority students, enrolled full time, able to demonstrate financial need, and U.S. or Canadian citizens. Along with their application, they must submit a 1- to 2-page essay describing their leadership abilities and experiences, their community and volunteer involvement, their goals as a health care executive, and how this scholarship can help them achieve their career goals.

Financial data The stipend is $5,000.

Duration 1 year.

Additional information The program was established and named in honor of Dr. Albert W. Dent, the foundation's first African American fellow and president emeritus of Dillard University.

Number awarded Varies each year; the sponsor awards up to 20 scholarships through this and its other scholarship program.

Deadline March of each year.

[540]
AMBASSADOR MINERVA JEAN FALCON HAWAI'I SCHOLARSHIP

Hawai'i Community Foundation
Attn: Scholarship Department
827 Fort Street Mall
Honolulu, HI 96813
(808) 566-5570   Toll Free: (888) 731-3863
Fax: (808) 521-6286
E-mail: scholarships@hcf-hawaii.org
Web: hcf.scholarships.ngwebsolutions.com

Summary To provide financial assistance to Hawaii residents of Filipino ancestry who are interested in attending college in the state.

Eligibility This program is open to Hawaii residents of Filipino ancestry who are enrolled in or planning to enroll in an accredited 2- or 4-year college or university in the state. Applicants must be full-time students at the undergraduate or graduate level and able to demonstrate academic achievement (GPA of 2.7 or higher), good moral character, and financial need. Along with their application, they must submit a short statement indicating their reasons for attending college, their planned course of study, their career goals, and what community service means to them. They must also submit a 2-page essay on how they plan to be involved in the community as a Filipino-American student.

Financial data The amounts of the awards depend on the availability of funds and the need of the recipient. Recently, the average value of the scholarships awarded by the foundation was $2,800.

Duration 1 year.

Additional information This scholarship was first offered in 2001.

Number awarded Varies each year.

Deadline February of each year.

[541]
AMELIA KEMP MEMORIAL SCHOLARSHIP

Women of the Evangelical Lutheran Church in America
Attn: Scholarships
8765 West Higgins Road
Chicago, IL 60631-4101
(773) 380-2741   Toll Free: (800) 638-3522, ext. 2741
Fax: (773) 380-2419   E-mail: valora.starr@elca.org
Web: www.womenoftheelca.org

Summary To provide financial assistance to Asian American and other lay women of color who are members of Evangelical Lutheran Church of America (ELCA) congregations and who wish to study on the undergraduate, graduate, professional, or vocational school level.

Eligibility This program is open to ELCA lay women of color who are at least 21 years of age and have experienced an interruption of at least 2 years in their education since high school. Applicants must have been admitted to an educational institution to prepare for a career in other than ordained ministry. U.S. citizenship is required.

Financial data The maximum stipend is $1,000 per year.

Duration 1 year; recipients may reapply for 1 additional year.

Number awarded 1 or more each year.

Deadline February of each year.

[542]
AMERICAN ANTHROPOLOGICAL ASSOCIATION MINORITY DISSERTATION FELLOWSHIP PROGRAM

American Anthropological Association
Attn: Committee on Minority Issues in Anthropology
2300 Clarendon Boulevard, Suite 1301
Arlington, VA 22201
(703) 528-1902   Fax: (703) 528-3546
E-mail: arussell@aaanet.org
Web: www.aaanet.org/cmtes/minority/Minfellow.cfm

Summary To provide funding to Asian Americans and other minorities who are working on a Ph.D. dissertation in anthropology.

Eligibility This program is open to Asian American, Native American, African American, Latino(a), and Pacific Islander doctoral students who have been admitted to degree candidacy in anthropology. Applicants must be U.S. citizens, enrolled in a full-time academic program leading to a doctoral degree in anthropology, and members of the American Anthropological Association. They must have a record of outstanding academic success, have had their dissertation proposal approved by their dissertation committee prior to application, be writing a dissertation in an area of anthropological research, and need funding to complete the dissertation. Along with their application, they must submit a cover letter, a research plan summary, a curriculum vitae, a statement regarding employment, a disclosure statement providing information about other sources of available and pending financial support, 3 letters of recommendation, and an official transcript from their doctoral program. Selection is based on the quality of the submitted information and the judged likelihood that the applicant will have a good chance of completing the dissertation.

Financial data The grant is $10,000. Funds are sent in 2 installments (in September and in January) directly to the recipient.

Duration 1 year; nonrenewable.

Number awarded 1 each year.

Deadline February of each year.

[543]
AMERICAN ASSOCIATION OF CHINESE IN TOXICOLOGY AND CHARLES RIVER BEST ABSTRACT AWARD

Society of Toxicology
Attn: American Association of Chinese in Toxicology
  Special Interest Group
1821 Michael Faraday Drive, Suite 300
Reston, VA 20190-5348
(703) 438-3115   Fax: (703) 438-3113
E-mail: sothq@toxicology.org
Web: www.toxicology.org/ai/af/awards_details.aspx?id=98

Summary To recognize and reward graduate student and postdoctoral members of the Society of Toxicology (SOT) who are of Chinese ethnic origin and present outstanding papers at the annual meeting.

Eligibility This award is available to SOT members who are graduate students or postdoctoral fellows of Chinese descent (having 1 or more parents of Chinese descent). Candidates must have an accepted abstract for the SOT annual meeting. Along with the abstract, they must submit a cover letter outlining the significance of the work to the field of toxicology.

Financial data The prizes are $500 for first, $300 for second, and $200 for third.

Duration The prizes are presented annually.

Number awarded 3 each year.

Deadline December of each year.

[544]
AMERICAN ASSOCIATION OF JAPANESE UNIVERSITY WOMEN SCHOLARSHIP PROGRAM

American Association of Japanese University Women
Attn: Scholarship Committee
3543 West Boulevard
Los Angeles, CA 90016
E-mail: aajuwcholar@gmail.com
Web: www.aajuw.org/new-page-3

Summary To provide financial assistance to female students currently enrolled in upper-division or graduate classes in California.

Eligibility This program is open to women enrolled at accredited colleges or universities in California as juniors, seniors, or graduate students. Applicants must be involved in U.S.-Japan relations, cultural exchanges, and leadership development in the areas of their designated field of study. Along with their application, they must submit a current resume, an official transcript of the past 2 years of college work, 2 letters of recommendation, and an essay (up to 2 pages in English or 1,200 characters in Japanese) on what they hope to accomplish in their field of study and how that will contribute to better U.S.-Japan relations.

Financial data The stipend is $2,000.

Duration 1 year.

Additional information The association was founded in 1970 to promote the education of women as well as to contribute to U.S.-Japan relations, cultural exchanges, and leadership development.

Number awarded 1 to 3 each year. Since this program was established, it has awarded nearly $100,000 worth of scholarships to 110 women.

Deadline September of each year.

[545]
AMERICAN BAR ASSOCIATION LEGAL OPPORTUNITY SCHOLARSHIP

American Bar Association
Attn: Fund for Justice and Education
321 North Clark Street, 21st Floor
Chicago, IL 60654-7598
(312) 988-5927   Fax: (312) 988-6392
E-mail: legalosf@staff.abanet.org
Web: www.americanbar.org

Summary To provide financial assistance to Asian American and other racial and ethnic minority students who are interested in attending law school.

Eligibility This program is open to racial and ethnic minority college graduates who are interested in attending an ABA-accredited law school. Only students beginning law school may apply; students who have completed 1 or more semesters of law school are not eligible. Applicants must have a cumulative GPA of 2.5 or higher and be citizens or permanent residents of the United States. Along with their application, they must submit a 1,000-word statement describing their personal and family background, community service activities, and other connections to their racial and ethnic minority community. Financial need is also considered in the selection process.

Financial data The stipend is $5,000 per year.

Duration 1 year; may be renewed for 2 additional years if satisfactory performance in law school has been achieved.

Additional information This program began in the 2000-01 academic year.

Number awarded Approximately 20 each year.

Deadline February of each year.

[546]
AMERICAN EDUCATIONAL RESEARCH ASSOCIATION MINORITY FELLOWSHIPS IN EDUCATION RESEARCH

American Educational Research Association
Attn: Fellowships Program
1430 K Street, N.W., Suite 1200
Washington, DC 20005
(202) 238-3200   Fax: (202) 238-3250
E-mail: fellowships@aera.net
Web: www.aera.net

Summary To provide funding to Asian American and other minority doctoral students writing their dissertation on educational research.

Eligibility This program is open to U.S. citizens and permanent residents who have advanced to candidacy and successfully defended their Ph.D./Ed.D. dissertation research proposal. Applicants must plan to work full time on their dissertation in educational research, the humanities, or social or behavioral science disciplinary or interdisciplinary fields, such as economics, political science, psychology, or sociology. This program is targeted for members of groups historically underrepresented in higher education (Asian Americans, African Americans, American Indians, Alaskan Natives, Native Hawaiian or Pacific Islanders, and Hispanics or Latinos). Selection is based on scholarly achievements and publications, letters of recommendation, quality and significance of the proposed research, and commitment of the applicant's faculty mentor to the goals of the program.

Financial data The grant is $20,000, including up to $1,000 for travel to the sponsor's annual conference.

Duration 1 year; nonrenewable.

Additional information This program began in 1991.

Number awarded Up to 3 each year.

Deadline October of each year.

[547]
AMERICAN EPILEPSY SOCIETY PREDOCTORAL RESEARCH FELLOWSHIPS

American Epilepsy Society
135 South LaSalle Street, Suite 2850
Chicago, IL 60603
(312) 883-3800   Fax: (312) 896-5784
E-mail: info@aesnet.org
Web: www.aesnet.org

Summary To provide funding to doctoral candidates, especially Asian Americans and other minorities, who are interested in conducting dissertation research related to epilepsy.

Eligibility This program is open full-time doctoral students conducting dissertation research with an epilepsy-related theme under the guidance of a mentor with expertise in epilepsy research. Applicants must have a defined research plan and access to institutional resources to conduct the proposed project. Selection is based on the applicant's potential and commitment to develop as an independent and productive epilepsy researcher, academic record, and research experience; the mentor's research qualifications; the research training plan; and the quality of the research facilities, resources, and training opportunities. Applications are especially encouraged from women, members of minority groups, and people with disabilities. U.S. citizenship is not required, but all research must be conducted in the United States.

Financial data Grants range up $30,000, including $29,000 as stipend and $1,000 for travel support and complimentary registration to attend the sponsor's annual meeting.

Duration 1 year; nonrenewable.

Additional information In addition to the funding provided by the American Epilepsy Society, support is available from the TESS Research Foundation for applications focused on epilepsy due to SLC13A5 mutations; the LGS Foundation for applications focused on Lennox-Gastaut-Syndrome; the PCDH19 Alliance for applications focused on epilepsy due to PCDH19 mutations; the Dravet Syndrome Foundation for applications focused on Dravet Syndrome; Wishes for Elliott for applications focused on epilepsy due to SCN8A mutations; and the TS Alliance for applications focused on epilepsy associated with tuberous sclerosis complex (TSC).

Number awarded Varies each year.

Deadline Letters of intent must be submitted by October of each year; final proposals are due in January.

[548]
AMERICAN MUSEUM OF NATURAL HISTORY GRADUATE STUDENT FELLOWSHIP PROGRAM

American Museum of Natural History
Attn: Richard Gilder Graduate School
Central Park West at 79th Street
New York, NY 10024-5192
(212) 769-5055   E-mail: Fellowships-rggs@amnh.org
Web: www.amnh.org

Summary To provide financial assistance to doctoral students in selected programs at designated universities, especially Asian Americans and other minorities, who are interested in utilizing the resources of the American Museum of Natural History in their training and research program.

Eligibility This program is open to doctoral students in scientific disciplines practiced at the museum. The applicant's university exercises educational jurisdiction over the program and awards the degree; the museum curator serves as a graduate adviser, co-major professor, or major professor. Both U.S. citizens and noncitizens are eligible to apply. Candidates for a master's degree are not eligible. The museum encourages women, minorities, persons with disabilities, and Vietnam Era and disabled veterans to apply.

Financial data Fellowships provide a stipend and health insurance.

Duration 1 year; may be renewed up to 3 additional years.

Additional information The cooperating universities (and their relevant programs) are Columbia University, in anthropology, vertebrate and invertebrate paleontology, earth and planetary sciences, and evolutionary, ecological, and environmental biology; Cornell University in entomology; the Graduate Center of City University of New York in earth and planetary sciences, paleontology, and evolutionary biology; New York University in molecular biology; and Stony Brook University in astronomy and astrophysics. Students must apply simultaneously to the museum and to 1 of the cooperating universities.

Number awarded Varies each year.

Deadline December of each year.

[549]
AMERICAN NURSES ASSOCIATION MINORITY FELLOWSHIP PROGRAM

American Nurses Association
Attn: SAMHSA Minority Fellowship Programs
8515 Georgia Avenue, Suite 400
Silver Spring, MD 20910-3492
(301) 628-5247   Toll Free: (800) 274-4ANA
Fax: (301) 628-5339   E-mail: janet.jackson@ana.org
Web: www.emfp.org

Summary To provide financial assistance to Asian American and other minority nurses who are doctoral candidates interested in psychiatric, mental health, and substance abuse issues that impact the lives of ethnic minority people.

Eligibility This program is open to nurses who have a master's degree and are members of an ethnic or racial minority group, including but not limited to Asians and Asian Americans, Blacks or African Americans, Hispanics or Latinos, American Indians and Alaska Natives, and Native Hawaiians and other Pacific Islanders. Applicants must be enrolled full time in an accredited doctoral nursing program. They must be certified as a Mental Health Nurse Practitioner, Mental Health Clinical Nurse Specialist, or Mental Health Nurse. U.S. citizenship or permanent resident status and membership in the American Nurses Association are required. Selection is based on commitment to a career in substance abuse in psychiatric/mental health issues affecting minority populations.

Financial data The program provides an annual stipend of $22,476 and tuition assistance up to $5,000.

Duration 3 to 5 years.

Additional information Funds for this program are provided by the Substance Abuse and Mental Health Services Administration (SAMHSA).

Number awarded 1 or more each year.

Deadline March of each year.

[550]
AMERICAN NURSES ASSOCIATION MINORITY FELLOWSHIP PROGRAM YOUTH

American Nurses Association
Attn: SAMHSA Minority Fellowship Programs
8515 Georgia Avenue, Suite 400
Silver Spring, MD 20910-3492
(301) 628-5247   Toll Free: (800) 274-4ANA
Fax: (301) 628-5339   E-mail: janet.jackson@ana.org
Web: www.emfp.org

Summary To provide financial assistance to Asian American and other minority nurses who are interested in working on a master's degree in psychiatric/mental health nursing for service to young people.

Eligibility This program is open to nurses who are members of the American Nurses Association and members of an ethnic or racial minority group, including but not limited to Asians and Asian Americans, Blacks or African Americans, Hispanics or Latinos, American Indians and Alaska Natives, and Native Hawaiians and other Pacific Islanders. Applicants must be enrolled full time in an accredited master's degree behavioral health (psychiatric/mental health/substance abuse) nursing program. They must intend to apply for certification to become a Psychiatric Mental Health Nurse Practitioners, a fellowship-approved certification in substance abuse, or another sub-specialty that is associated with behavioral health services for children, adolescents, and youth transitioning into adulthood (ages 16 through 25). U.S. citizenship or permanent resident status is required. Selection is based on commitment to a career that provides behavioral health services to young people.

Financial data The stipend is $11,500 per year. Funds are disbursed directly to the fellow.

Duration 1 year; may be renewed.

Additional information Funds for this program are provided by the Substance Abuse and Mental Health Services Administration (SAMHSA).

Number awarded 1 or more each year.

Deadline March of each year.

[551]
AMERICAN POLITICAL SCIENCE ASSOCIATION MINORITY FELLOWS PROGRAM

American Political Science Association
Attn: Diversity and Inclusion Programs
1527 New Hampshire Avenue, N.W.
Washington, DC 20036-1206
(202) 349-9362   Fax: (202) 483-2657
E-mail: kmealy@apsanet.org
Web: www.apsanet.org/mfp

Summary To provide financial assistance to Asian American and other minorities interested in working on a doctoral degree in political science.

Eligibility This program is open to Asian Pacific Americans, African Americans, Latino(a)s, and Native Americans who are in their senior year at a college or university or currently enrolled in a master's degree program. Applicants must be planning to enroll in a doctoral program in political science to prepare for a career in teaching and research. They must be U.S. citizens and able to demonstrate financial need. Along with their application, they must submit a 500-word personal statement that includes why they are interested in attending graduate school in political science, what specific fields within the discipline they plan to study, and how they intend to contribute to research within the discipline. Selection is based on interest in teaching and potential for research in political science.

Financial data The stipend is $2,000 per year.

Duration 2 years.

Additional information In addition to the fellows who receive stipends from this program, students who are selected as fellows without stipend are recommended for admission and financial support to every doctoral political science program in the country. This program was established in 1969.

Number awarded Up to 12 fellows receive stipends each year.

Deadline March or October of each year.

[552]
AMERICAN SOCIETY OF INDIAN ENGINEERS SCHOLARSHIP PROGRAM

American Society of Indian Engineers
Attn: Scholarship Program
P.O. Box 741007
Houston, TX 77274
E-mail: asiehouston@gmail.com
Web: www.asiehouston.org/?s=scholarship

Summary To provide financial assistance to residents of any state who are of Indian origin and are working on an undergraduate or graduate degree in engineering or architecture at a college in the Houston area of Texas.

Eligibility This program is open to residents of any state who are of Indian origin and currently enrolled at a college or university in the greater Houston metropolitan area. Applicants must be working full time on an associate, bachelor's, or graduate degree in engineering or architecture. Along with their application, they must submit an essay about themselves, their achievements, career goals, and activities. Selection is based on that essay (50%), GPA (25%), and financial need (25%). An interview may also be required.

Financial data The stipend is $1,000.

Duration 1 year.

Number awarded Up to 10 each year.

Deadline September of each year.

[553]
AMERICAN SPEECH-LANGUAGE-HEARING FOUNDATION SCHOLARSHIP FOR INTERNATIONAL STUDENTS

American Speech-Language-Hearing Foundation
Attn: Programs Administrator
2200 Research Boulevard
Rockville, MD 20850-3289
(301) 296-8703   Toll Free: (800) 498-2071, ext. 8703
Fax: (301) 296-8567
E-mail: foundationprograms@asha.org
Web: www.ashfoundation.org

Summary To provide financial assistance to Asian American and other minority and international students who are interested in working on a graduate degree in communication sciences and disorders.

Eligibility This program is open to full-time international and minority graduate students who are enrolled in communication sciences and disorders programs. Applicants must submit an essay, up to 5 pages in length, on a topic that relates to the future of leadership in the discipline. Selection is based on academic promise and outstanding academic achievement.

Financial data The stipend is $5,000. Funds must be used for educational support (e.g., tuition, books, school living expenses), not for personal or conference travel.

Duration   The award is granted annually.

Additional information   This program is supported by the Kala Singh Memorial Fund.

Number awarded   Up to 3 each year.

Deadline   May of each year.

[554]
AMERICAN SPEECH-LANGUAGE-HEARING FOUNDATION SCHOLARSHIP FOR MINORITY STUDENTS

American Speech-Language-Hearing Foundation
Attn: Programs Administrator
2200 Research Boulevard
Rockville, MD 20850-3289
(301) 296-8703   Toll Free: (800) 498-2071, ext. 8703
Fax: (301) 296-8567
E-mail: foundationprograms@asha.org
Web: www.ashfoundation.org

Summary   To provide financial assistance to Asian American and other minority graduate students in communication sciences and disorders programs.

Eligibility   This program is open to full-time graduate students who are enrolled in communication sciences and disorders programs, with preference given to U.S. citizens who are members of a racial or ethnic minority group. Applicants must submit an essay, up to 5 pages in length, on a topic that relates to the future of leadership in the discipline. Selection is based on academic promise and outstanding academic achievement.

Financial data   The stipend is $5,000. Funds must be used for educational support (e.g., tuition, books, school living expenses), not for personal or conference travel.

Duration   1 year.

Number awarded   Up to 3 each year.

Deadline   May of each year.

[555]
AMERICAN THEOLOGICAL LIBRARY ASSOCIATION DIVERSITY SCHOLARSHIP

American Theological Library Association
Attn: Diversity Committee
300 South Wacker Drive, Suite 2100
Chicago, IL 60606-6701
(312) 454-5100   Toll Free: (888) 665-ATLA
Fax: (312) 454-5505   E-mail: memberrep@atla.com
Web: www.atla.com

Summary   To provide funding to Asian American and other library students from underrepresented groups who are members of the American Theological Library Association (ATLA) interested in working on a master's degree in theological librarianship.

Eligibility   This program is open to ATLA members from underrepresented groups (religious, racial, ethnic, or gender) who are enrolled at an ALA-accredited master's degree program in library and information studies. Applicants must submit personal statements on what diversity means to them, why their voice has not yet been heard, how they will increase diversity in their immediate context, and how they plan to increase diversity and participate fully in the ATLA.

Financial data   The stipend is $2,400.

Duration   1 year.

Number awarded   1 each year.

Deadline   April of each year.

[556]
ANHEUSER-BUSCH NAPABA LAW FOUNDATION PRESIDENTIAL SCHOLARSHIPS

National Asian Pacific American Bar Association
Attn: NAPABA Law Foundation
1612 K Street, N.W., Suite 510
Washington, DC 20006
(202) 775-9555   Fax: (202) 775-9333
E-mail: nlfstaff@napaba.org
Web: www.napaba.org/?page=NLF_scholarships

Summary   To provide financial assistance to law students interested in serving the Asian Pacific American community.

Eligibility   This program is open to students at ABA-accredited law schools in the United States. Applicants must demonstrate leadership potential to serve the Asian Pacific American community upon graduation. Along with their application, they must submit a 500-word essay that covers 1) the most significant experiences in their background that have shaped and demonstrated their commitment to serving the needs of Asian Pacific Americans; and 2) how they intend to serve the needs of the Asian Pacific American community in their future legal career. Selection is based on that essay, academic achievement, leadership, and commitment to serving the Asian Pacific American community. U.S. citizenship or permanent resident status is required.

Financial data   The stipend is $7,500.

Duration   1 year.

Additional information   This program is supported by Anheuser-Busch Companies, Inc.

Number awarded   2 each year.

Deadline   August of each year.

[557]
APA/DIVISION 39 GRANT

American Psychological Foundation
750 First Street, N.E.
Washington, DC 20002-4242
(202) 336-5843   Fax: (202) 336-5812
E-mail: foundation@apa.org
Web: www.apa.org/apf/funding/division-39.aspx

Summary   To provide funding to psychologists who wish to conduct psychoanalytical research related to Asian Americans and other underserved populations.

Eligibility   This program is open to psychologists who have a demonstrated knowledge of psychoanalytical principles. Applicants may be, but are not required to be, practicing psychoanalytic therapists. Preference is given to graduate students involved in dissertation research, early-career professionals, and/or those who demonstrate a long-term interest in research related to underserved populations. The research may be of an empirical, theoretical, or clinical nature. Selection is based on conformance with stated program goals and qualifications; quality and potential impact of both previous and proposed research projects; originality, innovation, and contribution to the field with both previous and proposed research projects; and applicant's demonstrated interest in research related to underserved populations. The sponsor encourages applications from individuals who represent diversity in race, ethnicity, gender, age, disability, and sexual orientation.

Financial data The grant is $4,000.

Duration 1 year.

Additional information This program, which began in 2014, is sponsored by the American Psychological Association's Division 39 (Psychoanalysis).

Number awarded 1 each year.

Deadline July of each year.

[558]
APA MINORITY MEDICAL STUDENT SUMMER MENTORING PROGRAM

American Psychiatric Association
Attn: Division of Diversity and Health Equity
1000 Wilson Boulevard, Suite 1825
Arlington, VA 22209-3901
(703) 907-8653   Toll Free: (888) 35-PSYCH
Fax: (703) 907-7852   E-mail: mking@psych.org
Web: www.psychiatry.org/minority-fellowship

Summary To provide funding to Asian American and other minority medical students who are interested in working on a summer project with a psychiatrist mentor.

Eligibility This program is open to minority medical students who are interested in psychiatric issues. Minorities include Asian Americans, American Indians, Alaska Natives, Native Hawaiians, Hispanic/Latinos, and African Americans. Applicants must be interested in working with a psychiatrist mentor, primarily on clinical work with underserved minority populations and mental health care disparities. Work settings may be in a research, academic, or clinical environment. Most of them are inner-city or rural and deal with psychiatric subspecialties, particularly substance abuse and geriatrics. Selection is based on interest of the medical student and specialty of the mentor, practice setting, and geographic proximity of the mentor to the student. U.S. citizenship or permanent resident status is required.

Financial data Fellowships provide $1,500 for living and out-of-pocket expenses directly related to the conduct of the fellowship.

Duration Summer months.

Additional information This program is funded by the Substance Abuse and Mental Health Services Administration.

Number awarded Varies each year.

Deadline March of each year.

[559]
APABA-SV AND BALIF JOINT SCHOLARSHIP

Asian Pacific American Bar Association of the Silicon Valley
Attn: Scholarship and Fellowship Committee
P.O. Box 60988
Palo Alto, CA 94306
E-mail: apabasv@gmail.com
Web: www.apabasv.com/awards-scholarships

Summary To provide financial assistance to students from any state who are enrolled at law schools in the San Francisco Bay area and have served the Asian Pacific American and LGBT communities.

Eligibility This program is open to students currently enrolled at law schools in the San Francisco Bay area who have 1) demonstrated leadership and service to the Asian Pacific American community and the LGBT community; 2) overcome personal hardships or challenges; and 3) shown excellence and achievement in law school. Applicants must submit a 2-page essay explaining how they satisfy those requirements. Finalists are interviewed.

Financial data The stipend is $3,000.

Duration 1 year.

Additional information This program began in 2013 with support from the Charity Foundation of the Asian Pacific American Bar Association of the Silicon Valley (APABA-SV) and the Bay Area Lawyers for Individual Freedom (BALIF).

Number awarded 1 each year.

Deadline June of each year.

[560]
APABA-SV EQUAL JUSTICE SCHOLARSHIPS

Asian Pacific American Bar Association of the Silicon Valley
Attn: Scholarship and Fellowship Committee
P.O. Box 60988
Palo Alto, CA 94306
E-mail: apabasv@gmail.com
Web: www.apabasv.com/awards-scholarships

Summary To provide financial assistance to students from any state who are enrolled at law schools in the San Francisco Bay area and have been involved in the Asian Pacific American community.

Eligibility This program is open to students currently enrolled at law schools in the San Francisco Bay area who have 1) demonstrated leadership and service to the Asian Pacific American community in the United States; 2) overcome personal hardships or challenges; and 3) shown excellence and achievement in law school. Applicants must submit a 2-page essay explaining how they satisfy those requirements. Strong preference is given to students who will be interning at a nonprofit organization that serves the Asian Pacific American community and who can demonstrate financial need. Finalists are interviewed.

Financial data The stipend is $5,000.

Duration 1 year.

Additional information This program is funded by the law firm Lee, Tran & Liang.

Number awarded Up to 2 each year.

Deadline June of each year.

[561]
APAGS COMMITTEE FOR THE ADVANCEMENT OF RACIAL AND ETHNIC DIVERSITY (CARED) GRANT PROGRAM

American Psychological Association
Attn: American Psychological Association of Graduate Students
750 First Street, N.E.
Washington, DC 20002-4242
(202) 336-6014   Fax: (202) 336-5694
E-mail: apags@apa.org
Web: www.apa.org/about/awards/apags-cema.aspx

Summary To provide funding to graduate students who are members of the American Psychological Association of Graduate Students (APAGS) and who wish to develop a project that increases membership and participation of Asian American and other ethnic minority students within the association.
Eligibility This program is open to members of APAGS who are enrolled at least half time in a master's or doctoral program at an accredited university. Applicants must be interested in developing a project to increase the membership and participation of ethnic minority graduate students within APAGS, advertise education and training opportunities for ethnic minorities, and enhance the recruitment and retention efforts for ethnic minority students in psychology. Examples include, but are not limited to, workshops, conferences, speaker series, mentorship programs, and the development of student organizations with a focus on multiculturalism or ethnic minority concerns.
Financial data The grant is $1,000.
Duration The grant is presented annually.
Additional information This grant was first awarded in 1997.
Number awarded 4 each year.
Deadline November of each year.

[562]
APALA SCHOLARSHIP

Asian Pacific American Librarians Association
Attn: Executive Director
P.O. Box 677593
Orlando, FL 32867-7593
(407) 823-5048   Fax: (407) 823-5865
E-mail: bbasco@mail.ucf.edu
Web: www.apalaweb.org/awards/apala-scholarship

Summary To provide financial assistance to members of the Asian Pacific American Librarians Association (APALA) who are working on a graduate library degree.
Eligibility This program is open to APALA members of Asian or Pacific Islander heritage who are enrolled or have been accepted into a master's program or doctoral degree program in library or information science at an ALA-accredited library school. Applicants must be citizens or permanent residents of the United States or Canada. They may be enrolled full or part time. Along with their application, they must submit a 1-page essay on either their vision of a librarian's role in the 21st century or the contributions they can make as an Asian or Pacific Islander librarian.
Financial data The stipend is $1,000.
Duration 1 year.
Number awarded 1 each year.
Deadline April of each year.

[563]
APF GRADUATE STUDENT SCHOLARSHIPS

American Psychological Foundation
750 First Street, N.E.
Washington, DC 20002-4242
(202) 336-5843   Fax: (202) 336-5812
E-mail: foundation@apa.org
Web: www.apa.org/apf/funding/cogdop.aspx

Summary To provide funding for research to graduate students, especially Asian Americans and other minorities, in psychology.
Eligibility Each department of psychology that is a member in good standing of the Council of Graduate Departments of Psychology (COGDOP) may nominate up to 3 candidates for these scholarships. Nominations must include a completed application form, a letter of nomination from the department chair or director of graduate studies, a letter of recommendation from the nominee's graduate research adviser, a transcript of all graduate course work completed by the nominee, a curriculum vitae, and a brief outline of the nominee's thesis or dissertation research project. Selection is based on the context for the research, the clarity and comprehensibility of the research question, the appropriateness of the research design, the general importance of the research, and the use of requested funds. The sponsor encourages applications from individuals who represent diversity in race, ethnicity, gender, age, disability, and sexual orientation.
Financial data Awards range from $1,000 to $5,000 per year. A total of $28,000 is available for these scholarships each year.
Duration 1 year.
Additional information The highest rated nominees receive the Charles and Carol Spielberger Scholarship of $5,000, the Harry and Miriam Levinson Scholarship of $5,000 and the William and Dorothy Bevan Scholarship of $5,000. The next highest rated nominee receives the Ruth G. and Joseph D. Matarazzo Scholarship of $3,000. The next highest rated nominee receives the Clarence J. Rosecrans Scholarship of $2,000. The next highest rated nominees receive the William C. Howell Scholarship, the Dr. Judy Kuriansky Scholarship, and the Peter and Malina James and Dr. Louis P. James Legacy Scholarship of $1,000 each. Another 8 scholarships of $1,000 each, offered by the COGDOP, are also awarded.
Number awarded 16 each year: 3 at $5,000, 1 at $3,000, 1 at $2,000, and 11 at $1,000.
Deadline June of each year.

[564]
APIQWTC SCHOLARSHIP

Asian Pacific Islander Queer Women and Transgender
    Community
c/o Amy Sueyoshi
San Francisco State University
College of Ethnic Studies
1600 Holloway Avenue
San Francisco, CA 94132
(415) 405-0774   E-mail: sueyoshi@sfsu.edu
Web: www.apiqwtc.org/resources/apiqwtc-scholarship

Summary To provide financial assistance to Asian Pacific Islander (API) lesbian and bisexual women and transgender individuals who are high school seniors, undergraduates, or graduate students interested in working on a degree in any field at a college in any state.
Eligibility This program is open to API high school seniors and current undergraduate or graduate students in any field. Applicants must identify as a lesbian, bisexual, or queer woman or a transgender individual. Along with their application, they must submit a 2-page personal statement that covers their community involvement and future goals; how their

cultural heritage, sexual orientation, and/or gender identity has influenced their life; any activities in which they have been involved; any relevant experiences up to the present; and how they see themselves involved in the community in the future, either through their career or otherwise.

Financial data The stipend is $1,000.

Duration 1 year.

Additional information The Asian Pacific Islander Queer Women and Transgender Community (APIQWTC) is a community of more than 10 organizations in the San Francisco Bay area provide support and community for queer Asian and Pacific Islander individuals, but its scholarships are available to students from any state.

Number awarded 2 each year.

Deadline February of each year.

[565]
ARCHIE MOTLEY MEMORIAL SCHOLARSHIP FOR MINORITY STUDENTS

Midwest Archives Conference
c/o Rachel Howard
University of Louisville Libraries
Archives and Special Collections
Louisville, KY 40292
(502) 852-4476   E-mail: Rachel.howard@louisville.edu
Web: www.midwestarchives.org/motley

Summary To provide financial assistance to Asian American and other minority graduate students preparing for a career in archival administration.

Eligibility This program is open to graduate students of Asian, African, American Indian, Pacific Islander, or Latino descent who are enrolled or accepted for enrollment in a graduate, multi-course program in archival administration at a college or university in any state. The graduate program must offer at least 3 courses in archival administration or be listed in the current Directory of Archival Education of the Society of American Archivists (SAA). Applicants must have a GPA of 3.0 or higher. They may be residents of any state and attending school in any state. Along with their application, they must submit a 500-word essay on their interests and future goals in archival administration.

Financial data The stipend is $750.

Duration 1 year.

Additional information This program began in 2004.

Number awarded 2 each year.

Deadline February of each year.

[566]
ARKANSAS CONFERENCE ETHNIC AND LANGUAGE CONCERNS COMMITTEE SCHOLARSHIPS

United Methodist Church-Arkansas Conference
Attn: Committee on Ethnic and Language Concerns
800 Daisy Bates Drive
Little Rock, AR 72202
(501) 324-8045   Toll Free: (877) 646-1816
Fax: (501) 324-8018   E-mail: mallen@arumc.org
Web: www.arumc.org/docs-and-forms

Summary To provide financial assistance to Asian American and other ethnic minority Methodist students from Arkan-

sas who are interested in attending college or graduate school in any state.

Eligibility This program is open to ethnic minority undergraduate and graduate students who are active members of local congregations affiliated with the Arkansas Conference of the United Methodist Church (UMC). Applicants must be currently enrolled in an accredited institution of higher education in any state. Along with their application, they must submit an essay explaining how this scholarship will make them a leader in the UMC. Preference is given to students attending a UMC-affiliated college or university.

Financial data The stipend is $500 per semester ($1,000 per year) for undergraduates or $1,000 per semester ($2,000 per year) for graduate students.

Duration 1 year; may be renewed.

Number awarded 5 each year: 1 in each UMC Arkansas district.

Deadline February or September of each year.

[567]
ARL CAREER ENHANCEMENT PROGRAM

Association of Research Libraries
Attn: Director of Diversity Programs
21 Dupont Circle, N.W., Suite 800
Washington, DC 20036
(202) 296-2296   Fax: (202) 872-0884
E-mail: mpuente@arl.org
Web: www.arl.org

Summary To provide an opportunity for Asian Americans and members of other minority racial and ethnic groups to gain work experience at a library that is a member of the Association of Research Libraries (ARL).

Eligibility This program is open to members of racial and ethnic minority groups that are underrepresented as professionals in academic and research libraries (Asian, American Indian or Alaska Native, Black or African American, Native Hawaiian or other Pacific Islander, or Hispanic or Latino). Applicants must have completed at least 12 credit hours of an M.L.I.S. degree program at an ALA-accredited institution. They must be interested in an internship at 1 of 7 ARL member institutions. Along with their application, they must submit a 500-word essay on what attracts them to an internship opportunity in an ARL library, their professional interests as related to the internship, and their goals for the internship.

Financial data Fellows receive a stipend of $4,800 for the internship, housing reimbursement up to $2,500, relocation assistance up to $1,000, and financial support (approximately $1,400) to attend the annual ARL Leadership Institute.

Duration The internship lasts 6 to 12 weeks (or 240 hours).

Additional information This program is funded by the Institute of Museum and Library Services. Recently, the 7 participating ARL institutions were the University of Arizona, University of California at San Diego, University of Kentucky, University of Michigan, University of Washington, National Library of Medicine, and North Carolina State University.

Number awarded Varies each year; recently, 13 of these fellows were selected.

Deadline October of each year.

[568]
ARL INITIATIVE TO RECRUIT A DIVERSE WORKFORCE

Association of Research Libraries
Attn: Director of Diversity Programs
21 Dupont Circle, N.W., Suite 800
Washington, DC 20036
(202) 296-2296   Fax: (202) 872-0884
E-mail: mpuente@arl.org
Web: www.arl.org

Summary   To provide financial assistance to Asian Americans and members of other minority racial and ethnic groups who are interested in preparing for a career as an academic or research librarian.

Eligibility   This program is open to members of racial and ethnic minority groups that are underrepresented as professionals in academic and research libraries (Asian, American Indian or Alaska Native, Black or African American, Native Hawaiian or other Pacific Islander, or Hispanic or Latino). Applicants must be interested in working on an M.L.I.S. degree at an ALA-accredited program. They must be citizens or permanent residents of the United States (including Puerto Rico) or Canada.

Financial data   The stipend is $5,000 per year.

Duration   2 years.

Additional information   This program began in 2000. Funding is currently provided by the Institute of Museum and Library Services and by the contributions of 52 libraries that are members of the Association of Research Libraries (ARL).

Number awarded   Varies each year; recently, 15 were awarded.

Deadline   April of each year.

[569]
ARL/SAA MOSAIC SCHOLARSHIPS

Society of American Archivists
Attn: Chair, Awards Committee
17 North State Street, Suite 1425
Chicago, IL 60602-4061
(312) 606-0722   Toll Free: (866) 722-7858
Fax: (312) 606-0728   E-mail: info@archivists.org
Web: www2.archivists.org

Summary   To provide financial assistance to Asian American and other minority students who are working on a graduate degree in archival science.

Eligibility   This program is open to minority graduate students, defined as those of Asian, American Indian/Alaska Native, Black/African American, Hispanic/Latino, or Native Hawaiian/other Pacific Islander descent. Applicants must be enrolled or planning to enroll full or part time in a master's degree program or a multi-course program in archival science, archival management, digital archives, special collections, or a related program. They may have completed no more than half of the credit requirements for a degree. Along with their application, they must submit a 500-word essay outlining their interests and future goals in the archives profession. U.S. or Canadian citizenship or permanent resident status is required.

Financial data   The stipend is $10,000.

Duration   1 year.

Additional information   This program began in 2009. A second iteration of the program began in 2013 in partnership with the Association of Research Libraries (ARL) and financial support provided by the Institute of Museum and Library Sciences (IMLS).

Number awarded   1 or 2 each year.

Deadline   June of each year.

[570]
ARTTABLE MENTORED INTERNSHIPS FOR DIVERSITY IN THE VISUAL ARTS PROFESSIONS

ArtTable Inc.
1 East 53rd Street, Fifth Floor
New York, NY 10022
(212) 343-1735   Fax: (866) 363-4188
E-mail: info@arttable.org
Web: www.arttable.org/summermentoredinternship

Summary   To provide an opportunity for women who are Asian American or from other diverse backgrounds to gain mentored work experience during the summer and to prepare for a career as an art professional.

Eligibility   This program is open to women who are college seniors, recent graduates, or graduate students and interested in preparing for a career as a visual arts professional (including administrative director, art adviser, art appraiser, art critic, art dealer, art librarian, arts funder, arts lawyer, conservator, curator, editor, educator, fundraiser, management consultant, public relations consultant, writer). Applicants must be from a cultural or ethnic background that is underrepresented in the field. They must be interested in working during the summer with a mentor at an art museum or similar facility. U.S. citizenship or permanent resident status is required.

Financial data   The stipend is $3,000. The hosting institution or mentor receives $500 for administrative and other costs.

Duration   8 weeks during the summer.

Additional information   This program began in 2000. Support is provided by the Samuel H. Kress Foundation.

Number awarded   Varies each year; recently, 5 of these internships were awarded.

Deadline   February of each year.

[571]
ASA MINORITY FELLOWSHIP PROGRAM GENERAL FELLOWSHIP

American Sociological Association
Attn: Minority Affairs Program
1430 K Street, N.W., Suite 600
Washington, DC 20005-2504
(202) 383-9005, ext. 322   Fax: (202) 638-0882
TDD: (202) 638-0981 E-mail: minority.affairs@asanet.org
Web: www.asanet.org

Summary   To provide financial assistance to doctoral students in sociology who are Asian Americans or members of other minority groups.

Eligibility   This program is open to U.S. citizens, permanent residents, and noncitizen nationals who are Asian Americans (e.g., southeast Asians, Japanese, Chinese, Koreans), Pacific Islanders (e.g., Filipinos, Samoans, Hawaiians, Guamanians Blacks/African Americans, Latinos (e.g., Mexican

Americans, Puerto Ricans, Cubans), or American Indians or Alaskan Natives). Applicants must be entering or continuing students in sociology at the doctoral level. Along with their application, they must submit 3-page essays on 1) the reasons why they decided to undertake graduate study in sociology, their primary research interests, and why they hope to do with a Ph.D. in sociology; and 2) what led them to select the doctoral program they attend or hope to attend and how they see that doctoral program preparing them for a professional career in sociology. Selection is based on commitment to research, focus of research experience, academic achievement, writing ability, research potential, and financial need.

Financial data The stipend is $18,000 per year.

Duration 1 year; may be renewed up to 2 additional years.

Additional information This program, which began in 1974, is supported by individual members of the American Sociological Association (ASA) and by several affiliated organizations (Alpha Kappa Delta, Sociologists for Women in Society, the Association of Black Sociologists, the Midwest Sociological Society, and the Southwestern Sociological Association).

Number awarded Varies each year; since the program began, more than 500 of these fellowships have been awarded.

Deadline January of each year.

[572]
ASEI GRADUATE SCHOLARSHIPS

American Society of Engineers of Indian Origin
Attn: Scholarship Program
P.O. Box 18215
Irvine, CA 92623
E-mail: scholarships@aseiusa.org
Web: www.aseiusa.org

Summary To provide financial assistance to graduate students of Indian origin (from India) who are working on a degree in engineering, computer science, or related areas.

Eligibility This program is open to graduate students of Indian origin (by birth, ancestry, or relation). Applicants must be enrolled full time at an ABET-accredited college or university in the United States and working on a degree in engineering, computer science, or an allied science and have a GPA of 3.5 or higher. They must be members of the American Society of Engineers of Indian Origin (ASEI). Selection is based on demonstrated ability, academic achievement (including GPA, honors, and awards), career objectives, faculty recommendations, involvement in science fair and campus activities, financial hardship, industrial exposure (including part-time work and internships), and involvement in ASEI and other community activities.

Financial data Stipends range from $500 to $1,000.

Duration 1 year.

Number awarded Several each year.

Deadline August of each year.

[573]
ASIAN AMERICAN ARCHITECTS/ENGINEERS ASSOCIATION STUDENT SCHOLARSHIPS

Asian American Architects/Engineers Association
Attn: Foundation
645 West Ninth Street, Unit 110-175
Los Angeles, CA 90015
(213) 896-9270   Fax: (213) 985-7404
E-mail: info@aaaesc.org
Web: www.aaaesc.org/foundation_student_scholarship

Summary To provide financial assistance to members of the Asian American Architects/Engineers Association (AAa/e) who are interested in working on an undergraduate or graduate degree at a school in southern California.

Eligibility This program is open to student members of AAa/e who are U.S. citizens, permanent residents, or noncitizens enrolled or planning to enroll full time at a college or university in southern California. Applicants must be graduating seniors, community college students, undergraduates, or graduate students working on or planning to work on a degree in architecture, civil engineering (environmental, geotechnical, structural, transportation), electrical engineering, mechanical engineering, landscape architecture, planning and urban design, or construction and construction management. Along with their application, they must submit 1) a 1-page personal statement on their involvement and service to the Asian Pacific Islander community, their interest in their field, and what makes them unique; 2) letters of recommendation from 2 faculty members or employers; and 3) a sample of their work, which may be a design or research project, a completed project, or a proposed project, including an assignment from a class, a senior project, or an assignment from work. For high school seniors and community college students, selection is based on personal statements (50%), recommendations (30%), and the work sample (20%); for undergraduate and graduate students, selection is based on the work sample (65%), personal statements (20%), and recommendations (15%).

Financial data Stipends range up to $5,000.

Duration 1 year.

Number awarded Varies each year; recently, 4 were awarded.

Deadline June of each year.

[574]
ASIAN AMERICAN BAR ASSOCIATION LAW OF THE GREATER BAY AREA FOUNDATION SCHOLARSHIPS

Asian American Bar Association of the Greater Bay Area
Attn: AABA Law Foundation
c/o Miriam Kim, Vice President
Munger, Tolles & Olson
560 Mission Street, 27th Floor
San Francisco, CA 94105
(415) 512-4041   E-mail: aaba.bayarea@gmail.com
Web: www.aaba-bay.com

Summary To provide financial assistance to Asian American residents of any state, especially those who are enrolled at law schools in the San Francisco Bay area, and planning to serve the Asian American community after graduation.

Eligibility This program is open to Asian American students from any state who are attending law schools in the Bay area and have demonstrated a strong commitment to serving the needs of the Asian American community. Students at other law schools may be eligible if they can demonstrate a commitment to serving the Asian American community in the Bay area. Applicants must submit a 3-page personal statement that covers 1) what they see as a pressing issue or concern facing the Asian American community and the role they see themselves playing in advocating or engaging in such an issue; 2) their experience in overcoming economic and other discriminatory barriers; and 3) the characteristics that have made prominent Asian Americans successful and how they would exhibit those same qualities. Selection is based on community service or public interest work for the Asian Pacific American (APA) community or other underrepresented communities; demonstrated leadership in the APA community; demonstrated financial need; and commitment to the Bay Area.

Financial data Stipends are at least $5,000.

Duration 1 year.

Additional information This program includes the Asian Pacific American Judges Scholarship, the Joe Morozumi Scholarship, the Raymond L. Ocampo Jr. Family Scholarship, and the AABA Law Foundation Scholarship.

Number awarded Varies each year; recently, 4 were awarded.

Deadline January of each year.

[575]
ASIAN AMERICAN GRANTS

American Baptist Churches USA
Attn: American Baptist Home Mission Societies
Office of Financial Aid for Studies
P.O. Box 851
Valley Forge, PA 19482-0851
(610) 768-2067   Toll Free: (800) ABC-3USA, ext. 2067
Fax: (610) 768-2470
E-mail: communications@abhms.org
Web: www.abhms.org

Summary To provide ministerial experience during the summer to Asian American Baptist seminarians.

Eligibility This program is open to Asian American seminarians who are interested in gaining local church experience in the summer months. Applicants must be U.S. citizens who have been a member of a church affiliated with American Baptist Churches USA for at least 1 year.

Financial data The grant is $500; the employing church is expected to match the grant.

Duration Summer months.

Number awarded Varies each year.

Deadline May of each year.

[576]
ASIAN AMERICAN LAWYERS ASSOCIATION OF MASSACHUSETTS SCHOLARSHIP

Asian American Lawyers Association of Massachusetts
c/o Vincent Lai
Proskauer Rose LLP
One International Place
Boston, MA 02110-2600
(617) 526-9600   Fax: (617) 526-9899
Web: www.aalam.org/membership_lawstudents.shtml

Summary To provide financial assistance to Asian American students from any state enrolled at law schools in Massachusetts.

Eligibility This program is open to students currently enrolled at law schools in Massachusetts who can demonstrate leadership potential, maturity and responsibility, and a commitment to making a contribution to the Asian Pacific American community. Applicants must submit a 500-word essay on how they, as a future Asian Pacific American lawyer, think they can best contribute to the Asian Pacific American community. Financial need is not considered in the selection process.

Financial data The stipend is $2,500.

Duration 1 year.

Number awarded 1 each year.

Deadline May of each year.

[577]
ASIAN AND PACIFIC AMERICAN LAWYERS ASSOCIATION OF NEW JERSEY SCHOLARSHIPS

Asian and Pacific American Lawyers Association of New
  Jersey
Attn: Scholarship Committee
494 Broad Street, Suite 210
Newark, NJ 07102
(973) 718-7347, ext. 121
Web: www.apalanj.org/foundation

Summary To provide financial assistance to students who are enrolled at law schools in New Jersey and who have demonstrated an interest in the Asian American community.

Eligibility This program is open to students currently enrolled at a law school in New Jersey either as a full-time first- or second-year student or as a part-time first-, second-, or third-year student. Applicants must submit 400-word essays on 1) the most pressing issue or concern they believe the Asian American community is facing today and the role they see themselves playing in advocating for that issue or concern; 2) their suggestions on how Asians and Pacific Islander Americans can stand up and be counted in the legal community and the community at large; and 3) who they see as a successful leader within the Asian American community and the characteristics that make the leader so successful. Selection is based on the essays, academic success, potential to contribute positively to the legal profession, and financial need.

Financial data The stipend is at least $1,000.

Duration 1 year.

Number awarded 3 each year: 1 at each law school in New Jersey.

Deadline April of each year.

[578]
ASIAN BAR ASSOCIATION OF WASHINGTON STUDENT SCHOLARSHIPS

Asian Bar Association of Washington
Attn: Student Scholarship Foundation
c/o Dainen Penta, President
Heahy Fjelstad Peryea
901 Fifth Avenue, Suite 820
Seattle, WA 98164
(206) 403-1933   Fax: (206) 858-6368
E-mail: ABAWScholarship@outlook.com
Web: www.abaw.org/scholarships.html

Summary To provide financial assistance to students of Asian heritage from any state who are attending law school in Washington.

Eligibility This program is open to students from any state currently attending law school in the state of Washington. Applicants must be a member of the Asian Pacific Islander (API) student organization at their school. Along with their application, they must submit a 1,000-word personal statement describing their contributions to the API community and their plans to contribute to that community following graduation from law school, a resume, a copy of their most recent law school transcript, and 2 letters of reference.

Financial data Stipends range from $500 to $6,000.

Duration 1 year.

Additional information This program includes the Yamashita Scholarship, the Sharon A. Sakamoto President's Scholarship, and the Northwest Minority Job Fair Scholarship.

Number awarded Varies each year; recently, 5 were awarded: 1 at $6,000, 1 at $4,000, 2 at $2,000, and 1 at $500.

Deadline September of each year.

[579]
ASIAN HERITAGE LAW SCHOOL SCHOLARSHIP

Infinity Law Group LLC
Attn: Gabriel Cheong
One Adams Place
859 Willard Street, Suite 400
Quincy, MA 02169
(619) 250-8236   E-mail: info@infinlaw.com
Web: www.infinlaw.com/scholarship

Summary To provide financial assistance for law school to students of Asian heritage.

Eligibility This program is open to U.S. citizens and others authorized to work in the United States who are of Asian heritage with at least 1 parent of Asian ancestry. Applicants must have been accepted to enter law school in the upcoming year. They must have an undergraduate GPA of 3.0 or higher. Along with their application, they must submit an essay of 1 to 3 pages describing how their background and experiences in the Asian American community has influenced their choice to go to law school and how they plan to use their law degree.

Financial data The stipend is $1,000.

Duration 1 year.

Additional information This program began in 2015.

Number awarded 1 each year.

Deadline January of each year.

[580]
ASIAN PACIFIC AMERICAN BAR ASSOCIATION OF COLORADO SCHOLARSHIPS

Asian Pacific American Bar Association of Colorado
c/o Justin Cohen, Secretary
Brownstein Hyatt Farber Schreck
410 17th Street, Suite 2200
Denver, CO 80202-4432
(303) 223-1254   Fax: (303) 223-1111
E-mail: jcohen@bhfs.com
Web: www.apaba-colorado.org/apaba-foundation

Summary To provide financial assistance to Asian American law students in Colorado.

Eligibility This program is open to students from any state currently enrolled at law schools in Colorado. Applicants must demonstrate a record of public service to the Asian community in the state.

Financial data The stipend is $1,000. The recipients' law schools must match the award, so the total is $2,000.

Duration 1 year.

Additional information This program began in 1996.

Number awarded 2 each year.

Deadline Deadline not specified.

[581]
ASIAN PACIFIC ISLANDER AMERICAN PUBLIC AFFAIRS ASSOCIATION COLLEGE SCHOLARSHIPS

Asian Pacific Islander American Public Affairs Association
Attn: Community Education Foundation
4000 Truxel Road, Suite 3
Sacramento, CA 95834
(916) 928-9988   Fax: (916) 678-7555
E-mail: info@apapa.org
Web: www.apapa.org/programs/youth-leadership

Summary To provide financial assistance to residents of California, especially those of Asian or Pacific Islander ancestry, who are attending college or graduate school in any state.

Eligibility This program is open to residents of California who are currently enrolled as an undergraduate or graduate student at an accredited 2- or 4-year college or university in any state. All students are eligible, but applications are especially encouraged from those who have Asian or Pacific Islander ancestry. They must have a GPA of 2.75 or higher. Along with their application, they must submit a personal statement demonstrating their commitment to the Asian Pacific Islander community. Selection is based on academic achievement, abilities, career goals, civic activities, leadership skills, and demonstrated commitment to the Asian Pacific Islander community. U.S. citizenship or permanent resident status is required.

Financial data The stipend is $1,000. Funds are paid directly to the student's institution.

Duration 1 year; nonrenewable.

Number awarded Varies each year; recently, 14 were awarded.

Deadline February of each year.

[582]
ASME GRADUATE TEACHING FELLOWSHIP

ASME International
Attn: Education Manager
Two Park Avenue, Floor 7
New York, NY 10016-5618
(212) 591-7559   Toll Free: (800) THE-ASME
Fax: (212) 591-7856   E-mail: lawreya@asme.org
Web: www.asme.org

Summary   To provide funding to members of the American Society of Mechanical Engineers (ASME), especially Asian Americans and other minorities, who are working on a doctorate in mechanical engineering.

Eligibility   This program is open to U.S. citizens or permanent residents who have an undergraduate degree from an ABET-accredited program, belong to the society as a student member, are currently employed as a teaching assistant with lecture responsibility, and are working on a Ph.D. in mechanical engineering. Along with their application, they must submit a statement about their interest in a faculty career. Applications from women and minorities are particularly encouraged.

Financial data   Fellowship stipends are $5,000 per year.

Duration   Up to 2 years.

Additional information   Recipients must teach at least 1 lecture course.

Number awarded   Up to 4 each year.

Deadline   February of each year.

[583]
ASSE DIVERSITY COMMITTEE GRADUATE SCHOLARSHIP

American Society of Safety Engineers
Attn: ASSE Foundation
Scholarship Award Program
520 North Northwest Highway
Park Ridge, IL 60068-2538
(847) 699-2929   Fax: (847) 296-3769
E-mail: assefoundation@asse.org
Web: foundation.asse.org/scholarships-and-grants

Summary   To provide financial assistance to graduate students who are Asian Americans or members of other diverse groups and working on a degree related to occupational safety.

Eligibility   This program is open to students who are working on a graduate degree in occupational safety, health, environment, industrial hygiene, occupational health nursing, or a closely-related field (e.g., industrial or environmental engineering). Applicants must be full- or part-time students who have completed at least 9 semester hours and have a GPA of 3.5 or higher. A goal of this program is to support individuals regardless of race, ethnicity, gender, religion, personal beliefs, age, sexual orientation, physical challenges, geographic location, university, or specific area of study. U.S. citizenship is not required. Membership in the American Society of Safety Engineers (ASSE) is not required, but preference is given to members.

Financial data   The stipend is $1,000 per year.

Duration   1 year; recipients may reapply.

Number awarded   1 each year.

Deadline   November of each year.

[584]
ATKINS NORTH AMERICA LEADERSHIP SCHOLARSHIP

Conference of Minority Transportation Officials
Attn: National Scholarship Program
100 M Street, S.E., Suite 917
Washington, DC 20003
(202) 506-2917   E-mail: info@comto.org
Web: www.comto.org/page/scholarships

Summary   To provide financial assistance to Asian American and other minority undergraduate and graduate students interested in working on a degree in transportation or a related field.

Eligibility   This program is open to minority 1) undergraduates who have completed at least 12 semester hours of study; and 2) graduate students. Applicants must be studying transportation, engineering, planning, or a related discipline. Along with their application they must submit a cover letter on their transportation-related career goals and life aspirations. Financial need is not considered in the selection process.

Financial data   The stipend is $3,000. Funds are paid directly to the recipient's college or university.

Duration   1 year.

Additional information   This program is sponsored by Atkins North America.

Number awarded   1 each year.

Deadline   April of each year.

[585]
BALFOUR PHI DELTA PHI MINORITY SCHOLARSHIP AWARD

Phi Delta Phi International Legal Fraternity
Attn: Executive Director
P.O. Box 11570
Fort Lauderdale, FL 33339
(202) 223-6801   Toll Free: (800) 368-5606
Fax: (202) 223-6808   E-mail: info@phideltaphi.org
Web: www.phideltaphi.org/?page=BalfourMinorityGuide

Summary   To provide financial assistance to Asian Americans and other minorities who are members of Phi Delta Phi International Legal Fraternity.

Eligibility   This program is open to law students who have been members of the legal fraternity for at least 1 year. Applicants must be minorities, defined to include Asian/Pacific Islanders, African Americans, American Indians/Alaskan Natives, Hispanic, or LGBT students. They must affirm that they intend to practice law in inner-cities of the United States, especially in New England. Along with their application, they must submit a 750-word essay on why they consider themselves qualified to serve as role models for minority youth. Priority is given to students at law schools in New England, especially Massachusetts.

Financial data   The stipend is $3,000.

Duration   1 year.

Additional information   This program began in 1997 with funding from the Lloyd G. Balfour Foundation.

Number awarded   1 each year.

Deadline   October of each year.

[586]
BASIC PSYCHOLOGICAL SCIENCE RESEARCH GRANT

American Psychological Association
Attn: American Psychological Association of Graduate Students
750 First Street, N.E.
Washington, DC 20002-4242
(202) 336-6014   E-mail: apags@apa.org
Web: www.apa.org/about/awards/apags-science.aspx

Summary To provide funding to members of the American Psychological Association of Graduate Students (APAGS) who are interested in conducting graduate research in psychological science, including those dealing specifically with diversity issues.

Eligibility This program is open to members of the association who are enrolled at least half time in a psychology or neuroscience graduate program at an accredited university. Applicants must be interested in conducting thesis, dissertation, or other research in psychological science. Along with their application, they must submit a curriculum vitae, letter of recommendation, and 3-page research proposal. The program includes grants specifically reserved for research focused on diversity, defined to include issues of age, sexual orientation, physical disability, socioeconomic status, race/ethnicity, workplace role/position, religious and spiritual orientation, and work/family concerns. Applicants for diversity grants must also submit 1 250-word statement that explains 1) how this research applies to one or more areas of diversity; and 2) how the overall merit and broader implications of this study contribute to our psychological understanding of diversity.

Financial data The stipend is $1,000.

Duration 1 year.

Additional information These grants were first awarded in 2009; the diversity component began in 2014.

Number awarded Approximately 12 each year, of which up to 3 are reserved for researchers specifically focusing on diversity issues.

Deadline November of each year.

[587]
BENTON-MEIER SCHOLARSHIPS

American Psychological Foundation
750 First Street, N.E.
Washington, DC 20002-4242
(202) 336-5843   Fax: (202) 336-5812
E-mail: foundation@apa.org
Web: www.apa.org/apf/funding/benton-meier.aspx

Summary To provide research funding to Asian American and other graduate students from diverse groups who are completing a dissertation related to neuropsychology.

Eligibility This program is open to students who have been admitted to candidacy for a doctoral degree in the area of neuropsychology. Applicants must submit statements documenting their research competence and area commitment, a budget and justification, and how the scholarship money will be used. Selection is based on conformance with stated program goals and the applicant's demonstrated scholarship and research competence. The sponsor encourages applications from individuals who represent diversity in race, ethnicity, gender, age, disability, and sexual orientation.

Financial data The grant is $2,500.

Duration 1 year.

Additional information This program replaces the Henry Hécaen Scholarship, first awarded in 1994, and the Manfred Meier Scholarship, first awarded in 1997.

Number awarded 2 each year.

Deadline May of each year.

[588]
BERYLE M. CHRISTESEN MEMORIAL SCHOLARSHIP

Hmong American Education Fund
P.O. Box 17468
St. Paul, MN 55117
(651) 592-1576   E-mail: scholarships@thehaef.org
Web: www.thehaef.org

Summary To provide financial assistance to Hmong undergraduate and graduate students from Minnesota who are working on a degree in education, especially art education.

Eligibility This program is open to students of Hmong descent who are residents of Minnesota and currently enrolled as full-time undergraduate or graduate students at 2- or 4-year colleges or universities in any state. Applicants must be U.S. citizens or permanent residents and have a GPA of 2.7 or higher. They must be working on a degree in education; preference is given to students preparing for a career in K-12 art education. Along with their application, they must submit a 1,500-word essay on their commitment to education, why they chose to go into education, and their community service. Selection is based on academic achievement.

Financial data The stipend is $1,000.

Duration 1 year; nonrenewable.

Number awarded 1 each year.

Deadline March of each year.

[589]
BILL BERNBACH DIVERSITY SCHOLARSHIPS

American Association of Advertising Agencies
Attn: AAAA Foundation
1065 Avenue of the Americas, 16th Floor
New York, NY 10018
(212) 262-2500   E-mail: bbscholarship@ddb.com
Web: www.aaaa.org

Summary To provide financial assistance to Asian American and other multicultural students interested in working on an undergraduate or graduate degree in advertising at designated schools.

Eligibility This program is open to Asian Americans, African Americans, Hispanic Americans, and Native Americans (including American Indians, Alaska Natives, Native Hawaiians, and other Pacific Islanders) who are interested in studying the advertising creative arts at designated institutions as a full-time student. Applicants must be working on or have already received an undergraduate degree and be able to demonstrate creative talent and promise. They must be U.S. citizens, nationals, or permanent residents. Along with their application, they must submit 10 samples of creative work in their respective field of expertise.

Financial data The stipend is $5,000.

Duration 1 year.

Additional information This program, which began in 1998, is currently sponsored by DDB Worldwide. The participating schools are the Art Center College of Design (Pasadena, California), Creative Circus (Atlanta, Georgia), Miami Ad School (Miami Beach, Florida), University of Oklahoma (Norman, Oklahoma), University of Texas at Austin, VCU Brandcenter (Richmond, Virginia), Savannah College of Art and Design (Savannah, Georgia), University of Oregon (Eugene), City College of New York, School of Visual Arts (New York, New York), Fashion Institute of Technology (New York, New York), and Howard University (Washington, D.C.).

Number awarded 3 each year.

Deadline May of each year.

[590]
BISHOP THOMAS HOYT, JR. FELLOWSHIP

St. John's University
Attn: Collegeville Institute for Ecumenical and Cultural
  Research
2475 Ecumenical Drive
P.O. Box 2000
Collegeville, MN 56321-2000
(320) 363-3366   Fax: (320) 363-3313
E-mail: staff@CollegevilleInstitute.org
Web: www.collegevilleinstitute.org

Summary To provide funding to Asian American and other students of color who wish to complete their doctoral dissertation while in residence at the Collegeville Institute for Ecumenical and Cultural Research of St. John's University in Collegeville, Minnesota.

Eligibility This program is open to people of color completing a doctoral dissertation in ecumenical and cultural research. Applicants must be interested in a residency at the Collegeville Institute for Ecumenical and Cultural Research of St. John's University. Along with their application, they must submit a 1,000-word description of the research project they plan to complete while in residence at the Institute.

Financial data The stipend covers the residency fee of $2,500, which includes housing and utilities.

Duration 1 year.

Additional information Residents at the Institute engage in research, publication, and education on the important intersections between faith and culture. They seek to discern and communicate the meaning of Christian identity and unity in a religiously and culturally diverse world.

Number awarded 1 each year.

Deadline January of each year.

[591]
BONG HAK HYUN MEMORIAL SCHOLARSHIPS

Philip Jaisohn Memorial Foundation
Attn: Scholarship Committee
6705 Old York Road
Philadelphia, PA 19126
(215) 224-2000, ext. 116   Fax: (215) 224-9164
E-mail: info@jaisohn.org
Web: www.jaisohn.com/scholarships

Summary To provide financial assistance to Korean American undergraduate and graduate students who are studying health care or medicine.

Eligibility This program is open to Korean American undergraduate and graduate students who are currently enrolled at a college or university in the United States and working on a degree in health care or a field of medicine. Applicants must be able to demonstrate excellence in community activities and financial need. Along with their application, they must submit an essay on either "Who is Dr. Jaisohn to Me," or "The Significance of Dr. Jaisohn's Ideal to Korean Americans." They must also submit a 100-word statement on how they can contribute to and be involved in the activities of the Philip Jaisohn Memorial Foundation. Selection is based on potential, passion, and leadership.

Financial data The stipend is $1,500.

Duration 1 year.

Number awarded 2 each year.

Deadline August of each year.

[592]
BOR-UEI CHEN SCHOLARSHIPS

Photonics Society of Chinese-Americans
c/o Norman Kwong, Scholarship Committee Chair
MACOM Technology Solutions
1500 Hughes Way
Long Beach, CA 90801
(818) 415-6160   E-mail: norman.kwong@binoptics.com
Web: www.psc-sc.org/psc/index.php/scholarship

Summary To provide financial assistance to Chinese American graduate students in the field of optical communications and photonic devices.

Eligibility This program is open to Chinese American graduate students at universities in the United States who are nominated by a member of the Photonics Society of Chinese-Americans. Nominees must be working on a degree in a field related to optical communications and photonic devices. Selection is based on the merits of the candidate's research work as documented by publications in technical journals, conference presentations, and recommendations from the candidate's sponsor or adviser.

Financial data The stipend is $1,000.

Duration 1 year.

Additional information This program began in 1995.

Number awarded 2 or 3 each year.

Deadline November of each year.

[593]
BREAKTHROUGH TO NURSING SCHOLARSHIPS

National Student Nurses' Association
Attn: Foundation
45 Main Street, Suite 606
Brooklyn, NY 11201
(718) 210-0705   Fax: (718) 210-0710
E-mail: nsna@nsna.org
Web: www.nsna.org

Summary To provide financial assistance to Asian American and other minority undergraduate and graduate students who wish to prepare for careers in nursing.

Eligibility This program is open to students currently enrolled in state-approved schools of nursing or pre-nursing associate degree, baccalaureate, diploma, generic master's, generic doctoral, R.N. to B.S.N., R.N. to M.S.N., or L.P.N./L.V.N. to R.N. programs. Graduating high school seniors are not eligible. Support for graduate education is provided only for a first degree in nursing. Applicants must be members of a racial or ethnic minority underrepresented among registered nurses (Asian, American Indian or Alaska Native, Hispanic or Latino, Native Hawaiian or other Pacific Islander, or Black or African American). They must be committed to providing quality health care services to underserved populations. Along with their application, they must submit a 200-word description of their professional and educational goals and how this scholarship will help them achieve those goals. Selection is based on academic achievement, financial need, and involvement in student nursing organizations and community health activities. U.S. citizenship or permanent resident status is required.

Financial data Stipends range from $1,000 to $2,000.

Duration 1 year.

Additional information Applications must be accompanied by a $10 processing fee.

Number awarded Varies each year; recently, 13 were awarded: 10 sponsored by the American Association of Critical-Care Nurses and 3 sponsored by the Mayo Clinic.

Deadline January of each year.

[594]
BRONSON T.J. TREMBLAY MEMORIAL SCHOLARSHIP

Colorado Nurses Foundation
Attn: Scholarships
P.O. Box 3406
Englewood, CO 80155
(303) 694-4728   Toll Free: (800) 205-6655
Fax: (303) 200-7099   E-mail: mail@cnfound.org
Web: www.coloradonursesfoundation.com/?page_id=1087

Summary To provide financial assistance to Asian American and other non-white male undergraduate and graduate nursing students in Colorado.

Eligibility This program is open to non-white male Colorado residents who have been accepted as a student in an approved nursing program in the state. Applicants may be 1) second-year students in an associate degree program; 2) junior or senior level B.S.N. undergraduate students; 3) R.N.s enrolled in a baccalaureate or higher degree program in a school of nursing; 4) R.N.s with a master's degree in nursing, currently practicing in Colorado and enrolled in a doctoral program; or 5) students in the second or third year of a Doctorate Nursing Practice (D.N.P.) or Ph.D. program. Undergraduates must have a GPA of 3.25 or higher and graduate students must have a GPA of 3.5 or higher. Selection is based on professional philosophy and goals, dedication to the improvement of patient care in Colorado, demonstrated commitment to nursing, potential for leadership, involvement in community and professional organizations, recommendations, GPA, and financial need.

Financial data The stipend is $1,000.

Duration 1 year.

Number awarded 1 each year.

Deadline October of each year.

[595]
BROWN AND CALDWELL MINORITY SCHOLARSHIP

Brown and Caldwell
Attn: HR/Scholarship Program
1527 Cole Boulevard, Suite 300
Lakewood, CO 80401
(303) 239-5400   Fax: (303) 239-5454
E-mail: scholarships@brwncald.com
Web: www.brownandcaldwell.com/Scholarships.asp?id=1

Summary To provide financial assistance to Asian American and other minority students working on an undergraduate or graduate degree in an environmental or engineering field.

Eligibility This program is open to members of minority groups (Asians, African Americans, Hispanics, Pacific Islanders, Native Americans, or Alaska Natives) who are full-time juniors, seniors, or graduate students at an accredited 4-year college or university. Applicants must have a GPA of 3.0 or higher and a declared major in civil, chemical, or environmental engineering or an environmental science (e.g., biology, ecology, geology, hydrogeology). They must be U.S. citizens or permanent residents. Along with their application, they must submit an essay (up to 250 words) on a topic that changes annually but relates to their personal development. Financial need is not considered in the selection process.

Financial data The stipend is $5,000.

Duration 1 year.

Number awarded 1 each year.

Deadline May of each year.

[596]
BRYAN CAVE/NAPABA LAW FOUNDATION COMMUNITY SERVICE SCHOLARSHIP

National Asian Pacific American Bar Association
Attn: NAPABA Law Foundation
1612 K Street, N.W., Suite 510
Washington, DC 20006
(202) 775-9555   Fax: (202) 775-9333
E-mail: nlfstaff@napaba.org
Web: www.napaba.org/?page=NLF_FI

Summary To provide an opportunity for law students to conduct a project in public interest law at nonprofit organizations that serve the Asian Pacific American community.

Eligibility This program is open to full- and part-time students at accredited law schools who are interested in working on a summer project that will benefit the Asian Pacific American community. Applicants must have obtained a summer law internship that they have arranged themselves with a public service, civic, or nonprofit organization or a corporation that is not a law firm. They must submit a 500-word personal statement explaining 1) how the upcoming internship will benefit the Asian Pacific American community; and 2) their past or present activities showing commitment to the public interest or the Asian Pacific American community.

Financial data The stipend is $2,500. Funds must be used to further the recipient's law school education.

Duration At least 8 weeks during the summer.

Additional information This program is funded by Bryan Cave LLP.

Number awarded 1 each year.

Deadline May of each year.

[597]
BUCKFIRE & BUCKFIRE MEDICAL SCHOOL DIVERSITY SCHOLARSHIP

Buckfire & Buckfire, P.C.
Attn: Scholarships
25800 Northwestern Highway, Suite 890
Southfield, MI 48075
(248) 569-4646   Toll Free: (800) 606-1717
Fax: (248) 569-6737 E-mail: marketing@buckfirelaw.com
Web: www.buckfirelaw.com/library/general

Summary To provide financial assistance to medical students who come from an Asian American or other minority background.

Eligibility This program is open to U.S. citizens who are members of an ethnic, racial, or other minority or who demonstrate a defined commitment to issues of diversity within their academic career. Applicants must have completed at least 1 semester at an accredited medical school and have a GPA of 3.0 or higher. Selection is based on academic achievement and an essay on how they will utilize their medical degree to promote diversity.

Financial data The stipend is $2,000.

Duration 1 year.

Additional information This program began in 2014.

Number awarded 1 each year.

Deadline May of each year.

[598]
CALA SCHOLARSHIP

Chinese American Librarians Association
c/o Raymond Wang, Scholarship Committee Co-Chair
Community College of Baltimore County
Essex Library, Room 102
7201 Rossville Boulevard
Baltimore, MD 21237
(443) 840-1898   Fax: (443) 840-1724
E-mail: rwang@ccbcmd.edu
Web: www.cala-web.org/node/1616

Summary To provide financial assistance to Chinese American students interested in working on a graduate degree in library or information science.

Eligibility This program is open to students enrolled full time in an accredited library school in North America and working on a master's or doctoral degree. Applicants must be of Chinese nationality or Chinese descent.

Financial data The stipend is $1,000.

Duration 1 year.

Additional information This program began in 2004.

Number awarded 1 each year.

Deadline April of each year.

[599]
CALIFORNIA BAR FOUNDATION 1L DIVERSITY SCHOLARSHIPS

State Bar of California
Attn: California Bar Foundation
180 Howard Street
San Francisco, CA 94105-1639
(415) 856-0780   Fax: (415) 856-0788
E-mail: scholarships@calbarfoundation.org
Web: www.calbarfoundation.org

Summary To provide financial assistance to residents of any state who are Asian Americans or members of other groups historically underrepresented in the legal profession and entering law school in California.

Eligibility This program to open to residents of any state who are entering their first year at a law school in California. Applicants must be able to contribute to greater diversity in the legal profession. Diversity includes a broad array of backgrounds and life experiences, including students from groups or with skills or attributes that are underrepresented in the legal profession. Students from socially and economically disadvantaged backgrounds are especially encouraged to apply. Along with their application, they must submit a 500-word essay describing their commitment to serving the community and, if applicable, any significant obstacles or hurdles they have overcome to attend law school. Financial need is considered in the selection process.

Financial data The stipend is $7,500.

Duration 1 year.

Additional information This program began in 2008. Each year, the foundation grants awards named after sponsors that donate funding for the scholarships.

Number awarded Varies each year; recently, 33 were awarded.

Deadline May of each year.

[600]
CALIFORNIA CAPITOL SUMMER INTERNSHIP PROGRAM

Asian Pacific Islander American Public Affairs Association
Attn: Community Education Foundation
4000 Truxel Road, Suite 3
Sacramento, CA 95834
(916) 928-9988   Fax: (916) 678-7555
E-mail: info@apapa.org
Web: www.apapa.org/programs/youth-leadership

Summary To provide summer work experience at an office of state government in Sacramento to undergraduate and graduate student residents of California who are of Asian or Pacific Islander background.

Eligibility This program is open to undergraduate and graduate students who are of Asian or Pacific Islander background and residents of California attending college in the state. Applicants must be interested in a summer internship in Sacramento at an office of state government. They must have a GPA of 2.75 or higher. Along with their application, they must submit a 2-page statement on their Asian or Pacific Islander background, community and public service involvement, academic and career goals, and future plans for public services and/or politics and government involvement. Selection is based on GPA, demonstrated leadership, interpersonal skills, written and verbal communication skills, and community service.

Financial data Interns receive a stipend of $1,000 upon successful completion of the program.

Duration 8 weeks, beginning in June.

Additional information Interns must also complete 40 community service hours for the sponsor's Sacramento chapter.

Number awarded Up to 20 each year.

Deadline February of each year.

[601]
CALIFORNIA COMMUNITY SERVICE-LEARNING PROGRAM

National Medical Fellowships, Inc.
Attn: Scholarship Program
347 Fifth Avenue, Suite 510
New York, NY 10016
(212) 483-8880   Toll Free: (877) NMF-1DOC
Fax: (212) 483-8897 E-mail: scholarships@nmfonline.org
Web: www.nmfonline.org

Summary To provide funding to Vietnamese, Cambodian, or other underrepresented medical students in California who wish to participate in a community service program for underserved areas of the state.

Eligibility This program is open to members of underrepresented minority groups (Vietnamese, Cambodian, African American, Hispanic/Latino, or Native American) who are U.S. citizens or DACA certified. Applicants must be currently enrolled in an accredited medical school in California. They must be interested in a self-directed service-learning experience that provides 200 hours of community service in medically-underserved areas of the state. Selection is based on demonstrated leadership early in career and commitment to serving medically underserved communities.

Financial data The stipend is $5,000.

Additional information Funding for this program, which began in 2013 and is administered by National Medical Fellowships (NMF), is provided by the California Wellness Foundation.

Number awarded 10 each year.

Deadline March of each year.

[602]
CALIFORNIA PLANNING FOUNDATION DIVERSITY IN PLANNING SCHOLARSHIP

American Planning Association-California Chapter
Attn: California Planning Foundation
c/o Kelly Main
California Polytechnic State University at San Luis Obispo
City and Regional Planning Department
Office 21-116B
San Luis Obispo, CA 93407-0283
(805) 756-2285   Fax: (805) 756-1340
E-mail: cpfapplications@gmail.com
Web: www.californiaplanningfoundation.org

Summary To provide financial assistance to Asian American and other undergraduate and graduate students in accredited planning programs at California universities who will increase diversity in the profession.

Eligibility This program is open to students entering their final year for an undergraduate or master's degree in an accredited planning program at a university in California. Applicants must be students who will increase diversity in the planning profession. Along with their application, they must submit 1) a 500-word personal statement explaining why planning is important to them, their potential contribution to the profession of planning in California, and how this scholarship would help them to complete their degree; 2) a 500-word description of their experience in planning (e.g., internships, volunteer experiences, employment); and 3) a 500-word essay on what they consider to be 1 of the greatest planning challenges in California today. Selection is based on academic performance, increasing diversity in the planning profession, commitment to serve the planning profession in California, and financial need.

Financial data The stipend is $3,000. The award includes a 1-year student membership in the American Planning Association (APA) and payment of registration for the APA California Conference.

Duration 1 year.

Additional information The accredited planning programs are at 3 campuses of the California State University system (California State Polytechnic University at Pomona, California Polytechnic State University at San Luis Obispo, and San Jose State University), 3 campuses of the University of California (Berkeley, Irvine, and Los Angeles), and the University of Southern California.

Number awarded 1 each year.

Deadline March of each year.

[603]
CAMS SCHOLARSHIP PROGRAM

Chinese American Medical Society
Attn: Scholarship Committee
265 Canal Street, Suite 515
New York, NY 10013
(212) 334-4760   Fax: (646) 304-6373
E-mail: jlove@camsociety.org
Web: www.chineseamericanmedicalsociety.cloverpad.org

Summary To provide financial assistance to Chinese and Chinese American students who are working on a degree in medicine or dentistry.

Eligibility This program is open to Chinese or Chinese American students who are currently enrolled in the first, second, or third year at an approved medical or dental school in the United States. Applicants must submit a personal statement that includes their career goals, a current vitae, 2 letters of recommendation, and documentation of financial need. Special consideration is given to applicants with research projects relating to health care of the Chinese.

Financial data The stipend is $5,000.

Duration 1 year; nonrenewable.

Additional information This program, which began in 1973, includes the Esther Lim Memorial Scholarship established in 1989, the Ruth Ru-yin Liu Memorial Scholarship established in 1996, the American Center for Chinese Medical Sciences Scholarship established in 2004 upon the dissolution of that organization, and the Jeng Family Fund Scholarship, established in 2013.

Number awarded Varies each year; recently, 4 were awarded.

Deadline April of each year.

[604]
CAMS SUMMER RESEARCH FELLOWSHIP

Chinese American Medical Society
Attn: Scholarship Committee
265 Canal Street, Suite 515
New York, NY 10013
(212) 334-4760   Fax: (646) 304-6373
E-mail: jlove@camsociety.org
Web: www.chineseamericanmedicalsociety.cloverpad.org

Summary To provide funding to Chinese American medical and dental students who are interested in conducting a summer research project.

Eligibility This program is open to Chinese or Chinese Americans who are enrolled in a medical or dental school in the United States and are interested in conducting a research project. The research can be basic science or clinical. A physician or dentist must sponsor and supervise the project. Special consideration is given to proposals involving Chinese American health issues.

Financial data The stipend is $400 per week.

Duration 6 to 10 weeks during the summer.

Additional information A written report is expected at the conclusion of the project.

Number awarded Varies each year.

Deadline April of each year.

[605]
CANFIT PROGRAM GRADUATE SCHOLARSHIPS

Communities-Adolescents-Nutrition-Fitness
Attn: Scholarship Program
P.O. Box 3989
Berkeley, CA 94703
(510) 644-1533, ext. 112   Toll Free: (800) 200-3131
Fax: (510) 843-9705   E-mail: info@canfit.org
Web: www.canfit.org/scholarships

Summary To provide financial assistance to Asian American and other minority graduate students who are working on a degree in nutrition, physical education, or public health in California.

Eligibility This program is open to Asian Americans, American Indians, Alaska Natives, African Americans, Pacific Islanders, and Latinos/Hispanics from California who are enrolled in 1) an approved master's or doctoral program in nutrition, public health, or physical education in the state; or 2) a pre-professional practice program approved by the American Dietetic Association at an accredited university in the state. Applicants must have completed 12 to 15 units of graduate course work and have a cumulative GPA of 3.0 or higher. Along with their application, they must submit 1) documentation of financial need; 2) letters of recommendation from 2 individuals; 3) a 1- to 2-page letter describing their academic goals and involvement in community nutrition and/or physical education activities; and 4) an essay of 500 to 1,000 words on a topic related to healthy foods for youth from low-income communities of color.

Financial data A stipend is awarded (amount not specified).

Number awarded 1 or more each year.

Deadline March of each year.

[606]
CAPABA EDUCATIONAL FOUNDATION SCHOLARSHIP

Connecticut Asian Pacific American Bar Association
Attn: CAPABA Educational Foundation
c/o Amy Lin Meyerson
20 Old Stage Coach Road
Weston, CT 06883
(203) 232-4322   Fax: (203) 548-9213
E-mail: amy@almesq.com
Web: www.capaba.org

Summary To provide financial assistance to Asian Pacific American (APA) law students from Connecticut.

Eligibility This program is open to members of the APA community in Connecticut who are attending a law school in the state. Applicants must submit 1) a brief essay on how they have served the needs of the APA community; 2) a brief essay on how they think they can best contribute to the APA community as a lawyer; and 3) an essay of 500 to 1,000 words on a legal reform that they consider the most pressing issue facing the APA community. Selection is based on leadership potential, excellence in academia, and a firm commitment and involvement with the APA community in Connecticut.

Financial data The stipend is $1,000.

Duration 1 year.

Additional information This program began in 2010.

Number awarded Up to 2 each year.

Deadline September of each year.

[607]
CAPAL FEDERAL INTERNSHIP PROGRAM

Conference on Asian Pacific American Leadership
Attn: Scholarship Committee
P.O. Box 65073
Washington, DC 20035-5073
(877) 892-5427   Fax: (877) 892-5427
E-mail: scholarships@capal.org
Web: www.capal.org

Summary To provide funding for summer internships with designated federal agencies to Asian Pacific American undergraduate and graduate students.

Eligibility This program is open to Asian Pacific American (APA) undergraduate and graduate students who are working on a degree in any field. Applicants must be interested in a summer internship at a federal agency; recently, those included the Office of Personnel Management (OPM) and several agencies within the U.S. Department of Agriculture (Rural Development, Forest Service, Agricultural Research Service, and Food Safety and Inspection Service). Along with their application, they must submit a 750-word essay on 2 of the following topics: 1) their long-term career goals and how the summer internship experience will advance those; 2) their previous educational, community work, and internship experiences and how those experiences have influenced their long-term career goals; or 3) how they will use the experiences and knowledge that they gain during their summer in Washington to better serve the APA community and their local community. Selection is based on demonstrated commitment to public service, including service to the APA community; potential to benefit from the internship; demonstrated leadership and potential for continued growth in leadership skills; relevance of the proposed internship to overall public sector goals; academic achievement; and financial need. U.S. citizenship or permanent resident status is required.

Financial data Interns receive $3,000 as a stipend and $500 to help pay travel expenses.

Duration At least 6 weeks during the summer.

Additional information Assignments are available in Washington, D.C. or at sites nationwide.

Number awarded Varies each year; recently, 15 were awarded.

Deadline March of each year.

[608]
CAPAL PUBLIC SERVICE SCHOLARSHIPS

Conference on Asian Pacific American Leadership
Attn: Scholarship Committee
P.O. Box 65073
Washington, DC 20035-5073
(877) 892-5427   Fax: (877) 892-5427
E-mail: scholarships@capal.org
Web: www.capal.org

Summary To provide funding for summer internships in Washington, D.C. to Asian Pacific American undergraduate and graduate students.

Eligibility This program is open to Asian Pacific American (APA) undergraduate and graduate students who have secured an unpaid public sector internship within the Washington, D.C. metropolitan area at a federal government agency, a Capitol Hill legislative office, or a nonprofit organization. Applicants must demonstrate a desire to build skills and develop their commitment to public service and the APA community. Along with their application, they must submit a 750-word essay on 2 of the following topics: 1) their long-term career goals and how the summer internship experience will advance those; 2) their previous educational, community work, and internship experiences and how those experiences have influenced their long-term career goals; or 3) how they will use the experiences and knowledge that they gain during their summer in Washington to better serve the APA community and their local community. Selection is based on demonstrated commitment to public service, including service to the APA community; potential to benefit from the internship; demonstrated leadership and potential for continued growth in leadership skills; relevance of the proposed internship to overall public sector goals; academic achievement; and financial need.

Financial data Awardees receive a stipend of $3,500 to help pay expenses during their internship.

Duration At least 6 weeks during the summer.

Additional information This program began in 1992. Recipients must agree to have a Community Action Plan (CAP) proposed, approved, and presented before their departure from Washington, D.C. at the end of the summer.

Number awarded Varies each year; recently, 7 were awarded.

Deadline March of each year.

[609]
CAPAL-MAASU PUBLIC SERVICE SCHOLARSHIPS

Conference on Asian Pacific American Leadership
Attn: Scholarship Committee
P.O. Box 65073
Washington, DC 20035-5073
(877) 892-5427   Fax: (877) 892-5427
E-mail: scholarships@capal.org
Web: www.capal.org

Summary To provide funding for summer internships in Washington, D.C. to Asian Pacific American undergraduate and graduate students who are attending schools that are members of the Midwest Asian American Students Union (MAASU).

Eligibility This program is open to Asian Pacific American (APA) undergraduate and graduate students who have secured an unpaid public sector internship within the Washington, D.C. metropolitan area at a federal government agency, a Capitol Hill legislative office, or a nonprofit organization. Applicants must demonstrate a desire to build skills and develop their commitment to public service and the APA community. They must be attending an MAASU college or university in Colorado, Illinois, Indiana, Iowa, Kansas, Michigan, Minnesota, Missouri, Nebraska, North Dakota, Ohio, Oklahoma, South Dakota, or Wisconsin. Along with their application, they must submit a 750-word essay on 2 of the following topics: 1) their long-term career goals and how the summer internship experience will advance those; 2) their previous educational, community work, and internship experiences and how those experiences have influenced their long-term career goals; or 3) how they will use the experiences and knowledge that they gain during their summer in Washington to better serve the APA community and their local community. Selection is based on demonstrated commitment to public service, including service to the APA community; potential to benefit from the internship; demonstrated leadership and potential for continued growth in leadership skills; relevance of the proposed internship to overall public sector goals; academic achievement; and financial need.

Financial data The awardee receives a stipend of $3,500 to help pay expenses during the internship.

Duration At least 6 weeks during the summer.

Additional information Recipients must agree to have a Community Action Plan (CAP) proposed, approved, and presented before their departure from Washington, D.C. at the end of the summer.

Number awarded 1 each year.

Deadline March of each year.

[610]
CARL A. SCOTT BOOK FELLOWSHIPS

Council on Social Work Education
Attn: Chair, Carl A. Scott Memorial Fund
1701 Duke Street, Suite 200
Alexandria, VA 22314-3457
(703) 683-8080   Fax: (703) 683-8099
E-mail: info@cswe.org
Web: www.cswe.org

Summary To provide financial assistance to Asian American and other ethnic minority social work students in their last year of study for a baccalaureate or master's degree.

Eligibility This program is open to students from ethnic groups of color (Asian American, African American/Black, Hispanic/Latino, Native Hawaiian or other Pacific Islander, or American Indian/Alaska Native) who are in the last year of study for a social work degree in an accredited baccalaureate or master's degree program. Applicants must have a cumulative GPA of 3.0 or higher and be enrolled full time. They must demonstrate a commitment to work for equity and social justice in social work.

Financial data The stipend is $500.

Duration This is a 1-time award.

Number awarded 2 each year.

Deadline May of each year.

[611]
CARMEN E. TURNER SCHOLARSHIPS

Conference of Minority Transportation Officials
Attn: National Scholarship Program
100 M Street, S.E., Suite 917
Washington, DC 20003
(202) 506-2917   E-mail: info@comto.org
Web: www.comto.org/page/scholarships

Summary To provide financial assistance for college or graduate school to members of the Conference of Minority Transportation Officials (COMTO) and their families.

Eligibility This program is open to undergraduate and graduate students who have been members or whose parents, guardians, or grandparents have been members of COMTO for at least 1 year. Applicants must be working on a degree in a field related to transportation and have a GPA of 2.5 or higher. Along with their application they must submit a cover letter on their transportation-related career goals and life aspirations. Financial need is not considered in the selection process.

Financial data The stipend is $3,500. Funds are paid directly to the recipient's college or university.

Duration 1 year.

Number awarded 1 each year.

Deadline April of each year.

[612]
CARRINGTON-HSIA-NIEVES SCHOLARSHIP FOR MIDWIVES OF COLOR

American College of Nurse-Midwives
Attn: ACNM Foundation, Inc.
8403 Colesville Road, Suite 1550
Silver Spring, MD 20910-6374
(240) 485-1850   Fax: (240) 485-1818
E-mail: foundation@acnmf.org
Web: www.midwife.org

Summary To provide financial assistance to Asian American and other midwives of color who are members of the American College of Nurse-Midwives (ACNM) and engaged in doctoral or postdoctoral study.

Eligibility This program is open to ACNM members of color who are certified nurse midwives (CNM) or certified midwives (CM). Applicants must be enrolled in a program of doctoral or postdoctoral education. Along with their application, they must submit brief statements on their 5-year academic career plans, their intended use of the funds, and their intended future participation in the local, regional, and/or

national activities of the ACNM and in activities that otherwise contribute substantially to midwifery research, education, or practice.

Financial data The stipend is $5,000.

Duration 1 year.

Number awarded 1 each year.

Deadline October of each year.

[613]
CATHY L. BROCK SCHOLARSHIP

Institute for Diversity in Health Management
Attn: Membership and Education Specialist
155 North Wacker Avenue
Chicago, IL 60606
(312) 422-2658   E-mail: cbiddle@aha.org
Web: www.diversityconnection.org

Summary To provide financial assistance to Asian American and other graduate students in health care management, especially financial operations, who will contribute to ethnic diversity in the profession.

Eligibility This program is open to U.S. citizens who represent ethnically diverse cultural backgrounds. Applicants must be enrolled in the first or second year of a master's degree program in health administration or a comparable program and have a GPA of 3.0 or higher. Along with their application, they must submit 1) a personal statement of 1 to 2 pages on their interest in health care management and their career goals; 2) an essay on what they see as the most challenging issue facing America's hospitals and health systems; and 3) a 500-word essay on their interest and background in health care finance. Selection is based on academic achievement, commitment to a career in health care finance, and financial need.

Financial data The stipend is $1,000.

Duration 1 year.

Number awarded 1 each year.

Deadline January of each year.

[614]
CAY DRACHNIK MINORITIES FUND

American Art Therapy Association, Inc.
Attn: Scholarships and Grants Committee
4875 Eisenhower Avenue, Suite 240
Alexandria, VA 22304
Toll Free: (888) 290-0878   E-mail: info@arttherapy.org
Web: www.arttherapy.org/aata-awards.html

Summary To help to pay for the books needed by Asian American and other minority students who are members of the American Art Therapy Association (AATA).

Eligibility This program is open to minority student AATA members accepted or enrolled in a graduate art therapy program approved by the association. Applicants must be able to demonstrate financial need. Along with their application, they must submit a 2-page essay that contains a brief biography and a statement of how they see their role in the future of art therapy.

Financial data The fund provides $900 for the purchase of books.

Duration 1 year.

Number awarded 1 each year.

Deadline March of each year.

[615]
CH2M HILL PARTNERSHIP SCHOLARSHIP

Women's Transportation Seminar
Attn: WTS Foundation
1701 K Street, N.W., Suite 800
Washington, DC 20006
(202) 955-5085   Fax: (202) 955-5088
E-mail: wts@wtsinternational.org
Web: www.wtsinternational.org/education/scholarships

Summary To provide financial assistance to women graduate students, especially Asian Americans and other minorities, interested in preparing for a career in transportation.

Eligibility This program is open to women who are enrolled in a graduate degree program in a transportation-related field (e.g., transportation engineering, planning, finance, or logistics). Applicants must have at least a 3.0 GPA and be interested in a career in transportation. Along with their application, they must submit a 750-word statement about their career goals after graduation and why they think they should receive the scholarship award. Applications must be submitted first to a local chapter; the chapters forward selected applications for consideration on the national level. Minority women are particularly encouraged to apply. Selection is based on transportation involvement and goals, job skills, and academic record.

Financial data The stipend is $10,000.

Duration 1 year.

Additional information This program is sponsored by CH2M Hill. Local chapters may also award additional funding to winners in their area.

Number awarded 1 each year.

Deadline Applications must be submitted by November to a local WTS chapter.

[616]
CHARLES B. RANGEL GRADUATE FELLOWSHIP PROGRAM

Howard University
Attn: Ralph J. Bunche International Affairs Center
2218 Sixth Street, N.W.
Washington, DC 20059
(202) 806-4367   Toll Free: (877) 633-0002
Fax: (202) 806-5424 E-mail: rangelprogram@howard.edu
Web: www.rangelprogram.org

Summary To provide financial assistance for graduate study in a field related to the work of the Foreign Service, especially to Asian American and members of other underrepresented minority groups.

Eligibility This program is open to U.S. citizens who are either graduating college seniors or recipients of an undergraduate degree. Applicants must be planning to enter graduate school to work on a master's degree in international affairs or other area of interest to the Foreign Service of the U.S. Department of State (e.g., public administration, public policy, business administration, foreign languages, economics, political science, or communications). They must have a GPA of 3.2 or higher. The program encourages applications from members of minority groups historically underrepresented in the Foreign Service and those who can demonstrate financial need.

Financial data The program provides a stipend of $20,000 per year for tuition and fees, $15,000 per year for room, board, books, and other education-related expenses, and a stipend of $10,000 per year for housing, transportation, and related expenses for summer internships.

Duration 2 years.

Additional information This program is offered jointly by Howard University and the U.S. Department of State. Fellows are provided an internship working on international issues for members of Congress during the summer after they are selected and before they begin graduate study. They are provided a second internship at a U.S. embassy overseas during the summer before their second year of graduate study. Fellows who complete the program and Foreign Service entry requirements receive appointments as Foreign Service Officers. Each fellow who obtains a master's degree is committed to at least 5 years of service as a Foreign Service Officer. If recipients do not complete the program successfully or do not fulfill the 3-year service obligation, they may be subject to a reimbursement obligation.

Number awarded 20 each year.

Deadline January of each year.

[617]
CHER YEE LEE AND MA VANG SCHOLARSHIP

Hmong American Education Fund
P.O. Box 17468
St. Paul, MN 55117
(651) 592-1576   E-mail: scholarships@thehaef.org
Web: www.thehaef.org

Summary To provide financial assistance to Hmong residents of Minnesota who come from a large family and are interested in attending college or graduate school in any state.

Eligibility This program is open to residents of Minnesota who identify themselves as a person of Hmong descent and come from a family of 5 or more siblings. Applicants must be high school seniors, GED recipients, or current undergraduate or graduate students enrolled or planning to enroll full time at a 2- or 4-year college or university in any state. They must be U.S. citizens or permanent residents. Along with their application, they must submit transcripts and a 1,500-word essay on their commitment to education; their family, their struggles, and their triumphs; and how coming from a large family influenced their educational goals and overall life.

Financial data The stipend is $1,000.

Duration 1 year; nonrenewable.

Number awarded 1 each year.

Deadline March of each year.

[618]
CHERZONG V. VANG SCIENCE AND ENGINEERING SCHOLARSHIP

Hmong American Education Fund
P.O. Box 17468
St. Paul, MN 55117
(651) 592-1576   E-mail: scholarships@thehaef.org
Web: www.thehaef.org

Summary To provide financial assistance to Hmong residents of Minnesota who are working on an undergraduate or graduate degree in science or engineering at a college in any state.

Eligibility This program is open to residents of Minnesota who identify themselves as a person of Hmong descent. Applicants must be enrolled as full-time undergraduate or graduate students at a 2- or 4-year college or university in any state and working on a degree in science or engineering. They must be U.S. citizens or permanent residents and have a GPA of 3.3 or higher. Along with their application, they must submit transcripts and a 1,500-word essay on their commitment to education, the sciences, and/or engineering; their knowledge of the Hmong people; and their community service. Selection is based on academic achievement.

Financial data The stipend is $500.

Duration 1 year; nonrenewable.

Number awarded 1 each year.

Deadline March of each year.

[619]
CHINESE AMERICAN ASSOCIATION OF MINNESOTA SCHOLARSHIPS

Chinese American Association of Minnesota
Attn: Scholarship Program
P.O. Box 582584
Minneapolis, MN 55458-2584
E-mail: info@caam.org
Web: www.caam.org/scholarships

Summary To provide financial assistance to Minnesota residents of Chinese descent who are interested in attending college or graduate school in any state.

Eligibility This program is open to Minnesota residents of Chinese descent who are enrolled or planning to enroll full time at a postsecondary school, college, or graduate school in any state. Applicants must submit an essay on the role their Chinese heritage has played in their work, study, and accomplishments. Selection is based on academic record, leadership qualities, and community service; financial need is also considered for some awards. Membership in the Chinese American Association of Minnesota (CAAM) is not required. Priority is given to applicants who have not previously received a CAAM scholarship.

Financial data The stipend is $1,000.

Duration 1 year.

Additional information Recipients who are not CAAM members are expected to become members for at least 2 years.

Number awarded 1 or more each year.

Deadline November of each year.

[620]
CHINESE AMERICAN PHYSICIANS SOCIETY SCHOLARSHIP PROGRAM FOR U.S. MEDICAL STUDENTS

Chinese American Physicians Society
c/o Lawrence Ng, M.D., Award Committee Chair
101 Callan Avenue, Suite 401
San Leandro, CA 94577
(510) 357-7077   Fax: (510) 357-4363
E-mail: admin@caps-ca.org
Web: www.caps-ca.org/scholarship.html

Summary To provide financial assistance to medical students in the United States, especially those willing to serve Chinese communities after graduation.

Eligibility This program is open to students attending or planning to attend a U.S. medical school. Applicants may be from any location and of any sex, race, or color. Preference is given to those willing to serve Chinese communities after graduation. Along with their application, they must submit a 500-word essay on a topic that changes annually; recently, students who asked to write on how they use their time wisely. Selection is based on the essay, academic achievement, financial need, and community service.

Financial data Stipends range from $2,000 to $5,000 per year.

Duration 1 year; may be renewed.

Number awarded Varies each year; recently, 8 were awarded.

Deadline February of each year.

[621]
CHIPS QUINN SCHOLARS PROGRAM

Newseum Institute
Attn: Chips Quinn Scholars Program
555 Pennsylvania Avenue, N.W.
Washington, DC 20001
(202) 292-6271   Fax: (202) 292-6275
E-mail: kcatone@freedomforum.org
Web: www.newseuminstitute.org

Summary To provide work experience to Asian American and other minority college students and recent graduates who are majoring in journalism.

Eligibility This program is open to students of color who are college juniors, seniors, graduate students, or recent graduates with journalism majors or career goals in newspapers. Candidates must be nominated or endorsed by journalism faculty, campus media advisers, editors of newspapers, or leaders of minority journalism associations. Along with their application, they must submit a resume, transcripts, 2 letters of recommendation, and an essay of 200 to 400 words on why they want to be a Chips Quinn Scholar. Reporters and copy editors must also submit 6 samples of published articles they have written; photographers must submit 15 to 25 photographs on a DVD; multimedia journalists and graphic designers should submit 6 to 10 samples of their work on a DVD. Applicants must have a car and be available to work as a full-time intern during the spring or summer. U.S. citizenship or permanent resident status is required. Campus newspaper experience is strongly encouraged.

Financial data Students chosen for this program receive a travel stipend to attend a Multimedia training program in

Nashville, Tennessee prior to reporting for their internship, a $500 housing allowance from the Freedom Forum, and a competitive salary during their internship.

Duration Internships are for 10 to 12 weeks, in spring or summer.

Additional information This program began in 1991 in memory of the late John D. Quinn Jr., managing editor of the *Poughkeepsie Journal.* Funding is provided by the Freedom Forum, formerly the Gannett Foundation. After graduating from college and obtaining employment with a newspaper, alumni of this program are eligible to apply for fellowship support to attend professional journalism development activities.

Number awarded Approximately 70 each year. Since the program began, more than 1,300 scholars have been selected.

Deadline September of each year.

[622]
CHIYOKO AND THOMAS SHIMAZAKI SCHOLARSHIP

Japanese American Citizens League
Attn: National Scholarship Awards
1765 Sutter Street
San Francisco, CA 94115
(415) 345-1075   Fax: (415) 345-1077
E-mail: pwada@jacl.org
Web: www.jacl.org/jacl-national-scholarship-program

Summary To provide financial assistance to student members of the Japanese American Citizens League (JACL) who are interested in preparing for a career in medicine.

Eligibility This program is open to JACL members who are interested in preparing for a career in the medical field. Applicants must submit information on their involvement in JACL and a 2-page essay on a topic that changes annually but relates to Japanese Americans. Selection is based on that essay, academic history, JACL involvement, school activities, work history, scholastic honors, and community involvement.

Financial data Stipends generally average more than $2,000.

Duration 1 year; nonrenewable.

Number awarded At least 1 each year.

Deadline March of each year.

[623]
CLA SCHOLARSHIP FOR MINORITY STUDENTS IN MEMORY OF EDNA YELLAND

California Library Association
1055 East Colorado Boulevard, Fifth Floor
Pasadena, CA 91106
(626) 204-4071   E-mail: info@cla-net.org
Web: www.cla-net.org/?page=110

Summary To provide financial assistance to Asian American and other students of ethnic minority origin in California who are attending graduate school in any state to prepare for a career in library or information science.

Eligibility This program is open to California residents who are members of ethnic minority groups (Asian American, American Indian/Alaska Native, African American/Black, Latino/Hispanic, or Pacific Islander). Applicants must have completed at least 1 course in a master's program at an accredited graduate library school in any state. Evidence of

financial need and U.S. citizenship or permanent resident status must be submitted. Finalists are interviewed.

Financial data The stipend is $2,500.

Duration 1 academic year.

Additional information This fellowship is named for the executive secretary of the California Library Association from 1947 to 1963 who worked to promote the goals of the California Library Association and the profession. Until 1985, it was named the Edna Yelland Memorial Scholarship.

Number awarded 3 each year.

Deadline July of each year.

[624]
COMMERCIAL AND FEDERAL LITIGATION SECTION DIVERSITY FELLOWSHIP

The New York Bar Foundation
One Elk Street
Albany, NY 12207
(518) 487-5651   Fax: (518) 487-5699
E-mail: moclair@tnybf.org
Web: www.tnybf.org/fellandschol

Summary To provide an opportunity for residents of any state who are Asian Americans or students from other diverse backgrounds and attending law school in New York to gain summer work experience in a litigation position in the public sector in the state.

Eligibility This program is open to Asian/Pacific Islander, Black/African American, Latino/a, or Native American/Alaskan Native students from any state who are enrolled in the first year at a law school in New York. Applicants must have demonstrated an interest in commercial and federal litigation. They must be interested in working in a litigation position during the summer in the public sector in New York. Selection is based on content and quality of application materials, demonstrated interest in litigation, work experience, academic record, leadership experience, extracurricular activities, community service, quality of written expression, maturity, integrity, and professionalism.

Financial data The stipend is $6,000.

Duration 10 weeks during the summer.

Additional information This program began in 2007 with support from the Commercial and Federal Litigation Section of the New York State Bar Association. It is administered by The New York Bar Foundation.

Number awarded 1 each year.

Deadline January of each year.

[625]
COMMITMENT TO DIVERSITY IN MEDICAL EDUCATION AWARDS

Student Osteopathic Medical Association
Attn: SOMA Foundation
142 East Ontario Street
Chicago, IL 60611
(312) 202-8193   Toll Free: (800) 621-1773
Fax: (312) 202-8200
E-mail: scholarships-grants@somafoundation.org
Web: www.somafoundation.org

Summary To recognize and reward members of the Student Osteopathic Medical Association (SOMA) who are Asian Americans or other students who can demonstrate commitment to diversity issues and their relationship to professional medical education.

Eligibility This program is open to SOMA members who are in their second, third, or fourth year of studies at an accredited college or school of osteopathic medicine. Applicants must have demonstrated leadership in their chapter in implementing programs, events, or presentations pertaining to topics of ethnicity, race, religion, sexual orientation, and gender. Along with their application, they must submit a 1,000-word statement on why they believe diversity in medical education is important and how one can promote multiculturalism awareness.

Financial data The award is $500.

Duration The awards are presented annually.

Number awarded 2 each year.

Deadline January of each year.

[626]
COMMITTEE ON ETHNIC MINORITY RECRUITMENT SCHOLARSHIP

United Methodist Church-California-Pacific Annual
  Conference
Attn: Board of Ordained Ministry
1720 East Linfield Street
Glendora, CA 91740
(626) 824-2284   E-mail: admin@bom.calpacumc.org
Web: www.calpacumc.org/ordainedministry/scholarships

Summary To provide financial assistance to Asian American and members of other ethnic minority groups in the California-Pacific Annual Conference of the United Methodist Church (UMC) who are attending a seminary in any state to qualify for ordination as an elder or deacon.

Eligibility This program is open to members of ethnic minority groups in the UMC California-Pacific Annual Conference who are enrolled at a seminary in any state approved by the UMC University Senate. Applicants must have been approved as certified candidates by their district committee and be seeking Probationary Deacon or Elder's Orders. They may apply for 1 or more types of assistance: tuition scholarships, grants for books and school supplies (including computers), or emergency living expense grants.

Financial data Tuition stipends are $1,000 per year; books and supplies grants range up to $1,000 per year; emergency living expense grants depend on need and the availability of funds.

Duration 1 year; may be renewed up to 2 additional years.

Additional information The California-Pacific Annual Conference includes churches in southern California, Hawaii, Guam, and Saipan.

Number awarded Varies each year.

Deadline August of each year for fall term; December of each year for spring term.

[627]
COMPUTATIONAL CHEMISTRY AND MATERIALS SCIENCE SUMMER INSTITUTE

Lawrence Livermore National Laboratory
Physical and Life Sciences Directorate
Attn: Director of Student Programs
7000 East Avenue, L-452
Livermore, CA 94550
(925) 422-6351   E-mail: kulp2@llnl.gov
Web: www-pls.llnl.gov

Summary To provide an opportunity for doctoral students, especially Asian Americans and other minorities, to work on summer research projects on computational materials science and chemistry at Lawrence Livermore National Laboratory (LLNL).

Eligibility This program is open to full-time doctoral students who are interested in working on research projects involving computational materials and chemistry. Applicants must be interested in working at LLNL as a guest of an LLNL host scientist on a computational project. They must be enrolled in a Ph.D. program at a U.S. or foreign university. U.S. citizenship is not required. Selection is based on academic record, aptitude, research interests, and recommendations of instructors. Strong preference is given to students with exceptional academic records and potential for making outstanding contributions to applied science. Women and minorities are encouraged to apply.

Financial data The stipend ranges from $4,100 to $4,900 per month, depending on number of school years completed. Living accommodations and arrangements are the responsibility of the intern.

Duration 8 to 10 weeks, during the summer.

Number awarded 10 to 15 each year.

Deadline February of each year.

[628]
CORA AGUDA MANAYAN FUND

Hawai'i Community Foundation
Attn: Scholarship Department
827 Fort Street Mall
Honolulu, HI 96813
(808) 566-5570   Toll Free: (888) 731-3863
Fax: (808) 521-6286
E-mail: scholarships@hcf-hawaii.org
Web: hcf.scholarships.ngwebsolutions.com

Summary To provide financial assistance to Hawaii residents of Filipino ancestry who are interested in attending graduate school in the state to prepare for a career in the health field.

Eligibility This program is open to Hawaii residents of Filipino ancestry who are interested in enrolling full time in a graduate health-related program at a college in the state. Applicants must be able to demonstrate academic achievement (GPA of 3.0 or higher), good moral character, and financial need. Along with their application, they must submit a short statement indicating their reasons for attending college, their planned course of study, their career goals, and what community service means to them.

Financial data The amounts of the awards depend on the availability of funds and the need of the recipient. Recently, the average value of the scholarships awarded by the foundation was $2,800.

Duration 1 year.

Number awarded Varies each year; recently, 10 were awarded.

Deadline February of each year.

[629]
CORRIS BOYD SCHOLARS PROGRAM

Association of University Programs in Health
  Administration
Attn: Prizes, Fellowships and Scholarships
2000 14th Street North, Suite 780
Arlington, VA 22201
(703) 894-0940, ext. 122   Fax: (703) 894-0941
E-mail: lmeckley@aupha.org
Web: www.aupha.org

Summary To provide financial assistance to Asian American and other minority students entering graduate schools affiliated with the Association of University Programs in Health Administration (AUPHA).

Eligibility This program is open to students of color (Asian Americans, African Americans, American Indians, Alaska Natives, Latino/Hispanic, Native Hawaiians, Pacific Islanders) who have been accepted to a master's degree program in health care management at an AUPHA member institution. Applicants must be U.S. citizens or permanent residents and have a GPA of 3.0 or higher. Along with their application, they must submit a personal statement explaining why they are choosing to prepare for a career in health administration. Selection is based on leadership qualities, academic achievement, community involvement, and commitment to health care and health care management as a career path; financial need may be considered if all other factors are equal.

Financial data The stipend is $40,000.

Duration 1 year.

Additional information This program began in 2006.

Number awarded 2 each year.

Deadline April of each year.

[630]
DALMAS A. TAYLOR MEMORIAL SUMMER MINORITY POLICY FELLOWSHIP

Society for the Psychological Study of Social Issues
208 I Street, N.E.
Washington, DC 20002-4340
(202) 675-6956   Toll Free: (877) 310-7778
Fax: (202) 675-6902   E-mail: awards@spssi.org
Web: www.spssi.org

Summary To enable Asian American or other graduate students of color to be involved in the public policy activities of the American Psychological Association (APA) during the summer.

Eligibility This program is open to graduate students who are members of an ethnic minority group (including, but not limited to, Asian American, African American, Alaskan Native, American Indian, Hispanic, and Pacific Islander) and/or have demonstrated a commitment to a career in psychology or a related field with a focus on ethnic minority issues. Applicants must be interested in spending a summer in Washington, D.C. to work on public policy issues in conjunction with the Minority Fellowship Program of the APA. Their application must indicate why they are interested in the fellowship, their previous and current research experiences, their interest and involvement in ethnic minority psychological issues, and how the fellowship would contribute to their career goals.

Financial data The stipend is $3,000. The sponsor also provides travel expenses and up to $1,500 for living expenses.

Duration 8 to 12 weeks.

Additional information This program began in 2000. The sponsor is Division 9 of the APA.

Number awarded 1 each year.

Deadline February of each year.

[631]
DAVE CALDWELL SCHOLARSHIP

American Water Works Association
Attn: Scholarship Coordinator
6666 West Quincy Avenue
Denver, CO 80235-3098
(303) 794-7771   Toll Free: (800) 926-7337
Fax: (303) 347-0804   E-mail: scholarships@awwa.org
Web: www.awwa.org

Summary To provide financial assistance to Asian American and other minority students interested in working on a graduate degree in the field of water supply and treatment.

Eligibility This program is open to minority and female students working on a graduate degree in the field of water supply and treatment at a college or university in Canada, Guam, Mexico, Puerto Rico, or the United States. Students who have been accepted into graduate school but have not yet begun graduate study are encouraged to apply. Applicants must submit a 2-page resume, official transcripts, 3 letters of recommendation, a proposed curriculum of study, a 1-page statement of educational plans and career objectives demonstrating an interest in the drinking water field, and a 3-page proposed plan of research. Selection is based on academic record and potential to provide leadership in applied research and consulting in the drinking water field.

Financial data The stipend is $10,000.

Duration 1 year; nonrenewable.

Additional information Funding for this program comes from the engineering firm Brown and Caldwell.

Number awarded 1 each year.

Deadline January of each year.

[632]
DAVID EATON SCHOLARSHIP

Unitarian Universalist Association
Attn: Ministerial Credentialing Office
24 Farnsworth Street
Boston, MA 02210-1409
(617) 948-6403   Fax: (617) 742-2875
E-mail: mcoadministrator@uua.org
Web: www.uua.org

Summary To provide financial assistance to Asian American and other minority women preparing for the Unitarian Universalist (UU) ministry.

Eligibility This program is open to women from historically marginalized groups who are currently enrolled or planning to enroll full or at least half time in a UU ministerial training program with aspirant or candidate status. Applicants must be citizens of the United States or Canada. Priority is given first to those who have demonstrated outstanding ministerial ability and secondarily to students with the greatest financial need (especially persons of color).

Financial data The stipend ranges from $1,000 to $15,000 per year.

Duration 1 year.

Number awarded 1 or 2 each year.

Deadline April of each year.

[633]
DAVID IBATA PRINT SCHOLARSHIP

Asian American Journalists Association-Chicago Chapter
c/o Lorene Yue
Crain's Chicago Business
150 North Michigan Avenue, 16th Floor
Chicago, IL 60601
E-mail: chicagoaaja@gmail.com
Web: www.aajachicago.wordpress.com

Summary To provide funding to members of the Asian American Journalists Association (AAJA) who are interested in a summer internship at a Chicago publication.

Eligibility This program is open to AAJA members who are college sophomores, juniors, seniors, graduate students or recent graduates. Applicants must be interested in an internship at Crain's Chicago Business. Along with their application, they must submit a resume that includes their job experience in journalism and 5 clips.

Financial data AAJA-Chicago awards a $2,500 stipend for the internship and Crain's Chicago Business matches that with a grant of $2,500.

Duration 10 to 12 weeks during the summer.

Number awarded 1 each year.

Deadline December of each year.

[634]
DAVID SANKEY MINORITY SCHOLARSHIP IN METEOROLOGY

National Weather Association
Attn: Executive Director
3100 Monitor Avenue, Suite 123
Norman, OK 73072
(405) 701-5167   Fax: (405) 701-5227
E-mail: exdir@nwas.org
Web: www.nwas.org

Summary To provide financial assistance to Asian Americans and members of other underrepresented groups working on an undergraduate or graduate degree in meteorology.

Eligibility This program is open to members of underrepresented ethnic groups who are either entering their sophomore or higher year of undergraduate study or enrolled as graduate students. Applicants must be working on a degree in meteorology. Along with their application, they must submit a 1-page statement explaining why they are applying for this scholarship. Selection is based on that statement, academic achievement, and 2 letters of recommendation.

Financial data The stipend is $1,000.

Duration 1 year.

Additional information This program began in 2002.

Number awarded 1 each year.

Deadline April of each year.

[635]
DAVID TAMOTSU KAGIWADA MEMORIAL SCHOLARSHIP

Christian Church (Disciples of Christ)
Attn: Disciples Home Missions
130 East Washington Street
P.O. Box 1986
Indianapolis, IN 46206-1986
(317) 713-2652   Toll Free: (888) DHM-2631
Fax: (317) 635-4426   E-mail: mail@dhm.disciples.org
Web: www.discipleshomemissions.org

Summary To provide financial assistance to Asians and Pacific Islanders interested in preparing for a career in the ministry of the Christian Church (Disciples of Christ).

Eligibility This program is open to ministerial students of Asian and Pacific Islander descent who are members of a Christian Church (Disciples of Christ) congregation in the United States or Canada. Applicants must plan to prepare for the ordained ministry, be working on an M.Div. or equivalent degree, provide evidence of financial need, be enrolled full time at an accredited school or seminary, provide a transcript of academic work, and be under the care of a regional Commission on the Ministry or in the process of coming under care.

Financial data A stipend is awarded (amount not specified).

Duration 1 year; recipients may reapply.

Number awarded Varies each year.

Deadline March of each year.

[636]
DEEP CARBON OBSERVATORY DIVERSITY GRANTS

American Geosciences Institute
Attn: Grant Coordinator
4220 King Street
Alexandria, VA 22302-1502
(703) 379-2480   Fax: (703) 379-7563
E-mail: hrhp@agiweb.org
Web: www.americangeosciences.org

Summary To provide funding to geoscientists who are Filipinos or members of other underrepresented ethnic groups and interested in participating in research and other activities of the Deep Carbon Observatory (DCO) project.

Eligibility This program is open to traditionally underrepresented geoscientists (e.g., Filipinos, African Americans, Native Americans, Native Alaskans, Hispanics, Latinos, Latinas, Native Hawaiians, Native Pacific Islanders, of mixed racial/ethnic backgrounds) who are U.S. citizens or permanent residents. Applicants must be interested in participating in the DCO, a global research program focused on understanding carbon in Earth, and must have research interests that are aligned with its mission. They may be doctoral students, postdoctoral researchers, or early-career faculty members or research staff.

Financial data Grants average $5,000.

Duration 1 year.

Additional information This program is funded by the Alfred P. Sloan Foundation.

Number awarded 4 or 5 each year.

Deadline April of each year.

[637]
DELAWARE ATHLETIC TRAINERS' ASSOCIATION ETHNIC DIVERSITY ADVISORY COMMITTEE SCHOLARSHIP

Delaware Athletic Trainers' Association
c/o Education Committee Chair
University of Delaware
159 Fred Rust Ice Arena
Newark, DE 19716
(302) 831-6402   E-mail: kaminski@udel.edu
Web: www.delata.org/scholarship-applications.html

Summary To provide financial assistance to Asian American and other ethnic minority members of the National Athletic Trainers' Association (NATA) from Delaware who are working on an undergraduate or graduate degree in the field.

Eligibility This program is open to NATA members who are members of ethnic diversity groups and residents of Delaware or attending college in that state. Applicants must be enrolled full time in an undergraduate athletic training education program or a graduate athletic training program and have a GPA of 2.5 or higher. They must intend to prepare for the profession of athletic training. Along with their application, they must submit an 800-word statement on their athletic training background, experience, philosophy, and goals. Selection is based equally on academic performance and athletic training clinical achievement.

Financial data A stipend is awarded (amount not specified).

Duration 1 year.

Number awarded 1 or more each year.

Deadline February of each year.

[638]
DISSERTATION FELLOWSHIPS OF THE CONSORTIUM FOR FACULTY DIVERSITY

Consortium for Faculty Diversity at Liberal Arts Colleges
c/o Gettysburg College
Provost's Office
300 North Washington Street
Campus Box 410
Gettysburg, PA 17325
(717) 337-6796   E-mail: sgockows@gettysburg.edu
Web: www.gettysburg.edu

Summary To provide an opportunity for doctoral candidates who are Asian Americans or others who will promote diversity to work on their dissertation while in residence at selected liberal arts colleges.

Eligibility This program is open to U.S. citizens and permanent residents who have completed all the requirements for the Ph.D. or M.F.A. except the dissertation. Applicants must be interested in a residency at a member institution of the Consortium for Faculty Diversity at Liberal Arts Colleges during which they will complete their dissertation. They must be able to contribute to diversity at the institution.

Financial data Dissertation fellows receive a stipend based on the average salary paid to instructors at the participating college. Modest funds are made available to finance the fellow's proposed research, subject to the usual institutional procedures.

Duration 1 year.

Additional information The following schools are participating in the program: Allegheny College, Amherst College, Bard College, Bowdoin College, Bryn Mawr College, Bucknell University, Carleton College, Centenary College of Louisiana, Centre College, College of the Holy Cross, Colorado College, Denison University, DePauw University, Dickinson College, Gettysburg College, Grinnell College, Gustavus Adolphus College, Hamilton College, Haverford College, Hobart and William Smith Colleges, Juniata College, Lafayette College, Lawrence University, Luther College, Macalester College, Mount Holyoke College, Muhlenberg College, Oberlin College, Pitzer College, Pomona College, Reed College, Scripps College, Skidmore College, Smith College, Southwestern University, St. Lawrence University, St. Olaf College, Swarthmore College, The College of Wooster, Trinity College, University of Richmond, Vassar College, and Wellesley College. Fellows are expected to teach at least 1 course in each academic term of residency, participate in departmental seminars, and interact with students.

Number awarded Varies each year.

Deadline October of each year.

[639]
DIVERSIFYING HIGHER EDUCATION FACULTY IN ILLINOIS

Illinois Board of Higher Education
Attn: DFI Program
431 East Adams Street, Second Floor
Springfield, IL 62701-1404
(217) 782-2551   Fax: (217) 782-8548
TDD: (888) 261-2881   E-mail: DFI@ibhe.org
Web: www.ibhe.state.il.us/DFI/default.htm

Summary To provide fellowship/loans to Asian American and other minority students interested in enrolling in graduate school programs in Illinois to prepare for a career in higher education.

Eligibility This program is open to U.S. citizens and permanent residents who 1) are residents of Illinois and have received a baccalaureate degree from an educational institution in the state; or 2) have received a baccalaureate degree from an accredited educational institution in any state and have lived in Illinois for at least the 3 previous years. Applicants must be members of a minority group traditionally underrepresented in graduate school enrollment in Illinois (Asian Americans, African Americans, Hispanic Americans, Alaskan Natives, American Indians, Native Alaskans, Native Hawaiians, or other Pacific Islanders) and have been admitted to a graduate program in the state to work on a doctoral or master's degree and prepare for a career in teaching or administration at an Illinois postsecondary institution or Illinois higher education governing board. They must have a GPA of 2.75 or higher in the last 60 hours of undergraduate work or 3.2 or higher in at least 9 hours of graduate study. Along with their application, they must submit statements on 1) their professional goals (including their intended employment setting, intended position in Illinois higher education, plans for achieving their intended goals, and current and/or past experiences that would be helpful in achieving their intended goals; and 2) their underrepresented status (including how their underrepresented status influenced their personal and academic development and why they should be awarded a fellowship designated specifically for underrepresented groups in higher education). Financial need is considered in the selection process.

Financial data   Stipends are $10,000 for new fellows or $13,000 per year for renewal fellows. Some participating institutions also provide a tuition waiver or scholarship. This is a fellowship/loan program. Recipients must agree to accept a position, in teaching or administration, at an Illinois postsecondary educational institution, on an Illinois higher education governing or coordinating board, or at a state agency in an education-related position. Recipients failing to fulfill the conditions of the award are required to repay 20% of the total award.

Duration   Up to 2 years for master's degree students; up to 4 years for doctoral students.

Additional information   The Illinois General Assembly established this program in 2004 as a successor to 2 earlier programs (both established in 1985); the Illinois Consortium for Educational Opportunity Program (ICEOP) and the Illinois Minority Graduate Incentive Program (IMGIP).

Number awarded   Varies each year; recently, 111 new and renewal fellows were receiving support through this program.

Deadline   February of each year.

[640]
DIVERSITY IN PSYCHOLOGY AND LAW RESEARCH AWARD

American Psychological Association
Attn: Division 41 (American Psychology-Law Society)
c/o Kathy Gaskey, Administrative Officer
P.O. Box 11488
Southport, NC 28461-3936
(910) 933-4018   Fax: (910) 933-4018
E-mail: apls@ec.rr.com
Web: www.apadivisions.org

Summary   To provide funding to student members of the American Psychology-Law Society (AP-LS) who are interested in conducting a research project related to diversity.

Eligibility   This program is open to undergraduate and graduate student members of AP-LS who are interested in conducting research on issues related to psychology, law, multiculturalism, and/or diversity (e.g., research pertaining to psycholegal issues on race, gender, culture, sexual orientation). Students from underrepresented groups are strongly encouraged to apply; underrepresented groups include, but are not limited to: racial and ethnic minorities; first-generation college students; lesbian, gay, bisexual, and transgender students; and students with physical disabilities. Applicants must submit a project description that includes a statement of the research problem, the project's likely impact on the field of psychology and law broadly, methodology, budget, and an overview of relevant literature. Selection is based on the impact of the project on diversity and multiculturalism and the expected completion within the allocated time.

Financial data   The grant is $1,000.

Duration   The project must be completed within 1 year.

Number awarded   Up to 5 each year.

Deadline   November of each year.

[641]
DIVERSITY SUMMER FELLOWSHIP IN HEALTH LAW

The New York Bar Foundation
One Elk Street
Albany, NY 12207
(518) 487-5651   Fax: (518) 487-5699
E-mail: moclair@tnybf.org
Web: www.tnybf.org/fellandschol

Summary   To provide an opportunity for Asian American and other diverse residents of any state attending law school in New York to gain work experience in health law with an attorney or facility in the state.

Eligibility   This program is open to diverse students from any state who are enrolled at a law school in New York. They must be interested in working on health law with a health care attorney or facility in New York. Along with their application, they must submit a writing sample on any topic, preferably health law. Selection is based on content and quality of application materials, demonstrated interest in health law, work experience, academic record, leadership experience, extracurricular activities, community service, quality of written expression, maturity, integrity, and professionalism.

Financial data   The stipend is $5,000.

Duration   8 weeks during the summer.

Additional information   This program began in 2011 by the Health Law Section of the New York State Bar Association. It is administered by The New York Bar Foundation.

Number awarded   2 each year.

Deadline   December of each year.

[642]
DOCTORAL DIVERSITY FELLOWSHIPS IN SCIENCE, TECHNOLOGY, ENGINEERING, AND MATHEMATICS

State University of New York
Attn: Office of Diversity, Equity and Inclusion
State University Plaza, T1000A
353 Broadway
Albany, NY 12246
(518) 320-1189   E-mail: carlos.medina@suny.edu
Web: system.suny.edu/odei/diversity-programs

Summary   To provide financial assistance to Asian American and other residents of any state who are working on a doctoral degree in a field of science, technology, engineering, or mathematics (STEM) at campuses of the State University of New York (SUNY) and contribute to the diversity of the student body.

Eligibility   This program is open to U.S. citizens and permanent residents who are residents of any state and enrolled as doctoral students at any of the participating SUNY institutions. Applicants must be working on a degree in a field of STEM. They must be able to demonstrate how they will contribute to the diversity of the student body, primarily by having overcome a disadvantage or other impediment to success in higher education. Economic disadvantage, although not a requirement, may be the basis for eligibility. Membership in a racial or ethnic group that is underrepresented at the applicant's school or program may serve as a plus factor in making awards, but may not form the sole basis of selection.

Financial data The stipend is $20,000 per year. A grant of $2,000 to support research and professional development is also provided.

Duration 3 years; may be renewed for up to 2 additional years.

Number awarded 2 each year.

Deadline March of each year.

[643]
DOCTORAL/POST-DOCTORAL FELLOWSHIP PROGRAM IN LAW AND SOCIAL SCIENCE

American Bar Foundation
Attn: Administrative Assistant for Academic Affairs and
   Research Administration
750 North Lake Shore Drive
Chicago, IL 60611-4403
(312) 988-6517   Fax: (312) 988-6579
E-mail: aehrhardt@abfn.org
Web: www.americanbarfoundation.org

Summary To provide research funding to scholars, especially Asian Americans and other minorities, who are completing or have completed doctoral degrees in fields related to law, the legal profession, and legal institutions.

Eligibility This program is open to Ph.D. candidates in the social sciences who have completed all doctoral requirements except the dissertation. Applicants who have completed the dissertation are also eligible. Doctoral and proposed research must be in the general area of sociolegal studies or in social scientific approaches to law, the legal profession, or legal institutions and legal processes. Applications must include 1) a dissertation abstract or proposal with an outline of the substance and methods of the research; 2) 2 letters of recommendation; and 3) a curriculum vitae. Minority candidates are especially encouraged to apply.

Financial data The stipend is $30,000. Fellows may request up to $1,500 to reimburse expenses associated with research, travel to meet with advisers, or travel to conferences at which papers are presented. Relocation expenses of up to $2,500 may be reimbursed on application.

Duration 12 months, beginning in September.

Additional information Fellows are offered access to the computing and word processing facilities of the American Bar Foundation and the libraries of Northwestern University and the University of Chicago. This program was established in 1996. Fellowships must be held in residence at the American Bar Foundation. Appointments to the fellowship are full time; fellows are not permitted to undertake other work.

Number awarded 1 or more each year.

Deadline December of each year.

[644]
DON H. LIU SCHOLARS PROGRAM

Asian American Bar Association of New York
Attn: Scholars Program
45 Rockefeller Plaza, 20th Floor
New York, NY 10111
(212) 332-2478   Fax: (718) 228-7206
E-mail: DonHLiuScholars@gmail.com
Web: www.aabany.org/?page=447

Summary To provide financial assistance to Asian Americans entering law school in designated eastern states.

Eligibility This program is open to U.S. citizens and permanent residents of Asian descent who are the first in their immediate family to work on a graduate or professional degree. Applicants must be enrolled full time at a law school in Connecticut, Delaware, Maryland, Massachusetts, New Jersey, New York, Pennsylvania, or Washington, D.C. They must intend to practice in the private sector in the New York City metropolitan area following graduation. Selection is based on demonstrated academic and/or leadership accomplishments or promise through work and/or other activities. Financial need is considered in the selection process.

Financial data The stipend is $15,000.

Duration 1 year.

Additional information This program began in 2014.

Number awarded 2 each year.

Deadline January of each year.

[645]
DR. DAVID MONASH/HARRY LLOYD AND ELIZABETH PAWLETTE MARSHALL MEDICAL STUDENT SERVICE SCHOLARSHIPS

National Medical Fellowships, Inc.
Attn: Scholarship Program
347 Fifth Avenue, Suite 510
New York, NY 10016
(212) 483-8880   Toll Free: (877) NMF-1DOC
Fax: (212) 483-8897 E-mail: scholarships@nmfonline.org
Web: www.nmfonline.org

Summary To provide funding for a community health project to Vietnamese, Cambodian, and other underrepresented medical students in Chicago who are committed to remaining in the area and working to reduce health disparities.

Eligibility This program is open to residents of any state who are currently enrolled in their second through fourth year at a medical school in Chicago. U.S. citizenship is required. Applicants must be interested in conducting a community health project in an underserved community. They must identify as an underrepresented minority student in health care (defined as Vietnamese, Cambodian, African American, Hispanic/Latino, American Indian, Alaska Native, Native Hawaiian, or Pacific Islander) and/or socioeconomically disadvantaged student. Along with their application, they must submit documentation of financial status; a short biography; a resume; 2 letters of recommendation; a personal statement of 500 to 1,000 words on their personal and professional motivation for a medical career, their commitment to primary care and service in a health and/or community setting, their motivation for working to reduce health disparities, and their commitment to improving health care; a personal statement of 500 to 1,000 words on the experiences that are preparing them to practice in an underserved community; and a 150- to 350-word description of their proposed community service project. Selection is based on demonstrated leadership early in career and commitment to serving medically underserved communities in Chicago.

Financial data The stipend is $5,000.

Duration 1 year.

Additional information This program began in 2010 with support from the Chicago Community Trust.

Number awarded 6 each year.

Deadline May of each year.

[646]
DR. HARIHARA MEHENDALE GRADUATE STUDENT BEST ABSTRACT AWARD

Society of Toxicology
Attn: Association of Scientists of Indian Origin Special
  Interest Group
1821 Michael Faraday Drive, Suite 300
Reston, VA 20190-5348
(703) 438-3115   Fax: (703) 438-3113
E-mail: sothq@toxicology.org
Web: www.toxicology.org/ai/af/awards_details.aspx?id=142

Summary To recognize and reward graduate student members of the Society of Toxicology (SOT) who are of Indian origin and present outstanding papers at the annual meeting.

Eligibility This award is available to graduate students of Indian origin who are members of SOT and its Association of Scientists of Indian Origin (ASIO). Candidates must have an accepted abstract of a research poster or platform presentation for the SOT annual meeting. Along with the abstract, they must submit a cover letter outlining the significance of their research to the field of toxicology and how this award will help them to further their career goals.

Financial data A plaque and a cash award (amount not specified) are presented.

Duration The award is presented annually.

Additional information This award was established in 2008.

Number awarded 1 each year.

Deadline December of each year.

[647]
DR. KIYOSHI SONODA MEMORIAL SCHOLARSHIP

Japanese American Citizens League
Attn: National Scholarship Awards
1765 Sutter Street
San Francisco, CA 94115
(415) 345-1075   Fax: (415) 345-1077
E-mail: pwada@jacl.org
Web: www.jacl.org/jacl-national-scholarship-program

Summary To provide financial assistance to student members of the Japanese American Citizens League (JACL) who are interested in preparing for a career in dentistry.

Eligibility This program is open to JACL members who are enrolled or planning to enroll at a school of dentistry. Applicants must submit information on their involvement in JACL and a 2-page essay on a topic that changes annually but relates to Japanese Americans. Selection is based on that essay, academic history, JACL involvement, school activities, work history, scholastic honors, and community involvement.

Financial data Stipends generally average more than $2,000.

Duration 1 year; nonrenewable.

Number awarded At least 1 each year.

Deadline March of each year.

[648]
DR. KOU BLIAXA AND SONG VANG ANY DISCIPLINE SCHOLARSHIP

Hmong American Education Fund
P.O. Box 17468
St. Paul, MN 55117
(651) 592-1576   E-mail: scholarships@thehaef.org
Web: www.thehaef.org

Summary To provide financial assistance to Hmong undergraduate and graduate students from Minnesota who are working on a degree in any field.

Eligibility This program is open to students of Hmong descent who are residents of Minnesota and currently enrolled as full-time undergraduate or graduate students at 2- or 4-year colleges or universities in any state. Applicants must be U.S. citizens or permanent residents and have a GPA of 3.0 or higher. They may be working on a degree in any field. Along with their application, they must submit a 1,500-word essay on their commitment to education, their financial need, how this scholarship can help them, and their community service.

Financial data The stipend is $500.

Duration 1 year; nonrenewable.

Number awarded 1 each year.

Deadline March of each year.

[649]
DR. KOU BLIAXA AND SONG VANG MEDICAL AND DENTAL SCHOLARSHIPS

Hmong American Education Fund
P.O. Box 17468
St. Paul, MN 55117
(651) 592-1576   E-mail: scholarships@thehaef.org
Web: www.thehaef.org

Summary To provide financial assistance to Hmong residents of Minnesota who have been accepted to a medical or dental school in any state.

Eligibility This program is open to students of Hmong descent who are residents of Minnesota and have been accepted as a full-time student at a medical or dental school in any state. Applicants must be U.S. citizens or permanent residents and have a GPA of 3.0 or higher. Along with their application, they must submit a 1,500-word essay on their commitment to education, medicine, or dentistry; their financial need; how this scholarship can help them; and their community service.

Financial data The stipend is $500.

Duration 1 year; nonrenewable.

Number awarded 2 each year.

Deadline March of each year.

[650]
DR. LAXMAN DESAI GRADUATE STUDENT BEST ABSTRACT AWARD

Society of Toxicology
Attn: Association of Scientists of Indian Origin Special
  Interest Group
1821 Michael Faraday Drive, Suite 300
Reston, VA 20190-5348
(703) 438-3115   Fax: (703) 438-3113
E-mail: sothq@toxicology.org
Web: www.toxicology.org/ai/af/awards_details.aspx?id=144

Summary To recognize and reward graduate student members of the Society of Toxicology (SOT) who are of Indian origin and present outstanding papers at the annual meeting.

Eligibility This award is available to graduate students of Indian origin who are members of SOT and its Association of Scientists of Indian Origin (ASIO). Candidates must have an accepted abstract of a research poster or platform presentation for the SOT annual meeting. Along with the abstract, they must submit a cover letter outlining the significance of their research to the field of toxicology and how this award will help them to further their career goals.

Financial data A plaque and a cash award (amount not specified) are presented.

Duration The award is presented annually.

Additional information This award was established in 2009.

Number awarded 1 each year.

Deadline December of each year.

[651]
DR. NANCY FOSTER SCHOLARSHIP PROGRAM

National Oceanic and Atmospheric Administration
Attn: Office of National Marine Sanctuaries
1305 East-West Highway
N/ORM 6 SSMC4, Room 11146
Silver Spring, MD 20910
(301) 713-7245   Fax: (301) 713-9465
E-mail: fosterscholars@noaa.gov
Web: fosterscholars.noaa.gov/aboutscholarship.html

Summary To provide financial assistance to graduate students, especially Asian Americans and other minorities, who are interested in working on a degree in fields related to marine sciences.

Eligibility This program is open to U.S. citizens, particularly women and members of minority groups, currently working on or intending to work on a master's or doctoral degree in oceanography, marine biology, or maritime archaeology, including all science, engineering, and resource management of ocean and coastal areas. Applicants must submit a description of their academic, research, and career goals, and how their proposed course of study or research will help them to achieve those goals. They must be enrolled full time and have a GPA of 3.3 or higher. As part of their program, they must be interested in participating in a summer research collaboration at a facility of the National Oceanic and Atmospheric Administration (NOAA). Selection is based on academic record and a statement of career goals and objectives (20%); quality of project and applicability to program priorities (30%); recommendations and/or endorsements (15%); addi-

tional relevant experience related to diversity of education, extracurricular activities, honors and awards, written and oral communication skills, and interpersonal skills (20%); and financial need (15%).

Financial data The program provides a stipend of $30,000 per academic year, a tuition allowance of up to $12,000 per academic year, and up to $10,000 of support for a 4- to 6-week research collaboration at a NOAA facility is provided.

Duration Master's degree students may receive up to 2 years of stipend and tuition support and 1 research collaboration (for a total of $94,000). Doctoral students may receive up to 4 years of stipend and tuition support and 2 research collaborations (for a total of $188,000).

Additional information This program began in 2001.

Number awarded Varies each year; recently, 3 were awarded.

Deadline December of each year.

[652]
DRI LAW STUDENT DIVERSITY SCHOLARSHIP

DRI-The Voice of the Defense Bar
Attn: Deputy Executive Director
55 West Monroe Street, Suite 2000
Chicago, IL 60603
(312) 795-1101   Fax: (312) 795-0747
E-mail: dri@dri.org
Web: www.dri.org/About

Summary To provide financial assistance to Asian American and other minority law students.

Eligibility This program is open to full-time students entering their second or third year of law school who are African American, Hispanic, Asian, Native American, women, or other students who will come from backgrounds that would add to the cause of diversity, including sexual orientation. Applicants must submit an essay, up to 1,000 words, on a topic that changes annually but relates to the work of defense attorneys. Selection is based on that essay, demonstrated academic excellence, service to the profession, service to the community, and service to the cause of diversity. Students affiliated with the American Association for Justice as members, student members, or employees are not eligible. Finalists are invited to participate in personal interviews.

Financial data The stipend is $10,000.

Duration 1 year.

Additional information This program began in 2004.

Number awarded 2 each year.

Deadline May of each year.

[653]
EASTERN REGION KOREAN AMERICAN COLLEGE/GRADUATE SCHOLARSHIPS

Korean American Scholarship Foundation
Eastern Region
1952 Gallows Road, Suite 310
Vienna, VA 22182
(703) 748-5935   Fax: (703) 748-1874
E-mail: erc.scholarship@kasf.org
Web: www.kasf.org/eastern

Summary To provide financial assistance to Korean American students from any state who are working on an undergraduate or graduate degree in any field at a school in eastern states.

Eligibility   This program is open to Korean Americans who are high school seniors or full-time undergraduate or graduate students currently enrolled or planning to enroll at a college or university in an eastern state. Applicants may reside anywhere in the United States, provided they attend school in the sponsor's eastern region: Delaware, District of Columbia, Indiana, Kentucky, Maryland, North Carolina, Pennsylvania, Virginia, and West Virginia. They must have a GPA of 3.0 or higher. Both U.S. citizens and foreign nationals are eligible. Selection is based on academic achievement (25%), extracurricular activities (10%), an essay (10%), recommendations (10%), financial need (40%), and extra credit for having extraordinary circumstances (5%).

Financial data   Stipends range up to $5,000.

Duration   1 year; renewable.

Number awarded   Varies each year; recently, 46 were awarded.

Deadline   July of each year.

[654]
EDSA MINORITY SCHOLARSHIP

Landscape Architecture Foundation
Attn: Leadership in Landscape Scholarship Program
1129 20th Street, N.W., Suite 202
Washington, DC 20036
(202) 331-7070   Fax: (202) 331-7079
E-mail: scholarships@lafoundation.org
Web: www.lafoundation.org

Summary   To provide financial assistance to Asian American and other minority college students who are interested in studying landscape architecture.

Eligibility   This program is open to Asian American, African American, Hispanic, Native American, and minority college students of other cultural and ethnic backgrounds. Applicants must be entering their final 2 years of undergraduate study in landscape architecture or working on a graduate degree in that field. Along with their application, they must submit a 500-word essay on a design or research effort they plan to pursue (explaining how it will contribute to the advancement of the profession and to their ethnic heritage), 3 work samples, and 2 letters of recommendation. Selection is based on professional experience, community involvement, extracurricular activities, and financial need.

Financial data   The stipend is $5,000.

Additional information   This scholarship was formerly designated the Edward D. Stone, Jr. and Associates Minority Scholarship.

Number awarded   1 each year.

Deadline   February of each year.

[655]
EDUCATIONAL FOUNDATION OF THE COLORADO SOCIETY OF CERTIFIED PUBLIC ACCOUNTANTS MINORITY SCHOLARSHIPS

Colorado Society of Certified Public Accountants
Attn: Educational Foundation
7887 East Belleview Avenue, Suite 200
Englewood, CO 80111
(303) 773-2877   Toll Free: (800) 523-9082 (within CO)
Fax: (303) 773-6344
Web: www.cocpa.org

Summary   To provide financial assistance to Asian American and other minority upper-division and graduate students in Colorado who are majoring in accounting.

Eligibility   This program is open to Colorado minority residents (Asian American, Black or African American, Hispanic or Latino, Native American) who are upper-division or graduate students at colleges and universities in the state and have completed at least 6 semester hours of accounting courses. Applicants must have a GPA of at least 3.0 overall and 3.25 in accounting classes. They must be U.S. citizens or noncitizens legally living and studying in Colorado with a valid visa that enables them to become employed. Financial need is not considered in the selection process.

Financial data   The stipend is $2,500. Funds are paid directly to the recipient's school to be used for books, C.P.A. review materials, tuition, fees, and dormitory room and board.

Duration   1 year; recipients may reapply.

Number awarded   1 or more each year.

Deadline   May of each year for fall semester or quarter; November of each year for winter quarter or spring semester.

[656]
EDWARD S. ROTH SCHOLARSHIP

Society of Manufacturing Engineers
Attn: SME Education Foundation
One SME Drive
P.O. Box 930
Dearborn, MI 48121-0930
(313) 425-3300   Toll Free: (866) 547-6333
Fax: (313) 425-3411   E-mail: foundation@sme.org
Web: www.smeef.org

Summary   To provide financial assistance to Asian American and other students enrolled or planning to work on a bachelor's or master's degree in manufacturing engineering at selected universities.

Eligibility   This program is open to U.S. citizens who are graduating high school seniors or currently-enrolled undergraduate or graduate students. Applicants must be enrolled or planning to enroll as a full-time student at 1 of 13 selected 4-year universities to work on a bachelor's or master's degree in manufacturing engineering. They must have a GPA of 3.0 or higher. Preference is given to 1) students demonstrating financial need; 2) minority students; and 3) students participating in a co-op program. Along with their application, they must submit a brief statement about why they chose their major, their career and educational objectives, and how this scholarship will help them attain those objectives.

Financial data   Stipends range from $1,000 to $6,000 and recently averaged approximately $2,000.

Duration   1 year; may be renewed.

Additional information The eligible institutions are California Polytechnic State University at San Luis Obispo, California State Polytechnic State University at Pomona, University of Miami (Florida), Bradley University (Illinois), Central State University (Ohio), Miami University (Ohio), Boston University, Worcester Polytechnic Institute (Massachusetts), University of Massachusetts, St. Cloud State University (Minnesota), University of Texas at Rio Grande Valley, Brigham Young University (Utah), and Utah State University.

Number awarded 2 each year.

Deadline January of each year.

[657]
EIICHI MATSUSHITA MEMORIAL SCHOLARSHIP FUND

Evangelical Lutheran Church in America
Congregational and Synodical Mission
Attn: Program Director for Asian and Pacific Islander
 Ministries
8765 West Higgins Road
Chicago, IL 60631
(773) 380-2834   Toll Free: (800) 638-3522
Fax: (773) 380-2833
E-mail: Pongsak.Limthongviratn@elca.org
Web: www.asianlutherans.net/scholarship

Summary To provide financial assistance to Asian/Pacific Islanders who wish to receive seminary training to become ordained Lutheran pastors or certified lay teachers.

Eligibility This program is open to students who are of Asian or Pacific Islander background and are attending a Lutheran seminary, have been endorsed by the appropriate synodical or district commissions, have demonstrated financial need, and have received partial financial support from their home congregations. Applicants must include a 250-word statement on their commitment to Asian/Pacific Islander ministry.

Financial data The stipend is $750.

Duration 1 year; may be renewed.

Additional information The scholarship was established by Asian Lutherans in North America.

Number awarded 2 each year.

Deadline September of each year.

[658]
EIZO AND TOYO SAKUMOTO TRUST SCHOLARSHIPS

Hawai'i Community Foundation
Attn: Scholarship Department
827 Fort Street Mall
Honolulu, HI 96813
(808) 566-5570   Toll Free: (888) 731-3863
Fax: (808) 521-6286
E-mail: scholarships@hcf-hawaii.org
Web: hcf.scholarships.ngwebsolutions.com

Summary To provide financial assistance to Hawaii residents of Japanese ancestry who are interested in attending graduate school in the state.

Eligibility This program is open to Hawaiian residents of Japanese ancestry who are enrolled or planning to enroll at an accredited college or university in the state. Applicants must be full-time graduate students and able to demonstrate

academic achievement (GPA of 3.5 or higher), good moral character, and financial need. They must have been born in Hawaii. Along with their application, they must submit a short statement indicating their reasons for attending college, their planned course of study, their career goals, and what community service means to them.

Financial data The amounts of the awards depend on the availability of funds and the need of the recipient. Recently, the average value of the scholarships awarded by the foundation was $2,800.

Duration 1 year.

Number awarded Varies each year; recently, 30 were awarded.

Deadline February of each year.

[659]
ELIZABETH MUNSTERBERG KOPPITZ CHILD PSYCHOLOGY GRADUATE FELLOWSHIPS

American Psychological Foundation
750 First Street, N.E.
Washington, DC 20002-4242
(202) 336-5843   Fax: (202) 336-5812
E-mail: foundation@apa.org
Web: www.apa.org/apf/funding/koppitz.aspx

Summary To provide funding to doctoral students, especially Asian Americans and members of other underrepresented groups, interested in conducting research in child psychology.

Eligibility This program is open to graduate students who have progressed academically through the qualifying examinations, usually after the third or fourth year of doctoral study. Applicants must be interested in conducting psychological research that promotes the advancement of knowledge and learning in the field of child psychology. Selection is based on conformance with stated program goals, magnitude of incremental contribution, quality of proposed work, and applicant's demonstrated scholarship and research competence. The sponsor encourages applications from individuals who represent diversity in race, ethnicity, gender, age, disability, and sexual orientation.

Financial data The grant is $25,000.

Duration 1 year.

Additional information This fellowship was first awarded in 2003.

Number awarded Varies each year; recently, 6 were selected.

Deadline November of each year.

[660]
ELLIOTT C. ROBERTS SCHOLARSHIP

Institute for Diversity in Health Management
Attn: Membership and Education Specialist
155 North Wacker Avenue
Chicago, IL 60606
(312) 422-2658   E-mail: cbiddle@aha.org
Web: www.diversityconnection.org

Summary To provide financial assistance to Asian American and other graduate students in health care management who will contribute to ethnic diversity in the profession.

Eligibility This program is open to U.S. citizens who represent ethnically diverse cultural backgrounds. Applicants must be enrolled in the second year of a master's degree program in health administration or a comparable program and have a GPA of 3.0 or higher. Along with their application, they must submit 1) a personal statement of 1 to 2 pages on their interest in health care management and their career goals; 2) an essay on what they see as the most challenging issue facing America's hospitals and health systems; and 3) a 500-word essay on their interest and background in health care finance. Selection is based on academic achievement, commitment to community service, and financial need.

Financial data   The stipend is $1,000.

Duration   1 year.

Number awarded   1 each year.

Deadline   January of each year.

[661]
ELLIS INJURY LAW DIVERSITY SCHOLARSHIPS

Ellis Law Corporation
Attn: Scholarship
883 North Douglas Street
El Segundo, CA 90245
Toll Free: (888) 559-7672
E-mail: scholarships@alelaw.com
Web: www.ellisinjurylaw.com/scholarships

Summary   To provide financial assistance to pre-law and law students who either are Asian Americans or members of another ethnic minority group or have been involved in diversity issues.

Eligibility   This program is open to students accepted or enrolled at 1) a 4-year college or university with the intention of working on a law degree; and 2) an ABA-accredited law school. Applicants must be either members of an ethnic/racial minority or individuals who have made a demonstrative commitment to diversity within their school and/or community. They must have a GPA of 3.0 or higher. Along with their application, they must submit an essay of 1,500 to 2,000 words answering 3 questions about recent Supreme Court decisions regarding affirmative action. Selection is based on that essay and transcripts.

Financial data   The stipend is $1,000.

Duration   1 year.

Additional information   This program began in 2014.

Number awarded   3 each year.

Deadline   December of each year.

[662]
EMERGING ARCHIVAL SCHOLARS PROGRAM

Archival Education and Research Institute
Center for Information as Evidence
c/o UCLA Graduate School of Education and Information
    Studies
Office of External Relations
2043 Moore Hall
Los Angeles, CA 90095-1521
(310) 206-0375   Fax: (310) 794-5324
Web: aeri.gseis.ucla.edu/fellowships.htm

Summary   To provide an opportunity for Asian American and other minority undergraduate and graduate students to learn more about the field of archival studies and to be exposed to research in the field.

Eligibility   This program is open to undergraduates who have completed their junior year and to students who have completed the first year of a master's degree program. Applicants must be Asian/Pacific Islander, African American, Hispanic/Latino, Native American, Puerto Rican, or any other person who will add diversity to the field of archival studies. They must have a GPA of 3.0 or higher, but they may be working on a degree in any field and are not required to have prior knowledge of or experience in archival studies. U.S. citizenship or permanent resident status is required. Applicants must be interested in attending the week-long Archival Education and Research Institute (AERI), held at a different university each summer, where they are assigned both a faculty research mentor and a Ph.D. student mentor who introduce them to doctoral research and careers in archival studies.

Financial data   Grants provide payment of round-trip travel, accommodation, and most meals.

Duration   These grants are offered annually.

Additional information   This program, first offered in 2009, is supported by the Institute of Museum and Library Services. Scholars who indicate an interest in continuing on to a doctoral program in archival studies after completing the AERI may be invited to participate in a supervised research project that will last up to 1 year and to present results of their research in a poster session at the AERI of the following year.

Number awarded   Up to 7 each year.

Deadline   April of each year.

[663]
ENDOWMENT FOR SOUTH ASIAN STUDENTS OF INDIAN DESCENT

Pennsylvania Medical Society
Attn: Foundation
777 East Park Drive
P.O. Box 8820
Harrisburg, PA 17105-8820
(717) 558-7854
Toll Free: (800) 228-7823, ext. 7854 (within PA)
Fax: (717) 558-7818
E-mail: studentservices-foundation@pamedsoc.org
Web: www.foundationpamedsoc.org

Summary   To provide financial assistance to south Asian Indian residents of Pennsylvania who are enrolled at a medical school in the state.

Eligibility   This program is open to South Asian Indians or descendants of South Asian Indian immigrants to the United States who have been Pennsylvania residents for at least 12 months. Applicants must be entering the second, third, or fourth year of full-time study at an accredited allopathic or osteopathic medical school in Pennsylvania. They must submit a 1-page essay explaining why they chose to become a physician and what contributions they expect to make to the health profession. Financial need is considered in the selection process.

Financial data   The stipend is $2,000. Funds are paid directly to the recipient's medical school through the appropriate channels.

Duration   1 year.

Additional information   This program began in 2003.

Number awarded   1 each year.

Deadline   September of each year.

[664]
ENVIRONMENT AND NATURAL RESOURCES FELLOWSHIPS

Harvard University
John F. Kennedy School of Government
Belfer Center for Science and International Affairs
Attn: STPP Fellowship Coordinator
79 John F. Kennedy Street, Mailbox 53
Cambridge, MA 02138
(617) 495-1498   Fax: (617) 495-8963
E-mail: patricia_mclaughlin@hks.harvard.edu
Web: belfercenter.ksg.harvard.edu

Summary To provide funding to professionals, postdoctorates, and doctoral students, especially Asian Americans and other minorities, interested in conducting research on environmental and natural resource issues at the Belfer Center for Science and International Affairs at Harvard University in Cambridge, Massachusetts.

Eligibility The postdoctoral fellowship is open to recent recipients of the Ph.D. or equivalent degree, university faculty members, and employees of government, military, international, humanitarian, and private research institutions who have appropriate professional experience. Applicants for predoctoral fellowships must have passed their general examinations. Scholars from a wide range of disciplinary and multi-disciplinary fields and those holding a Ph.D. in engineering or in the natural sciences are strongly encouraged to apply. The program especially encourages applications from women, minorities, and citizens of all countries. All applicants must be interested in conducting research on projects of the Environment and Natural Resources (ENRP) Program. Recently, those included projects on energy technology innovation, sustainable energy development in China, managing the atom, and the geopolitics of energy.

Financial data The stipend is $37,500 for postdoctoral research fellows or $25,000 for predoctoral research fellows. Fellows who renew their grant receive a monthly stipend of $3,750 for postdoctoral fellows or $2,500 for predoctoral fellows. Stipends for advanced research fellows vary. Health insurance is also provided.

Duration 10 months; may be renewed on a month-by-month basis.

Additional information Fellows are expected to devote some portion of their time to collaborative endeavors, as arranged by the appropriate program or project director. Predoctoral fellows are expected to contribute to the program's research activities, as well as work on (and ideally complete) their dissertations. Postdoctoral research fellows are also expected to complete a book, monograph, or other significant publication during their period of residence.

Number awarded A limited number each year.

Deadline January of each year.

[665]
EPISCOPAL ASIAMERICA MINISTRIES THEOLOGICAL EDUCATION SCHOLARSHIPS

Episcopal Church Center
Attn: Domestic and Foreign Missionary Society
Scholarship Committee
815 Second Avenue, Fifth Floor
New York, NY 10017-4503
(212) 716-6168   Toll Free: (800) 334-7676
Fax: (212) 867-0395
E-mail: ahercules@episcopalchurch.org
Web: www.episcopalchurch.org

Summary To provide financial assistance to Asian and Pacific Island Americans interested in seeking ordination and serving in a ministry involving Asians and Pacific Islanders in the Episcopal Church.

Eligibility This program is open to Asian and Pacific Island students pursuing theological education, including diocesan programs as well as seminary education. Applicants must be a member of an Asian or Pacific Island constituency in the Episcopal Church and have begun the process of seeking ordination through a local Episcopal diocese. They must intend to serve in a ministry of the Episcopal Church involving Asian or Pacific Island Americans. Scholarships are presented both for full- and part-time study.

Financial data The maximum stipend is $10,000 per year.

Duration 1 year; may be renewed up to 3 additional years.

Additional information This program receives support from several funds of the sponsoring agency: the Susan R. Bonsall Scholarship Fund (established in 1901), the William B. Foote Educational Fund (established in 1919), the Daniel Albert Pierce Fund (established in 1920), the Rev. Arthur Mann Memorial Fund (established in 1926), the Theological Education Scholarship Fund (established in 1983), and the Gates Austill Fund (established by an outside trust).

Number awarded Varies each year; recently, 4 of these scholarships, with a value of $19,000, were awarded.

Deadline April of each year.

[666]
ESTHER KATZ ROSEN FUND GRANTS

American Psychological Foundation
750 First Street, N.E.
Washington, DC 20002-4242
(202) 336-5843   Fax: (202) 336-5812
E-mail: foundation@apa.org
Web: www.apa.org/apf/funding/rosen.aspx

Summary To provide funding to graduate students and early-career psychologists, especially Asian Americans and other minorities, interested in conducting research or other projects on psychological issues relevant to giftedness in children.

Eligibility This program is open to 1) graduate students at universities in the United States and Canada who have advanced to candidacy; and 2) psychologists who completed their doctoral degree within the past 10 years. Applicants must be interested in engaging in activities related to identified gifted and talented children and adolescents, including research, pilot projects, research-based programs, or projects aimed at improving the quality of education in psychological science and its application in secondary schools for high ability students. Selection is based on conformance with stated program goals and qualifications, quality and impact of proposed work, innovation and contribution to the field, and applicant's demonstrated competence and capability to execute the proposed work. The sponsor encourages applications from individuals who represent diversity in race, ethnicity, gender, age, disability, and sexual orientation.

Financial data Grants range from $1,000 to $50,000.

Duration 1 year.

Additional information The Esther Katz Rosen Fund was established in 1974. In 2013, the sponsor combined the Rosen Graduate Student Fellowship, the Rosen Early Career Research Grant, and the Pre-College Grant program into this single program.

Number awarded Varies each year; recently, 2 were awarded.

Deadline February of each year.

[667]
ESTHER NGAN-LING CHOW AND MAREYJOYCE GREEN SCHOLARSHIP

Sociologists for Women in Society
Attn: Administrative Officer
University of Kansas
Department of Sociology
1415 Jayhawk Boulevard, Room 716
Lawrence, KS 66045
(785) 864-9405   E-mail: swsao@outlook.com
Web: www.socwomen.org

Summary To provide funding to Asian Americans and other women of color who are conducting dissertation research in sociology.

Eligibility This program is open to women from a racial/ethnic group that faces discrimination in the United States. Applicants must be in the early stages of writing a doctoral dissertation in sociology on a topic relating to the concerns that women of color face domestically and/or internationally. They must be able to demonstrate financial need. Both domestic and international students are eligible to apply. Along with their application, they must submit a personal statement that details their short- and long-term career and research goals; a resume or curriculum vitae; 2 letters of recommendation; and a 5-page dissertation proposal that includes the purpose of the research, the work to be accomplished through support from this scholarship, and a time line for completion.

Financial data The stipend is $15,000. An additional grant of $500 is provided to enable the recipient to attend the winter meeting of Sociologists for Women in Society (SWS), and travel expenses to attend the summer meeting are reimbursed.

Duration 1 year.

Additional information This program began in 2007 and was originally named the Women of Color Dissertation Scholarship.

Number awarded 1 each year.

Deadline March of each year.

[668]
ETHNIC IN-SERVICE TRAINING FUND FOR CLINICAL PASTORAL EDUCATION (EIST-CPE)

United Methodist Church
Attn: General Board of Higher Education and Ministry
Office of Loans and Scholarships
1001 19th Avenue South
P.O. Box 340007
Nashville, TN 37203-0007
(615) 340-7342   Fax: (615) 340-7367
E-mail: umscholar@gbhem.org
Web: www.gbhem.org

Summary To provide financial assistance to United Methodist Church clergy and candidates for ministry who are Asian Americans or members of other minority groups interested in preparing for a career as a clinical pastor.

Eligibility This program is open to U.S. citizens and permanent residents who are members of ethnic or racial minority groups and have been active, full members of a United Methodist Church for at least 1 year prior to applying. Applicants must be United Methodist clergy, certified candidates for ministry, or seminary students accepted into an accredited Clinical Pastor Education (CPE) or an accredited American Association of Pastoral Counselors (AAPC) program. They must be preparing for a career as a chaplain, pastoral counselor, or in pastoral care.

Financial data Grants range up to $2,000.

Duration 1 year.

Number awarded 1 each year.

Deadline February of each year.

[669]
EXTERNSHIP IN ADDICTION PSYCHIATRY

American Psychiatric Association
Attn: Minority Medical Student Awards
1000 Wilson Boulevard, Suite 1825
Arlington, VA 22209-3901
(703) 907-7894   Toll Free: (888) 357-7849
Fax: (703) 907-1087   E-mail: Mfpstudents@psych.org
Web: www.psychiatry.org

Summary To provide an opportunity for Asian American and other minority medical students to spend an elective residency learning about substance abuse disorders, prevention, and early intervention.

Eligibility This program is open to student members of the American Psychiatric Association (APA) who come from racial/ethnic minorities and are currently enrolled at accredited U.S. medical school. Applicants must be interested in working with a mentor at a designated site to gain exposure to how psychiatrists treat patients with substance abuse disorders and participate in an interactive didactic experiential learning program. Mentors and sites are selected where there is an approved substance abuse training program and a significant number of substance abuse disorder patients from minority and underserved populations. U.S. citizenship or permanent resident status is required.

Financial data The program provides a stipend of $1,500 for living expenses and funding for travel to and from the mentoring site.

Duration 1 month during the summer.

Number awarded 6 each year.

Deadline March of each year.

[670]
FACS GRADUATE FELLOWSHIPS

National Association of Teacher Educators for Family and Consumer Sciences
c/o Debra Price, Fellowship Committee Chair
116 East Summit Street
Bolivar, MO 65613
(417) 327-6636   E-mail: debraprice81@gmail.com
Web: www.natefacs.org/Pages/awards.html

Summary To provide financial assistance to Asian American and other graduate students in family and consumer science education.

Eligibility This program is open to graduate students working on a master's or doctoral degree in family and consumer sciences education. Applicants must submit an autobiographical sketch (up to 3 pages in length) presenting their professional goals, including information on the institution where they are studying or planning to study, areas or emphases of study, possible research topic, and other pertinent information regarding their plans. Selection is based on likelihood of completing the degree, likelihood of contribution to family and consumer sciences education, previous academic work, professional association involvement, professional experience (including scholarly work), and references. At least 1 fellowship is reserved for a minority (African American, Hispanic American, Native American, or Asian American) candidate.

Financial data Stipends range from $2,000 to $4,000.

Duration 1 year.

Additional information The sponsor is an affiliate of the Family and Consumer Sciences (FACS) Division of the Association for Career and Technical Education (ACTE).

Number awarded Varies each year.

Deadline September of each year.

[671]
FARM CREDIT EAST SCHOLARSHIPS

Farm Credit East
Attn: Scholarship Program
240 South Road
Enfield, CT 06082
(860) 741-4380   Toll Free: (800) 562-2235
Fax: (860) 741-4389
E-mail: specialoffers@famcrediteast.com
Web: www.farmcrediteast.com

Summary To provide financial assistance to residents of designated northeastern states, especially Asian Americans and other minorities, who plan to attend school in any state to work on an undergraduate or graduate degree in a field related to agriculture, forestry, or fishing.

Eligibility This program is open to residents of Connecticut, Maine, Massachusetts, New Jersey, Rhode Island, and portions of New York and New Hampshire. Applicants must be working on or planning to work on an associate, bachelor's, or graduate degree in production agriculture, agribusiness, the forest products industry, or commercial fishing at a college or university in any state. They must submit a 200-word essay on why they wish to prepare for a career in agriculture, forestry, or fishing. Selection is based on the essay, extracurricular activities (especially farm work experience and activities indicative of an interest in preparing for a career in agriculture or agribusiness), and interest in agriculture. The program includes diversity scholarships reserved for members of minority groups (Asian, Black or African American, American Indian or Alaska Native, Native Hawaiian or other Pacific Islander, or Hispanic or Latino).

Financial data The stipend is $1,500. Funds are paid directly to the student to be used for tuition, room and board, books, and other academic charges.

Duration 1 year; nonrenewable.

Additional information Recipients are given priority for an internship with the sponsor in the summer following their junior year. Farm Credit East was formerly named First Pioneer Farm Credit.

Number awarded Varies each year; recently, 32, including several diversity scholarships, were awarded.

Deadline April of each year.

[672]
FBANC FOUNDATION LEGAL SCHOLARSHIP

Filipino Bar Association of Northern California
Attn: Foundation
268 Bush Street, Suite 2928
San Francisco, CA 94104
E-mail: fbancinfo@gmail.com
Web: www.fbanc.org

Summary To provide financial assistance to entering or continuing students at law schools in northern California who are interested in serving the Filipino American community.

Eligibility This program is open to currently-enrolled and entering students at northern California law school who have a tie to the Filipino American community and intend to provide legal services to that community after graduation from law school. Applicants must submit a current transcript or admit letter, a resume, a list of their involvement in activities of the Filipino Bar Association of Northern California (FBANC), and a 2-page essay on 1) an obstacle or adversity they have faced and how that experience has affected their decision to attend law school or their career plans after law school; and 2) barriers that Filipino and Filipino Americans experience regarding the legal system and ways that those barriers can be addressed to increase the community's access to justice. Selection is based on that essay, academic standing, demonstrated interest in issues affecting the Filipino American community, and their desire to serve the Filipino American community.

Financial data The stipend is $2,500.

Duration 1 year.

Number awarded 2 each year.

Deadline April of each year.

[673]
FELLOWSHIPS FOR LATINO/A, ASIAN AND FIRST NATIONS DOCTORAL STUDENTS

Forum for Theological Exploration
Attn: Fellowship Program
160 Clairemont Avenue, Suite 300
Decatur, GA 30030
(678) 369-6755   Fax: (678) 369-6757
E-mail: dhutto@fteleaders.org
Web: www.fteleaders.org

Summary To provide funding to Latino/as, Asians, and members of First Nations who are working on a doctoral degree in religious, theological, or biblical studies.

Eligibility This program is open to students of Latino/a, Asian, or First Nations descent who are U.S. or Canadian citizens or permanent residents working full time on a Ph.D. or Th.D. degree. Applicants must be past the course work stage; they are not required to have been advanced to candidacy, but they must have had their dissertation topic approved and be in a position to devote full time to writing. Students who are working on a Doctor of Ministry (D.Min.) degree are not eligible.

Financial data The stipend is $25,000.

Duration 1 year.

Additional information Fellows also receive reimbursement of expenses to attend the sponsor's Christian Leadership Forum. This sponsor was formerly named the The Fund for Theological Education, Inc.

Number awarded Varies each year; recently, 12 were awarded.

Deadline January of each year.

[674]
FILIPINO NURSES' ORGANIZATION OF HAWAI'I SCHOLARSHIP

Hawai'i Community Foundation
Attn: Scholarship Department
827 Fort Street Mall
Honolulu, HI 96813
(808) 566-5570   Toll Free: (888) 731-3863
Fax: (808) 521-6286
E-mail: scholarships@hcf-hawaii.org
Web: hcf.scholarships.ngwebsolutions.com

Summary To provide financial assistance to Hawaii residents of Filipino ancestry who are interested in attending college in any state to prepare for a career as a nurse.

Eligibility This program is open to Hawaii residents of Filipino ancestry who are enrolled or planning to enroll full time at a college or university in any state and work on an undergraduate or graduate degree in nursing. Applicants must be able to demonstrate academic achievement (GPA of 2.7 or higher), good moral character, and financial need. Along with their application, they must submit a short statement indicating their reasons for attending college, their planned course of study, their career goals, and what community service means to them.

Financial data The amounts of the awards depend on the availability of funds and the need of the recipient. Recently, the average value of the scholarships awarded by the foundation was $2,800.

Duration 1 year.

Number awarded Varies each year; recently, 2 were awarded.

Deadline February of each year.

[675]
FIRST TRANSIT SCHOLARSHIP

Conference of Minority Transportation Officials
Attn: National Scholarship Program
100 M Street, S.E., Suite 917
Washington, DC 20003
(202) 506-2917   E-mail: info@comto.org
Web: www.comto.org/page/scholarships

Summary To provide financial assistance to Asian American and other minority upper-division and graduate students in engineering or other field related to transportation.

Eligibility This program is open to minority juniors, seniors, and graduate students in transporation, planning, engineering or other technical transportation-related disciplines. Applicants must submit a cover letter on their transportation-related career goals and life aspirations. Financial need is not considered in the selection process.

Financial data The stipend is $6,000. Funds are paid directly to the recipient's college or university.

Duration 1 year.

Additional information This program is sponsored by First Transit Inc.

Number awarded 1 each year.

Deadline April of each year.

[676]
F.J. MCGUIGAN DISSERTATION AWARD

American Psychological Foundation
750 First Street, N.E.
Washington, DC 20002-4242
(202) 336-5843   Fax: (202) 336-5812
E-mail: foundation@apa.org
Web: www.apa.org/apf/funding/mcguigan-dissertation.aspx

Summary To provide funding to doctoral candidates, especially Asian Americans and members of other underrepresented groups interested in conducting research on the materialistic understanding of the human mind.

Eligibility This program is open to graduate students enrolled full time in a psychology program at an accredited college or university in the United States or Canada. Applicants must be interested in conducting dissertation research that addresses an aspect of mental function (e.g., cognition, affect, motivation) and seeks to understand the mind from both a neural and behavioral perspective. Selection is based on conformance with stated program goals, quality of proposed work, and applicant's demonstrated scholarship and research competence. The sponsor encourages applications from individuals who represent diversity in race, ethnicity, gender, age, disability, and sexual orientation.

Financial data The grant is $2,000.

Duration 1 year.

Additional information This grant was first awarded in 2009.

Number awarded 1 each year.

Deadline May of each year.

[677]
FLORIDA LIBRARY ASSOCIATION MINORITY SCHOLARSHIPS

Florida Library Association
541 East Tennessee Street, Suite 103
Tallahassee, FL 32308
(850) 270-9205   Fax: (850) 270-9405
E-mail: flaexecutivedirector@comcast.net
Web: www.flalib.org/scholarships.php

Summary   To provide financial assistance to Asian American and other minority students working on a graduate degree in library and information science in Florida.

Eligibility   This program is open to residents of Florida who are working on a graduate degree in library and information science at schools in the state. Applicants must be members of a minority group: Asian/Pacific Islander, Black/African American, American Indian/Alaska Native, or Hispanic/Latino. They must have some experience in a Florida library, must be a member of the Florida Library Association, and must commit to working in a Florida library for at least 1 year after graduation. Along with their application, they must submit 1) a list of activities, honors, awards, and/or offices held during college and outside college; 2) an essay of 1 to 2 pages on why they are entering librarianship; and 3) an essay of 1 to 2 pages on their career goals with respect to Florida libraries. Financial need is considered in the selection process.

Financial data   The stipend is $2,000.

Duration   1 year.

Number awarded   1 each year.

Deadline   January of each year.

[678]
FLOW PANGARAP SCHOLARSHIP

Filipino Lawyers of Washington
Attn: Scholarship Committee
c/o Dennis G.M. Narciso
The Narciso Law Firm, PLLC
P.O. Box 14366
Mill Creek, WA 98082-2366
E-mail: students@filipinolawyers.org
Web: www.filipinolawyers.org/scholarship

Summary   To provide financial assistance to students from any state who are enrolled at law schools in the Pacific Northwest and have a record of service to the Filipino community.

Eligibility   This program is open to residents of any state currently enrolled at law schools in the Pacific Northwest. Applicants are not required to be of Filipino ancestry, but they must have a demonstrated significant commitment to community service, particularly service to the Filipino or Filipino American community. Along with their application, they must submit a 1,000-word essay on how they have demonstrated leadership and commitment to the community and how they intend to use their law degree to enhance the lives of those they will serve. Selection is based on the essay, academic achievement, work experience, activities, post-law school goals, and service to the Filipino or Filipino American community.

Financial data   Stipends range from $500 to $3,000.

Duration   1 year.

Number awarded   Up to 3 each year.

Deadline   September of each year.

[679]
FRANCIS M. KEVILLE MEMORIAL SCHOLARSHIP

Construction Management Association of America
Attn: CMAA Foundation
7926 Jones Branch Drive, Suite 800
McLean, VA 22101-3303
(703) 677-3361   E-mail: foundation@cmaanet.org
Web: www.cmaafoundation.org

Summary   To provide financial assistance to Asian American and other minority undergraduate and graduate students working on a degree in construction management.

Eligibility   This program is open to women and members of minority groups who are enrolled as full-time undergraduate or graduate students. Applicants must have completed at least 1 year of study and have at least 1 full year remaining for a bachelor's or master's degree in construction management or a related field. Along with their application, they must submit essays on why they are interested in a career in construction management and why they should be awarded this scholarship. Selection is based on that essay (20%), academic performance (40%), recommendation of the faculty adviser (15%), and extracurricular activities (25%); a bonus of 5% is given to student members of the Construction Management Association of America (CMAA).

Financial data   The stipend is $5,000. Funds are disbursed directly to the student's university.

Duration   1 year.

Number awarded   1 each year.

Deadline   April of each year.

[680]
FRANKLIN C. MCLEAN AWARD

National Medical Fellowships, Inc.
Attn: Scholarship Program
347 Fifth Avenue, Suite 510
New York, NY 10016
(212) 483-8880   Toll Free: (877) NMF-1DOC
Fax: (212) 483-8897 E-mail: scholarships@nmfonline.org
Web: www.nmfonline.org

Summary   To provide financial assistance to Vietnamese, Cambodians, and other minority medical students who demonstrate academic achievement.

Eligibility   This program is open to Vietnamese, Cambodians, African Americans, Hispanics/Latinos, Native Americans, and Pacific Islanders who are entering their senior year of medical school. They must be U.S. citizens or DACA students. Selection is based on academic achievement, leadership, and community service.

Financial data   The stipend is $5,000.

Duration   1 year.

Additional information   This program began in 1968.

Number awarded   1 each year.

Deadline   September of each year.

[681]
GAIUS CHARLES BOLIN DISSERTATION AND POST-MFA FELLOWSHIPS

Williams College
Attn: Dean of the Faculty
880 Main Street
Hopkins Hall, Third Floor
P.O. Box 141
Williamstown, MA 01267
(413) 597-4351   Fax: (413) 597-3553
E-mail: gburda@williams.edu
Web: faculty.williams.edu

Summary To provide financial assistance to Asian Americans and members of other underrepresented groups who are interested in teaching courses at Williams College while working on their doctoral dissertation or building their post-M.F.A. professional portfolio.

Eligibility This program is open to members of underrepresented groups, including ethnic minorities, first-generation college students, women in predominantly male fields, and scholars with disabilities. Applicants must be 1) doctoral candidates in any field who have completed all work for a Ph.D. except for the dissertation; or 2) artists who completed an M.F.A. degree within the past 2 years and are building their professional portfolio. They must be willing to teach a course at Williams College. Along with their application, they must submit a full curriculum vitae, a graduate school transcript, 3 letters of recommendation, a copy of their dissertation prospectus or samples of their artistic work, and a description of their teaching interests within a department or program at Williams College. U.S. citizenship or permanent resident status is required.

Financial data Fellows receive $38,000 for the academic year, plus housing assistance, office space, computer and library privileges, and a research allowance of up to $4,000.

Duration 2 years.

Additional information Bolin fellows are assigned a faculty adviser in the appropriate department. This program was established in 1985. Fellows are expected to teach a 1-semester course each year. They must be in residence at Williams College for the duration of the fellowship.

Number awarded 2 each year.

Deadline November of each year.

[682]
GAPA FOUNDATION SCHOLARSHIP

Gay Asian Pacific Alliance
Attn: GAPA Foundation
P.O. Box 22482
San Francisco, CA 94122
(415) 857-GAPA
E-mail: scholarship@gapafoundation.org
Web: www.gapafoundation.org/scholarships

Summary To provide financial assistance to lesbian, gay, bisexual, and transgender (LGBT) Asian and Pacific Islanders who are interested in attending college in any state.

Eligibility This program is open to high school seniors, college students, graduate school students, and vocational school students who identify both as Asian/Pacific Islander (API) and LGBT. Applicants must have a GPA of 2.5 or higher and a history of activism within either the API and/or the LGBT communities. They are not required to be members of either community, although preference is given to those who are members of both. Along with their application, they must submit 1) a brief statement about a significant challenge in their life that has helped shape them into the person they are today; 2) a brief statement about how they are currently active in the API and/or LGBTQ community; and 3) a 500-word essay describing a significant challenge facing the API/LGBT community today and what they would do to help solve this issue if they had the resources. Interviews may be scheduled (in person for applicants who live in the San Francisco Bay area, by phone for those who live elsewhere).

Financial data The stipend is $1,000.

Duration 1 year.

Additional information This program began in 1997 as the George Choy Memorial Scholarship.

Number awarded Up to 4 each year.

Deadline July of each year.

[683]
GENERAL VANG PAO SCHOLARSHIP

Hmong American Education Fund
P.O. Box 17468
St. Paul, MN 55117
(651) 592-1576   E-mail: scholarships@thehaef.org
Web: www.thehaef.org

Summary To provide financial assistance to Hmong undergraduate and graduate students who demonstrate leadership.

Eligibility This program is open to students of Hmong descent who are currently enrolled as full-time undergraduate or graduate students at 2- or 4-year colleges or universities in any state. Applicants must be U.S. citizens or permanent residents and have a GPA of 3.0 or higher. Along with their application, they must submit a 1,500-word essay on their commitment to education, their leadership qualities, their financial need, how this scholarship can help them, and their community service. Selection is based on academic excellence, leadership qualities, commitment to helping their community, and financial need.

Financial data The stipend is $2,500.

Duration 1 year; nonrenewable.

Number awarded 1 each year.

Deadline March of each year.

[684]
GENERATION GOOGLE SCHOLARSHIPS FOR CURRENT UNIVERSITY STUDENTS

Google Inc.
Attn: Scholarships
1600 Amphitheatre Parkway
Mountain View, CA 94043-8303
(650) 253-0000   Fax: (650) 253-0001
E-mail: generationgoogle@google.com
Web: www.google.com

Summary To provide financial assistance to members of underrepresented groups, including Filipinos, enrolled as undergraduate or graduate students in a computer-related field.

Eligibility This program is open to students enrolled as full-time undergraduate or graduate students at a college or university in the United States or Canada. Applicants must be members of a group underrepresented in computer science: Filipinos/Native Hawaiians/Pacific Islanders, African Americans, Hispanics, or American Indians. They must be working on a degree in computer science, computer engineering, or a closely-related field. Selection is based on academic achievement, leadership, and passion for computer science and technology.

Financial data The stipend is $10,000 per year for U.S. students or $C5,000 for Canadian students.

Duration 1 year; may be renewed.

Additional information Recipients are also invited to attend Google's Computer Science Summer Institute at Mountain View, California, Seattle, Washington, or Cambridge, Massachusetts in the summer.

Number awarded Varies each year.

Deadline February of each year.

[685]
GE-NMF PRIMARY CARE LEADERSHIP PROGRAM

National Medical Fellowships, Inc.
Attn: Scholarship Program
347 Fifth Avenue, Suite 510
New York, NY 10016
(212) 483-8880   Toll Free: (877) NMF-1DOC
Fax: (212) 483-8897   E-mail: pclpinfo@nmfonline.org
Web: www.nmfonline.org

Summary To provide funding to underrepresented medical and nursing students, including Vietnamese and Cambodians, who wish to participate in a summer mentored clinical experience in selected communities.

Eligibility This program is open to members of underrepresented minority groups (Vietnamese, Cambodian, African American, Hispanic/Latino, American Indian, Native Hawaiian, Alaska Native, or Native Pacific Islander) and/or socioeconomically disadvantaged students. U.S. citizenship is required. Applicants must be currently enrolled in an accredited medical school or graduate-level nursing degree program. They must be interested in a mentored clinical service-learning experience that includes a site-specific independent project at a community health center in Atlanta, Boston/Lynn, Chicago, Houston, Los Angeles, Miami, Mound Bayou (Mississippi), New York, Phoenix, Rochester (New York), or Seattle. Along with their application, they must submit documentation of financial status; a short biography; a resume; 2 letters of recommendation; and a 500-word personal statement on their experiences working in or being part of a medically underserved population and how those experiences have impacted their educational path, professional aspirations, and decision to apply to this program.

Financial data The stipend is $5,000. Funds are expected to cover travel, living, and lodging expenses.

Duration Scholars are required to complete 200 clinical service-learning hours within a 6- to 8-week period during the summer following receipt of the award.

Additional information Funding for this program, which began in 2012 and is administered by National Medical Fellowships (NMF), is provided by the GE Foundation.

Number awarded Varies each year, recently, 59 were granted: 2 in Atlanta, 2 in Boston/Lynn, 8 in Chicago, 5 in

Houston, 12 in Los Angeles, 8 in Miami, 2 in Bound Bayou, 2 in New York, 8 in Phoenix, 4 in Rochester, and 6 in Seattle.

Deadline March of each year.

[686]
GEOLOGICAL SOCIETY OF AMERICA GRADUATE STUDENT RESEARCH GRANTS

Geological Society of America
Attn: Program Officer-Grants, Awards and Recognition
3300 Penrose Place
P.O. Box 9140
Boulder, CO 80301-9140
(303) 357-1060   Toll Free: (888) 443-4472, ext. 1060
Fax: (303) 357-1070   E-mail: awards@geosociety.org
Web: www.geosociety.org/grants/gradgrants.htm

Summary To provide funding to graduate student members of the Geological Society of America (GSA), especially Asian Americans and other minorities, interested in conducting research at universities in the United States, Canada, Mexico, or Central America.

Eligibility This program is open to GSA members working on a master's or doctoral degree at a university in the United States, Canada, Mexico, or Central America. Applicants must be interested in conducting geological research. Minorities, women, and persons with disabilities are strongly encouraged to apply. Selection is based on the scientific merits of the proposal, the capability of the investigator, and the reasonableness of the budget.

Financial data Grants range up to $2,500 and recently averaged $1,851. Funds can be used for the cost of travel, room and board in the field, services of a technician or field assistant, funding of chemical and isotope analyses, or other expenses directly related to the fulfillment of the research contract. Support is not provided for the purchase of ordinary field equipment, for maintenance of the families of the grantees and their assistants, as reimbursement for work already accomplished, for institutional overhead, for adviser participation, or for tuition costs.

Duration 1 year.

Additional information In addition to general grants, GSA awards a number of specialized grants.

Number awarded Varies each year; recently, the society awarded nearly 400 grants worth more than $723,000 through this and all of its specialized programs.

Deadline January of each year.

[687]
GEORGE A. STRAIT MINORITY SCHOLARSHIP ENDOWMENT

American Association of Law Libraries
Attn: Chair, Scholarships Committee
105 West Adams Street, Suite 3300
Chicago, IL 60603
(312) 939-4764   Fax: (312) 431-1097
E-mail: scholarships@aall.org
Web: www.aallnet.org

Summary To provide financial assistance to Asian American and other minority college seniors or college graduates who are interested in becoming law librarians.

Eligibility This program is open to college graduates with meaningful law library experience who are members of minority groups and intend to have a career in law librarianship. Applicants must be degree candidates at an ALA-accredited library school or an ABA-accredited law school. Along with their application, they must submit a personal statement that discusses their interest in law librarianship, reason for applying for this scholarship, career goals as a law librarian, and any other pertinent information.

Financial data The stipend is $3,500.

Duration 1 year.

Additional information This program, established in 1990, is currently supported by Thomson Reuters.

Number awarded Varies each year; recently, 6 were awarded.

Deadline March of each year.

[688]
GERBER SCHOLARSHIP IN PEDIATRICS

National Medical Fellowships, Inc.
Attn: Scholarship Program
347 Fifth Avenue, Suite 510
New York, NY 10016
(212) 483-8880   Toll Free: (877) NMF-1DOC
Fax: (212) 483-8897 E-mail: scholarships@nmfonline.org
Web: www.nmfonline.org

Summary To provide financial assistance to underrepresented minority medical students, including Vietnamese and Cambodians, who are interested in pediatrics.

Eligibility This program is open to Vietnamese, Cambodians, African Americans, Hispanics/Latinos, Native Americans, and Pacific Islanders who are enrolled in medical school. Applicants must be interested in pediatrics with an emphasis on nutrition. They must be U.S. citizens or DACA students. Selection is based on leadership, commitment to serving medically underserved communities, and financial need.

Financial data The stipend is $5,000.

Duration 1 year.

Additional information This program, which began in 1997, is supported by Gerber.

Number awarded 2 each year.

Deadline September of each year.

[689]
GLOBAL MISSION CHURCH SCHOLARSHIP

Global Mission Church
Attn: Scholarship Committee
13421 Georgia Avenue
Silver Spring, MD 20906
(301) 460-1656   Fax: (301) 460-7925
E-mail: gmcscholarship@gmcusa.org
Web: www.gmcusa.org

Summary To provide financial assistance to Korean Americans attending a seminary or graduate school to prepare for a career in full-time Christian ministry.

Eligibility This program is open to full-time Korean American graduate students who have finished at least 1 semester at a seminary or graduate school in any state. Applicants must be preparing for a career in full-time ministry. Along with their application, they must submit a statement of personal testimony, a letter of recommendation from the pastor of their

seminary church, a transcript from their seminary, and information on their financial need.

Financial data The stipend is $1,000.

Duration 1 year.

Number awarded 1 or more each year.

Deadline June of each year.

[690]
GO RED MULTICULTURAL SCHOLARSHIP FUND

American Heart Association
Attn: Go Red for Women
7272 Greenville Avenue
Dallas, TX 75231-4596
Toll Free: (800) AHA-USA1
E-mail: GoRedScholarship@heart.org
Web: www.goredforwomen.org

Summary To provide financial assistance to Asian American and other women from multicultural backgrounds who are preparing for a career in a field of health care.

Eligibility This program is open to women who are currently enrolled at an accredited college, university, health care institution, or program and have a GPA of 3.0 or higher. Applicants must be U.S. citizens or permanent residents of Asian/Pacific Islander, Hispanic, African American, or other minority origin. They must be working on an undergraduate or graduate degree as preparation for a career as a nurse, physician, or allied health care worker. Selection is based on community involvement, a personal essay, transcripts, and 2 letters of recommendation.

Financial data The stipend is $2,500.

Duration 1 year.

Additional information This program, which began in 2012, is supported by Macy's.

Number awarded 16 each year.

Deadline December of each year.

[691]
GOLDSTEIN AND SCHNEIDER SCHOLARSHIPS BY THE MACEY FUND

Society for Industrial and Organizational Psychology Inc.
Attn: SIOP Foundation
440 East Poe Road, Suite 101
Bowling Green, OH 43402
(419) 353-0032   Fax: (419) 352-2645
E-mail: siopfoundation@siop.org
Web: www.siop.org/SIOPAwards/thornton.aspx

Summary To provide funding to Asian American and other minority student members of the Society for Industrial and Organizational Psychology (SIOP) who are conducting doctoral research.

Eligibility This program is open to student affiliate members of SIOP who are enrolled full time in a doctoral program in industrial and organizational (I/O) psychology or a closely-related field at an accredited college or university. Applicants must be members of an ethnic minority group (Asian/Pacific American, Native American/Alaskan Native, African/Caribbean American, or Latino/Hispanic American). They must have an approved dissertation plan that has potential to make significant theoretical and application contributions to the field of I/O psychology.

Financial data The stipend is $3,000. Students may elect to have the funds paid to them directly or to be deposited into a "professional development" account at their university.

Duration 1 academic year.

Additional information The SIOP is Division 14 of the American Psychological Association. This program consists of the Benjamin Schneider Scholarship (offered in odd-numbered years) and the Irwin L. Goldstein Scholarship (offered in even-numbered years).

Number awarded 1 each year.

Deadline October of each year.

[692]
GORDON STAFFORD SCHOLARSHIP IN ARCHITECTURE

Stafford King Wiese Architects
Attn: Scholarship Selection Committee
622 20th Street
Sacramento, CA 95811
(916) 930-5900   Fax: (916) 290-0100
E-mail: info@skwaia.com
Web: www.skwarchitects.com/about/scholarship

Summary To provide financial assistance to Asian Americans and members of other minority groups from California interested in studying architecture at a college in any state.

Eligibility This program is open to California residents currently enrolled at accredited schools of architecture in any state as first-year new or first-year transfer students and working on a bachelor's or 5-year master's degree. Applicants must be able to demonstrate minority status (defined as Pacific Asian, Asian Indian, Black, Hispanic, or Native American). They must submit a 500-word statement expressing their desire to prepare for a career in architecture. Finalists are interviewed and must travel to Sacramento, California at their own expense for the interview.

Financial data The stipend is $3,000 per year. That includes $1,500 deposited in the recipient's school account and $1,500 paid to the recipient directly.

Duration 1 year; may be renewed up to 4 additional years.

Additional information This program began in 1995.

Number awarded Up to 5 each year.

Deadline June of each year.

[693]
GRADUATE FELLOWSHIP IN THE HISTORY OF SCIENCE

American Geophysical Union
Attn: History of Geophysics
2000 Florida Avenue, N.W.
Washington, DC 20009-1277
(202) 777-7522   Toll Free: (800) 966-2481
Fax: (202) 328-0566
E-mail: HistoryofGeophysics@agu.org
Web: education.agu.org

Summary To provide funding to doctoral candidates, especially Asian Americans and members of other underrepresented groups, who are conducting dissertation research in the history of geophysics.

Eligibility This program is open to doctoral candidates at U.S. institutions who have passed all preliminary examinations. Applicants must be completing a dissertation in the history of the geophysical sciences, including topics related to atmospheric sciences, biogeosciences, geodesy, geomagnetism and paleomagnetism, hydrology, ocean sciences, planetary sciences, seismology, space physics, aeronomy, tectonophysics, volcanology, geochemistry, and petrology. They must submit a cover letter with a curriculum vitae, undergraduate and graduate transcripts, a 10-page description of the dissertation topic and proposed research plan, and 3 letters of recommendation. U.S. citizenship or permanent resident status is required. Applications are encouraged from women, minorities, and students with disabilities who are traditionally underrepresented in the geophysical sciences.

Financial data The grant is $5,000; funds are to be used to assist with the costs of travel to obtain archival or research materials.

Duration 1 year.

Number awarded 1 each year.

Deadline September of each year.

[694]
GRADUATE RESEARCH FELLOWSHIP PROGRAM OF THE NATIONAL SCIENCE FOUNDATION

National Science Foundation
Directorate for Education and Human Resources
Attn: Division of Graduate Education
4201 Wilson Boulevard, Room 875S
Arlington, VA 22230
(703) 331-3542   Toll Free: (866) NSF-GRFP
Fax: (703) 292-9048   E-mail: info@nsfgrfp.org
Web: www.nsf.gov/funding/pgm_summ.jsp?pims_id=6201

Summary To provide financial assistance to graduate students, especially Asian Americans and members of other underrepresented groups, who are interested in working on a master's or doctoral degree in fields supported by the National Science Foundation (NSF).

Eligibility This program is open to U.S. citizens, nationals, and permanent residents who wish to work on research-based master's or doctoral degrees in a field of science, technology, engineering, or mathematics (STEM) supported by NSF (including astronomy, chemistry, computer and information sciences and engineering, geosciences, engineering, life sciences, materials research, mathematical sciences, physics, psychology, social sciences, or STEM education and learning). Other work in medical, dental, law, public health, or practice-oriented professional degree programs, or in joint science-professional degree programs, such as M.D./Ph.D. and J.D./Ph.D. programs, is not eligible. Applications normally should be submitted during the senior year in college or in the first year of graduate study; eligibility is limited to those who have completed no more than 12 months of graduate study since completion of a baccalaureate degree. Applicants who have already earned an advanced degree in science, engineering, or medicine (including an M.D., D.D.S., or D.V.M.) are ineligible. Selection is based on 1) intellectual merit of the proposed activity: strength of the academic record, proposed plan of research, previous research experience, references, appropriateness of the choice of institution; and 2) broader impacts of the proposed activity: how well does the activity advance discovery and understanding, how well does it broaden the participation of underrepresented groups (e.g., women, minorities, persons with disabilities, veterans), to what extent will it enhance the infrastructure for research and education, will the results be disseminated broadly to enhance scientific and technological understanding, what may be the benefits of the proposed activity to society).

Financial data The stipend is $32,000 per year; an additional $12,000 cost-of-education allowance is provided to the recipient's institution.

Duration Up to 3 years, usable over a 5-year period.

Number awarded Approximately 2,000 each year.

Deadline October of each year.

[695]
GREAT LAKES SECTION IFT DIVERSITY SCHOLARSHIP

Institute of Food Technologists-Great Lakes Section
c/o Andrea Kirk, Scholarship Chair
Post Foods, LLC
275 Cliff Street
Battle Creek, MI 49014
E-mail: greatlakesift@gmail.com
Web: www.greatlakesift.org/student-scholarships

Summary To provide financial assistance to Asian Americans and other minority members of the Great Lakes Section of the Institute of Food Technologists (IFT) from any state who are working on an undergraduate or graduate degree related to food technology at a college in Michigan.

Eligibility This program is open to minority residents of any state who are members of the IFT Great Lakes Section (GLS) and working full time on an undergraduate or graduate degree in food science, nutrition, food engineering, food packaging, or related fields at a college or university in Michigan. Applicants must have a GPA of 3.0 or higher and plans for a career in the food industry. Along with their application, they must submit a 1-page personal statement that covers their academic program, future plans and career goals, extracurricular activities (including involvement in community, university, GLS, or national IFT activities), and work experience. Financial need is not considered in the selection process.

Financial data The stipend is $1,000.

Duration 1 year; nonrenewable.

Number awarded 1 each year.

Deadline February of each year.

[696]
GREENSPOON MARDER DIVERSITY SCHOLARSHIP PROGRAM FOR LAW STUDENTS

Community Foundation of Sarasota County
Attn: Grants and Scholarships Coordinator
2635 Fruitville Road
P.O. Box 49587
Sarasota, FL 34230-6587
(941) 556-7114   Fax: (941) 952-7115
E-mail: eyoung@cfsarasota.org
Web: www.cfsarasota.org

Summary To provide financial assistance to Asian American and other minority students from any state attending designated law schools (most of which are in Florida).

Eligibility This program is open to racial and ethnic minority students from any state who are members of groups traditionally underrepresented in the legal profession. Applicants must be entering their second year of full-time study at the University of Florida Levin College of Law, Florida State University College of Law, Stetson University College of Law, Nova Southeastern University Shepard Broad Law Center, St. Thomas University School of Law, Howard University College of Law, Texas Southern University Thurgood Marshall School of Law, Florida Coastal School of Law, or Florida International University College of Law. They must have a GPA of 2.6 or higher. Along with their application, they must submit a 1,000-word personal statement that describes their personal strengths, their contributions through community service, any special or unusual circumstances that may have affected their academic performance, or their personal and family history of educational or socioeconomic disadvantage; it should include aspects of their minority racial or ethnic identity that are relevant to their application. Applicants may also include information about their financial circumstances if they wish to have those considered in the selection process. U.S. citizenship or permanent resident status is required.

Financial data The stipend is $2,500 per semester.

Duration 1 semester (the spring semester of the second year of law school); may be renewed 1 additional semester (the fall semester of the third year).

Additional information This program was established by the Florida law firm Ruden McClosky, which was acquired by the firm Greenspoon Marder in 2011. It is administered by the Community Foundation of Sarasota County, but the law firm selects the recipients.

Number awarded 1 or more each year.

Deadline July of each year.

[697]
HANA SCHOLARSHIPS

United Methodist Church
Attn: General Board of Higher Education and Ministry
Office of Loans and Scholarships
1001 19th Avenue South
P.O. Box 340007
Nashville, TN 37203-0007
(615) 340-7342   Fax: (615) 340-7367
E-mail: umscholar@gbhem.org
Web: www.gbhem.org

Summary To provide financial assistance to upper-division and graduate Methodist students who are of Hispanic, Asian, Native American, or Pacific Islander ancestry.

Eligibility This program is open to full-time juniors, seniors, and graduate students at accredited colleges and universities in the United States who have been active, full members of a United Methodist Church (UMC) for at least 3 years prior to applying. Applicants must have at least 1 parent who is Asian, Hispanic, or Native American. They must be able to demonstrate involvement in their Hispanic, Asian, or Native American (HANA) community in the UMC. Selection is based on that involvement, academic ability (GPA of at least 2.85), and financial need. U.S. citizenship or permanent resident status is required.

Financial data Stipends range from $1,000 to $3,000.

Duration 1 year; recipients may reapply.

Number awarded 50 each year.

Deadline February of each year.

[698]
HEALTH RESEARCH AND EDUCATIONAL TRUST SCHOLARSHIPS

New Jersey Hospital Association
Attn: Health Research and Educational Trust
760 Alexander Road
P.O. Box 1
Princeton, NJ 08543-0001
(609) 275-4224   Fax: (609) 452-8097
E-mail: jhritz@njha.com
Web: www.njha.com/education/scholarships

Summary To provide financial assistance to New Jersey residents, especially Asian Americans and other minorities, who are working on an undergraduate or graduate degree in a field related to health care administration at a school in any state.

Eligibility This program is open to residents of New Jersey enrolled in an upper-division or graduate program in hospital or health care administration, public administration, nursing, or other allied health profession at a school in any state. Graduate students working on an advanced degree to prepare to teach nursing are also eligible. Applicants must have a GPA of 3.0 or higher and be able to demonstrate financial need. Along with their application, they must submit a 2-page essay (on which 50% of the selection is based) describing their academic plans for the future. Minorities and women are especially encouraged to apply.

Financial data The stipend is $2,000.

Duration 1 year.

Additional information This program began in 1983.

Number awarded Varies each year; recently, 3 were awarded.

Deadline June of each year.

[699]
HELEN LEE SCHOLARSHIP

Philip Jaisohn Memorial Foundation
Attn: Scholarship Committee
6705 Old York Road
Philadelphia, PA 19126
(215) 224-2000, ext. 116   Fax: (215) 224-9164
E-mail: info@jaisohn.org
Web: www.jaisohn.com/scholarships

Summary To provide financial assistance to Korean American undergraduate and graduate students who demonstrate significant financial need.

Eligibility This program is open to Korean American undergraduate and graduate students who are currently enrolled at a college or university in the United States. Applicants must be able to demonstrate academic excellence, leadership and service to their school and community, and financial need. Along with their application, they must submit a 100-word essay on either "Who is Dr. Jaisohn to Me," or "The Significance of Dr. Jaisohn's Ideal to Korean Americans." They must also submit a brief statement on how they can contribute to and be involved in the activities of the Philip Jaisohn Memorial Foundation. Selection is based primarily on financial need.

Financial data The stipend is $2,000.

Duration 1 year.

Number awarded 2 each year.

Deadline August of each year.

[700]
HELENE M. OVERLY MEMORIAL GRADUATE SCHOLARSHIP

Women's Transportation Seminar
Attn: WTS Foundation
1701 K Street, N.W., Suite 800
Washington, DC 20006
(202) 955-5085   Fax: (202) 955-5088
E-mail: wts@wtsinternational.org
Web: www.wtsinternational.org/education/scholarships

Summary To provide financial assistance to women graduate students, especially Asian Americans and other minorities, interested in preparing for a career in transportation.

Eligibility This program is open to women who are enrolled in a graduate degree program in a transportation-related field (e.g., transportation engineering, planning, finance, or logistics). Applicants must have at least a 3.0 GPA and be interested in a career in transportation. Along with their application, they must submit a 750-word statement about their career goals after graduation and why they think they should receive the scholarship award. Applications must be submitted first to a local chapter; the chapters forward selected applications for consideration on the national level. Minority women are particularly encouraged to apply. Selection is based on transportation involvement and goals, job skills, and academic record.

Financial data The stipend is $10,000.

Duration 1 year.

Additional information This program began in 1981. Local chapters may also award additional funding to winners in their area.

Number awarded 1 each year.

Deadline Applications must be submitted by November to a local WTS chapter.

[701]
HENRY AND CHIYO KUWAHARA CREATIVE ARTS AWARD

Japanese American Citizens League
Attn: National Scholarship Awards
1765 Sutter Street
San Francisco, CA 94115
(415) 345-1075   Fax: (415) 345-1077
E-mail: pwada@jacl.org
Web: www.jacl.org/jacl-national-scholarship-program

Summary To provide financial assistance to undergraduate and graduate student members of the Japanese American Citizens League (JACL) interested in completing a project in the creative arts.

Eligibility This program is open to JACL members who are working on an undergraduate or graduate degree in the creative arts. Professional artists are not eligible. Applicants must submit a detailed proposal for a project they wish to create, including a time plan, anticipated date of completion, and itemized budget. They must also submit information on their involvement in JACL and a 2-page essay on a topic that changes annually but relates to Japanese Americans. Selection is based on that essay, academic history, JACL involvement, school activities, work history, scholastic honors, and community involvement. Preference is given to students who are interested in creative projects that reflect the Japanese American experience and culture.

Financial data Stipends generally average more than $2,000.

Duration 1 year; nonrenewable.

Number awarded At least 1 each year.

Deadline March of each year.

[702]
HENRY AND CHIYO KUWAHARA MEMORIAL SCHOLARSHIPS

Japanese American Citizens League
Attn: National Scholarship Awards
1765 Sutter Street
San Francisco, CA 94115
(415) 345-1075   Fax: (415) 345-1077
E-mail: pwada@jacl.org
Web: www.jacl.org/jacl-national-scholarship-program

Summary To provide financial assistance for undergraduate or graduate study to members of the Japanese American Citizens League (JACL).

Eligibility This program is open to JACL members who are high school seniors, undergraduates, or graduate students. Applicants must be attending or planning to attend a college, university, trade school, or business college. They must submit information on their involvement in JACL and a 2-page essay on a topic that changes annually but relates to Japanese Americans. Selection is based on that essay, academic history, JACL involvement, school activities, work history, scholastic honors, and community involvement.

Financial data Stipends generally average more than $2,000.

Duration 1 year; nonrenewable.

Number awarded 6 each year: 2 each to entering freshmen, continuing undergraduates, and entering or currently-enrolled graduate students.

Deadline February of each year for graduating high school seniors; March of each year for current undergraduate or graduate students.

[703]
HENRY L. DIAMOND B&D LAW CLERK

Environmental Law Institute
2000 L Street, N.W., Suite 620
Washington, DC 20036
(202) 939-380037   Fax: (202) 939-3868
E-mail: law@eli.org
Web: www.eli.org/jobs/beveridge-diamond-acoel-law-clerks

Summary To provide law students, especially Asian Americans and other minorities, with summer work experience at the Environmental Law Institute (ELI) in Washington, D.C.

Eligibility This program is open to law students, especially first-year students, who have an interest in environmental law. Applicants must be interested in working during the summer at ELI on its domestic and international projects and publications (such as the *Environmental Law Reporter*). Along with their application they must submit a resume (including college and law school transcripts), references, transcripts, a writing sample, and a cover letter that explains how the applicant will

contribute to the diversity of environmental law, management, and policy. Minority candidates are encouraged to apply.

Financial data The stipend is $5,000.

Duration At least 10 weeks during the summer.

Additional information This program is supported by the law firm Beveridge & Diamond, P.C.

Number awarded 1 each year.

Deadline Applications may be submitted at any time.

[704]
HENRY P. DAVID GRANTS FOR RESEARCH AND INTERNATIONAL TRAVEL IN HUMAN REPRODUCTIVE BEHAVIOR AND POPULATION STUDIES

American Psychological Foundation
750 First Street, N.E.
Washington, DC 20002-4242
(202) 336-5843   Fax: (202) 336-5812
E-mail: foundation@apa.org
Web: www.apa.org/apf/funding/david.aspx

Summary To provide funding to young psychologists, especially Asian Americans and other minorities, who are interested in conducting research on reproductive behavior.

Eligibility This program is open to doctoral students in psychology working on a dissertation and young psychologists who have no more than 10 years of postgraduate experience. Applicants must be interested in conducting research on human reproductive behavior or an area related to population concerns. Along with their application, they must submit a current curriculum vitae, 2 letters of recommendation, and an essay of 1 to 2 pages on their interest in human reproductive behavior or in population studies. The sponsor encourages applications from individuals who represent diversity in race, ethnicity, gender, age, disability, and sexual orientation.

Financial data The grant is $1,500.

Duration The grant is presented annually.

Additional information Every third year (2017, 1020), the program also provides support for a non-U.S. reproductive health/population science professional to travel to and participate in the Psychosocial Workshop, held in conjunction with the Population Association of America annual meeting.

Number awarded 2 in the years when the program offers support to a non-U.S. professional to travel to the United States; 1 in other years.

Deadline November of each year.

[705]
HERBERT W. NICKENS MEDICAL STUDENT SCHOLARSHIPS

Association of American Medical Colleges
Attn: Division of Diversity Policy and Programs
655 K Street, N.W., Suite 100
Washington, DC 20001-2399
(202) 862-6203   Fax: (202) 828-1125
E-mail: nickensawards@aamc.org
Web: www.aamc.org/initiatives/awards/nickens-student

Summary To provide financial assistance to medical students, including Asian Americans, who have demonstrated efforts to address the health-care needs of minorities.

Eligibility This program is open to U.S. citizens and permanent residents entering their third year of study at a U.S. allopathic medical school. Each medical school may nominate 1 student for these awards. The letter must describe the nominee's 1) academic achievement through the first and second year, including special awards and honors, clerkships or special research projects, and extracurricular activities in which the student has shown leadership abilities; 2) leadership efforts to eliminate inequities in medical education and health care; 3) demonstrated leadership efforts in addressing the educational, societal, and health-care needs of minorities; and 4) awards and honors, special research projects, and extracurricular activities in which the student has shown leadership abilities. Nominees must submit a curriculum vitae and a 2-page essay that discusses their leadership efforts in eliminating inequities in medical education and health care for minorities.

Financial data The stipend is $5,000.

Duration 1 year.

Number awarded 5 each year.

Deadline April of each year.

[706]
HERMAN G. GREEN, PHD MEMORIAL SCHOLARSHIP

South Carolina Professional Association for Access and
Equity
Attn: Financial Secretary
P.O. Box 71297
North Charleston, SC 29415
(843) 670-4890   E-mail: anderson4569@bellsouth.net
Web: www.scpaae.org/#!scholarships/c11tv

Summary To provide financial assistance to graduate students at colleges and universities in South Carolina who are Asian Americans or otherwise recognized as underrepresented minorities on their campus.

Eligibility This program is open to residents of any state who have completed at least 9 semester hours of graduate study at a college or university in South Carolina. Applicants must be recognized as an underrepresented ethnic minority on their campus. They must have a GPA of 3.5 or higher. Along with their application, they must submit 1) a personal letter on their public service, academic and career goals, honors and awards, leadership skills and organization participation, community service, and a statement of why they would like to receive this scholarship; and 2) a paragraph defining access and equity and describing how they can assist in achieving access and equity within South Carolina. Financial need is not considered in the selection process.

Financial data The stipend is $1,200.

Duration 1 year.

Number awarded 1 or more each year.

Deadline February of each year.

[707]
HIGH SCHOOL AND COLLEGE STUDENT ESSAY, POETRY AND VIDEO CONTEST

Go For Broke National Education Center
355 East First Street, Suite 200
Los Angeles, CA 90012
(310) 222-5711   Fax: (310) 222-5700
E-mail: chris@goforbroke.org
Web: www.goforbroke.org

Summary To recognize and reward college and high school students who submit outstanding essays, poetry, or videos relating to the World War II experience of Japanese American soldiers.

Eligibility This contest is open to high school (grades 9-12) and college (undergraduate and graduate) students. Applicants must submit an essay or poem of 250 to 500 words or a video 3 to 5 minutes in length. The topic of the entries may be 1) the Japanese American World War II soldier experience and its relevance to our lives today; 2) a specific Japanese American World War II soldier and elements of his experience that are most meaningful to the student; or 3) what the Japanese American World War II experience can teach us about the Constitution, rights, and responsibilities.

Financial data Awards are $1,000 for winners and $250 for other finalists.

Duration The contest is held annually.

Additional information This contest began in 2013.

Number awarded Awards are presented to 6 winners and 10 other finalists.

Deadline June of each year.

[708]
HILO CHINESE SCHOOL SCHOLARSHIP

Hawai'i Community Foundation
Attn: Scholarship Department
827 Fort Street Mall
Honolulu, HI 96813
(808) 566-5570   Toll Free: (888) 731-3863
Fax: (808) 521-6286
E-mail: scholarships@hcf-hawaii.org
Web: hcf.scholarships.ngwebsolutions.com

Summary To provide financial assistance to residents of Hawaii of Chinese ancestry who are working on an undergraduate or graduate degree in any field at a college in any state.

Eligibility This program is open to residents of Hawaii who are currently enrolled full time at an accredited 2- or 4-year college or university in any state. First preference is given to descendants of Hilo Chinese School alumni; second preference is given to students of Chinese ancestry. Applicants must be working on an undergraduate or graduate degree in any field. They must have a GPA of 2.5 or higher be able to demonstrate financial need. Along with their application, they must submit a short statement indicating their reasons for attending college, their planned course of study, their career goals, and what community service means to them.

Financial data The amounts of the awards depend on the availability of funds and the need of the recipient. Recently, the average value of the scholarships awarded by the foundation was $2,800.

Duration 1 year.

Additional information The Hilo Chinese School opened in 1930 to teach Chinese language. When the school closed, a trust was established to support this program.

Number awarded 1 or more each year.

Deadline February of each year.

[709]
HMONG HOME HEALTH CARE SCHOLARSHIPS

Hmong American Education Fund
P.O. Box 17468
St. Paul, MN 55117
(651) 592-1576   E-mail: scholarships@thehaef.org
Web: www.thehaef.org

Summary To provide financial assistance to Hmong residents of Minnesota who are interested in attending college or graduate school in any state to study health care or social services.

Eligibility This program is open to residents of Minnesota who identify themselves as a person of Hmong descent. Applicants must be high school seniors, GED recipients, or current undergraduate or graduate students enrolled or planning to enroll full time at a 2- or 4-year college or university in any state. They must be U.S. citizens or permanent residents and have a GPA of 3.2 or higher. Their field of study must be health care, social services, or a related field. Along with their application, they must submit transcripts and a 1,500-word essay on their educational accomplishments, community service, financial need, and how this scholarship can help them.

Financial data The stipend is $750.

Duration 1 year; nonrenewable.

Additional information Support for this program is provided by Hmong Home Health Care, Inc.

Number awarded 2 each year.

Deadline March of each year.

[710]
HOLLY A. CORNELL SCHOLARSHIP

American Water Works Association
Attn: Scholarship Coordinator
6666 West Quincy Avenue
Denver, CO 80235-3098
(303) 794-7771   Toll Free: (800) 926-7337
Fax: (303) 347-0804   E-mail: scholarships@awwa.org
Web: www.awwa.org

Summary To provide financial assistance to Asian American and other minority students interested in working on an master's degree in the field of water supply and treatment.

Eligibility This program is open to minority and female students working on a master's degree in the field of water supply and treatment at a college or university in Canada, Guam, Mexico, Puerto Rico, or the United States. Students who have been accepted into graduate school but have not yet begun graduate study are encouraged to apply. Applicants must submit a 2-page resume, official transcripts, 3 letters of recommendation, a proposed curriculum of study, a 1-page statement of educational plans and career objectives demonstrating an interest in the drinking water field, and a 3-page proposed plan of research. Selection is based on academic record and potential to provide leadership in the field of water supply and treatment.

Financial data The stipend is $7,500.

Duration 1 year; nonrenewable.

Additional information Funding for this program, which began in 1990, comes from the consulting firm CH2M Hill.

Number awarded 1 each year.

Deadline January of each year.

[711]
HONORABLE THOMAS TANG INTERNATIONAL MOOT COURT COMPETITION SCHOLARSHIPS

National Asian Pacific American Bar Association
Attn: NAPABA Law Foundation
1612 K Street, N.W., Suite 510
Washington, DC 20006
(202) 775-9555   Fax: (202) 775-9333
E-mail: thomastang@napaba.org
Web: www.napaba.org/?page=TTMCPC

Summary To recognize and reward law students who participate in a moot court competition sponsored by the National Asian Pacific American Bar Association (NAPABA).

Eligibility This competition is open to students at ABA-accredited law schools who have completed the first year of study. All students are eligible, but a goal of the program is to reach out to Asian Pacific American law students and provide them with an opportunity to showcase their writing and oral advocacy skills. Applicants must enter the competition as teams of 2 students each.

Financial data A total of $10,000 is awarded in prizes each year.

Duration The competition is held annually.

Additional information This competition began in 1993. The entry fee is $200 per team.

Number awarded Generally 6 each year: 2 for members of the first-place team, 2 for members of the second-place team, 1 for best brief, and 1 for best oralist.

Deadline August of each year.

[712]
HOWARD MAYER BROWN FELLOWSHIP

American Musicological Society
6010 College Station
Brunswick, ME 04011-8451
(207) 798-4243   Toll Free: (877) 679-7648
Fax: (207) 798-4254   E-mail: ams@ams-net.org
Web: www.ams-net.org/fellowships/hmb.php

Summary To provide financial assistance to Asian American and other minority students who are working on a doctoral degree in the field of musicology.

Eligibility This program is open to members of minority groups historically underrepresented in the field of musicology. In the United States, that includes Asian Americans, African Americans, Native Americans, and Hispanic Americans. In Canada, it refers to aboriginal people and visible minorities. Applicants must have completed at least 1 year of full-time academic work at an institution with a graduate program in musicology and be planning to complete a Ph.D. degree in the field. There are no restrictions on research area, age, or sex. U.S. or Canadian citizenship or permanent resident status is required.

Financial data The stipend is $20,000.

Duration 1 year; nonrenewable.

Additional information This fellowship was first awarded in 1995.

Number awarded 1 each year.

Deadline December of each year.

[713]
H.R. CHUNG LEADERSHIP SCHOLARSHIP

Philip Jaisohn Memorial Foundation
Attn: Scholarship Committee
6705 Old York Road
Philadelphia, PA 19126
(215) 224-2000, ext. 116   Fax: (215) 224-9164
E-mail: info@jaisohn.org
Web: www.jaisohn.com/scholarships

Summary To provide financial assistance to Korean American undergraduate and graduate students who demonstrate involvement in extracurricular, athletic, and community activities.

Eligibility This program is open to Korean American undergraduate and graduate students who are currently enrolled at a college or university in the United States. Applicants must be able to demonstrate academic excellence, leadership and service to their school and community, and financial need. Along with their application, they must submit a 100-word essay on either "Who is Dr. Jaisohn to Me," or "The Significance of Dr. Jaisohn's Ideal to Korean Americans." They must also submit a brief statement on how they can contribute to and be involved in the activities of the Philip Jaisohn Memorial Foundation. Selection is based primarily on leadership in extracurricular activities, varsity sports, or community involvement.

Financial data The stipend is $1,500.

Duration 1 year.

Number awarded 1 each year.

Deadline August of each year.

[714]
HSIAO MEMORIAL ECONOMICS SCHOLARSHIP

Asian Pacific Fund
Attn: Scholarship Coordinator
465 California Street, Suite 809
San Francisco, CA 94104
(415) 395-9985 E-mail: scholarship@asianpacificfund.org
Web: www.asianpacificfund.org

Summary To provide financial assistance to Asian graduate students from any state who are working on a Ph.D. degree in economics.

Eligibility This program is open to graduate students at colleges and universities in the United States who are working on a Ph.D. degree in economics. Preference is given to students preparing for a career in academia. Applicants must be of at least 50% Asian heritage; preference is given to students of Chinese descent. They must have a GPA of 3.0 or higher and be able to demonstrate financial need. U.S. citizens, permanent residents, and foreign nationals are all eligible. Preference is given to applicants whose research interests would benefit Asians, Asian Americans, or persons in social or economic need.

Financial data The stipend is $1,000.

Duration 1 year; nonrenewable.

Number awarded 1 each year.

Deadline May of each year.

[715]
HUGH J. ANDERSEN MEMORIAL SCHOLARSHIPS

National Medical Fellowships, Inc.
Attn: Scholarship Program
347 Fifth Avenue, Suite 510
New York, NY 10016
(212) 483-8880   Toll Free: (877) NMF-1DOC
Fax: (212) 483-8897 E-mail: scholarships@nmfonline.org
Web: www.nmfonline.org

Summary To provide financial assistance to Vietnamese, Cambodian, and other underrepresented minority medical students at schools in Minnesota.

Eligibility This program is open to Vietnamese, Cambodians, African Americans, Hispanics/Latinos, Native Americans, and Pacific Islanders who are entering the second or third year of medical school. Applicants must be Minnesota residents enrolled at an accredited medical school in Minnesota. They must be U.S. citizens or DACA students. Selection is based on leadership, commitment to serving medically underserved communities, and financial need.

Financial data The stipend is $5,000.

Duration 1 year.

Additional information This program began in 1982.

Number awarded 2 each year.

Deadline September of each year.

[716]
IBM PHD FELLOWSHIP PROGRAM

IBM Corporation
Attn: University Relations
1133 Westchester Avenue
White Plains, NY 10604
Toll Free: (800) IBM-4YOU   TDD: (800) IBM-3383
E-mail: phdfellow@us.ibm.com
Web: www.research.ibm.com

Summary To provide funding and work experience to students, especially Asian Americans and other minorities, who are working on a Ph.D. in a research area of broad interest to IBM.

Eligibility Students nominated for this fellowship should be enrolled full time at an accredited college or university in any country and should have completed at least 1 year of graduate study in computer science or engineering, electrical or mechanical engineering, physical sciences (chemistry, material sciences, physics), mathematical sciences, public sector and business sciences, or service science, management, and engineering (SSME). Focus areas that receive special consideration include technology that creates new business or social value, cognitive computing research, cloud and distributed computing technology and solutions, or fundamental science and technology. Applicants should be planning a career in research. Nominations must be made by a faculty member and endorsed by the department head. The program values diversity, and encourages nominations of women, minorities, and others who contribute to that diversity. Selection is based on the applicants' potential for research excellence, the degree to which their technical interests align with those of IBM, and academic progress to date. Preference is given to students who have had an IBM internship or have closely collaborated with technical or services people from IBM.

Financial data Fellowships pay tuition, fees, and a stipend of $17,500 per year.

Duration 1 year; may be renewed up to 2 additional years, provided the recipient is renominated, interacts with IBM's technical community, and demonstrates continued progress and achievement.

Additional information Recipients are offered an internship at 1 of the IBM Research Division laboratories and are given an IBM computer.

Number awarded Varies each year; recently, 57 were awarded.

Deadline October of each year.

[717]
ILLINOIS MINORITY REAL ESTATE SCHOLARSHIP

Illinois Association of Realtors
Attn: Illinois Real Estate Educational Foundation
522 South Fifth Street
P.O. Box 2607
Springfield, IL 62708
Toll Free: (866) 854-REEF   Fax: (217) 529-5893
E-mail: lclayton@iar.org
Web: www.ilreef.org

Summary To provide financial assistance to Illinois residents who are Asian Americans or members of other minority groups and preparing for a career in real estate.

Eligibility This program is open to residents of Illinois who are Asian, African American, Hispanic or Latino, or Native American. Applicants must be interested in preparing for a career in real estate by pursuing: 1) courses to meet Illinois broker license requirements; 2) course work to meet Illinois broker license requirement; 3) course work required for Illinois appraisal licensing/certification; 4) professional development unrelated to obtaining license/certification; or 5) an undergraduate or graduate program of study. Along with their application, they must submit information on their employment history, transcripts, evidence of financial need, and an essay that describes their career goals and explains why they believe they should receive scholarship assistance through this program.

Financial data The maximum stipend is $500.

Duration Funds must be used within 24 months of the award date.

Number awarded 1 or more each year.

Deadline Applications may be submitted at any time, but they must be received at least 12 weeks prior to the beginning of the school term for which financial assistance is requested.

[718]
ILLINOIS NURSES FOUNDATION CENTENNIAL SCHOLARSHIP

Illinois Nurses Association
Attn: Illinois Nurses Foundation
P.O. Box 636
Manteno, IL 60950
(815) 468-8804   Fax: (773) 304-1419
E-mail: info@ana-illinois.org
Web: www.ana-illinois.org

Summary To provide financial assistance to nursing undergraduate and graduate students who are Asian Americans or members of other underrepresented groups.

Eligibility This program is open to students working on an associate, bachelor's, or master's degree at an accredited NLNAC or CCNE school of nursing. Applicants must be members of a group underrepresented in nursing (Asians, African Americans, Hispanics, American Indians, or males). Undergraduates must have earned a passing grade in all nursing courses taken to date and have a GPA of 2.85 or higher. Graduate students must have completed at least 12 semester hours of graduate work and have a GPA of 3.0 or higher. All applicants must be willing to 1) act as a spokesperson to other student groups on the value of the scholarship to continuing their nursing education; and 2) be profiled in any media or marketing materials developed by the Illinois Nurses Foundation. Along with their application, they must submit a narrative of 250 to 500 words on how they, as nurses, plan to affect policy at either the state or national level that impacts on nursing or health care generally, or how they believe they will impact the nursing profession in general.

Financial data A stipend is awarded (amount not specified).

Duration 1 year.

Number awarded 1 or more each year.

Deadline March of each year.

[719]
INDIANA CLEO FELLOWSHIPS

Indiana Supreme Court
Attn: Division of State Court Administration
30 South Meridian Street, Suite 500
Indianapolis, IN 46204
(317) 232-2542   Toll Free: (800) 452-9963
Fax: (317) 233-6586   E-mail: ashley.rozier@courts.in.gov
Web: www.in.gov/judiciary/cleo/2402.htm

Summary To provide financial assistance to Asian American and other minority and disadvantaged college seniors from any state interested in attending law school in Indiana.

Eligibility This program is open to residents of Indiana who attend college in the state or attend college out of state and are recommended by the admissions officer at a law school in the state. Applicants must be minority, low income, first-generation college, or limited English proficiency college seniors who have applied to an Indiana law school. Selected applicants are invited to participate in the Indiana Conference for Legal Education Opportunity (Indiana CLEO) Summer Institute, held at a law school in the state. Admission to that program is based on GPA, LSAT scores, 3 letters of recommendation, a resume, a personal statement, and financial need. Students who successfully complete the Institute and are admitted to an Indiana law school receive these fellowships.

Financial data All expenses for the Indiana CLEO Summer Institute are paid. The fellowship stipend is $9,000 per year.

Duration The Indiana CLEO Summer Institute lasts 6 weeks. Fellowships are for 1 year and may be renewed up to 2 additional years.

Additional information The first Summer Institute was held in 1997.

Number awarded 30 students are invited to participate in the summer institute; the number of those selected to receive a fellowship varies each year.

Deadline February of each year.

[720]
INTELLECTUAL PROPERTY LAW SECTION WOMEN AND MINORITY SCHOLARSHIP

State Bar of Texas
Attn: Intellectual Property Law Section
c/o Bhaveeni D. Parmar, Scholarship Selection
  Committee
Law Office of Bhaveeni Parmar PLLC
4447 North Central Expressway, Suite 110-295
Dallas, Texas 75205
E-mail: bhaveeni@parmarlawoffice.com
Web: www.texasbariplaw.org

Summary To provide financial assistance to Asian American and other minority students at law schools in Texas who plan to practice intellectual property law.

Eligibility This program is open to women and members of minority groups (Asian Americans, African Americans, Hispanics, and Native Americans) from any state who are currently enrolled at an ABA-accredited law school in Texas. Applicants must be planning to practice intellectual property law in Texas. Along with their application, they must submit a 2-page essay explaining why they plan to prepare for a career in intellectual property law in Texas, any qualifications they believe are relevant for their consideration for this scholarship, and (optionally) any issues of financial need they wish to have considered.

Financial data The stipend is $5,000.

Duration 1 year.

Number awarded 2 each year: 1 to a women and 1 to a minority.

Deadline May of each year.

[721]
INTERFAITH SPIRITUALITY SCHOLARSHIP

Unitarian Universalist Association
Attn: Ministerial Credentialing Office
24 Farnsworth Street
Boston, MA 02210-1409
(617) 948-6403   Fax: (617) 742-2875
E-mail: mcoadministrator@uua.org
Web: www.uua.org

Summary To provide financial assistance to seminary students, especially Asian Americans and other persons of color, who are preparing for the Unitarian Universalist (UU) ministry and are interested in interfaith understanding.

Eligibility This program is open to seminary students who are enrolled full or at least half time in a UU ministerial training program with candidate status. Applicants must have demonstrated 1) an interest in and desire to integrate interfaith understanding into their ministry; and 2) a commitment to guiding others on their own spiritual path. They must be citizens of the United States or Canada. Priority is given first to those who have demonstrated outstanding ministerial ability and secondarily to students with the greatest financial need (especially persons of color).

Financial data The stipend ranges from $1,000 to $15,000 per year.

Duration 1 year.

Number awarded 1 each year.

Deadline April of each year.

[722]
INTERMOUNTAIN SECTION AWWA DIVERSITY SCHOLARSHIP

American Water Works Association-Intermountain
  Section
Attn: Member Services Coordinator
3430 East Danish Road
Sandy, UT 84093
(801) 712-1619, ext. 2   Fax: (801) 487-6699
E-mail: nicoleb@ims-awwa.org
Web: ims-awwa.site-ym.com/group/StudentPO

Summary To provide financial assistance to Asian American and other minority undergraduate and graduate students working on a degree in the field of water quality, supply, and treatment at a university in the Intermountain West.

Eligibility This program is open to 1) women; and 2) students who identify as Asian, Hispanic or Latino, Black or African American, Native Hawaiian or other Pacific Islander, or American Indian or Alaska Native. Applicants must be entering or enrolled in an undergraduate or graduate program at a college or university in the Intermountain West (defined to include all or portions of Arizona, Colorado, Idaho, Montana, Nevada, New Mexico, Utah, or Wyoming) that relates to water quality, supply, or treatment. Along with their application, they must submit a 2-page essay on their academic interests and career goals and how those relate to water quality, supply, or treatment. Selection is based on that essay, letters of recommendation, and potential to contribute to the field of water quality, supply, and treatment in the Intermountain West.

Financial data The stipend is $1,000. The winner also receives a 1-year student membership in the Intermountain Section of the American Water Works Association (AWWA).

Duration 1 year; nonrenewable.

Number awarded 1 each year.

Deadline November of each year.

[723]
INTERNATIONAL COMMUNICATIONS INDUSTRIES FOUNDATION SCHOLARSHIPS

InfoComm International
International Communications Industries Foundation
11242 Waples Mill Road, Suite 200
Fairfax, VA 22030
(703) 273-7200   Toll Free: (800) 659-7469
Fax: (703) 278-8082   E-mail: jhardwick@infocomm.org
Web: www.infocomm.org

Summary To provide financial assistance to undergraduate and graduate students who are interested in preparing for a career in the audiovisual (AV) industry, especially Asian Americans and other minorities.

Eligibility This program is open to second-year students at 2-year colleges, juniors and seniors at 4-year institutions, and graduate students. Applicants must have a GPA of 2.75 or higher and be majoring or planning to major in audiovisual subjects or related fields, including audio, video, audiovisual, radio/television/film, or other field related to a career in the audiovisual industry. Students in other programs, such as journalism, may be eligible if they can demonstrate a relationship to career goals in the AV industry. Minority and women candidates are especially encouraged to apply. Selection is based on essays about their career interests, presentation of the application, GPA, AV-related experience, work experience, and letters of recommendation.

Financial data The stipend is $4,000. Funds are sent directly to the school.

Duration 1 year.

Additional information InfoComm International, formerly the International Communications Industries Association, established the International Communications Industries Foundation (ICIF) to manage its charitable and educational activities.

Number awarded Varies each year.

Deadline April of each year.

[724]
INTERNATIONAL SECURITY AND COOPERATION PREDOCTORAL FELLOWSHIPS

Stanford University
Center for International Security and Cooperation
Attn: Fellowships Coordinator
Encina Hall, Room C206-10
616 Serra Street
Stanford, CA 94305-6165
(650) 723-9625   Fax: (650) 724-5683
E-mail: CISACfellowship@stanford.edu
Web: cisac.fsi.stanford.edu/docs/cisac_fellowship_program

Summary To provide funding to doctoral students, especially Asian Americans and other minorities, who are interested in working on a dissertation on international security problems at Stanford University's Center for International Security and Cooperation.

Eligibility This program is open to students currently enrolled in doctoral programs at academic institutions in the United States who would benefit from access to the facilities offered by the center. Applicants may be working in any discipline of the social sciences, humanities, natural sciences, law, or engineering that relates to international security problems. Relevant topics include nuclear weapons policy and nonproliferation; nuclear energy; cybersecurity, cyberwarfare, and the future of the Internet; war and civil conflict; global governance, migration and transnational flows, from norms to criminal trafficking; biosecurity and global health; implications of geostrategic shifts; insurgency, terrorism, and homeland security; and consolidating peace after conflict. The sponsor welcomes applications from women, minorities, and citizens of all countries.

Financial data The stipend ranges from $25,000 to $28,000. Medical insurance is available for those who do not have coverage.

Duration 9 to 11 months.

Additional information Fellows are expected to complete dissertation chapters or their dissertation during their fellowship. They should not plan to spend any time conducting research abroad or in other parts of the country.

Number awarded Varies each year; recently, 9 were awarded.

Deadline January of each year.

[725]
IRTS BROADCAST SALES ASSOCIATE PROGRAM

International Radio and Television Society Foundation
Attn: Director, Special Projects
1697 Broadway, 10th Floor
New York, NY 10019
(212) 867-6650   Toll Free: (888) 627-1266
Fax: (212) 867-6653   E-mail: submit@irts.org
Web: 406.144.myftpupload.com

Summary To provide summer work experience to Asian American and other minority graduate students interested in working in broadcast sales in the New York City area.

Eligibility This program is open to graduating college seniors and students already enrolled in graduate school who are members of a minority (African American, Hispanic/Latino, Asian/Pacific Islander, American Indian/Alaskan Native) group. Applicants must be interested in working during the summer in a sales training program traditionally reserved for actual station group employees. They must be a communications major or have demonstrated a strong interest in the field through extracurricular activities or other practical experience, but they are not required to have experience in broadcast sales.

Financial data Travel, housing, and a living allowance are provided.

Duration 9 weeks during the summer.

Additional information The program consists of a 1-week orientation to the media and entertainment business, followed by an 8-week internship experience in the sales division of a network stations group.

Number awarded Varies each year.

Deadline February of each year.

[726]
IRTS SUMMER FELLOWSHIP PROGRAM

International Radio and Television Society Foundation
Attn: Director, Special Projects
420 Lexington Avenue, Suite 1601
New York, NY 10170-0101
(212) 867-6650   Toll Free: (888) 627-1266
Fax: (212) 867-6653   E-mail: apply@irts.org
Web: irtsfoundation.org/summer-fellowship-program

Summary To provide summer work experience to upper-division and graduate students, especially Asian Americans and other minorities, who are interested in working during the summer in broadcasting and related fields in the New York City area.

Eligibility This program is open to juniors, seniors, and graduate students at 4-year colleges and universities. Applicants must either be a communications major or have demonstrated a strong interest in the field through extracurricular activities or other practical experience. Minority (Asian/Pacific

Islander, African American, Hispanic/Latino, American Indian/Alaskan Native) students are especially encouraged to apply.

Financial data Travel, housing, and a living allowance are provided.

Duration 9 weeks during the summer.

Additional information The first week consists of a comprehensive orientation to broadcasting, cable, advertising, and new media. Then, the participants are assigned an 8-week fellowship. This full-time "real world" experience in a New York-based corporation allows them to reinforce or redefine specific career goals before settling into a permanent job. Fellows have worked at all 4 major networks, at local New York City radio and television stations, and at national rep firms, advertising agencies, and cable operations. This program includes fellowships reserved for students at designated universities (University of Pennsylvania, Brooklyn College, City College of New York, College of the Holy Cross) and the following named awards: the Thomas S. Murphy Fellowship (sponsored by ABC National Television Sales), the Helen Karas Memorial Fellowship, the Mel Karmazin Fellowship, the Neil Postman Memorial Summer Fellowship, the Ari Bluman Memorial Summer Fellowship (sponsored by Group M), the Thom Casadonte Memorial Fellowship (sponsored by Bloomberg), the Joanne Mercado Memorial Fellowship (sponsored by Nielsen), the Donald V. West Fellowship (sponsored by the Library of American Broadcasting Foundation), the Leslie Moonves Fellowship (sponsored by CBS Television Station Sales, and the Sumner M. Redstone Fellowship (sponsored by CBS Television Station Sales). Other sponsors include the National Academy of Television Arts & Sciences, Fox Networks, NBCUniversal, and Unilever.

Number awarded Varies; recently, 30 were awarded.

Deadline November of each year.

[727]
ISAAC J. "IKE" CRUMBLY MINORITIES IN ENERGY GRANT

American Association of Petroleum Geologists
Foundation
Attn: Grants-in-Aid Program
1444 South Boulder Avenue
P.O. Box 979
Tulsa, OK 74101-0979
(918) 560-2644   Toll Free: (855) 302-2743
Fax: (918) 560-2642   E-mail: foundation@aapg.org
Web: foundation.aapg.org

Summary To provide funding to Asian American and other minority graduate students who are interested in conducting research related to earth science aspects of the petroleum industry.

Eligibility This program is open to women and ethnic minorities (Asian, Black, Hispanic, or Native American, including American Indian, Eskimo, Hawaiian, or Samoan) who are working on a master's or doctoral degree. Applicants must be interested in conducting research related to the search for and development of petroleum and energy-minerals resources and to related environmental geology issues. Selection is based on student's academic and employment history (10 points), scientific merit of proposal (30 points), suitability to program objectives (30 points), financial merit of proposal (20 points), and endorsement by faculty or department adviser (10 points).

Financial data Grants range from $500 to $3,000. Funds are to be applied to research-related expenses (e.g., a summer of field work). They may not be used to purchase capital equipment or to pay salaries, tuition, room, or board.

Duration 1 year. Doctoral candidates may receive a 1-year renewal.

Number awarded 1 each year.

Deadline February of each year.

[728]
JACK L. STEPHENS GRADUATE SCHOLARSHIP

Conference of Minority Transportation Officials-Fort
Lauderdale Chapter
Attn: Scholarship Committee
Victor Garcia, South Florida Regional Transportation
Authority
801 N.W. 33rd Street
Pompano Beach, FL 33064
(954) 788-7925   Toll Free: (800) GO SFRTA
Fax: (854) 788-7961   TDD: (800) 273-7545
E-mail: victorgarcia@comtoftlauderdale.org
Web: www.comtoftlauderdale.org/scholarship-program

Summary To provide financial assistance to Asian American and other minority students working on a transportation-related graduate degree at a college in Florida.

Eligibility This program is open to minority students currently enrolled at accredited colleges and universities in Florida. Applicants must be working on a master's or doctoral degree in a transportation-related field and have a GPA of 2.5 or higher. They must be U.S. citizens or permanent residents. Along with their application, they must submit an essay of 500 to 750 words on their transportation-related career goals and life aspirations. Financial need is not considered in the selection process.

Financial data The stipend is $2,500.

Duration 1 year; nonrenewable.

Additional information This program began in 2015.

Number awarded 1 each year.

Deadline April of each year.

[729]
JACOB WILLIAMS SCHOLARSHIP

United Methodist Foundation of Indiana
8401 Fishers Center Drive
Fishers, IN 46038-2318
(317) 788-7879   Toll Free: (877) 391-8811
Fax: (317) 788-0089
E-mail: foundation@UMFIndiana.org
Web: www.umfindiana.org/endowments

Summary To provide financial assistance to Asian American and other ethnic minority ministerial students from Indiana who are attending a seminary in any state that is approved by the United Methodist Church (UMC).

Eligibility This program is open to members of ethnic minority groups who are candidates for ordination and certified by a District Committee of the Indiana Conference of the UMC. Applicants must be enrolled full time at an approved seminary in any state. They must be seeking ordination as a deacon or elder. Along with their application, they must submit documentation of financial need and a statement of their vocational goals.

Financial data Stipends are awarded at the rate of $100 per credit hour (per semester) and $200 per projected decade of service remaining (per semester).

Duration 1 year; may be renewed.

Number awarded 1 or more each year.

Deadline May of each year for fall semester; October of each year for spring semester.

[730]
JAISOHN JOURNALISM SCHOLARSHIP

Philip Jaisohn Memorial Foundation
Attn: Scholarship Committee
6705 Old York Road
Philadelphia, PA 19126
(215) 224-2000, ext. 116   Fax: (215) 224-9164
E-mail: info@jaisohn.org
Web: www.jaisohn.com/scholarships

Summary To provide financial assistance to Korean American undergraduate and graduate students who are working on a degree in journalism.

Eligibility This program is open to Korean American undergraduate and graduate students who are currently enrolled at a college or university in the United States. Applicants must be working on a degree in journalism. They must be able to demonstrate academic excellence, leadership and service to their school and community, and financial need. Along with their application, they must submit a 100-word essay on either "Who is Dr. Jaisohn to Me," or "The Significance of Dr. Jaisohn's Ideal to Korean Americans." They must also submit a brief statement on how they can contribute to and be involved in the activities of the Philip Jaisohn Memorial Foundation.

Financial data The stipend is $1,000.

Duration 1 year.

Number awarded 1 each year.

Deadline August of each year.

[731]
JAMES B. MORRIS SCHOLARSHIPS

James B. Morris Scholarship Fund
Attn: Scholarship Selection Committee
P.O. Box 12145
Des Moines, IA 50312
(515) 864-0922
Web: www.morrisscholarship.org

Summary To provide financial assistance to Asian American and other minority undergraduate, graduate, and law students from Iowa.

Eligibility This program is open to minority students (Asian/Pacific Islanders, African Americans, Hispanics, or Native Americans) who are interested in working on an undergraduate or graduate degree. Applicants must be either Iowa residents attending a college or university anywhere in the United States or non-Iowa residents who are attending a college or university in Iowa. Along with their application, they must submit an essay of 250 to 500 words on why they are applying for this scholarship, activities or organizations in which they are involved, and their future plans. Selection is based on the essay, academic achievement (GPA of 2.5 or

higher), community service, and financial need. U.S. citizenship is required.

Financial data The stipend ranges from $1,000 to $2,500 per year.

Duration 1 year; may be renewed.

Additional information This fund was established in 1978 in honor of the J.B. Morris family, who founded the Iowa branch of the National Association for the Advancement of Colored People and published the *Iowa Bystander* newspaper. The program includes the Ann Chapman Scholarships, the Vincent Chapman, Sr. Scholarships, the Catherine Williams Scholarships, and the Brittany Hall Memorial Scholarships. Support for additional scholarships is provided by EMC Insurance Group and Wells Fargo Bank.

Number awarded Varies each year; recently, 22 were awarded.

Deadline February of each year.

[732]
JAMES CARLSON MEMORIAL SCHOLARSHIP

Oregon Office of Student Access and Completion
Attn: Scholarship Processing Coordinator
1500 Valley River Drive, Suite 100
Eugene, OR 97401-2146
(541) 687-7422   Toll Free: (800) 452-8807, ext. 7422
Fax: (541) 687-7414   TDD: (800) 735-2900
E-mail: cheryl.a.connolly@state.or.us
Web: app.oregonstudentaid.gov/Catalog/Default.aspx

Summary To provide financial assistance to Oregon residents, especially Asian Americans and members of other diverse groups, who are majoring in education on the undergraduate or graduate school level at a school in any state.

Eligibility This program is open to residents of Oregon who are U.S. citizens or permanent residents and enrolled at a college or university in any state. Applicants must be either 1) college seniors or fifth-year students majoring in elementary or secondary education; or 2) graduate students working on an elementary or secondary certificate. Full-time enrollment and financial need are required. Priority is given to 1) students who come from diverse environments and submit an essay of 250 to 350 words on their experience living or working in diverse environments; 2) dependents of members of the Oregon Education Association; and 3) applicants committed to teaching autistic children.

Financial data Stipends for scholarships offered by the Oregon Office of Student Access and Completion (OSAC) range from $1,000 to $10,000 but recently averaged $4,368.

Duration 1 year; nonrenewable.

Additional information This program is administered by the OSAC with funds provided by the Oregon Community Foundation.

Number awarded Varies each year; recently, 3 were awarded.

Deadline February of each year.

[733]
JAMES E. WEBB INTERNSHIPS

Smithsonian Institution
Attn: Office of Fellowships and Internships
470 L'Enfant Plaza, Suite 7102
P.O. Box 37012, MRC 902
Washington, DC 20013-7012
(202) 633-7070   Fax: (202) 633-7069
E-mail: siofi@si.edu
Web: www.smithsonianofi.com

Summary To provide internship opportunities throughout the Smithsonian Institution to Asian American and other minority upper-division and graduate students in business or public administration.

Eligibility This program is open to minorities who are juniors, seniors, or graduate students majoring in areas of business or public administration (finance, human resource management, accounting, or general business administration). Applicants must have a GPA of 3.0 or higher. They must seek placement in offices, museums, and research institutes within the Smithsonian Institution.

Financial data Interns receive a stipend of $600 per week and a travel allowance.

Duration 10 weeks during the summer, fall, or spring.

Number awarded Varies each year; recently, 8 of these internships were awarded.

Deadline January of each year for summer or fall; September of each year for spring.

[734]
JAMES ECHOLS SCHOLARSHIP

California Association for Health, Physical Education,
   Recreation and Dance
Attn: Chair, Scholarship Committee
1501 El Camino Avenue, Suite 3
Sacramento, CA 95815-2748
(916) 922-3596   Toll Free: (800) 499-3596 (within CA)
Fax: (916) 922-0133   E-mail: reception@cahperd.org
Web: www.cahperd.org

Summary To provide financial assistance to Asian American and other minority student members of the California Association for Health, Physical Education, Recreation and Dance.

Eligibility This program is open to California residents who have been members of the association for at least 60 days and are attending a 2- or 4-year college or university in the state. Applicants must be undergraduate or graduate students working on a degree in health education, physical education, recreation, or dance and have completed at least 60 semester hours of college work. Selection is based on scholastic proficiency (a GPA of 3.0 or higher); leadership ability in school, community, and professional activities; and personal qualities of enthusiasm, cooperativeness, responsibility, initiative, and ability to work with others. This scholarship is awarded to the highest-ranked minority (Asian, African American, Latino, or Native American) applicant.

Financial data The stipend is $1,000.

Duration 1 year.

Number awarded 1 each year.

Deadline November of each year.

[735]
JANE C. WALDBAUM ARCHAEOLOGICAL FIELD SCHOOL SCHOLARSHIP

Archaeological Institute of America
c/o Boston University
656 Beacon Street, Sixth Floor
Boston, MA 02215-2006
(617) 358-4184   Fax: (617) 353-6550
E-mail: fellowships@aia.bu.edu
Web: www.archaeological.org/grants/708

Summary To provide funding to upper-division and graduate students, especially Asian Americans and other minorities, who are interested in participating in an archaeological field project in the United States or any other country.

Eligibility This program is open to junior and senior undergraduates and first-year graduate students who are currently enrolled at a college or university in the United States or Canada. Minority and disadvantaged students are encouraged to apply. Applicants must be interested in participating in an archaeological excavation or survey project in any country. They may not have previously participated in an archaeological excavation. Students majoring in archaeology or related disciplines are especially encouraged to apply.

Financial data The grant is $1,000.

Duration At least 1 month during the summer.

Additional information These scholarships were first awarded in 2007.

Number awarded Varies each year; recently, 15 were awarded.

Deadline February of each year.

[736]
JANE SONG MEMORIAL SCHOLARSHIPS

Philip Jaisohn Memorial Foundation
Attn: Scholarship Committee
6705 Old York Road
Philadelphia, PA 19126
(215) 224-2000, ext. 116   Fax: (215) 224-9164
E-mail: info@jaisohn.org
Web: www.jaisohn.com/scholarships

Summary To provide financial assistance to Korean American undergraduate and graduate students who are studying nursing.

Eligibility This program is open to Korean American undergraduate and graduate students who are currently enrolled at a college or university in the United States and working on a degree in nursing or other field of patient care. Applicants must be able to demonstrate excellence in community activities and financial need. Along with their application, they must submit an essay on either "Who is Dr. Jaisohn to Me," or "The Significance of Dr. Jaisohn's Ideal to Korean Americans." They must also submit a 100-word statement on how they can contribute to and be involved in the activities of the Philip Jaisohn Memorial Foundation. Selection is based on potential, passion, and leadership.

Financial data The stipend is $1,500.

Duration 1 year.

Number awarded 2 each year.

Deadline August of each year.

[737]
JAPANESE AMERICAN ASSOCIATION OF NEW YORK HONJO SCHOLARSHIP

Japanese American Association of New York, Inc.
Attn: Scholarship Committee
49 West 45th Street, 11th Floor
New York, NY 10036
(212) 840-6942   Fax: (212) 840-0616
E-mail: info@jaany.org
Web: www.jaany.org/honjo_scholarship.html

Summary   To provide financial assistance to graduate students of Japanese descent who are working on a degree at a school in the New York area in any field that will promote U.S.-Japan relations.

Eligibility   This program is open to graduate students of Japanese descent enrolled full time at a college or university in the New York area. Applicants may be working on a degree in any field (except medicine, music, studio art, or performing arts) that furthers U.S.-Japan relations. Along with their application, they must submit a resume, 2 letters of recommendation, undergraduate and graduate transcripts, and an essay of 500 to 750 words on how their current course of study will help further U.S.-Japan relations.

Financial data   The stipend ranges from $3,500 to $10,000.

Duration   1 year.

Additional information   This program is supported by the Honjo Foundation.

Number awarded   1 each year.

Deadline   February of each year.

[738]
JAPANESE AMERICAN ASSOCIATION OF NEW YORK MUSIC SCHOLARSHIP AWARDS

Japanese American Association of New York, Inc.
Attn: Scholarship Committee
49 West 45th Street, 11th Floor
New York, NY 10036
(212) 840-6942   Fax: (212) 840-0616
E-mail: info@jaany.org
Web: www.jaany.org/music_scholarship.html

Summary   To recognize and reward Japanese and Japanese American students who participate in a music competition.

Eligibility   This music competition is open to students who are Japanese or Americans of Japanese descent. Recently, the competition was limited to ensembles from trio to quintet; applicants performed 1 piece from the Classical era and another from the Romantic era or the 20th century at the recital in New York.

Financial data   Awards range from $2,000 to $5,000.

Duration   The competition is held annually.

Number awarded   2 each year.

Deadline   September of each year.

[739]
JAPANESE AMERICAN BAR ASSOCIATION EDUCATIONAL FOUNDATION SCHOLARSHIPS

Japanese American Bar Association
Attn: JABA Educational Foundation
P.O. Box 71961
Los Angeles, CA 90071
(323) 221-8900   E-mail: JEFscholarship@gmail.com
Web: www.jabaonline.org/scholarships

Summary   To provide financial assistance to law students who have participated in the Asian Pacific Islander (API) community.

Eligibility   This program is open to students currently enrolled in law school. Applicants must demonstrate an intention to practice law in southern California. Along with their application, they must submit a 500-word personal statement discussing their commitment to community service, involvement with the Japanese American and/or API community, and plans for using their law degree. Selection is based on service to the Asian Pacific American community, academic achievement, adversities overcome, desire to practice law in the southern California area, and financial need.

Financial data   The stipend is $2,000.

Duration   1 year.

Additional information   This program, which began in 1984, includes the Justice John F. Aiso Scholarship, the Justice Stephen K. Tamura Scholarship, and the Lim Ruger Foundation Scholarship (established in 2007).

Number awarded   3 each year.

Deadline   January of each year.

[740]
JAPANESE AMERICAN VETERANS ASSOCIATION MEMORIAL SCHOLARSHIPS

Japanese American Veterans Association
c/o Terry Shima, Outreach and Education Committee Chair
415 Russell Avenue, Number 1005
Gaithersburg, MD 20877
(301) 987-6746   E-mail: ttshima@comcast.net
Web: www.javadc.org

Summary   To provide financial assistance for college or graduate school to relatives of Japanese American veterans and military personnel.

Eligibility   This program is open to graduating high school seniors and students currently working on an undergraduate or graduate degree at a college, university, or school of specialized study. Applicants must be related, by blood or marriage, to 1) a person who served with the 442nd Regimental Combat Team, the 100th Infantry Battalion, or other unit associated with those; 2) a person who served in the U.S. Military Intelligence Service during or after World War II; 3) a person of Japanese ancestry who is serving or has served in the U.S. armed forces and been honorable discharged; or 4) a member of the Japanese American Veterans Association (JAVA) whose membership extends back at least 1 year.

Financial data   The stipend is $1,500.

Duration   1 year; recipients may reapply.

Additional information   These scholarships, first awarded in 2008, include the following named awards: the Orville C. Shirey Memorial Scholarship, the Joseph Ichiuji Memorial

Scholarship, the Phil and Douglas Ishio Scholarship, the Kiyoko Tsuboi Taubkin Scholarship, the Ranger Grant Hirabayashi Memorial Scholarship, the Victor and Teru Matsui Scholarship, the Betty Shima Scholarship, the Mitsugi Kasai Scholarship, and the U.S. Senator Daniel K. Inouye Scholarship.

Number awarded   10 each year.

Deadline   April of each year.

[741]
JAPANESE MEDICAL SOCIETY OF AMERICA SCHOLARSHIPS

Japanese Medical Society of America, Inc.
100 Park Avenue, Suite 1600
New York, NY 10017
(212) 351-5038   Fax: (212) 351-5047
E-mail: info@jmsa.org
Web: www.jmsa.org/student-members/about-scholarships

Summary   To provide funding to Japanese American medical school students, residents, and fellows who are interested in working on a project.

Eligibility   This program is open to Japanese Americans who are currently enrolled as medical students, residents, or fellows. Applicants must be proposing to conduct a project that will benefit the Japanese Medical Society of America (JMSA) and the Japanese community. Along with their application, they must submit a 1-page essay about themselves and what they will do to contribute to the JMSA. Selection is based on academic excellence and interest in JMSA.

Financial data   Stipends depend on the availability of funds, but have ranged from $2,500 to $20,000. Support is provided primarily for tuition, but a portion of the funds may be used to carry out the proposed project.

Duration   1 year.

Additional information   This program receives support from a number of sponsors, including the Honjo Foundation, Nishioka Foundation, Mitsui USA, Nippon Life, and Toyota USA.

Number awarded   Varies each year; recently, 11 were awarded.

Deadline   December of each year.

[742]
JAY LEE SOCIAL SERVICE SCHOLARSHIP

Philip Jaisohn Memorial Foundation
Attn: Scholarship Committee
6705 Old York Road
Philadelphia, PA 19126
(215) 224-2000, ext. 116   Fax: (215) 224-9164
E-mail: info@jaisohn.org
Web: www.jaisohn.com/scholarships

Summary   To provide financial assistance to Korean American undergraduate and graduate students who have participated in social service activities.

Eligibility   This program is open to Korean American undergraduate and graduate students who are currently enrolled at a college or university in the United States. Applicants must be able to demonstrate excellence in community service activities and financial need. Along with their application, they must submit a 100-word essay on either "Who is Dr. Jaisohn to Me," or "The Significance of Dr. Jaisohn's Ideal to

Korean Americans." They must also submit a brief statement on how they can contribute to and be involved in the activities of the Philip Jaisohn Memorial Foundation. Selection is based on community service and future potential.

Financial data   The stipend is $1,000.

Duration   1 year.

Number awarded   1 each year.

Deadline   August of each year.

[743]
JEAN LU STUDENT SCHOLARSHIP AWARD

Society of Toxicology
Attn: American Association of Chinese in Toxicology
  Special Interest Group
1821 Michael Faraday Drive, Suite 300
Reston, VA 20190-5348
(703) 438-3115   Fax: (703) 438-3113
E-mail: sothq@toxicology.org
Web: www.toxicology.org/ai/af/awards_details.aspx?id=126

Summary   To provide funding for research to graduate student members of the Society of Toxicology (SOT) who are of Chinese ethnic origin and working on a Ph.D. in the field.

Eligibility   This program is open to Chinese students (born in China or, if born in the United States, having 1 or more parents of Chinese descent) who are SOT members. Applicants must be enrolled full time in a Ph.D. program in toxicology and have been advanced to candidacy. Selection is based on academic achievement, demonstration of leadership, relevance of thesis to toxicology, and letters of recommendation. Finalists are interviewed by telephone.

Financial data   The stipend is $1,000. Funds may be used for payment of tuition and/or other educational and research-related expenses, including travel.

Duration   1 year.

Additional information   This program began in 2008.

Number awarded   1 each year.

Deadline   December of each year.

[744]
JEANNE SPURLOCK RESEARCH FELLOWSHIP IN SUBSTANCE ABUSE AND ADDICTION FOR MINORITY MEDICAL STUDENTS

American Academy of Child and Adolescent Psychiatry
Attn: Department of Research, Training, and Education
3615 Wisconsin Avenue, N.W.
Washington, DC 20016-3007
(202) 587-9663   Fax: (202) 966-5894
E-mail: training@aacap.org
Web: www.aacap.org

Summary   To provide funding to Asian American and other minority medical students who are interested in working during the summer on the topics of drug abuse and addiction with a child and adolescent psychiatrist researcher-mentor.

Eligibility   This program is open to Asian American, African American, Native American, Alaska Native, Mexican American, Hispanic, and Pacific Islander students in accredited U.S. medical schools. Applicants must present a plan for a program of research training in drug abuse and addiction that involves significant contact with a mentor who is an experienced child and adolescent psychiatrist researcher. The plan should include program planning discussions; instruction in research planning and implementation; regular meetings with the mentor, laboratory director, and research group; and assigned readings. The mentor must be a member of the American Academy of Child and Adolescent Psychiatry (AACAP). Research assignments may include responsibility for part of the observation or evaluation, developing specific aspects of the research mechanisms, conducting interviews or tests, using rating scales, and psychological or cognitive testing of subjects. The training plan also should include discussion of ethical issues in research, such as protocol development, informed consent, collection and storage of raw data, safeguarding data, bias in analyzing data, plagiarism, protection of patients, and ethical treatment of animals. U.S. citizenship or permanent resident status is required.

Financial data The stipend is $4,000. Fellows also receive reimbursement of travel expenses to attend the annual meeting of the American Academy of Child and Adolescent Psychiatry.

Duration 12 weeks during the summer.

Additional information Upon completion of the training program, the student is required to submit a brief paper summarizing the research experience. The fellowship pays expenses for the fellow to attend the academy's annual meeting and present this paper. This program is co-sponsored by the National Institute on Drug Abuse.

Number awarded Up to 5 each year.

Deadline February of each year.

[745]
JIM McKAY SCHOLARSHIP PROGRAM

National Collegiate Athletic Association
Attn: Jim McKay Scholarship Program Staff Liaison
700 West Washington Street
P.O. Box 6222
Indianapolis, IN 46206-6222
(317) 917-6683　　　　　　Fax: (317) 917-6888
E-mail: lthomas@ncaa.org
Web: www.ncaa.org/jim-mckay-scholarship-program

Summary To provide financial assistance to student-athletes, especially Asian Americans and other minorities, who are interested in attending graduate school to prepare for a career in sports communications.

Eligibility This program is open to college seniors planning to enroll full time in a graduate degree program and to students already enrolled full time in graduate study at an institution that is a member of the National Collegiate Athletic Association (NCAA). Applicants must have competed in intercollegiate athletics as a member of a varsity team at an NCAA member institution and have an overall undergraduate cumulative GPA of 3.5 or higher. They must be preparing for a career in the sports communications industry. Women and minorities are especially encouraged to apply. Neither financial need nor U.S. citizenship are required. Nominations must be submitted by the faculty athletics representative or chief academic officer at the institution in which the student is or was an undergraduate.

Financial data The stipend is $10,000.

Duration 1 year; nonrenewable.

Additional information This program began in 2008.

Number awarded 2 each year: 1 female and 1 male.

Deadline January of each year.

[746]
J.K. SASAKI MEMORIAL SCHOLARSHIPS

West Los Angeles United Methodist Church
Attn: Scholarship Committee
1913 Purdue Avenue
Los Angeles, CA 90025
(310) 479-1379　　　　　　Fax: (310) 478-7756
E-mail: wlaumc@aol.com
Web: www.wlaumc.org

Summary To provide financial assistance to Japanese American and other Asian American seminary students who are preparing for ordained ministry in the United Methodist Church.

Eligibility This program is open to Japanese American and other Asian American students at Protestant seminaries in the United States. Applicants must be planning to serve a Japanese American or Asian American congregation of the United Methodist Church as an ordained minister. They must have a GPA of 2.5 or higher. Along with their application, they must submit 2 essays (of 500 words each) on 1) their motivations for preparing for a career in the United Methodist Church; and 2) their concerns for the local church and the United Methodist Church with issues related to Asian Americans and/or Pacific Islanders.

Financial data Stipends range from $250 to $1,000.

Duration 1 year; recipients may reapply.

Additional information This program began in 1972 and given its current name in 2006.

Number awarded 1 or more each year.

Deadline February of each year.

[747]
JOANN JETER MEMORIAL DIVERSITY SCHOLARSHIP

Associates Foundation
Attn: Claudia Perot, Scholarship Committee Chair
JCD 6
P.O. Box 3621
Portland, OR 97208-3621
(503) 230-3754
Web: www.theassociatesonline.org

Summary To provide financial assistance to Asian American and other students who reflect elements of diversity and are interested in working on an undergraduate or graduate degree in any field.

Eligibility This program is open to students who are enrolled or planning to enroll as a full-time undergraduate or graduate student at an accredited 4-year college or university or a full-time student at a 2-year college enrolled in a program leading to an academic degree. Applicants must be from a diverse background, including first-generation college student, cultural and/or ethnic minority background, low-income, or other clearly articulated aspects of diversity as presented in an essay.

Financial data The stipend ranges from $500 to $1,000.

Duration 1 year.

Number awarded Varies each year; recently, 3 were awarded.

Deadline April of each year.

[748]
JOHN A. MAYES EDAC SCHOLARSHIP

National Athletic Trainers' Association
Attn: Ethnic Diversity Advisory Committee
1620 Valwood Parkway, Suite 115
Carrollton, TX 75006
(214) 637-6282   Toll Free: (800) 879-6282
Fax: (214) 637-2206
Web: www.nata.org

Summary To provide financial aid to Asian American and other ethnically diverse graduate students who are preparing for a career as an athletic trainer.

Eligibility This program is open to members of ethnically diverse groups who have been accepted into an entry-level master's athletic training degree program or into a doctoral-level athletic training and/or sports medicine degree program. Applicants must be sponsored by a certified athletic trainer who is a member of the National Athletic Trainers' Association (NATA). They must have a cumulative undergraduate GPA of 3.2 or higher. First priority is given to a student working on an entry-level athletic training master's degree; second priority is given to a student entering the second year of an athletic training master's degree program; third priority is given to a student working on a doctoral degree in athletic training or sports medicine. Special consideration is given to applicants who have been members of NATA for at least 2 years.

Financial data The stipend is $2,300.

Duration 1 year.

Additional information This program began in 2009.

Number awarded 1 each year.

Deadline February of each year.

[749]
JOHN AND MURIEL LANDIS SCHOLARSHIPS

American Nuclear Society
Attn: Scholarship Coordinator
555 North Kensington Avenue
La Grange Park, IL 60526-5535
(708) 352-6611   Toll Free: (800) 323-3044
Fax: (708) 352-0499   E-mail: outreach@ans.org
Web: committees.ans.org/need/apply.html

Summary To provide financial assistance to undergraduate or graduate students, especially Asian Americans and other minorities, who are interested in preparing for a career in nuclear-related fields and can demonstrate financial need.

Eligibility This program is open to undergraduate and graduate students at colleges or universities located in the United States who are preparing for, or planning to prepare for, a career in nuclear science, nuclear engineering, or a nuclear-related field. Qualified high school seniors are also eligible. Applicants must have greater than average financial need and have experienced circumstances that render them disadvantaged. Along with their application, they must submit an essay on their academic and professional goals, experiences that have affected those goals, etc. Selection is based on that essay, academic achievement, letters of recommendation, and financial need. Women and members of minority groups are especially urged to apply. U.S. citizenship is not required.

Financial data The stipend is $5,000, to be used to cover tuition, books, fees, room, and board.

Duration 1 year; nonrenewable.

Number awarded Up to 9 each year.

Deadline January of each year.

[750]
JOHN MCLENDON MEMORIAL MINORITY POSTGRADUATE SCHOLARSHIP AWARD

National Association of Collegiate Directors of Athletics
Attn: NACDA Foundation
24651 Detroit Road
Westlake, OH 44145
(440) 788-7474   Fax: (440) 892-4007
E-mail: knewman@nacda.com
Web: www.nacda.com/mclendon/scholarship.html

Summary To provide financial assistance to Asian American and other minority college seniors who are interested in working on a graduate degree in athletics administration.

Eligibility This program is open to minority college students who are seniors, are attending school on a full-time basis, have a GPA of 3.2 or higher, intend to attend graduate school to earn a degree in athletics administration, and are involved in college or community activities. Also eligible are college graduates who have at least 2 years' experience in an athletics administration position. Candidates must be nominated by an official of a member institution of the National Association of Collegiate Directors of Athletics (NACDA) or (for college graduates) a supervisor.

Financial data The stipend is $10,000.

Duration 1 year.

Additional information Recipients must maintain full-time status during the senior year to retain their eligibility. They must attend NACDA-member institutions.

Number awarded 5 each year.

Deadline Nominations must be submitted by April of each year.

[751]
JOHN STANFORD MEMORIAL WLMA SCHOLARSHIP

Washington Library Association-School Library Division
c/o Susan Kaphammer, Scholarship Chair
521 North 24th Avenue
Yakima, WA 98902
(509) 972-5999   E-mail: scholarships@wlma.org
Web: www.wla.org/school-scholarships

Summary To provide financial assistance to Asian Americans and other ethnic minorities in Washington who are interested in attending a school in any state to prepare for a library media career.

Eligibility This program is open to residents of Washington who are working toward a library media endorsement or graduate degree in the field at a school in any state. Applicants must be members of an ethnic minority group. They must be working or planning to work in a school library. Along with their application, they must submit a 3-page letter that includes a description of themselves and their achievements to date, their interest and work in the library field, their personal and professional activities, their goals and plans for further education and professional development, how they expect the studies funded by this award to impact their professional practice and contributions to the Washington school library community, and their financial need.

Financial data   The stipend is $1,000.

Duration   1 year.

Additional information   The School Library Division of the Washington Library Association was formerly the Washington Library Media Association (WLMA).

Number awarded   1 each year.

Deadline   May of each year.

[752]
JOHNSON & JOHNSON/AACN MINORITY NURSE FACULTY SCHOLARS PROGRAM

American Association of Colleges of Nursing
One Dupont Circle, N.W., Suite 530
Washington, DC 20036
(202) 463-6930   Fax: (202) 785-8320
E-mail: scholarship@aacn.nche.edu
Web: www.aacn.nche.edu/students/scholarships/minority

Summary   To provide fellowship/loans to Asian American and other minority students who are working on a graduate degree in nursing to prepare for a career as a faculty member.

Eligibility   This program is open to members of racial and ethnic minority groups (Asian American, Alaska Native, American Indian, Black or African American, Native Hawaiian or other Pacific Islander, or Hispanic or Latino) who are enrolled full time at a school of nursing. Applicants must be working on 1) a doctoral nursing degree (e.g., Ph.D., D.N.P.); or 2) a clinically-focused master's degree in nursing (e.g., M.S.N., M.S.). They must commit to 1) serve in a teaching capacity at a nursing school for a minimum of 1 year for each year of support they receive; 2) provide 6-month progress reports to the American Association of Colleges of Nursing (AACN) throughout the entire funding process and during the payback period; 3) agree to work with an assigned mentor throughout the period of the scholarship grant; and 4) attend an annual leadership training conference to connect with their mentor, fellow scholars, and colleagues. Selection is based on ability to contribute to nursing education; leadership potential; development of goals reflecting education, research, and professional involvement; ability to work with a mentor/adviser throughout the award period; proposed research and/or practice projects that are significant and show commitment to improving nursing education and clinical nursing practice in the United States; proposed research and/or clinical education professional development plan that exhibits quality, feasibility, and innovativeness; and evidence of commitment to a career in nursing education and to recruiting, mentoring, and retaining other underrepresented minority nurses. Preference is given to students enrolled in doctoral nursing programs. Applicants must be U.S. citizens, permanent residents, refugees, or qualified immigrants.

Financial data   The stipend is $18,000 per year. The award includes $1,500 that is held in escrow to cover the costs for the recipient to attend the leadership training conference. Recipients are required to sign a letter of commitment that they will provide 1 year of service in a teaching capacity at a nursing school in the United States for each year of support received; if they fail to complete that service requirement, they must repay all funds received.

Duration   1 year; may be renewed 1 additional year.

Additional information   This program, established in 2007, is sponsored by the Johnson & Johnson Campaign for Nursing's Future.

Number awarded   5 each year.

Deadline   April of each year.

[753]
JONATHAN T.Y. YEH MEMORIAL STUDENT PRIZE

American Folklore Society
Attn: Timothy Lloyd, Executive Director
Indiana University
Eigenmann Hall
1900 East Tenth Street
Bloomington, IN 47406
(812) 856-2379   Fax: (812) 856-2483
E-mail: timlloyd@indiana.edu
Web: www.afsnet.org/?page=YehAward

Summary   To recognize and reward outstanding student papers on a subject dealing with Asian and/or Asian American folklore.

Eligibility   This competition is open to full-time undergraduate and graduate students under 30 years of age. Applicants must submit a 10- to 12-page research paper dealing with Asian and/or Asian American folklore studies. They must be able to demonstrate prospects for publication of their scholarly work and a dedication to research and/or teaching folklore studies.

Financial data   The prize is $500.

Duration   The prize is awarded annually.

Additional information   This prize is awarded by the Transnational Asia/Pacific Section of the American Folklore Society (AFS).

Number awarded   1 each year.

Deadline   May of each year.

[754]
JOSEPHINE FORMAN SCHOLARSHIP

Society of American Archivists
Attn: Chair, Awards Committee
17 North State Street, Suite 1425
Chicago, IL 60602-4061
(312) 606-0722   Toll Free: (866) 722-7858
Fax: (312) 606-0728   E-mail: info@archivists.org
Web: www2.archivists.org

Summary   To provide financial assistance to Asian American and other minority graduate students working on a degree in archival science.

Eligibility   This program is open to members of minority groups (Asian, American Indian/Alaska Native, Black/African American, Hispanic/Latino, or Native Hawaiian/other Pacific Islander) currently enrolled in or accepted to a graduate program or a multi-course program in archival administration. The program must offer at least 3 courses in archival science and students may have completed no more than half of the credit requirements toward their graduate degree. Selection is based on potential for scholastic and personal achievement and commitment both to the archives profession and to advancing diversity concerns within it. U.S. citizenship or permanent resident status is required.

Financial data   The stipend is $10,000.

Duration 1 year.

Additional information Funding for this program, established in 2011, is provided by the General Commission on Archives and History of the United Methodist Church.

Number awarded 1 each year.

Deadline February of each year.

[755]
JOSIAH MACY JR. FOUNDATION SCHOLARSHIPS

National Medical Fellowships, Inc.
Attn: Scholarship Program
347 Fifth Avenue, Suite 510
New York, NY 10016
(212) 483-8880   Toll Free: (877) NMF-1DOC
Fax: (212) 483-8897 E-mail: scholarships@nmfonline.org
Web: www.nmfonline.org

Summary To provide financial assistance to Vietnamese, Cambodians, and other underrepresented minority medical students who demonstrate financial need.

Eligibility This program is open to Vietnamese, Cambodians, African Americans, Hispanics/Latinos, Native Americans, and Pacific Islanders who are entering their second or third year of medical school. They must be U.S. citizens or DACA students. Selection is based on leadership, commitment to serving medically underserved communities, and financial need.

Financial data A stipend is awarded (amount not specified).

Duration 1 year.

Additional information This program is sponsored by the Josiah Macy Jr. Foundation.

Number awarded 4 each year.

Deadline September of each year.

[756]
JOURNEY TOWARD ORDAINED MINISTRY SCHOLARSHIP

United Methodist Church
Attn: General Board of Higher Education and Ministry
Office of Loans and Scholarships
1001 19th Avenue South
P.O. Box 340007
Nashville, TN 37203-0007
(615) 340-7344   Fax: (615) 340-7367
E-mail: umscholar@gbhem.org
Web: www.gbhem.org

Summary To provide financial assistance to Asian American and other minority United Methodist students preparing for ministry at a Methodist-related institution.

Eligibility This program is open to members of racial or ethnic minority groups who are 30 years of age or younger and have been active, full members of a United Methodist Church for at least 2 years prior to applying. Applicants must be enrolled as full-time undergraduate or graduate students at a United Methodist-related institution in a program that leads to ordained ministry. Undergraduates must have a GPA of 2.85 or higher and graduate students must have a GPA of 3.0 or higher.

Financial data The stipend is $5,000.

Duration 1 year.

Number awarded 1 or more each year.

Deadline February of each year.

[757]
JTBF SUMMER JUDICIAL INTERNSHIP PROGRAM

Just the Beginning Foundation
c/o Maria Shade Harris, Chief Operating Officer
233 South Wacker Drive, Suite 6600
Chicago, IL 60606
(312) 258-5930   E-mail: mharris@jtb.org
Web: www.jtb.org/about/our-programs

Summary To provide work experience to Asian American and other minority and economically disadvantaged law students who plan to seek judicial clerkships after graduation.

Eligibility This program is open to students currently enrolled in their second or third year of law school who are members of minority or economically disadvantaged groups. Applicants must intend to work as a clerk in the federal or state judiciary upon graduation or within 5 years of graduation.

Financial data Program externs receive a summer stipend in an amount determined by the sponsor.

Duration Students must perform at least 35 hours per week of work for at least 8 weeks during the summer.

Additional information This program began in 2005. Law students are matched with federal and state judges across the country who provide assignments to the participants that will enhance their legal research, writing, and analytical skills (e.g., drafting memoranda). Students are expected to complete at least 1 memorandum of law or other key legal document each semester of the externship. Course credit may be offered, but students may not receive academic credit and a stipend simultaneously.

Number awarded Varies each year.

Deadline January of each year.

[758]
JUDGE EDWARD Y. KAKITA SCHOLARSHIP

Japanese American Bar Association
Attn: JABA Educational Foundation
P.O. Box 71961
Los Angeles, CA 90071
(323) 221-8900   E-mail: JEFscholarship@gmail.com
Web: www.jabaonline.org/scholarships

Summary To provide financial assistance to law students who have participated in the Asian Pacific Islander (API) community and are interested in international law, commercial litigation, and/or corporate law.

Eligibility This program is open to students currently enrolled in law school. Applicants must demonstrate an intention to practice law in southern California. Along with their application, they must submit a 500-word personal statement discussing their commitment to community service, involvement with the Japanese American and/or API community, and interest in international law, commercial litigation, and/or corporate law. Selection is based on service to the Asian Pacific American community; academic achievement; overcoming adversity; desire to practice law in the southern California area; desire to practice in the areas of international law, commercial litigation, and/or corporate law; and financial need.

Financial data   The stipend is $2,000.

Duration   1 year.

Additional information   This program began in 2006.

Number awarded   1 each year.

Deadline   January of each year.

[759]
JUDGE WILLIAM M. MARUTANI FELLOWSHIP

Philadelphia Bar Association
Attn: Foundation
1101 Market Street, 11th Floor
Philadelphia, PA 19107-2911
(215) 238-6347   Fax: (215) 238-1159
E-mail: jhilburnholmes@philabarfoundation.org
Web: www.philabarfoundation.org

Summary   To provide financial assistance to Asian Pacific American residents of any state who are enrolled at law schools in Pennsylvania, especially the Philadelphia area, and interested in a summer internship.

Eligibility   This program is open to Asian Pacific American first- or second-year law students at Dickinson School of Law, Rutgers-Camden University School of Law, Temple University James E. Beasley School of Law, University of Pennsylvania School of Law, Villanova University School of Law, Drexel University College of Law, Widener University School of Law, Duquesne University School of Law, and University of Pittsburgh School of Law. Applicants must be interested in taking a summer internship position with federal, state, or municipal government offices or agencies (including the judiciary) or nonprofit public interest organizations in the Greater Philadelphia area. Along with their application, they must submit a 2-page essay describing a life experience they have had or a personal/professional aspiration that would reflect the spirit and professional legacy of Judge William M. Marutani. Selection is based on that essay, law school transcripts, past and present work and community service experience, prior accomplishments and awards, and character.

Financial data   The stipend is $5,000.

Duration   10 weeks during the summer.

Additional information   This program was established by the Asian Pacific American Bar Association of Pennsylvania in conjunction with the Philadelphia Bar Foundation.

Number awarded   1 each year.

Deadline   March of each year.

[760]
JUDICIAL INTERN OPPORTUNITY PROGRAM

American Bar Association
Attn: Section of Litigation
321 North Clark Street
Chicago, IL 60654-7598
(312) 988-6348   Fax: (312) 988-6234
E-mail: Gail.Howard@americanbar.org
Web: www.americanbar.org

Summary   To provide an opportunity for Asian American and other minority and economically disadvantaged law students to gain experience as judicial interns in selected courts during the summer.

Eligibility   This program is open to first- and second-year students at ABA-accredited law schools who are 1) members of racial or ethnic groups that are traditionally underrepresented in the legal profession (Asians, African Americans, Hispanics/Latinos, Native Americans); 2) students with disabilities; 3) students who are economically disadvantaged; or 4) students who identify themselves as lesbian, gay, bisexual, or transgender. Applicants must be interested in a judicial internship at courts in selected areas and communities. They may indicate a preference for the area in which they wish to work, but they may not specify a court or a judge. Along with their application, they must submit a current resume, a 10-page legal writing sample, and a 2-page statement of interest that outlines their qualifications for the internship. Screening interviews are conducted by staff of the American Bar Association, either in person or by telephone. Final interviews are conducted by the judges with whom the interns will work. Some spots are reserved for students with an interest in intellectual property law.

Financial data   The stipend is $2,000.

Duration   6 weeks during the summer.

Additional information   Recently, internships were available in the following locations: Chicago along with surrounding cities and circuits throughout Illinois; Houston, Dallas, and the southern and eastern districts of Texas; Miami, Florida; Phoenix, Arizona; Los Angeles, California; New York City; Philadelphia, Pennsylvania; San Francisco, California; Seattle, Washington; and Washington, D.C. Some internships in Chicago, Los Angeles, Texas, and Washington, D.C. are reserved for students with an interest in intellectual property law.

Number awarded   Varies each year; recently, 194 of these internships were awarded, including 31 at courts in Illinois, 17 in Dallas, 14 in Houston, 14 in Miami, 17 in Phoenix, 23 in Los Angeles, 30 in San Francisco, 10 in New York, 12 in Philadelphia, 8 in Seattle, and 18 in Washington, D.C.

Deadline   January of each year.

[761]
JULIE CUNNINGHAM LEGACY SCHOLARSHIP

Conference of Minority Transportation Officials
Attn: National Scholarship Program
100 M Street, S.E., Suite 917
Washington, DC 20003
(202) 506-2917   E-mail: info@comto.org
Web: www.comto.org/page/scholarships

Summary   To provide financial assistance to Asian American and other minority graduate students who are working on a degree in transportation to prepare for a leadership role in that industry.

Eligibility   This program is open to minorities who are working on a graduate degree with an interest in leadership in transportation. Applicants must have a GPA of 3.0 or higher. They must be able to demonstrate strong leadership skills, active commitment to community service and diversity, and a commitment to the Conference of Minority Transportation Officials (COMTO) on a local or national level. Along with their application they must submit a cover letter on their transportation-related career goals and life aspirations. Financial need is not considered in the selection process.

Financial data   The stipend is $7,500. Funds are paid directly to the recipient's college or university.

Duration 1 year.
Number awarded 1 each year.
Deadline April of each year.

[762]
JUSTIN HARUYAMA MINISTERIAL SCHOLARSHIP

Japanese American United Church
Attn: Haruyama Scholarship Committee
255 Seventh Avenue
New York, NY 10001
(212) 242-9444   Fax: (212) 242-5274
E-mail: ministryjauc@gmail.com
Web: www.jauc.org/haruyama

Summary To provide financial assistance to Protestant seminary students who are interested in serving Japanese American congregations.

Eligibility This program is open to students of Japanese ancestry who are enrolled full time at an accredited Protestant seminary in the United States. Applicants must be working on a ministerial degree in order to serve Japanese American congregations. Along with their application, they must submit 2 letters of recommendation, a transcript of grades, information on their financial situation, and a brief statement of their spiritual journey.

Financial data The stipend is $500.

Duration 1 year; may be renewed.

Number awarded Varies each year; recently, 6 were awarded.

Deadline May of each year.

[763]
KAISER PERMANENTE COLORADO DIVERSITY SCHOLARSHIP PROGRAM

Kaiser Permanente
Attn: Diversity Development Department
10065 East Harvard Avenue, Suite 400
Denver, CO 80231
Toll Free: (877) 457-4772
E-mail: co-diversitydevelopment@kp.org

Summary To provide financial assistance to Colorado residents who are Asian Pacific Americans or members of other diverse groups and interested in working on an undergraduate or graduate degree in a health care field at a public college in the state.

Eligibility This program is open to all residents of Colorado, including those who identify as 1 or more of the following: Asian Pacific, African American, Latino, lesbian, gay, bisexual, transgender, intersex, Native American, U.S. veteran, and/or a person with a disability. Applicants must be enrolled or planning to enroll full time at a publicly-funded college, university, or technical school in Colorado as 1) a graduating high school senior with a GPA of 2.7 or higher; 2) a GED recipient with a GED score of 520 or higher; 3) an undergraduate student; or 4) a graduate or doctoral student. They must be preparing for a career in health care (e.g., athletic training, audiology, cardiovascular perfusion technology, clinical medical assisting, cytotechnology, dental assisting, dental hygiene, diagnostic medicine, dietetics, emergency medical technology, medicine, nursing, occupational therapy, pharmacy, phlebotomy, physical therapy, physician assistant, radiology, respiratory therapy, social work, sports medicine, surgical technology). Selection is based on academic achievement, character qualities, community outreach and volunteering, and financial need.

Financial data Stipends range from $1,400 to $2,600 per year.

Duration 1 year; may be renewed.

Number awarded Varies each year; recently, 17 were awarded.

Deadline March of each year.

[764]
KALPANA CHAWLA SCHOLARSHIP AWARD

American Society of Engineers of Indian Origin
Attn: Scholarship Program
P.O. Box 18215
Irvine, CA 92623
E-mail: scholarships@aseiusa.org
Web: www.aseiusa.org

Summary To provide financial assistance to graduate students of Indian origin (from India) who are working on a degree in aerospace engineering.

Eligibility This program is open to graduate students of Indian origin (by birth, ancestry, or relation). Applicants must be enrolled full time at an accredited college or university in the United States and working on a degree in aerospace engineering with a GPA of 3.7 or higher. They must be members of the American Society of Engineers of Indian Origin (ASEI) Selection is based on academic achievement, technical expertise, and leadership excellence.

Financial data The stipend is $2,000.

Duration 1 year.

Additional information This program began in 2003 to honor Kalpana Chawla, an astronaut who lost her life on the Columbia shuttle.

Number awarded 1 each year.

Deadline August of each year.

[765]
KAY LONGCOPE SCHOLARSHIP AWARD

National Lesbian & Gay Journalists Association
2120 L Street, N.W., Suite 850
Washington, DC 20037
(202) 588-9888   Fax: (202) 588-1818
E-mail: info@nlgfa.org
Web: www.nlgja.org/resources/longcope

Summary To provide financial assistance to Asian American and other lesbian, gay, bisexual, and transgender (LGBT) undergraduate and graduate students of color who are interested in preparing for a career in journalism.

Eligibility This program is open to LGBT students of color who are current or incoming undergraduate or graduate students at a college, university, or community college. Applicants must be planning a career in journalism and be committed to furthering the sponsoring organization's mission of fair and accurate coverage of the LGBT community. They must demonstrate an awareness of the issues facing the LGBT community and the importance of fair and accurate news coverage. For undergraduates, a declared major in journalism and/or communications is desirable but not required; non-journalism majors may demonstrate their commitment to a journalism career through work samples, internships, and work on a school news publication, online news service, or broadcast affiliate. Graduate students must be enrolled in a journalism program. Along with their application, they must submit a 1-page resume, 5 work samples, official transcripts, 3 letters of recommendation, and a 750-word news story on a designated subject involving the LGBT community. U.S. citizenship or permanent resident status is required. Selection is based on journalistic and scholastic ability.

Financial data   The stipend is $3,000.

Duration   1 year.

Additional information   This program began in 2008.

Number awarded   1 each year.

Deadline   May of each year.

[766]
KENNETH B. AND MARNIE P. CLARK FUND

American Psychological Foundation
750 First Street, N.E.
Washington, DC 20002-4242
(202) 336-5843   Fax: (202) 336-5812
E-mail: foundation@apa.org
Web: www.apa.org/apf/funding/clark-fund.aspx

Summary   To provide funding to psychologists, especially Asian Americans and members of other groups that will contribute to diversity, who wish to conduct a project related to academic achievement in children.

Eligibility   This program is open to psychologists who wish to conduct research or development activities that promote the understanding of the relationship between self-identity and academic achievement with an emphasis on children in grade levels K-8. Eligibility alternates between graduate students in odd-numbered years and early-career (within 10 years of completion of postdoctoral work) psychologists. Selection is based on conformance with stated program goals and qualifications; quality and potential impact of proposed work; originality, innovation, and contribution to the field with the proposed project; and applicant's demonstrated competence and capability to execute the proposed work. The sponsor encourages applications from individuals who represent diversity in race, ethnicity, gender, age, disability, and sexual orientation.

Financial data   The grant is $10,000.

Duration   1 year.

Additional information   This program began in 2012.

Number awarded   1 each year.

Deadline   June of each year.

[767]
KENNETH B. CHANG MEMORIAL SCHOLARSHIPS

Korean American Bar Association of Southern California
c/o Joann H. Lee
Legal Aid Foundation of Los Angeles
1102 Crenshaw Boulevard
Los Angeles, CA 90019
(323) 801-7976   E-mail: kabascholarship@gmail.com
Web: www.kabasocal.org/about-us/scholarships

Summary   To provide financial assistance to students from any state who are enrolled at law schools in southern Califor-

nia and have been active in the Asian Pacific Islander and/or Korean American community.

Eligibility   This program is open to students from any state currently enrolled at law schools in southern California. Applicants must be able to demonstrate a commitment to serving the Korean American community and/or Asian Pacific Islander community through past, current, or future contributions. Students are evaluated on the basis of their written applications and an interview. Financial need may also be a factor.

Financial data   Stipends range from $1,000 to $2,000.

Duration   1 year.

Additional information   This program is supported by the law firm of Kim Ruger & Kim.

Number awarded   Varies each year.

Deadline   April of each year.

[768]
KENTUCKY LIBRARY ASSOCIATION SCHOLARSHIP FOR MINORITY STUDENTS

Kentucky Library Association
c/o Executive Director
5932 Timber Ridge Drive, Suite 101
Prospect, KY 40059
(502) 223-5322   Fax: (502) 223-4937
E-mail: info@kylibasn.org
Web: www.klaonline.org/scholarships965.cfm

Summary   To provide financial assistance to Asian Americans or members of othr minority groups who are residents of Kentucky or attending school there and are working on an undergraduate or graduate degree in library science.

Eligibility   This program is open to members of minority groups (defined as American Indian, Alaskan Native, Black, Hispanic, Pacific Islander, or other ethnic group) who are entering or continuing at a graduate library school accredited by the American Library Association (ALA) or an undergraduate library program accredited by the National Council for Teacher Education (NCATE). Applicants must be residents of Kentucky or a student in a library program in the state. Along with their application, they must submit a statement of their career objectives, why they have chosen librarianship as a career, and their reasons for applying for this scholarship. Selection is based on that statement, cumulative undergraduate and graduate GPA (if applicable), academic merit and potential, and letters of recommendation. U.S. citizenship or permanent resident status is required.

Financial data   The stipend is $1,000.

Duration   1 year; nonrenewable.

Number awarded   1 or more each year.

Deadline   June of each year.

[769]
KENTUCKY MINORITY EDUCATOR RECRUITMENT AND RETENTION SCHOLARSHIPS

Kentucky Department of Education
Attn: Office of Next-Generation Learners
500 Mero Street, 19th Floor
Frankfort, KY 40601
(502) 564-1479   Fax: (502) 564-4007
TDD: (502) 564-4970
E-mail: jennifer.baker@education.ky.gov
Web: www.education.ky.gov

Summary To provide forgivable loans to Asian Americans and other minority undergraduate and graduate students enrolled in Kentucky public institutions who want to become teachers.

Eligibility This program is open to residents of Kentucky who are undergraduate or graduate students pursuing initial teacher certification at a public university or community college in the state. Applicants must have a GPA of 2.75 or higher and either maintain full-time enrollment or be a part-time student within 18 semester hours of receiving a teacher education degree. They must be U.S. citizens and meet the Kentucky definition of a minority student.

Financial data Stipends are $5,000 per year at the 8 state universities in Kentucky or $2,000 per year at community and technical colleges. This is a scholarship/loan program. Recipients are required to teach 1 semester in Kentucky for each semester or summer term the scholarship is received. If they fail to fulfill that requirement, the scholarship converts to a loan payable at 6% annually.

Duration 1 year; may be renewed up to 3 additional years.

Additional information The Kentucky General Assembly established this program in 1992.

Number awarded Varies each year.

Deadline Each state college of teacher education sets its own deadline.

[770]
KOREAN AMERICAN BAR ASSOCIATION OF WASHINGTON SCHOLARSHIP

Korean American Bar Association of Washington
c/o Pia Kamimura, Scholarship Chair
Two Dogs Barking Productions
704 Court A
Tacoma, WA 98402
(253) 970-1900   E-mail: piakim@gmail.com
Web: www.kaba-washington.org/for-students

Summary To provide financial assistance to students from any state who are enrolled at law schools in Washington and have a record of service to the Korean community.

Eligibility This program is open to residents of any state currently enrolled at law schools in Washington. Applicants are not required to be of Korean ancestry, but they must have a demonstrated significant commitment to community service, particularly service to the Korean or Korean American community. Along with their application, they must submit a 2-page essay on either 1) what they see as a challenge facing the Korean American community and how their contribution to the legal profession can help address those challenges; or 2) the challenges they believe minorities and the greater minority bar face in the legal profession today and how their involvement with the sponsoring organization can help address those challenges. Selection is based on the essay, community service and involvement, personal goals and achievements, and an interview.

Financial data The stipend ranges from $1,000 to $4,000.

Duration 1 year.

Number awarded 1 to 3 each year.

Deadline January of each year.

[771]
KOREAN AMERICAN CHRISTIAN SCHOLARSHIP FOUNDATION OF GREATER WASHINGTON SCHOLARSHIPS

Korean American Christian Scholarship Foundation of
  Greater Washington
7024 Highland Meadows Court
Alexandria, VA 22315
E-mail: sangkuenpark@gmail.com
Web: www.kapastorscholarship.org/?page_id=2

Summary To provide financial assistance to theology students who plan to become pastors serving Korean Americans.

Eligibility This program is open to Christian students who are entering or attending an approved theological seminary. Applicants must have a clear purpose to serve the second and third generations of Korean Americans. They must be U.S. citizens or permanent residents living in any state. Along with their application, they must submit a letter of recommendation (in Korean or English) from their senior pastor, transcripts, a testimony of faith, and information on financial status.

Financial data A stipend is awarded (amount not specified).

Duration 1 year.

Number awarded 10 to 12 each year.

Deadline April of each year.

[772]
KOREAN HONOR SCHOLARSHIP

Embassy of the Republic of Korea in the USA
2320 Massachusetts Avenue, N.W.
Washington, DC 20008
(202) 939-5679   Fax: (202) 342-1597
Web: usa.mofa.go.kr

Summary To provide financial assistance to undergraduate and graduate students of Korean or Korean American heritage.

Eligibility This program is open to students of Korean or Korean American heritage. Applicants must be entering or enrolled full time in an undergraduate or graduate degree program at a college or university in the United States or Canada. They must have a GPA of 3.5 or higher (3.0 or higher for students in music or art). Along with their application, they must submit a 600-word essay (in English) on a topic that changes annually but relates to their Korean heritage. Selection is based on that essay, academic achievement, awards, honors, performances, extracurricular activities, and a letter of recommendation. Students with disabilities are especially encouraged to apply.

Financial data The stipend is $3,000 or $1,000.

Duration 1 year; nonrenewable.

Additional information This program began in 1981 when the government of the Republic of Korea donated $1 million to commemorate the 100th anniversary of the establishment of diplomatic relations between Korea and the United States. Subsequent donations have added to the fund.

Number awarded 1 at $3,000 and approximately 35 each year at $1,000 (including 2 or 3 for students in music or art and 1 or 2 for students with disabilities). Since the program began, it has awarded more than 3,000 of these scholarships.

Deadline June of each year.

[773]
KOREAN NURSES ASSOCIATION OF SOUTHERN CALIFORNIA REGISTERED NURSE EDUCATION SCHOLARSHIPS

Korean Nurses Association of Southern California
1254 West Sixth Street, Suite 809
Los Angeles, CA 90017
(213) 434-1019   E-mail: kanascrn@gmail.com
Web: www.koamrn.org

Summary To provide financial assistance to Korean nurses in California who wish to attend college in southern California to work on a bachelor's or graduate degree.

Eligibility This program is open to Korean registered nurses who are enrolled or entering a baccalaureate or higher degree nursing program in southern California. Applicants must be citizens or permanent residents of the United States. Along with their application, they must submit a 1-page essay on their reasons for selecting nursing as a career, including their professional goals and objectives. Selection is based on that essay, work experience in nursing and related fields, community service and volunteer work experience, cumulative GPA, and letters of recommendation. Priority consideration is given to members of the Korean Nurses Association of Southern California and their immediate family members.

Financial data A stipend is awarded (amount not specified).

Duration 1 year; may be renewed 1 additional year.

Number awarded 1 or more each year.

Deadline November of each year.

[774]
KOREAN TOXICOLOGISTS ASSOCIATION IN AMERICA BEST PRESENTATIONS BY GRADUATE STUDENT AND POSTDOCTORAL TRAINEE AWARD

Society of Toxicology
Attn: Korean Toxicologists Association in America Special
   Interest Group
1821 Michael Faraday Drive, Suite 300
Reston, VA 20190-5348
(703) 438-3115   Fax: (703) 438-3113
E-mail: sothq@toxicology.org
Web: www.toxicology.org/ai/af/awards_details.aspx?id=125

Summary To recognize and reward graduate students and postdoctoral trainees who present outstanding papers at a session of the Korean Toxicologists Association in America (KTAA) at the annual meeting of the Society of Toxicology (SOT).

Eligibility This award is available to graduate students and postdoctoral trainees who have an accepted abstract of a research poster or platform presentation for a KTAA session at the SOT annual meeting. Along with the abstract, they must submit a letter of nomination from their major adviser.

Financial data A plaque and a cash award (amount not specified) are presented.

Duration The awards are presented annually.

Additional information These awards are presented jointly by KTAA and the Korean Institute of Toxicology (KIT).

Number awarded 2 each year.

Deadline January of each year.

[775]
KOREAN-AMERICAN ADVENTIST SCHOLARSHIP FOUNDATION

Korean-American Adventist Scholarships
c/o Korean Adventist Press
619 South New Hampshire Avenue
Los Angeles, CA 90005
(213) 388-6100   E-mail: sdascholarship@gmail.com
Web: www.sdascholarship.org/?page_id=15

Summary To provide financial assistance to Korean-American Adventists who are interested in working on an undergraduate or graduate degree in any field.

Eligibility This program is open to Korean-American Adventists who are high school seniors or students currently enrolled in college or graduate school. Applicants must have a GPA of 3.0 or higher. Along with their application, they must submit a 1- to 2-page personal essay that describes their personal history, life passions, long-term goals, and financial situation. Their pastor must provide an evaluation of their spiritual dedication, motivation, citizenship, church activities, academic achievement, and financial need.

Financial data The stipend is $1,000.

Duration 1 year.

Additional information This program began in 2004.

Number awarded 20 each year.

Deadline May of each year.

[776]
KSEA-KUSCO SCHOLARSHIPS FOR GRADUATE STUDENTS

Korean-American Scientists and Engineers Association
Attn: Scholarship Committee
1952 Gallows Drive, Suite 300
Vienna, VA 22182
(703) 748-1221   Fax: (703) 748-1331
E-mail: hq@ksea.org
Web: scholarship.ksea.org/InfoGraduate.aspx

Summary To provide financial assistance to graduate student members of the Korean-American Scientists and Engineers Association (KSEA) studying Korea-U.S. science and technology cooperation.

Eligibility This program is open to graduate students at colleges and universities in the United States who are either 1) of Korean heritage; or 2) non-ethnic Korean students working on a degree related to Korea-U.S. science and technology cooperation. Applicants must be KSEA members working on a degree in science, engineering, or a related field. Along with their application, they must submit an essay of 600 to 800 words on a topic that changes annually but relates to cooperation in science. Selection is based on that essay (25%), KSEA activities and community service (25%), recommendation letters (20%), and academic performance (30%).

Financial data The stipend is $1,500.

Duration 1 year.

Additional information This program, established in 2005, is supported by the Korea-US Science Cooperation Center (KUSCO).

Number awarded Approximately 20 each year.

Deadline March of each year.

[777]
LAGRANT FOUNDATION GRADUATE SCHOLARSHIPS

Lagrant Foundation
Attn: Senior Talent Acquisition and Fundraising Manager
633 West Fifth Street, 48th Floor
Los Angeles, CA 90071
(323) 469-8680, ext. 223   Fax: (323) 469-8683
E-mail: erickainiguez@lagrant.com
Web: www.lagrantfoundation.org

Summary To provide financial assistance to Asian American and other minority graduate students who are working on a degree in advertising, public relations, or marketing.

Eligibility This program is open to Asian American/Pacific Islanders, African Americans, Hispanics/Latinos, and Native Americans/American Indians who are full-time graduate students at an accredited institution. Applicants must have a GPA of 3.2 or higher and be working on a master's degree in advertising, marketing, or public relations. They must have at least 2 academic semesters remaining to complete their degree. Along with their application, they must submit 1) a 1- to 2-page essay outlining their career goals; why it is important to increase ethnic representation in the fields of advertising, marketing, and public relations; and the role of an advertising, marketing, or public relations practitioner; 2) a paragraph describing the graduate school and/or community activities in which they are involved; 3) a brief paragraph describing any honors and awards they have received; 4) a letter of reference; 5) a resume; and 6) an official transcript. U.S. citizenship or permanent resident status is required.

Financial data The stipend is $5,000.

Duration 1 year.

Number awarded Varies each year; recently, 19 were awarded.

Deadline February of each year.

[778]
LAURENCE R. FOSTER MEMORIAL SCHOLARSHIPS

Oregon Office of Student Access and Completion
Attn: Scholarship Processing Coordinator
1500 Valley River Drive, Suite 100
Eugene, OR 97401-2146
(541) 687-7422   Toll Free: (800) 452-8807, ext. 7422
Fax: (541) 687-7414   TDD: (800) 735-2900
E-mail: cheryl.a.connolly@state.or.us
Web: app.oregonstudentaid.gov/Catalog/Default.aspx

Summary To provide financial assistance to residents of Oregon, especially Asian Americans and others from diverse

backgrounds, who are enrolled at a college or graduate school in any state to prepare for a public health career.

Eligibility This program is open to residents of Oregon who are enrolled at least half time at a 4-year college or university in any state to prepare for a career in public health (not private practice). Preference is given first to applicants from diverse environments; second to persons employed in, or graduate students working on a degree in, public health; and third to juniors and seniors majoring in a health program (e.g., nursing, medical technology, physician assistant). Applicants must be able to demonstrate financial need. Along with their application, they must submit essays of 250 to 350 words on 1) what public health means to them; 2) the public health aspect they intend to practice and the health and population issues impacted by that aspect; and 3) their experience living or working in diverse environments.

Financial data Stipends for scholarships offered by the Oregon Office of Student Access and Completion (OSAC) range from $1,000 to $10,000 but recently averaged $4,368.

Duration 1 year.

Additional information This program is administered by the OSAC with funds provided by the Oregon Community Foundation.

Number awarded Varies each year; recently, 6 were awarded.

Deadline February of each year.

[779]
LAW SCHOLARSHIPS OF THE JAPANESE AMERICAN CITIZENS LEAGUE

Japanese American Citizens League
Attn: National Scholarship Awards
1765 Sutter Street
San Francisco, CA 94115
(415) 345-1075   Fax: (415) 345-1077
E-mail: pwada@jacl.org
Web: www.jacl.org/jacl-national-scholarship-program

Summary To provide financial assistance to student members of the Japanese American Citizens League (JACL) who are interested in preparing for a career in law.

Eligibility This program is open to JACL members who are currently enrolled or planning to enroll at an accredited law school. Applicants must submit information on their involvement in JACL and a 2-page essay on a topic that changes annually but relates to Japanese Americans. Selection is based on that essay, academic history, JACL involvement, school activities, work history, scholastic honors, and community involvement.

Financial data Stipends generally average more than $2,000.

Duration 1 year; nonrenewable.

Additional information This program consists of the following named awards: the Grace Andow Memorial Scholarship, the Mary Reiko Osaka Memorial Scholarship, the Sho Sato Memorial Scholarship, and the Thomas T. Hayashi Memorial Scholarship.

Number awarded 4 each year.

Deadline March of each year.

[780]
LEADERSHIP FOR DIVERSITY SCHOLARSHIP

California School Library Association
Attn: CSL Foundation
6444 East Spring Street, Number 237
Long Beach, CA 90815-1553
Toll Free: (888) 655-8480   Fax: (888) 655-8480
E-mail: info@csla.net
Web: www.csla.net/awards-2/scholarships

Summary   To provide financial assistance to students who reflect the diversity of California's population and are interested in earning a credential as a library media teacher in the state.

Eligibility   This program is open to students who are Asian Americans or members of other traditionally underrepresented groups enrolled in a college or university library media teacher credential program in California. Applicants must intend to work as a library media teacher in a California school library media center for a minimum of 3 years. Along with their application, they must submit a 250-word statement on what they can contribute to the profession, their commitment to serving the needs of multicultural and multilingual students, and their financial need.

Financial data   The stipend is $1,500.

Duration   1 year.

Number awarded   1 each year.

Deadline   September of each year.

[781]
LEADERSHIP LEGACY SCHOLARSHIP FOR GRADUATES

Women's Transportation Seminar
Attn: WTS Foundation
1701 K Street, N.W., Suite 800
Washington, DC 20006
(202) 955-5085   Fax: (202) 955-5088
E-mail: wts@wtsinternational.org
Web: www.wtsinternational.org/education/scholarships

Summary   To provide financial assistance to graduate women, especially Asian Americans and other minorities, interested in a career in transportation.

Eligibility   This program is open to women who are working on a graduate degree in transportation or a transportation-related field (e.g., transportation engineering, planning, business management, finance, or logistics). Applicants must have a GPA of 3.0 or higher and be interested in a career in transportation. Along with their application, they must submit a 1,000-word statement about their vision of how their education will give them the tools to better serve their community's needs and transportation issues. Applications must be submitted first to a local chapter; the chapters forward selected applications for consideration on the national level. Minority women are especially encouraged to apply. Selection is based on transportation involvement and goals, job skills, and academic record; financial need is not considered.

Financial data   The stipend is $5,000.

Duration   1 year.

Additional information   This program began in 2008. Each year, it focuses on women with a special interest; recently, it was reserved for women who have a specific interest in addressing the impact of transportation on sustainabil-

ity, land use, environmental impact, security, and quality of life issues internationally.

Number awarded   1 each year.

Deadline   Applications must be submitted by November to a local WTS chapter.

[782]
LEON BRADLEY SCHOLARSHIPS

American Association of School Personnel Administrators
Attn: Scholarship Program
11863 West 112th Street, Suite 100
Overland Park, KS 66210
(913) 327-1222   Fax: (913) 327-1223
E-mail: aaspa@aaspa.org
Web: www.aaspa.org/leon-bradley-scholarship

Summary   To provide financial assistance to Asian American and other minority undergraduates, paraprofessionals, and graduate students preparing for a career in teaching and school leadership at colleges in designated southeastern states.

Eligibility   This program is open to members of minority groups (Asian, American Indian, Alaskan Native, Pacific Islander, Black, Hispanic, Middle Easterner) currently enrolled full time at a college or university in Alabama, Florida, Georgia, Kentucky, North Carolina, South Carolina, Tennessee, or Virginia. Applicants must be 1) undergraduates in their final year (including student teaching) of an initial teaching certification program; 2) paraprofessional career-changers in their final year (including student teaching) of an initial teaching certification program; or 3) graduate students who have served as a licensed teacher and are working on a school administrator credential. They must have an overall GPA of 3.0 or higher. Priority is given to applicants who 1) can demonstrate work experience that has been applied to college expenses; 2) have received other scholarship or financial aid support; or 3) are seeking initial certification and/or endorsement in a state-identified critical area.

Financial data   Stipends are $2,500 for undergraduates in their final year, $1,500 for paraprofessionals in their final year, and $1,500 for graduate students.

Duration   1 year.

Number awarded   4 each year: 1 undergraduate, 1 paraprofessional, and 2 graduate students.

Deadline   May of each year.

[783]
LIBRARY AND INFORMATION TECHNOLOGY ASSOCIATION MINORITY SCHOLARSHIPS

American Library Association
Attn: Library and Information Technology Association
50 East Huron Street
Chicago, IL 60611-2795
(312) 280-4270   Toll Free: (800) 545-2433, ext. 4270
Fax: (312) 280-3257   TDD: (888) 814-7692
E-mail: lita@ala.org
Web: www.ala.org/lita/awards

Summary   To provide financial assistance to Asian American and other minority graduate students interested in preparing for a career in library automation.

Eligibility   This program is open to U.S. or Canadian citizens who are interested in working on a master's degree in library/information science and preparing for a career in the field of library and automated systems. Applicants must be a member of 1 of the following ethnic groups: Asian, Pacific Islander, American Indian, Alaskan Native, African American, or Hispanic. They may not have completed more than 12 credit hours of course work for their degree. Selection is based on academic excellence, leadership potential, evidence of a commitment to a career in library automation and information technology, and prior activity and experience in those fields. Financial need is considered when all other factors are equal.

Financial data Stipends are $3,000 or $2,500. Funds are paid directly to the recipient.

Duration 1 year.

Additional information This program includes scholarships funded by Online Computer Library Center (OCLC) and by Library Systems & Services, Inc. (LSSI).

Number awarded 2 each year: 1 at $3,000 (funded by OCLC) and 1 at $2,500 (funded by LSSI).

Deadline February of each year.

[784]
LIBRARY OF CONGRESS JUNIOR FELLOWS PROGRAM

Library of Congress
Library Services
Attn: Junior Fellows Program Coordinator
101 Independence Avenue, S.E., Room LM-642
Washington, DC 20540-4600
(202) 707-6610   Fax: (202) 707-6269
E-mail: jrfell@loc.gov
Web: www.loc.gov/hr/jrfellows/index.html

Summary To provide summer work experience at the Library of Congress (LC) to upper-division and graduate students and to recent graduates, especially Asian Americans and members of other underrepresented groups.

Eligibility This program is open to U.S. citizens with subject expertise in the following areas: collections preservation; geography and maps; humanities, art, and culture; information technology; library sciences; or chemistry and science. Applicants must 1) be juniors or seniors at an accredited college or university; 2) be graduate students; or 3) have completed their degree in the past year. Women, minorities, and persons with disabilities are strongly encouraged to apply. Selection is based on academic achievement, letters of recommendation, and an interview.

Financial data Fellows are paid a taxable stipend of $3,000.

Duration 10 weeks, beginning in either May or June. Fellows work a 40-hour week.

Additional information Fellows work with primary source materials and assist selected divisions at LC in the organization and documentation of archival collections, production of finding aids and bibliographic records, preparation of materials for preservation and service, completion of bibliographical research, and digitization of LC's historical collections.

Number awarded Varies each year; recently, 38 were awarded.

Deadline January of each year.

[785]
LILY PABILONA EMERGING ENTREPRENEUR SCHOLARSHIP

Against the Grain Productions
3523 McKinney Avenue, Suite 231
Dallas, TX 75204
E-mail: outreach@againstthegrainproductions.com
Web: www.againstthegrainproductions.com

Summary To provide financial assistance to Asian and Pacific Island students working on an undergraduate or graduate degree in entrepreneurship.

Eligibility This program is open to high school seniors and current full-time students at accredited 2- and 4-year colleges and universities and vocational schools. Applicants must be of at least 50% Asian and/or Pacific Islander ethnicity and U.S. citizens, nationals, or permanent residents. They must be working on a degree in entrepreneurship and have a GPA of 3.0 or higher. Selection is based on an essay, academic performance, leadership and community service, letters of recommendation, and an interview.

Financial data The stipend is $5,000. Funds are disbursed directly to the educational institution.

Duration 1 year.

Additional information This program began in 2016.

Number awarded 2 each year.

Deadline May of each year.

[786]
LINDA YU BROADCAST SCHOLARSHIP

Asian American Journalists Association-Chicago Chapter
c/o Susanna Song
CBS 2 Broadcast Center
22 West Washington Street
Chicago, IL 60602
E-mail: ssong@cbs.com
Web: www.aajachicago.wordpress.com

Summary To provide funding to members of the Asian American Journalists Association (AAJA) who are interested in a summer internship at a Chicago television station.

Eligibility This program is open to AAJA members who are college juniors, seniors, or graduate students. Applicants must be interested in a broadcast news internship at a Chicago television station. Along with their application, they must submit a resume that includes their job experience in journalism and 5 writing samples.

Financial data The stipend is $2,500.

Duration 10 to 12 weeks during the summer.

Number awarded 1 each year.

Deadline December of each year.

[787]
LIONEL C. BARROW MINORITY DOCTORAL STUDENT SCHOLARSHIP

Association for Education in Journalism and Mass Communication
Attn: Communication Theory and Methodology Division
234 Outlet Pointe Boulevard, Suite A
Columbia, SC 29210-5667
(803) 798-0271   Fax: (803) 772-3509
E-mail: aejmc@aejmc.org
Web: www.aejmc.us

Summary To provide financial assistance to Asian Americans and other minorities who are interested in working on a doctorate in mass communication.
Eligibility This program is open to minority students enrolled in a Ph.D. program in journalism and/or mass communication. Applicants must submit 2 letters of recommendation, a resume, and a brief letter outlining their research interests and career plans. Membership in the association is not required, but applicants must be U.S. citizens or permanent residents. Selection is based on the likelihood that the applicant's work will contribute to communication theory and/or methodology.
Financial data The stipend is $2,000.
Duration 1 year.
Additional information This program began in 1972.
Number awarded 1 each year.
Deadline May of each year.

[788]
LIZETTE PETERSON-HOMER INJURY PREVENTION GRANT AWARD

American Psychological Foundation
750 First Street, N.E.
Washington, DC 20002-4242
(202) 336-5843   Fax: (202) 336-5812
E-mail: foundation@apa.org
Web: www.apa.org/apf/funding/peterson-homer.aspx

Summary To provide funding to graduate students and faculty, especially Asian Americans and members of other diverse groups, interested in conducting research related to the prevention of injuries in children.
Eligibility This program is open to graduate students and faculty interested in conducting research that focuses on the prevention of physical injury in children and young adults through accidents, violence, abuse, or suicide. Applicants must submit a 100-word abstract, description of the project, detailed budget, curriculum vitae, and letter from the supporting faculty supervisor (if the applicant is a student). Selection is based on conformance with stated program goals, magnitude of incremental contribution, quality of proposed work, and applicant's demonstrated scholarship and research competence. The sponsor encourages applications from individuals who represent diversity in race, ethnicity, gender, age, disability, and sexual orientation.
Financial data Grants up to $5,000 are available.
Additional information This program began in 1999 as the Rebecca Routh Coon Injury Research Award. The current name was adopted in 2003. It is supported by Division 54 (Society of Pediatric Psychology) of the American Psychological Association and the American Psychological Foundation.
Number awarded 1 each year.
Deadline September of each year.

[789]
LOS ANGELES CHAPTER OF AAJA SCHOLARSHIPS

Asian American Journalists Association-Los Angeles
  Chapter
Attn: Frank Buckley, Scholarship Chair
KTLA-TV
5800 Sunset Boulevard
Los Angeles, CA 90028
E-mail: aajalaawards@gmail.com
Web: www.aaja-la.org/category/programs/scholarships

Summary To provide financial assistance to Asian/Pacific Islander students in the Los Angeles area who are interested in careers in journalism.
Eligibility This program is open to Asian/Pacific Islander full-time students who are planning a career in radio, photography, print, news design, television, or multimedia journalism. Applicants must be attending a college or university in the Los Angeles area (Los Angeles, Orange, Riverside, San Bernardino, or Ventura counties). Membership in the Asian American Journalists Association (AAJA) is encouraged for applicants and required for recipients. Selection is based on academic achievement, commitment to the field of journalism, journalistic ability, sensitivity to Asian American and Pacific Islander issues, and financial need.
Financial data The stipend is $2,500.
Duration 1 year; may be renewed.
Number awarded Several each year.
Deadline January of each year.

[790]
LTK ENGINEERING SCHOLARSHIP

Conference of Minority Transportation Officials
Attn: National Scholarship Program
100 M Street, S.E., Suite 917
Washington, DC 20003
(202) 506-2917   E-mail: info@comto.org
Web: www.comto.org/page/scholarships

Summary To provide financial assistance to Asian American and other minority upper-division and graduate students in engineering or other field related to transportation.
Eligibility This program is open to full-time minority juniors, seniors, and graduate students in engineering or other technical transportation-related disciplines. Applicants must have a GPA of 3.0 or higher. Along with their application they must submit a cover letter on their transportation-related career goals and life aspirations. Financial need is not considered in the selection process.
Financial data The stipend is $6,000. Funds are paid directly to the recipient's college or university.
Duration 1 year.
Additional information This program is sponsored by LTK Engineering Services.
Number awarded 1 each year.
Deadline April of each year.

[791]
LTK ENGINEERING TRANSPORTATION PLANNING SCHOLARSHIP

Conference of Minority Transportation Officials
Attn: National Scholarship Program
100 M Street, S.E., Suite 917
Washington, DC 20003
(202) 506-2917   E-mail: info@comto.org
Web: www.comto.org/page/scholarships

Summary To provide financial assistance to Asian American and other minority upper-division and graduate students in planning or other field related to transportation.

Eligibility This program is open to full-time minority juniors, seniors, and graduate students in planning of other technical transportation-related disciplines. Applicants must have a GPA of 3.0 or higher. Along with their application they must submit a cover letter on their transportation-related career goals and life aspirations. Financial need is not considered in the selection process.

Financial data The stipend is $5,000. Funds are paid directly to the recipient's college or university.

Duration 1 year.

Additional information This program is sponsored by LTK Engineering Services.

Number awarded 1 each year.

Deadline April of each year.

[792]
M. DICK OSUMI CIVIL RIGHTS AND PUBLIC INTEREST SCHOLARSHIP

Japanese American Bar Association
Attn: JABA Educational Foundation
P.O. Box 71961
Los Angeles, CA 90071
(323) 221-8900   E-mail: JEFscholarship@gmail.com
Web: www.jabaonline.org/scholarships

Summary To provide financial assistance to law students who have participated in the Asian Pacific Islander (API) community and are interested in civil rights, public interest law, and/or public policy.

Eligibility This program is open to students currently enrolled in law school. Applicants must demonstrate an intention to practice law in southern California. Along with their application, they must submit a 500-word personal statement discussing their commitment to community service, involvement with the Japanese American and/or API community, and interest in the areas of civil rights, public interest law, and/or public policy. Selection is based on service to the Asian Pacific American community; academic achievement; overcoming adversity; desire to practice law in the southern California area; desire to practice in the areas of civil rights, public interest law, and/or public policy; and financial need.

Financial data The stipend is $2,000.

Duration 1 year.

Number awarded 1 each year.

Deadline January of each year.

[793]
MAGOICHI AND SHIZUKO KATO MEMORIAL SCHOLARSHIP

Japanese American Citizens League
Attn: National Scholarship Awards
1765 Sutter Street
San Francisco, CA 94115
(415) 345-1075   Fax: (415) 345-1077
E-mail: pwada@jacl.org
Web: www.jacl.org/jacl-national-scholarship-program

Summary To provide financial assistance for graduate study, especially in medicine or the ministry, to members of the Japanese American Citizens League (JACL).

Eligibility This program is open to JACL members who are attending or planning to attend an accredited college or university as a graduate student. Applicants must submit information on their involvement in JACL and a 2-page essay on a topic that changes annually but relates to Japanese Americans. Selection is based on that essay, academic history, JACL involvement, school activities, work history, scholastic honors, and community involvement. Preference is given to applicants planning a career in medicine or the ministry.

Financial data Stipends generally average more than $2,000.

Duration 1 year; nonrenewable.

Number awarded 1 each year.

Deadline March of each year.

[794]
MARILYN A. JACKSON MEMORIAL AWARD

Omaha Presbyterian Seminary Foundation
7101 Mercy Road, Suite 216
Omaha, NE 68106-2616
(402) 397-5138   Toll Free: (888) 244-6714
Fax: (402) 397-4944   E-mail: opsf@opsf-omaha.org
Web: www.omahapresbyterianseminaryfoundation.org

Summary To provide financial assistance to students at Presbyterian theological seminaries who are willing to serve in designated states, especially Asian Americans and members of other ethnic minority groups.

Eligibility This program is open to members of a Presbyterian Church, under the care of a presbytery as a candidate/inquirer, and accepted or enrolled to work on a master's degree in divinity at 1 of the following 10 Presbyterian theological institutions: Austin Presbyterian Theological Seminary (Austin, Texas); Columbia Theological Seminary (Decatur, Georgia); University of Dubuque Theological Seminary (Dubuque, Iowa); Johnson C. Smith Theological Seminary (Atlanta, Georgia); Louisville Presbyterian Theological Seminary (Louisville, Kentucky); McCormick Theological Seminary (Chicago, Illinois); Pittsburgh Theological Seminary (Pittsburgh, Pennsylvania); Princeton Theological Seminary (Princeton, New Jersey); San Francisco Theological Seminary (San Anselmo, California); or Union Theological Seminary and Presbyterian School of Christian Education (Richmond, Virginia). Applicants must be willing to serve in a small Presbyterian church for 5 years in Colorado, Iowa, Kansas, Minnesota, Missouri, Montana, Nebraska, North Dakota, Oklahoma, South Dakota, Utah, Wisconsin, or Wyoming. Along with their application, they must submit answers to 7 questions about themselves and their commitment to pastoral service. Preference is given to members of ethnic minority groups from the following synods: Lakes and Prairies (Iowa, Minnesota, Nebraska, North Dakota, South Dakota, Wisconsin), Mid-America (Delaware, Maryland, North Carolina, Virginia, Washington, D.C.), Rocky Mountains (Colorado, Montana, Utah, Wyoming), and Sun (Arkansas, Louisiana, Oklahoma, Texas). Financial need is considered in the selection process.

Financial data The stipend is $7,500.

Duration 1 year.

Number awarded 1 each year.

Deadline April of each year.

[795]
MARJORIE BOWENS-WHEATLEY SCHOLARSHIPS

Unitarian Universalist Association
Attn: UU Women's Federation
258 Harvard Street
Brookline, MA 02446
(617) 838-6989   E-mail: uuwf@uua.org
Web: www.uuwf.org

Summary To provide financial assistance to Asian American and other women of color who are working on an undergraduate or graduate degree to prepare for Unitarian Universalist ministry or service.

Eligibility This program is open to women of color who are either 1) aspirants or candidates for the Unitarian Universalist ministry; or 2) candidates in the Unitarian Universalist Association's professional religious education or music leadership credentialing programs. Applicants must submit a 1- to 2-page narrative that covers their call to UU ministry, religious education, or music leadership; their passions; how their racial/ethnic/cultural background influences their goals for their calling; and how the work of the program's namesake relates to their dreams and plans for their UU service.

Financial data The stipend is $1,500.

Duration 1 year.

Additional information This program began in 2009.

Number awarded Varies each year; recently, 2 were awarded.

Deadline March of each year.

[796]
MARK ANDO AND ITO FAMILY SCHOLARSHIP

Far West Athletic Trainers' Association
c/o Ned Bergert, Scholarship Chair
4942 Casa Oro Drive
Yorba Linda, CA 92886
(714) 501-3858   E-mail: nhbergert@gmail.com
Web: www.fwatad8.org/committees/scholarships-committee

Summary To provide financial assistance to members of the National Athletic Trainers Association (NATA) from any state who are of Asian descent and working on an undergraduate or graduate degree in its District 8.

Eligibility This program is open to students of Asian descent from any state who are enrolled as undergraduate or graduate students at colleges and universities in California, Guam, Hawaii, or Nevada and preparing for a career as an athletic trainer. Applicants must be student members of NATA and a District 8 member of NATA working on a bachelor's, master's, or doctoral degree in athletic training. They must

have a GPA of 3.2 or higher and a record of distinction in their athletic training program, academic major, institution, intercollegiate athletics, and higher education. Along with their application, they must submit a statement on their athletic training background, experience, philosophy, and goals. Financial need is not considered in the selection process.

Financial data The stipend is $1,500.

Duration 1 year.

Additional information FWATA serves as District 8 of NATA.

Number awarded 1 each year.

Deadline February of each year.

[797]
MARK T. BANNER SCHOLARSHIP FOR LAW STUDENTS

Richard Linn American Inn of Court
c/o Amy Ziegler, Scholarship Chair
Green Burns & Crain
300 South Wacker Drive, Suite 2500
Chicago, IL 60606
(312) 987-2926   Fax: (312) 360-9315
E-mail: marktbannerscholarship@linninn.org
Web: www.linninn.org/Pages/scholarship.shtml

Summary To provide financial assistance to law students who are Asian Americans of members of other groups historically underrepresented in intellectual property law.

Eligibility This program is open to students at ABA-accredited law schools in the United States who are members of groups historically underrepresented (by race, sex, ethnicity, sexual orientation, or disability) in intellectual property law. Applicants must submit a 3-page statement on how ethics, civility, and professionalism have been their focus; how diversity has impacted them; and their commitment to a career in intellectual property law. Selection is based on academic merit; written and oral communication skills; leadership qualities; community involvement; commitment, qualities and actions toward ethics, civility and professionalism; and commitment to a career in IP law.

Financial data The stipend is $5,000.

Duration 1 year.

Number awarded 1 each year.

Deadline November of each year.

[798]
MARTHA AND ROBERT ATHERTON MINISTERIAL SCHOLARSHIP

Unitarian Universalist Association
Attn: Ministerial Credentialing Office
24 Farnsworth Street
Boston, MA 02210-1409
(617) 948-6403   Fax: (617) 742-2875
E-mail: mcoadministrator@uua.org
Web: www.uua.org

Summary To provide financial assistance to seminary students, especially Asian Americans and other persons of color, who are preparing for the Unitarian Universalist (UU) ministry.

Eligibility This program is open to second- or third-year seminary students currently enrolled full or at least half time in a UU ministerial training program with aspirant or candidate status. Applicants must respect hard work as a foundation of a full life and appreciate the freedom, political system, and philosophical underpinnings of our country. They should be citizens of the United States or Canada. Priority is given first to those who have demonstrated outstanding ministerial ability and secondarily to students with the greatest financial need (especially persons of color).

Financial data The stipend ranges from $1,000 to $15,000 per year.

Duration 1 year.

Additional information This program began in 1997.

Number awarded 1 or 2 each year.

Deadline April of each year.

[799]
MARTIN LUTHER KING, JR. MEMORIAL SCHOLARSHIP FUND

California Teachers Association
Attn: CTA Foundation for Teaching and Learning
1705 Murchison Drive
P.O. Box 921
Burlingame, CA 94011-0921
(650) 697-1400   E-mail: scholarships@cta.org
Web: www.cta.org

Summary To provide financial assistance for college or graduate school to Asian Pacific Americans and other racial and ethnic minorities who are members of the California Teachers Association (CTA), children of members, or members of the Student CTA.

Eligibility This program is open to members of racial or ethnic minority groups (Asians/Pacific Islanders, African Americans, American Indians/Alaska Natives, and Hispanics) who are 1) active CTA members; 2) dependent children of active, retired, or deceased CTA members; or 3) members of Student CTA. Applicants must be interested in preparing for a teaching career in public education or already engaged in such a career.

Financial data Stipends vary each year; recently, they ranged up to $6,000.

Duration 1 year.

Number awarded Varies each year; recently, 24 were awarded: 1 to a CTA member, 10 to children of CTA members, and 13 to Student CTA members.

Deadline February of each year.

[800]
MARTIN LUTHER KING JR. SCHOLARSHIP AWARDS

American Correctional Association
Attn: Scholarship Award Committee
206 North Washington Street, Suite 200
Alexandria, VA 22314
(703) 224-0000   Toll Free: (800) ACA-JOIN
Fax: (703) 224-0179   E-mail: execoffice@aca.org
Web: www.aca.org

Summary To provide financial assistance for undergraduate or graduate study to Asian Americans and other minorities interested in a career in the criminal justice field.

Eligibility Members of the American Correctional Association (ACA) may nominate a minority person for these awards. Nominees do not need to be ACA members, but they must

have been accepted to or be enrolled in an undergraduate or graduate program in criminal justice at a 4-year college or university. Along with the nomination package, they must submit a 250-word essay describing their reflections on the ideals and philosophies of Dr. Martin Luther King and how they have attempted to emulate those qualities in their lives. They must provide documentation of financial need, academic achievement, and commitment to the principles of Dr. King.

Financial data A stipend is awarded (amount not specified). Funds are paid directly to the recipient's college or university.

Duration 1 year.

Number awarded 1 each year.

Deadline May of each year.

[801]
MARY WOLFSKILL TRUST FUND INTERNSHIP

Library of Congress
Library Services
Attn: Junior Fellows Program Coordinator
101 Independence Avenue, S.E., Room LM-642
Washington, DC 20540-4600
(202) 707-9929   Fax: (202) 707-6269
E-mail: jfla@loc.gov
Web: www.loc.gov

Summary To provide summer work experience in the Manuscript Division of the Library of Congress (LC) to upper-division and graduate students, especially Asian Americans and other minorities.

Eligibility This program is open to undergraduate and graduate students who have expertise in library science or collections conservation and preservation. Applicants must be interested in gaining an introductory knowledge of the principles, concepts, and techniques of archival management through a summer internship in the LC Manuscript Division. They should be able to demonstrate an ability to communicate effectively in writing and have knowledge of integrated library systems, basic library applications, and other information technologies. Knowledge of American history is beneficial. Applications from minorities and students at smaller and lesser-known schools are particularly encouraged. U.S. citizenship is required.

Financial data The stipend is $3,000.

Duration 10 weeks during the summer. Fellows work a 40-hour week.

Number awarded 1 each year.

Deadline January of each year.

[802]
MATHEMATICA SUMMER FELLOWSHIPS

Mathematica Policy Research, Inc.
Attn: Human Resources
600 Alexander Park
P.O. Box 2393
Princeton, NJ 08543-2393
(609) 799-3535   Fax: (609) 799-0005
E-mail: humanresources@mathematica-mpr.com
Web: www.mathematica-mpr.com

Summary To provide an opportunity for graduate students in social policy fields, especially Asian Americans and other minorities, who wish to work on an independent summer research project at an office of Mathematica Policy Research, Inc.

Eligibility This program is open to students enrolled in a master's or Ph.D. program in public policy or a social science. Applicants must be interested in conducting independent research on a policy issue of relevance to the economic and social problems of minority groups or individuals with disabilities. They are placed with a mentor in 1 of the following divisions: health research, human services research, or survey research. The proposed research must relate to the work of Mathematica, but fellows do not work on Mathematica projects. Qualified minority students and students with disabilities are encouraged to apply.

Financial data The stipend is $10,000. Fellows also receive $500 for project-related expenses.

Duration 3 months during the summer.

Additional information Mathematica offices are located in Ann Arbor (Michigan), Cambridge (Massachusetts), Chicago (Illinois), Oakland (California), Princeton (New Jersey), and Washington, D.C. Fellows may indicate their choice of location, but they are assigned to the office where the work of the research staff meshes best with their topic and interests.

Number awarded Up to 5 each year.

Deadline March of each year.

[803]
MCGUIREWOODS/NLF INTERNSHIP PROGRAM

National Asian Pacific American Bar Association
Attn: NAPABA Law Foundation
1612 K Street, N.W., Suite 510
Washington, DC 20006
(202) 775-9555　　　　　　　Fax: (202) 775-9333
E-mail: aasaria@napaba.org
Web: www.napaba.org/?page=NLF_FI

Summary To provide funding to undergraduate and law students interested in a summer internship at the National Asian Pacific American Bar Association (NAPABA) and its Law Foundation (NLF).

Eligibility This program is open to 1) undergraduates interested in working on issues that affect Asian Pacific Americans; and 2) law students interested in working as a clerk. Assignments for undergraduates require working 50% of their time on NAPABA projects and 50% on NLF projects. Assignments for law students require full-time work for NAPABA. Tasks involve promoting justice, equity, and opportunity for Asian Pacific Americans; fostering professional development, legal scholarship, advocacy, and community involvement; and developing and supporting programs to educate the legal profession and Asian Pacific American communities about legal issues affecting those communities.

Financial data The stipend for the law clerk is $4,50. The stipend for the fundraising and policy intern is $3,000.

Duration 10 weeks during the summer.

Additional information These internships were first awarded in 2010 with support from McGuireWoods LLP.

Number awarded 2 each year: 1 law clerk and 1 fundraising and policy intern.

Deadline March of each year.

[804]
MCKINNEY FAMILY FUND SCHOLARSHIP

Cleveland Foundation
Attn: Scholarship Processing
1422 Euclid Avenue, Suite 1300
Cleveland, OH 44115-2001
(216) 861-3810　　　　　　　Fax: (216) 861-1729
E-mail: mbaker@clevefdn.org
Web: www.clevelandfoundation.org

Summary To provide financial assistance to residents of Ohio, especially Asian Americans or members of other minority groups, who are interested in attending college or graduate school in any state.

Eligibility This program is open to U.S. citizens who have been residents of Ohio for at least 2 years. Applicants must be high school seniors or graduate students and interested in working full or part time on an associate, bachelor's, master's, or doctoral degree at an accredited college or university in any state. They must have a GPA of 2.5 or higher. Preference is given to applicants of minority descent. Selection is based on evidence of sincerity toward obtaining an academic credential. Financial need may be used as a tiebreaker.

Financial data The stipend is $2,000 per year. Funds are paid directly to the school and must be applied to tuition, fees, books, supplies, and equipment required for course work.

Duration 1 year; may be renewed up to 3 additional.

Number awarded 1 or more each year.

Deadline March of each year.

[805]
MEDICAL STUDENT ELECTIVE IN HIV PSYCHIATRY

American Psychiatric Association
Attn: Office of HIV Psychiatry
1000 Wilson Boulevard, Suite 1825
Arlington, VA 22209-3901
(703) 907-8668　　　　　　Toll Free: (888) 357-7849
Fax: (703) 907-1087　　　　　E-mail: aids@psych.org
Web: www.psychiatry.org

Summary To provide an opportunity for Asian American and other minority medical students to spend an elective residency learning about HIV psychiatry.

Eligibility This program is open to medical students entering their fourth year at an accredited M.D. or D.O. degree-granting institution. Preference is given to minority candidates and those who have primary interests in services related to HIV/AIDS and substance abuse and its relationship to the mental health or the psychological well-being of ethnic minorities. Applicants should be interested in a psychiatry, internal medicine, pediatrics, or research career. They must be interested in participating in a program that includes intense training in HIV mental health (including neuropsychiatry), a clinical and/or research experience working with a mentor, and participation in the Committee on AIDS of the American Psychiatric Association (APA). U.S. citizenship is required.

Financial data A small stipend is provided (amount not specified).

Duration 1 month.

Additional information The heart of the program is in establishing a mentor relationship at 1 of several sites, becoming involved with a cohort of medical students interested in HIV medicine/psychiatry, participating in an interactive didactic/experimental learning program, and developing expertise in areas related to ethnic minority mental health research or psychiatric services. Students selected for the program who are not APA members automatically receive membership.

Number awarded   Varies each year.

Deadline   March of each year.

[806]
MEDICAL STUDENT TRAINING IN AGING RESEARCH PROGRAM

American Federation for Aging Research
Attn: Executive Director
55 West 39th Street, 16th Floor
New York, NY 10018
(212) 703-9977   Toll Free: (888) 582-2327
Fax: (212) 997-0330   E-mail: grants@afar.org
Web: www.afar.org/research/funding/mstar

Summary   To enable medical students, especially Asian Americans or members of other underrepresented groups, who have completed at least 1 year at an American medical school to attend a short training session in clinical geriatrics and aging research at selected training centers.

Eligibility   This program is open to allopathic and osteopathic medical students in good standing who have completed at least 1 year of medical school and are citizens, nationals, or permanent residents of the United States. Applicants must be interested in a summer experience in aging-related research and geriatrics either at a National Training Center supported by the National Institute on Aging (NIA) or at their home institution. Selection is based on academic excellence, interest in geriatrics, and potential for success. Applications are especially encouraged from students who are members of ethnic or racial groups underrepresented in aging and geriatric research, students with disabilities, and students whose background and experience are likely to diversify the research or medical questions being addressed.

Financial data   The stipend is $1,980 per month.

Duration   8 to 12 weeks during the summer.

Additional information   This program began in 1994. Major funding is provided by the NIA, the John A. Hartford Foundation, the MetLife Foundation, and the Jean and Louis Dreyfus Foundation. It is administered by the American Federation for Aging Research (AFAR) and NIA. Scholars attend training sessions with top experts in geriatrics and/or gerontology and other disciplines (e.g., physiology, molecular biology, neurology, and epidemiology). The training sessions are conducted at designated National Training Centers; for a complete list, including all partnership institutions, contact AFAR.

Number awarded   Approximately 130 each year.

Deadline   January of each year.

[807]
MENTAL HEALTH AND SUBSTANCE ABUSE FELLOWSHIP PROGRAM

Council on Social Work Education
Attn: Minority Fellowship Program
1701 Duke Street, Suite 200
Alexandria, VA 22314-3457
(703) 683-2050   Fax: (703) 683-8099
E-mail: mfpy@cswe.org
Web: www.cswe.org

Summary   To provide financial assistance to Asian Americans and other racial minority members interested in preparing for a clinical career in the mental health fields.

Eligibility   This program is open to U.S. citizens, noncitizen nationals, and permanent residents who have been underrepresented in the field of social work. These include but are not limited to the following groups: Asian/Pacific Islanders (e.g., Chinese, East Indians, South Asians, Filipinos, Hawaiians, Japanese, Koreans, and Samoans), American Indians/Alaskan Natives, Blacks, and Hispanics (e.g., Mexicans/Chicanos, Puerto Ricans, Cubans, Central or South Americans). Applicants must be interested in and committed to a career in mental health and/or substance abuse with specialization in the delivery of services of ethnic and racial minority groups. They must have a degree in social work and be accepted to or enrolled in a full-time master's or doctoral degree program. Selection is based on evidence of strong fit with and commitment to behavioral health services for underserved racial/ethnic populations; life experiences relevant to and/or volunteer or work experience with racial/ethnic populations; high quality scholarly writing showing ability to think and write at the doctoral level; academic evidence of ability to achieve timely degree completion; and fit of the sponsor's mission with the applicant's behavioral health services or research agenda.

Financial data   The program provides a monthly stipend (amount not specified), specialized training, and support for professional development.

Duration   1 academic year; renewable for 2 additional years if funds are available and the recipient makes satisfactory progress toward the degree objectives.

Additional information   The program has been funded since 1978 by the Center for Mental Health Services (CMHS), the Center for Substance Abuse Prevention (CSAP), and the Center for Substance Abuse Treatment (CSAT) within the Substance Abuse and Mental Health Services Administration. The master's degree program was added in 2014.

Number awarded   Varies each year; recently, 40 master's degree students, 12 new doctoral fellows and 12 returning doctoral fellows were appointed.

Deadline   February of each year.

[808]
MICHIGAN ACCOUNTANCY FOUNDATION FIFTH/ GRADUATE YEAR SCHOLARSHIP PROGRAM

Michigan Association of Certified Public Accountants
Attn: Michigan Accountancy Foundation
5480 Corporate Drive, Suite 200
P.O. Box 5068
Troy, MI 48007-5068
(248) 267-3680   Toll Free: (888) 877-4CPE (within MI)
Fax: (248) 267-3737   E-mail: MAF@micpa.org
Web: www.mafonline.org/?page_id=35

Summary　To provide financial assistance to students at Michigan colleges and universities, especially Asian Americans and members of other underrepresented groups, who are working on a degree in accounting.

Eligibility　This program is open to students enrolled full time at accredited Michigan colleges and universities with a declared concentration in accounting. Applicants must be seniors planning to enter the fifth or graduate year of their school's program. They must intend to or have successfully passed the Michigan C.P.A. examination and intend to practice public accounting in the state. Along with their application, they must submit 500-word statements about 1) examples of their leadership roles and extracurricular activities, community involvement and volunteerism, how they are financing their education, and the accomplishments of which they are most proud; and 2) their professional goals for the next 5 years and any special circumstances they wish to have considered. Special consideration is given to applicants who are single parents, physically challenged, minority, or self-supporting. U.S. citizenship or eligibility for permanent employment in the United States is required.

Financial data　The stipend is $3,000; funds are disbursed directly to the recipient's college or university.

Duration　1 year.

Additional information　This program includes the William E. Balhoff Leadership Scholarship, the Jeff Bergeron Leadership Scholarship, the Robert A. Bogan Scholarship (limited to a student from the metropolitan Detroit area), the Kenneth Bouyer Leadership Scholarship, the Peggy A. Dzierzawski Leadership Scholarship, the George Johnson Leadership Scholarship, the Thomas McTavish Leadership Scholarship, the Randy Paschke Leadership Scholarship, and the Governor Rick Snyder Leadership Scholarship.

Number awarded　15 to 20 each year.

Deadline　January of each year.

[809]
MICHIGAN AUTO LAW DIVERSITY SCHOLARSHIP

Michigan Auto Law
Attn: Natalie Lombardo
30101 Northwestern Highway
Farmington Hills, MI 48334
(248) 353-7575　　　　　　　　Fax: (248) 353-4504
E-mail: bwarner@ michiganautolaw.com
Web: www.michiganautolaw.com

Summary　To provide financial assistance to law students who are Asian Americans or others who will contribute to diversity of their school's student body.

Eligibility　This program is open to students entering their first, second, or third year at an accredited law school in the United States. Applicants must be a member of an ethnic or racial minority or demonstrate a defined commitment to issues of diversity within their academic career. They must be U.S. citizens and have a GPA of 3.0 or higher. Selection is based on transcripts and an essay describing their efforts to encourage greater racial or ethnic diversity within the student body of their law school and/or undergraduate program.

Financial data　The stipend is $2,000.

Duration　1 year.

Number awarded　1 each year.

Deadline　April of each year.

[810]
MIDWESTERN REGION KOREAN AMERICAN SCHOLARSHIPS

Korean American Scholarship Foundation
Midwestern Region
c/o Augie Lee, Scholarship Committee Chair
379 Hollow Hill Drive
Wauconda, IL 60010
(847) 721-9930　　　　E-mail: mwrc.scholarship@kasf.org
Web: www.kasf.org/midwestern

Summary　To provide financial assistance to Korean American students from any state who are working on or planning to work on an undergraduate or graduate degree in any field at a school in the Midwest.

Eligibility　This program is open to Korean American students who are currently enrolled or planning to enroll at a college or university in the midwestern states as full-time undergraduate or graduate students. Applicants may reside anywhere in the United States as long as they attend school in the midwestern region: Illinois, Iowa, Kansas, Michigan, Minnesota, Missouri, Nebraska, North Dakota, South Dakota, and Wisconsin. They must have a GPA of 3.0 or higher. Both U.S. citizens and foreign nationals are eligible. Selection is based on academic achievement (25%), extracurricular activities (10%), an essay (10%), recommendations (10%), financial need (40%), and extra credit for having extraordinary circumstances (5%).

Financial data　Stipends range from $1,000 to $2,000.

Duration　1 year; renewable.

Number awarded　Varies each year; recently, 14 were awarded.

Deadline　July of each year.

[811]
MIDWIVES OF COLOR-WATSON MIDWIFERY STUDENT SCHOLARSHIP

American College of Nurse-Midwives
Attn: ACNM Foundation, Inc.
8403 Colesville Road, Suite 1550
Silver Spring, MD 20910-6374
(240) 485-1850　　　　　　　　Fax: (240) 485-1818
E-mail: foundation@acnmf.org
Web: www.midwife.org

Summary　To provide financial assistance for midwifery education to Asian Americans and other students of color who belong to the American College of Nurse-Midwives (ACNM).

Eligibility　This program is open to ACNM members of color who are currently enrolled in an accredited basic midwife education program and have successfully completed 1 academic or clinical semester/quarter or clinical module. Applicants must submit they must submit a 150-word essay on their 5-year midwifery career plans; a 150-word essay on their intended future participation in the local, regional, and/or national activities of the ACNM; a 150-word essay on their need for financial assistance; and a 100-word statement on how they would use the funds if they receive the scholarship.

Selection is based on academic excellence, leadership potential, and financial need.

Financial data The stipend is $3,000.

Duration 1 year.

Number awarded Varies each year; recently, 3 were awarded.

Deadline February of each year.

[812]
MIKE M. MASAOKA CONGRESSIONAL FELLOWSHIP

Japanese American Citizens League
Attn: Washington Office
1629 K Street, N.W., Suite 400
Washington, DC 20006
(202) 223-1240   Fax: (202) 296-8082
E-mail: pouchida@jacl.org
Web: www.jacl.org/internships-and-fellowships

Summary To provide an opportunity for graduate student members of the Japanese American Citizens League (JACL) to gain work experience on the staff of a member of Congress.

Eligibility This program is open to U.S. citizens who are graduating college seniors or students in a graduate or professional program. Applicants must be JACL members who are interested in working in Washington on the staff of a member of Congress. Preference is given to those having a demonstrated commitment to Asian American issues, particularly those affecting the Japanese American community. Along with their application, they must submit essays on their career goals and how this award would further those goals.

Financial data The stipend ranges from $2,200 to $2,500 per month.

Duration 6 to 8 months.

Number awarded 1 each year.

Deadline July of each year.

[813]
MILDRED COLODNY DIVERSITY SCHOLARSHIP FOR GRADUATE STUDY IN HISTORIC PRESERVATION

National Trust for Historic Preservation
Attn: Scholarship Coordinator
2600 Virginia Avenue, N.W., Suite 1000
Washington, DC 20037
(202) 588-6124   Toll Free: (800) 944-NTHP, ext. 6124
Fax: (202) 588-6038   E-mail: david_field@nthp.org
Web: www.preservationnation.org

Summary To provide financial assistance for study, conference attendance, and summer work experience to graduate students, especially Asian Americans and others from diverse groups, who are interested in working on a degree in a field related to historic preservation.

Eligibility This program is open to students in their final year of undergraduate study intending to enroll in a graduate program in historic preservation and graduate students enrolled in or intending to enroll in historic preservation programs; these programs may be in a department of history, architecture, American studies, urban planning, museum studies, or a related field with a primary emphasis on historic preservation. The program of study must be at a U.S. college,

university, or other institution and students must be eligible to work in the United States. Applications are especially encouraged from people who will contribute to diversity in the field of historic preservation. The sponsor defines diversity to include people of all races, creeds, genders, ages, sexual orientations, religions, physical characteristics and abilities, veteran status, and economic or social backgrounds. Selection is based on financial need, undergraduate academic performance, promise shown for future achievement, commitment to working in preservation in the United States following graduation, and potential to help increase diversity within the preservation movement.

Financial data The program provides a stipend of up to $15,000 that covers graduate school tuition, a summer internship with the sponsor following the student's first year of study, and the student's attendance at a National Preservation Conference.

Duration 1 year; nonrenewable.

Additional information Internships may be completed at 1) the sponsor's Washington, D.C. office; 2) a regional office or historic museum site; or 3) the offices of 1 of the sponsor's partner organizations.

Number awarded 1 each year.

Deadline February of each year.

[814]
MILLER JOHNSON WEST MICHIGAN DIVERSITY LAW SCHOOL SCHOLARSHIP

Grand Rapids Community Foundation
Attn: Education Program Officer
185 Oakes Street S.W.
Grand Rapids, MI 49503-4008
(616) 454-1751, ext. 103   Fax: (616) 454-6455
E-mail: rbishop@grfoundation.org
Web: www.grfoundation.org/scholarshipslist

Summary To provide financial assistance to Asian American and other minorities from Michigan who are attending law school in any state.

Eligibility This program is open to U.S. citizens who are students of color (Asian, African American, Hispanic, Native American, Pacific Islander) and residents of Michigan. Applicants must be attending an accredited law school in any state. They must have a GPA of 3.0 or higher and be able to demonstrate financial need.

Financial data The stipend is $5,000. Funds are paid directly to the recipient's institution.

Duration 1 year.

Number awarded 1 each year.

Deadline March of each year.

[815]
MINORITIES IN GOVERNMENT FINANCE SCHOLARSHIP

Government Finance Officers Association
Attn: Scholarship Committee
203 North LaSalle Street, Suite 2700
Chicago, IL 60601-1210
(312) 977-9700   Fax: (312) 977-4806
Web: www.gfoa.org

Summary To provide financial assistance to Asian American and other minority upper-division and graduate students who are preparing for a career in state and local government finance.

Eligibility This program is open to upper-division and graduate students who are preparing for a career in public finance by working on a degree in public administration, accounting, finance, political science, economics, or business administration (with a specific focus on government or nonprofit management). Applicants must be members of a minority group, citizens or permanent residents of the United States or Canada, and able to provide a letter of recommendation from a representative of their school. Selection is based on career plans, academic record, plan of study, letters of recommendation, and GPA. Financial need is not considered.

Financial data The stipend is $6,000.

Duration 1 year.

Additional information This program defines minorities as Blacks or African Americans, American Indians or Alaskan Natives, Hispanics or Latinos, Native Hawaiians or other Pacific Islanders, or Asians.

Number awarded 1 each year.

Deadline February of each year.

[816]
MINORITY FACULTY DEVELOPMENT SCHOLARSHIP AWARD IN PHYSICAL THERAPY

American Physical Therapy Association
Attn: Honors and Awards Program
1111 North Fairfax Street
Alexandria, VA 22314-1488
(703) 684-APTA   Toll Free: (800) 999-APTA, ext. 8082
Fax: (703) 684-7343   TDD: (703) 683-6748
E-mail: honorsandawards@apta.org
Web: www.apta.org

Summary To provide financial assistance to Asian American and other minority faculty members in physical therapy who are interested in working on a post-professional doctoral degree.

Eligibility This program is open to U.S. citizens and permanent residents who are members of the following minority groups: Asian, African American or Black, Native Hawaiian or other Pacific Islander, American Indian or Alaska Native, or Hispanic/Latino. Applicants must be full-time faculty members, teaching in an accredited or developing professional physical therapist education program, who will have completed the equivalent of 2 full semesters of post-professional doctoral course work. They must possess a license to practice physical therapy in a U.S. jurisdiction and be enrolled as a student in an accredited post-professional doctoral program whose content has a demonstrated relationship to physical therapy. Along with their application, they must submit a personal essay on their professional goals, including their plans to contribute to the profession and minority services. Selection is based on contributions in the area of minority affairs and services and contributions to the profession of physical therapy. Preference is given to members of the American Physical Therapy Association (APTA).

Financial data A stipend is awarded (amount not specified).

Duration 1 year.

Additional information This program began in 1999.

Number awarded 1 or more each year.

Deadline November of each year.

[817]
MINORITY FELLOWSHIPS IN ENVIRONMENTAL LAW

New York State Bar Association
Attn: Environmental Law Section
One Elk Street
Albany, NY 12207
(518) 463-3200   Fax: (518) 487-5517
E-mail: lbataille@nysba.org
Web: www.nysba.org

Summary To provide an opportunity for Asian American and other minority law students from New York to gain summer work experience in environmental law.

Eligibility This program is open to law students who are Asian, Pacific Islander African American, Latino, Native American, or Alaskan Native. Applicants must be residents of New York or attending law school in that state. They must be interested in a summer internship working on legal matters for a government environmental agency or public interest environmental organization in New York State. Selection is based on interest in environmental issues, academic record (undergraduate and/or law school), personal qualities, leadership abilities, and financial need.

Financial data The stipend is $6,000.

Duration At least 10 weeks during the summer.

Additional information This program began in 1992.

Number awarded 1 each year.

Deadline December of each year.

[818]
MINORITY MEDICAL STUDENT SUMMER EXTERNSHIP IN ADDICTION PSYCHIATRY

American Psychiatric Association
Attn: Division of Diversity and Health Equity
1000 Wilson Boulevard, Suite 1825
Arlington, VA 22209-3901
(703) 907-8653   Toll Free: (888) 35-PSYCH
Fax: (703) 907-7852   E-mail: mking@psych.org
Web: www.psychiatry.org/minority-fellowship

Summary To provide funding to Asian American and other minority medical students who are interested in working on a research externship during the summer with a mentor who specializes in addiction psychiatry.

Eligibility This program is open to minority medical students who have a specific interest in services related to substance abuse treatment and prevention. Minorities include Asian Americans, American Indians, Alaska Natives, Native Hawaiians, Hispanics/Latinos, and African Americans. Applicants must be interested in working with a mentor who specializes in addiction psychiatry. Work settings provide an emphasis on working clinically with or studying underserved minority populations and issues of co-occurring disorders, substance abuse treatment, and mental health disparity. Most of them are in inner-city or rural settings.

Financial data Externships provide $1,500 for travel expenses to go to the work setting of the mentor and up to another $1,500 for out-of-pocket expenses directly related to the conduct of the externship.

Duration I month during the summer.

Additional information Funding for this program is provided by the Substance Abuse and Mental Health Services Administration (SAMHSA).

Number awarded 10 each year.

Deadline March of each year.

[819]
MINORITY TEACHERS OF ILLINOIS SCHOLARSHIP PROGRAM

Illinois Student Assistance Commission
Attn: Scholarship and Grant Services
1755 Lake Cook Road
Deerfield, IL 60015-5209
(847) 948-8550   Toll Free: (800) 899-ISAC
Fax: (847) 831-8549   TDD: (800) 526-0844
E-mail: isac.studentservices@isac.illinois.gov
Web: www.isac.org

Summary To provide scholarship/loans to Asian American and other minority students in Illinois who plan to become teachers at the preschool, elementary, or secondary level.

Eligibility Applicants must be Illinois residents, U.S. citizens or eligible noncitizens, members of a minority group (Asian American, African American/Black, Hispanic American, or Native American), and high school graduates or holders of a General Educational Development (GED) certificate. They must be enrolled at least half time as an undergraduate or graduate student, have a GPA of 2.5 or higher, not be in default on any student loan, and be enrolled or accepted for enrollment in a teacher education program.

Financial data Grants up to $5,000 per year are awarded. This is a scholarship/loan program. Recipients must agree to teach full time 1 year for each year of support received. The teaching agreement may be fulfilled at a public, private, or parochial preschool, elementary school, or secondary school in Illinois; at least 30% of the student body at those schools must be minority. It must be fulfilled within the 5-year period following the completion of the undergraduate program for which the scholarship was awarded. The time period may be extended if the recipient serves in the U.S. armed forces, enrolls full time in a graduate program related to teaching, becomes temporarily disabled, is unable to find employment as a teacher at a qualifying school, or takes additional courses on at least a half-time basis to obtain certification as a teacher in Illinois. Recipients who fail to honor this work obligation must repay the award with 5% interest.

Duration 1 year; may be renewed for a total of 8 semesters or 12 quarters.

Number awarded Varies each year.

Deadline Priority consideration is given to applications received by February of each year.

[820]
MINORU YASUI MEMORIAL SCHOLARSHIP

Japanese American Citizens League
Attn: National Scholarship Awards
1765 Sutter Street
San Francisco, CA 94115
(415) 345-1075   Fax: (415) 345-1077
E-mail: pwada@jacl.org
Web: www.jacl.org/jacl-national-scholarship-program

Summary To provide financial assistance for graduate study in selected fields to members of the Japanese American Citizens League (JACL).

Eligibility This program is open to JACL members who are attending or planning to attend an accredited college or university as a graduate student. Applicants must submit information on their involvement in JACL and a 2-page essay on a topic that changes annually but relates to Japanese Americans. Selection is based on that essay, academic record, JACL involvement, school activities, work history, scholastic honors, and community involvement. Preference is given to applicants with a strong interest in human and civil rights; fields of study may also include sociology, law, or education.

Financial data Stipends generally average more than $2,000.

Duration 1 year; nonrenewable.

Number awarded At least 1 each year.

Deadline March of each year.

[821]
MIRIAM WEINSTEIN PEACE AND JUSTICE EDUCATION AWARD

Philanthrofund Foundation
Attn: Scholarship Committee
1409 Willow Street, Suite 109
Minneapolis, MN 55403-2241
(612) 870-1806   Toll Free: (800) 435-1402
Fax: (612) 871-6587   E-mail: info@PfundOnline.org
Web: www.pfundonline.org/scholarships.html

Summary To provide financial assistance to Asian American and other minority students from Minnesota who have supported gay, lesbian, bisexual, and transgender (GLBT) activities and are interested in working on a degree in education.

Eligibility This program is open to residents of Minnesota and students attending a Minnesota educational institution who are members of a religious, racial, or ethnic minority. Applicants must be self-identified as GLBT or from a GLBT family and have demonstrated a commitment to peace and justice issues. They may be attending or planning to attend trade school, technical college, college, or university (as an undergraduate or graduate student). Preference is given to students who have completed at least 2 years of college and are working on a degree in education. Selection is based on the applicant's 1) affirmation of GLBT or allied identity; 2) evidence of experience and skills in service and leadership; and 3) evidence of service, leading, and working for change in GLBT communities, including serving as a role model, mentor, and/or adviser.

Financial data The stipend is $3,000. Funds must be used for tuition, books, fees, or dissertation expenses.

Duration 1 year.

Number awarded 1 each year.

Deadline January of each year.

[822]
MLA/NLM SPECTRUM SCHOLARSHIPS

Medical Library Association
Attn: Grants Coordinator
65 East Wacker Place, Suite 1900
Chicago, IL 60601-7246
(312) 419-9094, ext. 15   Fax: (312) 419-8950
E-mail: awards@mail.mlahq.org
Web: www.mlanet.org/p/cm/ld/fid=449

Summary   To provide financial assistance to Asian Americans and members of other minority groups interested in preparing for a career as a medical librarian.

Eligibility   This program is open to members of minority groups (Asians, African Americans, Hispanics, Native Americans, and Pacific Islanders) who are attending library schools accredited by the American Library Association (ALA). Applicants must be interested in preparing for a career as a health sciences information professional.

Financial data   The stipend is $3,250.

Duration   1 year.

Additional information   This program, established in 2001, is jointly sponsored by the Medical Library Association (MLA) and the National Library of Medicine (NLM) of the U.S. National Institutes of Health (NIH). It operates as a component of the Spectrum Initiative Scholarship program of the ALA.

Number awarded   2 each year.

Deadline   February of each year.

[823]
MLA SCHOLARSHIP FOR MINORITY STUDENTS

Medical Library Association
Attn: Grants Coordinator
65 East Wacker Place, Suite 1900
Chicago, IL 60601-7246
(312) 419-9094, ext. 15   Fax: (312) 419-8950
E-mail: awards@mail.mlahq.org
Web: www.mlanet.org/p/cm/ld/fid=304

Summary   To assist Asian American and other minority students interested in preparing for a career in medical librarianship.

Eligibility   This program is open to racial minority students (Asians, Blacks or African Americans, Hispanics or Latinos, Aboriginals, North American Indians or Alaskan Natives, Native Hawaiians, or other Pacific Islanders) who are entering an ALA-accredited graduate program in librarianship or who have completed less than half of their academic requirements for a master's degree in library science. They must be interested in preparing for a career in medical librarianship. Selection is based on academic record, letters of reference, professional potential, and the applicant's statement of career objectives. U.S. or Canadian citizenship or permanent resident status is required.

Financial data   The stipend is $5,000.

Duration   1 year.

Additional information   This program began in 1973.

Number awarded   1 each year.

Deadline   November of each year.

[824]
MOSS ADAMS FOUNDATION SCHOLARSHIP

Educational Foundation for Women in Accounting
Attn: Foundation Administrator
136 South Keowee Street
Dayton, OH 45402
(937) 424-3391   Fax: (937) 222-5749
E-mail: info@efwa.org
Web: www.efwa.org/scholarships_graduate.php

Summary   To provide financial support to women, including Asian American and other minority women, who are working on an accounting degree.

Eligibility   This program is open to women who are enrolled in an accounting degree program at an accredited college or university. Applicants must meet 1 of the following criteria: 1) women pursuing a fifth-year requirement either through general studies or within a graduate program; 2) women returning to school as current or reentry juniors or seniors; or 3) minority women. Selection is based on aptitude for accounting and business, commitment to the goal of working on a degree in accounting (including evidence of continued commitment after receiving this award), clear evidence that the candidate has established goals and a plan for achieving those goals (both personal and professional), financial need, and a demonstration of how the scholarship will impact her life. U.S. citizenship is required.

Financial data   The stipend is $1,000.

Duration   1 year.

Additional information   This program was established by Rowling, Dold & Associates LLP, a woman-owned C.P.A. firm based in San Diego. It was renamed when that firm merged with Moss Adams LLP.

Number awarded   2 each year: 1 to an undergraduate and 1 to a graduate student.

Deadline   April of each year.

[825]
MSCPA MINORITY SCHOLARSHIPS

Missouri Society of Certified Public Accountants
Attn: MSCPA Educational Foundation
540 Maryville Centre Drive, Suite 200
P.O. Box 958868
St. Louis, MO 63195-8868
(314) 997-7966   Toll Free: (800) 264-7966 (within MO)
Fax: (314) 997-2592   E-mail: dhull@mocpa.org
Web: www.mocpa.org/students/scholarships

Summary   To provide financial assistance to Asian American and other minority residents of Missouri who are working on an undergraduate or graduate degree in accounting at a university in the state.

Eligibility   This program is open to members of minority groups underrepresented in the accounting profession (Black/African American, Hispanic/Latino, Native American, Asian American) who are currently working full time on an undergraduate or graduate degree in accounting at a college or university in Missouri. Applicants must either be residents of Missouri or the children of members of the Missouri Society of Certified Public Accountants (MSCPA). They must be U.S. citizens, have completed at least 30 semester hours of college work, have a GPA of 3.3 or higher, and be student members of the MSCPA. Selection is based on the GPA, involvement in MSCPA, educator recommendations, and leadership potential. Financial need is not considered.

Financial data The stipend is $1,250 per year.

Duration 1 year; may be renewed.

Number awarded Varies each year; recently, 3 were awarded.

Deadline February of each year.

[826]
MSIPP INTERNSHIPS

Department of Energy
Office of Environmental Management
Savannah River National Laboratory
Attn: MSIPP Program Manager
Building 773-41A, 232
Aiken, SC 29808
(803) 725-9032   E-mail: connie.yung@srnl.doe.gov
Web: srnl.doe.gov/msipp/internships.htm

Summary To provide an opportunity for undergraduate and graduate students at Minority Serving Institutions (MSIs) to work on a summer research project at designated National Laboratories of the U.S. Department of Energy (DOE).

Eligibility This program is open to full-time undergraduate and graduate students enrolled at an accredited MSI. Applicants must be interested in working during the summer on a research project at a participating DOE National Laboratory. They must be working on a degree in a field of science, technology, engineering, or mathematics (STEM); the specific field depends on the particular project on which they wish to work. Their GPA must be 3.0 or higher. U.S. citizenship is required.

Financial data The stipend depends on the cost of living at the location of the host laboratory.

Duration 10 weeks during the summer.

Additional information This program is administered at the Savannah River National Laboratory (SRNL) in Aiken, South Carolina, which serves as the National Laboratory for the DOE Office of Environmental Management. The other participating National Laboratories are Argonne National Laboratory (ANL) in Argonne, Illinois, Idaho National Laboratory (INL) in Idaho Falls, Idaho, Los Alamos National Laboratory (LANL) in Los Alamos, New Mexico, Oak Ridge National Laboratory (ORNL) in Oak Ridge, Tennessee, and Pacific Northwest National Laboratory (PNNL) in Richland, Washington. The program began in 2016.

Number awarded Varies each year. Recently, the program offered 11 research projects at SRNL, 12 at ANL, 1 at INL, 7 at LANL, 4 at ORNL, and 7 at PNNL.

Deadline March of each year.

[827]
MULTICULTURAL AUDIENCE DEVELOPMENT INITIATIVE INTERNSHIPS

Metropolitan Museum of Art
Attn: Internship Programs
1000 Fifth Avenue
New York, NY 10028-0198
(212) 570-3710   Fax: (212) 570-3782
E-mail: mmainterns@metmuseum.org
Web: www.metmuseum.org

Summary To provide summer work experience at the Metropolitan Museum of Art to college undergraduates, graduate students, and recent graduates who are Asian Americans or from other diverse backgrounds.

Eligibility This program is open to members of diverse groups who are undergraduate juniors and seniors, students currently working on a master's degree, or individuals who completed a bachelor's or master's degree within the past year. Ph.D. students may be eligible to apply during the first 12 months of their program, provided they have not yet achieved candidacy. Students from various academic backgrounds are encouraged to apply, but they must be interested in preparing for a career in the arts and museum fields. Freshmen and sophomores are not eligible.

Financial data The stipend is $3,750.

Duration 10 weeks, beginning in June.

Additional information Interns are assigned to departmental projects (curatorial, administration, or education) at the Metropolitan Museum of Art; other assignments may include giving gallery talks and working at the Visitor Information Center. The assignment is for 35 hours a week. The internships are funded by the Multicultural Audience Initiative at the museum.

Number awarded 1 or more each year.

Deadline January of each year.

[828]
NAPABA LAW FOUNDATION PUBLIC INTEREST INTERNSHIPS

National Asian Pacific American Bar Association
Attn: NAPABA Law Foundation
1612 K Street, N.W., Suite 510
Washington, DC 20006
(202) 775-9555   Fax: (202) 775-9333
E-mail: nlfstaff@napaba.org
Web: www.napaba.org/?page=NLF_FI

Summary To provide funding to law students interested in a summer internship at a public interest organization that serves the Asian Pacific American community.

Eligibility Applications for grants must be submitted by public interest organizations that provide either direct legal services or impact litigation on behalf of the Asian Pacific American community. Once host organizations have been selected, the National Asian Pacific American Bar Association (NAPABA) Law Foundation solicits applicants through its web site, newsletter, and Facebook page. Interested law students apply directly to host organizations, which select 3 to 5 finalists. The NAPABA Law Foundation then selects the students who will work as interns at each host organization.

Financial data The host organization receives a grant of $6,000; all funds must be used as salary for the intern. The host organization is responsible for any administrative fees, payroll processing fees, federal withholding, taxes, etc.

Duration 10 weeks during the summer.

Additional information These internships were first awarded in 2011.

Number awarded At least 2 each year.

Deadline Potential host organizations must submit their applications by January of each year. Interested students must apply by April of each year.

[829]
NASA EDUCATION AERONAUTICS SCHOLARSHIP AND ADVANCED STEM TRAINING AND RESEARCH FELLOWSHIP

National Aeronautics and Space Administration
Attn: National Scholarship Deputy Program Manager
Office of Education and Public Outreach
Ames Research Center
Moffett Field, CA 94035
(650) 604-6958　　E-mail: elizabeth.a.cartier@nasa.gov
Web: nspires.nasaprs.com

Summary　To provide financial assistance to Asian Americans and members of other underrepresented groups interested in working on a graduate degree in fields of science, technology, engineering, and mathematics (STEM) of interest to the U.S. National Aeronautics and Space Administration (NASA).

Eligibility　This program (identified as AS&ASTAR) is open to students who have a bachelor's degree and have historically been underrepresented in NASA-related fields (women, minorities, persons with disabilities, and veterans). Applicants must be working on a research-based master's or doctoral degree in a NASA-related field of STEM, including chemistry, computer and information science and engineering, geosciences (e.g., geophysics, hydrology, oceanography, paleontology, planetary science), engineering (e.g., aeronautical, aerospace, biomedical, chemical, civil, computer, electrical, electronic, environmental, industrial, materials, mechanical, nuclear, ocean, optical, systems), life sciences (e.g., biochemistry, cell biology, environmental biology, genetics, neurosciences, physiology), materials research, mathematical sciences, or physics and astronomy). They must arrange with a researcher at a NASA Center to serve as a technical adviser in collaboration with the student's faculty adviser. Research must be conducted at a NASA Center as a team project involving the student, the faculty adviser, and the NASA technical adviser. In the selection process, consideration is given to the proposed use of NASA facilities, content, and people. Applications must include a plan for a Center-Based Research Experience (CBRE) to be conducted during the summer at the NASA facility. Students must be U.S. citizens and have a GPA of 3.0 or higher.

Financial data　Grants provide a stipend of $25,000 for master's degree students or $30,000 for doctoral candidates, $10,000 for tuition offset and fees, $8,000 as a CBRE allowance, $1,000 as a health insurance allowance, $4,500 as a faculty adviser allowance, and $1,500 as a fellow professional development allowance.

Duration　1 year; may be renewed up to 2 additional years.

Additional information　The participating NASA facilities are Ames Research Center (Moffett Field, California), Armstrong Flight Research Center (Edwards, California), Glenn Research Center (Cleveland, Ohio), Goddard Space Flight Center (Greenbelt, Maryland), Jet Propulsion Laboratory (Pasadena, California), Johnson Space Center (Houston, Texas), Kennedy Space Center (Kennedy Space Center, Florida), Langley Research Center (Hampton, Virginia), Marshall Space Flight Center (Marshall Space Flight Center, Alabama), and Stennis Space Center (Stennis Space Center, Mississippi).

Number awarded　At least 13 each year.

Deadline　June of each year.

[830]
NASP GRADUATE STUDENT RESEARCH GRANTS

National Association of School Psychologists
Attn: Research Committee
4340 East-West Highway, Suite 402
Bethesda, MD 20814
(301) 657-0270　　　　　　Toll Free: (866) 331-NASP
Fax: (301) 657-0275　　　　TDD: (301) 657-4155
E-mail: walcottc@ecu.edu
Web: www.nasponline.org

Summary　To provide funding for research to graduate student members of the National Association of School Psychologists (NASP).

Eligibility　This program is open to students who are NASP members enrolled in a regionally-accredited doctoral or non-doctoral school psychology program in the United States. Applicants must be interested in conducting thesis or dissertation research that furthers the mission and goals of NASP and has the potential to impact the field positively. Priority is given to applications for research on the following topics: critical shortages in school psychology; the role of school psychologists as qualified mental and behavioral health providers; nationwide recognition and implementation of the NASP Practice Model; or leadership skills and qualities of school psychologists.

Financial data　The grant is $1,000.

Duration　1 year.

Number awarded　3 each year, including at least 1 for thesis research and 1 for dissertation research.

Deadline　September of each year.

[831]
NASP-ERT MINORITY SCHOLARSHIP PROGRAM

National Association of School Psychologists
Attn: Education and Research Trust
4340 East-West Highway, Suite 402
Bethesda, MD 20814
(301) 657-0270　　　　　　Toll Free: (866) 331-NASP
Fax: (301) 657-0275　　　　TDD: (301) 657-4155
E-mail: kbritton@naspweb.org
Web: www.nasponline.org

Summary　To provide financial assistance to Asian American and other minority graduate students who are members of the National Association of School Psychologists (NASP) and enrolled in a school psychology program.

Eligibility　This program is open to minority students who are NASP members enrolled full or part time in a regionally-accredited school psychology program in the United States. Applicants must have a GPA of 3.0 or higher. Doctoral candidates are not eligible. Applications must be accompanied by 1) a resume that includes undergraduate and/or graduate schools attended, awards and honors, student and professional activities, work and volunteer experiences, research and publications, workshops or other presentations, and any special skills, training, or experience, such as bilingualism, teaching experience, or mental health experience; and 2) a statement, up to 1,000 words, of professional goals. Selection is based on adherence to instructions; completeness of the application; applicant's experience, interests and growth as reflected on their resume; applicant's professional goals statement; recommendations; financial standing; and degree of scholarship. U.S. citizenship is required.

Financial data The stipend is $5,000 per year.

Duration 1 year; may be renewed up to 2 additional years.

Additional information This program, which began in 1995, includes the Deborah Peek Crockett Minority Scholarship Award, the Wayne Gressett Memorial Minority Scholarship Award, and the Pearson Minority Scholarship Award.

Number awarded Varies each year; recently, 4 were awarded.

Deadline November of each year.

[832]
NASSIRI & JUNG FOUNDATION PUBLIC INTEREST SCHOLARSHIP

Filipino Bar Association of Northern California
Attn: Foundation
268 Bush Street, Suite 2928
San Francisco, CA 94104
E-mail: fbancinfo@gmail.com
Web: www.fbanc.org

Summary To provide financial assistance to entering or continuing students at law schools in northern California who are interested in serving the Filipino American community.

Eligibility This program is open to currently-enrolled and entering students at northern California law school who have a tie to the Filipino American community and intend to provide legal services to that community after graduation from law school. Applicants must submit a current transcript or admit letter, a resume, a list of their involvement in activities of the Filipino Bar Association of Northern California (FBANC), and a 2-page essay on 1) an obstacle or adversity they have faced and how that experience has affected their decision to attend law school or their career plans after law school; and 2) barriers that Filipino and Filipino Americans experience regarding the legal system and ways that those barriers can be addressed to increase the community's access to justice. Selection is based on that essay, academic standing, demonstrated interest in issues affecting the Filipino American community, and their desire to serve the Filipino American community.

Financial data The stipend is $3,000.

Duration 1 year.

Additional information This program is funded by the Nassiri & Jung Foundation.

Number awarded 1 each year.

Deadline April of each year.

[833]
NATIONAL DEFENSE SCIENCE AND ENGINEERING GRADUATE FELLOWSHIP PROGRAM

American Society for Engineering Education
Attn: NDSEG Fellowship Program
1818 N Street, N.W., Suite 600
Washington, DC 20036-2479
(202) 649-3831   Fax: (202) 265-8504
E-mail: ndseg@asee.org
Web: ndseg.asee.org/about_ndseg

Summary To provide financial assistance to doctoral students in areas of science and engineering, especially Asian

Americans and other minorities, that are of potential military importance.

Eligibility This program is open to U.S. citizens and nationals entering or enrolled in the early stages of a doctoral program in aeronautical and astronautical engineering; biosciences, including toxicology; chemical engineering; chemistry; civil engineering; cognitive, neural, and behavioral sciences; computer and computational sciences; electrical engineering; geosciences, including terrain, water, and air; materials science and engineering; mathematics; mechanical engineering; naval architecture and ocean engineering; oceanography; or physics, including optics. Applicants must be enrolled or planning to enroll as full-time students. Applications are particularly encouraged from women, members of ethnic minority groups (Asians, American Indians, African Americans, Hispanics or Latinos, Native Hawaiians and other Pacific Islanders, and Alaska Natives), and persons with disabilities. Selection is based on all available evidence of ability, including academic records, letters of recommendation, and GRE scores.

Financial data The annual stipend is $30,500 for the first year, $31,000 for the second year; and $31,500 for the third year; the program also pays the recipient's institution full tuition and required fees (not to include room and board). Medical insurance is covered up to $1,000 per year.

Duration 3 years, as long as satisfactory academic progress is maintained.

Additional information This program is sponsored by the High Performance Computing Modernization Program within the Department of Defense, the Army Research Office, the Air Force Office of Scientific Research, and the Office of Naval Research. Recipients do not incur any military or other service obligation.

Number awarded Approximately 200 each year.

Deadline December of each year.

[834]
NATIONAL MEDICAL FELLOWSHIPS EMERGENCY SCHOLARSHIP FUND

National Medical Fellowships, Inc.
Attn: Scholarship Program
347 Fifth Avenue, Suite 510
New York, NY 10016
(212) 483-8880   Toll Free: (877) NMF-1DOC
Fax: (212) 483-8897 E-mail: scholarships@nmfonline.org
Web: www.nmfonline.org

Summary To provide financial assistance to Vietnamese, Cambodians, and other minority medical students who are facing financial emergencies.

Eligibility This program is open to U.S. citizens who are enrolled in the third or fourth year of an accredited M.D. or D.O. degree-granting program in the United States and are facing extreme financial difficulties because of unforeseen training-related expenses. The emergency must be sudden, unexpected, and unbudgeted. Applicants must be Vietnamese, Cambodians, African Americans, Latinos, Native Hawaiians, Alaska Natives, American Indians, or Pacific Islanders who permanently reside in the United States. They must be interested in primary care practice in underserved communities.

Financial data Assistance ranges up to $5,000.

Duration 1 year; nonrenewable.

Additional information This program began in 2008.

Number awarded Varies each year; recently, 3 were awarded.

Deadline Applications may be submitted at any time.

[835]
NATIONAL URBAN FELLOWS PROGRAM

National Urban Fellows, Inc.
Attn: Program Director
1120 Avenue of the Americas, Fourth Floor
New York, NY 10036
(212) 730-1700   Fax: (212) 730-1823
E-mail: info@nuf.org
Web: www.nuf.org/fellows-overview

Summary To provide mid-career public sector professionals, especially Asian Americans and other people of color, with an opportunity to strengthen leadership skills through a master's degree program coupled with a mentorship.

Eligibility This program is open to U.S. citizens who have a bachelor's degree, have at 5 to 7 years of professional work experience with 2 years in a management capacity, have demonstrated leadership capacity with potential for further growth, have a GPA of 3.0 or higher, and can demonstrate a commitment to public service. Applicants must submit a 1-page autobiographical statement, a 2-page personal statement, and a 2-page statement on their career goals. They may be of any racial or ethnic background, but the program's goal is to increase the number of competent administrators from underrepresented ethnic and cultural groups at all levels of public and private urban management organizations. Semifinalists are interviewed.

Financial data The stipend is $25,000. Fellows are required to pay a $500 registration fee and a $7,500 co-investment tuition payment upon acceptance and enrollment in the program.

Duration 14 months.

Additional information The program begins with a summer semester of study at Bernard M. Baruch College of the City University of New York. Following this, fellows spend 9 months in mentorship assignments with a senior administrator in a government agency, a major nonprofit, or a foundation. The final summer is spent in another semester of study at Baruch College. Fellows who successfully complete all requirements are granted a master's of public administration from that college. A $150 processing fee must accompany each application.

Number awarded Approximately 40 to 50 each year.

Deadline December of each year.

[836]
NAVAL RESEARCH LABORATORY SUMMER RESEARCH PROGRAM FOR HBCU/MI UNDERGRADUATES AND GRADUATES

Naval Research Laboratory
Attn: Personnel Operations Branch
4555 Overlook Avenue, S.W.
Washington, DC 20375-5320
(202) 767-8313
Web: www.nrl.navy.mil/hbcu/description

Summary To provide research experience at the Naval Research Laboratory (NRL) to undergraduate and graduate students in fields of science, technology, engineering, and mathematics (STEM) at minority institutions.

Eligibility This program is open to undergraduate and graduate students who have completed at least 1 year of study at an Historically Black College or University (HBCU), Minority Institution (MI), or Tribal College or University (TCU). Applicants must be working on a degree in a field of STEM and have a cumulative GPA of 3.0 or higher. They must be interested in participating in a research program at NRL under the mentorship of a senior staff scientist. U.S. citizenship or permanent resident status is required.

Financial data The stipend is $810 per week for undergraduates or $1,050 per week for graduate students. Subsidized housing is provided at a motel in the area.

Duration 10 weeks during the summer.

Additional information This program is conducted in accordance with a planned schedule and a working agreement between NRL, the educational institution, and the student.

Number awarded Varies each year.

Deadline February of each year.

[837]
NBCC MINORITY FELLOWSHIP PROGRAM

National Board for Certified Counselors
Attn: NBCC Foundation
3 Terrace Way
Greensboro, NC 27403
(336) 232-0376   Fax: (336) 232-0010
E-mail: foundation@nbcc.org
Web: nbccf-mfpdr.applicantstack.com/x/detail/a2b3qvixcgjm

Summary To provide financial assistance to doctoral candidates, especially Asian Americans and those from other racially and ethnically diverse populations, and who are interested in working on a degree in mental health and/or substance abuse counseling.

Eligibility This program is open to U.S. citizens and permanent residents who are enrolled full time in an accredited doctoral degree mental health and/or substance abuse and addictions counseling program. Applicants must have a National Certified Counselor or equivalent credential. They must commit to provide mental health and substance abuse services to racially and ethnically diverse populations. Asian Americans, African Americans, Alaska Natives, American Indians, Hispanics/Latinos, Native Hawaiians, and Pacific Islanders are especially encouraged to apply. Applicants must be able to commit to providing substance abuse and addictions counseling services to underserved minority populations for at least 2 years after graduation.

Financial data The stipend is $20,000.

Duration 1 year.

Additional information This program began in 2012 with support from the Substance Abuse and Mental Health Services Administration.

Number awarded 23 each year.

Deadline June of each year.

[838]
NBCC MINORITY FELLOWSHIP PROGRAM (MASTER'S ADDICTIONS)

National Board for Certified Counselors
Attn: NBCC Foundation
3 Terrace Way
Greensboro, NC 27403
(336) 232-0376   Fax: (336) 232-0010
E-mail: foundation@nbcc.org
Web: nbccf-mfp.applicantstack.com/x/detail/a2hlw8mozup7

Summary To provide financial assistance to students, especially Asian Americans and members of other racially and ethnically diverse populations, who are interested in working on a master's degree in substance abuse and addictions counseling.

Eligibility This program is open to U.S. citizens and permanent residents who are enrolled full time in an accredited master's degree substance abuse and addictions counseling program. Applicants must demonstrate knowledge of and experience with racially and ethnically diverse populations. They must be able to commit to applying for the National Certified Counselor credential prior to graduation and to providing substance abuse and addictions counseling services to underserved minority transition-age youth populations (16-25 years of age) for at least 2 years after graduation. Asian Americans, African Americans, Alaska Natives, American Indians, Hispanics/Latinos, Native Hawaiians, and Pacific Islanders are especially encouraged to apply.

Financial data The stipend is $11,000.

Duration 1 year.

Additional information This program began in 2012 with support from the Substance Abuse and Mental Health Services Administration.

Number awarded 40 each year.

Deadline June of each year.

[839]
NBCC MINORITY FELLOWSHIP PROGRAM (MASTER'S MENTAL HEALTH)

National Board for Certified Counselors
Attn: NBCC Foundation
3 Terrace Way
Greensboro, NC 27403
(336) 232-0376   Fax: (336) 232-0010
E-mail: foundation@nbcc.org
Web: nbccf-mfp.applicantstack.com/x/detail/a2hlw8m1394v

Summary To provide financial assistance to students who have knowledge of and experience with Asian Americans or members of other racially and ethnically diverse populations and are interested in working on a master's degree in mental health counseling.

Eligibility This program is open to U.S. citizens and permanent residents who are enrolled full time in an accredited master's degree mental health counseling program. Applicants must demonstrate knowledge of and experience with racially and ethnically diverse populations. They must be able to commit to applying for the National Certified Counselor credential prior to graduation and to providing mental health counseling services to underserved minority transition-age youth populations (16-25 years of age) for at least 2 years after graduation. Asian Americans, African Americans,

Alaska Natives, American Indians, Hispanics/Latinos, Native Hawaiians, and Pacific Islanders are especially encouraged to apply.

Financial data The stipend is $5,000.

Duration 1 year.

Additional information This program is supported by the Substance Abuse and Mental Health Services Administration.

Number awarded 40 each year.

Deadline June of each year.

[840]
NCAA ETHNIC MINORITY ENHANCEMENT POSTGRADUATE SCHOLARSHIP FOR CAREERS IN ATHLETICS

National Collegiate Athletic Association
Attn: Office for Diversity and Inclusion
700 West Washington Street
P.O. Box 6222
Indianapolis, IN 46206-6222
(317) 917-6683   Fax: (317) 917-6888
E-mail: lthomas@ncaa.org
Web: www.ncaa.org

Summary To provide funding to Asian American and other ethnic minority graduate students who are interested in preparing for a career in intercollegiate athletics.

Eligibility This program is open to members of minority groups who have been accepted into a program at a National Collegiate Athletic Association (NCAA) member institution that will prepare them for a career in intercollegiate athletics (athletics administrator, coach, athletic trainer, or other career that provides a direct service to intercollegiate athletics). Applicants must be U.S. citizens, have performed with distinction as a student body member at their respective undergraduate institution, have a cumulative undergraduate GPA of 3.2 or higher, and be entering the first semester or term of full-time postgraduate study. Selection is based on the applicant's involvement in extracurricular activities, course work, commitment to preparing for a career in intercollegiate athletics, and promise for success in that career. Financial need is not considered.

Financial data The stipend is $7,500; funds are paid to the college or university of the recipient's choice.

Duration 1 year; nonrenewable.

Number awarded 13 each year.

Deadline February of each year.

[841]
NCPACA GRADUATE SCHOLARSHIPS

National Council of Philippine American Canadian Accountants
c/o Ed Ortiz, Scholarship Chair
333 South Des Plaines Street, Suite 2-N
Chicago, IL 60661
(312) 876-1900   Fax: (312) 876-1911
E-mail: ecortiz@ecortiz.com
Web: www.ncpacafoundation.com/shout-out.html

Summary To provide financial assistance to graduate students in accounting and related fields who are connected to the National Council of Philippine American Canadian Accountants (NCPACA).

Eligibility This program is open to full-time graduate students at a 4-year college or university in the United States or Canada. Applicants must be 1) enrolled in an accounting program; 2) have been an accounting major as an undergraduate and be accepted to a master's-level accounting, business administration, finance, or taxation program; or 3) have any undergraduate major and be accepted to a master's-level accounting program. They must submit a 500-word essay on 1) why they want to become a CPA and how attaining that licensure will contribute to their goals; and 2) how they could reach other college and/or high school students to promote the CPA profession. Selection is based primarily on academic achievement; financial need is evaluated as a secondary consideration.

Financial data The stipend is $5,000. Payments are sent directly to the recipient's school.

Duration 1 year.

Additional information Recipients must attend the annual conference of the NCPACA.

Number awarded 1 or more each year.

Deadline July of each year.

[842]
NEIGHBORHOOD DIABETES EDUCATION PROGRAM

National Medical Fellowships, Inc.
Attn: Scholarship Program
347 Fifth Avenue, Suite 510
New York, NY 10016
(212) 483-8880   Toll Free: (877) NMF-1DOC
Fax: (212) 483-8897 E-mail: scholarships@nmfonline.org
Web: www.nmfonline.org

Summary To provide funding to Vietnamese, Cambodian, and other underrepresented medical and nursing students who wish to participate in a neighborhood diabetes education project in New York City.

Eligibility This program is open to members of underrepresented minority groups (Vietnamese, Cambodian, African American, Hispanic/Latino, or Native American) who are U.S. citizens. Applicants must be currently enrolled in an accredited medical school or graduate-level nursing degree program in Connecticut, New Jersey, New York, or Pennsylvania. They must be interested in a mentored service-learning experience that provides 200 hours of proactive diabetes education at a variety of community sites and health care settings in New York City. Selection is based on demonstrated leadership early in career and commitment to serving medically underserved communities.

Financial data The stipend is $5,000.

Additional information Funding for this program, which began in 2015 and is administered by National Medical Fellowships (NMF), is provided by the Empire BlueCross BlueShield Foundation.

Number awarded 10 each year.

Deadline March of each year.

[843]
NELLIE STONE JOHNSON SCHOLARSHIP

Nellie Stone Johnson Scholarship Program
P.O. Box 40309
St. Paul, MN 55104
(651) 738-1404   Toll Free: (866) 738-5238
E-mail: info@nelliestone.org
Web: www.nelliestone.org/scholarship-program

Summary To provide financial assistance to Asian American and other racial minority union members and their families who are interested in working on an undergraduate or graduate degree in any field at a Minnesota state college or university.

Eligibility This program is open to students in undergraduate and graduate programs at a 2- or 4-year institution that is a component of Minnesota State Colleges and Universities (MnSCU). Applicants must be a minority (Asian, American Indian, Alaska Native, Black/African American, Chicano(a) or Latino(a), Native Hawaiian, or Pacific Islander) and a union member or the child, grandchild, or spouse of a minority union member. They must submit a 2-page essay about their background, educational goals, career goals, and commitment to the causes of human or civil rights. Undergraduates must have a GPA of 2.0 or higher; graduate students must have a GPA of 3.0 or higher. Preference is given to Minnesota residents. Selection is based on the essay, commitment to human or civil rights, extracurricular activities, volunteer activities, community involvement, academic standing, and union verification.

Financial data Stipends are $1,200 per year for full-time students or $500 per year for part-time students.

Duration 1 year; may be renewed up to 3 additional years for students working on a bachelor's degree, 1 additional year for students working on a master's degree, or 1 additional year for students in a community or technical college program.

Number awarded Varies each year; recently, 18 were awarded.

Deadline May of each year.

[844]
NEW LIFE CHURCH ANNUAL SCHOLARSHIPS

New Life Church of Chicago
Attn: Scholarship Committee
1200 West Northwest Highway
Palatine, IL 60067
(847) 359-5200   Fax: (847) 359-8409
E-mail: scholarship@NLChicago.org
Web: www.newlife-chicago.org/zbxe/main_banner/56490

Summary To provide financial assistance for college, graduate school, or seminary to Korean Americans who are either the child of a pastor or studying theology.

Eligibility This program is open to Korean Americans who are either 1) the child of a pastor or missionary and currently enrolled in college or graduate school; or 2) currently studying theology at a seminary or graduate school. Applicants must have completed at least 15 credit hours of undergraduate study or 8 credit hours as a graduate student and have a GPA of 3.0 or higher. Selection is based on transcripts, 2 letters of recommendation, a 500-word personal testimony and vision statement, and financial need.

Financial data The stipend is $1,500.

Duration 1 year.

Additional information This program began in 2002.

Number awarded 12 each year.

Deadline October of each year.

[845]
NEW YORK COMMUNITY TRUST/NMF MEDICAL EDUCATION AND POLICY SCHOLARSHIP

National Medical Fellowships, Inc.
Attn: Scholarship Program
347 Fifth Avenue, Suite 510
New York, NY 10016
(212) 483-8880   Toll Free: (877) NMF-1DOC
Fax: (212) 483-8897 E-mail: scholarships@nmfonline.org
Web: www.nmfonline.org

Summary To provide funding for medical education or health policy research to Vietnamese, Cambodians, and other underrepresented minority students at designated medical schools in New York City.

Eligibility This program is open to Vietnamese, Cambodians, African Americans, Hispanics/Latinos, Native Americans, and Pacific Islanders who are enrolled at Montefiore Medical Center, Icahn School of Medicine at Mount Sinai, or Columbia University's College of Physicians and Surgeons. Applicants must be interested in conducting medical education or health policy research. They must be U.S. citizens or DACA students. Selection is based on leadership, commitment to serving medically underserved communities, and financial need.

Financial data The stipend is $6,000.

Duration 1 year.

Additional information This program is sponsored by the New York Community Trust.

Number awarded 1 each year.

Deadline September of each year.

[846]
NEW YORK COMMUNITY TRUST/NMF MEDICAL RESEARCH SCHOLARSHIPS

National Medical Fellowships, Inc.
Attn: Scholarship Program
347 Fifth Avenue, Suite 510
New York, NY 10016
(212) 483-8880   Toll Free: (877) NMF-1DOC
Fax: (212) 483-8897 E-mail: scholarships@nmfonline.org
Web: www.nmfonline.org

Summary To provide funding for community health research to Vietnamese, Cambodians, and other underrepresented minority students at medical schools in New York City.

Eligibility This program is open to Vietnamese, Cambodians, African Americans, Hispanics/Latinos, Native Americans, and Pacific Islanders who are entering their second through fourth year at a medical school in New York City. Applicants must be interested in conducting community health research that addresses health inequities in the city. They must be U.S. citizens or DACA students. Selection is based on leadership, commitment to serving medically underserved communities, and financial need.

Financial data The stipend is $6,000.

Duration 1 year.

Additional information This program was established by the New York Community Trust in 2013.

Number awarded 2 each year.

Deadline September of each year.

[847]
NEW YORK EXCEPTIONAL UNDERGRADUATE/ GRADUATE STUDENT SCHOLARSHIP

Conference of Minority Transportation Officials
Attn: National Scholarship Program
100 M Street, S.E., Suite 917
Washington, DC 20003
(202) 506-2917   E-mail: info@comto.org
Web: www.comto.org/page/scholarships

Summary To provide financial assistance to Asian American or other minority students who are members or relatives of members of the Conference of Minority Transportation Officials (COMTO) in New York and working on an undergraduate or graduate degree in transportation.

Eligibility This program is open to minorities who have been members or relatives of members of COMTO in New York for at least 1 year. Applicants must be enrolled full time at an accredited college, university, or vocational/technical institute and working on an undergraduate or graduate degree in a transportation-related discipline. They must have a GPA of 3.5 or higher. Along with their application they must submit a cover letter on their transportation-related career goals and life aspirations. Financial need is not considered in the selection process.

Financial data The stipend is $5,000. Funds are paid directly to the recipient's college or university.

Duration 1 year.

Number awarded 1 each year.

Deadline April of each year.

[848]
NJLA DIVERSITY SCHOLARSHIP

New Jersey Library Association
c/o Kassundra Miller, Scholarship Committee Co-Chair
Wood-Ridge Memorial Library
231 Hackensack Street
Wood-Ridge, NJ 07075
(201) 438-2455   Fax: (201) 438-8399
E-mail: miller@woodridge.bccls.org
Web: www.njlamembers.org/scholarship

Summary To provide financial assistance to New Jersey residents who are Asian Americans or members of other minority groups and interested in working on a graduate or postgraduate degree in public librarianship at a school in any state.

Eligibility This program is open to residents of New Jersey and individuals who have worked in a New Jersey library for at least 12 months. Applicants must be members of a minority group (Asian/Pacific Islander, African American, Latino/Hispanic, or Native American/Native Alaskan). They must be enrolled or planning to enroll at an ALA-accredited school of library science in any state to work on a graduate or postgraduate degree in librarianship. Along with their application, they must submit an essay of 150 to 250 words explaining their choice of librarianship as a profession. An interview is required. Selection is based on academic ability and financial need.

Financial data   The stipend is $850.

Duration   1 year.

Number awarded   1 each year.

Deadline   February of each year.

[849]
NLF SCHOLARSHIPS

National Asian Pacific American Bar Association
Attn: NAPABA Law Foundation
1612 K Street, N.W., Suite 510
Washington, DC 20006
(202) 775-9555   Fax: (202) 775-9333
E-mail: nlfstaff@napaba.org
Web: www.napaba.org/?page=NLF_scholarships

Summary   To provide financial assistance to law students interested in serving the Asian Pacific American community.

Eligibility   This program is open to students at ABA-accredited law schools in the United States. Applicants must demonstrate leadership potential to serve the Asian Pacific American community upon graduation. Along with their application, they must submit a 500-word essay that covers 1) the most significant experiences in their background that have shaped and demonstrated their commitment to serving the needs of Asian Pacific Americans; and 2) how they intend to serve the needs of the Asian Pacific American community in their future legal career. Selection is based on that essay, academic achievement, leadership, and commitment to bettering the Asian Pacific American community. U.S. citizenship or permanent resident status is required.

Financial data   The stipend is $2,500 for named scholarships or $2,000 for others.

Duration   1 year.

Additional information   This program began in 1995. In 2003, 1 of the scholarships was named the Chris Nakamura Scholarship in honor of a leader of the Asian Pacific American legal community in Arizona. The Lim Ruger Scholarship was established in 2004 with support from the law firm of Lim, Ruger & Kim of Los Angeles. Other named scholarships include the Low Family Scholarship, established in 2014, and the Locke Lord/NLF Scholarship, established in 2015 by Locke Lord LLP.

Number awarded   4 named scholarships and 8 to 10 others are awarded each year.

Deadline   August of each year.

[850]
NMF NATIONAL ALUMNI COUNCIL SCHOLARSHIP PROGRAM

National Medical Fellowships, Inc.
Attn: Scholarship Program
347 Fifth Avenue, Suite 510
New York, NY 10016
(212) 483-8880   Toll Free: (877) NMF-1DOC
Fax: (212) 483-8897 E-mail: scholarships@nmfonline.org
Web: www.nmfonline.org

Summary   To provide financial assistance to Vietnamese, Cambodians, and other underrepresented minority medical students who are committed to the health of underserved communities.

Eligibility   This program is open to Vietnamese, Cambodians, African Americans, Hispanics/Latinos, Native Americans, and Pacific Islanders who are entering their fourth year of medical school. Applicants must have demonstrated commitment to the health of underserved communities through community service and leadership potential at an early stage in their professional careers. They must be U.S. citizens or DACA students. Financial need is considered in the selection process.

Financial data   The stipend is $5,000.

Duration   1 year.

Number awarded   8 each year.

Deadline   September of each year.

[851]
NONG KHAI JUNIOR VANG SCHOLARSHIP

Hmong American Education Fund
P.O. Box 17468
St. Paul, MN 55117
(651) 592-1576   E-mail: scholarships@thehaef.org
Web: www.thehaef.org

Summary   To provide financial assistance to Hmong undergraduate and graduate students who demonstrate academic achievement.

Eligibility   This program is open to students of Hmong descent who are currently enrolled as full-time undergraduate or graduate students at 2- or 4-year colleges or universities in any state. Applicants must be U.S. citizens or permanent residents and have a GPA of 3.0 or higher. Along with their application, they must submit a 1,500-word essay on their commitment to education, their financial need, how this scholarship can help them, and their community service. Selection is based on commitment to academic achievement, drive to achieve their goals, commitment to helping their community, and financial need.

Financial data   The stipend is $500.

Duration   1 year; nonrenewable.

Number awarded   1 each year.

Deadline   March of each year.

[852]
NORTH AMERICAN TAIWANESE MEDICAL ASSOCIATION SCHOLARSHIPS

North American Taiwanese Medical Association
  Foundation
Attn: Director
7923 Garden Grove Boulevard
Garden Grove, CA 92841
(714) 898-2275   Fax: (714) 373-2659
E-mail: hsu0316@hotmail.com
Web: www.natma.org/scholarshipinfo.html

Summary   To provide financial assistance for additional study to Taiwanese American medical, dental, and allied health graduate students, residents, or fellows.

Eligibility   This program is open to medical, dental, and allied health students, residents, or fellows who are of Taiwanese American descent. Applicants must have completed at least 1 year of graduate school study and be enrolled in a program of training at an accredited U.S. institution or program. Along with their application, they must submit a 1-page essay on ways that the sponsor can increase awareness of the services and benefits that it provides to its members and the greater community, a transcript, and 2 letters of recommendation.

Financial data The stipend is $2,000.

Duration 1 year.

Number awarded 3 each year.

Deadline June of each year.

[853]
NORTH TEXAS EXCEPTIONAL UNDERGRADUATE/GRADUATE STUDENT SCHOLARSHIP

Conference of Minority Transportation Officials
Attn: National Scholarship Program
100 M Street, S.E., Suite 917
Washington, DC 20003
(202) 506-2917   E-mail: info@comto.org
Web: www.comto.org/page/scholarships

Summary To provide financial assistance to Asian American and other minority residents of Texas who are working on an undergraduate or graduate degree in transportation.

Eligibility This program is open to minorities who are residents of Texas enrolled at an accredited college, university, or vocational/technical institute and working on an undergraduate or graduate degree in a transportation-related discipline. Applicants must have a GPA of 2.5 or higher. Along with their application they must submit a cover letter on their transportation-related career goals and life aspirations. Financial need is not considered in the selection process. Membership in the Conference of Minority Transportation Officials (COMTO) is considered a plus but is not required.

Financial data The stipend is $4,500. Funds are paid directly to the recipient's college or university.

Duration 1 year.

Number awarded 1 each year.

Deadline April of each year.

[854]
NORTHEASTERN REGION KOREAN AMERICAN SCHOLARSHIPS

Korean American Scholarship Foundation
Northeastern Region
Attn: Scholarship Committee Chair
1411 Broadway, Fourth Floor
New York, NY 10018
E-mail: nerc.scholarship@kasf.org
Web: www.kasf.org/northeastern

Summary To provide financial assistance to Korean American students from any state who are working on an undergraduate or graduate degree in any field at a school in northeastern states.

Eligibility This program is open to residents of any state who are 1) U.S. citizens of Korean heritage; 2) Korean citizens who have a valid visa to study in the United States; and 3) citizens of any other country who are of Korean heritage and have a valid visa to study in the United States. Applicants must be enrolled or planning to enroll as a full-time undergraduate or graduate student at a college or university in Connecticut, Maine, Massachusetts, New Hampshire, New Jersey, New York, Ohio, Rhode Island, or Vermont. Selection is based on academic achievement, school and community

activities, letters of recommendation, a personal essay, and financial need.

Financial data Stipends range from $1,000 to $2,000.

Duration 1 year; renewable.

Number awarded Varies each year; recently, 67 were awarded.

Deadline July of each year.

[855]
NOTRE DAME INSTITUTE FOR ADVANCED STUDY GRADUATE STUDENT FELLOWSHIPS

University of Notre Dame
Institute for Advanced Study
Attn: Programs Administrator
1124 Flanner Hall
Notre Dame, IN 46556
(574) 631-1305   Fax: (574) 631-8997
E-mail: csherman@nd.edu
Web: ndias.nd.edu/fellowships/graduate-student

Summary To provide funding to Asian American or other underrepresented graduate students who are interested in conducting research on topics of interest to the Notre Dame Institute for Advanced Study (NDIAS) while in residence at the institute.

Eligibility This program is open to graduate students in all disciplines, including the arts, engineering, the humanities, law, and the natural, social, and physical sciences. Applicants must be interested in conducting research that furthers the work of the NDIAS, defined as cultivating "the contemplative ideal that is an essential factor in the Catholic intellectual tradition and vital for the progression of scholarship." They must be able to demonstrate excellent records of scholarly, artistic, or research accomplishment in their field; ability to interact with other fellows and to engage in collegial discussions of research presentations; a willingness to contribute to a cooperative community of scholars; and projects that touch on normative, integrative, or ultimate questions, especially as they involve the Catholic intellectual tradition. Applications are especially encouraged from traditionally underrepresented groups. There are no citizenship requirements; non-U.S. nationals are welcome to apply.

Financial data The grant is $25,000, including a $1,000 research account, office facilities, a computer and printer, access to libraries and other facilities, and twice-weekly institute seminars and events.

Duration 1 academic year.

Number awarded Varies each year; recently, 2 were awarded.

Deadline October of each year.

[856]
NSCA MINORITY SCHOLARSHIPS

National Strength and Conditioning Association
Attn: NSCA Foundation
1885 Bob Johnson Drive
Colorado Springs, CO 80906-4000
(719) 632-6722, ext. 152   Toll Free: (800) 815-6826
Fax: (719) 632-6367   E-mail: foundation@nsca.org
Web: www.nsca.com/foundation/nsca-scholarships

Summary To provide financial assistance to Asian American and other minorities who are interested in working on an undergraduate or graduate degree in strength training and conditioning.

Eligibility This program is open to Asian Americans, Blacks, Hispanics, and Native Americans who are 17 years of age and older. Applicants must have been accepted into an accredited postsecondary institution to work on an undergraduate or graduate degree in the strength and conditioning field. Along with their application, they must submit a 500-word essay on their personal and professional goals and how receiving this scholarship will assist them in achieving those goals. Selection is based on that essay, academic achievement, strength and conditioning experience, honors and awards, community involvement, letters of recommendation, and involvement in the National Strength and Conditioning Association (NSCA).

Financial data The stipend is $1,500.

Duration 1 year.

Additional information The NSCA is a nonprofit organization of strength and conditioning professionals, including coaches, athletic trainers, physical therapists, educators, researchers, and physicians. This program was first offered in 2003.

Number awarded Varies each year; recently, 5 were awarded.

Deadline March of each year.

[857]
NWSA WOMEN OF COLOR CAUCUS-*FRONTIERS* STUDENT ESSAY AWARD

National Women's Studies Association
Attn: Women of Color Caucus
11 East Mount Royal Avenue, Suite 100
Baltimore, MD 21202
(410) 528-0355   Fax: (410) 528-0357
E-mail: awards@nwsa.org
Web: www.nwsa.org/content.asp?admin=Y&contentid=16

Summary To recognize and reward essays on feminist issues written by Asian American or other women of color graduate students and recent postdoctorates who are members of the National Women's Studies Association (NWSA).

Eligibility This competition is open to women of color (defined as those of Asian, Pacific Islander, African, Middle East, American Indian, Alaskan Native or Latin American descent) who are currently enrolled in a graduate or professional program. Recipients of Ph.D.s who completed their degree requirements within the past year are also eligible. Applicants must submit a scholarly essay that provides critical theoretical discussions and/or analyses of issues and experiences of women and girls of color. They must be members of the NWSA.

Financial data The award is $500.

Duration The award is presented annually.

Number awarded 1 each year.

Deadline May of each year.

[858]
OACTA LAW STUDENT DIVERSITY SCHOLARSHIPS

Ohio Association of Civil Trial Attorneys
17 South High Street, Suite 200
Columbus, OH 43215
(614) 228-4727   E-mail: oacta@assnoffices.com
Web: www.oacta.org/About/diversity_scholarship.aspx

Summary To provide financial assistance to Asian Americans and other minorities who are enrolled at law schools in Ohio.

Eligibility This program is open to students entering their second or third year at a law school in Ohio. Applicants must be women or members of minority ethnic or racial groups (Asian, Pan Asian, African American, Hispanic, or Native American). Along with their application, they must submit a law school transcript and a cover letter that addresses their academic, personal, and professional accomplishments and why they should be selected as a recipient of this scholarship. Selection is based on academic achievement in law school, professional interest in civil defense practice, service to community, and service to the cause of diversity.

Financial data The stipend is $1,250.

Duration 1 year.

Number awarded Up to 3 each year.

Deadline April of each year.

[859]
OHIO SOCIETY OF CPAS COLLEGE SCHOLARSHIP PROGRAM

Ohio Society of CPAs
Attn: Ohio CPA Foundation
535 Metro Place South
P.O. Box 1810
Dublin, OH 43017-7810
(614) 764-2727, ext. 344
Toll Free: (800) 686-2727, ext. 344
Fax: (614) 764-5880   E-mail: oscpa@ohio-cpa.com
Web: www.ohiocpa.com

Summary To provide financial assistance to undergraduate and graduate student members of the Ohio Society of CPAs, especially Asian Americans and members of other underrepresented groups, who are working on a degree in accounting at colleges and universities in the state.

Eligibility This program is open to U.S. citizens who are Ohio residents working on undergraduate or graduate degrees in accounting at colleges and universities in the state in order to complete the 150 hours required for the C.P.A. examination. Applicants must have completed at least 30 hours of college credit and have a GPA of 3.0 or higher. Awards are available to 3 categories of students: 1) 2-year awards, for students at community colleges or other 2-year institutions; 2) 4-year awards, for students at 4-year colleges and universities; and 3) diversity awards, for students from underrepresented ethnic, racial, or cultural groups.

Financial data The stipend is $2,000.

Duration 1 year; nonrenewable.

Number awarded Varies each year; recently, 20 were awarded.

Deadline November of each year.

[860]
OKLAHOMA CAREERTECH FOUNDATION TEACHER RECRUITMENT/RETENTION SCHOLARSHIP FOR TEACHERS

Oklahoma CareerTech Foundation
Attn: Administrator
1500 West Seventh Avenue
Stillwater, OK 74074-4364
(405) 743-5453   Fax: (405) 743-5541
E-mail: leden@careertech.ok.gov
Web: www.okcareertech.org

Summary To provide financial assistance to residents of Oklahoma who are Asian Americans or reflect the diversity of the state in other ways and are interested in attending a college or university in the state to earn a credential or certification for a career in the Oklahoma CareerTech system.

Eligibility This program is open to residents of Oklahoma who are incumbent CareerTech teachers working toward a CareerTech credential or certification at an institution of higher education in the state. Applicants must reflect the ethnic diversity of the state. Along with their application, they must submit brief statements on their interest and commitment to the CareerTech teaching profession and their financial need.

Financial data The stipend ranges from $500 per semester to $1,500 per year.

Duration 1 semester; may be renewed, provided the recipient maintains a GPA of 2.5 or higher.

Number awarded 1 or more each year.

Deadline May of each year.

[861]
OLIVER GOLDSMITH, M.D. SCHOLARSHIP

Kaiser Permanente Southern California
Attn: Residency Administration and Recruitment
393 East Walnut Street, Fifth Floor
Pasadena, CA 91188
Toll Free: (877) 574-0002   Fax: (626) 405-6581
E-mail: socal.residency@kp.org
Web: residency-scal-kaiserpermanente.org

Summary To provide financial assistance to Asian American and other medical students who will help bring diversity to the profession.

Eligibility This program is open to students entering their third or fourth year of allopathic or osteopathic medical school. Members of all ethnic and racial groups are encouraged to apply, but applicants must have demonstrated their commitment to diversity through community service, clinical volunteering, or research. They may be attending medical school in any state, but they must intend to practice in southern California and they must be available to participate in a mentoring program and a clerkship at a Kaiser Permanente facility in that region.

Financial data The stipend is $5,000.

Duration 1 year.

Additional information This program began in 2004.

Number awarded 12 each year.

Deadline January of each year.

[862]
OLYMPIA BROWN AND MAX KAPP AWARD

Unitarian Universalist Association
Attn: Ministerial Credentialing Office
24 Farnsworth Street
Boston, MA 02210-1409
(617) 948-6403   Fax: (617) 742-2875
E-mail: mcoadministrator@uua.org
Web: www.uua.org

Summary To provide financial assistance to Unitarian Universalist (UU) candidates for the ministry, especially Asian Americans and other persons of color) who submit a project on an aspect of Universalism.

Eligibility This program is open to students currently enrolled full or at least half time in a UU ministerial training program with candidate status. Applicants are primarily citizens of the United States or Canada. Along with their application, they may submit a paper, sermon, or a special project on an aspect of Unitarian Universalism. Priority is given first to those who have demonstrated outstanding ministerial ability and secondarily to students with the greatest financial need (especially persons of color).

Financial data The stipend is $2,500.

Duration 1 year.

Number awarded 1 each year.

Deadline April of each year.

[863]
OPERATION JUMP START III SCHOLARSHIPS

American Association of Advertising Agencies
Attn: AAAA Foundation
1065 Avenue of the Americas, 16th Floor
New York, NY 10018
(212) 262-2500   E-mail: ameadows@aaaa.org
Web: www.aaaa.org

Summary To provide financial assistance to Asian American and other multicultural art directors and copywriters interested in working on an undergraduate or graduate degree in advertising.

Eligibility This program is open to Asian Americans, African Americans, Hispanic Americans, and Native Americans who are U.S. citizens or permanent residents. Applicants must be incoming graduate students at 1 of 6 designated portfolio schools or full-time juniors at 1 of 2 designated colleges. They must be able to demonstrate extreme financial need, creative talent, and promise. Along with their application, they must submit 10 samples of creative work in their respective field of expertise.

Financial data The stipend is $5,000 per year.

Duration Most awards are for 2 years.

Additional information Operation Jump Start began in 1997 and was followed by Operation Jump Start II in 2002. The current program began in 2006. The 6 designated portfolio schools are the AdCenter at Virginia Commonwealth University, the Creative Circus in Atlanta, the Portfolio Center in Atlanta, the Miami Ad School, the University of Texas at Austin, and Pratt Institute. The 2 designated colleges are the Minneapolis College of Art and Design and the Art Center College of Design at Pasadena, California.

Number awarded 20 each year.

Deadline Deadline not specified.

[864]
OREGON STATE BAR SCHOLARSHIPS

Oregon State Bar
Attn: Diversity and Inclusion Department
16037 S.W. Upper Boones Ferry Road
P.O. Box 231935
Tigard, OR 97281-1935
(503) 620-0222
Toll Free: (800) 452-8260, ext. 338 (within OR)
Fax: (503) 684-1366   TDD: (503) 684-7416
E-mail: cling@osbar.org
Web: www.osbar.org/diversity/programs.html#scholar

Summary   To provide financial assistance to entering and continuing students from any state enrolled at law schools in Oregon, especially Asian Americans and others who will help the Oregon State Bar achieve its diversity and inclusion objectives.

Eligibility   This program is open to students entering or continuing at 1 of the law schools in Oregon (Willamette, University of Oregon, and Lewis and Clark). Preference is given to students who will contribute to the Oregon State Bar's diversity and inclusion program, defined to include age, culture, disability, ethnicity, gender and gender identity or expression, geographic location, national origin, race, religion, sex, sexual orientation, and socio-economic status. Along with their application, they must submit a 500-word personal statement on either 1) how their status as a person of diversity has influenced their decision to become a lawyer and how will it influence them throughout their legal professional career; or 2) a challenge they have faced, how they met the challenge, and how that experience will affect the decisions they will make as a legal professional. They must also submit a sample of their legal writing. Selection is based on the personal statement (35%), legal writing ability (25%), academic achievement (15%), work experience and honors (10%), and financial need (15%).

Financial data   The stipend is $2,000 per year. Funds are credited to the recipient's law school tuition account.

Duration   1 year; recipients may reapply.

Number awarded   10 each year.

Deadline   March of each year.

[865]
OREGON-IDAHO CONFERENCE UMC ETHNIC MINORITY LEADERSHIP AWARDS

United Methodist Church-Oregon-Idaho Conference
Attn: Scholarship Coordinator
1505 S.W. 18th Avenue
Portland, OR 97201-2524
(503) 226-7031   Toll Free: (800) J-WESLEY
E-mail: linda@umoi.org
Web: www.umoi.org/scholarships

Summary   To provide financial assistance to Asian American and other ethnic minority Methodists from Oregon and Idaho who are interested in attending a college or graduate school in any state.

Eligibility   This program is open to members of ethnic minority groups (Asian, African American, Native American, Pacific Islander, or Hispanic) who have belonged to a congregation affiliated with the Oregon-Idaho Conference of the United Methodist Church (UMC) for at least 1 year. Applicants must be enrolled or planning to enroll full time as an undergraduate or graduate student at a 2- or 4-year college or university in any state. Along with their application, they must submit personal statements on 1) their faith development; and 2) where they sense God is calling the church in the present and future. Selection is based primarily on demonstrated leadership excellence and/or the potential for leadership excellence in the UMC and in community projects or activities, but other factors, including financial need, are also considered.

Financial data   The stipend is $750.

Duration   1 year.

Number awarded   1 each year.

Deadline   April of each year.

[866]
ORGANIC CHEMISTRY GRADUATE STUDENT FELLOWSHIPS

American Chemical Society
Division of Organic Chemistry
1155 16th Street, N.W.
Washington, DC 20036
(202) 872-4401   Toll Free: (800) 227-5558, ext. 4401
E-mail: division@acs.org
Web: www.organicdivision.org/?nd=graduate_fellowship

Summary   To provide funding for research to members of the Division of Organic Chemistry of the American Chemical Society (ACS), especially Asian Americans and other minorities, who are working on a doctoral degree in organic chemistry.

Eligibility   This program is open to members of the division who are entering the third or fourth year of a Ph.D. program in organic chemistry. Applicants must submit 3 letters of recommendation, a resume, and a short essay on a research area of their choice. U.S. citizenship or permanent resident status is required. Selection is based primarily on evidence of research accomplishment. Applications from women and minorities are especially encouraged.

Financial data   The stipend is $26,000; that includes $750 for travel support to present a poster of their work at the National Organic Symposium.

Duration   1 year.

Additional information   This program began in 1982. It includes the Emmanuil Troyansky Fellowship. Current corporate sponsors include Organic Syntheses, Boehringer Ingelheim, and Amgen.

Number awarded   Varies each year; recently, 5 were awarded.

Deadline   May of each year.

[867]
PA STUDENT SCHOLARSHIPS

American Academy of Physician Assistants
Attn: Physician Assistant Foundation
2318 Mill Road, Suite 1300
Alexandria, VA 22314-6868
(703) 836-2272   Fax: (703) 684-1924
E-mail: pafoundation@aapa.org
Web: www.pa-foundation.org

Summary   To provide financial assistance to student members of the American Academy of Physician Assistants

(AAPA) who are Asian Americans or other underrepresented minorities or economically and/or educationally disadvantaged.

Eligibility This program is open to AAPA student members attending a physician assistant program accredited by the Commission on Accreditation of Allied Health Education Programs. Applicants must qualify as 1) an underrepresented minority (Asian other than Chinese, Filipino, Japanese, Korean, Asian Indian, or Thai, American Indian, Alaska Native, Black or African American, Hispanic or Latino, Native Hawaiian or other Pacific Islander); 2) economically disadvantaged (with income below a specified level); or 3) educationally disadvantaged (from a high school with low SAT scores, from a school district in which less than half of graduates go on to college, has a diagnosed physical or mental impairment, English is not their primary language, the first member of their family to attend college). They must have completed at least 1 semester of PA studies.

Financial data Stipends are $2,500, $2,000, or $1,000.

Duration 1 year; nonrenewable.

Additional information This program includes the AAPA Past Presidents Scholarship, the Bristol-Myers Squibb Endowed Scholarship, the National Commission on Certification of Physician Assistants Endowed Scholarships, the Procter & Gamble Endowed Scholarship, and the PA Foundation Scholarships.

Number awarded Varies each year; recently, 32 were awarded: 3 at $2,500, 27 at $2,000, and 2 at $1,000.

Deadline January of each year.

[868]
PATRICIA G. ARCHBOLD PREDOCTORAL SCHOLAR AWARD

National Hartford Center of Gerontological Nursing
 Excellence
Attn: Hartford Institute for Geriatric Nursing
NYU Rory Myers College of Nursing
433 First Avenue, Fifth Floor
New York, NY 10010
(202) 779-1439   E-mail: nhcgne@nyu.edu
Web: www.nhcgne.org

Summary To provide funding to nurses who are Asian Americans or members of other underrepresented minority groups who are interested in working on a doctoral degree in gerontological nursing.

Eligibility This program is open to registered nurses who are members of underrepresented minority groups (Asians, American Indians, Alaska Natives, Blacks or African Americans, Hispanics or Latinos/Latinas, Native Hawaiians or other Pacific Islanders) and have been admitted to a doctoral program as a full-time student. The institution they plan to attend must be a member of the National Hartford Center of Gerontological Nursing Excellence (NHCGNE). Applicants must plan an academic research career in geriatric nursing. They must identify a mentor/adviser with whom they will work and whose program of research in geriatric nursing is a good match with their own research interest area. Selection is based on potential for substantial long-term contributions to the knowledge base in geriatric nursing; leadership potential; evidence of commitment to a career in academic geriatric nursing; and evidence of involvement in educational,

research, and professional activities. U.S. citizenship or permanent resident status is required.

Financial data The stipend is $50,000 per year. An additional stipend of $5,000 is available to fellows whose research includes the study of pain in the elderly.

Duration 2 years.

Additional information This program began in 2001 with funding from the John A. Hartford Foundation. In 2004, the Mayday Fund added support to scholars who focus on the study of pain in the elderly. Until 2013 it was known as the Building Academic Geriatric Nursing Capacity Program.

Number awarded 1 or more each year.

Deadline January of each year.

[869]
PATRICIA M. LOWRIE DIVERSITY LEADERSHIP SCHOLARSHIP

Association of American Veterinary Medical Colleges
Attn: Diversity Committee
1101 Vermont Avenue, N.W., Suite 301
Washington, DC 20005-3536
(202) 371-9195, ext. 147   Toll Free: (877) 862-2740
Fax: (202) 842-0773   E-mail: lgreenhill@aavmc.org
Web: www.aavmc.org

Summary To provide financial assistance to veterinary students who are Asian Americans or have promoted diversity in the profession in other ways.

Eligibility This program is open to second-, third-, and fourth-year students at veterinary colleges in the United States. Applicants must have a demonstrated record of contributing to enhancing diversity and inclusion through course projects, co-curricular activities, outreach, domestic and community engagement, research, and/or an early reputation for influencing others to be inclusive. Along with their application, they must submit a 3-page personal statement that describes 1) why diversity and inclusion are important to them personally and professionally; 2) how they intend to continue contributing to diversity and inclusion efforts in the veterinary profession after graduation; and 3) what it might mean to be honored as a recipient of this scholarship. They must also indicate how they express their race and/or ethnicity (Asian, American Indian or Alaskan, Black or African American, Hispanic, Native Hawaiian or Pacific Islander, or White) and how they express their gender (male, female, transgender spectrum, or other). Selection is based primarily on documentation of a demonstrated commitment to promoting diversity in academic veterinary medicine; consideration is also given to academic achievement, the student's broader community service record, and financial need.

Financial data The stipend is $6,000.

Duration 1 year; nonrenewable.

Additional information This program began in 2013.

Number awarded 1 each odd-numbered year.

Deadline October of each even-numbered year.

[870]
PATRICK D. MCJULIEN MINORITY GRADUATE SCHOLARSHIP

Association for Educational Communications and
  Technology
Attn: ECT Foundation
320 West Eighth Street, Suite 101
Bloomington, IN 47404-3745
(812) 335-7675   Toll Free: (877) 677-AECT
Fax: (812) 335-7678   E-mail: aect@aect.org
Web: aectorg.yourwebhosting.com

Summary To provide financial assistance to Asian American and other minority members of the Association for Educational Communications and Technology (AECT) working
on a graduate degree in the field of educational communications and technology.

Eligibility This program is open to AECT members who
are members of minority groups. Applicants must be full-time
graduate students enrolled in a degree-granting program in
educational technology at the master's (M.S.), specialist
(Ed.S.), or doctoral (Ph.D., Ed.D.) levels. They must have a
GPA of 3.0 or higher.

Financial data The stipend is $500.
Duration 1 year.
Number awarded 1 each year.
Deadline May of each year.

[871]
PAUL STEPHEN LIM ASIAN-AMERICAN PLAYWRITING AWARDS

John F. Kennedy Center for the Performing Arts
Education Department
Attn: Kennedy Center American College Theater Festival
2700 F Street, N.W.
Washington, DC 20566
(202) 416-8864   Fax: (202) 416-8860
E-mail: ghenry@kennedy-center.org
Web: web.kennedy-center.org

Summary To recognize and reward outstanding Asian
America student playwrights.

Eligibility Students at any accredited junior or senior college in the United States are eligible to compete, provided
their college agrees to participate in the Kennedy Center
American College Theater Festival (KCACTF). Undergraduate students must be carrying at least 6 semester hours,
graduate students must be enrolled in at least 3 semester
hours, and continuing part-time students must be enrolled in
a regular degree or certificate program. This award is presented to the author of the best play on any subject who is of
Asian heritage.

Financial data The winning playwright receives a cash
award of $1,000 for a full-length play or $500 for a 1-act play.
Other benefits include appropriate membership in the Dramatists Guild and an all-expense paid professional development
opportunity.

Duration The awards are presented annually.
Additional information This program, which began in
2011, is part of the Michael Kanin Playwriting Awards Program. The sponsoring college or university must pay a registration fee of $275 for each production.

Number awarded 2 each year.
Deadline November of each year.

[872]
PEGGY PETERMAN SCHOLARSHIP

Tampa Bay Times
Attn: Director of Corporate Giving
490 First Avenue South
St. Petersburg, FL 33701
(727) 893-8780   Toll Free: (800) 333-7505, ext. 8780
Fax: (727) 892-2257   E-mail: waclawek@tampabay.com
Web: www.tampabay.com

Summary To provide financial assistance to Asian American and other minority undergraduate and graduate students
who are interested in preparing for a career in the newspaper
industry and who accept an internship at the *Tampa Bay
Times.*

Eligibility This program is open to minority college sophomores, juniors, seniors, and graduate students from any state
who are interested in preparing for a career in the newspaper
industry. Applicants must be interested in an internship at the
Tampa Bay Times and must apply for that at the same time as
they apply for this scholarship. They should have experience
working on a college publication and at least 1 professional
internship.

Financial data The stipend is $5,000.
Duration Internships are for 12 weeks during the summer.
Scholarships are for 1 year.
Number awarded 1 each year.
Deadline October of each year.

[873]
PFATS-NFL CHARITIES MINORITY SCHOLARSHIPS

Professional Football Athletic Trainers Society
c/o Britt Brown, ATC, Associate Athletic Trainer
Dallas Cowboys
One Cowboys Parkway
Irving, TX 75063
(972) 497-4992   E-mail: bbrown@dallascowboys.net
Web: www.pfats.com/about/scholarships

Summary To provide financial assistance to Asian American and other ethnic minority undergraduate and graduate
students working on a degree in athletic training.

Eligibility This program is open to ethnic minority students
who are working on an undergraduate or graduate degree in
athletic training. Applicants must have a GPA of 2.5 or higher.
Along with their application, they must submit a cover letter, a
curriculum vitae, and a letter of recommendation from their
supervising athletic trainer. Female athletic training students
are encouraged to apply.

Financial data A stipend is awarded (amount not speci-
fied).
Duration 1 year.
Additional information Recipients also have an opportu-
nity to work at summer training camp of a National Football
League (NFL) team. Support for this program, which began in
1993, is provided by NFL Charities.
Number awarded 1 or more each year.
Deadline March of each year.

[874]
PHI TAU PHI MID-AMERICA CHAPTER SCHOLARSHIPS

Phi Tau Phi Scholastic Honor Society-Mid-America
  Chapter
c/o Arthur Yuan, Scholarship Committee Chair
John Marshall Law School
315 South Plymouth Court
Chicago, IL 60604
E-mail: ayuan@jmls.edu
Web: www.phitauphima.org/awards.html

Summary To provide financial assistance to undergraduate and graduate students of Chinese heritage at colleges and universities in selected midwestern states.

Eligibility This program is open to undergraduate and graduate students enrolled at colleges and universities in Illinois, Indiana, Iowa, Kansas, Michigan, Minnesota, Ohio, Texas, and Wisconsin who have a GPA of 3.5 or higher. Applicants must be of Chinese descent and interested in and committed to Chinese heritage and culture. They must be entering their junior or senior year of undergraduate study or their second year or higher of graduate work. Along with their application, they must submit a 500-word essay on their professional goals and achievements.

Financial data The stipend is $1,000.

Duration 1 year.

Additional information Phi Tau Phi, first organized in 1921 in China and reestablished in 1964 in the United States, is a relatively small honor society of scholars, mainly of Chinese heritage, in various disciplines of science, technology, art, and the humanities.

Number awarded 4 each year.

Deadline July of each year.

[875]
PHI TAU PHI WEST AMERICA CHAPTER SCHOLARSHIP AWARDS

Phi Tau Phi Scholastic Honor Society-West America
  Chapter
c/o Jason Cong, President
University of California at Los Angeles
Computer Science
4711 BH
P.O. Box 951596
Los Angeles, CA 90095-1596
(310) 206-2775   E-mail: cong@cs.ucla.edu
Web: ptp.cms.caltech.edu/scholarship.html

Summary To provide financial assistance to upper-division and graduate students of Chinese heritage from any state at colleges and universities in southern California.

Eligibility This program is open to juniors, seniors, and graduate students from any state enrolled at accredited institutions of higher education in southern California. Applicants must be of Chinese heritage or have a demonstrated interest in Chinese and culture. They must have a GPA of 3.4 or higher. Along with their application, they must submit a 1-page essay on their professional goals, achievements, and interest in Chinese culture. Financial need is not considered in the selection process.

Financial data The stipend is $1,000.

Duration 1 year.

Additional Information Phi Tau Phi, first organized in 1921 in China and reestablished in 1964 in the United States, is a relatively small honor society of scholars, mainly of Chinese heritage, in various disciplines of science, technology, art, and the humanities.

Number awarded Varies each year; recently, 4 were awarded: 2 to undergraduates and 2 to graduate students.

Deadline August of each year.

[876]
PHILIPPINE NURSES ASSOCIATION HAWAII FOUNDATION SCHOLARSHIP FUND

Hawai'i Community Foundation
Attn: Scholarship Department
827 Fort Street Mall
Honolulu, HI 96813
(808) 566-5570   Toll Free: (888) 731-3863
Fax: (808) 521-6286
E-mail: scholarships@hcf-hawaii.org
Web: hcf.scholarships.ngwebsolutions.com

Summary To provide financial assistance to residents of Hawaii who are of Filipino ancestry and interested in working on an undergraduate or graduate degree in nursing at a college in any state.

Eligibility This program is open to residents of Hawaii who are of Filipino ancestry and enrolled or planning to enroll full time at a 2- or 4-year college or university in any state. Applicants must be interested in working on an undergraduate or graduate degree in nursing. They must be able to demonstrate academic achievement (GPA of 3.5 or higher), good moral character, and financial need. Along with their application, they must submit a short statement indicating their reasons for attending college, their planned course of study, their career goals, and what community service means to them.

Financial data The amounts of the awards depend on the availability of funds and the need of the recipient. Recently, the average value of the scholarships awarded by the foundation was $2,800.

Duration 1 year.

Additional information The Philippine Nurses Association Hawaii Foundation established this program in 2005.

Number awarded Varies each year.

Deadline February of each year.

[877]
PHILIPPINE NURSES ASSOCIATION OF AMERICA SCHOLARSHIP

Philippine Nurses Association of America
Attn: PNAA Foundation
1883 East Maple Road
Troy, MI 48083
(248) 588-8881
Web: www.mypnaafoundation.org/untitled-cmgc

Summary To provide financial assistance for graduate study to members of the Philippine Nurses Association of America (PNAA).

Eligibility This program is open to PNAA members who are enrolled or admitted at an accredited program for a master's degree in nursing, post-master's study, or doctoral degree. Applicants must be endorsed by their PNAA chapter president. Along with their application, they must submit a

150-word essay on their professional career goals and how this scholarship will help them attain those goals. Selection is based on that essay, academic record, 2 letters of recommendation, and a resume.

Financial data The stipend is $1,000 per year.

Duration 1 year; may be renewed, provided the recipient maintains a GPA of 3.0 or higher.

Number awarded Varies each year; recently, 6 were awarded.

Deadline May of each year.

[878]
PHILIPPINE NURSES ASSOCIATION OF NORTHERN CALIFORNIA GRADUATE NURSING STUDENT SCHOLARSHIP

Philippine Nurses Association of Northern California, Inc.
c/o Tess Estrin, Scholarship Committee Chair
11 Duval Drive
South San Francisco, CA 94080
E-mail: tessestrin@gmail.com
Web: www.pnanorthcal.org

Summary To provide financial assistance to Filipino Americans from any state enrolled in a graduate nursing program at a school in northern California.

Eligibility This program is open to Filipino American residents of any state who are currently enrolled in the first year or higher of an accredited graduate nursing program in northern California. Applicants must have a GPA of 3.0 or higher and a record of participation in extracurricular or community activities. They must have demonstrated leadership ability or potential both within and outside the clinical setting. Along with their application, they must submit brief statements on their strengths and opportunities for improvement, their career goals, why they need a scholarship, how they can contribute to the goals of the Philippine Nurses Association of Northern California (PNANC), and an accomplishment or activity as a nursing student that has impacted their life or the life of another person. Preference is given to members of PNANC.

Financial data The stipend is $1,000.

Duration 1 year.

Additional information The recipient must commit to participate in at least 4 PNANC activities during the following 2 years.

Number awarded 1 each year.

Deadline October of each year.

[879]
PHILLIPS EXETER ACADEMY DISSERTATION YEAR FELLOWSHIP

Phillips Exeter Academy
Attn: Dean of Multicultural Affairs
20 Main Street
Exeter, NH 03833-2460
(603) 772-4311   Fax: (603) 777-4393
E-mail: teaching_opportunities@exeter.edu
Web: www.exeter.edu

Summary To provide an opportunity for doctoral candidates who are Asian Americans or from other diverse backgrounds to work on their dissertation during a residency at Phillips Exeter Academy in Exeter, New Hampshire.

Eligibility This program is open to Ph.D. candidates in any discipline who are in the completion stage of their dissertation. Applicants must be prepared to devote full time to their writing during a residency at the academy. Along with their application, they must submit a curriculum vitae, 2 letters of reference, a 2- to 3-page synopsis of the dissertation, and a 500-word statement of purpose testifying to the appropriateness of the fellowship. Candidates who are interested in potentially teaching in an independent school setting and who are underrepresented in higher education are particularly encouraged to apply.

Financial data This program provides a stipend ($14,310), research and travel funds up to $1,000, room and board, benefits, access to facilities and resources of the school, and professional development opportunities.

Duration 1 academic year.

Additional information Fellows do not have any regular or prescribed duties. During the tenure of the program, fellows may not have any other full- or part-time job.

Number awarded 1 each year.

Deadline March of each year.

[880]
PNAGA ANNUAL SCHOLARSHIP FOR GRADUATE NURSING STUDIES

Philippine Nurses Association of Georgia
c/o Merlyn Walker, Treasurer
3216 Christian Springs Drive
Lithonia, GA 30038
(404) 910-3764   E-mail: thepnaga@gmail.com
Web: sites.google.com/site/thepnaga/scholarships

Summary To provide financial assistance for graduate study to members of the Philippine Nurses Association of Georgia (PNAGA).

Eligibility This program is open to PNAGA members who are currently enrolled in a graduate nursing program in any state. Applicants must submit a resume or curriculum vitae, a letter of recommendation, and a 150-word essay on their professional career goals.

Financial data The stipend is $1,000.

Duration 1 year.

Number awarded 1 or more each year.

Deadline April of each year.

[881]
PORTER PHYSIOLOGY DEVELOPMENT AWARDS

American Physiological Society
Attn: Education Office
9650 Rockville Pike, Room 3111
Bethesda, MD 20814-3991
(301) 634-7132   Fax: (301) 634-7098
E-mail: education@the-aps.org
Web: www.the-aps.org

Summary To provide financial assistance to Asian Americans and other minorities who are members of the American Physiological Society (APS) interested in working on a doctoral degree in physiology.

Eligibility This program is open to U.S. citizens and permanent residents who are members of racial or ethnic minority groups (Asian, Hispanic or Latino, American Indian or Alaska Native, Black or African American, or Native Hawaiian or other Pacific Islander). Applicants must be currently enrolled in or accepted to a doctoral program in physiology at a university as full-time students. They must be APS members and have actively participated in its work. Selection is based on the applicant's potential for success (academic record, statement of interest, previous awards and experiences, letters of recommendation); applicant's proposed training environment (including quality of preceptor); and applicant's research and training plan (clarity and quality).

Financial data The stipend is $28,300 per year. No provision is made for a dependency allowance or tuition and fees.

Duration 1 year; may be renewed for 1 additional year and, in exceptional cases, for a third year.

Additional information This program is supported by the William Townsend Porter Foundation (formerly the Harvard Apparatus Foundation). The first Porter Fellowship was awarded in 1920. In 1966 and 1967, the American Physiological Society established the Porter Physiology Development Committee to award fellowships to minority students engaged in graduate study in physiology. The highest ranked applicant for these fellowships is designated the Eleanor Ison Franklin Fellow.

Number awarded Varies each year; recently, 6 were awarded.

Deadline January of each year.

[882]
PREDOCTORAL FELLOWSHIP IN MENTAL HEALTH AND SUBSTANCE ABUSE SERVICES

American Psychological Association
Attn: Minority Fellowship Program
750 First Street, N.E.
Washington, DC 20002-4242
(202) 336-6127   Fax: (202) 336-6012
TDD: (202) 336-6123   E-mail: mfp@apa.org
Web: www.apa.org

Summary To provide financial assistance to doctoral students committed to providing mental health and substance abuse services to Asian Americans and other ethnic minority populations.

Eligibility Applicants must be U.S. citizens, nationals, or permanent residents, enrolled full time in an accredited doctoral program, and committed to a career in psychology related to ethnic minority mental health and substance abuse services. Members of ethnic minority groups (Asian Americans, African Americans, Hispanics/Latinos, American Indians, Alaskan Natives, Native Hawaiians, and other Pacific Islanders) are especially encouraged to apply. Preference is given to students specializing in clinical, school, and counseling psychology. Selection is based on commitment to ethnic minority behavioral health services or policy, knowledge of ethnic minority behavioral health services, the fit between career goals and training environment selected, potential as a future leader in ethnic minority psychology as demonstrated through accomplishments and goals, scholarship and grades, and letters of recommendation.

Financial data The stipend varies but is based on the amount established by the National Institutes of Health for predoctoral students; recently that was $23,376 per year.

Duration 1 academic or calendar year; may be renewed for up to 2 additional years.

Additional information Funding is provided by the U.S. Substance Abuse and Mental Health Services Administration.

Number awarded Varies each year.

Deadline January of each year.

[883]
PRESBYTERIAN WOMEN OF COLOR GRANTS

Presbyterian Church (USA)
Attn: Office of Financial Aid for Service
100 Witherspoon Street
Louisville, KY 40202-1396
(502) 569-5224   Toll Free: (888) 728-7228, ext. 5224
Fax: (502) 569-8766   TDD: (800) 833-5955
E-mail: finaid@pcusa.org
Web: www.presbyterianmission.org

Summary To provide financial assistance to graduate students who are Asian Americans or other women of color and Presbyterian Church (USA) members interested in preparing for church occupations.

Eligibility This program is open to women of color who are full-time graduate students at a PCUSA seminary or accredited theological institution approved by their Committee on Preparation for Ministry. Applicants must be working on 1) an M.Div. degree and enrolled as an inquirer or candidate by a PCUSA presbytery; or 2) an M.A.C.E. degree and preparing for a church occupation. They must be PCUSA members, U.S. citizens or permanent residents, able to demonstrate financial need, and recommended by the financial aid officer at their theological institution. Along with their application, they must submit a 1,000-word essay on what they believe God is calling them to do in ministry.

Financial data Stipends range from $1,000 to $3,000 per year. Funds are intended as supplements to students who have been awarded a Presbyterian Study Grant but still demonstrate remaining financial need.

Duration 1 year; may be renewed up to 2 additional years.

Number awarded Varies each year; the sponsor awards approximately 130 grants for this and 3 related programs each year.

Deadline June of each year.

[884]
PRIMARY CARE RESOURCE INITIATIVE FOR MISSOURI

Missouri Department of Health and Senior Services
Attn: Primary Care and Rural Health
P.O. Box 570
Jefferson City, MO 65102-0570
(573) 751-6219   Toll Free: (800) 891-7415
Fax: (573) 522-8146   E-mail: info@health.mo.gov
Web: health.mo.gov/living/families/primarycare/primo

Summary To provide scholarship/loans to residents of Missouri, especially Asian Americans and other minorities, who are interested in working as a health care professional in an underserved area of the state following graduation.

Eligibility This program is open to residents of Missouri who have lived for 1 or more years in the state for purposes other than attending an educational institution. Applicants must have been accepted by or currently be attending a Missouri school offering a course of study leading to a degree in

1) primary care medicine; 2) dentistry; 3) dental hygiene; 4) psychiatry; 5) psychology; 6) licensed clinical social work; or 7) licensed professional counseling. Physicians and dentists in primary care residency programs are also eligible. Priority is given to residents of medically underserved areas in Missouri, minority group members, and previous recipients.

Financial data   Loans range from $5,000 to $20,000 per year. This is a scholarship/loan program. Loans of 5 years or more are forgiven at the rate of 20% per year for qualifying employment in an area of defined need (a geographic area or a population that is experiencing a shortage of primary health care providers in Missouri). Loans for less than 5 years are forgiven on a year-for-year basis. If the loan is not forgiven by service, it must be repaid within 60 months at 9.5% interest.

Duration   Full-time undergraduate students may receive up to 4 loans. Part-time medical students may receive loans for up to 4 or 6 years, depending on the length of their program. Physicians and dentists in primary care residency programs may receive up to 3 years of loans.

Additional information   This program is also known as the PRIMO Loan Program.

Number awarded   Varies each year; recently, a total of 32 of these loans were granted.

Deadline   April of each year.

[885]
PRUDENTIAL FINANCIAL SUMMER INTERNSHIP

National Asian Pacific American Bar Association
Attn: Prudential Internship Selection Committee
1612 K Street, N.W., Suite 510
Washington, DC 20006
(202) 775-9555   Fax: (202) 775-9333
E-mail: rglenn@napaba.org
Web: www.napaba.org/?page=NLF_FI

Summary   To provide an opportunity for law students who are members of the National Asian Pacific American Bar Association (NAPABA) to gain work experience during a summer internship at Prudential Financial in Newark, New Jersey.

Eligibility   This program is open to NAPABA members who have completed the first year at an accredited law school with a GPA of 3.0 or higher. Applicants must be interested in a summer internship at Prudential Financial in Newark, New Jersey. They should have business-related experience or interest.

Financial data   The stipend is approximately $10,000.

Duration   10 weeks during the summer.

Number awarded   1 each year.

Deadline   January of each year.

[886]
PSI CHI DIVERSITY ARTICLE AWARDS

Psi Chi
825 Vine Street
P.O. Box 709
Chattanooga, TN 37401-0709
(423) 756-2044   Fax: (877) 774-2443
E-mail: awards@psichi.org
Web: www.psichi.org/?page=diversityinfo

Summary   To recognize and reward undergraduate and graduate student members of Psi Chi (an honor society in psychology) who submit outstanding articles on issues of diversity for publication in society journals.

Eligibility   This program is open to undergraduate and graduate students who have either 1) had an article published in the *Psi Chi Journal of Psychological Research* ; or 2) submitted an article for publication in *Eye on Psi Chi*. The article must relate to issues of diversity, defined to include ethnic minorities, LGBTQ, gender, economic factors, mental disability, physical disability, or nontraditional students. Selection is based on content-originality and impact, research or practitioner, results or outcomes, scholarship content, and relevance (50%); focus-diversity goals and objectives are strongly developed, order of ideas is explicitly and consistently clear, logical, and effective, and conclusions are well-formulated and supported by the results or outcomes (35%); and language-style and mechanics (15%).

Financial data   The awards are $600.

Duration   The awards are presented annually.

Number awarded   2 each year: 1 for an article published in the *Psi Chi Journal of Psychological Research* and 1 for an article submitted to *Eye on Psi Chi*.

Deadline   October of each year.

[887]
PUBLIC HONORS FELLOWSHIPS OF THE OREGON STATE BAR

Oregon State Bar
Attn: Diversity and Inclusion Department
16037 S.W. Upper Boones Ferry Road
P.O. Box 231935
Tigard, OR 97281-1935
(503) 620-0222
Toll Free: (800) 452-8260, ext. 338 (within OR)
Fax: (503) 684-1366   TDD: (503) 684-7416
E-mail: cling@osbar.org
Web: www.osbar.org/diversity/programs.html#honors

Summary   To provide law students in Oregon with summer work experience in public interest law, especially Asian Americans and others who will help the Oregon State Bar achieve its diversity and inclusion objectives.

Eligibility   This program is open to students at law schools in Oregon who are not in the first or final year of study. Each school may nominate up to 5 students. Nominees must have demonstrated a career goal in public interest or public sector law. Preference is given to students who will contribute to the Oregon State Bar's diversity and inclusion program, defined to include age, culture, disability, ethnicity, gender and gender identity or expression, geographic location, national origin, race, religion, sex, sexual orientation, and socio-economic status. They must be interested in working in a law office during the summer; the employment should be in Oregon, although exceptions will be made if the job offers the student special experience not available within the state. Along with their application, they must submit a 500-word personal statement on either 1) how their status as a person of diversity has influenced their decision to become a lawyer and how will it influence them throughout their legal professional career; or 2) a challenge they have faced, how they met the challenge, and how that experience will affect the decisions they will make as a legal professional. They must also submit a sample of their legal writing. Selection is based on the personal statement (35%), legal writing ability (25%), academic achievement (15%), work experience and honors (10%), and financial need (15%). The information on those students is forwarded to prospective employers in Oregon and they arrange to interview the selectees.

Financial data Fellows receive a stipend of $5,000.

Duration 3 months during the summer.

Additional information There is no guarantee that all students selected by the sponsoring organization will receive fellowships at Oregon law firms.

Number awarded 6 each year: 2 from each of the law schools.

Deadline Each law school sets its own deadline.

[888]
PUBLIC POLICY AND INTERNATIONAL AFFAIRS FELLOWSHIPS

Public Policy and International Affairs Fellowship Program
c/o University of Minnesota
Humphrey School of Public Affairs
130 Humphrey School
301 19th Avenue South
Minneapolis, MN 55455
Toll Free: (877) 774-2001   E-mail: hadd0029@umn.edu
Web: www.ppiaprogram.org/ppia

Summary To provide financial assistance to Asian Americans and students from other underrepresented groups who have completed a specified summer institute and are interested in preparing for graduate study in the fields of public policy and/or international affairs.

Eligibility This program is open to people of color historically underrepresented in public policy and international affairs. Applicants must be U.S. citizens or permanent residents interested in a summer institute in public policy and international affairs. They must first apply directly to the summer institute. Following participation in that institute, they apply for graduate study in fields of their choice at 41 designated universities. For a list of participating institutions, contact the sponsor.

Financial data The participating programs in public policy and/or international affairs have agreed to waive application fees and grant fellowships of at least $5,000 to students who have participated in the summer institutes.

Duration 1 summer and 1 academic year.

Additional information This program was established in 1981 when the Alfred P. Sloan Foundation provided a grant to the Association for Public Policy Analysis and Management (APPAM). From 1981 through 1988, participants were known as Sloan Fellows. From 1889 through 1995, the program was supported by the Ford Foundation and administered by the Woodrow Wilson National Fellowship Administration, so participants were known as Woodrow Wilson Fellows in Public Policy and International Affairs. Beginning in 1995, the program's name was shortened to the Public Policy and International Affairs Fellowship Program (PPIA) and the Association of Professional Schools of International Affairs (APSIA) also became an institutional sponsor. In 1999, the Ford Foundation ended its support for PPIA effective with the student cohort that participated in summer institutes in 1999. The APPAM and APSIA incorporated PPIA as an independent organization and have continued to sponsor it. Since summer of 2001, summer institutes have been held at 5 universities:

the Summer Program in Public Policy and International Affairs at the Gerald R. Ford School of Public Policy at the University of Michigan, the Humphrey School Junior Institute at the Humphrey School of Public Affairs at the University of Minnesota (which serves as host of the program), the UCP-PIA Junior Summer Institute at the Richard and Rhoda Goldman School of Public Policy at the University of California at Berkeley, the PPIA Junior Summer Institute at the Woodrow Wilson School of Public and International Affairs at Princeton University, and the PPIA Junior Summer Institute at the Heinz School of Public Policy and Management at Carnegie Mellon University. For information on those institutes, contact the respective school. Additional support is currently provided by the Foundation for Child Development and the William T. Grant Foundation.

Number awarded Varies each year.

Deadline Each of the 5 participating universities that offer summer institutes and each of the 41 universities that accept students for graduate study sets its own deadline.

[889]
RACE RELATIONS MULTIRACIAL STUDENT SCHOLARSHIP

Christian Reformed Church
Attn: Office of Race Relations
1700 28th Street, S.E.
Grand Rapids, MI 49508
(616) 224-5883   Toll Free: (877) 864-3977
Fax: (616) 224-0834   E-mail: elugo@crcna.org
Web: www.crcna.org/race/scholarships

Summary To provide financial assistance to Asian American and other minority undergraduate and graduate students interested in attending colleges related to the Christian Reformed Church in North America (CRCNA).

Eligibility This program is open to students of color in the United States and Canada. Normally, applicants are expected to be members of CRCNA congregations who plan to pursue their educational goals at Calvin Theological Seminary or any of the colleges affiliated with the CRCNA. They must be interested in training for the ministry of racial reconciliation in church and/or in society. Along with their application, they must submit paragraphs about their personal history and family, Christian faith, and Christian leadership goals. Students who have no prior history with the CRCNA must attend a CRCNA-related college or seminary for a full academic year before they are eligible to apply for this program. Students entering their sophomore year must have earned a GPA of 2.0 or higher as freshmen; students entering their junior year must have earned a GPA of 2.3 or higher as sophomores; students entering their senior year must have earned a GPA of 2.6 or higher as juniors.

Financial data First-year students receive $500 per semester. Other levels of students may receive up to $2,000 per academic year.

Duration 1 year.

Additional information This program was first established in 1971 and revised in 1991. Recipients are expected to train to engage actively in the ministry of racial reconciliation in church and in society. They must be able to work in the United States or Canada upon graduating and must consider working for 1 of the agencies of the CRCNA.

Number awarded Varies each year; recently, 31 students received a total of $21,000 in support.

Deadline March of each year.

[890]
RACIAL ETHNIC PASTORAL LEADERSHIP PROGRAM

Synod of Southern California and Hawaii
Attn: Racial Ethnic Pastoral Leadership Program
14225 Roscoe Boulevard
Panorama, CA 91402
(213) 483-3840, ext. 112　　　　Fax: (818) 891-0212
E-mail: ntucker@synod.org
Web: www.synod.org/#repl

Summary To provide financial assistance to Asian Americans and members of other racial minority groups in the Presbyterian Church (USA) Synod of Southern California and Hawaii who are preparing for a career as a pastor or other church vocation.

Eligibility Applicants must be under care of their church's Session and enrolled with a Presbytery within the Synod of Southern California and Hawaii. They must be members of racial ethnic groups interested in becoming a Presbyterian pastor or other church worker (e.g., commissioned ruling elder, certified Christian educator) and serving in a racial ethnic ministry within the PCUSA. Racial ethnic persons who already have an M.Div. degree, are from another denomination in correspondence with the PCUSA, and are seeking to meet PCUSA requirements for ordination or transfer may also be eligible if they plan to serve in a racial ethnic congregation or an approved specialized ministry. Applicants must submit documentation of financial need, recommendations from the appropriate presbytery committee or session, a current transcript, and essays on their goals and objectives. They must be enrolled full or part time in a PCUSA seminary or other seminary approved by the Committee on Preparation for Ministry of their Presbytery.

Financial data The stipend is $5,000 per year.

Duration 1 year; may be renewed.

Additional information This program began in 1984.

Number awarded Varies each year; recently, 5 students were receiving support from this program. Since the program began, it has awarded $372,375 to approximately 335 seminarians.

Deadline April of each year.

[891]
RACIAL ETHNIC SUPPLEMENTAL GRANTS

Presbyterian Church (USA)
Attn: Office of Financial Aid for Service
100 Witherspoon Street
Louisville, KY 40202-1396
(502) 569-5224　　　Toll Free: (888) 728-7228, ext. 5224
Fax: (502) 569-8766　　　TDD: (800) 833-5955
E-mail: finaid@pcusa.org
Web: www.presbyterianmission.org

Summary To provide financial assistance to Asian American and other minority graduate students who are Presbyterian Church (USA) members interested in preparing for church occupations.

Eligibility This program is open to racial/ethnic graduate students (Asian American, African American, Hispanic American, Native American, or Alaska Native) who are enrolled full time at a PCUSA seminary or accredited theological institution approved by their Committee on Preparation for Ministry. Applicants must be working on 1) an M.Div. degree and enrolled as an inquirer or candidate by a PCUSA presbytery; or 2) an M.A.C.E. degree and preparing for a church occupation. They must be PCUSA members, U.S. citizens or permanent residents, able to demonstrate financial need, and recommended by the financial aid officer at their theological institution. Along with their application, they must submit a 1,000-word essay on what they believe God is calling them to do in ministry.

Financial data Stipends range from $500 to $1,000 per year. Funds are intended as supplements to students who have been awarded a Presbyterian Study Grant but still demonstrate remaining financial need.

Duration 1 year; may be renewed up to 2 additional years.

Number awarded Varies each year; the sponsor awards approximately 130 grants for this and 3 related programs each year.

Deadline June of each year.

[892]
RAILROAD AND MINE WORKERS MEMORIAL SCHOLARSHIP

Japanese American Citizens League
Attn: National Scholarship Awards
1765 Sutter Street
San Francisco, CA 94115
(415) 345-1075　　　　Fax: (415) 345-1077
E-mail: pwada@jacl.org
Web: www.jacl.org/jacl-national-scholarship-program

Summary To provide financial assistance for graduate study in any field to members of the Japanese American Citizens League (JACL).

Eligibility This program is open to JACL members who are attending or planning to attend an accredited college or university as a graduate student. Applicants must submit information on their involvement in JACL and a 2-page essay on a topic that changes annually but relates to Japanese Americans. Selection is based on that essay, academic history, JACL involvement, school activities, work history, scholastic honors, and community involvement.

Financial data Stipends generally average more than $2,000.

Duration 1 year; nonrenewable.

Additional information This program was established to honor the Japanese American railroad and mine workers who lost their jobs during World War II.

Number awarded At least 1 each year.

Deadline March of each year.

[893]
RALPH W. SHRADER DIVERSITY SCHOLARSHIPS

Armed Forces Communications and Electronics
  Association
Attn: AFCEA Educational Foundation
4400 Fair Lakes Court
Fairfax, VA 22033-3899
(703) 631-6138   Toll Free: (800) 336-4583, ext. 6138
Fax: (703) 631-4693   E-mail: scholarship@afcea.org
Web: www.afcea.org

Summary To provide financial assistance to master's degree students, especially Asian Americans and other minorities, in fields related to communications and electronics.

Eligibility This program is open to U.S. citizens working on a master's degree at an accredited college or university in the United States. Applicants must be enrolled full time and studying computer science, engineering (chemical, electrical, electronic, communications, or systems), mathematics, physics, technology management, information technology, or other field directly related to the support of U.S. national security or intelligence enterprises. At least 1 of these scholarships is set aside for a woman or a minority. Selection is based primarily on academic excellence.

Financial data The stipend is $3,000. Funds are paid directly to the recipient.

Duration 1 year.

Additional information This program is sponsored by Booz Allen Hamilton.

Number awarded Up to 5 each year, at least 1 of which is for a woman or minority candidate.

Deadline May of each year.

[894]
RAMA SCHOLARSHIP FOR THE AMERICAN DREAM

American Hotel & Lodging Educational Foundation
Attn: Manager of Foundation Programs
1250 I Street, N.W., Suite 1100
Washington, DC 20005-5904
(202) 289-3180   Fax: (202) 289-3199
E-mail: foundation@ahlef.org
Web: www.ahlef.org

Summary To provide financial assistance to Asian American and other minority undergraduate and graduate students working on a degree in hotel management at designated schools.

Eligibility This program is open to U.S. citizens and permanent residents enrolled as full- or part-time undergraduate or graduate students with a GPA of 2.5 or higher. Applicants must be attending 1 of 13 designated hospitality management schools, which select the recipients. Preference is given to students of Asian-Indian descent and other minority groups and to JHM Hotel employees and their dependents.

Financial data The stipend varies at each of the participating schools, but ranges from $1,000 to $3,000.

Duration 1 year.

Additional information This program was established by JHM Hotels, Inc. in 1998. The participating institutions are Bethune-Cookman University, California State Polytechnic University at Pomona, Cornell University, Florida International University, Georgia State University, Greenville Technical College, Howard University, Johnson & Wales University (Charlotte, North Carolina), New York University, University of Central Florida, University of Houston, University of South Carolina, and Virginia Polytechnic Institute and State University.

Number awarded Varies each year; recently, 20 were awarded. Since the program was established, it has awarded more than $726,000 to 446 recipients.

Deadline April of each year.

[895]
RAMSEY COUNTY BAR FOUNDATION LAW STUDENT SCHOLARSHIP

Ramsey County Bar Foundation
Attn: Diversity Committee
E-1401 First National Bank Building
332 Minnesota Street
St. Paul, MN 55101
(651) 222-0846   Fax: (651) 223-8344
E-mail: Cheryl@ramseybar.org
Web: www.ramseybar.org/news/law-student-scholarship

Summary To provide financial assistance to Asian Americans and members of other groups traditionally underrepresented in the legal profession who are attending law school in Minnesota.

Eligibility This program is open to residents of any state who are currently enrolled at a Minnesota law school. Applicants must be a member of a group traditionally underrepresented in the legal profession, including race, sex, ethnicity, sexual orientation, or disability. They must contribute meaningfully to diversity in their community, have a record of academic or professional achievement, and display leadership qualities through past work experience, community involvement, or student activities.

Financial data The stipend ranges up to $6,000.

Duration 1 year.

Number awarded 1 each year.

Deadline February of each year.

[896]
RANDY GERSON MEMORIAL GRANT

American Psychological Foundation
750 First Street, N.E.
Washington, DC 20002-4242
(202) 336-5843   Fax: (202) 336-5812
E-mail: foundation@apa.org
Web: www.apa.org/apf/funding/gerson.aspx

Summary To provide funding to graduate students, especially Asian Americans and members of other underrepresented groups, who are interested in conducting research in the psychology of couple and/or family dynamics and/or multi-generational processes.

Eligibility This program is open to full-time graduate students in psychology. Applicants must be proposing a project that advances the systemic understanding of couple and/or family dynamics and/or multi-generational processes. Work that advances theory, assessment, or clinical practice in those areas is eligible. Preference is given to projects that use or contribute to the development of Bowen family systems.

Selection is based on conformance with stated program goals, magnitude of incremental contribution, quality of proposed work, and applicant's competence to execute the project. The sponsor encourages applications from individuals who represent diversity in race, ethnicity, gender, age, disability, and sexual orientation.

Financial data   The grant is $6,000.

Duration   The grant is presented annually.

Additional information   This grant was first awarded in 1998.

Number awarded   1 each year.

Deadline   January of each year.

[897]
RAYMOND L. OCAMPO JR. SCHOLARSHIP

Filipino Bar Association of Northern California
Attn: Foundation
268 Bush Street, Suite 2928
San Francisco, CA 94104
E-mail: fbancinfo@gmail.com
Web: www.fbanc.org

Summary   To provide financial assistance to entering or continuing students at law schools in northern California who are interested in serving the Filipino American community.

Eligibility   This program is open to currently-enrolled and entering students at northern California law school who have a tie to the Filipino American community and intend to provide legal services to that community after graduation from law school. Applicants must submit a current transcript or admit letter, a resume, a list of their involvement in activities of the Filipino Bar Association of Northern California (FBANC), and a 2-page essay on 1) an obstacle or adversity they have faced and how that experience has affected their decision to attend law school or their career plans after law school; and 2) barriers that Filipino and Filipino Americans experience regarding the legal system and ways that those barriers can be addressed to increase the community's access to justice. Selection is based on that essay, academic standing, demonstrated interest in issues affecting the Filipino American community, and their desire to serve the Filipino American community.

Financial data   The stipend is $5,000.

Duration   1 year.

Additional information   This program began in 2000 as a result of a gift from Raymond L. Ocampo, Jr., who founded the Filipino Bar Association of Northern California in 1980.

Number awarded   1 each year.

Deadline   April of each year.

[898]
RDW GROUP, INC. MINORITY SCHOLARSHIP FOR COMMUNICATIONS

Rhode Island Foundation
Attn: Donor Services Administrator
One Union Station
Providence, RI 02903
(401) 427-4011   Fax: (401) 331-8085
E-mail: rbogert@rifoundation.org
Web: www.rifoundation.org

Summary   To provide financial assistance to Rhode Island Asian American and other undergraduate and graduate students of color interested in preparing for a career in communications at a school in any state.

Eligibility   This program is open to undergraduate and graduate students at colleges and universities in any state who are Rhode Island residents of color. Applicants must intend to work on a degree in communications (including computer graphics, art, cinematography, or other fields that would prepare them for a career in advertising). They must be able to demonstrate financial need and a commitment to a career in communications. Along with their application, they must submit an essay (up to 300 words) on the impact they would like to have on the communications field.

Financial data   The stipend is approximately $2,000 per year.

Duration   1 year; recipients may reapply.

Additional information   This program is sponsored by the RDW Group, Inc.

Number awarded   1 each year.

Deadline   April of each year.

[899]
RESOURCES FOR THE FUTURE SUMMER INTERNSHIPS

Resources for the Future
Attn: Internship Coordinator
1616 P Street, N.W., Suite 600
Washington, DC 20036-1400
(202) 328-5020   Fax: (202) 939-3460
E-mail: IC@rff.org
Web: www.rff.org

Summary   To provide internships to undergraduate and graduate students, especially Asian Americans and other minorities, who are interested in working on research projects in public policy during the summer.

Eligibility   This program is open to undergraduate and graduate students (with priority to graduate students) interested in an internship at Resources for the Future (RFF). Applicants must be working on a degree in the social and natural sciences and have training in economics and quantitative methods or an interest in public policy. They should display strong writing skills and a desire to analyze complex environmental policy problems amenable to interdisciplinary methods. The ability to work without supervision in a careful and conscientious manner is essential. Women and minority candidates are strongly encouraged to apply. Both U.S. and non-U.S. citizens are eligible, if the latter have proper work and residency documentation.

Financial data   The stipend is $375 per week for graduate students or $350 per week for undergraduates. Housing assistance is not provided.

Duration   10 weeks during the summer; beginning and ending dates can be adjusted to meet particular student needs.

Number awarded   Varies each year.

Deadline   March of each year.

[900]
RETAIL REAL ESTATE DIVERSITY SCHOLARSHIP

International Council of Shopping Centers
Attn: ICSC Foundation
1221 Avenue of the Americas, 41st Floor
New York, NY 10020-1099
(646) 728-3628   Fax: (732) 694-1690
E-mail: foundation@icsc.org
Web: www.icsc.org

Summary To provide financial assistance to Asian American and other minority graduate students who are members of the International Council of Shopping Centers (ICSC) and preparing for a career as a retail real estate professional.

Eligibility This program is open to U.S. citizens who are graduate student members of ICSC and working on a degree related to the retail real estate profession. Applicants must be a member of an underrepresented ethnic minority group (Asian or Pacific Islander, American Indian or Alaskan Native, African American, Hispanic, Caribbean). They must have a GPA of 3.0 or higher and be enrolled full time or enrolled part time while working.

Financial data The stipend is $2,500.

Duration 1 year.

Number awarded 1 or more each year.

Deadline January of each year.

[901]
REVEREND H. JOHN AND ASAKO YAMASHITA MEMORIAL SCHOLARSHIP

Japanese American Citizens League
Attn: National Scholarship Awards
1765 Sutter Street
San Francisco, CA 94115
(415) 345-1075   Fax: (415) 345-1077
E-mail: pwada@jacl.org
Web: www.jacl.org/jacl-national-scholarship-program

Summary To provide financial assistance for graduate study in education to members of the Japanese American Citizens League (JACL).

Eligibility This program is open to JACL members who are attending or planning to attend an accredited college or university as a graduate student. Applicants must demonstrate a concern for education, social justice, and service to their communities. They must submit information on their involvement in JACL and a 2-page essay on a topic that changes annually but relates to Japanese Americans. Selection is based on that essay, academic history, JACL involvement, school activities, work history, scholastic honors, and community involvement.

Financial data Stipends generally average more than $2,000.

Duration 1 year; nonrenewable.

Number awarded At least 1 each year.

Deadline March of each year.

[902]
RICHARD D. HAILEY SCHOLARSHIP

American Association for Justice
Attn: AAJ Education
777 Sixth Street, N.W., Suite 200
Washington, DC 20001
(202) 684-9563   Toll Free: (800) 424-2725
Fax: (202) 965-0355   E-mail: education@justice.org
Web: www.justice.org

Summary To provide financial assistance for law school to Asian American and other minority student members of the American Association for Justice (AAJ).

Eligibility This program is open to Asian American, African American, Hispanic, Native American, and biracial members of the association who are entering the first, second, or third year of law school. Applicants must submit a 500-word essay on how they meet the selection criteria: commitment to the association, involvement in student chapter and minority caucus activities, desire to represent victims, interest and proficiency of skills in trial advocacy, and financial need.

Financial data The stipend is $1,000.

Duration 1 year.

Additional information The American Association for Justice was formerly the Association of Trial Lawyers of America.

Number awarded Up to 6 each year.

Deadline May of each year.

[903]
ROBERT E. WONE FELLOWSHIP

Asian Pacific American Bar Association Educational Fund
P.O. Box 2209
Washington, DC 20013-2209
Fax: (202) 598-1233   E-mail: aefboard@gmail.com
Web: www.aefdc.com/fellowships

Summary To provide funding to law students from any state who are interested in interning during the summer with a public interest organization that benefits either the Asian Pacific American community or the metropolitan Washington, D.C. community at large.

Eligibility This program is open to law students who have obtained an unpaid internship with a public interest organization (e.g., government organizations and other nonprofits serving the public interest). The organization must serve either the greater Washington, D.C. area or the Asian Pacific American community. Applicants must submit an essay, up to 500 words, on the internship, how it will benefit the Asian Pacific American community or the metropolitan Washington, D.C. area, and how their past and/or present activities show commitment to the public interest and/or the Asian Pacific American community. Preference is given to applicants interning at direct service organizations. Selection is based primarily on the essay, but the applicant's maturity and responsibility are also considered.

Financial data The stipend is $4,500.

Duration At least 10 weeks or a total of 400 hours during the summer.

Additional information This program began in 2007.

Number awarded 1 each year.

Deadline April of each year.

[904]
ROBERT T. MATSUI ANNUAL WRITING COMPETITION

Asian Pacific American Bar Association Educational Fund
P.O. Box 2209
Washington, DC 20013-2209
Fax: (202) 598-1233   E-mail: aefboard@gmail.com
Web: www.aefdc.com/matsui-writing-competition

Summary   To recognize and reward law students who submit outstanding articles on topics of interest to the Asian Pacific American legal community.

Eligibility   This competition is open to law students in the United States. Applicants must submit an original law review article, up to 10,000 words in length, that has not been published. The topic must relate to Asian Pacific Americans and the law.

Financial data   The award is $1,500.

Duration   The award is presented annually.

Additional information   This competition was established in 2005. The winning entry is published by the *Asian Pacific American Law Journal* at the University of California, Los Angeles School of Law.

Number awarded   1 each year.

Deadline   May of each year.

[905]
ROBERT TOIGO FOUNDATION FELLOWSHIPS

Robert Toigo Foundation
Attn: Fellowship Program Administrator
180 Grand Avenue, Suite 450
Oakland, CA 94612
(510) 763-5771   Fax: (510) 763-5778
E-mail: info@toigofoundation.org
Web: www.toigofoundation.org

Summary   To provide financial assistance to Asian American and other minority students working on a master's degree in business administration or a related field.

Eligibility   This program is open to members of minority groups (South Asian American, Asian American/Pacific Islander, African American, Hispanic/Latino, or Native American/Alaskan Native) who are entering or enrolled in a program for an M.B.A., J.D./M.B.A., master's in real estate, or master's in finance. Applicants must be preparing for a career in finance, including (but not limited to) investment management, investment banking, corporate finance, real estate, private equity, venture capital, business development, pension fund investment, or financial services consulting. U.S. citizenship or permanent resident status is required.

Financial data   The stipend is $2,500 per year.

Duration   Up to 2 years.

Additional information   The application fee is $50.

Number awarded   Approximately 50 to 60 each year.

Deadline   March of each year.

[906]
ROSA L. PARKS COLLEGE SCHOLARSHIP

Conference of Minority Transportation Officials
Attn: National Scholarship Program
100 M Street, S.E., Suite 917
Washington, DC 20003
(202) 506-2917   E-mail: info@comto.org
Web: www.comto.org/page/scholarships

Summary   To provide financial assistance to Asian American and other students who have a tie to the Conference of Minority Transportation Officials (COMTO) and are interested in working on an undergraduate or master's degree in transportation.

Eligibility   This program is open to 1) undergraduates who have completed at least 60 semester credit hours in a transportation discipline; and 2) students working on a master's degree in transportation who have completed at least 15 credits. Applicants must be or have a parent, guardian, or grandparent who has been a COMTO member for at least 1 year. They must have a GPA of 3.0 or higher. Along with their application they must submit a cover letter on their transportation-related career goals and life aspirations. Financial need is not considered in the selection process.

Financial data   The stipend is $4,500. Funds are paid directly to the recipient's college or university.

Duration   1 year.

Number awarded   1 each year.

Deadline   April of each year.

[907]
ROY H. POLLACK SCHOLARSHIP

Unitarian Universalist Association
Attn: Ministerial Credentialing Office
24 Farnsworth Street
Boston, MA 02210-1409
(617) 948-6403   Fax: (617) 742-2875
E-mail: mcoadministrator@uua.org
Web: www.uua.org

Summary   To provide financial assistance to seminary students, especially Asian Americans and other persons of color who are preparing for the Unitarian Universalist (UU) ministry.

Eligibility   This program is open to seminary students who are enrolled full or at least half time in their second or third year in a UU ministerial training program with candidate status. Applicants must be citizens of the United States or Canada. Priority is given first to those who have demonstrated outstanding ministerial ability and secondarily to students with the greatest financial need (especially persons of color).

Financial data   The stipend ranges from $1,000 to $15,000 per year.

Duration   1 year.

Additional information   This program began in 1998.

Number awarded   Varies each year; recently, 2 were awarded.

Deadline   April of each year.

[908]
ROY SCRIVNER MEMORIAL RESEARCH GRANTS

American Psychological Foundation
750 First Street, N.E.
Washington, DC 20002-4242
(202) 336-5843   Fax: (202) 336-5812
E-mail: foundation@apa.org
Web: www.apa.org/apf/funding/scrivner.aspx

Summary To provide funding to graduate students, especially Asian Americans and members of other underrepresented groups, who are interested in conducting dissertation research on lesbian, gay, bisexual, and transgender (LGBT) family psychology and therapy.

Eligibility This program is open to doctoral candidates who are interested in conducting empirical research in all fields of the behavioral and social sciences that focus on LGBT family psychology and LGBT family therapy. Proposals are especially encouraged for empirical studies that address the following: problems faced by LGBT families such as those associated with cultural, racial, socioeconomic, and family structure diversity; successful coping mechanisms such as sources of support and resilience for family members; and clinical issues and interventions in the domain of LGBT. Selection is based on conformance with stated program goals; quality of proposed work, including research plan and expected outcome; applicant's demonstrated scholarship and competence, and appropriateness of proposed budget. The sponsor encourages applications from individuals who represent diversity in race, ethnicity, gender, age, disability, and sexual orientation.

Financial data The grant is $15,000.

Duration 1 year.

Number awarded 1 each year.

Deadline October of each year.

[909]
R.P. AND J.L. CARR SOCIAL JUSTICE SCHOLARSHIP

OCA Asian Pacific American Advocates-Wisconsin
  Chapter
c/o Albert Chen, Scholarship Committee Chair
120 North 73rd Street
Milwaukee, WI 53213
(414) 258-2410   E-mail: albertchen@aol.com
Web: www.ocawi.org/www/scholarships.html

Summary To provide financial assistance to members of the Wisconsin Chapter of OCA Asian Pacific American Advocates (OCA-WI) who are interested in working on a graduate degree in a field related to peace and social justice.

Eligibility This program is open to OCA-WI members who are enrolled or planning to enroll full time in a graduate program at an accredited college or university in any state. Applicants must be interested in working on a degree in a field related to peace and social justice (e.g., law, public policy, political science, community development). Along with their application, they must submit a 2-page personal statement that describes themselves, their field of study, pertinent personal history, and professional plans. U.S. citizenship or permanent resident status is required.

Financial data The stipend is $2,000.

Duration 1 year; nonrenewable.

Additional information This program began in 2008.

Number awarded 1 each year.

Deadline March of each year.

[910]
RURAL OPPORTUNITY FELLOWSHIPS OF THE OREGON STATE BAR

Oregon State Bar
Attn: Diversity and Inclusion Department
16037 S.W. Upper Boones Ferry Road
P.O. Box 231935
Tigard, OR 97281-1935
(503) 620-0222
Toll Free: (800) 452-8260, ext. 338 (within OR)
Fax: (503) 684-1366   TDD: (503) 684-7416
E-mail: cling@osbar.org
Web: www.osbar.org/diversity/programs.html#rural

Summary To provide summer work experience in rural areas to law students in Oregon who are Asian Americans or in other ways will help the Oregon State Bar achieve its diversity and inclusion objectives.

Eligibility This program is open to students at law schools in Oregon who are interested in working for a public employer or nonprofit organization in rural areas of the state during the summer. The program defines rural areas as anywhere along the Oregon coast, anywhere east of the Cascade Mountains, or anywhere south of Roseburg. Applicants must contribute to the Oregon State Bar's diversity and inclusion program, defined to include age, culture, disability, ethnicity, gender and gender identity or expression, geographic location, national origin, race, religion, sex, sexual orientation, and socio-economic status. They must be planning to practice in Oregon. Along with their application, they must submit a 500-word personal statement on either 1) how their status as a person of diversity has influenced their decision to become a lawyer and how will it influence them throughout their legal professional career; or 2) a challenge they have faced, how they met the challenge, and how that experience will affect the decisions they will make as a legal professional. They must also submit a sample of their legal writing. Selection is based on the personal statement (35%), legal writing ability (25%), academic achievement (15%), work experience and honors (10%), and financial need (15%).

Financial data Fellows receive a stipend of $8,360.

Duration 3 months during the summer.

Number awarded 2 each year.

Deadline January of each year.

[911]
RUTH D. PETERSON FELLOWSHIPS FOR RACIAL AND ETHNIC DIVERSITY

American Society of Criminology
Attn: Awards Committee
1314 Kinnear Road, Suite 212
Columbus, OH 43212-1156
(614) 292-9207   Fax: (614) 292-6767
E-mail: asc@asc41.com
Web: www.asc41.com

Summary To provide financial assistance to Asian American or other ethnic minority doctoral students in criminology and criminal justice.
Eligibility This program is open to students of color, especially members of ethnic groups underrepresented in the field of criminology and criminal justice, including (but not limited to) Asians, Blacks, Indigenous peoples, and Latina/os. Applicants must have been accepted into a doctoral program in the field. Along with their application, they must submit an up-to-date curriculum vitae; a personal statement on their race or ethnicity; copies of undergraduate and graduate transcripts; a statement of need and prospects for other financial assistance; a letter describing career plans, salient experiences, and nature of interest in criminology and criminal justice; and 3 letters of reference.
Financial data The stipend is $6,000.
Duration 1 year.
Additional information This program began in 1988 as the American Society of Criminology Graduate Fellowships for Ethnic Minorities. Its current name was adopted in 2016.
Number awarded 3 each year.
Deadline February of each year.

[912]
RUTH WEBB MINORITY SCHOLARSHIP

California Academy of Physician Assistants
2318 South Fairview Street
Santa Ana, CA 92704-4938
(714) 427-0321   Fax: (714) 427-0324
E-mail: capa@capanet.org
Web: www.capanet.org

Summary To provide financial assistance to Asian American or other minority student members of the California Academy of Physician Assistants (CAPA) enrolled in physician assistant programs in California.
Eligibility This program is open to student members of CAPA enrolled in primary care physician assistant programs in California. Applicants must be members of a minority group (Asian/Pacific Islander, African American, Hispanic, or Native American/Alaskan Native). They must have maintained good academic standing and conducted activities to promote the physician assistant profession. Along with their application, they must submit an essay describing the activities they have performed to promote the physician assistant profession, the importance of representing minorities in their community, and why they should be awarded this scholarship. Financial need is considered in the selection process.
Financial data The stipend is $2,000.
Duration 1 year.
Number awarded 1 each year.
Deadline December of each year.

[913]
RYU FAMILY FOUNDATION SCHOLARSHIP GRANTS

Ryu Family Foundation, Inc.
Attn: Jenny Kang
186 Parish Drive
Wayne, NJ 07470
(646) 250-0317   E-mail: RyuFoundation@gmail.com
Web: www.ryufoundation.org

Summary To provide financial assistance to Korean and Korean American students in the Northeast who are working on an undergraduate or graduate degree in any field.
Eligibility This program is open to Korean Americans (U.S. citizens) and Koreans (with or without permanent resident status). Applicants must be enrolled full time and working on an undergraduate or graduate degree; have a GPA of 3.5 or higher; be able to document financial need; and be either residing or attending college in 1 of the following 10 northeastern states: Connecticut, Delaware, Maine, Massachusetts, New Hampshire, New Jersey, New York, Pennsylvania, Rhode Island, or Vermont. Along with their application, they must submit a 500-word essay on a subject that changes annually; recently, students were asked to write on 1 of the following: 1) what they would you like to do to change the world for the better; 2) something they have done in the past that has made a difference in their family; or 3) a book or article they have read that has inspired them.
Financial data A stipend is awarded (amount not specified). Checks are made out jointly to the recipient and the recipient's school.
Duration 1 year; may be renewed.
Number awarded Approximately 18 each year.
Deadline November of each year.

[914]
SABA-DC PUBLIC INTEREST FELLOWSHIPS

South Asian Bar Association of Washington DC
Attn: Secretary
P.O. Box 65349
Washington, DC 20035
(703) 683-9600   E-mail: sabadcsecretary@gmail.com
Web: www.sabadc.org/publicinterestfellowship

Summary To provide funding to students from any state enrolled at law schools in the Washington, D.C. area who have accepted an unpaid internship and are either south Asians or interested in the south Asian community.
Eligibility This program is open to first- and second-year students from any state who are enrolled at law schools in the Washington, D.C. area. Applicants must have accepted an unpaid legal internship in the area. They must either 1) be of south Asian descent; or 2) have accepted an internship that specifically focuses on the needs of the local south Asian community. The internship must relate to public interest law and may be with a nonprofit organization, legal services organization, district attorney or public defender, government agency, or public service law firm. Along with their application, they must submit an essay that describes their previous service and/or plans to serve the South Asian community in the District of Columbia area, why they believe public interest work is important or relevant to the South Asian community, the organization where they will be working and the community it serves, what their duties will be, the reason why they applied to the organization where they plan to intern, how this experience will benefit them as a public interest attorney, and they immediate career and professional goals. Selection is based on that essay, commitment to public service, academic achievement, and financial need.
Financial data Recently, the stipend was $5,000.
Duration Summer months.

Number awarded Several each year.

Deadline April of each year.

[915]
SABA-NC FOUNDATION PUBLIC INTEREST FELLOWSHIPS

South Asian Bar Association of Northern California
Attn: SABA-NC Foundation Secretary
P.O. Box 2733
San Francisco, CA 94126
E-mail: foundation.sabanc@gmail.com
Web: www.southasianbar.org/saba-foundation/fellowships

Summary To provide summer work experience in public interest law that will benefit the South Asian community of northern California, especially to students at law schools in the area.

Eligibility This program is open to students from any state enrolled at an ABA-accredited law school at least part time who can demonstrate dedication and commitment to public interest work benefiting the South Asian community in northern California. Strong preference is given to applicants enrolled at law schools in northern California and employed at an organization in the area doing work that directly impacts the South Asian community. Selection is based on academic achievement, essays on the applicant's involvement in the South Asian community and the northern California community at large, commitment to public service, financial need, and other personal circumstances. Interviews may be required.

Financial data The stipend ranges up to $5,000.

Duration Summer months.

Additional information This program started in 2005.

Number awarded Varies each year; recently, 4 were awarded.

Deadline April of each year.

[916]
SAJA SCHOLARSHIPS

South Asian Journalists Association
Attn: Zainab Imam, Secretary
c/o Columbia Journalism School
Pulitzer Hall
2950 Broadway
New York, NY 10027
E-mail: secretary@saja.org
Web: www.saja.org/scholarships

Summary To provide financial assistance for undergraduate and graduate study to journalism students of south Asian descent.

Eligibility This program is open to students of south Asian descent (including Bangladesh, Bhutan, India, Maldives, Nepal, Pakistan, and Sri Lanka; Indo-Caribbeans are also eligible). Applicants must be serious about preparing for a journalism career and must provide evidence they plan to do so through courses, internships, or freelancing. They may be 1) high school seniors about to enroll in an accredited college or university; 2) current students in an accredited college or university in the United States or Canada; or 3) students enrolled or about to enter a graduate program in the United States or Canada. Applicants with financial hardship are given special consideration. Selection is based on interest in journalism, writing skills, participation in the sponsoring organization, reasons for entering journalism, and financial need.

Financial data The stipends are $2,000 for high school seniors, $3,000 for undergraduates, or $5,000 for graduate students.

Duration 1 year.

Additional information Recipients are expected to give back to the South Asian Journalists Association (SAJA) by volunteering at the annual convention or at other events during the year.

Number awarded Varies each year; recently, 11 were awarded: a to a high school senior, 6 to undergraduates, and 4 to graduate students.

Deadline March of each year.

[917]
SAM CHU LIN SCHOLARSHIP

Asian American Journalists Association-Los Angeles
  Chapter
Attn: Frank Buckley, Scholarship Chair
KTLA-TV
5800 Sunset Boulevard
Los Angeles, CA 90028
E-mail: aajalaawards@gmail.com
Web: www.aaja-la.org/category/programs/scholarships

Summary To provide financial assistance to Asian/Pacific Islander students in the Los Angeles area who are interested in careers in broadcast journalism.

Eligibility This program is open to Asian/Pacific Islander full-time students who are planning a career in broadcast journalism. Applicants must be attending a college or university in the Los Angeles area (Los Angeles, Orange, Riverside, San Bernardino, or Ventura counties). Membership in the Asian American Journalists Association (AAJA) is encouraged for applicants and required for recipients. Selection is based on academic achievement, commitment to the field of journalism, journalistic ability, sensitivity to Asian American and Pacific Islander issues, and financial need.

Financial data The stipend is $2,500.

Duration 1 year; may be renewed.

Number awarded 1 each year.

Deadline January of each year.

[918]
SARASOTA COUNTY BAR ASSOCIATION DIVERSITY SCHOLARSHIP

Community Foundation of Sarasota County
Attn: Grants and Scholarships Coordinator
2635 Fruitville Road
P.O. Box 49587
Sarasota, FL 34230-6587
(941) 556-7114   Fax: (941) 952-7115
E-mail: eyoung@cfsarasota.org
Web: www.cfsarasota.org

Summary To provide financial assistance and work experience in Sarasota County, Florida to law students from any state who are Asian Americans or will add to the diversity of the legal profession in other ways.

Eligibility This program is open to first- through third-year law students of traditionally underrepresented backgrounds (e.g., race, color, religion, national origin, ethnicity, age, gender, sexual orientation, physical disability, socioeconomic background). Applicants must be interested in practicing law after graduation and in obtaining summer placement in private law firms or government agencies in Sarasota County. They may be attending law school in any state but they should have or have had family, school, or community ties to the county. Along with their application, they must submit a 250-word essay describing how their particular background would help the Sarasota County Bar Association achieve its goal of making the local legal community more diverse.

Financial data   Students receive a salary for their summer employment and a stipend of $5,000, sent directly to their law school, upon completion of their employment.

Duration   1 summer for employment and 1 year for law school enrollment.

Additional information   This program, also known as the Richard R. Garland Diversity Scholarship, is sponsored by the Sarasota County Bar Association.

Number awarded   1 or more each year.

Deadline   February of each year.

[919]
SASP ADVANCED STUDENT DIVERSITY SCHOLARSHIPS

American Psychological Association
Attn: Division 16 (School Psychology)
750 First Street, N.E.
Washington, DC 20002-4242
(202) 336-6165   Fax: (202) 218-3599
TDD: (202) 336-6123   E-mail: cchambers@apa.org
Web: www.apadivisions.org/division-16/awards/sasp.aspx

Summary   To provide financial assistance to continuing graduate student members of the Student Affiliates in School Psychology (SASP) of Division 16 (School Psychology) of the American Psychological Association (APA), especially Asian Americans and other students from other underrepresented cultural backgrounds.

Eligibility   This program is open to SASP members who come from underrepresented cultural backgrounds. Applicants must be working on a graduate degree to prepare for a career as a school psychologist. They must be entering their third, fourth, or fifth year of graduate study.

Financial data   The stipend is $1,000.

Duration   1 year; nonrenewable.

Number awarded   1 each year.

Deadline   April of each year.

[920]
SASP INCOMING STUDENT DIVERSITY SCHOLARSHIPS

American Psychological Association
Attn: Division 16 (School Psychology)
750 First Street, N.E.
Washington, DC 20002-4242
(202) 336-6165   Fax: (202) 218-3599
TDD: (202) 336-6123   E-mail: cchambers@apa.org
Web: www.apadivisions.org/division-16/awards/sasp.aspx

Summary   To provide financial assistance to entering graduate student members of the Student Affiliates in School Psychology (SASP) of Division 16 (School Psychology) of the American Psychological Association (APA) who are Asian

Americans or from other underrepresented cultural backgrounds.

Eligibility   This program is open to SASP members who come from underrepresented cultural backgrounds. Applicants must be working on a graduate degree to prepare for a career as a school psychologist. They must be entering their first or second year of graduate study.

Financial data   The stipend is $500.

Duration   1 year; nonrenewable.

Number awarded   2 each year.

Deadline   April of each year.

[921]
SCHOLARSHIP FOR A THEOLOGICAL LIBRARIANSHIP COURSE

American Theological Library Association
Attn: Diversity Committee
300 South Wacker Drive, Suite 2100
Chicago, IL 60606-6701
(312) 454-5100   Toll Free: (888) 665-ATLA
Fax: (312) 454-5505   E-mail: memberrep@atla.com
Web: www.atla.com

Summary   To provide funding to library students from Asian American or other underrepresented groups who are members of the American Theological Library Association (ATLA) and interested in taking a course in theological librarianship.

Eligibility   This program is open to ATLA members from underrepresented groups (religious, racial, ethnic, or gender) who wish to attend a theological librarianship course at an ALA-accredited master's program in library and information studies. Applicants must submit personal statements on what diversity means to them, why their voice has not yet been heard, how their voice will add diversity to the theological librarianship course, how they will increase diversity in their immediate context, and how they plan to increase diversity and participate fully in the ATLA.

Financial data   The stipend is $1,200.

Duration   Up to 1 year.

Number awarded   1 each year.

Deadline   April of each year.

[922]
SCHOLARSHIPS FOR MINORITY ACCOUNTING STUDENTS

American Institute of Certified Public Accountants
Attn: Academic and Career Development Division
220 Leigh Farm Road
Durham, NC 27707-8110
(919) 402-4931   Fax: (919) 419-4705
E-mail: scholarships@aicpa.org
Web: www.aicpa.org

Summary   To provide financial assistance to Asian Americans and other minorities interested in studying accounting at the undergraduate or graduate school level.

Eligibility   This program is open to minority undergraduate and graduate students, enrolled full time, who have a GPA of 3.3 or higher (both cumulatively and in their major) and intend to pursue a C.P.A. credential. The program defines minority students as those whose heritage is Asian American, Black or African American, Hispanic or Latino, or Native American. Undergraduates must have completed at least 30 semester hours, including at least 6 semester hours of a major in accounting. Graduate students must be working on a master's degree in accounting, finance, taxation, or a related program. Applicants must be U.S. citizens or permanent residents and student affiliate members of the American Institute of Certified Public Accountants (AICPA). Along with their application, they must submit 500-word essays on 1) why they want to become a C.P.A. and how attaining that licensure will contribute to their goals; and 2) how they would spread the message about accounting and the C.P.A. profession in their community and school. In the selection process, some consideration is given to financial need.

Financial data Stipends range up to $5,000 per year. Funds are disbursed directly to the recipient's school.

Duration 1 year; may be renewed up to 3 additional years or until completion of a bachelor's or master's degree, whichever is earlier.

Additional information This program began in 1969. Additional support is provided by the Accounting Education Foundation of the Texas Society of Certified Public Accountants, the New Jersey Society of Certified Public Accountants, Robert Half International, and the Virgin Islands Society of Certified Public Accountants.

Number awarded Varies each year; recently, 97 students received funding through this program.

Deadline March of each year.

[923]
SCIENCE, TECHNOLOGY, AND PUBLIC POLICY FELLOWSHIPS

Harvard University
John F. Kennedy School of Government
Belfer Center for Science and International Affairs
Attn: STPP Fellowship Coordinator
79 John F. Kennedy Street, Mailbox 53
Cambridge, MA 02138
(617) 495-1498   Fax: (617) 495-8963
E-mail: patricia_mclaughlin@hks.harvard.edu
Web: belfercenter.ksg.harvard.edu

Summary To provide funding to professionals, postdoctorates, and doctoral students, especially Asian Americans and other minorities, who are interested in conducting research in science, technology, and public policy areas of concern to the Belfer Center for Science and International Affairs at Harvard University in Cambridge, Massachusetts.

Eligibility The postdoctoral fellowship is open to recent recipients of the Ph.D. or equivalent degree, university faculty members, and employees of government, military, international, humanitarian, and private research institutions who have appropriate professional experience. Applicants for predoctoral fellowships must have passed their general examinations. Scholars from a wide range of disciplinary and multi-disciplinary fields and those holding a Ph.D. in engineering or in the natural sciences are strongly encouraged to apply. The program especially encourages applications from women, minorities, and citizens of all countries. All applicants must be interested in conducting research on projects of the Science, Technology, and Public Policy (STPP) Program. Recently, those included projects on Internet policy and regulatory reform, energy technology innovation, water and energy resources, sustainable energy development in China, technology and innovation, solar geoengineering and climate policy, technological innovation and globalization, agricultural innovation in Africa, managing the atom, and the geopolitics of energy.

Financial data The stipend is $37,500 for postdoctoral research fellows or $25,000 for predoctoral research fellows. Fellows who renew their grant receive a monthly stipend of $3,750 for postdoctoral fellows or $2,500 for predoctoral fellows. Stipends for advanced research fellows vary. Health insurance is also provided.

Duration 10 months; may be renewed on a month-by-month basis.

Additional information Fellows are expected to devoted some portion of their time to collaborative endeavors, as arranged by the appropriate program or project director. Predoctoral fellows are expected to contribute to the program's research activities, as well as work on (and ideally complete) their dissertations. Postdoctoral research fellows are also expected to complete a book, monograph, or other significant publication during their period of residence.

Number awarded A limited number each year.

Deadline January of each year.

[924]
SCOTT AND PAUL PEARSALL SCHOLARSHIP

American Psychological Foundation
750 First Street, N.E.
Washington, DC 20002-4242
(202) 336-5843   Fax: (202) 336-5812
E-mail: foundation@apa.org
Web: www.apa.org/apf/funding/pearsall.aspx

Summary To provide funding to graduate students, especially Asian Americans and members of other underrepresented groups, who are interested in conducting research on the psychological effect of stigma on people with disabilities.

Eligibility This program is open to full-time graduate students at accredited universities in the United States and Canada. Applicants must be interested in conducting research that seeks to increase the public's understanding of the psychological pain and stigma experiences by adults living with physical disabilities, such as cerebral palsy. Selection is based on conformance with stated program goals and the quality of proposed work. The sponsor encourages applications from individuals who represent diversity in race, ethnicity, gender, age, disability, and sexual orientation. Preference is given to proposals that contain a plan to disseminate findings to the public.

Financial data The grant is $10,000.

Duration 1 year.

Additional information This program began in 2013.

Number awarded 2 each year.

Deadline September of each year.

[925]
SECTION OF BUSINESS LAW DIVERSITY CLERKSHIP PROGRAM

American Bar Association
Attn: Section of Business Law
321 North Clark Street
Chicago, IL 60654-7598
(312) 988-5588   Fax: (312) 988-5578
E-mail: businesslaw@americanbar.org
Web: www.americanbar.org

Summary To provide summer work experience in business law to Asian American and other underrepresented student members of the American Bar Association (ABA) and its Section of Business Law who will help the section to fulfill its goal of promoting diversity.

Eligibility This program is open to first- and second-year students at ABA-accredited law schools who are interested in a summer business court clerkship. Applicants must 1) be a member of an underrepresented group (student of color, woman, student with disabilities, gay, lesbian, bisexual, or transgender); or 2) have overcome social or economic disadvantages, such as a physical disability, financial constraints, or cultural impediments to becoming a law student. They must be able to demonstrate financial need. Along with their application, they must submit a 500-word essay that covers why they are interested in this clerkship program, what they would gain from the program, how it would positively influence their future professional goals as a business lawyer, and how they meet the program's criteria. Membership in the ABA and its Section of Business Law are required.

Financial data The stipend is $6,000.

Duration Summer months.

Additional information This program began in 2008. Assignments vary, but have included business courts in Delaware, Illinois, Maryland, Pennsylvania, and South Carolina.

Number awarded 9 each year.

Deadline January of each year.

[926]
SELECTED PROFESSIONS FELLOWSHIPS FOR WOMEN OF COLOR

American Association of University Women
Attn: AAUW Educational Foundation
1111 16th Street, N.W.
Washington, DC 20036-4873
(202) 785-7700   Toll Free: (800) 326-AAUW
Fax: (202) 872-1425   TDD: (202) 785-7777
E-mail: aauw@applyists.com
Web: www.aauw.org

Summary To aid Asian Americans and other women of color who are in their final year of graduate training in the fields of business administration, law, or medicine.

Eligibility This program is open to women who are working full time on a degree in fields in which women of color have been historically underrepresented: business administration (M.B.A.), law (J.D.), or medicine (M.D., D.O.). They must be Asian Americans, African Americans, Mexican Americans, Puerto Ricans and other Hispanics, Native Americans, Alaska Natives, or Pacific Islanders. U.S. citizenship or permanent resident status is required. Applicants in business administration must be entering their second year of study;

applicants in law must be entering their third year of study; applicants in medicine may be entering their third or fourth year of study. Special consideration is given to applicants who 1) demonstrate their intent to enter professional practice in disciplines in which women are underrepresented, to serve underserved populations and communities, or to pursue public interest areas; and 2) are nontraditional students. Selection is based on professional promise and personal attributes (50%), academic excellence and related academic success indicators (40%), and financial need (10%).

Financial data Stipends range from $5,000 to $18,000.

Duration 1 year, beginning in July.

Additional information The filing fee is $35.

Number awarded Varies each year; recently, a total of 25 Selected Professions Fellowships were awarded.

Deadline January of each year.

[927]
SEO CAREER LAW PROGRAM

Sponsors for Educational Opportunity
Attn: Career Program
55 Exchange Place
New York, NY 10005
(212) 979-2040   Toll Free: (800) 462-2332
Fax: (646) 706-7113
E-mail: careerprogram@seo-usa.org
Web: www.seo-usa.org/Career/Corporate_Law

Summary To provide summer work experience to students of color interested in studying law.

Eligibility This program is open to Asian Americans and other students of color who are college seniors or recent graduates planning to attend law school in the United States. Applicants must be interested in a summer internship at a participating law firm that specializes in corporate law, including initial public offerings of stock, mergers and acquisitions, joint ventures, corporate reorganizations, cross-border financing, including securities, tax, bankruptcy, antitrust, real estate and white-collar crime. They must have a cumulative GPA of 3.0 or higher. Personal interviews are required.

Financial data Interns receive a competitive stipend of up to $1,300 per week.

Duration 10 weeks during the summer.

Additional information This program began in 1980. Internships are available in New York City, Washington, D.C., Houston, Los Angeles, San Francisco, Menlo Park, Palo Alto, or Atlanta.

Number awarded Varies each year.

Deadline February of each year.

[928]
SERVICES FOR TRANSITION AGE YOUTH FELLOWSHIP

American Psychological Association
Attn: Minority Fellowship Program
750 First Street, N.E.
Washington, DC 20002-4242
(202) 336-6127   Fax: (202) 336-6012
TDD: (202) 336-6123   E-mail: mfp@apa.org
Web: www.apa.org/pi/mfp/psychology/stay/index.aspx

Summary To provide financial assistance to master's degree students, especially Asian Americans and other minorities, who are committed to providing mental health services to ethnic minority youth.

Eligibility Applicants must be U.S. citizens, nationals, or permanent residents, enrolled full time in a terminal master's degree program that will prepare them to provide mental health services to ethnic minority transition age youth (16 through 25 years of age) and their families. Their program must be housed in the same department as an APA-accredited doctoral program. They are not required to identify as ethnic minorities, but members of such groups (African Americans, Hispanics/Latinos, American Indians, Alaskan Natives, Asian Americans, Native Hawaiians, and other Pacific Islanders) are especially encouraged to apply. Along with their application, they must submit a 2-page essay on their interests and career goals in psychology. Students enrolled in counseling, marriage and family therapy, and addiction programs are not eligible.

Financial data The stipend is $6,000.

Duration 1 year.

Additional information Funding is provided by the U.S. Substance Abuse and Mental Health Services Administration.

Number awarded Varies each year; recently, 24 were awarded.

Deadline January of each year.

[929]
SHEILA SUEN LAI SCHOLARSHIP OF LIBRARY AND INFORMATION SCIENCE

Chinese American Librarians Association
c/o Raymond Wang, Scholarship Committee Co-Chair
Community College of Baltimore County
Essex Library, Room 102
7201 Rossville Boulevard
Baltimore, MD 21237
(443) 840-1898   Fax: (443) 840-1724
E-mail: rwang@ccbcmd.edu
Web: www.cala-web.org/node/1616

Summary To provide financial assistance to Chinese American students interested in working on a graduate degree in library or information science.

Eligibility This program is open to students enrolled full time in an accredited library school in North America and working on a master's or doctoral degree. Applicants must be of Chinese nationality or Chinese descent.

Financial data The stipend is $500.

Duration 1 year.

Additional information The program was established in 1989.

Number awarded 1 each year.

Deadline April of each year.

[930]
SIA YANG SCHOLARSHIP

Hmong American Education Fund
P.O. Box 17468
St. Paul, MN 55117
(651) 592-1576   E-mail: scholarships@thehaef.org
Web: www.thehaef.org

Summary To provide financial assistance to Hmong and southeast Asian refugees from of any state who have lost a parent through death and are interested in working on an undergraduate or graduate degree in any field.

Eligibility This program is open to students of Hmong or other southeast Asian refugee descent who are high school seniors, GED recipients, or current full-time undergraduate or graduate students at 2- or 4-year colleges or universities in any state. Applicants must be U.S. citizens or permanent residents. They must have lost at least 1 parent through death. Along with their application, they must submit a 1,500-word essay on their commitment to education, how losing a parent or both parents has impacted them, and their community service. Selection is based on academic achievement.

Financial data The stipend is $1,000.

Duration 1 year; nonrenewable.

Number awarded 1 each year.

Deadline March of each year.

[931]
SLA NEW ENGLAND DIVERSITY LEADERSHIP DEVELOPMENT SCHOLARSHIP

SLA New England
c/o Khalilah Gambrell, Diversity Chair
EBSCO Information Services
10 Estes Street
Ipswich, MA 01938
(978) 356-6500   Toll Free: (800) 653-2726
Fax: (978) 356-6565   E-mail: gambrell9899@gmail.com
Web: newengland.sla.org/member-benefits/stipends

Summary To provide financial assistance for library science tuition or attendance at the annual conference of the Special Libraries Association (SLA) to members of SLA New England who are Asian Americans or represent another diverse population.

Eligibility This program is open to SLA New England members who are of Asian American, Black (African American), Hispanic, Pacific Islander American, Native Alaskan, or Native Hawaiian heritage. Applicants must be seeking funding for SLA annual meeting attendance, tuition reimbursement for a library science program, or tuition reimbursement for a course directly related to the library and information science field. Along with their application, they must submit a 500-word essay on how they will encourage and celebrate diversity within the SLA New England community.

Financial data The award covers actual expenses up to $1,500.

Duration This is a 1-time award.

Number awarded 1 each year.

Deadline April of each year.

[932]
SMITHSONIAN MINORITY AWARDS PROGRAM

Smithsonian Institution
Attn: Office of Fellowships and Internships
470 L'Enfant Plaza, Suite 7102
P.O. Box 37012, MRC 902
Washington, DC 20013-7012
(202) 633-7070   Fax: (202) 633-7069
E-mail: siofi@si.edu
Web: www.smithsonianofi.com

Summary To provide funding to Asian American and other minority undergraduate and graduate students interested in conducting research at the Smithsonian Institution.

Eligibility This program is open to members of U.S. minority groups underrepresented in the Smithsonian's scholarly programs. Applicants must be undergraduates or beginning graduate students interested in conducting research in the Institution's disciplines and in the museum field. They must be U.S. citizens or permanent residents and have a GPA of 3.0 or higher.

Financial data Students receive a grant of $600 per week.

Duration Up to 10 weeks.

Additional information Recipients must carry out independent research projects in association with the Smithsonian's research staff. Eligible fields of study currently include animal behavior, ecology, and environmental science (including an emphasis on the tropics); anthropology (including archaeology); astrophysics and astronomy; earth sciences and paleobiology; evolutionary and systematic biology; history of science and technology; history of art (especially American, contemporary, African, Asian, and 20th-century art); American crafts and decorative arts; social and cultural history of the United States; and folklife. Students are required to be in residence at the Smithsonian for the duration of the fellowship.

Number awarded Varies each year; recently, 25 were granted: 2 for fall, 19 for summer, and 4 for spring.

Deadline January of each year for summer and fall residency; September of each year for spring residency.

[933]
SMITHSONIAN MINORITY STUDENT INTERNSHIP

Smithsonian Institution
Attn: Office of Fellowships and Internships
470 L'Enfant, Suite 7102
P.O. Box 37012, MRC 902
Washington, DC 20013-7012
(202) 633-7070   Fax: (202) 633-7069
E-mail: siofi@si.edu
Web: www.smithsonianofi.com/minority-internship-program

Summary To provide Asian American and other minority undergraduate or graduate students with the opportunity to work on research or museum procedure projects in specific areas of history, art, or science at the Smithsonian Institution.

Eligibility Internships are offered to minority students who are actively engaged in undergraduate or graduate study or have graduated within the past 4 months. Applicants must be U.S. citizens or permanent residents who have an overall GPA of 3.0 or higher. Applicants must be interested in conducting research in any of the following fields of interest to the Smithsonian: animal behavior, ecology, and environmental science (including an emphasis on the tropics); anthropology (including archaeology); astrophysics and astronomy; earth sciences and paleobiology; evolutionary and systematic biology; history of science and technology; history of art (especially American, contemporary, African, Asian, and 20th-century art); American crafts and decorative arts; social and cultural history of the United States; and folklife.

Financial data The program provides a stipend of $600 per week; travel allowances may also be offered.

Duration 10 weeks during the summer or academic year.

Number awarded Varies each year.

Deadline January of each year for summer or fall; September of each year for spring.

[934]
SOCIETY FOR THE STUDY OF SOCIAL PROBLEMS RACIAL/ETHNIC MINORITY GRADUATE SCHOLARSHIP

Society for the Study of Social Problems
Attn: Executive Officer
University of Tennessee
901 McClung Tower
Knoxville, TN 37996-0490
(865) 689-1531   Fax: (865) 689-1534
E-mail: sssp@utk.edu
Web: www.sssp1.org

Summary To provide funding to Asian American and other ethnic and racial minority members of the Society for the Study of Social Problems (SSSP) who are interested in conducting research for their doctoral dissertation.

Eligibility This program is open to SSSP members who are Asian or Asian American, Black or African American, Hispanic or Latino, Native Hawaiian or other Pacific Islander, or American Indian or Alaska Native. Applicants must have completed all requirements for a Ph.D. (course work, examinations, and approval of a dissertation prospectus) except the dissertation. They must have a GPA of 3.25 or higher and be able to demonstrate financial need. Their field of study may be any of the social and/or behavioral sciences that will enable them to expand their perspectives in the investigation into social problems. U.S. citizenship or permanent resident status is required.

Financial data The stipend is $15,000. Additional grants provide $500 for the recipient to 1) attend the SSSP annual meeting prior to the year of the work to receive the award; and 2) attend the meeting after the year of the award to present a report on the work completed.

Duration 1 year.

Number awarded 1 each year.

Deadline January of each year.

[935]
SOCIETY OF BIBLICAL LITERATURE REGIONAL SCHOLARS AWARDS

Society of Biblical Literature
c/o The Luce Center
825 Houston Mill Road, Suite 350
Atlanta, GA 30329
(404) 727-3100   Fax: (404) 727-3101
E-mail: sblexec@sbl-site.org
Web: www.sbl-site.org/membership/SBLAwards.aspx

Summary To provide funding for annual meeting attendance or professional development to members of the Society of Biblical Literature (SBL) at the doctoral or recent postdoctoral level, especially Asian Americans and other minorities.

Eligibility This award is available to SBL members who are Ph.D. candidates or who completed a Ph.D. within the past 4 years. Applicants must present at an SBL regional meeting an original work of their own scholarship and must submit a copy of the paper, along with a curriculum vitae, to the regional coordinator for their SBL region. Members of the selection committee attend the oral presentation and evaluate it on the basis of clear articulation of argument advanced, even and engaging delivery, clear pronunciation and style appropriate to oral presentation, and creative and appropriate use of presentation materials. The written papers are evaluated as oral presentations, not as research articles, on the basis of the following criteria: clarity of expression and argumentation, demonstrated knowledge and critical use of scholarly resources and publications, use and knowledge of the primary sources, and originality of ideas and solutions. Women and minorities are encouraged to apply.

Financial data The award is $1,000. Funds may be used to support attendance at the SBL annual meeting or to promote future scholarship and professional development.

Duration The awards are presented annually.

Number awarded Up to 6 each year.

Deadline Each of the 11 SBL regions establishes its own deadline.

[936]
SOONGOOK CHOI SCHOLARSHIPS

Christian Church (Disciples of Christ)
Attn: Disciples Home Missions
130 East Washington Street
P.O. Box 1986
Indianapolis, IN 46206-1986
(317) 713-2652   Toll Free: (888) DHM-2631
Fax: (317) 635-4426   E-mail: mail@dhm.disciples.org
Web: www.discipleshomemissions.org

Summary To provide financial assistance to Asians and Pacific Islanders interested in preparing for a career in the ministry of the Christian Church (Disciples of Christ).

Eligibility This program is open to ministerial students of Asian and Pacific Islander descent who are members of a Christian Church (Disciples of Christ) congregation in the United States or Canada. Applicants must plan to prepare for the ordained ministry in a multiracial community, be working on an M.Div. or equivalent degree, provide evidence of financial need, be enrolled full time in an accredited school or seminary, provide a transcript of academic work, and be under the care of a regional Commission on the Ministry or in the process of coming under care.

Financial data A stipend is awarded (amount not specified).

Duration 1 year; may be renewed.

Additional information This program began in 2004.

Number awarded 1 each year.

Deadline March of each year.

[937]
SOUTH ASIAN BAR ASSOCIATION OF NEW YORK PUBLIC INTEREST FELLOWSHIPS

South Asian Bar Association of New York
c/o Uday Luthra, Vice President of Public Interest Fellowship
Ernst & Young Tax Practice
5 Times Square
New York, NY 10036-6530
(212) 773-3000   Fax: (773) 773-6350
E-mail: sabanyfellowship@gmail.com
Web: www.sabany.org

Summary To provide funding to law students from any state who have ties to the South Asian community and have accepted an unpaid summer internship in New York.

Eligibility This program is open to first- and second-year students at law schools in any state who have accepted an unpaid public interest legal internship in New York or the New York City metropolitan region (including Bergen, Essex, Hudson, Middlesex, Morris, Passaic, and Union counties in New Jersey and Fairfield County in Connecticut). Applicants must either 1) be of south Asian descent; or 2) have accepted an internship that specifically focuses on the needs of the local south Asian community. Selection is based on a 200-word job description that includes the mission of the host organization, the community it serves, and the specific work they will perform (40 points); a 500-word personal statement that explains why they selected the proposed internship and their interest in public service law (50 points); and financial need (10 points).

Financial data Recently, stipends averaged $2,700.

Duration At least 10 weeks during the summer.

Additional information These fellowships were first awarded in 2004.

Number awarded Varies each year; recently, 5 were awarded.

Deadline March of each year.

[938]
SOUTHERN CALIFORNIA CHINESE LAWYERS ASSOCIATION FELLOWSHIPS

Southern California Chinese Lawyers Association
c/o Faith Santoso
Asian Americans Advancing Justice
1145 Wilshire Boulevard, Second Floor
Los Angeles, CA 90017
(213) 977-7500
E-mail: fsantoso@advancingjustice-la.org
Web: www.sccla.org/page-1426592/3256338

Summary To provide an opportunity for students from any state enrolled at law schools in southern California to gain work experience at an Asian Pacific American organization.

Eligibility This program is open to Asian Pacific American students at law schools in southern California. Applicants must be interested in gaining work experience at the Legal Services Unit of Asian Americans Advancing Justice in Los Angeles, which provides free legal services to low-income individuals. They must be available to work 2 full days (15 hours) per week for 10 weeks.

Financial data The stipend is $2,000.

Duration 10 weeks.

Number awarded 2 to 4 each year.
Deadline March of each year.

[939]
SOUTHERN CALIFORNIA CHINESE LAWYERS ASSOCIATION SCHOLARSHIPS

Southern California Chinese Lawyers Association
c/o Faith Santoso
Asian Americans Advancing Justice
1145 Wilshire Boulevard, Second Floor
Los Angeles, CA 90017
(213) 977-7500
E-mail: fsantoso@advancingjustice-la.org
Web: www.sccla.org/page-1426592/3256338

Summary To provide financial assistance to Asian Pacific American students from any state enrolled at law schools in southern California.

Eligibility This program is open to Asian Pacific American students at law schools in southern California. Applicants may be in any year of law school, including entering first-year students and fourth-year evening students. Selection is based on academic accomplishment, financial need, and/or potential contribution to the Chinese American community.

Financial data The stipend is $1,000.

Duration 1 year.

Additional information This program includes the following named scholarships: the Ming Y. Moy Memorial Scholarship, the Justice Elwood Lui Scholarship, the Lee Gum Low Presidential Scholarship, the Judge Jack B. Tso Scholarship, the George S. Lee Scholarship, and the Margaret and Ned Good Scholarships.

Number awarded Several each year.

Deadline March of each year.

[940]
SOUTHERN REGION KOREAN AMERICAN SCHOLARSHIPS

Korean American Scholarship Foundation
Southern Region
Attn: Scholarship Committee Chair
6065 Sweet Creek Road
Johns Creek, GA 30097
E-mail: src.scholarship@kasf.org
Web: www.kasf.org/southern

Summary To provide financial assistance to Korean American students from any state who are working on or planning to work on an undergraduate or graduate degree in any field at a school in southern states.

Eligibility This program is open to Korean American students who are enrolled or planning to enroll at a college or university in the southern states as full-time undergraduate or graduate students. Applicants may reside anywhere in the United States, but they must attend school in the southern region: Alabama, Florida, Georgia, South Carolina, and Tennessee. Both U.S. citizens and foreign nationals are eligible. Selection is based on academic achievement (GPA of 3.0 or higher), school activities, community service, and financial need.

Financial data Stipends are $1,000 for undergraduate, graduate, or professional students or $500 for high school students.

Duration 1 year; renewable.

Number awarded Varies each year; recently, 26 college and graduate scholarships and 6 high school scholarships were awarded.

Deadline July of each year.

[941]
SOUTHERN REGIONAL EDUCATION BOARD DISSERTATION AWARDS

Southern Regional Education Board
Attn: Coordinator, Institute and Scholar Services
592 Tenth Street N.W.
Atlanta, GA 30318-5776
(404) 879-5516   Fax: (404) 872-1477
E-mail: tammy.wright@sreb.org
Web: www.sreb.org/types-awards

Summary To provide funding to Asian American and other minority students who wish to complete a Ph.D. dissertation, especially in fields of science, technology, engineering, or mathematics (STEM), while in residence at a university in the southern states.

Eligibility This program is open to U.S. citizens and permanent residents who are members of racial/ethnic minority groups (Native Americans, Hispanic Americans, Asian Americans, and African Americans) and have completed all requirements for a Ph.D. except the dissertation. Applicants must be enrolled at a designated college or university in the following 11 states: Alabama, Arkansas, Georgia, Kentucky, Louisiana, Maryland, Mississippi, South Carolina, Tennessee, Virginia, or West Virginia. Enrollment at a graduate school in 5 of those states (Georgia, Mississippi, South Carolina, Tennessee, and Virginia) is available only to residents of those states. Residents of any state in the country may attend a university in the other 5 states. Preference is given to students in STEM disciplines with particularly low minority representation, although all academic fields are eligible. Applicants must be in a position to write full time and must expect to complete their dissertation within the year of the fellowship. Eligibility is limited to individuals who plan to become full-time faculty members at a college or university upon completion of their doctoral degree. The program is not open to students working on other doctoral degrees (e.g., M.D., D.B.A., D.D.S., J.D., D.V.M., Ed.D., Pharm.D., D.N.P., D.P.T.).

Financial data Fellows receive waiver of tuition and fees (in or out of state), a stipend of $20,000, a $500 research allowance, and reimbursement of expenses for attending the Compact for Faculty Diversity's annual Institute on Teaching and Mentoring.

Duration 1 year; nonrenewable.

Additional information This program began in 1993 as part of the Compact for Faculty Diversity, supported by the Pew Charitable Trusts and the Ford Foundation. It currently operates at universities in 10 of the member states of the Southern Regional Education Board (SREB): Alabama, Arkansas, Georgia, Kentucky, Louisiana, Mississippi, South Carolina, Tennessee, Virginia, and West Virginia; the other 6 member states (Delaware, Florida, Maryland, North Carolina, Oklahoma, and Texas) do not participate.

Number awarded Varies each year.

Deadline March of each year.

[942]
SOUTHWESTERN REGION KOREAN AMERICAN SCHOLARSHIPS

Korean American Scholarship Foundation
Southern Region
Attn: Scholarship Committee Chair
P.O. Box 420242
Houston, TX 77242
E-mail: swrc.scholarship@kasf.org
Web: www.kasf.org/southwestern

Summary To provide financial assistance to Korean American students from any state who are working on or planning to work on an undergraduate or graduate degree in any field at a school in southwestern states.

Eligibility This program is open to residents of any state who are 1) U.S. citizens of Korean heritage; 2) Korean citizens who have a valid visa to study in the United States; and 3) citizens of any other country who are of Korean heritage and have a valid visa to study in the United States. Applicants must be enrolled or planning to enroll as a full-time undergraduate or graduate student at a college or university in Arkansas, Louisiana, Mississippi, Oklahoma, or Texas. Selection is based on academic performance, extracurricular activities, community service, letters of recommendation, an essay, character and integrity, and financial need.

Financial data Stipends range from $1,000 to $2,000.

Duration 1 year; nonrenewable.

Number awarded Varies each year; recently, 27 were awarded.

Deadline July of each year.

[943]
SPECTRUM SCHOLARSHIP PROGRAM

American Library Association
Attn: Office for Diversity
50 East Huron Street
Chicago, IL 60611-2795
(312) 280-5048   Toll Free: (800) 545-2433, ext. 5048
Fax: (312) 280-3256   TDD: (888) 814-7692
E-mail: spectrum@ala.org
Web: www.ala.org/offices/diversity/spectrum

Summary To provide financial assistance to Asian American and other minority students interested in working on a degree in librarianship.

Eligibility This program is open to ethnic minority students (Asian, African American or Black, Native Hawaiian or other Pacific Islander, Latino or Hispanic, and American Indian or Alaska Native). Applicants must be U.S. or Canadian citizens or permanent residents who have completed no more than a third of the requirements for a master's or school library media degree. They must be enrolled full or part time at an ALA-accredited school of library and information studies or an ALA-recognized NCATE school library media program. Selection is based on academic leadership, outstanding service, commitment to a career in librarianship, statements indicating the nature of the applicant's library and other work experience, letters of reference, and personal presentation.

Financial data The stipend is $5,000.

Duration 1 year; nonrenewable.

Additional information This program began in 1998. It is administered by a joint committee of the American Library Association (ALA).

Number awarded Varies each year; recently, 69 were awarded.

Deadline February of each year.

[944]
SREB DOCTORAL AWARDS

Southern Regional Education Board
Attn: Coordinator, Institute and Scholar Services
592 Tenth Street N.W.
Atlanta, GA 30318-5776
(404) 879-5516   Fax: (404) 872-1477
E-mail: tammy.wright@sreb.org
Web: www.sreb.org/types-awards

Summary To provide financial assistance to Asian American and other minority students who wish to work on a doctoral degree, especially in fields of science, technology, engineering, or mathematics (STEM), at designated universities in the southern states.

Eligibility This program is open to U.S. citizens and permanent residents who are members of racial/ethnic minority groups (Asian Americans, Native Americans, Hispanic Americans, and African Americans) and have or will receive a bachelor's or master's degree. Applicants must be entering or enrolled in the first year of a Ph.D. program at a designated college or university in the following 11 states: Alabama, Arkansas, Georgia, Kentucky, Louisiana, Maryland, Mississippi, South Carolina, Tennessee, Virginia, West Virginia. Enrollment at a graduate school in 5 of those states (Georgia, Mississippi, South Carolina, Tennessee, and Virginia) is available only to residents of those states. Residents of any state in the country may attend a university in the other 5 states. Applicants must indicate an interest in becoming a full-time college or university professor. The program does not support students working on other doctoral degrees (e.g., M.D., D.B.A., D.D.S., J.D., D.V.M., Ed.D., Pharm.D., D.N.P., D.P.T.). Preference is given to applicants in STEM disciplines with particularly low minority representation, although all academic fields are eligible.

Financial data Scholars receive a waiver of tuition and fees (in or out of state) for up to 5 years, an annual stipend of $20,000 for 3 years, an annual allowance of $500 for research and professional development activities, and reimbursement of travel expenses to attend the Compact for Faculty Diversity's annual Institute on Teaching and Mentoring.

Duration Up to 5 years.

Additional information This program began in 1993 as part of the Compact for Faculty Diversity, supported by the Pew Charitable Trusts and the Ford Foundation.

Number awarded Varies each year; recently, the program was supporting more than 300 scholars.

Deadline March of each year.

[945]
STANFORD CHEN INTERNSHIP GRANTS

Asian American Journalists Association
Attn: Student Programs Coordinator
5 Third Street, Suite 1108
San Francisco, CA 94103
(415) 346-2051, ext. 102   Fax: (415) 346-6343
E-mail: programs@aaja.org
Web: www.aaja.org/apply-for-a-scholarship-now

Summary To provide supplemental grants to student members of the Asian American Journalists Association (AAJA) working as interns at small or medium-size news organizations.

Eligibility This program is open to AAJA members who are college juniors, seniors, or graduate students with a serious intent to prepare for a career in journalism (print, online, broadcast, or photography). Applicants must have already secured an internship with a print company (daily circulation less than 100,000) or broadcast company (market smaller than the top 50). Along with their application, they must submit a 200-word essay on the kind of experience they expect as an intern at a small to medium-size media company, their career goals, and why AAJA's mission is important to them; a resume; verification of the internship; a letter of recommendation; and a statement of financial need.

Financial data The grant is $1,750. Funds are to be used for living expenses or transportation.

Duration Summer months.

Additional information This program began in 1998.

Number awarded Varies each year; recently, 4 were awarded.

Deadline April of each year.

[946]
STANTON NUCLEAR SECURITY FELLOWSHIP

Stanford University
Center for International Security and Cooperation
Attn: Fellowships Coordinator
Encina Hall, Room C206-10
616 Serra Street
Stanford, CA 94305-6165
(650) 723-9625   Fax: (650) 724-5683
E-mail: CISACfellowship@stanford.edu
Web: cisac.fsi.stanford.edu/docs/cisac_fellowship_program

Summary To provide funding to doctoral candidates and junior scholars, especially Asian Americans and other minorities, who are interested in conducting research on nuclear security issues at Stanford University's Center for International Security and Cooperation.

Eligibility This program is open to doctoral candidates, recent postdoctorates, and junior faculty. Applicants must be interested in conducting research on nuclear security issues while in residence at the center. The sponsor welcomes applications from women, minorities, and citizens of all countries.

Financial data The stipend ranges from $25,000 to $28,000 for doctoral candidates or from $48,000 to $66,000 for postdoctorates, depending on experience. Medical insurance is available for those who do not have coverage.

Duration 9 to 11 months.

Additional information Fellows are expected to write a dissertation chapter or chapters, publishable article or articles, and/or make significant progress on turning a thesis into a book manuscript. They should not plan to spend any time conducting research abroad or in other parts of the country.

Number awarded Varies each year; recently, 3 were awarded: 1 doctoral candidate, 1 recent postdoctorate, and 1 junior faculty member.

Deadline January of each year.

[947]
SUMMER AFFIRMATIVE ACTION INTERNSHIP PROGRAM

Wisconsin Office of State Employment Relations
Attn: Division of Affirmative Action Workforce Planning
101 East Wilson Street, Fourth Floor
P.O. Box 7855
Madison, WI 53707-7855
(608) 266-6475   Fax: (608) 267-1020
E-mail: OSERDAA@wi.gov
Web: oser.state.wi.us/category.asp?linkcatid=342

Summary To provide an opportunity for Asian Americans and members of other underrepresented groups to gain summer work experience with agencies of the state of Wisconsin.

Eligibility This program is open to women, ethnic/racial minorities (Asian, Black or African American, Native Hawaiian or other Pacific Islander, American Indian or Alaska Native, or Hispanic or Latino), and persons with disabilities. Applicants must be sophomores, juniors, seniors, or graduate students at an accredited 4-year college or university or second-year students in the second year of a 2-year technical or vocational school program. They must be 1) Wisconsin residents enrolled full time at a school in Wisconsin or any other state; or 2) residents of other states who are enrolled full time at a school in Wisconsin.

Financial data Most internships provide a competitive stipend.

Duration Summer months.

Additional information This program began in 1974. Internships are available in criminal justice, engineering, finance/accounting, human resources, information technology, legal research, library science, public administration, recreational leadership, research analyst, social work, vocational/rehabilitation therapy, and various other government jobs.

Number awarded Varies each year. Since the program was established, it has placed more than 3,100 students with more than 30 different agencies and universities throughout the state.

Deadline February of each year.

[948]
SUMMER INTERNSHIPS IN NUCLEAR FORENSICS AND ENVIRONMENTAL RADIOCHEMISTRY

Lawrence Livermore National Laboratory
Physical and Life Sciences Directorate
Attn: Director of Student Programs
7000 East Avenue, L-452
Livermore, CA 94550
(925) 422-6351   E-mail: kulp2@llnl.gov
Web: www-pls.llnl.gov

Summary To provide an opportunity for graduate students, especially Asian Americans and other minorities, to work on summer research projects on nuclear forensics and environmental radiochemistry at Lawrence Livermore National Laboratory (LLNL).

Eligibility This program is open to full-time master's and doctoral students who are interested in working on research projects at LLNL involving nuclear forensics, nuclear chemistry, and environmental radiochemistry. Applicants must be U.S. citizens. Selection is based on academic record, aptitude, research interests, and recommendations of instructors. Strong preference is given to students with exceptional academic records and potential for making outstanding contributions to applied science. Women and minorities are encouraged to apply.

Financial data The stipend ranges from $4,100 to $4,900 per month, depending on number of school years completed. Living accommodations and arrangements are the responsibility of the intern.

Duration 8 weeks, during the summer.

Number awarded 10 to 15 each year.

Deadline February of each year.

[949]
SUMMER TRANSPORTATION INTERNSHIP PROGRAM FOR DIVERSE GROUPS

Department of Transportation
Attn: Summer Transportation Internship Program for
  Diverse Groups
Eighth Floor E81-105
1200 New Jersey Avenue, S.E.
Washington, DC 20590
(202) 366-2907   E-mail: Crystal.Taylor@dot.gov
Web: www.fhwa.dot.gov/education/stipdg.cfm

Summary To enable Asian American and other diverse undergraduate, graduate, and law students to gain work experience during the summer at facilities of the U.S. Department of Transportation (DOT).

Eligibility This program is open to all qualified applicants, but it is designed to provide women, persons with disabilities, and members of diverse social and ethnic groups with summer opportunities in transportation. Applicants must be U.S. citizens currently enrolled in a degree-granting program of study at an accredited institution of higher learning at the undergraduate (community or junior college, university, college, or Tribal College or University) or graduate level. Undergraduates must be entering their junior or senior year; students attending a Tribal or community college must have completed their first year of school; law students must be entering their second or third year of school. Students who will graduate during the spring or summer are not eligible unless they have been accepted for enrollment in graduate school. The program accepts applications from students in all majors who are interested in working on transportation-related topics and issues. Preference is given to students with a GPA of 3.0 or higher. Undergraduates must submit a 1-page essay on their transportation interests and how participation in this program will enhance their educational and career plans and goals. Graduate students must submit a writing sample representing their educational and career plans and goals. Law students must submit a legal writing sample.

Financial data The stipend is $4,000 for undergraduates or $5,000 for graduate and law students. The program also provides housing and reimbursement of travel expenses from interns' homes to their assignment location.

Duration 10 weeks during the summer.

Additional information Assignments are at the DOT headquarters in Washington, D.C., a selected modal administration, or selected field offices around the country.

Number awarded 80 to 100 each year.

Deadline January of each year.

[950]
SUNY GRADUATE DIVERSITY FELLOWSHIP PROGRAM

State University of New York
Attn: Office of Diversity, Equity and Inclusion
State University Plaza, T1000A
353 Broadway
Albany, NY 12246
(518) 320-1189   E-mail: carlos.medina@suny.edu
Web: system.suny.edu/odei/diversity-programs

Summary To provide financial assistance to graduate students at campuses of the State University of New York (SUNY) who are Asian Americans or will contribute to the diversity of the student body in other ways.

Eligibility This program is open to U.S. citizens and permanent residents who are entering or enrolled full-time graduate or professional students at any of the participating SUNY colleges. Applicants must be able to demonstrate how they will contribute to the diversity of the student body for the program for which they are applying, including having overcome a disadvantage or other impediment to success in higher education. Economic disadvantage, although not a requirement, may be the basis for eligibility. Membership in a racial or ethnic group that is underrepresented in the graduate or professional program involved may serve as a plus factor in making awards, but may not form the sole basis of selection. Awards are granted in the following priority order: 1) new graduate students who are being recruited but have not yet accepted admission to a graduate program; 2) Graduate Opportunity Waiver Program students who can be awarded a stipend to supplement their waiver to tuition; 3) currently-enrolled doctoral candidates who have completed all degree requirements except the dissertation; and 4) graduate assistants and teaching assistants who can receive a supplement to their current stipends to enhance their retention in graduate studies.

Financial data Stipends range from $7,500 to $10,000.

Duration 1 year; renewable.

Number awarded Varies each year; recently, this program awarded nearly $6 million in fellowships to 511 graduate students on 24 SUNY campuses. Of the recipients 32% were Latinos, 34% African Americans, 17% Whites, 5% Asians, and 5% Native Americans.

Deadline Deadline not specified.

[951]
SUSAN M. JACKSON MINISTERIAL SCHOLARS FUND

Unitarian Universalist Association
Attn: Ministerial Credentialing Office
24 Farnsworth Street
Boston, MA 02210-1409
(617) 948-6403   Fax: (617) 742-2875
E-mail: mcoadministrator@uua.org
Web: www.uua.org

Summary To provide financial assistance to seminary students preparing for the Unitarian Universalist (UU) ministry who are Asian Americans or other persons of color and can demonstrate enthusiasm about their faith.

Eligibility This program is open to seminary students who are enrolled full or at least half time in a UU ministerial training program with candidate status. Applicants must be citizens of the United States or Canada. They must be able to demonstrate their enthusiasm about Unitarian Universalist ideas and conclusions, drawn from their faith, that influence their lives. Priority is given first to those who have demonstrated outstanding ministerial ability and secondarily to students with the greatest financial need (especially persons of color).

Financial data The stipend ranges from $1,000 to $15,000 per year.

Duration 1 year.

Number awarded 1 each year.

Deadline April of each year.

[952]
SYNOD OF LAKES AND PRAIRIES RACIAL ETHNIC SCHOLARSHIPS

Synod of Lakes and Prairies
Attn: Committee on Racial Ethnic Ministry
2115 Cliff Drive
Eagen, MN 55122-3327
(651) 357-1140   Toll Free: (800) 328-1880, ext. 202
Fax: (651) 357-1141   E-mail: mkes@lakesandprairies.org
Web: www.lakesandprairies.org

Summary To provide financial assistance to Asian American and other minority residents of the Presbyterian Church (USA) Synod of Lakes and Prairies who are working on an undergraduate or graduate degree at a college or seminary in any state as preparation for service to the church.

Eligibility This program is open to members of Presbyterian churches who reside within the Synod of Lakes and Prairies (Iowa, Minnesota, Nebraska, North Dakota, South Dakota, and Wisconsin). Applicants must be members of ethnic minority groups studying at least half time for service in the Presbyterian Church (USA) as a teaching elder, ordained minister, commissioned ruling elder, lay professional, or volunteer. They must be in good academic standing, making progress toward an undergraduate or graduate degree, and able to demonstrate financial need. Along with their application, they must submit essays of 200 to 500 words on 1) what the church needs to do to be faithful to its mission in the world today; and 2) the people, practices, or events that influence their commitment to Christ in ways that renew their fair and strengthen their service.

Financial data Stipends range from $850 to $3,500.

Duration 1 year.

Number awarded Varies each year; recently, 9 were awarded.

Deadline September of each year.

[953]
TAIWANESE AMERICAN FOUNDATION OF BOSTON UNIVERSITY FELLOWSHIP PROGRAM

Taiwanese American Foundation of Boston
c/o C.Y. Wang
15 Crescent Road
Lexington, MA 02421
E-mail: info@taf-boston.org
Web: www.taf-boston.org/program.htm

Summary To provide funding to graduate students interested in conducting research or other projects related to Taiwanese studies.

Eligibility This program is open to graduate students whose study or research is related to the advancement of 1) any social, cultural, socioeconomic, literary, environmental, educational, or scientific interest of Taiwan or 2) any issue of public policy or foreign relations impacting Taiwan. To apply, they must submit a curriculum vitae or resume, a detailed proposal of the thesis to be written or project to be undertaken (up to 5 pages), 2 letters of recommendation, a statement of plans and commitments after the fellowship program, a report of funding resources that the proposed study or research has already received, and a list of publications or papers presented (if applicable).

Financial data The maximum grant is $6,000.

Duration 1 year.

Additional information Recipients must submit a final report on their study or research, including an explanation of how grant funds were spent.

Number awarded 1 or more each year.

Deadline January or August of each year.

[954]
TEXAS CHAPTER AAJA SCHOLARSHIPS

Asian American Journalists Association-Texas Chapter
c/o Alanna Quillen, President
KTBS 3 News
312 East Kings Highway
Shreveport, LA 71104
(318) 861-5800   E-mail: alanna.quillen@gmail.com
Web: www.aajatexas.org/programs/student-programs

Summary To provide financial assistance to students from designated southwestern states who are working on an undergraduate or graduate degree in journalism and can demonstrate an awareness of Asian American issues.

Eligibility This program is open to graduating high school seniors, undergraduates, and graduate students who are either 1) residents of Arkansas, Louisiana, New Mexico, Oklahoma, or Texas; or 2) attending or planning to attend an accredited college or university in those states. Applicants are not required to be members of the Asian American Journalists Association (AAJA). Along with their application, they must submit a 250-word autobiography that explains why they are interested in a career in journalism, a 500-word essay on the role of ethnic diversity in news coverage (both for the subjects of the news events and the journalists involved), their most recent official transcript, 2 letters of recommendation, and a resume. Work samples to be submitted are 3 legible clips from print journalism students; 3 to 5 prints or slides with captions or descriptions from print photojournalism students; 3 to 5 samples of work from design journalism students; 2 taped VHS or DVD excerpts with corresponding scripts from television broadcast students; 2 edited VHS or DVD excepts from television photojournalism students; 3 taped cassette excerpts with corresponding scripts from radio broadcast students; or 3 legible online articles from web journalism students. Selection is based on commitment to journalism, awareness of Asian American issues, journalistic ability, and scholastic ability.

Financial data The stipend is $1,000.

Duration 1 year.

Additional information Scholarship winners are also given a 1-year free membership in the AAJA Texas chapter.

Number awarded 2 each year.

Deadline May of each year.

[955]
TEXAS YOUNG LAWYERS ASSOCIATION DIVERSITY SCHOLARSHIP PROGRAM

Texas Young Lawyers Association
Attn: Diversity Committee
1414 Colorado, Fourth Floor
P.O. Box 12487
Austin, TX 78711-2487
(512) 427-1529   Toll Free: (800) 204-2222, ext. 1529
Fax: (512) 427-4117   E-mail: btrevino@texasbar.com
Web: www.tyla.org

Summary To provide financial assistance to residents of any state who are Asian Americans or members of other diverse groups and attending law school in Texas.

Eligibility This program is open to members of recognized diverse groups, including diversity based on gender, national origin, race, ethnicity, sexual orientation, gender identity, disability, socioeconomic status, and geography. Applicants must be attending an ABA-accredited law school in Texas. Along with their application, they must submit a brief essay on 1) why they believe diversity is important to the practice of law; and 2) what the Texas Young Lawyers Association and the State Bar of Texas can do to promote and support diversity in the legal profession. Selection is based on those essays, academic performance, demonstrated commitment to diversity, letters of recommendation, and financial need.

Financial data The stipend is $1,000.

Duration 1 year.

Number awarded At least 9 each year: at least 1 at each accredited law school in Texas.

Deadline October of each year.

[956]
THE LEADERSHIP INSTITUTE SCHOLARSHIPS

The Leadership Institute for Women of Color Attorneys, Inc.
Attn: Scholarship Chair
1266 West Paces Ferry Road, N.W., Suite 263
Atlanta, GA 30327
(404) 443-5715   E-mail: hhorton@mcquirewoods.com
Web: www.leadingwomenofcolor.org

Summary To provide financial assistance to Asian American and other women of color who are attending law school.

Eligibility This program is open to women of color who have completed at least 1 year at an accredited law school and have a GPA of 3.0 or higher. Applicants must be U.S. citizens who can demonstrate a commitment to the legal profession. Along with their application, they must submit brief statements on their work experience, extracurricular activities, why they think it is important for women of color to serve in the legal profession, what they believe is necessary for success in the legal profession, and what they plan to do with their law degree.

Financial data The stipend is $3,000.

Duration 1 year.

Number awarded 5 each year.

Deadline December of each year.

[957]
THE REV. J.K. FUKUSHIMA SCHOLARSHIP

Montebello Plymouth Congregational Church
144 South Greenwood Avenue
Montebello, CA 90640
(323) 721-5568   Fax: (323) 721-7955
E-mail: mpccucc@gmail.com
Web: www.montebelloucc.org

Summary To provide financial assistance to undergraduate and graduate students who are preparing for a career in Christian ministry and can demonstrate a commitment to the Asian American community.

Eligibility This program is open to 1) third- or fourth-year college students; and 2) graduate and professional students who have not completed a bachelor's or master's degree in theological studies. Applicants must be enrolled or have been accepted at an accredited school of theology. They must be working on a degree that will provide them with the skills and understanding necessary to further the development of Christian ministries. Along with their application, they must submit an essay on their commitment to the Asian American community.

Financial data The stipend is $500.

Duration 1 year.

Number awarded 1 or more each year.

Deadline May of each year.

[958]
THOMAS G. NEUSOM SCHOLARSHIPS

Conference of Minority Transportation Officials
Attn: National Scholarship Program
100 M Street, S.E., Suite 917
Washington, DC 20003
(202) 506-2917   E-mail: info@comto.org
Web: www.comto.org/page/scholarships

Summary To provide financial assistance for college or graduate school to Asian American and other minority members of the Conference of Minority Transportation Officials (COMTO) and their families.

Eligibility This program is open to undergraduate and graduate students who have been members of COMTO or whose parents, guardians, or grandparents have been members for at least 1 year. Applicants must be working (either full or part time) on a degree in a field related to transportation and have a GPA of 2.5 or higher. Along with their application they must submit a cover letter on their transportation-related career goals and life aspirations. Financial need is not considered in the selection process.

Financial data The stipend is $5,500. Funds are paid directly to the recipient's college or university.

Duration 1 year.

Number awarded 1 each year.

Deadline April of each year.

[959]
THOMAS R. PICKERING FOREIGN AFFAIRS FELLOWSHIPS

The Washington Center for Internships
Attn: Foreign Affairs Fellowship Program
1333 16th Street, N.W.
Washington, DC 20036-2205
(202) 238-7900   Fax: (202) 238-7700
E-mail: info@twc.org
Web: www.twc.edu

Summary To provide forgivable loans to undergraduate and graduate students, especially Asian Americans or members of other underrepresented groups, who are interested in preparing for a career with the Department of State's Foreign Service.

Eligibility This program is open to U.S. citizens who are entering their senior year of undergraduate study or their first year of graduate study. Applicants must be planning to work on a 2-year full-time master's degree program relevant to the work of the U.S. Foreign Service, including public policy, international affairs, public administration, business, economics, political science, sociology, or foreign languages. They must be preparing for a career in the Foreign Service. Applications are especially encouraged from women, members of minority groups historically underrepresented in the Foreign Service, and students with financial need.

Financial data The program pays for tuition, room, board, books, mandatory fees, and 1 round-trip ticket from the fellow's residence to academic institution, to a maximum of $37,500 per academic year.

Duration 2 years: the senior year of undergraduate study and the first year of graduate study for college seniors; the first 2 years of graduate school for entering graduate students.

Additional information This program is funded by the State Department and administered by The Washington Center for Internships. Fellows must commit to a minimum of 5 years of service in an appointment as a Foreign Service Officer following graduation and successful completion of the Foreign Service examination. If they fail to fulfill that commitment, they must refund all money received.

Number awarded Approximately 40 each year: 20 college seniors and 20 entering graduate students.

Deadline January of each year.

[960]
THZ FO FARM SCHOLARSHIP

Hawai'i Community Foundation
Attn: Scholarship Department
827 Fort Street Mall
Honolulu, HI 96813
(808) 566-5570   Toll Free: (888) 731-3863
Fax: (808) 521-6286
E-mail: scholarships@hcf-hawaii.org
Web: hcf.scholarships.ngwebsolutions.com

Summary To provide financial assistance to Hawaii residents of Chinese descent who are interested in working on an undergraduate or graduate degree in any field at a school in any state.

Eligibility This program is open to residents of Hawaii who are of Chinese ancestry and interested in studying any field as full-time undergraduate or graduate students at an accredited 2- or 4-year college or university in any state. Applicants must be able to demonstrate academic achievement (GPA of 2.7 or higher), good moral character, and financial need. Along with their application, they must submit a short statement indicating their reasons for attending college, their planned course of study, their career goals, and what community service means to them.

Financial data The amounts of the awards depend on the availability of funds and the need of the recipient. Recently, the average value of the scholarships awarded by the foundation was $2,800.

Duration 1 year.

Number awarded Varies each year; recently, 6 were awarded.

Deadline February of each year.

[961]
TONGAN CULTURAL SOCIETY SCHOLARSHIPS

Hawai'i Community Foundation
Attn: Scholarship Department
827 Fort Street Mall
Honolulu, HI 96813
(808) 566-5570   Toll Free: (888) 731-3863
Fax: (808) 521-6286
E-mail: scholarships@hcf-hawaii.org
Web: hcf.scholarships.ngwebsolutions.com

Summary To provide financial assistance to Hawaii residents of Tongan ancestry who are interested in attending college or graduate school in the state.

Eligibility This program is open to Hawaii residents of Tongan ancestry who are enrolled or planning to enroll at an accredited 4-year college or university in Hawaii. Applicants must be full-time undergraduate or graduate students and able to demonstrate academic achievement (GPA of 2.7 or higher), good moral character, and financial need. Along with their application, they must submit a short statement indicating their reasons for attending college, their planned course of study, their career goals, and what community service means to them.

Financial data The amounts of the awards depend on the availability of funds and the need of the recipient. Recently, the average value of the scholarships awarded by the foundation was $2,800.

Duration 1 year.

Number awarded Varies each year; recently, 3 were awarded.

Deadline February of each year.

[962]
TOUBY LYFOUNG MEMORIAL SCHOLARSHIP

Hmong American Education Fund
P.O. Box 17468
St. Paul, MN 55117
(651) 592-1576 E-mail: scholarships@thehaef.org
Web: www.thehaef.org

Summary To provide financial assistance to Hmong residents of any state who come from a lower middle class family and are interested in working on an undergraduate or graduate degree in any field.

Eligibility This program is open to students of Hmong descent who are high school seniors, GED recipients, or current full-time undergraduate or graduate students at 2- or 4-year colleges or universities in any state. Applicants must be U.S. citizens or permanent residents and have a GPA of 3.4 or higher. They must come from a lower middle class family. Along with their application, they must submit a 1,500-word essay on their commitment to education, their leadership qualities, their financial need, how this scholarship can help them, and their community service. Selection is based on academic excellence, leadership qualities, commitment to helping their community, and financial need or need based on hardship.

Financial data The stipend is $1,000.

Duration 1 year; nonrenewable.

Number awarded 1 each year.

Deadline March of each year.

[963]
TRAILBLAZER SCHOLARSHIP

Conference of Minority Transportation Officials
Attn: National Scholarship Program
100 M Street, S.E., Suite 917
Washington, DC 20003
(202) 506-2917 E-mail: info@comto.org
Web: www.comto.org/page/scholarships

Summary To provide financial assistance for college or graduate school to Asian American and other minority members of the Conference of Minority Transportation Officials (COMTO) and their families.

Eligibility This program is open to undergraduate and graduate students who have been members of COMTO or whose parents, guardians, or grandparents have been members for at least 1 year. Applicants must be working (either full or part time) on a degree in a field related to transportation and have a GPA of 2.5 or higher. Along with their application they must submit a cover letter on their transportation-related career goals and life aspirations. Financial need is not considered in the selection process.

Financial data The stipend is $2,500. Funds are paid directly to the recipient's college or university.

Duration 1 year.

Number awarded 1 each year.

Deadline April of each year.

[964]
TRANSAMERICA RETIREMENT SOLUTIONS LEADERS IN HEALTH CARE SCHOLARSHIP

Institute for Diversity in Health Management
Attn: Membership and Education Specialist
155 North Wacker Avenue
Chicago, IL 60606
(312) 422-2658 E-mail: cbiddle@aha.org
Web: www.diversityconnection.org

Summary To provide financial assistance to graduate students in health care management who are Asian Americans or will contribute to ethnic diversity in the profession in other ways.

Eligibility This program is open to U.S. citizens who represent ethnically diverse cultural backgrounds. Applicants must be enrolled in the second year of a master's degree program in health administration or a comparable program and have a GPA of 3.0 or higher. Along with their application, they must submit 1) a personal statement of 1 to 2 pages on their interest in health care management and their career goals; 2) an essay on what they see as the most challenging issue facing America's hospitals and health systems; and 3) a 500-word essay on their interest and background in health care finance. Selection is based on academic achievement, commitment to community service, and financial need.

Financial data The stipend is $5,000.

Duration 1 year.

Additional information This program began in 2007 as the Diversified Investment Advisors Leaders in Healthcare Scholarship. Its current name became effective in 2013 when Transamerica Retirement Solutions assumed sponsorship.

Number awarded 2 each year.

Deadline January of each year.

[965]
UNITED HEALTH FOUNDATION/NMF DIVERSE MEDICAL SCHOLARS PROGRAM

National Medical Fellowships, Inc.
Attn: Scholarship Program
347 Fifth Avenue, Suite 510
New York, NY 10016
(212) 483-8880 Toll Free: (877) NMF-1DOC
Fax: (212) 483-8897 E-mail: scholarships@nmfonline.org
Web: www.nmfonline.org

Summary To provide financial assistance to Vietnamese, Cambodians, and other underrepresented minority students at medical schools in designated areas who are interested in conducting a community health project.

Eligibility This program is open to Vietnamese, Cambodians, African Americans, Hispanics/Latinos, Native Americans, and Pacific Islanders who are currently enrolled at an accredited medical school in the greater New York City metropolitan area (including Connecticut, New Jersey, New York, and Pennsylvania), Florida (Orlando, Tampa, and greater Miami), Arizona (Phoenix), New Mexico (Albuquerque), Tennessee (Nashville), Texas (San Antonio), Wisconsin (Milwaukee), or Georgia (Atlanta). Applicants must have demonstrated leadership and a commitment to serving medically underserved communities. They must be interested in conducting a self-directed health project of 200 hours at a site of choice in an underserved community in the same area as their medical school. U.S. citizenship or DACA status is required.

Financial data The grant is $7,000.

Duration 1 year; recipients may apply for a second year of funding.

Additional information This program, sponsored by United Health Foundation, began in 2007.

Number awarded 30 each year.

Deadline October of each year.

[966]
UNITED HEALTHCARE/LAWYERS COLLABORATIVE FOR DIVERSITY CLERKSHIP

Lawyers Collaborative for Diversity
Attn: Program Coordinator
P.O. Box 230637
Hartford, CT 06123-0637
(860) 275-0668
E-mail: kdavis@lawyerscollaborativefordiversity.org
Web: www.lcdiversity.com/scholarships.htm

Summary To provide summer work experience at United Healthcare Services in Hartford, Connecticut to Asian Americans and other underrepresented students at law schools in Connecticut and western Massachusetts.

Eligibility This program is open to women and students of color in their first year at law schools in Connecticut or western Massachusetts. Applicants must be interested in a summer internship at United Healthcare Services in Harford, Connecticut. Along with their application, they must submit 500-word essays on 1) why they should be selected for this opportunity; and 2) their thoughts about diversity in Connecticut's legal community.

Financial data The stipend is $5,000.

Duration 8 weeks during the summer.

Additional information This program is sponsored by United HealthCare Services, Inc.

Number awarded 1 each year.

Deadline February of each year.

[967]
UNITED METHODIST FOUNDATION THEOLOGICAL AND PROFESSIONAL SCHOOL MERIT SCHOLARS PROGRAM

United Methodist Higher Education Foundation
Attn: Scholarships Administrator
60 Music Square East, Suite 350
P.O. Box 340005
Nashville, TN 37203-0005
(615) 649-3974   Toll Free: (800) 811-8110
Fax: (615) 649-3980
E-mail: umhefscholarships@umhef.org
Web: www.umhef.org

Summary To provide financial assistance to students preparing for ordination at seminaries affiliated with the United Methodist Church, especially Asian Americans and other ethnic minorities.

Eligibility This program is open to first- through third-year students working on a master's degree at the 14 United Methodist-related theological and professional schools. Applicants must be U.S. citizens or permanent residents and active members of the United Methodist Church for at least 1 year

prior to application. They must be planning to enroll full time and have a GPA of 3.0 or higher. Preference is given to ethnic minority and first generation college students. Financial need is considered in the selection process.

Financial data The stipend is $3,000.

Duration 1 year; nonrenewable.

Additional information Students may obtain applications from their school.

Number awarded 42 each year: 1 to a member of each class at each school.

Deadline Nominations from schools must be received by September of each year.

[968]
UNITED METHODIST WOMEN OF COLOR SCHOLARS PROGRAM

United Methodist Church
Attn: General Board of Higher Education and Ministry
Office of Loans and Scholarships
1001 19th Avenue South
P.O. Box 340007
Nashville, TN 37203-0007
(615) 340-7342   Fax: (615) 340-7367
E-mail: umscholar@gbhem.org
Web: www.gbhem.org

Summary To provide financial assistance to Methodist Asian American and other women of color who are working on a doctoral degree to prepare for a career as an educator at a United Methodist seminary.

Eligibility This program is open to women of color (have at least 1 parent who is Asian, African American, African, Hispanic, Native American, Alaska Native, or Pacific Islander) who have an M.Div. degree. Applicants must have been active, full members of a United Methodist Church for at least 3 years prior to applying. They must be enrolled full time in a degree program at the Ph.D. or Th.D. level to prepare for a career teaching at a United Methodist seminary.

Financial data The maximum stipend is $10,000 per year.

Duration 1 year; may be renewed up to 3 additional years.

Number awarded Varies each year; recently, 10 were awarded.

Deadline January of each year.

[969]
UPS/NLF GOLD MOUNTAIN SCHOLARSHIPS

National Asian Pacific American Bar Association
Attn: NAPABA Law Foundation
1612 K Street, N.W., Suite 510
Washington, DC 20006
(202) 775-9555   Fax: (202) 775-9333
E-mail: nlfstaff@napaba.org
Web: www.napaba.org/?page=NLF_scholarships

Summary To provide financial assistance to law students who are the first in their family to attend law school and interested in serving the Asian Pacific American community.

Eligibility This program is open to students at ABA-accredited law schools in the United States who are the first in their family to attend law school. Applicants must demonstrate leadership potential to serve the Asian Pacific American community upon graduation. Along with their application, they must submit a 500-word essay that covers 1) the most significant experiences in their background that have shaped and demonstrated their commitment to serving the needs of Asian Pacific Americans; and 2) how they intend to serve the needs of the Asian Pacific American community in their future legal career. Selection is based on that essay, academic achievement, leadership, and commitment to bettering the Asian Pacific American community. U.S. citizenship or permanent resident status is required.

Financial data The stipend is $5,000.

Duration 1 year.

Additional information This program is supported by the UPS Foundation and administered by the National Asian Pacific American Bar Association (NAPABA) Law Foundation.

Number awarded 2 each year.

Deadline August of each year.

[970]
UTC/LCD DIVERSITY SCHOLARS PROGRAM

Lawyers Collaborative for Diversity
Attn: Program Coordinator
P.O. Box 230637
Hartford, CT 06123-0637
(860) 275-0668
E-mail: kdavis@lawyerscollaborativefordiversity.org
Web: www.lcdiversity.com/scholarships.htm

Summary To provide financial assistance and summer work experience to Asian American and other underrepresented students at law schools in Connecticut and western Massachusetts.

Eligibility This program is open to women and people of color from any state who are currently enrolled in the first year at a law school in Connecticut or western Massachusetts. Applicants must be available to work as an intern during the summer following their first year. Along with their application, they must submit 500-word essays on 1) why diversity is important to them and how the Connecticut legal community can improve diversity in the legal profession; and 2) why they should be selected for this program.

Financial data The program provides a stipend of $2,000 per year for the second and third years of law school, a paid internship during the summer after the first year at a member firm of the Lawyers Collaborative for Diversity (LCD), and an unpaid internship with a legal department of United Technologies Corporation during that same summer.

Duration The scholarship is for 2 years; the paid internship is for 5 weeks during the summer; the unpaid internship is for 3 weeks during the summer.

Additional information This program is sponsored by United Technologies Corporation (UTC).

Number awarded 2 each year.

Deadline January of each year.

[971]
VAMA SCHOLARSHIP PROGRAM

Vietnamese American Medical Association
Attn: Scholarship Committee
1926 S.W. Green Oaks Boulevard
Arlington, TX 76017
(682) 667-1016   Fax: (817) 468-1852
E-mail: scholarship@vamausa.org
Web: www.vamausa.org/content/scholarships

Summary To provide financial assistance to medical students who are interested in serving the Vietnamese American community.

Eligibility This program is open to students enrolled in their third year at an accredited medical school in the United States. Applicants must be able to demonstrate a strong interest in serving the Vietnamese American community when they complete their training. Along with their application, they must submit a letter from the financial aid office of their medical school verifying the amount of other assistance they are receiving, a letter of recommendation, their medical school transcript, and a 600-word essay describing the reason why they wish to serve Vietnamese community in the United States, including the specific location where they plan to practice. Preference is given to applicants who demonstrate the greatest financial need.

Financial data The stipend is $1,000.

Duration 1 year.

Number awarded Varies each year.

Deadline May of each year.

[972]
VAZQUEZ PRIDE IN HEALTH SCHOLARSHIP

Pride Foundation
Attn: Educational Programs Director
2014 East Madison Street, Suite 300
Seattle, WA 98122
(206) 323-3318   Toll Free: (800) 735-7287
Fax: (206) 323-1017
E-mail: scholarships@pridefoundation.org
Web: www.pridefoundation.org

Summary To provide financial assistance for advanced study in health care to lesbian, gay, bisexual, transgender, or queer (LGBTQ) students of color who live in the Northwest.

Eligibility This program is open to residents of Alaska, Idaho, Montana, Oregon, or Washington who are studying or planning to study medicine, public health, and/or community health. Preference is given to LGBTQ students of color, students who are transgender/gender queer, or students who are from rural areas or plan to practice in rural communities. Selection is based on demonstrated commitment to social justice and LGBTQ concerns, leadership in their communities, the ability to be academically and personally successful, and (to some extent) financial need.

Financial data Recently, the average stipend for all scholarships awarded by the foundation was approximately $3,400. Funds are paid directly to the recipient's school.

Duration 1 year; recipients may reapply.

Number awarded 1 each year. Since it began offering scholarships in 1993, the foundation has awarded a total of more than $3.5 million to nearly 1,400 recipients.

Deadline January of each year.

[973]
VICTOR GRIFOLS ROURA SCHOLARSHIP

National Medical Fellowships, Inc.
Attn: Scholarship Program
347 Fifth Avenue, Suite 510
New York, NY 10016
(212) 483-8880   Toll Free: (877) NMF-1DOC
Fax: (212) 483-8897 E-mail: scholarships@nmfonline.org
Web: www.nmfonline.org

Summary To provide financial assistance to Vietnamese, Cambodians, and other underrepresented minority students at medical schools in the Los Angeles metropolitan area.

Eligibility This program is open to Vietnamese, Cambodians, African Americans, Hispanics/Latinos, Native Americans, and Pacific Islanders who are entering their second or third year at a medical school in the Los Angeles metropolitan area. Applicants must demonstrate an interest in hematology (diseases of the blood). They must be U.S. citizens or DACA students. Selection is based on leadership, commitment to serving medically underserved communities, and financial need.

Financial data The stipend is $7,500.

Duration 1 year.

Additional information This program began in 2013.

Number awarded 1 each year.

Deadline September of each year.

[974]
VIETNAMESE AMERICAN BAR ASSOCIATION OF NORTHERN CALIFORNIA SCHOLARSHIPS

Vietnamese American Bar Association of Northern
  California
Attn: Scholarships
772 North First Street
San Jose, CA 95112
(408) 975-9321   E-mail: scholarship@vabanc.org
Web: www.vabanc.org/index.php/navigation-menu/about

Summary To provide financial assistance to Vietnamese law students, especially those who are committed to serving the Vietnamese American community in northern California.

Eligibility This program is open to Vietnamese law students from any state. Priority is given to those who can demonstrate either 1) a commitment to serving the Vietnamese American community in northern California; or 2) a desire to engage in public interest or social justice work through postgraduate work or a summer position. Applicants must submit an 800-word personal statement on 1) what they see as a pressing concern facing the Vietnamese American community and how they see themselves contributing to or engaging in such an issue; and/or 2) their contributions to or activism within the Vietnamese American community; and/or 3) their experiences in overcoming socioeconomic and/or other barriers.

Financial data The stipend is $2,000.

Duration 1 year.

Additional information This program began in 2002. Recipients are required to attend the sponsor's annual scholarship dinner. No support is provided for transportation or lodging expenses to attend the dinner.

Number awarded 2 each year.

Deadline July of each year.

[975]
VIETNAMESE AMERICAN BAR ASSOCIATION OF THE GREATER WASHINGTON DC AREA SCHOLARSHIP

Vietnamese American Bar Association of the Greater
  Washington DC Area
410 Kentucky Avenue, S.E.
Washington, DC 20003
E-mail: vabadc@gmail.com
Web: www.vabadc.com

Summary To provide financial assistance to students at law schools in the greater Washington, D.C. area who are committed to serving the Vietnamese American community.

Eligibility This program is open to residents of any state who are currently enrolled at a law school in the greater Washington, D.C. area. Applicants must be able to demonstrate a commitment to serving the Vietnamese American community. Along with their application, they must submit a 750-word essay on 1 of the following topics: 1) how they plan to serve the needs of Vietnamese Americans in their legal career; 2) their experiences in serving the Vietnamese American community; or 3) how they have overcome barriers to achieve their academic and/or career goals. Selection is based on the essay, academic performance, and community service.

Financial data The stipend is $1,500.

Duration 1 year.

Additional information This program began in 2009.

Number awarded 2 each year.

Deadline March of each year.

[976]
VINCENT CHIN MEMORIAL SCHOLARSHIP

Asian American Journalists Association
Attn: Student Programs Coordinator
5 Third Street, Suite 1108
San Francisco, CA 94103
(415) 346-2051, ext. 102   Fax: (415) 346-6343
E-mail: programs@aaja.org
Web: www.aaja.org/apply-for-a-scholarship-now

Summary To provide financial assistance to student members of the Asian American Journalists Association (AAJA) who are high school seniors, undergraduates, or graduate students and interested in preparing for a career in journalism.

Eligibility This program is open to AAJA members who are working or planning to work full time on an undergraduate or graduate degree in journalism. Applicants must submit a brief essay on their choice of 4 topics: 1) could the attack that killed Vincent Chin happen again; 2) how Asian Americans are a single people; 3) should Asian Americans protest or conform in the face of incidents such as the murder of Vincent Chin; or 4) who was Lily Chin. Selection is based on academic achievement, commitment to journalism, sensitivity to Asian American and Pacific Islander issues, demonstrated journalistic ability, and financial need.

Financial data The stipend is $500.

Duration 1 year.

Number awarded 1 each year.

Deadline May of each year.

[977]
VIOLET AND CYRIL FRANKS SCHOLARSHIP

American Psychological Foundation
750 First Street, N.E.
Washington, DC 20002-4242
(202) 336-5843   Fax: (202) 336-5812
E-mail: foundation@apa.org
Web: www.apa.org/apf/funding/franks.aspx

Summary To provide funding to doctoral students, especially Asian Americans and members of other underrepresented groups, who are interested in conducting research related to mental illness.

Eligibility This program is open to full-time graduate students who are interested in conducting a research project that uses a psychological perspective to help understand and reduce stigma associated with mental illness. Applicants must identify the project's goal, the prior research that has been conducted in the area, whom the project will serve, the in intended outcomes and how the project will achieve those, and the total cost of the project. Selection is based on conformance with stated program goals, quality of proposed work, and applicant's demonstrated scholarship and competence. The sponsor encourages applications from individuals who represent diversity in race, ethnicity, gender, age, disability, and sexual orientation.

Financial data The grant is $5,000.

Duration 1 year.

Additional information This grant was first awarded in 2007.

Number awarded 1 each year.

Deadline May of each year.

[978]
VIRGINIA NURSE PRACTITIONER/NURSE MIDWIFE SCHOLARSHIP PROGRAM

Virginia Department of Health
Attn: Office of Minority Health and Public Health Policy
Workforce Incentive Programs
109 Governor Street, Suite 714 West
Richmond, VA 23219
(804) 864-7435   Fax: (804) 864-7440
E-mail: IncentivePrograms@vdh.virginia.gov
Web: www.vdh.virginia.gov

Summary To provide forgivable loans to nursing students, especially Asian Americans and other minorities, in Virginia who are willing to work as nurse practitioners and/or midwives in the state following graduation.

Eligibility This program is open to U.S. citizens, nationals, immigrants, and political refugees who are enrolled or accepted for enrollment full or part time at a nurse practitioner program or a nurse midwifery program in Virginia. Applicants must have been residents of Virginia for at least 1 year. They must have a cumulative GPA of at least 2.5 in undergraduate and/or graduate courses. Along with their application, they must submit a narrative that includes the significance of this scholarship for their educational goals, any school or community activities, and any skill-set that is pertinent to the nursing profession. Preference is given to 1) residents of designated medically underserved areas of Virginia; 2) students enrolled in family practice, obstetrics and gynecology, pediatric, adult health, and geriatric nurse practitioner programs; and 3) minority students.

Financial data The stipend is $5,000 per year. Recipients must agree to serve in a designated medically underserved area of Virginia for a period of years equal to the number of years of scholarship support received. The required service must begin within 2 years of the recipient's graduation and must be in a facility that provides services to persons who are unable to pay for the service and that participates in all government-sponsored insurance programs designed to assure full access to medical care service for covered persons. If the recipient fails to complete the course of study, or pass the licensing examination, or provide the required service, all scholarship funds received must be repaid with interest and a penalty.

Duration 1 year; may be renewed for 1 additional year.

Number awarded Up to 5 each year.

Deadline June of each year.

[979]
VIRGINIA TEACHING SCHOLARSHIP LOAN PROGRAM

Virginia Department of Education
Division of Teacher Education and Licensure
Attn: Director of Teacher Education
P.O. Box 2120
Richmond, VA 23218-2120
(804) 371-2475   Toll Free: (800) 292-3820
Fax: (804) 786-6759
E-mail: JoAnne.Carver@doe.virginia.gov
Web: www.doe.virginia.gov

Summary To provide scholarship/loans to undergraduate and graduate students, especially Asian Americans and other minorities, in Virginia who are interested in a career in teaching.

Eligibility This program is open to Virginia residents who are enrolled full or part time as a sophomore, junior, senior, or graduate student in a state-approved teacher preparation program in Virginia, who were in the top 10% of their high school class, and have a GPA of 2.7 or higher. Applicants must meet 1 or more of the following criteria: 1) are enrolled in a program leading to endorsement in a critical shortage area; 2) are a male in an elementary or middle school education program; 3) are a minority teaching candidate in any endorsement area; or 4) are a student in an approved teacher education program leading to an endorsement in career and technical education. They must agree to engage in full-time teaching following graduation in 1) designated teacher shortage areas within Virginia; 2) a school with a high concentration of students eligible for free or reduced lunch; 3) within a school division with a shortage of teachers; or 4) in a rural or urban region of the state with a teacher shortage.

Financial data The maximum scholarship/loan is $10,000 per year for full-time students or a prorated amount for part-time students. Loans are forgiven by qualified teaching of 1 year for each year of support received. If the recipient fails to fulfill the teaching service requirement, the loan must be repaid with interest.

Duration 1 year; may be renewed.

Additional information Critical shortage teaching areas in Virginia are currently identified as special education, career and technical education (including technology education, trade and industrial education, business education, and family and consumer sciences), mathematics (6-12), foreign language (preK-12), English, middle school (6-8), elementary education (preK-6), history and social sciences, health and physical education (preK-12), and school counselor (preK-12).

Number awarded   Varies each year.

Deadline   Deadline not specified.

[980]
VISION SCHOLARSHIP AWARD

Arumdaun Presbyterian Church
Attn: Vision Scholarship Committee
1 Arumdaun Street
Bethpage, NY 11714
(516) 349-5559   E-mail: arumdaunvision@gmail.com
Web: www.arumdaunchurch.org/visionscholarship

Summary   To provide financial assistance to Korean American Christians from designated northeastern states who attending seminary.

Eligibility   This program is open to Korean American Christians who live or attend seminary in Connecticut, Massachusetts, New Jersey, New York, Pennsylvania, or Rhode Island. Applicants must be enrolled full time in an M.Div. program with a vision of serving in youth ministry. They must be U.S. citizens or permanent residents. Along with their application, they must submit information on their financial situation and a 2-page essay on their vision as a Christian leader.

Financial data   The stipend is $2,000.

Duration   1 year.

Number awarded   1 or more each year.

Deadline   June of each year.

[981]
WALTER O. SPOFFORD, JR. MEMORIAL INTERNSHIP

Resources for the Future
Attn: Coordinator for Academic Programs
1616 P Street, N.W., Suite 600
Washington, DC 20036-1400
(202) 328-5020   Fax: (202) 939-3460
E-mail: spofford-award@rff.org
Web: www.rff.org

Summary   To provide summer internships to graduate students interested in working on Chinese environmental issues at Resources for the Future (RFF).

Eligibility   This program is open to first- or second-year graduate students in the social or natural sciences. Applicants must have a special interest in Chinese environmental issues and outstanding policy analysis and writing skills. They must be interested in a summer internship in Washington, D.C. at RFF. Both U.S. and non-U.S. citizens (especially Chinese students) are eligible, if the latter have proper work and residency documentation.

Financial data   The stipend is $375 per week. Housing assistance is not provided.

Duration   10 weeks during the summer.

Number awarded   1 each year.

Deadline   February of each year.

[982]
WARNER NORCROSS & JUDD LAW SCHOOL SCHOLARSHIP

Grand Rapids Community Foundation
Attn: Education Program Officer
185 Oakes Street S.W.
Grand Rapids, MI 49503-4008
(616) 454-1751, ext. 103   Fax: (616) 454-6455
E-mail: rbishop@grfoundation.org
Web: www.grfoundation.org/scholarshipslist

Summary   To provide financial assistance to Asian Americans and other minorities from Michigan who are attending law school.

Eligibility   This program is open to students of color who are attending or planning to attend an accredited law school. Applicants must be residents of Michigan or attending law school in the state. They must be U.S. citizens or permanent residents and have a GPA of 2.5 or higher. Financial need is considered in the selection process.

Financial data   The stipend is $5,000. Funds are paid directly to the recipient's institution.

Duration   1 year.

Additional information   Funding for this program is provided by the law firm Warner Norcross & Judd LLP.

Number awarded   1 each year.

Deadline   March of each year.

[983]
WAYNE ANTHONY BUTTS SCHOLARSHIP

National Medical Fellowships, Inc.
Attn: Scholarship Program
347 Fifth Avenue, Suite 510
New York, NY 10016
(212) 483-8880   Toll Free: (877) NMF-1DOC
Fax: (212) 483-8897 E-mail: scholarships@nmfonline.org
Web: www.nmfonline.org

Summary   To provide financial assistance to Vietnamese, Cambodian, and other underrepresented minority students at medical schools in the New York City metropolitan area.

Eligibility   This program is open to Vietnamese, Cambodians, African Americans, Hispanics/Latinos, Native Americans, and Pacific Islanders who are entering their first or second year of medical school. Applicants must be enrolled at a school in the New York City metropolitan area. They must be U.S. citizens or DACA students. Selection is based on leadership, commitment to serving medically underserved communities, and financial need.

Financial data   The stipend is $3,000.

Duration   1 year.

Additional information   This program began in 2013.

Number awarded   1 each year.

Deadline   September of each year.

[984]
WAYNE F. PLACEK GRANTS

American Psychological Foundation
750 First Street, N.E.
Washington, DC 20002-4242
(202) 336-5843   Fax: (202) 336-5812
E-mail: foundation@apa.org
Web: www.apa.org/apf/funding/placek.aspx

Summary To provide funding to pre- and postdoctoral scholars, especially Asian Americans and members of other underrepresented groups, who are interested in conducting research that will increase the general public's understanding of homosexuality and alleviate the stress experienced by gay men and lesbians.

Eligibility This program is open to scholars who have a doctoral degree (e.g., Ph.D., Psy.D., M.D.) and to graduate students in all fields of the behavioral and social sciences. Applicants must be interested in conducting empirical studies that address the following topics: prejudice, discrimination, and violence based on sexual orientation, including heterosexuals' attitudes and behaviors toward lesbian, gay, bisexual, and transgender (LGBT) people; family and workplace issues relevant to LGBT people; and subgroups of the LGBT population that have been historically underrepresented in scientific research. Selection is based on relevance to program goals, magnitude of incremental contribution, quality of proposed work, and applicant's demonstrated scholarship and research competence. The sponsor encourages applications from individuals who represent diversity in race, ethnicity, gender, age, disability, and sexual orientation.

Financial data The grant is $15,000.

Duration 1 year.

Additional information This program began in 1995.

Number awarded 1 or 2 each year.

Deadline February of each year.

[985]
WESTERN REGION KOREAN AMERICAN SCHOLARSHIPS

Korean American Scholarship Foundation
Western Region
Attn: Scholarship Committee
3540 Wilshire Boulevard, Suite 920
Los Angeles, CA 90010
(213) 380-KASF   Fax: (631) 380-5274
E-mail: wrc.scholarship@kasf.org
Web: www.kasf.org/westerrn

Summary To provide financial assistance to Korean American students from any state who are working on or planning to work on an undergraduate or graduate degree in any field at a school in western states.

Eligibility This program is open to residents of any state who are 1) U.S. citizens of Korean heritage; 2) Korean citizens who have a valid visa to study in the United States; and 3) citizens of any other country who are of Korean heritage and have a valid visa to study in the United States. Applicants must be enrolled or planning to enroll as a full-time undergraduate or graduate student at a college or university in Alaska, Arizona, California, Colorado, Hawaii, Idaho, Montana, Nevada, New Mexico, Oregon, Utah, Washington, or Wyoming. They must have a GPA of 3.0 or higher. Selection is based on academic achievement (25%), extracurricular activities (10%), an essay (10%), recommendations (10%), financial need (40%), and extra credit for having extraordinary circumstances (5%).

Financial data Stipends are at least $2,000.

Duration 1 year; renewable.

Number awarded Varies each year; recently, 50 were awarded.

Deadline July of each year.

[986]
WHAN SOON CHUNG SCHOLARSHIP

Philip Jaisohn Memorial Foundation
Attn: Scholarship Committee
6705 Old York Road
Philadelphia, PA 19126
(215) 224-2000, ext. 116   Fax: (215) 224-9164
E-mail: info@jaisohn.org
Web: www.jaisohn.com/scholarships

Summary To provide financial assistance to Korean American undergraduate and graduate students who are studying health care or medicine.

Eligibility This program is open to Korean American undergraduate and graduate students who are currently enrolled at a college or university in the United States and working on a degree in health care or a field of medicine. Applicants must be able to demonstrate excellence in community activities and financial need. Along with their application, they must submit an essay on either "Who is Dr. Jaisohn to Me," or "The Significance of Dr. Jaisohn's Ideal to Korean Americans." They must also submit a 100-word statement on how they can contribute to and be involved in the activities of the Philip Jaisohn Memorial Foundation. Selection is based on the applicant's desire to take Dr. Jaisohn as a role model to learn and spread his legacy.

Financial data The stipend is $1,500.

Duration 1 year.

Number awarded 1 each year.

Deadline August of each year.

[987]
WILEY W. MANUEL LAW FOUNDATION SCHOLARSHIPS

Wiley W. Manuel Law Foundation
c/o Law Offices of George Holland
1970 Broadway, Suite 1030
Oakland, CA 94612
(510) 465-4100
Web: www.wileymanuel.org/forms.html

Summary To provide financial assistance to Asian American and other minority students from any state enrolled at law schools in northern California.

Eligibility This program is open to minority students entering their third year at law schools in northern California. Applicants should exemplify the qualities of the late Justice Wiley Manuel, the first African American to serve on the California Supreme Court. Along with their application, they must submit a 250-word essay on why they should be awarded this scholarship. Financial need is also considered in the selection process.

Financial data The stipend is approximately $1,500.

Duration   1 year.

Number awarded   Varies each year; recently, 12 were awarded.

Deadline   August of each year.

[988]
WILLIAM AND CHARLOTTE CADBURY AWARD

National Medical Fellowships, Inc.
Attn: Scholarship Program
347 Fifth Avenue, Suite 510
New York, NY 10016
(212) 483-8880   Toll Free: (877) NMF-1DOC
Fax: (212) 483-8897 E-mail: scholarships@nmfonline.org
Web: www.nmfonline.org

Summary   To provide financial assistance to Vietnamese, Cambodian, and other underrepresented minority medical students who demonstrate academic achievement.

Eligibility   This program is open to Vietnamese, Cambodians, African Americans, Hispanics/Latinos, Native Americans, and Pacific Islanders who are entering their senior year of medical school. They must be U.S. citizens or DACA students. Selection is based on academic achievement, leadership, and community service.

Financial data   The stipend is $5,000.

Duration   1 year.

Additional information   This program began in 1977.

Number awarded   1 each year.

Deadline   September of each year.

[989]
WILLIAM G. ANDERSON, D.O. MINORITY SCHOLARSHIP

American Osteopathic Foundation
Attn: Director, Internal and External Affairs
142 East Ontario Street
Chicago, IL 60611-2864
(312) 202-8235   Toll Free: (866) 455-9383
Fax: (312) 202-8216   E-mail: ehart@aof-foundation.org
Web: www.aof.org

Summary   To provide financial assistance to Asian Pacific American and other minority students enrolled in colleges of osteopathic medicine.

Eligibility   This program is open to minority (Asian American, Pacific Islander, African American, Native American, or Hispanic) students entering their second, third, or fourth year at an accredited college of osteopathic medicine. Applicants must demonstrate 1) interest in osteopathic medicine, its philosophy, and its principles; 2) academic achievement; 3) leadership efforts in addressing the educational, societal, and health needs of minorities; 4) leadership efforts in addressing inequities in medical education and health care; 5) accomplishments, awards and honors, special projects, and extracurricular activities that demonstrate the applicant's ability to be a leader.

Financial data   The stipend is $7,500.

Duration   1 year.

Additional information   This program began in 1998.

Number awarded   1 each year.

Deadline   April of each year.

[990]
WILLIAM K. SCHUBERT M.D. MINORITY NURSING SCHOLARSHIP

Cincinnati Children's Hospital Medical Center
Attn: Office of Diversity and Inclusion, MLC 9008
3333 Burnet Avenue
Cincinnati, OH 45229-3026
(513) 803-6416   Toll Free: (800) 344-2462
Fax: (513) 636-5643   TDD: (513) 636-4900
E-mail: diversity@cchmc.org
Web: www.cincinnatichildrens.org

Summary   To provide financial assistance to Asian Americans and members of other underrepresented groups interested in working on a bachelor's or master's degree in nursing to prepare for licensure in Ohio.

Eligibility   This program is open to members of groups underrepresented in the nursing profession (males, Asians, American Indians or Alaska Natives, Blacks or African Americans, Hawaiian Natives or other Pacific Islanders, or Hispanics or Latinos). Applicants must be enrolled or accepted in a professional bachelor's or master's registered nurse program at an accredited school of nursing to prepare for initial licensure in Ohio. They must have a GPA of 2.75 or higher. Along with their application, they must submit a 750-word essay that covers 1) their long-range personal, educational, and professional goals; 2) why they chose nursing as a profession; 3) how their experience as a member of an underrepresented group has influenced a major professional and/or personal decision in their life; 4) any unique qualifications, experiences, or special talents that demonstrate their creativity; and 5) how their work experience has contributed to their personal development.

Financial data   The stipend is $2,750 per year.

Duration   1 year. May be renewed up to 3 additional years for students working on a bachelor's degree or 1 additional year for students working on a master's degree; renewal requires that students maintain a GPA of 2.75 or higher.

Number awarded   1 or more each year.

Deadline   April of each year.

[991]
WILLIAM RUCKER GREENWOOD SCHOLARSHIP

Association for Women Geoscientists-Potomac Chapter
Attn: Scholarships
P.O. Box 6644
Arlington, VA 22206-0644
E-mail: awgpotomacschol@hotmail.com
Web: www.awg.org/members/po_scholarships.htm

Summary   To provide financial assistance to Asian American and other minority women from any state working on an undergraduate or graduate degree in the geosciences at a college in the Potomac Bay region.

Eligibility   This program is open to minority women who are residents of any state and currently enrolled as full-time undergraduate or graduate geoscience majors at an accredited, degree-granting college or university in Delaware, the District of Columbia, Maryland, Virginia, or West Virginia. Selection is based on the applicant's 1) participation in geoscience or earth science educational activities; and 2) potential for leadership as a future geoscience professional.

Financial data The stipend is $1,000. The recipient also is granted a 1-year membership in the Association for Women Geoscientists (AWG).

Duration 1 year.

Number awarded 1 each year.

Deadline April of each year.

[992]
WISCONSIN LIBRARY ASSOCIATION DIVERSITY SCHOLARSHIP

Wisconsin Library Association
Attn: Scholarship Committee
4610 South Biltmore Lane, Suite 100
Madison, WI 53718-2153
(608) 245-3640   Fax: (608) 245-3646
E-mail: wla@wisconsinlibraries.org
Web: wla.wisconsinlibraries.org

Summary To provide financial assistance to Asian Pacific American and other minority residents of Wisconsin who are working on a master's degree in library and information science or library media at a school in the state.

Eligibility This program is open to members of racial and ethnic minority groups (Asians and Pacific Islanders, African Americans, Latinos or Hispanics, or Native Americans and Alaskan Natives) who are residents of Wisconsin. Applicants must have been admitted to a master's degree program in library and information science or in library media as a full- or part-time student at a college or university in the state. Along with their application, they must submit a 500-word essay describing 1) their background, experience, and career plans in the library profession; and 2) what this scholarship will mean to them. Selection is based on past academic performance, experience and background in library and library-related work, career plans in the library profession, and need and desire for the scholarship.

Financial data The stipend is $950.

Duration 1 year.

Number awarded 1 each year.

Deadline July of each year.

[993]
WOLVERINE BAR FOUNDATION SCHOLARSHIP

Wolverine Bar Association
Attn: Wolverine Bar Foundation
c/o Alexander Simpson, Scholarship Committee Co-Chair
Bodman PLC
201 West Big Beaver Road, Suite 500
Troy, MI 48084
(248) 743-6000   Fax: (248) 743-6002
E-mail: asimpson@bodmanlaw.com
Web: wolverinebar.org/Wolverine_Bar_Foundation.php

Summary To provide financial assistance for law school to Asian American and other minority students in Michigan.

Eligibility This program is open to minority law students who are either currently enrolled in a Michigan law school or are Michigan residents enrolled in an out-of-state law school. Applicants must be in at least their second year of law school. Selection is based on financial need, merit, and an interview.

Financial data The stipend is at least $500.

Duration 1 year; nonrenewable.

Additional Information The Wolverine Bar Association was established by a number of African American attorneys during the 1930s. It was the successor to the Harlan Law Club, founded in 1919 by attorneys in the Detroit area who were excluded from other local bar associations in Michigan.

Number awarded 1 or more each year.

Deadline March of each year.

[994]
WOMAN WHO MOVES THE NATION SCHOLARSHIP

Conference of Minority Transportation Officials
Attn: National Scholarship Program
100 M Street, S.E., Suite 917
Washington, DC 20003
(202) 506-2917   E-mail: info@comto.org
Web: www.comto.org/page/scholarships

Summary To provide financial assistance to Asian American and other minority women who are working on an undergraduate or graduate degree in specified fields to prepare for a management career in a transportation-related organization.

Eligibility This program is open to minority women who are working on an undergraduate or graduate degree with intent to lead in some capacity as a supervisor, manager, director, or other position in transit or a transportation-related organization. Applicants may be studying business, entrepreneurship, political science, or other specialized area. They must have a GPA of 3.0 or higher. Along with their application they must submit a cover letter on their transportation-related career goals and life aspirations. Financial need is not considered in the selection process.

Financial data The stipend is $5,000. Funds are paid directly to the recipient's college or university.

Duration 1 year.

Number awarded 1 each year.

Deadline April of each year.

[995]
WORKERS' RIGHTS SCHOLARSHIP

Ochoa|King
3737 Camino Del Rio South, Suite 407
San Diego, CA 92108
(619) 285-1662   Fax: (619) 285-1760
E-mail: info@union-attorneys.org
Web: www.union-attorneys.org/workers-rights-scholarship

Summary To provide financial assistance to law students in California, especially Asian Americans and members of other underrepresented groups, who can demonstrate a commitment to workers' rights.

Eligibility This program is open to students currently enrolled full time at a law school in California. Applicants must be preparing for a career in the labor movement, workers' rights, or public interest law. They must be able to demonstrate strong academic achievement and a demonstrated commitment to workers' rights. Along with their application, they must submit a 500-word statement explaining why they wish to prepare for a career in the labor movement and how their background and/or life experiences would improve diversity in the field of workers' rights. People of color, women, veterans, LGBTQ, and candidates with disabilities or from economically disadvantaged backgrounds are encouraged to apply.

Financial data The stipend is $500.

Duration 1 year.

Additional information This program began in 2012.

Number awarded 1 each year.

Deadline September of each year.

[996]
WORLD COMMUNION NATIONAL SCHOLARSHIPS

United Methodist Church
General Board of Global Ministries
Attn: Scholarship/Leadership Development Office
475 Riverside Drive, Room 1479
New York, NY 10115
(212) 870-3787   Toll Free: (800) UMC-GBGM
Fax: (212) 870-3654   E-mail: scholars@umcmission.org
Web: www.umcor.org/explore-our-work/Scholarships

Summary To provide financial assistance to Asian Americans and other students of color who are interested in attending graduate school to prepare for leadership in promoting the mission goals of the United Methodist Church.

Eligibility This program is open to U.S. citizens and permanent residents who are members of a community of color. Applicants must have applied to or been admitted to a master's, doctoral, or professional program at an institution of higher education in the United States. They must indicate a willingness to provide 5 years of Christian service after graduation in the areas of elimination of poverty, expansion of global health, leadership development, or congregational development. High priority is given to members of the United Methodist Church. Financial need is considered in the selection process.

Financial data The stipend ranges from $1,000 to $12,500, depending on the recipient's related needs and school expenses.

Duration 1 year.

Additional information These awards are funded by the World Communion Offering received in United Methodist Churches on the first Sunday in October.

Number awarded 5 to 10 each year.

Deadline November of each year.

[997]
WRITING COMPETITIVE TO PROMOTE DIVERSITY IN LAW SCHOOLS AND IN THE LEGAL PROFESSION

Law School Admission Council
Attn: Office of Diversity Initiatives
662 Penn Street
P.O. Box 40
Newtown, PA 18940-0040
(215) 968-1338   TDD: (215) 968-1169
E-mail: DiversityOffice@lsac.org
Web: www.lsac.org

Summary To recognize and reward law students who submit outstanding essays on what law schools can do to promote diversity.

Eligibility This competition is open to J.D. candidates in each year of study at law schools in the United States and Canada that are members of the Law School Admission Council (LSAC). Applicants must submit articles, up to 20 pages in length, on the techniques, resources and strategies law schools can utilize to recruit and retain students of color, students living with a disability, LGBTQ students, and other students who are from groups underrepresented in law schools and the legal profession. Selection is based on research and use of relevant sources and authorities; quality and clarity of legal analysis, persuasion, and writing; understanding, interpretations, and conclusions regarding diversity and the implications of diversity in this context; and compliance with all competition procedures.

Financial data The prize is $5,000.

Duration The prize is awarded annually.

Number awarded 3 each year: 1 to a student in each year of law school.

Deadline April of each year.

[998]
WSP/PARSONS BRINCKERHOFF WOMEN IN LEADERSHIP SCHOLARSHIP

Conference of Minority Transportation Officials
Attn: National Scholarship Program
100 M Street, S.E., Suite 917
Washington, DC 20003
(202) 506-2917   E-mail: info@comto.org
Web: www.comto.org/page/scholarships

Summary To provide financial assistance to Asian American and other minority women who are working on a master's degree in civil engineering or other transportation-related field.

Eligibility This program is open to minority women who are working full time on a master's degree in civil engineering with intent to prepare for a leadership role in transportation. They must have a GPA of 3.0 or higher. Along with their application they must submit a cover letter on their transportation-related career goals and life aspirations. Financial need is not considered in the selection process.

Financial data The stipend is $3,000. Funds are paid directly to the recipient's college or university.

Duration 1 year.

Additional information This program is sponsored by WSP USA, formerly Parsons Brinckerhoff, Inc.

Number awarded 1 each year.

Deadline April of each year.

[999]
XEROX TECHNICAL MINORITY SCHOLARSHIP PROGRAM

Xerox Corporation
Attn: Technical Minority Scholarship Program
150 State Street, Fourth Floor
Rochester, NY 14614
Toll Free: (877) 747-3625 E-mail: xtmsp@rballiance.com
Web: www.xerox.com/jobs/minority-scholarships/enus.html

Summary To provide financial assistance to Asian Americans and other minorities interested in undergraduate or graduate education in the sciences and/or engineering.

Eligibility This program is open to minorities (people of Asian, African American, Pacific Islander, Native American, Native Alaskan, or Hispanic descent) working full time on a bachelor's, master's, or doctoral degree in chemistry, computing and software systems, engineering (chemical, computer, electrical, imaging, manufacturing, mechanical, optical, or software), information management, laser optics, materials science, physics, or printing management science. Applicants must be U.S. citizens or permanent residents with a GPA of 3.0 or higher and attending a 4-year college or university.

Financial data Stipends range from $1,000 to $10,000.

Duration 1 year.

Number awarded Varies each year, recently, 128 were awarded.

Deadline September of each year.

[1000]
XIA THAO SCHOLARSHIP

Hmong American Education Fund
P.O. Box 17468
St. Paul, MN 55117
(651) 592-1576   E-mail: scholarships@thehaef.org
Web: www.thehaef.org

Summary To provide financial assistance to Hmong undergraduate and graduate students from Minnesota who demonstrate leadership.

Eligibility This program is open to students of Hmong descent who are residents of Minnesota and currently enrolled as full-time undergraduate or graduate students at 2- or 4-year colleges or universities in any state. Applicants must be U.S. citizens or permanent residents and have a GPA of 3.0 or higher. Along with their application, they must submit a 1,500-word essay on their commitment to education, their leadership qualities, their financial need, how this scholarship can help them, and their community service. Selection is based on academic excellence, leadership qualities, commitment to helping their community, and financial need.

Financial data The stipend is $500.

Duration 1 year; nonrenewable.

Number awarded 1 each year.

Deadline March of each year.

[1001]
YOUNG SOO CHOI STUDENT SCHOLARSHIP AWARD

Society of Toxicology
Attn: Korean Toxicologists Association in America Special Interest Group
1821 Michael Faraday Drive, Suite 300
Reston, VA 20190-5348
(703) 438-3115   Fax: (703) 438-3113
E-mail: sothq@toxicology.org
Web: www.toxicology.org/ai/af/awards_details.aspx?id=137

Summary To provide financial assistance to Korean students who are working on a graduate degree in toxicology.

Eligibility This program is open to Korean students (having been born in Korea or, if born in the United States, having 1 or more parents of Korean descent) who are enrolled or planning to enroll in a graduate program in toxicology or in a field of biomedical science related to toxicology. Applicants must

submit a description of their graduate program (including any research conducted or planned), copies of any abstracts prepared for presentations at professional meetings, a brief statement indicating how the scholarship will assist in their graduate training, and a letter of recommendation from their mentor. Selection is based on merit and financial need.

Financial data A stipend is awarded (amount not specified).

Duration 1 year.

Additional information This program began in 2008.

Number awarded 1 each year.

Deadline January of each year.

[1002]
ZOETIS/AAVMC VETERINARY STUDENT SCHOLARSHIP PROGRAM

Association of American Veterinary Medical Colleges
Attn: Associate Executive Director for Academic and Research Affairs
1101 Vermont Avenue, N.W., Suite 301
Washington, DC 20005-3536
(202) 371-9195, ext. 118   Toll Free: (877) 862-2740
Fax: (202) 842-0773   E-mail: tmashima@aavmc.org
Web: www.aavmc.org

Summary To provide financial assistance to veterinary students in all areas of professional interest, especially Asian Americans and other minorities.

Eligibility This program is open to second- and third-year students at veterinary colleges in the United States. Applicants may have a professional interest in any area, including food animal medicine, small animal clinical medicine, research, government services, public health, or organized veterinary medicine. Along with their application, they must submit a 3-page personal statement that describes 1) why diversity and inclusion are important to them personally and professionally; 2) how they intend to continue contributing to diversity and inclusion efforts in the veterinary profession after graduation; and 3) what it might mean to be honored as a recipient of this scholarship. They must also indicate how they express their race and/or ethnicity (American Indian or Alaskan, Asian, Black or African American, Hispanic, Native Hawaiian or Pacific Islander, or White) and how they express their gender (male, female, transgender spectrum, or other). Selection is based primarily on documentation of a demonstrated commitment to promoting diversity in academic veterinary medicine; consideration is also given to academic achievement, the student's broader community service record, and financial need.

Financial data The stipend is $2,000.

Duration 1 year; nonrenewable.

Additional information This program was established by Zoetis in 2010. That firm partnered with the Association of American Veterinary Medical Colleges (AAVMC) in 2014 to administer the program.

Number awarded Varies each year; recently, 452 were awarded.

Deadline November of each year.

Professionals/ Postdoctorates

Listed alphabetically by program title and described in detail here are 145 grants, awards, educational support programs, residencies, and other sources of "free money" available to professionals and postdoctorates of Asian origins (including those of subcontinent Asian and Pacific Islander descent). This funding can be used to support research, creative activities, formal academic classes, training courses, and/or residencies in the United States.

[1003]
AAJA AL NEUHARTH AWARD FOR INNOVATION IN INVESTIGATIVE JOURNALISM

Asian American Journalists Association
Attn: Program Associate
5 Third Street, Suite 1108
San Francisco, CA 94103
(415) 346-2051, ext. 104   Fax: (415) 346-6343
E-mail: DanielG@aaja.org
Web: www.aaja.org/category/membership/awards

Summary To recognize and reward journalists who have used digital tools for watchdog and investigative journalism and are nominated by members of the Asian American Journalism Association (AAJA).

Eligibility This award is available to journalists who have used digital tools to complete spot news, editorials, news analysis, columns, or features. The journalist's work must be submitted by an AAJA member, although members may submit their own work. Entries must be in English and published or aired between February of the previous year and February of the current year. Special consideration is given to journalism that helps a community understand and address important issues.

Financial data The award is $5,000.

Duration The award is presented annually.

Additional information This award is sponsored by the Gannett Foundation.

Number awarded 1 each year.

Deadline March of each year.

[1004]
AAPA-APF OKURA MENTAL HEALTH LEADERSHIP FOUNDATION FELLOWSHIP

American Psychological Foundation
750 First Street, N.E.
Washington, DC 20002-4242
(202) 336-5843   Fax: (202) 336-5812
E-mail: foundation@apa.org
Web: www.apa.org/apf/funding/okura-fellow.aspx

Summary To provide funding to members of the Asian American Psychological Association (AAPA) who are interested in conducting projects related to the Asian American and Pacific Islander (AAPI) community.

Eligibility This program is open to AAPA members who are interested in conducting psychological projects that will benefit the AAPI community. The emphasis of the program rotates among support for research (2015), support for training initiatives (2016), and support for service and practice initiatives (2017). Applicants must be within 10 years of completing their doctoral degree and be affiliated with a nonprofit organization. Selection is based on conformance with stated program goals and requirements; innovative and potential impact qualities; competence and capability of project leaders; and quality, viability, and promise of the proposed work.

Financial data The grant is $20,000.

Duration The grant is presented annually.

Additional information This program, established in 2009, is administered on behalf of AAPA by the American Psychological Foundation (APF), with funding provided by the Okura Mental Health Leadership Foundation.

Number awarded 1 each year.

Deadline September of each year.

[1005]
AAPINA GEROPSYCHIATRIC NURSING AWARD

Asian American/Pacific Islander Nurses Association
c/o Rei Serafica, Awards Committee Chair
University of Nevada at Las Vegas
School of Nursing
BHS 440
4505 South Maryland Parkway, Mail Code 3018
Las Vegas, NV 89154-3018
(702) 895-5746   Fax: (702) 895-4807
E-mail: reimund.serafica@unlv.edu
Web: www.aapina.org/ethnic-minority-nursing-award

Summary To provide funding to members of the Asian American/Pacific Islander Nurses Association (AAPINA) who are faculty members interested in conducting a pilot study on mental health issues of older Asian Americans or Pacific Islanders.

Eligibility This program is open to full-time faculty members at academic institutions who have been AAPINA members for at least 2 years. Applicants must be seeking funding for pilot or feasibility studies that focus on mental health issues of older Asian American or Pacific Islanders. Selection is based on significance of the study, investigators' experience and background, innovation, approach, and environment.

Financial data The grant is $1,000.

Duration 1 year.

Number awarded 1 each year.

Deadline February of each year.

[1006]
AAPINA RESEARCH GRANT PROGRAM

Asian American/Pacific Islander Nurses Association
c/o Rei Serafica, Awards Committee Chair
University of Nevada at Las Vegas
School of Nursing
BHS 440
4505 South Maryland Parkway, Mail Code 3018
Las Vegas, NV 89154-3018
(702) 895-5746   Fax: (702) 895-4807
E-mail: reimund.serafica@unlv.edu
Web: www.aapina.org/ethnic-minority-nursing-award

Summary To provide funding to members of the Asian American/Pacific Islander Nurses Association (AAPINA) who are faculty members interested in conducting a research project.

Eligibility This program is open to full-time faculty members at academic institutions who have been AAPINA members for at least 2 years. Applicants must be seeking funding for pilot or feasibility studies in preparation for larger grant applications. Selection is based on the proposal, potential for future funding, leadership skills, and participation in AAPINA.

Financial data The grant is $5,000.

Duration 1 year.

Number awarded 1 each year.

Deadline December of each year.

[1007]
AAUW CAREER DEVELOPMENT GRANTS

American Association of University Women
Attn: AAUW Educational Foundation
1111 16th Street, N.W.
Washington, DC 20036-4873
(202) 785-7700　　　Toll Free: (800) 326-AAUW
Fax: (202) 872-1425　　　TDD: (202) 785-7777
E-mail: aauw@applyists.com
Web: www.aauw.org

Summary To provide financial assistance to Asian American and other women of color who are seeking career advancement, career change, or reentry into the workforce.

Eligibility This program is open to women who are U.S. citizens or permanent residents, have earned a bachelor's degree, received their most recent degree more than 4 years ago, and are making career changes, seeking to advance in current careers, or reentering the workforce. Applicants must be interested in working toward a master's degree, second bachelor's or associate degree, professional degree (e.g., M.D., J.D.), certification program, or technical school certificate. They must be planning to undertake course work at an accredited 2- or 4-year college or university (or a technical school that is licensed, accredited, or approved by the U.S. Department of Education). Primary consideration is given to women of color and women pursuing their first advanced degree or credentials in nontraditional fields. Support is not provided for prerequisite course work or for Ph.D. course work or dissertations. Selection is based on demonstrated commitment to education and equity for women and girls, reason for seeking higher education or technical training, degree to which study plan is consistent with career objectives, potential for success in chosen field, documentation of opportunities in chosen field, feasibility of study plans and proposed time schedule, validity of proposed budget and budget narrative (including sufficient outside support), and quality of written proposal.

Financial data Grants range from $2,000 to $12,000. Funds may be used for tuition, fees, books, supplies, local transportation, dependent child care, or purchase of a computer required for the study program.

Duration 1 year, beginning in July; nonrenewable.

Additional information The filing fee is $35.

Number awarded Varies each year; recently, 63 of these grants, with a value of $670,000, were awarded.

Deadline December of each year.

[1008]
AES RESEARCH AND TRAINING FELLOWSHIP FOR CLINICIANS

American Epilepsy Society
135 South LaSalle Street, Suite 2850
Chicago, IL 60603
(312) 883-3800　　　Fax: (312) 896-5784
E-mail: info@aesnet.org
Web: www.aesnet.org

Summary To provide funding clinicians, especially Asian Americans and other minorities, who are interested in conducting research related to epilepsy.

Eligibility This program is open to clinical fellows, postdoctoral fellows, and newly appointed clinical faculty members who have an M.D., Ph.D., Sc.D., Pharm.D., R.N., or equivalent degree. Applicants must be interested in conducting research with an epilepsy-related theme under the guidance of a mentor with expertise in epilepsy research. They must have a defined research plan and access to institutional resources to conduct the proposed project with at least 50% of their time devoted to the fellowship. Physicians whose research will involve direct patient care or direct involvement with patients must have completed all residency training and be licensed to practice medicine at their institution. Selection is based on the applicant's potential and commitment to develop as an independent and productive epilepsy researcher, academic record, and research experience; the mentor's research qualifications; the research training plan; and the quality of the research facilities, resources, and training opportunities. Applications are especially encouraged from women, members of minority groups, and people with disabilities. U.S. citizenship is not required, but all research must be conducted in the United States.

Financial data Grants range up $50,000, including $49,000 as stipend and $1,000 for travel support and complimentary registration to attend the sponsor's annual meeting.

Duration 1 year; nonrenewable.

Additional information In addition to the funding provided by the American Epilepsy Society, support is available from the TESS Research Foundation for applications focused on epilepsy due to SLC13A5 mutations; the LGS Foundation for applications focused on Lennox-Gastaut-Syndrome; the PCDH19 Alliance for applications focused on epilepsy due to PCDH19 mutations; the Dravet Syndrome Foundation for applications focused on Dravet Syndrome; Wishes for Elliott for applications focused on epilepsy due to SCN8A mutations; and the TS Alliance for applications focused on epilepsy associated with tuberous sclerosis complex (TSC).

Number awarded Varies each year.

Deadline Letters of intent must be submitted by October of each year; final proposals are due in January.

[1009]
AMERICAN ASSOCIATION OF CHINESE IN TOXICOLOGY AND CHARLES RIVER BEST ABSTRACT AWARD

Society of Toxicology
Attn: American Association of Chinese in Toxicology
　Special Interest Group
1821 Michael Faraday Drive, Suite 300
Reston, VA 20190-5348
(703) 438-3115　　　Fax: (703) 438-3113
E-mail: sothq@toxicology.org
Web: www.toxicology.org/ai/af/awards_details.aspx?id=98

Summary To recognize and reward graduate student and postdoctoral members of the Society of Toxicology (SOT) who are of Chinese ethnic origin and present outstanding papers at the annual meeting.

Eligibility This award is available to SOT members who are graduate students or postdoctoral fellows of Chinese descent (having 1 or more parents of Chinese descent). Candidates must have an accepted abstract for the SOT annual meeting. Along with the abstract, they must submit a cover letter outlining the significance of the work to the field of toxicology.

Financial data The prizes are $500 for first, $300 for second, and $200 for third.

Duration The prizes are presented annually.

Number awarded 3 each year.

Deadline December of each year.

[1010]
AMERICAN ASSOCIATION OF CHINESE IN TOXICOLOGY DISTINGUISHED CHINESE TOXICOLOGIST LECTURESHIP AWARD

Society of Toxicology
Attn: American Association of Chinese in Toxicology
  Special Interest Group
1821 Michael Faraday Drive, Suite 300
Reston, VA 20190-5348
(703) 438-3115   Fax: (703) 438-3113
E-mail: sothq@toxicology.org
Web: www.toxicology.org/ai/af/awards_details.aspx?id=99

Summary To recognize and reward members of the Society of Toxicology (SOT) who are of Chinese ethnic origin and have made outstanding contributions to the field.

Eligibility This award is available to SOT members who are of Chinese ethnic origin. Nominees should have contributed significantly to the science of toxicology and have an exemplary professional life. Nominations must be submitted by at least 2 members of the American Association of Chinese in Toxicology Special Interest Group (AACT-SIG) of SOT.

Financial data The award consists of a plaque and a $500 honorarium.

Duration The award is presented annually.

Additional information The winner delivers an award lecture at an AACT-SIG session of the SOT annual meeting.

Number awarded 1 each year.

Deadline Nominations must be submitted by October of each year.

[1011]
AMERICAN ASSOCIATION OF OBSTETRICIANS AND GYNECOLOGISTS FOUNDATION RESEARCH AND TRAINING SCHOLARSHIPS

American Association of Obstetricians and Gynecologists
  Foundation
9 Newport Drive, Suite 200
Forest Hill, MD 21050
(443) 640-1051   Fax: (443) 640-1031
E-mail: info@aaogf.org
Web: www.aaogf.org/scholarship.asp

Summary To provide funding to physicians, especially Asian Americans and other minorities, who are interested in a program of research training in obstetrics and gynecology.

Eligibility Applicants must have an M.D. degree and be eligible for the certification process of the American Board of Obstetrics and Gynecology (ABOG). They must be interested in participating in research training conducted by 1 or more faculty mentors at an academic department of obstetrics and gynecology in the United States or Canada. The research training may be either laboratory-based or clinical, and should focus on fundamental biology, disease mechanisms, interventions or diagnostics, epidemiology, or translational research. Applicants for the scholarship co-sponsored by the Society for Maternal-Fetal Medicine (SMFM) must also be members or associate members of the SMFM. Women and minority candidates are strongly encouraged to apply. Selection is based on the scholarly, clinical, and research qualifications of the candidate; evidence of the candidate's commitment to an investigative career in academic obstetrics and gynecology in the United States or Canada; qualifications of the sponsoring department and mentor; overall quality of the mentoring plan; and quality of the research project.

Financial data The grant is $120,000 per year. Sufficient funds to support travel to the annual fellows' retreat must be set aside. The balance of the funds may be used for salary, technical support, and supplies.

Duration 1 year; may be renewed for 2 additional years, based on satisfactory progress of the scholar.

Additional information Scholars must devote at least 75% of their effort to the program of research training.

Number awarded 2 each year: 1 co-sponsored by ABOG and 1 co-sponsored by SMFM.

Deadline June of each year.

[1012]
AMERICAN EPILEPSY SOCIETY JUNIOR INVESTIGATOR RESEARCH AWARD

American Epilepsy Society
135 South LaSalle Street, Suite 2850
Chicago, IL 60603
(312) 883-3800   Fax: (312) 896-5784
E-mail: info@aesnet.org
Web: www.aesnet.org

Summary To provide funding to junior investigators, especially Asian Americans and other minorities, who are interested in conducting research related to epilepsy.

Eligibility This program is open to recently independent investigators who have an M.D., Ph.D., Pharm.D., R.N., or equivalent degree and an academic appointment at the level of assistant professor or equivalent. Applicants must be interested in conducting basic, translational, or clinical epilepsy research, including studies of disease mechanisms or treatments, epidemiological or behavioral studies, the development of new technologies, or health services and outcomes research. Applications are especially encouraged from women, members of minority groups, and people with disabilities. U.S. citizenship is not required, but all research must be conducted in the United States.

Financial data The grant is $50,000 per year for direct costs of research.

Duration 1 year; nonrenewable.

Additional information In addition to the funding provided by the American Epilepsy Society, support is available from the TESS Research Foundation for applications focused on epilepsy due to SLC13A5 mutations; the LGS Foundation for applications focused on Lennox-Gastaut-Syndrome; the PCDH19 Alliance for applications focused on epilepsy due to PCDH19 mutations; the Dravet Syndrome Foundation for applications focused on Dravet Syndrome; Wishes for Elliott for applications focused on epilepsy due to SCN8A mutations; and the TS Alliance for applications focused on epilepsy associated with tuberous sclerosis complex (TSC).

Number awarded Varies each year.

Deadline Letters of intent must be submitted by October of each year; final proposals are due in January.

[1013]
AMERICAN EPILEPSY SOCIETY POSTDOCTORAL RESEARCH FELLOWSHIPS

American Epilepsy Society
135 South LaSalle Street, Suite 2850
Chicago, IL 60603
(312) 883-3800   Fax: (312) 896-5784
E-mail: info@aesnet.org
Web: www.aesnet.org

Summary To provide funding to postdoctoral fellows, especially Asian Americans and other minorities, who are interested in conducting mentored research related to epilepsy.

Eligibility This program is open to postdoctoral fellows who have an M.D., Ph.D., Sc.D., Pharm.D., R.N., or equivalent degree. Applicants must be interested in conducting research with an epilepsy-related theme under the guidance of a mentor with expertise in epilepsy research. They must have a defined research plan and access to institutional resources to conduct the proposed project. Selection is based on the applicant's potential and commitment to develop as an independent and productive epilepsy researcher, academic record, and research experience; the mentor's research qualifications; the research training plan; and the quality of the research facilities, resources, and training opportunities. Applications are especially encouraged from women, members of minority groups, and people with disabilities. U.S. citizenship is not required, but all research must be conducted in the United States.

Financial data Grants range up $45,000, including $44,000 as stipend and $1,000 for travel support and complimentary registration to attend the sponsor's annual meeting.

Duration 1 year; nonrenewable.

Additional information In addition to the funding provided by the American Epilepsy Society, support is available from the TESS Research Foundation for applications focused on epilepsy due to SLC13A5 mutations; the LGS Foundation for applications focused on Lennox-Gastaut-Syndrome; the PCDH19 Alliance for applications focused on epilepsy due to PCDH19 mutations; the Dravet Syndrome Foundation for applications focused on Dravet Syndrome; Wishes for Elliott for applications focused on epilepsy due to SCN8A mutations; and the TS Alliance for applications focused on epilepsy associated with tuberous sclerosis complex (TSC).

Number awarded Varies each year.

Deadline Letters of intent must be submitted by October of each year; final proposals are due in January.

[1014]
AMERICAN NURSES ASSOCIATION MINORITY FELLOWSHIP PROGRAM

American Nurses Association
Attn: SAMHSA Minority Fellowship Programs
8515 Georgia Avenue, Suite 400
Silver Spring, MD 20910-3492
(301) 628-5247   Toll Free: (800) 274-4ANA
Fax: (301) 628-5339   E-mail: janet.jackson@ana.org
Web: www.emfp.org

Summary To provide financial assistance to Asian American and other minority nurses who are doctoral candidates interested in psychiatric, mental health, and substance abuse issues that impact the lives of ethnic minority people.

Eligibility This program is open to nurses who have a master's degree and are members of an ethnic or racial minority group, including but not limited to Asians and Asian Americans, Blacks or African Americans, Hispanics or Latinos, American Indians and Alaska Natives, and Native Hawaiians and other Pacific Islanders. Applicants must be enrolled full time in an accredited doctoral nursing program. They must be certified as a Mental Health Nurse Practitioner, Mental Health Clinical Nurse Specialist, or Mental Health Nurse. U.S. citizenship or permanent resident status and membership in the American Nurses Association are required. Selection is based on commitment to a career in substance abuse in psychiatric/mental health issues affecting minority populations.

Financial data The program provides an annual stipend of $22,476 and tuition assistance up to $5,000.

Duration 3 to 5 years.

Additional information Funds for this program are provided by the Substance Abuse and Mental Health Services Administration (SAMHSA).

Number awarded 1 or more each year.

Deadline March of each year.

[1015]
ANAC STUDENT DIVERSITY MENTORSHIP SCHOLARSHIP

Association of Nurses in AIDS Care
Attn: Awards Committee
3538 Ridgewood Road
Akron, OH 44333-3122
(330) 670-0101   Toll Free: (800) 260-6780
Fax: (330) 670-0109   E-mail: anac@anacnet.org
Web: www.nursesinaidscare.org

Summary To provide financial assistance to Asian American and other student nurses from minority groups who are interested in HIV/AIDS nursing and in attending the national conference of the Association of Nurses in AIDS Care (ANAC).

Eligibility This program is open to student nurses from a diverse racial or ethnic background, defined to include Asians/Pacific Islanders, African Americans, Hispanics/Latinos, and American Indians/Alaskan Natives. Candidates must have a genuine interest in HIV/AIDS nursing, be interested in attending the ANAC national conference, and desire to develop a mentorship relationship with a member of the ANAC Diversity Specialty Committee. They may be 1) prelicensure students enrolled in an initial R.N. or L.P.N./L.V.N. program (i.e. L.P.N./L.V.N., A.D.N., diploma, B.S./B.S.N.); or 2) current licensed R.N. students with an associate or diploma degree who are enrolled in a bachelor's degree program. Nominees may be recommended by themselves, nursing faculty members, or ANAC members, but their nomination must be supported by an ANAC member. Along with their nomination form, they must submit a 2,000-character essay describing their interest or experience in HIV/AIDS care and why they want to attend the ANAC conference.

Financial data Recipients are awarded a $1,000 scholarship (paid directly to the school), up to $599 in reimbursement of travel expenses to attend the ANAC annual conference, free conference registration, an award plaque, a free ticket to the awards ceremony at the conference, and a 2-year ANAC membership.

Duration 1 year.

Additional information The mentor will be assigned at the conference and will maintain contact during the period of study.

Number awarded 1 each year.

Deadline August of each year.

[1016]
ANISFIELD-WOLF BOOK AWARDS

Cleveland Foundation
1422 Euclid Avenue, Suite 1300
Cleveland, OH 44115-2001
(216) 861-3810   Fax: (216) 861-1729
E-mail: Hello@anisfield-wolf.org
Web: www.anisfield-wolf.org

Summary To recognize and reward recent books that have contributed to an understanding of racism or appreciation of the rich diversity of human cultures.

Eligibility Works published in English during the preceding year that "contribute to our understanding of racism or our appreciation of the rich diversity of human cultures" are eligible to be considered. Entries may be either scholarly or imaginative (fiction, poetry, memoir). Plays and screenplays are not eligible, nor are works in progress. Manuscripts and self-published works are not eligible, and no grants are made for completing or publishing manuscripts.

Financial data The prize is $10,000. If more than 1 author is chosen in a given year, the prize is divided equally among the winning books.

Duration The award is presented annually.

Additional information This program began in 1936.

Number awarded 2 each year: 1 for fiction or poetry and 1 for nonfiction, biography, or scholarly research.

Deadline December of each year.

[1017]
APA/DIVISION 39 GRANT

American Psychological Foundation
750 First Street, N.E.
Washington, DC 20002-4242
(202) 336-5843   Fax: (202) 336-5812
E-mail: foundation@apa.org
Web: www.apa.org/apf/funding/division-39.aspx

Summary To provide funding to psychologists who wish to conduct psychoanalytical research related to Asian Americans and other underserved populations.

Eligibility This program is open to psychologists who have a demonstrated knowledge of psychoanalytical principles. Applicants may be, but are not required to be, practicing psychoanalytic therapists. Preference is given to graduate students involved in dissertation research, early-career professionals, and/or those who demonstrate a long-term interest in research related to underserved populations. The research may be of an empirical, theoretical, or clinical nature. Selection is based on conformance with stated program goals and qualifications; quality and potential impact of both previous and proposed research projects; originality, innovation, and contribution to the field with both previous and proposed research projects; and applicant's demonstrated interest in research related to underserved populations. The sponsor encourages applications from individuals who represent diversity in race, ethnicity, gender, age, disability, and sexual orientation.

Financial data The grant is $4,000.

Duration 1 year.

Additional information This program, which began in 2014, is sponsored by the American Psychological Association's Division 39 (Psychoanalysis).

Number awarded 1 each year.

Deadline July of each year.

[1018]
APA/SAMHSA MINORITY FELLOWSHIP PROGRAM

American Psychiatric Association
Attn: Division of Diversity and Health Equity
1000 Wilson Boulevard, Suite 1825
Arlington, VA 22209-3901
(703) 907-8653   Toll Free: (888) 35-PSYCH
Fax: (703) 907-7852   E-mail: mking@psych.org
Web: www.psychiatry.org/minority-fellowship

Summary To provide educational enrichment to psychiatrists-in-training who are interested in providing quality and effective services to Asian Americans and other minorities.

Eligibility This program is open to residents who are in at least their second year of psychiatric training, members of the American Psychiatric Association (APA), and U.S. citizens or permanent residents. A goal of the program is to develop leadership to improve the quality of mental health care for members of ethnic minority groups (Asian Americans, American Indians, Native Alaskans, Native Hawaiians, Native Pacific Islanders, African Americans, and Hispanics/Latinos). Applicants must be interested in working with a component of the APA that is of interest to them and relevant to their career goals. Along with their application, they must submit a 2-page essay on how the fellowship would be utilized to alter their present training and ultimately assist them in achieving their career goals. Selection is based on commitment to serve ethnic minority populations, demonstrated leadership abilities, awareness of the importance of culture in mental health, and interest in the interrelationship between mental health/illness and transcultural factors.

Financial data Fellows receive a monthly stipend (amount not specified) and reimbursement of transportation, lodging, meals, and incidentals in connection with attendance at program-related activities. They are expected to use the funds to enhance their own professional development, improve training in cultural competence at their training institution, improve awareness of culturally relevant issues in psychiatry at their institution, expand research in areas relevant to minorities and underserved populations, enhance the current treatment modalities for minority patients and underserved individuals at their institution, and improve awareness in the surrounding community about mental health issues (particularly with regard to minority populations).

Duration 1 year; may be renewed 1 additional year.

Additional information Funding for this program is provided by the Substance Abuse and Mental Health Services Administration (SAMHSA). As part of their assignment to an APA component, fellows must attend the fall component meetings in September and the APA annual meeting in May. At those meeting, they can share their experiences as residents and minorities and discuss issues that impact on minority populations. This program is an outgrowth of the fellowships that were established in 1974 under a grant from the National Institute of Mental Health in answer to concerns about the underrepresentation of minorities in psychiatry.

Number awarded Varies each year; recently, 21 were awarded.

Deadline January of each year.

[1019]
APAICS FELLOWSHIP PROGRAM

Asian Pacific American Institute for Congressional
 Studies
Attn: Fellowship Program
1001 Connecticut Avenue, N.W., Suite 320
Washington, DC 20036
(202) 296-9200   Fax: (202) 296-9236
E-mail: fellowship@apaics.org
Web: www.apaics.org/congressional-fellows

Summary To provide an opportunity for recent graduates with an interest in issues affecting the Asian Pacific American community to work in the Executive or Legislative branch of the federal government or a nonprofit agency.

Eligibility Applicants must have a graduate or bachelor's degree from an accredited educational institution. They must have a demonstrated interest in the political process, public policy, and Asian American and Pacific Islander issues; relevant work or internship experience; evidence of leadership abilities; oral and written communication skills; a cumulative GPA of 3.0 or higher; and an interest in gaining work experience with the federal government or a nonprofit agency in Washington, D.C. U.S. citizenship or permanent resident status is required. Along with their application, they must submit a 750-word essay on the role of the Congressional Asian Pacific American Caucus (CAPAC) and why they want to be a part of it.

Financial data The stipend is $20,000. Funds are intended to cover housing and personal expenses. A separate stipend covers basic health insurance, and round-trip air transportation is provided.

Duration 9 months, starting in September.

Additional information This program is supported by Southwest Airlines.

Number awarded Varies each year; recently, 5 were awarded.

Deadline February of each year.

[1020]
APAICS SUMMER INTERNSHIPS

Asian Pacific American Institute for Congressional
 Studies
Attn: Summer Internship Program
1001 Connecticut Avenue, N.W., Suite 320
Washington, DC 20036
(202) 296-9200   Fax: (202) 296-9236
E-mail: internship@apaics.org
Web: www.apaics.org/summer-interns

Summary To provide an opportunity for undergraduate students and recent graduates with an interest in issues affecting the Asian Pacific Islander American communities to work in Washington, D.C. during the summer.

Eligibility This program is open to Asian American and Pacific Islander students currently enrolled in an accredited undergraduate institution; recent (within 90 days) graduates are also eligible. Applicants must be able to demonstrate interest in the political process, public policy issues, and Asian American and Pacific Islander community affairs; leadership abilities; and oral and written communication skills. They must be 18 years of age or older; U.S. citizens or permanent residents; and interested in working in Congress, federal agencies, or institutions that further the mission of the Asian Pacific American Institute for Congressional Studies (APAICS). Preference is given to students who have not previously had an internship in Washington, D.C.

Financial data The stipend is $2,000.

Duration 8 weeks, starting in June.

Additional information This program is sponsored by Southwest Airlines.

Number awarded Varies each year; recently, 20 interns were selected for this program.

Deadline January of each year.

[1021]
ARTTABLE MENTORED INTERNSHIPS FOR DIVERSITY IN THE VISUAL ARTS PROFESSIONS

ArtTable Inc.
1 East 53rd Street, Fifth Floor
New York, NY 10022
(212) 343-1735   Fax: (866) 363-4188
E-mail: info@arttable.org
Web: www.arttable.org/summermentoredinternship

Summary To provide an opportunity for women who are Asian American or from other diverse backgrounds to gain mentored work experience during the summer and to prepare for a career as an art professional.

Eligibility This program is open to women who are college seniors, recent graduates, or graduate students and interested in preparing for a career as a visual arts professional (including administrative director, art adviser, art appraiser, art critic, art dealer, art librarian, arts funder, arts lawyer, conservator, curator, editor, educator, fundraiser, management consultant, public relations consultant, writer). Applicants must be from a cultural or ethnic background that is underrepresented in the field. They must be interested in working during the summer with a mentor at an art museum or similar facility. U.S. citizenship or permanent resident status is required.

Financial data The stipend is $3,000. The hosting institution or mentor receives $500 for administrative and other costs.

Duration 8 weeks during the summer.

Additional information This program began in 2000. Support is provided by the Samuel H. Kress Foundation.

Number awarded Varies each year; recently, 5 of these internships were awarded.

Deadline February of each year.

[1022]
ASIAN AMERICAN STUDIES VISITING SCHOLAR AND VISITING RESEARCHER PROGRAM

University of California at Los Angeles
Institute of American Cultures
Asian American Studies Center
3230 Campbell Hall
P.O. Box 951546
Los Angeles, CA 90095-1546
(310) 825-2974   Fax: (310) 206-9844
E-mail: melanyd@ucla.edu
Web: www.iac.ucla.edu/fellowships_visitingscholar.html

Summary To provide funding to scholars interested in conducting research in Asian American studies at UCLA's Asian American Studies Center.

Eligibility Applicants must have completed a doctoral degree in Asian American or related studies. They must be interested in teaching or conducting research at UCLA's Asian American Studies Center. Visiting Scholar appointments are available to people who currently hold permanent academic appointments; Visiting Researcher appointments are available to postdoctorates who recently received their degree. UCLA faculty, students, and staff are not eligible. U.S. citizenship or permanent resident status is required.

Financial data Fellows receive a stipend of $35,000, health benefits, and up to $4,000 in research support. Visiting Scholars are paid through their home institution; Visiting Researchers receive their funds directly from UCLA.

Duration 9 months, beginning in October.

Additional information Fellows must teach or do research in the programs of the center. The award is offered in conjunction with UCLA's Institute of American Cultures (IAC).

Number awarded 1 each year.

Deadline January of each year.

[1023]
ASSOCIATION OF INDIAN NEUROLOGISTS IN AMERICA (AINA) LIFETIME ACHIEVEMENT AWARD

American Academy of Neurology
Attn: Association of Indian Neurologists in America
201 Chicago Avenue
Minneapolis, MN 55415
(612) 928-6062   Toll Free: (800) 879-1960
Fax: (612) 454-2746   E-mail: kmitchell@aan.com
Web: tools.aan.com

Summary To recognize and reward members of the American Academy of Neurology (AAN) who are of Indian ancestry and have made outstanding contributions to the profession.

Eligibility This award is presented to AAN members of Indian origin who have supported other Indian neurologists over a significant period of time in achieving meaningful progress. Letters of nomination must identify the nominee's success relating to the growth and prestige of neurologists of Indian origin, commitment to passing leadership skills and the value of involvement to peers and to the next generation of leaders, demonstration of exceptional dedication of time and effort for the greater good, commitment to team building and being a team player, and commitment to "bridge-building" for the Indian neurologic community and beyond through mutual partnerships and alliances.

Financial data The prize consists of $1,000 and a recognition plaque.

Duration The prize is awarded annually.

Number awarded 1 each year.

Deadline December of each year.

[1024]
BAXTER POSTDOCTORAL FELLOWSHIP

Marine Biological Laboratory
Attn: Division of Research
7 MBL Street
Woods Hole, MA 02543-1015
(508) 289-7173   Fax: (508) 457-1924
E-mail: research@mbl.edu
Web: www.mbl.edu/research/whitman-awards

Summary To provide funding to postdoctoral scientists, especially Asian Americans and members of other underrepresented groups, who wish to conduct summer research at the Marine Biological Laboratory (MBL) in Woods Hole, Massachusetts.

Eligibility This program is open to postdoctoral investigators in the biological and biomedical sciences who wish to conduct independent research at the MBL. Applicants must submit a statement of the potential impact of this award on their career development. The program encourages applications focused on 1) evolutionary, genetic, and genomic approaches in developmental biology with an emphasis on novel marine organisms; and 2) integrated imaging and computational approaches to illuminate cellular function and biology emerging from the study of marine and other organisms. Preference is given to early stage investigators, those new to the MBL, women, and minorities.

Financial data Grants range from $5,000 to $25,000, typically to cover laboratory rental and/or housing costs. Awardees are responsible for other costs, such as supplies, shared resource usage, affiliated staff who accompany them, or travel.

Duration 4 to 10 weeks during the summer.

Additional information This program is supported by Baxter International, Inc.

Number awarded 1 or 2 each year.

Deadline December of each year.

[1025]
BROADCAST NEWS INTERNSHIP GRANTS

Asian American Journalists Association
Attn: Student Programs Coordinator
5 Third Street, Suite 1108
San Francisco, CA 94103
(415) 346-2051, ext. 102   Fax: (415) 346-6343
E-mail: programs@aaja.org
Web: www.aaja.org/apply-for-a-scholarship-now

Summary To provide a supplemental grant to student and other members of the Asian American Journalists Association (AAJA) working as a summer intern at a radio or television broadcasting company.

Eligibility This program is open to AAJA members who are full-time college students or recent college graduates. Applicants must have secured a summer internship at a television or radio broadcasting company before they apply. Along with their application, they must submit a 200-word essay on why they want to prepare for a career in broadcast journalism, what they want to gain from the experience, and why AAJA's mission is important to them; a letter of recommendation; a resume; proof of age (at least 18 years); verification of an internship; and statement of financial need.

Financial data This program includes the Lloyd LaCuesta Scholarship Fund at $1,000 and the Sam Chu Lin Internship Grant at $500. Funds are to be used for living expenses or transportation.

Duration Summer months.

Number awarded 2 each year.

Deadline April of each year.

[1026]
BRONSON T.J. TREMBLAY MEMORIAL SCHOLARSHIP

Colorado Nurses Foundation
Attn: Scholarships
P.O. Box 3406
Englewood, CO 80155
(303) 694-4728   Toll Free: (800) 205-6655
Fax: (303) 200-7099   E-mail: mail@cnfound.org
Web: www.coloradonursesfoundation.com/?page_id=1087

Summary To provide financial assistance to Asian American and other non-white male undergraduate and graduate nursing students in Colorado.

Eligibility This program is open to non-white male Colorado residents who have been accepted as a student in an approved nursing program in the state. Applicants may be 1) second-year students in an associate degree program; 2) junior or senior level B.S.N. undergraduate students; 3) R.N.s enrolled in a baccalaureate or higher degree program in a school of nursing; 4) R.N.s with a master's degree in nursing, currently practicing in Colorado and enrolled in a doctoral program; or 5) students in the second or third year of a Doctorate Nursing Practice (D.N.P.) or Ph.D. program. Undergraduates must have a GPA of 3.25 or higher and graduate students must have a GPA of 3.5 or higher. Selection is based on professional philosophy and goals, dedication to the improvement of patient care in Colorado, demonstrated commitment to nursing, potential for leadership, involvement in community and professional organizations, recommendations, GPA, and financial need.

Financial data The stipend is $1,000.

Duration 1 year.

Number awarded 1 each year.

Deadline October of each year.

[1027]
BURR AND SUSIE STEINBACH FELLOWSHIP FUND

Marine Biological Laboratory
Attn: Division of Research
7 MBL Street
Woods Hole, MA 02543-1015
(508) 289-7173   Fax: (508) 457-1924
E-mail: research@mbl.edu
Web: www.mbl.edu/research/whitman-awards

Summary To provide funding to scientists, especially Asian Americans and members of other underrepresented groups, who have faculty positions and wish to conduct summer research at the Marine Biological Laboratory (MBL) in Woods Hole, Massachusetts.

Eligibility This program is open to faculty members who are interested in conducting summer research at the MBL. Applicants must submit a statement of the potential impact of this award on their career development. The program encourages applications focused on 1) evolutionary, genetic, and genomic approaches in developmental biology with an emphasis on novel marine organisms; and 2) integrated imaging and computational approaches to illuminate cellular function and biology emerging from the study of marine and other organisms. Preference is given to early stage investigators, those new to the MBL, women, and minorities.

Financial data Grants range from $5,000 to $25,000, typically to cover laboratory rental and/or housing costs. Awardees are responsible for other costs, such as supplies, shared resource usage, affiliated staff who accompany them, or travel.

Duration 4 to 10 weeks during the summer.

Number awarded 1 each year.

Deadline December of each year.

[1028]
BYRD FELLOWSHIP PROGRAM

Ohio State University
Byrd Polar and Climate Research Center
Attn: Fellowship Committee
Scott Hall Room 108
1090 Carmack Road
Columbus, OH 43210-1002
(614) 292-6531   Fax: (614) 292-4697
E-mail: contact@bpcrc.osu.edu
Web: bpcrc.osu.edu/byrdfellow

Summary To provide funding to postdoctorates, especially Asian Americans and members of other underrepresented groups, who are interested in conducting research on the Arctic or Antarctic areas at Ohio State University.

Eligibility This program is open to postdoctorates of superior academic background who are interested in conducting advanced research on either Arctic or Antarctic problems at the Byrd Polar and Climate Research Center at Ohio State University. Applicants must have received their doctorates within the past 5 years. Along with their application, they must submit a description of the specific research to be conducted during the fellowship and a curriculum vitae. Women, minorities, Vietnam-era veterans, disabled veterans, and individuals with disabilities are particularly encouraged to apply.

Financial data The stipend is $44,000 per year; an allowance of $5,000 for research and travel is also provided.

Duration 18 months.

Additional information This program was established by a major gift from the Byrd Foundation in memory of Rear Admiral Richard Evelyn Byrd and Marie Ames Byrd, his wife. Except for field work or other research activities requiring absence from campus, fellows are expected to be in residence at the university for the duration of the program.

Number awarded 1 each year.

Deadline March of each year.

[1029]
CAAM DOCUMENTARY FUND

Center for Asian American Media
Attn: Media Fund Director
145 Ninth Street, Suite 350
San Francisco, CA 94103-2641
(415) 863-0814　　　　　　　Fax: (415) 863-7428
E-mail: mediafund@caamedia.org
Web: www.caamedia.org/for-mediamakers/funding

Summary To provide funding to producers of public television documentaries that relate to the Asian American experience.

Eligibility This program is open to independent producers who are interested in developing and finishing public television documentaries on Asian American issues. Applicants must have previous film or television experience as demonstrated by a sample tape and must have artistic, budgetary, and editorial control. They must be 18 years of age or older and citizens or legal residents of the United States. All programs must be standard broadcast length and in accordance with PBS broadcast specifications. Ineligible projects include those for which the exclusive domestic television broadcast rights are not available; in the script development stage; intended solely for theatrical release or commercial in nature; in which the applicant is commissioned, employed, or hired by a commercial or public television station; that are thesis projects or student films co- or solely owned or copyrighted, or editorially or fiscally controlled by the school; that are foreign-based, owned, or controlled; or that are industrial or promotional projects. In the selection process, the following questions are considered: is the project a good match for American public television and its national audience; is the story idea compelling, engaging, original, and well-conceived; is the visual/stylistic treatment effective and distinctive; can the project be completed with a realistic timeline; will the project appeal not only to Asian American viewers, but also to a broader television audience; and does the sample tape show the skills and/or potential of the applicant to complete the proposed project.

Financial data Grants range from $15,000 to $50,000. Funding may be used either for production or completion activities.

Additional information This program was formerly known as the National Asian American Telecommunications Association Media Fund Grants. Funding is provided by the Corporation for Public Broadcasting.

Number awarded 5 to 10 grants are awarded each year.

Deadline February or September of each year.

[1030]
CARRINGTON-HSIA-NIEVES SCHOLARSHIP FOR MIDWIVES OF COLOR

American College of Nurse-Midwives
Attn: ACNM Foundation, Inc.
8403 Colesville Road, Suite 1550
Silver Spring, MD 20910-6374
(240) 485-1850　　　　　　　Fax: (240) 485-1818
E-mail: foundation@acnmf.org
Web: www.midwife.org

Summary To provide financial assistance to Asian American and other midwives of color who are members of the American College of Nurse-Midwives (ACNM) and engaged in doctoral or postdoctoral study.

Eligibility This program is open to ACNM members of color who are certified nurse midwives (CNM) or certified midwives (CM). Applicants must be enrolled in a program of doctoral or postdoctoral education. Along with their application, they must submit brief statements on their 5-year academic career plans, their intended use of the funds, and their intended future participation in the local, regional, and/or national activities of the ACNM and in activities that otherwise contribute substantially to midwifery research, education, or practice.

Financial data The stipend is $5,000.

Duration 1 year.

Number awarded 1 each year.

Deadline October of each year.

[1031]
CHANG-LIN TIEN EDUCATION LEADERSHIP AWARDS

Asian Pacific Fund
465 California Street, Suite 809
San Francisco, CA 94104
(415) 395-9985　　　　　　　E-mail: info@asianpacificfund.org
Web: asianpacificfund.org

Summary To recognize and reward Asian American administrators at colleges and universities who demonstrate outstanding leadership in higher education.

Eligibility This award is available to Asian Americans who are currently serving at the level of dean (or a position of comparable responsibility) or higher at a 4-year public or private college or university in the United States. Nominees should have demonstrated scholarly achievement, administrative experience, pride in their Asian and American heritage, dedication to excellence, and commitment to providing access to academic institutions for a diverse population of students. Self-nominations are not accepted.

Financial data Awards consist of an unrestricted grant of $10,000.

Duration The awards are presented annually.

Additional information These awards were first presented in 2007 to honor Dr. Chang-Lin Tien, the first Asian American to head a major research university as chancellor of UC Berkeley from 1990 to 1997.

Number awarded 2 each year.

Deadline Nominations must be submitted by April of each year.

[1032]
CHEST DIVERSITY COMMITTEE MINORITY INVESTIGATOR RESEARCH GRANT

American College of Chest Physicians
Attn: The CHEST Foundation
2595 Patriot Boulevard
Glenview, IL 60026
(224) 521-9527　　　　　　　Toll Free: (800) 343-2227
Fax: (224) 521-9801　　　　　E-mail: grants@chestnet.org
Web: www.chestnet.org

Summary To provide funding to Asian American and other minority physicians who are interested in conducting clinical or translational research on topics of interest to the American College of Chest Physicians (ACCP).

Eligibility This program is open to members of the ACCP who are members of an underrepresented group (Asian/ Pacific Island American, African American, Latin American, Hispanic American, Native American, women). Applicants must be interested in conducting a clinical or translational research project that contributes to the understanding of the pathophysiology or treatment of conditions or diseases related to pulmonary, cardiovascular, critical care, or sleep medicine. They may be at later career stages, but special consideration is given to those within 5 years of completing an advanced training program.

Financial data The grant is $25,000.

Duration 1 year, beginning in July.

Additional information This program is supported in part by AstraZeneca.

Number awarded 1 each year.

Deadline April of each year.

[1033]
CHIPS QUINN SCHOLARS PROGRAM

Newseum Institute
Attn: Chips Quinn Scholars Program
555 Pennsylvania Avenue, N.W.
Washington, DC 20001
(202) 292-6271   Fax: (202) 292-6275
E-mail: kcatone@freedomforum.org
Web: www.newseuminstitute.org

Summary To provide work experience to Asian American and other minority college students and recent graduates who are majoring in journalism.

Eligibility This program is open to students of color who are college juniors, seniors, graduate students, or recent graduates with journalism majors or career goals in newspapers. Candidates must be nominated or endorsed by journalism faculty, campus media advisers, editors of newspapers, or leaders of minority journalism associations. Along with their application, they must submit a resume, transcripts, 2 letters of recommendation, and an essay of 200 to 400 words on why they want to be a Chips Quinn Scholar. Reporters and copy editors must also submit 6 samples of published articles they have written; photographers must submit 15 to 25 photographs on a DVD; multimedia journalists and graphic designers should submit 6 to 10 samples of their work on a DVD. Applicants must have a car and be available to work as a full-time intern during the spring or summer. U.S. citizenship or permanent resident status is required. Campus newspaper experience is strongly encouraged.

Financial data Students chosen for this program receive a travel stipend to attend a Multimedia training program in Nashville, Tennessee prior to reporting for their internship, a $500 housing allowance from the Freedom Forum, and a competitive salary during their internship.

Duration Internships are for 10 to 12 weeks, in spring or summer.

Additional information This program began in 1991 in memory of the late John D. Quinn Jr., managing editor of the *Poughkeepsie Journal.* Funding is provided by the Freedom Forum, formerly the Gannett Foundation. After graduating from college and obtaining employment with a newspaper,

alumni of this program are eligible to apply for fellowship support to attend professional journalism development activities.

Number awarded Approximately 70 each year. Since the program began, more than 1,300 scholars have been selected.

Deadline September of each year.

[1034]
CIVIL SOCIETY INSTITUTE FELLOWSHIPS

Vermont Studio Center
80 Pearl Street
P.O. Box 613
Johnson, VT 05656
(802) 635-2727   Fax: (802) 635-2730
E-mail: info@vermontstudiocenter.org
Web: www.vermontstudiocenter.org/fellowships

Summary To provide funding to Asian American and other minority artists from the East Coast who are interested in a residency at the Vermont Studio Center in Johnson, Vermont.

Eligibility Eligible to apply for this support are painters, sculptors, printmakers, new and mixed-media artists, photographers who are members of a minority group and residents of the East Coast. Preference is given to applicants from New Haven (Connecticut), Jersey City (New Jersey), or Baltimore (Maryland). Applicants must be interested in a residency at the center in Johnson, Vermont. Visual artists must submit up to 20 slides or visual images of their work, poets must submit up to 10 pages, and other writers must submit 10 to 15 pages. Selection is based on artistic merit and financial need.

Financial data The residency fee of $3,950 covers studio space, room, board, lectures, and studio visits. The fellowship pays all residency fees plus a $500 travel stipend.

Duration 4 weeks.

Additional information This program is sponsored by the Institute for Civil Society.

Number awarded 3 each year (1 for each term).

Deadline February, June, or September of each year.

[1035]
DAVID IBATA PRINT SCHOLARSHIP

Asian American Journalists Association-Chicago Chapter
c/o Lorene Yue
Crain's Chicago Business
150 North Michigan Avenue, 16th Floor
Chicago, IL 60601
E-mail: chicagoaaja@gmail.com
Web: www.aajachicago.wordpress.com

Summary To provide funding to members of the Asian American Journalists Association (AAJA) who are interested in a summer internship at a Chicago publication.

Eligibility This program is open to AAJA members who are college sophomores, juniors, seniors, graduate students or recent graduates. Applicants must be interested in an internship at Crain's Chicago Business. Along with their application, they must submit a resume that includes their job experience in journalism and 5 clips.

Financial data AAJA-Chicago awards a $2,500 stipend for the internship and Crain's Chicago Business matches that with a grant of $2,500.

Duration 10 to 12 weeks during the summer.

Number awarded 1 each year.
Deadline December of each year.

[1036]
DEEP CARBON OBSERVATORY DIVERSITY GRANTS

American Geosciences Institute
Attn: Grant Coordinator
4220 King Street
Alexandria, VA 22302-1502
(703) 379-2480   Fax: (703) 379-7563
E-mail: hrhp@agiweb.org
Web: www.americangeosciences.org

Summary To provide funding to geoscientists who are Filipinos or members of other underrepresented ethnic groups and interested in participating in research and other activities of the Deep Carbon Observatory (DCO) project.

Eligibility This program is open to traditionally underrepresented geoscientists (e.g., Filipinos, African Americans, Native Americans, Native Alaskans, Hispanics, Latinos, Latinas, Native Hawaiians, Native Pacific Islanders, of mixed racial/ethnic backgrounds) who are U.S. citizens or permanent residents. Applicants must be interested in participating in the DCO, a global research program focused on understanding carbon in Earth, and must have research interests that are aligned with its mission. They may be doctoral students, postdoctoral researchers, or early-career faculty members or research staff.

Financial data Grants average $5,000.

Duration 1 year.

Additional information This program is funded by the Alfred P. Sloan Foundation.

Number awarded 4 or 5 each year.

Deadline April of each year.

[1037]
DOCTORAL/POST-DOCTORAL FELLOWSHIP PROGRAM IN LAW AND SOCIAL SCIENCE

American Bar Foundation
Attn: Administrative Assistant for Academic Affairs and
  Research Administration
750 North Lake Shore Drive
Chicago, IL 60611-4403
(312) 988-6517   Fax: (312) 988-6579
E-mail: aehrhardt@abfn.org
Web: www.americanbarfoundation.org

Summary To provide research funding to scholars, especially Asian Americans and other minorities, who are completing or have completed doctoral degrees in fields related to law, the legal profession, and legal institutions.

Eligibility This program is open to Ph.D. candidates in the social sciences who have completed all doctoral requirements except the dissertation. Applicants who have completed the dissertation are also eligible. Doctoral and proposed research must be in the general area of sociolegal studies or in social scientific approaches to law, the legal profession, or legal institutions and legal processes. Applications must include 1) a dissertation abstract or proposal with an outline of the substance and methods of the research; 2) 2 letters of recommendation; and 3) a curriculum vitae. Minority candidates are especially encouraged to apply.

Financial data The stipend is $30,000. Fellows may request up to $1,500 to reimburse expenses associated with research, travel to meet with advisers, or travel to conferences at which papers are presented. Relocation expenses of up to $2,500 may be reimbursed on application.

Duration 12 months, beginning in September.

Additional information Fellows are offered access to the computing and word processing facilities of the American Bar Foundation and the libraries of Northwestern University and the University of Chicago. This program was established in 1996. Fellowships must be held in residence at the American Bar Foundation. Appointments to the fellowship are full time; fellows are not permitted to undertake other work.

Number awarded 1 or more each year.

Deadline December of each year.

[1038]
DOROTHY BRACY/JANICE JOSEPH MINORITY AND WOMEN NEW SCHOLAR AWARD

Academy of Criminal Justice Sciences
7339A Hanover Parkway
P.O. Box 960
Greenbelt, MD 20768-0960
(301) 446-6300   Toll Free: (800) 757-ACJS
Fax: (301) 446-2819   E-mail: info@acjs.org
Web: www.acjs.org/Awards

Summary To recognize and reward Asian American and other junior scholars from underrepresented groups who have made outstanding contributions to the field of criminal justice.

Eligibility This award is available to members of the Academy of Criminal Justice Sciences (ACJS) who are members of a group that has experienced historical discrimination, including minorities and women. Applicants must have obtained a Ph.D. in a field of criminal justice within the past 7 years and be able to demonstrate a strong record as a new scholar in the areas of research, teaching, and service.

Financial data The award is $1,000.

Duration The award is presented annually.

Number awarded 1 each year.

Deadline October of each year.

[1039]
DR. DAVID MONASH/HARRY LLOYD AND ELIZABETH PAWLETTE MARSHALL RESIDENCY SCHOLARSHIPS

National Medical Fellowships, Inc.
Attn: Scholarship Program
347 Fifth Avenue, Suite 510
New York, NY 10016
(212) 483-8880   Toll Free: (877) NMF-1DOC
Fax: (212) 483-8897 E-mail: scholarships@nmfonline.org
Web: www.nmfonline.org

Summary To provide funding for repayment of student loans and other expenses to Vietnamese, Cambodian, and other underrepresented medical residents in Chicago who are committed to remaining in the area and working to reduce health disparities.

Eligibility This program is open to residents of any state who graduated from a medical school in Chicago and are currently engaged in a clinical residency program in the area in primary care, community/family medicine, or a related field. U.S. citizenship is required. Applicants must be seeking funding for repayment of student loans and other residency-related expenses. They must identify as an underrepresented minority student in health care (defined as Vietnamese, Cambodian, African American, Hispanic/Latino, American Indian, Alaska Native, Native Hawaiian, or Pacific Islander) and/or socioeconomically disadvantaged student. Along with their application, they must submit documentation of financial status; a short biography; a resume; 2 letters of recommendation; a personal statement of 500 to 1,000 words on their personal and professional motivation for a medical career, their commitment to primary care and service in a health and/or community setting, their motivation for working to reduce health disparities, and their commitment to improving health care; a personal statement of 500 to 1,000 words on the experiences that are preparing them to practice in an underserved community; and a copy of a residency contract from a Chicago clinical residency program. Selection is based on demonstrated leadership early in career and commitment to serving medically underserved communities in Chicago.

Financial data The grant is $25,000, of which 80% must be used to decrease medical school debt.

Duration 1 year.

Additional information This program began in 2010 with support from the Chicago Community Trust.

Number awarded 4 each year.

Deadline May of each year.

[1040]
DR. DHARM SINGH POSTDOCTORAL FELLOW BEST ABSTRACT AWARD

Society of Toxicology
Attn: Association of Scientists of Indian Origin Special
   Interest Group
1821 Michael Faraday Drive, Suite 300
Reston, VA 20190-5348
(703) 438-3115   Fax: (703) 438-3113
E-mail: sothq@toxicology.org
Web: www.toxicology.org/ai/af/awards_details.aspx?id=143

Summary To recognize and reward postdoctoral members of the Society of Toxicology (SOT) who are of Indian origin and present outstanding papers at the annual meeting.

Eligibility This award is available to postdoctoral fellows of Indian origin who are members of SOT and its Association of Scientists of Indian Origin (ASIO). Candidates must have an accepted abstract of a research poster or platform presentation for the SOT annual meeting. Along with the abstract, they must submit a cover letter outlining the significance of their research to the field of toxicology and how this award will help them to further their career goals.

Financial data A plaque and a cash award (amount not specified) are presented.

Duration The award is presented annually.

Additional information This award was established in 2008.

Number awarded 1 each year.

Deadline December of each year.

[1041]
DR. SUZANNE AHN AWARD FOR CIVIL RIGHTS AND SOCIAL JUSTICE FOR ASIAN AMERICANS

Asian American Journalists Association
Attn: Program Associate
5 Third Street, Suite 1108
San Francisco, CA 94103
(415) 346-2051, ext. 104   Fax: (415) 346-6343
E-mail: DanielG@aaja.org
Web: www.aaja.org/category/membership/awards

Summary To recognize and reward journalists who have published or broadcast outstanding coverage of Asian American Pacific Islander civil rights and social justice issues.

Eligibility This award is presented to journalists for excellence in coverage of civil rights of Asian American Pacific Islanders and/or issues of social justice. Nominees do not need to be Asians or members of the Asian American Journalists Association (AAJA). Their work must have been published (in newspapers, news services, web sites, magazines, books) or broadcast (on radio or TV). Book entries and documentaries must include a synopsis of the work, explaining how it specifically impacts social justice or civil rights in the Asian American Pacific Islander community. Submissions in other languages must come with an English translation.

Financial data The award consists of $5,000 and a plaque.

Duration The award is presented annually.

Additional information This award, first presented in 2003, is named for a Korean American physician, neurologist, and inventor. Nominations by non-members of AAJA must be accompanied by a $25 entry fee.

Number awarded 1 each year.

Deadline March of each year.

[1042]
DRS. ROSALEE G. AND RAYMOND A. WEISS RESEARCH AND PROGRAM INNOVATION GRANT

American Psychological Foundation
750 First Street, N.E.
Washington, DC 20002-4242
(202) 336-5843   Fax: (202) 336-5812
E-mail: foundation@apa.org
Web: www.apa.org/apf/funding/weiss.aspx

Summary To provide funding to professionals, especially Asian Americans and members of other diverse groups, interested in conducting projects that use psychology to solve social problems related to the priorities of the American Psychological Foundation (APF).

Eligibility This program is open to professionals at non-profit organizations engaged in research, education, and intervention projects and programs. Applicants must be interested in conducting an activity that uses psychology to solve social problems in the following priority areas: understanding and fostering the connection between mental and physical health; reducing stigma and prejudice; understanding and preventing violence to create a safer, more humane world; or addressing the long-term psychological needs of individuals and communities in the aftermath of disaster. Preference is given to psychologists within 10 years of completion of their doctorate; pilot projects that, if successful, would be strong candidates for support from major federal and foundation funding agencies; and "demonstration projects" that promise to generalize broadly to similar settings in other geographical areas and/or to other settings. Selection is based on the criticality of the proposed funding for the proposed work; clarity and comprehensiveness of methodology; innovative and potential impact qualities; and quality, viability, and promise of proposed work. The sponsor encourages applications from individuals who represent diversity in race, ethnicity, gender, age, disability, and sexual orientation.

Financial data The grant is $1,000.

Duration 1 year; nonrenewable.

Additional information This program began in 2003.

Number awarded 1 each year.

Deadline September of each year.

[1043]
E.E. JUST ENDOWED RESEARCH FELLOWSHIP FUND

Marine Biological Laboratory
Attn: Division of Research
7 MBL Street
Woods Hole, MA 02543-1015
(508) 289-7173   Fax: (508) 457-1924
E-mail: research@mbl.edu
Web: www.mbl.edu/research/whitman-awards

Summary To provide funding to Asian American and other minority scientists who wish to conduct summer research at the Marine Biological Laboratory (MBL) in Woods Hole, Massachusetts.

Eligibility This program is open to minority faculty members who are interested in conducting summer research at the MBL. Applicants must submit a statement of the potential impact of this award on their career development. The program encourages applications focused on 1) evolutionary, genetic, and genomic approaches in developmental biology with an emphasis on novel marine organisms; and 2) integrated imaging and computational approaches to illuminate cellular function and biology emerging from the study of marine and other organisms.

Financial data Grants range from $5,000 to $25,000, typically to cover laboratory rental and/or housing costs. Awardees are responsible for other costs, such as supplies, shared resource usage, affiliated staff who accompany them, or travel.

Duration 4 to 10 weeks during the summer.

Number awarded 1 each year.

Deadline December of each year.

[1044]
ENVIRONMENT AND NATURAL RESOURCES FELLOWSHIPS

Harvard University
John F. Kennedy School of Government
Belfer Center for Science and International Affairs
Attn: STPP Fellowship Coordinator
79 John F. Kennedy Street, Mailbox 53
Cambridge, MA 02138
(617) 495-1498   Fax: (617) 495-8963
E-mail: patricia_mclaughlin@hks.harvard.edu
Web: belfercenter.ksg.harvard.edu

Summary To provide funding to professionals, postdoctorates, and doctoral students, especially Asian Americans and other minorities, interested in conducting research on environmental and natural resource issues at the Belfer Center for Science and International Affairs at Harvard University in Cambridge, Massachusetts.

Eligibility The postdoctoral fellowship is open to recent recipients of the Ph.D. or equivalent degree, university faculty members, and employees of government, military, international, humanitarian, and private research institutions who have appropriate professional experience. Applicants for predoctoral fellowships must have passed their general examinations. Scholars from a wide range of disciplinary and multi-disciplinary fields and those holding a Ph.D. in engineering or in the natural sciences are strongly encouraged to apply. The program especially encourages applications from women, minorities, and citizens of all countries. All applicants must be interested in conducting research on projects of the Environment and Natural Resources (ENRP) Program. Recently, those included projects on energy technology innovation, sustainable energy development in China, managing the atom, and the geopolitics of energy.

Financial data The stipend is $37,500 for postdoctoral research fellows or $25,000 for predoctoral research fellows. Fellows who renew their grant receive a monthly stipend of $3,750 for postdoctoral fellows or $2,500 for predoctoral fellows. Stipends for advanced research fellows vary. Health insurance is also provided.

Duration 10 months; may be renewed on a month-by-month basis.

Additional information Fellows are expected to devote some portion of their time to collaborative endeavors, as arranged by the appropriate program or project director. Predoctoral fellows are expected to contribute to the program's research activities, as well as work on (and ideally complete) their dissertations. Postdoctoral research fellows are also expected to complete a book, monograph, or other significant publication during their period of residence.

Number awarded A limited number each year.

Deadline January of each year.

[1045]
ESTHER KATZ ROSEN FUND GRANTS

American Psychological Foundation
750 First Street, N.E.
Washington, DC 20002-4242
(202) 336-5843   Fax: (202) 336-5812
E-mail: foundation@apa.org
Web: www.apa.org/apf/funding/rosen.aspx

Summary To provide funding to graduate students and early-career psychologists, especially Asian Americans and other minorities, interested in conducting research or other projects on psychological issues relevant to giftedness in children.

Eligibility This program is open to 1) graduate students at universities in the United States and Canada who have advanced to candidacy; and 2) psychologists who completed their doctoral degree within the past 10 years. Applicants must be interested in engaging in activities related to identified gifted and talented children and adolescents, including research, pilot projects, research-based programs, or projects aimed at improving the quality of education in psychological science and its application in secondary schools for high ability students. Selection is based on conformance with stated program goals and qualifications, quality and impact of proposed work, innovation and contribution to the field, and applicant's demonstrated competence and capability to execute the proposed work. The sponsor encourages applications from individuals who represent diversity in race, ethnicity, gender, age, disability, and sexual orientation.

Financial data   Grants range from $1,000 to $50,000.

Duration   1 year.

Additional information   The Esther Katz Rosen Fund was established in 1974. In 2013, the sponsor combined the Rosen Graduate Student Fellowship, the Rosen Early Career Research Grant, and the Pre-College Grant program into this single program.

Number awarded   Varies each year; recently, 2 were awarded.

Deadline   February of each year.

[1046]
ETHNIC IN-SERVICE TRAINING FUND FOR CLINICAL PASTORAL EDUCATION (EIST-CPE)

United Methodist Church
Attn: General Board of Higher Education and Ministry
Office of Loans and Scholarships
1001 19th Avenue South
P.O. Box 340007
Nashville, TN 37203-0007
(615) 340-7342   Fax: (615) 340-7367
E-mail: umscholar@gbhem.org
Web: www.gbhem.org

Summary   To provide financial assistance to United Methodist Church clergy and candidates for ministry who are Asian Americans or members of other minority groups interested in preparing for a career as a clinical pastor.

Eligibility   This program is open to U.S. citizens and permanent residents who are members of ethnic or racial minority groups and have been active, full members of a United Methodist Church for at least 1 year prior to applying. Applicants must be United Methodist clergy, certified candidates for ministry, or seminary students accepted into an accredited Clinical Pastor Education (CPE) or an accredited American Association of Pastoral Counselors (AAPC) program. They must be preparing for a career as a chaplain, pastoral counselor, or in pastoral care.

Financial data   Grants range up to $2,000.

Duration   1 year.

Number awarded   1 each year.

Deadline   February of each year.

[1047]
FIRST BOOK GRANT PROGRAM FOR MINORITY SCHOLARS

Louisville Institute
Attn: Executive Director
1044 Alta Vista Road
Louisville, KY 40205-1798
(502) 992-5432   Fax: (502) 894-2286
E-mail: info@louisville-institute.org
Web: www.louisville-institute.org

Summary   To provide funding to Asian American and other scholars of color interested in completing a major research and book project that focuses on an aspect of Christianity in North America.

Eligibility   This program is open to members of racial/ethnic minority groups (Asian Americans, African Americans, Hispanics, Native Americans, Arab Americans, and Pacific Islanders) who have an earned doctoral degree (normally the Ph.D. or Th.D.). Applicants must be a non-tenured faculty member in a full-time, tenure-track position at an accredited institution of higher education (college, university, or seminary) in North America. They must be able to negotiate a full academic year free from teaching and committee responsibilities in order to engage in a scholarly research project leading to the publication of their first (or second) book focusing on an aspect of Christianity in North America. Selection is based on the intellectual quality of the research and writing project, its potential to contribute to scholarship in religion, and the potential contribution of the research to the vitality of North American Christianity.

Financial data   The grant is $40,000. Awards are intended to make possible a full academic year of sabbatical research and writing by providing up to half of the grantee's salary and benefits for that year. Funds are paid directly to the grantee's institution, but no indirect costs are allowed.

Duration   1 academic year; nonrenewable.

Additional information   The Louisville Institute is located at Louisville Presbyterian Theological Seminary and is supported by the Lilly Endowment. These grants were first awarded in 2003. Grantees may not accept other awards that provide a stipend during the tenure of this award, and they must be released from all teaching and committee responsibilities during the award year.

Number awarded   Varies each year; recently, 3 were awarded.

Deadline   January of each year.

[1048]
F.J. MCGUIGAN EARLY CAREER INVESTIGATOR RESEARCH PRIZE ON UNDERSTANDING THE HUMAN MIND

American Psychological Foundation
750 First Street, N.E.
Washington, DC 20002-4242
(202) 336-5843   Fax: (202) 336-5812
E-mail: foundation@apa.org
Web: www.apa.org/apf/funding/mcguigan-prize.aspx

Summary   To provide funding to young psychologists, especially Asian Americans and members of other underrepresented groups, interested in conducting research related to the human mind.

Eligibility   This program is open to investigators who have earned a doctoral degree in psychology or in a related field within the past 7 years. Nominees must have an affiliation with an accredited college, university, or other research institution. They must be engaged in research that seeks to explicate the concept of the human mind. The approach must be materialistic and should be primarily psychophysiological, but physiological and behavioral research may also qualify. Self-nominations are not accepted; candidates must be nominated by a senior colleague. The sponsor encourages nominations of individuals who represent diversity in race, ethnicity, gender, age, disability, and sexual orientation.

Financial data The grant is $25,000.

Duration These grants are awarded biennially, in even-numbered years.

Additional information The first grant under this program was awarded in 2002.

Number awarded 1 every other year.

Deadline February of even-numbered years.

[1049]
GAIUS CHARLES BOLIN DISSERTATION AND POST-MFA FELLOWSHIPS

Williams College
Attn: Dean of the Faculty
880 Main Street
Hopkins Hall, Third Floor
P.O. Box 141
Williamstown, MA 01267
(413) 597-4351   Fax: (413) 597-3553
E-mail: gburda@williams.edu
Web: faculty.williams.edu

Summary To provide financial assistance to Asian Americans and members of other underrepresented groups who are interested in teaching courses at Williams College while working on their doctoral dissertation or building their post-M.F.A. professional portfolio.

Eligibility This program is open to members of underrepresented groups, including ethnic minorities, first-generation college students, women in predominantly male fields, and scholars with disabilities. Applicants must be 1) doctoral candidates in any field who have completed all work for a Ph.D. except for the dissertation; or 2) artists who completed an M.F.A. degree within the past 2 years and are building their professional portfolio. They must be willing to teach a course at Williams College. Along with their application, they must submit a full curriculum vitae, a graduate school transcript, 3 letters of recommendation, a copy of their dissertation prospectus or samples of their artistic work, and a description of their teaching interests within a department or program at Williams College. U.S. citizenship or permanent resident status is required.

Financial data Fellows receive $38,000 for the academic year, plus housing assistance, office space, computer and library privileges, and a research allowance of up to $4,000.

Duration 2 years.

Additional information Bolin fellows are assigned a faculty adviser in the appropriate department. This program was established in 1985. Fellows are expected to teach a 1-semester course each year. They must be in residence at Williams College for the duration of the fellowship.

Number awarded 2 each year.

Deadline November of each year.

[1050]
GEORGE A. STRAIT MINORITY SCHOLARSHIP ENDOWMENT

American Association of Law Libraries
Attn: Chair, Scholarships Committee
105 West Adams Street, Suite 3300
Chicago, IL 60603
(312) 939-4764   Fax: (312) 431-1097
E-mail: scholarships@aall.org
Web: www.aallnet.org

Summary To provide financial assistance to Asian American and other minority college seniors or college graduates who are interested in becoming law librarians.

Eligibility This program is open to college graduates with meaningful law library experience who are members of minority groups and intend to have a career in law librarianship. Applicants must be degree candidates at an ALA-accredited library school or an ABA-accredited law school. Along with their application, they must submit a personal statement that discusses their interest in law librarianship, reason for applying for this scholarship, career goals as a law librarian, and any other pertinent information.

Financial data The stipend is $3,500.

Duration 1 year.

Additional information This program, established in 1990, is currently supported by Thomson Reuters.

Number awarded Varies each year; recently, 6 were awarded.

Deadline March of each year.

[1051]
GERALD OSHITA MEMORIAL FELLOWSHIP

Djerassi Resident Artists Program
Attn: Admissions
2325 Bear Gulch Road
Woodside, CA 94062-4405
(650) 747-1250   Fax: (650) 747-0105
E-mail: drap@djerassi.org
Web: www.djerassi.org/oshita.html

Summary To provide an opportunity for Asian Americans and other composers of color to participate in the Djerassi Resident Artists Program.

Eligibility This program is open to composers of Asian, African, Latino, or Native American ethnic background. Applicants must be interested in utilizing a residency to compose, study, rehearse, and otherwise advance their own creative projects.

Financial data The fellow is offered housing, meals, studio space, and a stipend of $2,500.

Duration 1 month, from late March through mid-November.

Additional information This fellowship was established in 1994. The program is located in northern California, 45 miles south of San Francisco, on 600 acres of rangeland, redwood forests, and hiking trails. There is a $45 non-refundable application fee.

Number awarded 1 each year.

Deadline February of each year.

[1052]
GERTRUDE AND MAURICE GOLDHABER DISTINGUISHED FELLOWSHIPS

Brookhaven National Laboratory
Attn: Bill Bookless
Building 460
40 Brookhaven Avenue
Upton, NY 11973
(631) 344-5734　　　　　E-mail: barkigia@bnl.gov
Web: www.bnl.gov/HR/goldhaber

Summary To provide funding to postdoctoral scientists, especially Asian Americans and other minorities, interested in conducting research at Brookhaven National Laboratory (BNL).

Eligibility This program is open to scholars who are no more than 3 years past receipt of the Ph.D. and are interested in working at BNL. Candidates must be interested in working in close collaboration with a member of the BNL scientific staff and qualifying for a scientific staff position at BNL upon completion of the appointment. The sponsoring scientist must have an opening and be able to support the candidate at the standard starting salary for postdoctoral research associates. The program especially encourages applications from minorities and women.

Financial data The program provides additional funds to bring the salary to $81,200 per year.

Duration 3 years.

Additional information This program is funded by Battelle Memorial Institute and the State University of New York at Stony Brook.

Number awarded Up to 2 each year.

Deadline June of each year.

[1053]
GLOBAL AMERICAN STUDIES POSTDOCTORAL FELLOWSHIPS

Harvard University
Charles Warren Center for Studies in American History
Emerson Hall, Fourth Floor
Cambridge, MA 02138
(617) 495-3591　　　　　Fax: (617) 496-2111
E-mail: cwc@fas.harvard.edu
Web: warrencenter.fas.harvard.edu/postdoc-fellowship

Summary To provide funding to recent postdoctoral scholars, especially Asian Americans and others who will contribute to diversity and are interested in conducting research in the Boston area on the history of the United States in the world.

Eligibility This program is open to scholars who completed a Ph.D. within the past 4 years. Applicants must be interested in conducting research in residence at Harvard on the history of the United States in the world and the world in the United States. Applications are welcomed from scholars with a variety of disciplinary backgrounds who bring a historical perspective to topics such as empire, migration, race, indigeneity, and ethnicity, and whose work investigates and/or interprets the history and experience in the United States of native peoples, or peoples of African, Asian, or Hispanic descent. The program especially welcomes applications from scholars who can contribute, through their research, teaching, and service, to the diversity and excellence of Harvard's academic community.

Financial data The maximum grant is $53,600.

Duration 1 year; may be renewed 1 additional year.

Additional information This program began in 2013. Fellows must remain in residence at the center for the duration of the program and teach 1 course per year.

Number awarded 2 each year.

Deadline December of each year.

[1054]
GLORIA E. ANZALDUA BOOK PRIZE

National Women's Studies Association
Attn: Book Prizes
11 East Mount Royal Avenue, Suite 100
Baltimore, MD 21202
(410) 528-0355　　　　　Fax: (410) 528-0357
E-mail: awards@nwsa.org
Web: www.nwsa.org

Summary To recognize and reward members of the National Women's Studies Association (NWSA) who have written outstanding books on women of color and transnational issues.

Eligibility This award is available to NWSA members who submit a book that was published during the preceding year. Entries must present groundbreaking scholarship in women's studies and make a significant multicultural feminist contribution to women of color and/or transnational studies.

Financial data The award provides an honorarium of $1,000 and lifetime membership in NWSA.

Duration The award is presented annually.

Additional information This award was first presented in 2008.

Number awarded 1 each year.

Deadline April of each year.

[1055]
HARVARD MEDICAL SCHOOL DEAN'S POSTDOCTORAL FELLOWSHIP

Harvard Medical School
Office for Diversity Inclusion and Community Partnership
Attn: Program Manager, Dean's Postdoctoral Fellowship
164 Longwood Avenue, Second Floor
Boston, MA 02115-5818
(617) 432-1083　　　　　Fax: (617) 432-3834
E-mail: brian_anderson@hms.harvard.edu
Web: www.hms.harvard.edu/dcp/deanspdfellowship

Summary To provide an opportunity for postdoctoral scholars in the social and basic sciences, especially Asian Americans and others from minority and disadvantaged backgrounds, to obtain research training at Harvard Medical School.

Eligibility This program is open to U.S. citizens and permanent residents who have completed an M.D., Ph.D., Sc.D., or equivalent degree in the basic or social sciences and have less than 4 years of relevant postdoctoral research experience. Applicants must be interested in a program of research training under the mentorship of a professor in 1 of the departments of Harvard Medical School: biological chemistry and molecular pharmacology, biomedical informatics, cell biology, genetics, global health and social medicine, health care policy, microbiology and immunobiology, neurobiology, stem cell and regenerative biology, or systems biology. Scientists from minority and disadvantaged backgrounds are especially encouraged to apply. Selection is based on academic achievement, scholarly promise, potential to add to the diversity of the Harvard Medical School community, and the likelihood that the application will become an independent scientist and societal leader.

Financial data Fellows receive a professional development allowance of $1,250 per year and a stipend that depends on the years of postdoctoral experience, ranging from $40,992 for zero to $47,820 for 4 years.

Duration 2 years.

Number awarded 2 each year.

Deadline Applications may be submitted at any time.

[1056]
HENRY P. DAVID GRANTS FOR RESEARCH AND INTERNATIONAL TRAVEL IN HUMAN REPRODUCTIVE BEHAVIOR AND POPULATION STUDIES

American Psychological Foundation
750 First Street, N.E.
Washington, DC 20002-4242
(202) 336-5843   Fax: (202) 336-5812
E-mail: foundation@apa.org
Web: www.apa.org/apf/funding/david.aspx

Summary To provide funding to young psychologists, especially Asian Americans and other minorities, who are interested in conducting research on reproductive behavior.

Eligibility This program is open to doctoral students in psychology working on a dissertation and young psychologists who have no more than 10 years of postgraduate experience. Applicants must be interested in conducting research on human reproductive behavior or an area related to population concerns. Along with their application, they must submit a current curriculum vitae, 2 letters of recommendation, and an essay of 1 to 2 pages on their interest in human reproductive behavior or in population studies. The sponsor encourages applications from individuals who represent diversity in race, ethnicity, gender, age, disability, and sexual orientation.

Financial data The grant is $1,500.

Duration The grant is presented annually.

Additional information Every third year (2017, 1020), the program also provides support for a non-U.S. reproductive health/population science professional to travel to and participate in the Psychosocial Workshop, held in conjunction with the Population Association of America annual meeting.

Number awarded 2 in the years when the program offers support to a non-U.S. professional to travel to the United States; 1 in other years.

Deadline November of each year.

[1057]
HUBBLE FELLOWSHIPS

Space Telescope Science Institute
Attn: Hubble Fellowship Program Office
3700 San Martin Drive
Baltimore, MD 21218
(410) 338-2474   Fax: (410) 338-4211
E-mail: hfinquiry@stsci.edu
Web: www.stsci.edu

Summary To provide funding to recent postdoctoral scientists, especially Asian Americans and other minorities, who are interested in conducting research related to the Hubble Space Telescope or related missions of the National Aeronautics and Space Administration (NASA).

Eligibility This program is open to postdoctoral scientists who completed their doctoral degree within the past 3 years in astronomy, physics, or related disciplines. Applicants must be interested in conducting research related to NASA Cosmic Origins missions: the Hubble Space Telescope, Herschel Space Observatory, James Webb Space Telescope, Stratospheric Observatory for Infrared Astronomy, or the Spitzer Space Telescope. They may U.S. citizens or English-speaking citizens of other countries with valid visas. Research may be theoretical, observational, or instrumental. Women and members of minority groups are strongly encouraged to apply.

Financial data Stipends are approximately $66,500 per year. Other benefits may include health insurance, relocation costs, and support for travel, equipment, and other direct costs of research.

Duration 3 years: an initial 1-year appointment and 2 annual renewals, contingent on satisfactory performance and availability of funds.

Additional information This program, funded by NASA, began in 1990 and was limited to work with the Hubble Space Telescope. A parallel program, called the Spitzer Fellowship, began in 2002 and was limited to work with the Spitzer Space Telescope. In 2009, those programs were combined into this single program, which was also broadened to include the other NASA Cosmic Origins missions. Fellows are required to be in residence at their host institution engaged in full-time research for the duration of the grant.

Number awarded Varies each year; recently, 17 were awarded.

Deadline October of each year.

[1058]
IDAHO FOLK AND TRADITIONAL ARTS APPRENTICESHIP AWARDS

Idaho Commission on the Arts
Attn: Traditional Arts
2410 North Old Penitentiary Road
P.O. Box 83720
Boise, ID 83720-0008
(208) 334-2119   Toll Free: (800) 278-3863
Fax: (208) 334-2488   E-mail: info@arts.idaho.gov
Web: www.arts.idaho.gov/grants/trap.aspx

Summary To provide funding to masters of traditional art forms in Idaho and apprentices who wish to learn from them.

Eligibility This program is open to traditional arts masters and apprentices who have been residents of Idaho for at least

1 year. Applicants must be interested in establishing a partnership in which the apprentice will learn by observation and practice within the family, tribe, occupational, or other group. Master artists should have learned skills informally and have received peer recognition for achieving the highest level of artistry according to community standards. Apprentices should have some background in the proposed art form, wish to learn from a recognized master, and be committed to continue practicing after the apprenticeship has ended. Art forms must represent shared cultural traditions of both applicants. Priority is given to art forms with few practitioners. In-family apprenticeships are encouraged. Selection is based on quality (master is recognized by peers and by community standards, the apprentice will benefit from working with the master at this time, the apprentice is committed to advancing his or her skills in the art form and carrying on the tradition); community (master and apprentice share the same cultural background, the art form is significant to their community, the art form is endangered within the particular traditional culture or there are few artists practicing it); and feasibility (the goals for the apprenticeship are clear, the budget is appropriate, the work plan provides appropriate time for interaction to achieve meaningful results).

Financial data The maximum grant is $3,000.

Duration From 4 to 10 months, depending on the particular art form and on the proposed work plan.

Number awarded Varies each year; recently, 7 of these fellowships were awarded.

Deadline January of each year.

[1059]
ILLINOIS MINORITY REAL ESTATE SCHOLARSHIP

Illinois Association of Realtors
Attn: Illinois Real Estate Educational Foundation
522 South Fifth Street
P.O. Box 2607
Springfield, IL 62708
Toll Free: (866) 854-REEF   Fax: (217) 529-5893
E-mail: lclayton@iar.org
Web: www.ilreef.org

Summary To provide financial assistance to Illinois residents who are Asian Americans or members of other minority groups and preparing for a career in real estate.

Eligibility This program is open to residents of Illinois who are Asian, African American, Hispanic or Latino, or Native American. Applicants must be interested in preparing for a career in real estate by pursuing: 1) courses to meet Illinois broker license requirements; 2) course work to meet Illinois broker license requirement; 3) course work required for Illinois appraisal licensing/certification; 4) professional development unrelated to obtaining license/certification; or 5) an undergraduate or graduate program of study. Along with their application, they must submit information on their employment history, transcripts, evidence of financial need, and an essay that describes their career goals and explains why they believe they should receive scholarship assistance through this program.

Financial data The maximum stipend is $500.

Duration Funds must be used within 24 months of the award date.

Number awarded 1 or more each year.

Deadline Applications may be submitted at any time, but they must be received at least 12 weeks prior to the beginning of the school term for which financial assistance is requested.

[1060]
INTERNATIONAL SECURITY AND COOPERATION POSTDOCTORAL FELLOWSHIPS

Stanford University
Center for International Security and Cooperation
Attn: Fellowships Coordinator
Encina Hall, Room C206-10
616 Serra Street
Stanford, CA 94305-6165
(650) 723-9625   Fax: (650) 724-5683
E-mail: CISACfellowship@stanford.edu
Web: cisac.fsi.stanford.edu/docs/cisac_fellowship_program

Summary To provide funding to postdoctorates, especially Asian Americans and other minorities, who are interested in conducting research on international security problems at Stanford University's Center for International Security and Cooperation.

Eligibility This program is open to scholars who have a Ph.D. or equivalent degree from the United States or abroad and would benefit from using the resources of the center. Applicants may be working in any discipline of the social sciences, humanities, natural sciences, law, or engineering that relates to international security problems. Relevant topics include nuclear weapons policy and nonproliferation; nuclear energy; cybersecurity, cyberwarfare, and the future of the Internet; war and civil conflict; global governance, migration and transnational flows, from norms to criminal trafficking; biosecurity and global health; implications of geostrategic shifts; insurgency, terrorism, and homeland security; and consolidating peace after conflict. The sponsor welcomes applications from women, minorities, and citizens of all countries.

Financial data The stipend ranges from $48,000 to $66,000, depending on experience. Medical insurance is available for those who do not have coverage.

Duration 9 to 11 months.

Additional information Fellows are expected to write a publishable article or articles and/or make significant progress on turning a thesis into a book manuscript. They should not plan to spend any time conducting research abroad or in other parts of the country.

Number awarded Varies each year; recently, 7 were awarded.

Deadline January of each year.

[1061]
INTERNATIONAL SECURITY AND COOPERATION PROFESSIONAL FELLOWSHIPS

Stanford University
Center for International Security and Cooperation
Attn: Fellowships Coordinator
Encina Hall, Room C206-10
616 Serra Street
Stanford, CA 94305-6165
(650) 723-9625   Fax: (650) 724-5683
E-mail: CISACfellowship@stanford.edu
Web: cisac.fsi.stanford.edu/docs/cisac_fellowship_program

Summary To provide funding to professionals who are interested in conducting research in residence on topics of interest to Stanford University's Center for International Security and Cooperation.

Eligibility This program is open to mid-career professionals in journalism, law, the military, government, or international organizations, either from the United States or abroad. Applicants must be interested in conducting research in any discipline of the social sciences, humanities, natural sciences, law, or engineering that relates to international security problems. Relevant topics include nuclear weapons policy and nonproliferation; nuclear energy; cybersecurity, cyberwarfare, and the future of the Internet; war and civil conflict; global governance, migration and transnational flows, from norms to criminal trafficking; biosecurity and global health; implications of geostrategic shifts; insurgency, terrorism, and homeland security; and consolidating peace after conflict. The sponsor welcomes applications from women, minorities, and citizens of all countries.

Financial data The stipend depends on experience and is determined on a case-by-case basis. Additional funds may be available for dependents and travel.

Duration 9 to 11 months.

Additional information Fellows are expected to write a publishable article during their fellowship. They should not plan to spend any time conducting research abroad or in other parts of the country.

Number awarded Varies each year; recently, 2 were awarded.

Deadline January of each year.

[1062]
JAMES A. RAWLEY PRIZE

Organization of American Historians
Attn: Award and Committee Coordinator
112 North Bryan Street
Bloomington, IN 47408-4141
(812) 855-7311   Fax: (812) 855-0696
E-mail: khamm@oah.org
Web: www.oah.org

Summary To recognize and reward authors of outstanding books dealing with race relations in the United States.

Eligibility This award is presented to the author of the outstanding book on the history of race relations in America. Entries must have been published during the current calendar year.

Financial data The award is $1,000 and a certificate.

Duration The award is presented annually.

Additional information This award was established in 1990.

Number awarded 1 each year.

Deadline September of each year.

[1063]
JAMES H. DUNN, JR. MEMORIAL FELLOWSHIP PROGRAM

Illinois Legislative Staff
Attn: Legislative Research Unit
222 South Chicago, Suite 301
Springfield, IL 62704-1894
(217) 782-6851   Fax: (217) 785-7572
E-mail: lru@ilga.gov
Web: www.ilga.gov/commission/lru/internships.html

Summary To provide recent college graduates, especially Asian Americans and members of other underrepresented groups, with work experience in Illinois state government.

Eligibility This program in open to residents of any state who have completed a bachelor's degree and are interested in working in the Illinois Governor's office or in various agencies under the Governor's jurisdiction. Applicants may have majored in any field, but they must be able to demonstrate a substantial commitment to excellence as evidenced by academic honors, leadership ability, extracurricular activities, and involvement in community or public service. Along with their application, they must submit 1) a 500-word personal statement on the qualities they will bring to the program, their career goals or plans, how their selection to this program would assist them in achieving those goals, and what they expect to gain from the program; and 2) a 1,000-word essay in which they identify and analyze a public issue that they feel has great impact on state government. A particular goal of the program is to achieve affirmative action through the nomination of qualified minorities, men, women, and persons with disabilities.

Financial data The stipend is $2,611 per month.

Duration 1 year, beginning in August.

Additional information Assignments are in Springfield and, to a limited extent, in Chicago or Washington, D.C.

Number awarded Varies each year.

Deadline February of each year.

[1064]
JAPANESE MEDICAL SOCIETY OF AMERICA SCHOLARSHIPS

Japanese Medical Society of America, Inc.
100 Park Avenue, Suite 1600
New York, NY 10017
(212) 351-5038   Fax: (212) 351-5047
E-mail: info@jmsa.org
Web: www.jmsa.org/student-members/about-scholarships

Summary To provide funding to Japanese American medical school students, residents, and fellows who are interested in working on a project.

Eligibility This program is open to Japanese Americans who are currently enrolled as medical students, residents, or fellows. Applicants must be proposing to conduct a project that will benefit the Japanese Medical Society of America (JMSA) and the Japanese community. Along with their application, they must submit a 1-page essay about themselves and what they will do to contribute to the JMSA. Selection is based on academic excellence and interest in JMSA.

Financial data Stipends depend on the availability of funds, but have ranged from $2,500 to $20,000. Support is provided primarily for tuition, but a portion of the funds may be used to carry out the proposed project.

Duration 1 year.

Additional information This program receives support from a number of sponsors, including the Honjo Foundation, Nishioka Foundation, Mitsui USA, Nippon Life, and Toyota USA.

Number awarded Varies each year; recently, 11 were awarded.

Deadline December of each year.

[1065]
JOEL ELKES RESEARCH AWARD

American College of Neuropsychopharmacology
Attn: Executive Office
5034-A Thoroughbred Lane
Brentwood, TN 37027
(615) 324-2360   Fax: (615) 523-1715
E-mail: acnp@acnp.org
Web: www.acnp.org/programs/awards.aspx

Summary To recognize and reward young scientists, especially Asian Americans and other minorities, who have contributed outstanding clinical or translational research to neuropsychopharmacology.

Eligibility This award is available to scientists who are younger than 50 years of age. Nominees must have made an outstanding clinical or translational contribution to neuropsychopharmacology. The contribution may be based on a single discovery or a cumulative body of work. Emphasis is placed on contributions that further understanding of self-regulatory processes as they affect mental function and behavior in disease and well-being. Membership in the American College of Neuropsychopharmacology (ACNP) is not required. Nomination of women and minorities is highly encouraged.

Financial data The award consists of an expense-paid trip to the ACNP annual meeting, a monetary honorarium, and a plaque.

Duration The award is presented annually.

Additional information This award was first presented in 1986.

Number awarded 1 each year.

Deadline Nominations must be submitted by June of each year.

[1066]
JOHN AND POLLY SPARKS EARLY CAREER GRANT FOR PSYCHOLOGISTS INVESTIGATING SERIOUS EMOTIONAL DISTURBANCE (SED)

American Psychological Foundation
750 First Street, N.E.
Washington, DC 20002-4242
(202) 336-5843   Fax: (202) 336-5812
E-mail: foundation@apa.org
Web: www.apa.org/apf/funding/sparks-early-career.aspx

Summary To provide funding to early-career psychologists, especially Asian Americans and members of other underrepresented groups, who are interested in conducting research on serious emotional disturbance in children.

Eligibility This program is open to young psychologists who completed a doctoral degree (Ed.D., Psy.D., Ph.D.) within the past 10 years. Applicants must be interested in conducting research in the area of early intervention and treatment for serious emotional disturbance in children. Selection is based on conformance with stated program goals and qualifications, quality and impact of proposed work, innovation and contribution to the field with proposed project, and applicant's demonstrated competence and capability to execute the proposed work. The sponsor encourages applications from individuals who represent diversity in race, ethnicity, gender, age, disability, and sexual orientation.

Financial data The grant is $17,000.

Duration 1 year.

Additional information This program began in 2013.

Number awarded 1 each year.

Deadline May of each year.

[1067]
JOHN MCLENDON MEMORIAL MINORITY POSTGRADUATE SCHOLARSHIP AWARD

National Association of Collegiate Directors of Athletics
Attn: NACDA Foundation
24651 Detroit Road
Westlake, OH 44145
(440) 788-7474   Fax: (440) 892-4007
E-mail: knewman@nacda.com
Web: www.nacda.com/mclendon/scholarship.html

Summary To provide financial assistance to Asian American and other minority college seniors who are interested in working on a graduate degree in athletics administration.

Eligibility This program is open to minority college students who are seniors, are attending school on a full-time basis, have a GPA of 3.2 or higher, intend to attend graduate school to earn a degree in athletics administration, and are involved in college or community activities. Also eligible are college graduates who have at least 2 years' experience in an athletics administration position. Candidates must be nominated by an official of a member institution of the National Association of Collegiate Directors of Athletics (NACDA) or (for college graduates) a supervisor.

Financial data The stipend is $10,000.

Duration 1 year.

Additional information Recipients must maintain full-time status during the senior year to retain their eligibility. They must attend NACDA-member institutions.

Number awarded 5 each year.

Deadline Nominations must be submitted by April of each year.

[1068]
JULIUS AXELROD MENTORSHIP AWARD

American College of Neuropsychopharmacology
Attn: Executive Office
5034-A Thoroughbred Lane
Brentwood, TN 37027
(615) 324-2360   Fax: (615) 523-1715
E-mail: acnp@acnp.org
Web: www.acnp.org/programs/awards.aspx

Summary To recognize and reward members of the American College of Neuropsychopharmacology (ACNP), especially Asian Americans and other minoritie, who have demonstrated outstanding mentoring of young scientists.

Eligibility This award is available to ACNP members who have made an outstanding contribution to neuropsychopharmacology by mentoring and developing young scientists into leaders in the field. Nominations must be accompanied by letters of support from up to 3 people who have been mentored by the candidate. Nomination of women and minorities is highly encouraged.

Financial data The award consists of a monetary honorarium and a plaque.

Duration The award is presented annually.

Additional information This award was first presented in 2004.

Number awarded 1 each year.

Deadline Nominations must be submitted by June of each year.

[1069]
KENNETH B. AND MARNIE P. CLARK FUND

American Psychological Foundation
750 First Street, N.E.
Washington, DC 20002-4242
(202) 336-5843   Fax: (202) 336-5812
E-mail: foundation@apa.org
Web: www.apa.org/apf/funding/clark-fund.aspx

Summary To provide funding to psychologists, especially Asian Americans and members of other groups that will contribute to diversity, who wish to conduct a project related to academic achievement in children.

Eligibility This program is open to psychologists who wish to conduct research or development activities that promote the understanding of the relationship between self-identity and academic achievement with an emphasis on children in grade levels K-8. Eligibility alternates between graduate students in odd-numbered years and early-career (within 10 years of completion of postdoctoral work) psychologists. Selection is based on conformance with stated program goals and qualifications; quality and potential impact of proposed work; originality, innovation, and contribution to the field with the proposed project; and applicant's demonstrated competence and capability to execute the proposed work. The sponsor encourages applications from individuals who represent diversity in race, ethnicity, gender, age, disability, and sexual orientation.

Financial data The grant is $10,000.

Duration 1 year.

Additional information This program began in 2012.

Number awarded 1 each year.

Deadline June of each year.

[1070]
KING-CHAVEZ-PARKS VISITING PROFESSORS PROGRAM

University of Michigan
Attn: Office of the Provost and Executive Vice President
 for Academic Affairs
503 Thompson Street
3084 Fleming Administration Building
Ann Arbor, MI 48109-1340
(734) 764-3982   Fax: (734) 764-4546
E-mail: provost@umich.edu
Web: www.provost.umich.edu

Summary To provide an opportunity for Asian American and other minority scholars to visit and teach at the University of Michigan.

Eligibility Outstanding minority (Asian/Pacific American, African American, Latino/a-Hispanic American, and Native American) scholars, performers, or practitioners are eligible to be nominated by University of Michigan faculty members to visit and lecture there. Nominations that include collaborations with other educational institutions in Michigan are of high priority.

Financial data Visiting Professors receive round-trip transportation and an appropriate honorarium.

Duration Visits range from 1 to 5 days.

Additional information This program was established in 1986. Visiting Professors are expected to lecture or teach at the university, offer at least 1 event open to the general public, and meet with minority campus/community groups, including local K-12 schools.

Number awarded Varies each year.

Deadline Nominations may be submitted at any time, but they must be received at least 30 days before a funding decision is required.

[1071]
KOREAN NURSES ASSOCIATION OF SOUTHERN CALIFORNIA REGISTERED NURSE EDUCATION SCHOLARSHIPS

Korean Nurses Association of Southern California
1254 West Sixth Street, Suite 809
Los Angeles, CA 90017
(213) 434-1019   E-mail: kanascrn@gmail.com
Web: www.koamrn.org

Summary To provide financial assistance to Korean nurses in California who wish to attend college in southern California to work on a bachelor's or graduate degree.

Eligibility This program is open to Korean registered nurses who are enrolled or entering a baccalaureate or higher degree nursing program in southern California. Applicants must be citizens or permanent residents of the United States. Along with their application, they must submit a 1-page essay on their reasons for selecting nursing as a career, including their professional goals and objectives. Selection is based on that essay, work experience in nursing and related fields, community service and volunteer work experience, cumulative GPA, and letters of recommendation. Priority consideration is given to members of the Korean Nurses Association of Southern California and their immediate family members.

Financial data A stipend is awarded (amount not specified).

Duration 1 year; may be renewed 1 additional year.

Number awarded 1 or more each year.

Deadline November of each year.

[1072]
KOREAN TOXICOLOGISTS ASSOCIATION IN AMERICA BEST PRESENTATIONS BY GRADUATE STUDENT AND POSTDOCTORAL TRAINEE AWARD

Society of Toxicology
Attn: Korean Toxicologists Association in America Special Interest Group
1821 Michael Faraday Drive, Suite 300
Reston, VA 20190-5348
(703) 438-3115　　　　　　　　Fax: (703) 438-3113
E-mail: sothq@toxicology.org
Web: www.toxicology.org/ai/af/awards_details.aspx?id=125

Summary To recognize and reward graduate students and postdoctoral trainees who present outstanding papers at a session of the Korean Toxicologists Association in America (KTAA) at the annual meeting of the Society of Toxicology (SOT).

Eligibility This award is available to graduate students and postdoctoral trainees who have an accepted abstract of a research poster or platform presentation for a KTAA session at the SOT annual meeting. Along with the abstract, they must submit a letter of nomination from their major adviser.

Financial data A plaque and a cash award (amount not specified) are presented.

Duration The awards are presented annually.

Additional information These awards are presented jointly by KTAA and the Korean Institute of Toxicology (KIT).

Number awarded 2 each year.

Deadline January of each year.

[1073]
KUN-PO SOO AWARD

American Psychiatric Association
Attn: American Psychiatric Foundation
1000 Wilson Boulevard, Suite 1825
Arlington, VA 22209-3901
(703) 907-8639　　　　　　　Toll Free: (888) 35-PSYCH
Fax: (703) 907-7852　　　E-mail: diversityatapa@psych.org
Web: www.americanpsychiatricfoundation.org

Summary To recognize and reward individuals who have made outstanding contributions toward understanding the impact and import of Asian cultural heritages in areas relevant to psychiatry.

Eligibility Nominees for this award need not be Asians, Americans, psychiatrists, or members of the American Psychiatric Association (APA). They should be engaged in research and scholarship in culture-specific mental health issues and treatment needs of Asian populations.

Financial data The honorarium is $1,000.

Duration The award is presented annually.

Additional information The winner is selected by the Council on Minority Mental Health and Mental Health Disparities of the American Psychiatric Association (APA) in consultation with the Caucus of Asian-American Psychiatrists. This

program was established in 1987 and funded in 1991. Until 1996, it was called the Asian American Award.

Number awarded 1 each year.

Deadline July of each year.

[1074]
LAURENCE R. FOSTER MEMORIAL SCHOLARSHIPS

Oregon Office of Student Access and Completion
Attn: Scholarship Processing Coordinator
1500 Valley River Drive, Suite 100
Eugene, OR 97401-2146
(541) 687-7422　　　　Toll Free: (800) 452-8807, ext. 7422
Fax: (541) 687-7414　　　　　　TDD: (800) 735-2900
E-mail: cheryl.a.connolly@state.or.us
Web: app.oregonstudentaid.gov/Catalog/Default.aspx

Summary To provide financial assistance to residents of Oregon, especially Asian Americans and others from diverse backgrounds, who are enrolled at a college or graduate school in any state to prepare for a public health career.

Eligibility This program is open to residents of Oregon who are enrolled at least half time at a 4-year college or university in any state to prepare for a career in public health (not private practice). Preference is given first to applicants from diverse environments; second to persons employed in, or graduate students working on a degree in, public health; and third to juniors and seniors majoring in a health program (e.g., nursing, medical technology, physician assistant). Applicants must be able to demonstrate financial need. Along with their application, they must submit essays of 250 to 350 words on 1) what public health means to them; 2) the public health aspect they intend to practice and the health and population issues impacted by that aspect; and 3) their experience living or working in diverse environments.

Financial data Stipends for scholarships offered by the Oregon Office of Student Access and Completion (OSAC) range from $1,000 to $10,000 but recently averaged $4,368.

Duration 1 year.

Additional information This program is administered by the OSAC with funds provided by the Oregon Community Foundation.

Number awarded Varies each year; recently, 6 were awarded.

Deadline February of each year.

[1075]
LEE & LOW BOOKS NEW VISIONS AWARD

Lee & Low Books
95 Madison Avenue, Suite 1205
New York, NY 10016
(212) 779-4400　　　　　　　　Fax: (212) 683-1894
E-mail: general@leeandlow.com
Web: www.leeandlow.com

Summary To recognize and reward outstanding unpublished fantasy or mystery books for young readers by Asian Americans or other writers of color.

Eligibility The contest is open to writers of color who are residents of the United States. Applicants must submit a manuscript of a fantasy, science fiction, or mystery book directed to readers at the middle grade or young adult level.

They may not previously have published a middle grade or young adult novel published.

Financial data The award is a $1,000 cash grant plus the standard publication contract, including the standard advance and royalties. The Honor Award winner receives a cash grant of $500.

Duration The competition is held annually.

Additional information This program began in 2012. Manuscripts may not be sent to any other publishers while under consideration for this award.

Number awarded 2 each year.

Deadline October of each year.

[1076]
LEE & LOW BOOKS NEW VOICES AWARD

Lee & Low Books
95 Madison Avenue, Suite 1205
New York, NY 10016
(212) 779-4400   Fax: (212) 683-1894
E-mail: general@leeandlow.com
Web: www.leeandlow.com

Summary To recognize and reward outstanding unpublished children's picture books by Asian Americans or other writers of color.

Eligibility The contest is open to writers of color who are residents of the United States and who have not previously published a children's picture book. Writers who have published in other venues, (e.g., children's magazines, young adult fiction and nonfiction) are eligible. Manuscripts previously submitted to the sponsor are not eligible. Submissions should be no more than 1,500 words and must address the needs of children of color by providing stories with which they can identify and relate and that promote a greater understanding of each other. Submissions may be fiction or nonfiction for children between the ages of 5 and 12. Folklore and animal stories are not considered. Up to 2 submissions may be submitted per entrant.

Financial data The award is a $1,000 cash grant plus the standard publication contract, including the standard advance and royalties. The Honor Award winner receives a cash grant of $500.

Duration The competition is held annually.

Additional information This program began in 2000. Manuscripts may not be sent to any other publishers while under consideration for this award.

Number awarded 2 each year.

Deadline September of each year.

[1077]
LEON BRADLEY SCHOLARSHIPS

American Association of School Personnel Administrators
Attn: Scholarship Program
11863 West 112th Street, Suite 100
Overland Park, KS 66210
(913) 327-1222   Fax: (913) 327-1223
E-mail: aaspa@aaspa.org
Web: www.aaspa.org/leon-bradley-scholarship

Summary To provide financial assistance to Asian American and other minority undergraduates, paraprofessionals, and graduate students preparing for a career in teaching and

school leadership at colleges in designated southeastern states.

Eligibility This program is open to members of minority groups (Asian, American Indian, Alaskan Native, Pacific Islander, Black, Hispanic, Middle Easterner) currently enrolled full time at a college or university in Alabama, Florida, Georgia, Kentucky, North Carolina, South Carolina, Tennessee, or Virginia. Applicants must be 1) undergraduates in their final year (including student teaching) of an initial teaching certification program; 2) paraprofessional career-changers in their final year (including student teaching) of an initial teaching certification program; or 3) graduate students who have served as a licensed teacher and are working on a school administrator credential. They must have an overall GPA of 3.0 or higher. Priority is given to applicants who 1) can demonstrate work experience that has been applied to college expenses; 2) have received other scholarship or financial aid support; or 3) are seeking initial certification and/or endorsement in a state-identified critical area.

Financial data Stipends are $2,500 for undergraduates in their final year, $1,500 for paraprofessionals in their final year, and $1,500 for graduate students.

Duration 1 year.

Number awarded 4 each year: 1 undergraduate, 1 paraprofessional, and 2 graduate students.

Deadline May of each year.

[1078]
LEROY C. MERRITT HUMANITARIAN FUND AWARD

LeRoy C. Merritt Humanitarian Fund
Attn: Secretary
50 East Huron Street
Chicago, IL 60611
(312) 280-4226   Toll Free: (800) 545-2433, ext. 4226
Fax: (312) 280-4227   E-mail: merrittfund@ala.org
Web: www.merrittfund.org

Summary To provide financial support to librarians facing discrimination based on race, sex, or other factors.

Eligibility The fund was established in 1970 to provide direct financial aid for the support, maintenance, medical care, legal fees, and welfare of librarians who are or have been "threatened with loss of employment or discharged because of their stand for the cause of intellectual freedom." In 1975, the scope of the fund was broadened to include librarians who had been discriminated against on the basis of gender, age, race, color, creed, sexual orientation, place of national origin, religion, disability, or defense of intellectual freedom. Applicants should describe their situation, including a brief explanation of its financial ramifications and of the amount of aid requested.

Financial data The amount awarded varies, depending upon the needs of the recipient.

Duration The award is granted annually.

Number awarded Varies each year.

Deadline Applications may be submitted at any time.

[1079]
LIBRARY OF CONGRESS JUNIOR FELLOWS PROGRAM

Library of Congress
Library Services
Attn: Junior Fellows Program Coordinator
101 Independence Avenue, S.E., Room LM-642
Washington, DC 20540-4600
(202) 707-6610   Fax: (202) 707-6269
E-mail: jrfell@loc.gov
Web: www.loc.gov/hr/jrfellows/index.html

Summary To provide summer work experience at the Library of Congress (LC) to upper-division and graduate students and to recent graduates, especially Asian Americans and members of other underrepresented groups.

Eligibility This program is open to U.S. citizens with subject expertise in the following areas: collections preservation; geography and maps; humanities, art, and culture; information technology; library sciences; or chemistry and science. Applicants must 1) be juniors or seniors at an accredited college or university; 2) be graduate students; or 3) have completed their degree in the past year. Women, minorities, and persons with disabilities are strongly encouraged to apply. Selection is based on academic achievement, letters of recommendation, and an interview.

Financial data Fellows are paid a taxable stipend of $3,000.

Duration 10 weeks, beginning in either May or June. Fellows work a 40-hour week.

Additional information Fellows work with primary source materials and assist selected divisions at LC in the organization and documentation of archival collections, production of finding aids and bibliographic records, preparation of materials for preservation and service, completion of bibliographical research, and digitization of LC's historical collections.

Number awarded Varies each year; recently, 38 were awarded.

Deadline January of each year.

[1080]
LILLA JEWEL AWARD FOR WOMEN ARTISTS

McKenzie River Gathering Foundation
Attn: Office Manager
1235 S.E. Morrison Street, Suite A
Portland, OR 97214
(503) 289-1517   Toll Free: (800) 489-6743
Fax: (503) 232-1731   E-mail: info@mrgfoundation.org
Web: www.mrgfoundation.org

Summary To recognize and reward Asian American and other women performance artists of color in Oregon who utilize the spoken word.

Eligibility Eligible to apply for this award are women artists in Oregon whose work relies on the spoken word and performance. Applicants must have demonstrated success as a spoken word artist and experience performing spoken word in front of a large audience. They must be interested in developing a work for presentation at the sponsoring organization's annual fundraising party. The performance may include music and mixed media. It should address progressive social, racial, economic, and/or environmental justice issues. Priority is given to women of color and those who identify as LGBT.

Financial data The award is $2,500.

Duration The award is presented annually.

Number awarded 1 each year.

Deadline November of each year.

[1081]
LIZETTE PETERSON-HOMER INJURY PREVENTION GRANT AWARD

American Psychological Foundation
750 First Street, N.E.
Washington, DC 20002-4242
(202) 336-5843   Fax: (202) 336-5812
E-mail: foundation@apa.org
Web: www.apa.org/apf/funding/peterson-homer.aspx

Summary To provide funding to graduate students and faculty, especially Asian Americans and members of other diverse groups, interested in conducting research related to the prevention of injuries in children.

Eligibility This program is open to graduate students and faculty interested in conducting research that focuses on the prevention of physical injury in children and young adults through accidents, violence, abuse, or suicide. Applicants must submit a 100-word abstract, description of the project, detailed budget, curriculum vitae, and letter from the supporting faculty supervisor (if the applicant is a student). Selection is based on conformance with stated program goals, magnitude of incremental contribution, quality of proposed work, and applicant's demonstrated scholarship and research competence. The sponsor encourages applications from individuals who represent diversity in race, ethnicity, gender, age, disability, and sexual orientation.

Financial data Grants up to $5,000 are available.

Additional information This program began in 1999 as the Rebecca Routh Coon Injury Research Award. The current name was adopted in 2003. It is supported by Division 54 (Society of Pediatric Psychology) of the American Psychological Association and the American Psychological Foundation.

Number awarded 1 each year.

Deadline September of each year.

[1082]
LOFT SPOKEN WORD IMMERSION GRANTS

The Loft Literary Center
Attn: Immersion Grant Program Director
1011 Washington Avenue South, Suite 200
Minneapolis, MN 55415
(612) 215-2585   Fax: (612) 215-2576
E-mail: bphi@loft.org
Web: www.loft.org/programs__awards/grants__awards

Summary To provide funding to Asian American and other spoken word poets of color who are interested in developing and implementing community learning and enrichment projects of their own design.

Eligibility This program is open to spoken word poets of color currently residing in the United States; the program defines poets of color to include Asians, South Asians, Asian Americans, Native Americans, Pacific Islanders, Africans, African Americans, Latino/as, Chicano/as, Arabs, Middle Easterners, and mixed race. Applicants must proposed to develop and implement a project that enriches their art as well as the community's. Proposal objectives and activities may include, but are not limited to, personal artistic growth; developing and teaching workshops or open mics in a non-traditional space; research and immersion into community-specific art forms; multidisciplinary and cross-community spoken word projects; ELL, bilingual, and multilingual immersion; or improving speaking, performance, and presentation skills. Tuition for non-degree granting programs (e.g., writers' conferences, community-based education) may be approved, but tuition for classes leading to a degree is not eligible. Selection is based on quality of a work sample; merit of the project design (originality, feasibility, clarity of the stated objectives, community immersion and enrichment, artistic growth of the artist); and the applicant's potential ability to complete the project.

Financial data The grant is $7,500.

Duration Projects must conclude within a year and a half.

Additional information Funding for this program comes from the Surdna Foundation.

Number awarded 4 each year, of whom 1 must be a resident of Minnesota.

Deadline October of each year.

[1083]
LONI DING AWARD FOR SOCIAL ISSUE DOCUMENTARY SHORT

Center for Asian American Media
Attn: James T. Yee Talent Development Program
145 Ninth Street, Suite 350
San Francisco, CA 94103-2641
(415) 863-0814   Fax: (415) 863-7428
E-mail: mediafund@caamedia.org
Web: www.caamedia.org/loni-ding-award

Summary To recognize and reward Asian American filmmakers who produce short features that relate to the experiences of underrepresented communities.

Eligibility This award is available to Asian American filmmakers whose work includes a short documentary that illuminates the experiences of Asian American and other underrepresented communities.

Financial data The award is $1,000.

Number awarded 1 each year.

Deadline Deadline not specified.

[1084]
LYMAN T. JOHNSON POSTDOCTORAL FELLOWSHIP

University of Kentucky
Attn: Vice President for Research
311 Main Building, 0032
Lexington, KY 40506-0032
(859) 257-5090   Fax: (859) 323-2800
E-mail: vprgrants@uky.edu
Web: www.research.uky.edu

Summary To provide an opportunity for recent postdoctorates, especially Asian Americans and other minorities, to conduct research at the University of Kentucky (U.K.).

Eligibility This program is open to U.S. citizens and permanent residents who have completed a doctoral degree within the past 2 years. Applicants must be interested in conducting an individualized research program under the mentorship of a U.K. professor. They should indicate, in their letter

of application, how their participation in this program would contribute to the compelling interest of diversity at U.K. Race, ethnicity, and national origin are among the factors that contribute to diversity. Selection is based on evidence of scholarship with competitive potential for a tenure-track faculty appointment at a research university, compatibility of specific research interests with those in doctorate-granting units at U.K., quality of the research proposal, support from mentor and references, and effect of the appointment on the educational benefit of diversity within the research or professional area.

Financial data The fellowship provides a stipend of $35,000 plus $5,000 for support of research activities.

Duration Up to 2 years.

Additional information In addition to conducting an individualized research program under the mentorship of a U.K. professor, fellows actively participate in research, teaching, and service to the university, their profession, and the community. This program began in 1992.

Number awarded 2 each year.

Deadline October of each year.

[1085]
MANY VOICES FELLOWSHIPS

Playwrights' Center
Attn: Artistic Programs Administrator
2301 East Franklin Avenue
Minneapolis, MN 55406-1024
(612) 332-7481, ext. 115   Fax: (612) 332-6037
E-mail: julia@pwcenter.org
Web: www.pwcenter.org/programs/many-voices-fellowships

Summary To provide funding to Asian Americans and other playwrights of color so they can spend a year in residence at the Playwrights' Center in Minneapolis.

Eligibility This program is open to playwrights of color who are citizens or permanent residents of the United States; residents of Minnesota and of other states are eligible. Applicants must be interested in playwriting and creating theater in a supportive artist community at the Playwrights' Center.

Financial data Fellows receive a $10,000 stipend, $2,500 for living expenses, and $1,500 in play development funds.

Duration 9 months, beginning in October.

Additional information This program, which began in 1994, is funded by the Jerome Foundation. Fellows must be in residence at the Playwrights' Center for the duration of the program.

Number awarded 2 each year: 1 to a resident of Minnesota and 1 to a resident of any state.

Deadline November of each year.

[1086]
MARIAM K. CHAMBERLAIN FELLOWSHIP IN WOMEN AND PUBLIC POLICY

Institute for Women's Policy Research
Attn: Fellowship Coordinator
1200 18th Street, N.W., Suite 301
Washington, DC 20036
(202) 785-5100   Fax: (202) 833-4362
E-mail: MKCfellowship@iwpr.org
Web: www.iwpr.org/about/fellowships

Summary To provide work experience at the Institute for Women's Policy Research (IWPR) to college graduates and graduate students, especially Asian Americans and members of other underrepresented groups, who are interested in economic justice for women.

Eligibility This program is open to scholars interested in conducting research projects on policies that affect women. Current topics of interest include the quality of women's jobs, including wages, paid sick leave, paid family leave, and workplace flexibility; increasing access to higher education and non-traditional jobs for low-income women and women with children; examining socioeconomic supports for women in job training programs, and for college students with children; the economic status of women and girls, women of color, and immigrant women across the United States. Applicants should have at least a bachelor's degree in social science (e.g., psychology, education, sociology, public policy), statistics, economics, mathematics, or women's studies. Graduate work is desirable but not required. They should have strong quantitative and library research skills and knowledge of women's issues. Familiarity with Microsoft Word and Excel is required; knowledge of STATA, SPSS, SAS, or graphics software is a plus. Members of underrepresented groups, based on race, color, religion, gender, national origin, age, disability, marital or veteran status, sexual orientation, or any other legally protected status, are especially encouraged to apply.

Financial data The stipend is $31,000 and includes health insurance and a public transportation stipend.

Duration 9 months, beginning in September.

Additional information The institute is a nonprofit, scientific research organization that works primarily on issues related to equal opportunity and economic and social justice for women. Research topics vary each year but relate to women and public policy.

Number awarded 1 each year.

Deadline February of each year.

[1087]
MARIE F. PETERS AWARD

National Council on Family Relations
Attn: Ethnic Minorities Section
1201 West River Parkway, Suite 200
Minneapolis, MN 55454-1115
(763) 781-9331   Toll Free: (888) 781-9331
Fax: (763) 781-9348   E-mail: info@ncfr.com
Web: www.ncfr.org

Summary To recognize and reward members of the National Council on Family Relations (NCFR) who have made significant contributions to the area of ethnic minority families.

Eligibility This award is available to members of NCFR who have demonstrated excellence in the area of ethnic minority families. Selection is based on leadership and/or mentoring, scholarship and/or service, research, publication, teaching, community service, contribution to the ethnic minorities section, and contribution to the NCFR.

Financial data The award is $500 and a plaque.

Duration The award is granted biennially, in odd-numbered years.

Additional information This award, which was established in 1983, is named after a prominent Black researcher and family sociologist who served in many leadership roles in NCFR. It is sponsored by the Ethnic Minorities Section of NCFR.

Number awarded 1 every other year.

Deadline April of odd-numbered years.

[1088]
MARTIN LUTHER KING, JR. MEMORIAL SCHOLARSHIP FUND

California Teachers Association
Attn: CTA Foundation for Teaching and Learning
1705 Murchison Drive
P.O. Box 921
Burlingame, CA 94011-0921
(650) 697-1400   E-mail: scholarships@cta.org
Web: www.cta.org

Summary To provide financial assistance for college or graduate school to Asian Pacific Americans and other racial and ethnic minorities who are members of the California Teachers Association (CTA), children of members, or members of the Student CTA.

Eligibility This program is open to members of racial or ethnic minority groups (Asians/Pacific Islanders, African Americans, American Indians/Alaska Natives, and Hispanics) who are 1) active CTA members; 2) dependent children of active, retired, or deceased CTA members; or 3) members of Student CTA. Applicants must be interested in preparing for a teaching career in public education or already engaged in such a career.

Financial data Stipends vary each year; recently, they ranged up to $6,000.

Duration 1 year.

Number awarded Varies each year; recently, 24 were awarded: 1 to a CTA member, 10 to children of CTA members, and 13 to Student CTA members.

Deadline February of each year.

[1089]
MINORITIES IN CANCER RESEARCH JANE COOK WRIGHT LECTURESHIP

American Association for Cancer Research
Attn: Scientific Awards
615 Chestnut Street, 17th Floor
Philadelphia, PA 19106-4404
(215) 446-7128   Toll Free: (866) 423-3965
Fax: (267) 765-1047   E-mail: awards@aacr.org
Web: www.aacr.org

Summary To recognize and reward investigators who, through leadership or by example, have furthered the advancement of Asian American or other minorities in cancer research.

Eligibility This award is available to investigators affiliated with institutions in any country involved in cancer research, cancer medicine, or cancer-related biomedical science. Nominees must have made meritorious contributions to the field of cancer research and, through leadership or by example, have furthered the advancement of minority investigators in cancer research. Selection is based on the nominee's contributions to cancer research and to the advancement of minorities; no consideration is given to age, race, gender, nationality, geographic location, or religious or political views.

Financial data The award consists of an honorarium of $5,000, a commemorative item, and support for the winner and a guest to attend the sponsor's annual meeting where the winner delivers a major lecture.

Duration The award is presented annually.

Additional information This award was established in 2006.

Number awarded 1 each year.

Deadline October of each year.

[1090]
MINORITY FACULTY DEVELOPMENT SCHOLARSHIP AWARD IN PHYSICAL THERAPY

American Physical Therapy Association
Attn: Honors and Awards Program
1111 North Fairfax Street
Alexandria, VA 22314-1488
(703) 684-APTA   Toll Free: (800) 999-APTA, ext. 8082
Fax: (703) 684-7343   TDD: (703) 683-6748
E-mail: honorsandawards@apta.org
Web: www.apta.org

Summary To provide financial assistance to Asian American and other minority faculty members in physical therapy who are interested in working on a post-professional doctoral degree.

Eligibility This program is open to U.S. citizens and permanent residents who are members of the following minority groups: Asian, African American or Black, Native Hawaiian or other Pacific Islander, American Indian or Alaska Native, or Hispanic/Latino. Applicants must be full-time faculty members, teaching in an accredited or developing professional physical therapist education program, who will have completed the equivalent of 2 full semesters of post-professional doctoral course work. They must possess a license to practice physical therapy in a U.S. jurisdiction and be enrolled as a student in an accredited post-professional doctoral program whose content has a demonstrated relationship to physical therapy. Along with their application, they must submit a personal essay on their professional goals, including their plans to contribute to the profession and minority services. Selection is based on contributions in the area of minority affairs and services and contributions to the profession of physical therapy. Preference is given to members of the American Physical Therapy Association (APTA).

Financial data A stipend is awarded (amount not specified).

Duration 1 year.

Additional information This program began in 1999.

Number awarded 1 or more each year.

Deadline November of each year.

[1091]
MULTICULTURAL AUDIENCE DEVELOPMENT INITIATIVE INTERNSHIPS

Metropolitan Museum of Art
Attn: Internship Programs
1000 Fifth Avenue
New York, NY 10028-0198
(212) 570-3710   Fax: (212) 570-3782
E-mail: mmainterns@metmuseum.org
Web: www.metmuseum.org

Summary To provide summer work experience at the Metropolitan Museum of Art to college undergraduates, graduate students, and recent graduates who are Asian Americans or from other diverse backgrounds.

Eligibility This program is open to members of diverse groups who are undergraduate juniors and seniors, students currently working on a master's degree, or individuals who completed a bachelor's or master's degree within the past year. Ph.D. students may be eligible to apply during the first 12 months of their program, provided they have not yet achieved candidacy. Students from various academic backgrounds are encouraged to apply, but they must be interested in preparing for a career in the arts and museum fields. Freshmen and sophomores are not eligible.

Financial data The stipend is $3,750.

Duration 10 weeks, beginning in June.

Additional information Interns are assigned to departmental projects (curatorial, administration, or education) at the Metropolitan Museum of Art; other assignments may include giving gallery talks and working at the Visitor Information Center. The assignment is for 35 hours a week. The internships are funded by the Multicultural Audience Initiative at the museum.

Number awarded 1 or more each year.

Deadline January of each year.

[1092]
NATIONAL ALUMNI CHAPTER GRANTS

Kappa Omicron Nu
Attn: Awards Committee
1749 Hamilton Road, Suite 106
Okemos, MI 48864
(517) 351-8335   Fax: (517) 351-8336
E-mail: info@kon.org
Web: www.kon.org/awards/grants.html

Summary To provide financial assistance to members of Kappa Omicron Nu, an honor society in the human sciences, especially Asian Americans and other minorities, who are interested in conducting research.

Eligibility This program is open to 1) individual scholars who are members of the society; and 2) research teams where the leader is a member of the society. Applicants must be interested in conducting research in family and consumer sciences or any of its related specializations. The research approach should be integrative in nature and shall make connections across specializations to pursue problems or questions. Special consideration is given to research that studies the cultural and religious differences affecting leadership, especially Asian, Hispanic, and Native American. Another topic of interest is the exploration of how minority students "strike out on their own" in career development.

Financial data The grant is $1,000.

Duration 1 year; multi-year funding may be accomplished by including a multi-year management plan in the initial proposal and reporting successful accomplishment of previous objectives annually.

Additional information The sponsor defines the "human sciences" to include athletic training, design, education, exercise science, family and consumer sciences, financial planning, food science and human nutrition, gerontology, health sciences, hotel/restaurant management, human development, interior design and human environment, kinesiology, leadership, merchandising management, policy analysis and management, social work, textiles and apparel, and wellness. Funding for these grants is provided by the National Alumni Chapter of Kappa Omicron Nu.

Number awarded   1 or more each year.

Deadline   February of each year.

[1093]
NATIONAL CENTER FOR ATMOSPHERIC RESEARCH POSTDOCTORAL FELLOWSHIPS

National Center for Atmospheric Research
Attn: Advanced Study Program
3090 Center Green Drive
P.O. Box 3000
Boulder, CO 80307-3000
(303) 497-1601   Fax: (303) 497-1646
E-mail: asp-apply@asp.ucar.edu
Web: www.asp.ucar.edu/pdfp/pd_announcement.php

Summary   To provide funding to recent doctorates, especially Asian Americans and other minorities, who wish to conduct research at the National Center for Atmospheric Research (NCAR) in Boulder, Colorado.

Eligibility   This program is open to recent Ph.D.s and Sc.D.s in atmospheric sciences as well as specialists from such disciplines as applied mathematics, biology, chemistry, computer science, economics, engineering, geography, geology, physics, and science education. Applicants must be interested in conducting research at the center in atmospheric sciences and global change. Selection is based on the applicant's scientific capability and potential, originality and independence, and the match between their interests and the research opportunities at the center. Applications from women and minorities are encouraged.

Financial data   The stipend is $60,500 in the first year and $62,000 in the second year. Fellows also receive life and health insurance, a relocation allowance, an allowance of $750 for moving and storing personal belongings, and scientific travel and registration fee reimbursement up to $3,500 per year.

Duration   2 years.

Additional information   NCAR is operated by the University Corporation for Atmospheric Research (a consortium of universities and research institutes) and sponsored by the National Science Foundation.

Number awarded   Varies; currently, up to 9 each year.

Deadline   January of each year.

[1094]
NATIONAL URBAN FELLOWS PROGRAM

National Urban Fellows, Inc.
Attn: Program Director
1120 Avenue of the Americas, Fourth Floor
New York, NY 10036
(212) 730-1700   Fax: (212) 730-1823
E-mail: info@nuf.org
Web: www.nuf.org/fellows-overview

Summary   To provide mid-career public sector professionals, especially Asian Americans and other people of color, with an opportunity to strengthen leadership skills through a master's degree program coupled with a mentorship.

Eligibility   This program is open to U.S. citizens who have a bachelor's degree, have at 5 to 7 years of professional work experience with 2 years in a management capacity, have demonstrated leadership capacity with potential for further growth, have a GPA of 3.0 or higher, and can demonstrate a commitment to public service. Applicants must submit a 1-page autobiographical statement, a 2-page personal statement, and a 2-page statement on their career goals. They may be of any racial or ethnic background, but the program's goal is to increase the number of competent administrators from underrepresented ethnic and cultural groups at all levels of public and private urban management organizations. Semifinalists are interviewed.

Financial data   The stipend is $25,000. Fellows are required to pay a $500 registration fee and a $7,500 co-investment tuition payment upon acceptance and enrollment in the program.

Duration   14 months.

Additional information   The program begins with a summer semester of study at Bernard M. Baruch College of the City University of New York. Following this, fellows spend 9 months in mentorship assignments with a senior administrator in a government agency, a major nonprofit, or a foundation. The final summer is spent in another semester of study at Baruch College. Fellows who successfully complete all requirements are granted a master's of public administration from that college. A $150 processing fee must accompany each application.

Number awarded   Approximately 40 to 50 each year.

Deadline   December of each year.

[1095]
NBCC MINORITY FELLOWSHIP PROGRAM

National Board for Certified Counselors
Attn: NBCC Foundation
3 Terrace Way
Greensboro, NC 27403
(336) 232-0376   Fax: (336) 232-0010
E-mail: foundation@nbcc.org
Web: nbccf-mfpdr.applicantstack.com/x/detail/a2b3qvixcgjm

Summary   To provide financial assistance to doctoral candidates, especially Asian Americans and those from other racially and ethnically diverse populations, and who are interested in working on a degree in mental health and/or substance abuse counseling.

Eligibility   This program is open to U.S. citizens and permanent residents who are enrolled full time in an accredited doctoral degree mental health and/or substance abuse and addictions counseling program. Applicants must have a National Certified Counselor or equivalent credential. They must commit to provide mental health and substance abuse services to racially and ethnically diverse populations. Asian Americans, African Americans, Alaska Natives, American Indians, Hispanics/Latinos, Native Hawaiians, and Pacific Islanders are especially encouraged to apply. Applicants must be able to commit to providing substance abuse and addictions counseling services to underserved minority populations for at least 2 years after graduation.

Financial data   The stipend is $20,000.

Duration   1 year.

Additional information This program began in 2012 with support from the Substance Abuse and Mental Health Services Administration.

Number awarded 23 each year.

Deadline June of each year.

[1096]
NEW INITIATIVES GRANTS

Kappa Omicron Nu
Attn: Awards Committee
1749 Hamilton Road, Suite 106
Okemos, MI 48864
(517) 351-8335   Fax: (517) 351-8336
E-mail: info@kon.org
Web: www.kon.org/awards/grants.html

Summary To provide financial assistance to members of Kappa Omicron Nu, an honor society in the human sciences, especially Asian Americans and other minorities, who are interested in conducting research.

Eligibility This program is open to 1) individual members of the society; and 2) research teams where the leader is a member of the society. Applicants must be interested in conducting research in family and consumer sciences or any of its related specializations. The research approach should be integrative in nature and must make connections across specializations to pursue problems or questions. Special consideration is given to research that studies the cultural and religious differences that affect leadership, especially Asian, Hispanic, and Native American. Another topic of interest is the exploration of how minority students "strike out on their own" in career development.

Financial data The maximum grant is $3,000.

Duration 1 year; multi-year funding may be accomplished by including a multi-year management plan in the initial proposal and reporting successful accomplishment of previous objectives annually.

Additional information The sponsor defines the "human sciences" to include athletic training, design, education, exercise science, family and consumer sciences, financial planning, food science and human nutrition, gerontology, health sciences, hotel/restaurant management, human development, interior design and human environment, kinesiology, leadership, merchandising management, policy analysis and management, social work, textiles and apparel, and wellness. Funding for these grants is provided by the New Initiatives Fund of Kappa Omicron Nu.

Number awarded 1 or more each year.

Deadline February of each year.

[1097]
NEW YORK FOUNDATION FOR THE ARTS ARTISTS' FELLOWSHIPS

New York Foundation for the Arts
20 Jay Street, Seventh Floor
Brooklyn, NY 11202
(212) 366-6900   Fax: (212) 366-1778
E-mail: fellowships@nyfa.org
Web: www.nyfa.org/Content/Show/Artists'%20Fellowships

Summary To provide funding for career development to creative artists living and working in the state of New York, especially Asian Americans and other from diverse backgrounds.

Eligibility Artists in New York who are more than 18 years of age are eligible to apply for this program if they are not currently enrolled in a degree program. Applicants must have lived in the state for at least 2 years at the time of application. They are required to submit, along with the application form, samples of current work. Awards are presented in a 3-year cycle with 5 fields each year: crafts/sculpture, printmaking/drawing/book arts, nonfiction literature, poetry, and digital/electronic arts (2017); fiction, folk/traditional arts, interdisciplinary work, painting, and video/film (2018); and architecture/environmental structures/design, choreography, music/sound, photography, and playwriting/screenwriting (2019). Selection is based on artistic excellence. The program is committed to supporting artists of diverse cultural, sexual, and ethnic backgrounds.

Financial data The grant is $7,000. Some special awards are larger.

Duration 1 year.

Additional information Since this program began in 1985, the sponsor has awarded more than $27 million to more than 4,000 artists. Named awards include the Geri Ashur Screenwriting Award (for $10,000), the Gregory Millard Fellowships (supported by the New York City Department of Cultural Affairs for artists in several categories), the Lily Auchincloss Foundation Fellow (painting), the Deutsche Bank Americas Foundation Fellow (painting), and the Basil H. Alkazzi Award for Excellence (which awards $40,000 to 2 painters). Major funding for this program is provided by the New York State Council on the Arts and the New York City Department of Cultural Affairs. Other support is provided by the Lily Auchincloss Foundation, Deutsche Bank Americas Foundation, and the Milton & Sally Avery Arts Foundation. Recipients must perform a public service activity coordinated by the Artists and Audiences Exchange.

Number awarded Varies each year; recently, 91 of these fellowships, worth $642,000, were awarded.

Deadline January of each year.

[1098]
NJLA DIVERSITY SCHOLARSHIP

New Jersey Library Association
c/o Kassundra Miller, Scholarship Committee Co-Chair
Wood-Ridge Memorial Library
231 Hackensack Street
Wood-Ridge, NJ 07075
(201) 438-2455   Fax: (201) 438-8399
E-mail: miller@woodridge.bccls.org
Web: www.njlamembers.org/scholarship

Summary To provide financial assistance to New Jersey residents who are Asian Americans or members of other minority groups and interested in working on a graduate or postgraduate degree in public librarianship at a school in any state.

Eligibility This program is open to residents of New Jersey and individuals who have worked in a New Jersey library for at least 12 months. Applicants must be members of a minority group (Asian/Pacific Islander, African American, Latino/Hispanic, or Native American/Native Alaskan). They must be enrolled or planning to enroll at an ALA-accredited school of library science in any state to work on a graduate or postgraduate degree in librarianship. Along with their application, they must submit an essay of 150 to 250 words explaining their choice of librarianship as a profession. An interview is required. Selection is based on academic ability and financial need.

Financial data The stipend is $850.

Duration 1 year.

Number awarded 1 each year.

Deadline February of each year.

[1099]
NORTH AMERICAN TAIWANESE MEDICAL ASSOCIATION SCHOLARSHIPS

North American Taiwanese Medical Association
  Foundation
Attn: Director
7923 Garden Grove Boulevard
Garden Grove, CA 92841
(714) 898-2275   Fax: (714) 373-2659
E-mail: hsu0316@hotmail.com
Web: www.natma.org/scholarshipinfo.html

Summary To provide financial assistance for additional study to Taiwanese American medical, dental, and allied health graduate students, residents, or fellows.

Eligibility This program is open to medical, dental, and allied health students, residents, or fellows who are of Taiwanese American descent. Applicants must have completed at least 1 year of graduate school study and be enrolled in a program of training at an accredited U.S. institution or program. Along with their application, they must submit a 1-page essay on ways that the sponsor can increase awareness of the services and benefits that it provides to its members and the greater community, a transcript, and 2 letters of recommendation.

Financial data The stipend is $2,000.

Duration 1 year.

Number awarded 3 each year.

Deadline June of each year.

[1100]
NOTRE DAME INSTITUTE FOR ADVANCED STUDY RESIDENTIAL FELLOWSHIPS

University of Notre Dame
Institute for Advanced Study
Attn: Programs Administrator
1124 Flanner Hall
Notre Dame, IN 46556
(574) 631-1305   Fax: (574) 631-8997
E-mail: csherman@nd.edu
Web: ndias.nd.edu/fellowships/residential

Summary To provide funding to scholars at all levels, especially Asian Americans and members of other underrepresented groups, who are interested in conducting research on topics of interest to the Notre Dame Institute for Advanced Study (NDIAS) while in residence at the institute.

Eligibility This program is open to faculty, scholars, public intellectuals, fellows from other institutes, and professional researchers in all disciplines, including the arts, engineering, the humanities, law, and the natural, social, and physical sciences. Applicants must be interested in conducting research that aligns with the intellectual orientation of the NDIAS,

which asks scholars "to include questions of values in their analyses, to integrate diverse disciplines, and to ask how their findings advance civilization." They must be able to demonstrate excellent records of scholarly, artistic, or research accomplishment in their field; ability to interact with other fellows and to engage in collegial discussions of research presentations; a willingness to contribute to a cooperative community of scholars; and projects that touch on normative, integrative, or ultimate questions, especially as the involve the Catholic intellectual tradition. Applications are especially encouraged from traditionally underrepresented groups. There are no citizenship requirements; non-U.S. nationals are welcome to apply.

Financial data The grant is $60,000 for a full academic year or prorated amounts for shorter periods. Other benefits include subsidized visiting faculty housing, research support up to $1,000, a private office at the institute, a computer and printer, access to university libraries and other facilities, and weekly institute seminars and events.

Duration Up to 1 academic year.

Number awarded Varies each year; recently, 14 were awarded.

Deadline October of each year.

[1101]
NWSA WOMEN OF COLOR CAUCUS-*FRONTIERS* STUDENT ESSAY AWARD

National Women's Studies Association
Attn: Women of Color Caucus
11 East Mount Royal Avenue, Suite 100
Baltimore, MD 21202
(410) 528-0355   Fax: (410) 528-0357
E-mail: awards@nwsa.org
Web: www.nwsa.org/content.asp?admin=Y&contentid=16

Summary To recognize and reward essays on feminist issues written by Asian American or other women of color graduate students and recent postdoctorates who are members of the National Women's Studies Association (NWSA).

Eligibility This competition is open to women of color (defined as those of Asian, Pacific Islander, African, Middle East, American Indian, Alaskan Native or Latin American descent) who are currently enrolled in a graduate or professional program. Recipients of Ph.D.s who completed their degree requirements within the past year are also eligible. Applicants must submit a scholarly essay that provides critical theoretical discussions and/or analyses of issues and experiences of women and girls of color. They must be members of the NWSA.

Financial data The award is $500.

Duration The award is presented annually.

Number awarded 1 each year.

Deadline May of each year.

[1102]
OKLAHOMA CAREERTECH FOUNDATION TEACHER RECRUITMENT/RETENTION SCHOLARSHIP FOR TEACHERS

Oklahoma CareerTech Foundation
Attn: Administrator
1500 West Seventh Avenue
Stillwater, OK 74074-4364
(405) 743-5453   Fax: (405) 743-5541
E-mail: leden@careertech.ok.gov
Web: www.okcareertech.org

Summary To provide financial assistance to residents of Oklahoma who are Asian Americans or reflect the diversity of the state in other ways and are interested in attending a college or university in the state to earn a credential or certification for a career in the Oklahoma CareerTech system.

Eligibility This program is open to residents of Oklahoma who are incumbent CareerTech teachers working toward a CareerTech credential or certification at an institution of higher education in the state. Applicants must reflect the ethnic diversity of the state. Along with their application, they must submit brief statements on their interest and commitment to the CareerTech teaching profession and their financial need.

Financial data The stipend ranges from $500 per semester to $1,500 per year.

Duration 1 semester; may be renewed, provided the recipient maintains a GPA of 2.5 or higher.

Number awarded 1 or more each year.

Deadline May of each year.

[1103]
ONLINE BIBLIOGRAPHIC SERVICES/ TECHNICAL SERVICES JOINT RESEARCH GRANT

American Association of Law Libraries
Attn: Online Bibliographic Services Special Interest
  Section
105 West Adams Street, Suite 3300
Chicago, IL 60603
(312) 939-4764   Fax: (312) 431-1097
E-mail: aallhq@aall.org
Web: www.aallnet.org

Summary To provide funding to members of the American Association of Law Libraries (AALL), especially Asian Americans and other minorities, who are interested in conducting a research project related to technical services in the United States, Canada, or any other country.

Eligibility This program is open to AALL members who are technical services law librarians. Preference is given to members of the Online Bibliographic Services and Technical Services Special Interest Sections, although members of other special interest sections are eligible if their work relates to technical services law librarianship. Applicants must be interested in conducting research that will enhance technical services law librarianship. Women and minorities are especially encouraged to apply. Preference is given to projects that can be completed in the United States or Canada, although foreign research projects are given consideration.

Financial data Grants range up to $1,000.

Duration 1 year.

Number awarded 1 or more each year.

Deadline March or September of each year.

[1104]
PATRICIA M. LOWRIE DIVERSITY LEADERSHIP SCHOLARSHIP

Association of American Veterinary Medical Colleges
Attn: Diversity Committee
1101 Vermont Avenue, N.W., Suite 301
Washington, DC 20005-3536
(202) 371-9195, ext. 147   Toll Free: (877) 862-2740
Fax: (202) 842-0773   E-mail: lgreenhill@aavmc.org
Web: www.aavmc.org

Summary To provide financial assistance to veterinary students who are Asian Americans or have promoted diversity in the profession in other ways.

Eligibility This program is open to second-, third-, and fourth-year students at veterinary colleges in the United States. Applicants must have a demonstrated record of contributing to enhancing diversity and inclusion through course projects, co-curricular activities, outreach, domestic and community engagement, research, and/or an early reputation for influencing others to be inclusive. Along with their application, they must submit a 3-page personal statement that describes 1) why diversity and inclusion are important to them personally and professionally; 2) how they intend to continue contributing to diversity and inclusion efforts in the veterinary profession after graduation; and 3) what it might mean to be honored as a recipient of this scholarship. They must also indicate how they express their race and/or ethnicity (Asian, American Indian or Alaskan, Black or African American, Hispanic, Native Hawaiian or Pacific Islander, or White) and how they express their gender (male, female, transgender spectrum, or other). Selection is based primarily on documentation of a demonstrated commitment to promoting diversity in academic veterinary medicine; consideration is also given to academic achievement, the student's broader community service record, and financial need.

Financial data The stipend is $6,000.

Duration 1 year; nonrenewable.

Additional information This program began in 2013.

Number awarded 1 each odd-numbered year.

Deadline October of each even-numbered year.

[1105]
PAUL HOCH DISTINGUISHED SERVICE AWARD

American College of Neuropsychopharmacology
Attn: Executive Office
5034-A Thoroughbred Lane
Brentwood, TN 37027
(615) 324-2360   Fax: (615) 523-1715
E-mail: acnp@acnp.org
Web: www.acnp.org/programs/awards.aspx

Summary To recognize and reward members of the American College of Neuropsychopharmacology (ACNP), especially Asian Americans and other minorities who have contributed outstanding service to the organization.

Eligibility This award is available to ACNP members who have made unusually significant contributions to the College. The emphasis of the award is on service to the organization, not on teaching, clinical, or research accomplishments. Any member or fellow of ACNP may nominate another member. Nomination of women and minorities is highly encouraged.

Financial data The award consists of an expense-paid trip to the ACNP annual meeting, a monetary honorarium, and a plaque.

Duration The award is presented annually.

Additional information This award was first presented in 1965.

Number awarded 1 each year.

Deadline Nominations must be submitted by June of each year.

[1106]
PAUL TOBENKIN MEMORIAL AWARD

Columbia University
Attn: Graduate School of Journalism
Program Manager, Professional Prizes
2950 Broadway
Mail Code 3805
New York, NY 10027
(212) 854-6468   Fax: (212) 854-3148
E-mail: cm3443@columbia.edu
Web: www.journalism.columbia.edu

Summary To recognize and reward outstanding newspaper writing that reflects the spirit of Paul Tobenkin, who fought all his life against racial and religious hatred, bigotry, bias, intolerance, and discrimination.

Eligibility Materials reflecting the spirit of Paul Tobenkin may be submitted by newspaper reporters in the United States, editors of their publications, or interested third parties. The items submitted must have been published during the previous calendar year in a weekly or daily newspaper.

Financial data The award is $1,500 plus a plaque.

Duration The award is presented annually.

Additional information This award was first presented in 1961.

Number awarded 1 or more each year.

Deadline March of each year.

[1107]
PEARSON EARLY CAREER GRANT

American Psychological Foundation
750 First Street, N.E.
Washington, DC 20002-4242
(202) 336-5843   Fax: (202) 336-5812
E-mail: foundation@apa.org
Web: www.apa.org/apf/funding/pearson.aspx

Summary To provide funding to early-career psychologists, especially Asian Americans and members of other underrepresented groups, who are interested in conducting a project in an area of critical society need.

Eligibility This program is open to psychologists who have an Ed.D., Psy.D., or Ph.D. from an accredited experience and no more than 10 years of postdoctoral experience. Applicants must be interested in conducting a project to improve areas of critical need in society, including (but not limited to) innovative scientifically-based clinical work with serious mental illness, serious emotional disturbance, incarcerated or homeless individuals, children with serious emotional disturbance (SED), or adults with serious mental illness (SMI). Selection is based on conformance with stated program goals and

qualifications, quality and impact of proposed work, innovation and contribution to the field with proposed project, applicant's demonstrated competence and capability to execute the proposed work. The sponsor encourages applications from individuals who represent diversity in race, ethnicity, gender, age, disability, and sexual orientation.

Financial data The grant is $12,000.

Duration 1 year.

Additional information This grant, supported by Pearson Education, was first awarded in 2010.

Number awarded 1 each year.

Deadline December of each year.

[1108]
PEN OPEN BOOK AWARD

PEN American Center
Attn: Literary Awards Associate
588 Broadway, Suite 303
New York, NY 10012
(212) 334-1660, ext. 4813   Fax: (212) 334-2181
E-mail: awards@pen.org
Web: www.pen.org/content/pen-open-book-award-5000

Summary To recognize and reward Asian American and othr authors of color from any country.

Eligibility This award is presented to an author of color (Asian, African, Arab, Caribbean, Latino, and Native American) whose book-length writings were published in the United States during the current calendar year. Works of fiction, literary nonfiction, biography/memoir, poetry, and other works of literary character are strongly preferred. U.S. citizenship or residency is not required. Nominations must be submitted by publishers or literary agents. Self-published books are not eligible.

Financial data The prize is $5,000.

Duration The prizes are awarded annually.

Additional information This prize was formerly known as the Beyond Margins Award. The entry fee is $75.

Number awarded 1 or 2 each year.

Deadline August of each year.

[1109]
POSTDOCTORAL FELLOWSHIP IN MENTAL HEALTH AND SUBSTANCE ABUSE SERVICES

American Psychological Association
Attn: Minority Fellowship Program
750 First Street, N.E.
Washington, DC 20002-4242
(202) 336-6127   Fax: (202) 336-6012
TDD: (202) 336-6123   E-mail: mfp@apa.org
Web: www.apa.org/pi/mfp/psychology/postdoc/index.aspx

Summary To provide financial assistance to postdoctoral scholars interested in a program of research training related to providing mental health and substance abuse services to Asian Americans and other ethnic minority populations.

Eligibility This program is open to U.S. citizens, nationals, and permanent residents who received a doctoral degree in psychology in the last 5 years. Applicants must be interested in participating in a program of training under a qualified sponsor for research and have a strong commitment to a career in ethnic minority behavioral health services or policy. Members of ethnic minority groups (Asian Americans, African

Americans, Hispanics/Latinos, American Indians, Alaskan Natives, Native Hawaiians, and other Pacific Islanders) are especially encouraged to apply. Selection is based on commitment to a career in ethnic minority mental health service delivery or public policy; qualifications of the sponsor; the fit between career goals and training environment selected; merit of the training proposal; potential as a future leader in ethnic minority psychology, demonstrated through accomplishments and goals; consistency between the applicant's work and the goals of the program; and letters of recommendation.

Financial data The stipend depends on the number of years of research experience and is equivalent to the standard postdoctoral stipend level of the National Institutes of Health (recently ranging from $47,484 for no years of experience to $58,510 for 7 or more years of experience).

Duration 1 academic or calendar year; may be renewed for 1 additional year.

Additional information Funding is provided by the U.S. Substance Abuse and Mental Health Services Administration.

Number awarded Varies each year.

Deadline January of each year.

[1110]
POSTDOCTORAL FELLOWSHIPS OF THE CONSORTIUM FOR FACULTY DIVERSITY

Consortium for Faculty Diversity at Liberal Arts Colleges
c/o Gettysburg College
Provost's Office
300 North Washington Street
Campus Box 410
Gettysburg, PA 17325
(717) 337-6796   E-mail: sgockows@gettysburg.edu
Web: www.gettysburg.edu

Summary To make available the facilities of liberal arts colleges to scholars who recently received their doctoral/advanced degree and will enhance diversity at their college.

Eligibility This program is open to scholars in the liberal arts and engineering who are U.S. citizens or permanent residents and received the Ph.D. or M.F.A. degree within the past 5 years. Applicants must be interested in a residency at a participating institution that is part of the Consortium for Faculty Diversity at Liberal Arts Colleges. They must be able to enhance diversity at the institution.

Financial data Fellows receive a stipend equivalent to the average salary paid by the host college to beginning assistant professors. Modest funds are made available to finance the fellow's proposed research, subject to the usual institutional procedures.

Duration 1 year.

Additional information The following schools are participating in the program: Allegheny College, Amherst College, Bard College, Bowdoin College, Bryn Mawr College, Bucknell University, Carleton College, Centenary College of Louisiana, Centre College, College of the Holy Cross, Colorado College, Denison University, DePauw University, Dickinson College, Gettysburg College, Grinnell College, Gustavus Adolphus College, Hamilton College, Haverford College, Hobart and William Smith Colleges, Juniata College, Lafayette College, Lawrence University, Luther College, Macalester College, Mount Holyoke College, Muhlenberg College, Oberlin College, Pitzer College, Pomona College, Reed College, Scripps College, Skidmore College, Smith College, Southwestern University, St. Lawrence University, St. Olaf College, Swarthmore College, The College of Wooster, Trinity College, University of Richmond, Vassar College, and Wellesley College. Fellows are expected to teach at least 60% of a regular full-time faculty member's load, participate in departmental seminars, and interact with students.

Number awarded Varies each year; recently, 23 of the 43 member institutions made a total of 51 appointments through this program.

Deadline October of each year.

[1111]
PRESIDENTIAL EARLY CAREER AWARDS FOR SCIENTISTS AND ENGINEERS

National Science and Technology Council
Executive Office of the President
Attn: Office of Science and Technology Policy
1650 Pennsylvania Avenue
Washington, DC 20504
(202) 456-4444   E-mail: NSTC@OST.eop.gov
Web: www.whitehouse.gov/administration/eop/ostp/nstc

Summary To recognize and reward the nation's most outstanding young science and engineering faculty members, especially Asian Americans and other minorities, by providing them with additional research funding.

Eligibility Eligible for these awards are U.S. citizens, nationals, and permanent residents who have been selected to receive research grants from other departments of the U.S. government. Recipients of designated research grant programs are automatically considered for these Presidential Early Career Awards for Scientists and Engineers (PECASE). Most of the participating programs encourage applications from racial/ethnic minority individuals, women, and persons with disabilities.

Financial data Awards carry a grant of at least $80,000 per year.

Duration 5 years.

Additional information The departments with research programs that nominate candidates for the PECASE program are include 1) the Department of Agriculture, primarily from the Agricultural Research Service; 2) the Department of Commerce, from the National Oceanic and Atmospheric Administration and the National Institute of Standards and Technology; 3) the Department of Defense, from the Office of Naval Research, the Air Force Office of Scientific Research Broad, and the Army Research Office; 4) the Department of Energy, from the national laboratories and the Office of Science; 5) the Department of Health and Human Services, from the National Institutes of Health; 6) the National Aeronautics and Space Administration, from programs funded through the traditional research grant process or the unsolicited proposal process; and 9) the National Science Foundation, from its Faculty Early Career Development (CAREER) Program. Other agencies that occasionally nominate recipients include the Department of Education, the Department of Interior, the Department of Transportation, the Department of Veterans Affairs, the Environmental Protection Agency, and the National Security Agency. For a list of the names, addresses, and telephone numbers of contact persons at each of the participating agencies, contact the Office of Science and Technology Policy.

Number awarded Varies each year; recently, 105 were granted.

Deadline Deadline not specified.

[1112]
PRIMARY CARE RESOURCE INITIATIVE FOR MISSOURI

Missouri Department of Health and Senior Services
Attn: Primary Care and Rural Health
P.O. Box 570
Jefferson City, MO 65102-0570
(573) 751-6219   Toll Free: (800) 891-7415
Fax: (573) 522-8146   E-mail: info@health.mo.gov
Web: health.mo.gov/living/families/primarycare/primo

Summary To provide scholarship/loans to residents of Missouri, especially Asian Americans and other minorities, who are interested in working as a health care professional in an underserved area of the state following graduation.

Eligibility This program is open to residents of Missouri who have lived for 1 or more years in the state for purposes other than attending an educational institution. Applicants must have been accepted by or currently be attending a Missouri school offering a course of study leading to a degree in 1) primary care medicine; 2) dentistry; 3) dental hygiene; 4) psychiatry; 5) psychology; 6) licensed clinical social work; or 7) licensed professional counseling. Physicians and dentists in primary care residency programs are also eligible. Priority is given to residents of medically underserved areas in Missouri, minority group members, and previous recipients.

Financial data Loans range from $5,000 to $20,000 per year. This is a scholarship/loan program. Loans of 5 years or more are forgiven at the rate of 20% per year for qualifying employment in an area of defined need (a geographic area or a population that is experiencing a shortage of primary health care providers in Missouri). Loans for less than 5 years are forgiven on a year-for-year basis. If the loan is not forgiven by service, it must be repaid within 60 months at 9.5% interest.

Duration Full-time undergraduate students may receive up to 4 loans. Part-time medical students may receive loans for up to 4 or 6 years, depending on the length of their program. Physicians and dentists in primary care residency programs may receive up to 3 years of loans.

Additional information This program is also known as the PRIMO Loan Program.

Number awarded Varies each year; recently, a total of 32 of these loans were granted.

Deadline April of each year.

[1113]
PRINT AND ONLINE NEWS INTERNSHIP GRANT

Asian American Journalists Association
Attn: Student Programs Coordinator
5 Third Street, Suite 1108
San Francisco, CA 94103
(415) 346-2051, ext. 102   Fax: (415) 346-6343
E-mail: programs@aaja.org
Web: www.aaja.org/apply-for-a-scholarship-now

Summary To provide a supplemental grant to members of the Asian American Journalists Association (AAJA) working as a summer intern at a print or online journalism company.

Eligibility This program is open to AAJA members who are full-time college students or recent college graduates. Applicants must have secured a summer internship at a print or online news outlet before they apply. Along with their application, they must submit a 200-word essay on why they want to prepare for a career in print or online journalism, what they want to gain from the experience, and why AAJA's mission is important to them; a letter of recommendation; a resume; proof of age (at least 18 years); verification of an internship; and statement of financial need.

Financial data The grant is $1,000. Funds are to be used for living expenses or transportation.

Duration Summer months.

Additional information This program began in 2006 as the William Woo Internship Fund.

Number awarded 1 each year.

Deadline April of each year.

[1114]
R. ROBERT & SALLY FUNDERBURG RESEARCH AWARD IN GASTRIC CANCER

American Gastroenterological Association
Attn: AGA Research Foundation
Research Awards Manager
4930 Del Ray Avenue
Bethesda, MD 20814-2512
(301) 222-4012   Fax: (301) 654-5920
E-mail: awards@gastro.org
Web: www.gastro.org

Summary To provide funding to established investigators, especially Asian American and other minorities, who are working on research that enhances fundamental understanding of gastric cancer pathobiology.

Eligibility This program is open to faculty at accredited North American institutions who have established themselves as independent investigators in the field of gastric biology, pursuing novel approaches to gastric mucosal cell biology, including the fields of gastric mucosal cell biology, regeneration and regulation of cell growth, inflammation as precancerous lesions, genetics of gastric carcinoma, oncogenes in gastric epithelial malignancies, epidemiology of gastric cancer, etiology of gastric epithelial malignancies, or clinical research in diagnosis or treatment of gastric carcinoma. Applicants must be individual members of the American Gastroenterological Association (AGA). Women and minority investigators are strongly encouraged to apply. Selection is based on the novelty, feasibility, and significance of the proposal. Preference is given to novel approaches.

Financial data The grant is $50,000 per year. Funds are to be used for the salary of the investigator. Indirect costs are not allowed.

Duration 2 years.

Number awarded 1 each year.

Deadline August of each year.

[1115]
RALPH J. BUNCHE AWARD

American Political Science Association
1527 New Hampshire Avenue, N.W.
Washington, DC 20036-1206
(202) 483-2512   Fax: (202) 483-2657
E-mail: apsa@apsanet.org
Web: www.apsanet.org

Summary   To recognize and reward outstanding scholarly books on ethnic/cultural pluralism.

Eligibility   Eligible to be nominated (by publishers or individuals) are scholarly political science books issued the previous year that explore issues of ethnic and/or cultural pluralism.

Financial data   The award is $1,000.

Duration   The award is presented annually.

Additional information   This award was first presented in 1978.

Number awarded   1 each year.

Deadline   February of each year.

[1116]
REGINALD F. LEWIS FELLOWSHIP FOR LAW TEACHING

Harvard Law School
Attn: Lewis Committee
Griswold Two South
1525 Massachusetts Avenue
Cambridge, MA 02138
(617) 495-3109
E-mail: LewisFellowship@law.harvard.edu
Web: hls.harvard.edu

Summary   To provide funding to law school graduates, especially Asian Americans and other of color, who are preparing for a career in law teaching and are interested in a program of research and training at Harvard Law School.

Eligibility   This program is open to recent graduates of law school who have demonstrated an interest in law scholarship and teaching. Applicants must be interested in spending time in residence at Harvard Law School where they will audit courses, attend workshops, and follow a schedule of research under the sponsorship of the committee. The program encourages the training of prospective law teachers who will enhance the diversity of the profession and especially encourages applications from candidates of color.

Financial data   The stipend is $50,000 per year.

Duration   2 years.

Number awarded   1 each year.

Deadline   January of each year.

[1117]
RESEARCH AND TRAINING PROGRAM ON POVERTY AND PUBLIC POLICY POSTDOCTORAL FELLOWSHIPS

University of Michigan
Gerald R. Ford School of Public Policy
Attn: National Poverty Center
Joan and Sanford Weill Hall
735 South State Street, Room 5100
Ann Arbor, MI 48109-3091
(734) 764-3490   Fax: (734) 763-9181
E-mail: npcinfo@umich.edu
Web: npc.umich.edu/opportunities/visiting

Summary   To provide funding to Asian American and other minority postdoctorates interested in conducting research and pursuing intensive training on poverty-related public policy issues at the University of Michigan.

Eligibility   This program is open to U.S. citizens and permanent residents who are members of a minority group that is underrepresented in the social sciences. Applicants must have received the Ph.D. degree within the past 5 years and be engaged in research on poverty and public policy. Along with their application, they must submit a research proposal that represents either a significant extension upon previous work or a new poverty research project; a 1- to 2-page statement that specifies the ways in which residence at the University of Michigan will foster their career development and research goals and provides information about how their racial/ethnic/regional/economic background qualifies them as a members of a group that is underrepresented in the social sciences; a curriculum vitae; and a sample of their scholarly writing. Preference is given to proposals that would benefit from resources available at the University of Michigan and from interactions with affiliated faculty.

Financial data   The stipend is $50,000 per calendar year.

Duration   1 or 2 years.

Additional information   This program is funded by the Ford Foundation. Fellows spend the year participating in a seminar on poverty and public policy and conducting their own research. Topics currently pursued include the effects of the recession and the American Recovery and Reinvestment Act of 2009 on workers, families, and children; evolution of the social safety net; longitudinal analyses of youth development; family formation and healthy marriages; immigration and poverty; investing in low-income families: the accumulation of financial assets and human capital; and qualitative and mixed-methods research on poverty. Fellows must be in residence at the University of Michigan for the duration of the program.

Number awarded   1 or more each year.

Deadline   January of each year.

[1118]
RESEARCH SCHOLAR AWARDS OF THE AMERICAN GASTROENTEROLOGICAL ASSOCIATION

American Gastroenterological Association
Attn: AGA Research Foundation
Research Awards Manager
4930 Del Ray Avenue
Bethesda, MD 20814-2512
(301) 222-4012   Fax: (301) 654-5920
E-mail: awards@gastro.org
Web: www.gastro.org/grants/research-scholar-award-rsa

Summary To provide research funding to young investigators, especially Asian Americans and other minorities, who are developing an independent career in an area of gastroenterology, hepatology, or related fields.

Eligibility Applicants must hold full-time faculty positions at North American universities or professional institutes at the time of application. They should be early in their careers (fellows and established investigators are not appropriate candidates). Candidates with an M.D. degree must have completed clinical training within the past 7 years and those with a Ph.D. must have completed their degree within the past 7 years. Membership in the American Gastroenterological Association (AGA) is required. Selection is based on significance, investigator, innovation, approach, environment, relevance to AGA mission, and evidence of institutional commitment. Women, minorities, and physician/scientist investigators are strongly encouraged to apply.

Financial data The grant is $90,000 per year. Funds are to be used for project costs, including salary, supplies, and equipment but excluding travel. Indirect costs are not allowed.

Duration 3 years.

Additional information At least 70% of the recipient's research effort should relate to the gastrointestinal tract or liver.

Number awarded Varies each year; recently, 5 were awarded.

Deadline August of each year.

[1119]
ROBERT L. FANTZ MEMORIAL AWARD FOR YOUNG PSYCHOLOGISTS

American Psychological Foundation
750 First Street, N.E.
Washington, DC 20002-4242
(202) 336-5843   Fax: (202) 336-5812
E-mail: foundation@apa.org
Web: www.apa.org/apf/funding/fantz.aspx

Summary To provide funding to promising young investigators in psychology, especially Asian Americans and other students who represent diversity.

Eligibility This program is open to young investigators in psychology or related disciplines. Candidates must show 1) evidence of basic scientific research or scholarly writing in perceptual-cognitive development and the development of selection attention; and 2) research and writing on the development of individuality, creativity, and free-choice of behavior. The sponsor encourages applications from individuals who represent diversity in race, ethnicity, gender, age, disability, and sexual orientation.

Financial data The award is $2,000. Funds are paid directly to the recipient's institution for equipment purchases, travel, computer resources, or other expenses related to the work recognized by the award.

Duration The award is presented annually.

Additional information This award was first presented in 1992.

Number awarded 1 each year.

Deadline Deadline not specified.

[1120]
ROBERT WOOD JOHNSON HEALTH POLICY FELLOWSHIPS

National Academy of Medicine
Attn: Health Policy Fellowships Program
500 Fifth Street, N.W.
Washington, DC 20001
(202) 334-1506   Fax: (202) 334-3862
E-mail: info@healthpolicyfellows.org
Web: www.healthpolicyfellows.org/apply

Summary To provide an opportunity to health professionals and behavioral and social scientists, especially Asian Americans and members of other underrepresented groups, who have an interest in health to participate in the formulation of national health policies while in residence at the National Academy of Medicine (NAM) in Washington, D.C.

Eligibility This program is open to mid-career professionals from academic faculties and nonprofit health care organizations who are interested in experiencing health policy processes at the federal level. Applicants must have a background in allied health professions, biomedical sciences, dentistry, economics or other social sciences, health services organization and administration, medicine, nursing, public health, social and behavioral health, or health law. They must be sponsored by the chief executive officer of an eligible nonprofit health care organization or academic institution. Selection is based on potential for leadership in health policy, potential for future growth and career advancement, professional achievements, interpersonal and communication skills, potential for significant contributions to building a Culture of Health, and individual plans for incorporating the fellowship experience into specific career goals. U.S. citizenship or permanent resident status is required. Applications are especially encouraged from candidates with diverse backgrounds of race, ethnicity, gender, age, disability, and socioeconomic status.

Financial data Total support for the Washington stay and continuing activities may not exceed $165,000. Grant funds may cover salary support at a level of up to $104,000 plus fringe benefits. Fellows are reimbursed for relocation expenses to and from Washington, D.C. No indirect costs are paid.

Duration The program lasts 1 year and includes an orientation in September and October; meetings in November and December with members of Congress, journalists, policy analysts, and other experts on the national political and governmental process; and working assignments from January through August. Fellows then return to their home institutions, but they receive up to 2 years of continued support for further development of health policy leadership skills.

Additional information This program, initiated in 1973, is funded by the Robert Wood Johnson Foundation.

Number awarded Up to 6 each year.

Deadline November of each year.

[1121]
ROME FOUNDATION FUNCTIONAL GI AND MOTILITY DISORDERS PILOT RESEARCH AWARD

American Gastroenterological Association
Attn: AGA Research Foundation
Research Awards Manager
4930 Del Ray Avenue
Bethesda, MD 20814-2512
(301) 222-4012   Fax: (301) 654-5920
E-mail: awards@gastro.org
Web: www.gastro.org

Summary To provide funding to investigators at all levels, especially Asian Americans and other minorities, who are interested in conducting pilot research related to functional gastrointestinal and motility disorders.

Eligibility This program is open to early stage and established investigators, postdoctoral research fellows, and combined research and clinical fellows. Applicants must be interested in conducting pilot research on the pathophysiology, diagnosis, and/or treatment of functional gastrointestinal or motility disorders. They must have an M.D. or Ph.D. degree and a full-time faculty position at a North American educational institution. Membership in the American Gastroenterological Association (AGA) is required. Selection is based on novelty, importance, feasibility, environment, and the overall likelihood that the project will lead to subsequent, more substantial grants in the areas of functional gastrointestinal and motility disorders research. Women and minorities are strongly encouraged to apply.

Financial data The grant is $50,000. Funds are to be used for project costs, including salary, supplies, and equipment but excluding travel. Indirect costs are not allowed.

Duration 1 year.

Additional information This program is sponsored by the Rome Foundation.

Number awarded Varies each year; recently, 2 were awarded.

Deadline January of each year.

[1122]
SALLY C. TSENG PROFESSIONAL DEVELOPMENT GRANT

Chinese American Librarians Association
c/o Jian Anna Xiong, Professional Development Grant
  Committee
Southern Illinois University at Carbondale
Library, MC 6632
605 Agriculture Drive
Carbondale, IL 62901
(618) 453-7108   E-mail: axiong@lib.siu.edu
Web: www.cala-web.org/node/205

Summary To provide funding to members of the Chinese American Librarians Association (CALA) who are interested in conducting a research project.

Eligibility This program is open to full-time librarians of Chinese descent who have been CALA members for at least 3 years. Applicants must be interested in conducting a

research project in library and information science for which they are qualified and which will result in the advancement of their professional status. Preference is given to members with 15 or fewer years of professional library experience.

Financial data The grant is $1,000.

Duration 1 year.

Number awarded 1 or 2 each year.

Deadline March of each year.

[1123]
SARA A. WHALEY BOOK PRIZE

National Women's Studies Association
Attn: Book Prizes
11 East Mount Royal Avenue, Suite 100
Baltimore, MD 21202
(410) 528-0355   Fax: (410) 528-0357
E-mail: awards@nwsa.org
Web: www.nwsa.org

Summary To recognize and reward members of the National Women's Studies Association (NWSA), especially Asian American and other women of color, who have written outstanding books on topics related to women and labor.

Eligibility This award is available to NWSA members who submit a book manuscript that relates to women and labor, including migration and women's paid jobs, illegal immigration and women's work, impact of AIDS on women's employment, trafficking of women and women's employment, women and domestic work, or impact of race on women's work. Both senior scholars (who have issued at least 2 books and published the entry within the past year) and junior scholars (who have a publication contract or a book in production) are eligible. Women of color of U.S. or international origin are encouraged to apply.

Financial data The award is $2,000.

Duration The awards are presented annually.

Additional information This award was first presented in 2008.

Number awarded 2 each year: 1 to a senior scholar and 1 to a junior scholar.

Deadline April of each year.

[1124]
SCHLUMBERGER FELLOWSHIP IN GEOSCIENCE COMMUNICATION

American Geosciences Institute
Attn: Critical Issues Program
4220 King Street
Alexandria, VA 22302-1502
(703) 379-2480   Fax: (703) 379-7563
E-mail: cipinfo@agiweb.org
Web: www.americangeosciences.org

Summary To provide geoscientists, especially Asian Americans and other minorities, with an opportunity to work on the Critical Issues Program (CIP) at the headquarters of the American Geosciences Institute (AGI).

Eligibility This program is open to geoscientists who have completed a master's or higher degree and are eligible to work in the United States. Applicants should have a broad geoscience background and excellent writing, graphical, and interpersonal communications skills. They must be interested in working on the CIP, including developing geoscience-based content for the CIP website, including webpage content, fact sheets, and other information products; working with technical experts to ensure the accuracy and impartiality of information products; promoting the program's products and services to decision makers and geoscientists via meetings, webinars, conferences, social media, regularly scheduled emails, and other channels; participating in planning, organizing, advertising webinars; providing input on the program's direction, planning, and communications strategy; and providing regular status reports on fellowship activities and achievements. Applications from women and minorities are especially encouraged.

Financial data The stipend is $4,000 per month.

Duration 12 months.

Number awarded 1 each year.

Deadline October of each year.

[1125]
SCIENCE, TECHNOLOGY, AND PUBLIC POLICY FELLOWSHIPS

Harvard University
John F. Kennedy School of Government
Belfer Center for Science and International Affairs
Attn: STPP Fellowship Coordinator
79 John F. Kennedy Street, Mailbox 53
Cambridge, MA 02138
(617) 495-1498   Fax: (617) 495-8963
E-mail: patricia_mclaughlin@hks.harvard.edu
Web: belfercenter.ksg.harvard.edu

Summary To provide funding to professionals, postdoctorates, and doctoral students, especially Asian Americans and other minorities, who are interested in conducting research in science, technology, and public policy areas of concern to the Belfer Center for Science and International Affairs at Harvard University in Cambridge, Massachusetts.

Eligibility The postdoctoral fellowship is open to recent recipients of the Ph.D. or equivalent degree, university faculty members, and employees of government, military, international, humanitarian, and private research institutions who have appropriate professional experience. Applicants for predoctoral fellowships must have passed their general examinations. Scholars from a wide range of disciplinary and multi-disciplinary fields and those holding a Ph.D. in engineering or in the natural sciences are strongly encouraged to apply. The program especially encourages applications from women, minorities, and citizens of all countries. All applicants must be interested in conducting research on projects of the Science, Technology, and Public Policy (STPP) Program. Recently, those included projects on Internet policy and regulatory reform, energy technology innovation, water and energy resources, sustainable energy development in China, technology and innovation, solar geoengineering and climate policy, technological innovation and globalization, agricultural innovation in Africa, managing the atom, and the geopolitics of energy.

Financial data The stipend is $37,500 for postdoctoral research fellows or $25,000 for predoctoral research fellows. Fellows who renew their grant receive a monthly stipend of $3,750 for postdoctoral fellows or $2,500 for predoctoral fellows. Stipends for advanced research fellows vary. Health insurance is also provided.

Duration 10 months; may be renewed on a month-by-month basis.

Additional information Fellows are expected to devoted some portion of their time to collaborative endeavors, as arranged by the appropriate program or project director. Predoctoral fellows are expected to contribute to the program's research activities, as well as work on (and ideally complete) their dissertations. Postdoctoral research fellows are also expected to complete a book, monograph, or other significant publication during their period of residence.

Number awarded A limited number each year.

Deadline January of each year.

[1126]
SHEILA SUEN LAI RESEARCH GRANT

Asian Pacific American Librarians Association
Attn: Executive Director
P.O. Box 677593
Orlando, FL 32867-7593
(407) 823-5048   Fax: (407) 823-5865
E-mail: bbasco@mail.ucf.edu
Web: www.apalaweb.org

Summary To provide research funding to members of the Asian Pacific American Librarians Association (APALA).

Eligibility Eligible to apply are APALA members in good standing who have been members for at least 1 year prior to applying. Applicants must have an M.L.S. or M.L.I.S. degree and currently be employed in a professional position in library science or a related field. They must be seeking funding to conduct research projects, attend research-related conferences and workshops, conduct research workshops and programs, or assist in research writing; attendance at professional association conferences is not supported. Current recipients of other APALA grants or scholarships are not eligible for this award.

Financial data Grants range up to $1,000.

Duration Grants are awarded annually.

Number awarded 1 or more each year.

Deadline February of each year.

[1127]
SHELBY CULLOM DAVIS CENTER FOR HISTORICAL STUDIES RESEARCH FELLOWSHIPS

Princeton University
Shelby Cullom Davis Center for Historical Studies
c/o Department of History
129 Dickinson Hall
Princeton, NJ 08544-1017
(609) 258-4997   Fax: (609) 258-5326
E-mail: davisctr@princeton.edu
Web: www.princeton.edu

Summary To provide funding to scholars, especially Asian Americans and members of other underrepresented groups, who are interested in conducting historical research at Princeton University's Center for Historical Studies.

Eligibility This program is open to scholars from any country who are interested in conducting research on a topic that changes biennially while in residence at the center. Recently, the center welcomed proposals for projects focusing on the theme "Risk and Fortune." Selection is based on the strength of the research projects, the relationship of those projects to the center's theme, previous scholarly work, and ability to contribute to the intellectual life and exchange of the center. Scholars who are non-U.S. nationals or who are members of traditionally underrepresented groups are encouraged to apply.

Financial data Fellows with no outside support receive the equivalent of their annual salary at their home university. Those with outside support that amounts to less their normal salary receive additional funds from the center to bring their salaries up to normal. Fellows from abroad whose base salary scale is below the normal American level receive a salary that is adjusted upward to take that into account. The center also pays the transportation costs for fellows without outside travel funds and their dependents, the cost of shipping books and papers for the fellows, $150 for shipping household goods each way, and research expenses (xeroxing, microfilming, typing, and travel) up to $2,000 per semester or $4,000 per year.

Duration 1 semester or 1 academic year.

Number awarded 5 to 6 each year.

Deadline November of each year.

[1128]
SLA NEW ENGLAND DIVERSITY LEADERSHIP DEVELOPMENT SCHOLARSHIP

SLA New England
c/o Khalilah Gambrell, Diversity Chair
EBSCO Information Services
10 Estes Street
Ipswich, MA 01938
(978) 356-6500   Toll Free: (800) 653-2726
Fax: (978) 356-6565   E-mail: gambrell9899@gmail.com
Web: newengland.sla.org/member-benefits/stipends

Summary To provide financial assistance for library science tuition or attendance at the annual conference of the Special Libraries Association (SLA) to members of SLA New England who are Asian Americans or represent another diverse population.

Eligibility This program is open to SLA New England members who are of Asian American, Black (African American), Hispanic, Pacific Islander American, Native Alaskan, or Native Hawaiian heritage. Applicants must be seeking funding for SLA annual meeting attendance, tuition reimbursement for a library science program, or tuition reimbursement for a course directly related to the library and information science field. Along with their application, they must submit a 500-word essay on how they will encourage and celebrate diversity within the SLA New England community.

Financial data The award covers actual expenses up to $1,500.

Duration This is a 1-time award.

Number awarded 1 each year.

Deadline April of each year.

[1129]
SMITHSONIAN MINORITY STUDENT INTERNSHIP

Smithsonian Institution
Attn: Office of Fellowships and Internships
470 L'Enfant, Suite 7102
P.O. Box 37012, MRC 902
Washington, DC 20013-7012
(202) 633-7070   Fax: (202) 633-7069
E-mail: siofi@si.edu
Web: www.smithsonianofi.com/minority-internship-program

Summary To provide Asian American and other minority undergraduate or graduate students with the opportunity to work on research or museum procedure projects in specific areas of history, art, or science at the Smithsonian Institution.

Eligibility Internships are offered to minority students who are actively engaged in undergraduate or graduate study or have graduated within the past 4 months. Applicants must be U.S. citizens or permanent residents who have an overall GPA of 3.0 or higher. Applicants must be interested in conducting research in any of the following fields of interest to the Smithsonian: animal behavior, ecology, and environmental science (including an emphasis on the tropics); anthropology (including archaeology); astrophysics and astronomy; earth sciences and paleobiology; evolutionary and systematic biology; history of science and technology; history of art (especially American, contemporary, African, Asian, and 20th-century art); American crafts and decorative arts; social and cultural history of the United States; and folklife.

Financial data The program provides a stipend of $600 per week; travel allowances may also be offered.

Duration 10 weeks during the summer or academic year.

Number awarded Varies each year.

Deadline January of each year for summer or fall; September of each year for spring.

[1130]
SOCIETY OF BIBLICAL LITERATURE REGIONAL SCHOLARS AWARDS

Society of Biblical Literature
c/o The Luce Center
825 Houston Mill Road, Suite 350
Atlanta, GA 30329
(404) 727-3100   Fax: (404) 727-3101
E-mail: sblexec@sbl-site.org
Web: www.sbl-site.org/membership/SBLAwards.aspx

Summary To provide funding for annual meeting attendance or professional development to members of the Society of Biblical Literature (SBL) at the doctoral or recent postdoctoral level, especially Asian Americans and other minorities.

Eligibility This award is available to SBL members who are Ph.D. candidates or who completed a Ph.D. within the past 4 years. Applicants must present at an SBL regional meeting an original work of their own scholarship and must submit a copy of the paper, along with a curriculum vitae, to the regional coordinator for their SBL region. Members of the selection committee attend the oral presentation and evaluate it on the basis of clear articulation of argument advanced, even and engaging delivery, clear pronunciation and style appropriate to oral presentation, and creative and appropriate use of presentation materials. The written papers are evaluated as oral presentations, not as research articles, on the basis of the following criteria: clarity of expression and argumentation, demonstrated knowledge and critical use of scholarly resources and publications, use and knowledge of the primary sources, and originality of ideas and solutions. Women and minorities are encouraged to apply.

Financial data The award is $1,000. Funds may be used to support attendance at the SBL annual meeting or to promote future scholarship and professional development.

Duration The awards are presented annually.

Number awarded Up to 6 each year.

Deadline Each of the 11 SBL regions establishes its own deadline.

[1131]
STANTON NUCLEAR SECURITY FELLOWSHIP

Stanford University
Center for International Security and Cooperation
Attn: Fellowships Coordinator
Encina Hall, Room C206-10
616 Serra Street
Stanford, CA 94305-6165
(650) 723-9625   Fax: (650) 724-5683
E-mail: CISACfellowship@stanford.edu
Web: cisac.fsi.stanford.edu/docs/cisac_fellowship_program

Summary To provide funding to doctoral candidates and junior scholars, especially Asian Americans and other minorities, who are interested in conducting research on nuclear security issues at Stanford University's Center for International Security and Cooperation.

Eligibility This program is open to doctoral candidates, recent postdoctorates, and junior faculty. Applicants must be interested in conducting research on nuclear security issues while in residence at the center. The sponsor welcomes applications from women, minorities, and citizens of all countries.

Financial data The stipend ranges from $25,000 to $28,000 for doctoral candidates or from $48,000 to $66,000 for postdoctorates, depending on experience. Medical insurance is available for those who do not have coverage.

Duration 9 to 11 months.

Additional information Fellows are expected to write a dissertation chapter or chapters, publishable article or articles, and/or make significant progress on turning a thesis into a book manuscript. They should not plan to spend any time conducting research abroad or in other parts of the country.

Number awarded Varies each year; recently, 3 were awarded: 1 doctoral candidate, 1 recent postdoctorate, and 1 junior faculty member.

Deadline January of each year.

[1132]
SUBSTANCE ABUSE FELLOWSHIP PROGRAM

American Psychiatric Association
Attn: Division of Diversity and Health Equity
1000 Wilson Boulevard, Suite 1825
Arlington, VA 22209-3901
(703) 907-8653   Toll Free: (888) 35-PSYCH
Fax: (703) 907-7852   E-mail: mking@psych.org
Web: www.psychiatry.org/minority-fellowship

Summary To provide educational enrichment to minority psychiatrists-in-training, especially Asian Americans and other minorities, and stimulate their interest in providing quality and effective services related to substance abuse to minorities and the underserved.

Eligibility This program is open to psychiatric residents who are members of the American Psychiatric Association (APA) and U.S. citizens or permanent residents. A goal of the program is to develop leadership to improve the quality of mental health care for members of ethnic minority groups (Asian Americans, American Indians, Native Alaskans, Native Hawaiians, Native Pacific Islanders, African Americans, and Hispanics/Latinos). Applicants must be in at least their fifth year of a substance abuse training program approved by an affiliated medical school or agency where a significant number of substance abuse patients are from minority and underserved groups. They must also be interested in working with a component of the APA that is of interest to them and relevant to their career goals. Along with their application, they must submit a 2-page essay on how the fellowship would be utilized to alter their present training and ultimately assist them in achieving their career goals. Selection is based on commitment to serve ethnic minority populations, demonstrated leadership abilities, awareness of the importance of culture in mental health, and interest in the interrelationship between mental health/illness and transcultural factors.

Financial data Fellows receive a monthly stipend (amount not specified) and reimbursement of transportation, lodging, meals, and incidentals in connection with attendance at program-related activities. They are expected to use the funds to enhance their own professional development, improve training in cultural competence at their training institution, improve awareness of culturally relevant issues in psychiatry at their institution, expand research in areas relevant to minorities and underserved populations, enhance the current treatment modalities for minority patients and underserved individuals at their institution, and improve awareness in the surrounding community about mental health issues (particularly with regard to minority populations).

Duration 1 year; may be renewed 1 additional year.

Additional information Funding for this program is provided by the Substance Abuse and Mental Health Services Administration (SAMHSA). As part of their assignment to an APA component, fellows must attend the fall component meetings in September and the APA annual meeting in May. At those meeting, they can share their experiences as residents and minorities and discuss issues that impact minority populations. This program is an outgrowth of the fellowships that were established in 1974 under a grant from the National Institute of Mental Health in answer to concerns about the underrepresentation of minorities in psychiatry.

Number awarded Varies each year; recently, 3 were awarded.

Deadline January of each year.

[1133]
SUMMER RESEARCH PROGRAM IN ECOLOGY

Harvard University
Harvard Forest
324 North Main Street
Petersham, MA 01366
(978) 724-3302   Fax: (978) 724-3595
E-mail: hfapps@fas.harvard.edu
Web: harvardforest.fas.harvard.edu/other-tags/reu

Summary To provide an opportunity for undergraduate students and recent graduates, especially Asian Americans and members of other diverse groups, to participate in a summer ecological research project at Harvard Forest in Petersham, Massachusetts.

Eligibility This program is open to undergraduate students and recent graduates interested in participating in a mentored research project at the Forest. The research may relate to the effects of natural and human disturbances on forest ecosystems, including global climate change, hurricanes, forest harvest, changing wildlife dynamics, or invasive species. Investigators come from many disciplines, and specific projects center on population and community ecology, paleoecology, land use history, aquatic ecology, biochemistry, soil science, ecophysiology, and atmosphere-biosphere exchanges. Students from diverse backgrounds are strongly encouraged to apply.

Financial data The stipend is $5,775. Free housing, meals, and travel reimbursement for 1 round trip are also provided.

Duration 11 weeks during the summer.

Additional information Funding for this program is provided by the National Science Foundation (as part of its Research Experience for Undergraduates program).

Number awarded Up to 25 each year.

Deadline February of each year.

[1134]
THEODORE BLAU EARLY CAREER AWARD FOR OUTSTANDING CONTRIBUTION TO PROFESSIONAL CLINICAL PSYCHOLOGY

American Psychological Foundation
750 First Street, N.E.
Washington, DC 20002-4242
(202) 336-5843   Fax: (202) 336-5812
E-mail: foundation@apa.org
Web: www.apa.org/apf/funding/blau.aspx

Summary To recognize and reward early-career clinical psychologists, especially Asian Americans and members of other diverse groups, who have made outstanding professional accomplishments.

Eligibility This award is available to clinical psychologists who are no more than 10 years past completion of their doctoral degree. Nominees must have a record of accomplishments that may include promoting the practice of clinical psychology through professional service; innovation in service delivery; novel application of applied research methodologies to professional practice; positive impact on health delivery systems; development of creative educational programs for practice; or other novel or creative activities advancing the service of the profession. Self-nominations are accepted. The sponsor encourages nominations of individuals who represent diversity in race, ethnicity, gender, age, disability, and sexual orientation.

Financial data The award is $4,000.

Duration The award is presented annually.

Additional information This award, first presented in 1998, is sponsored by Division 12 (Society of Clinical Psychology) of the American Psychological Association.

Number awarded 1 each year.

Deadline Nominations must be submitted by October of each year.

[1135]
THEODORE MILLON AWARD IN PERSONALITY PSYCHOLOGY

American Psychological Foundation
750 First Street, N.E.
Washington, DC 20002-4242
(202) 336-5843   Fax: (202) 336-5812
E-mail: foundation@apa.org
Web: www.apa.org/apf/funding/millon.aspx

Summary To recognize and reward psychologists, especially Asian Americans and members of other diverse groups, who have made outstanding contributions to the science of personality psychology.

Eligibility This award is available to psychologists engaged in advancing the science of personality psychology, including the areas of personology, personality theory, personality disorders, and personality measurement. Nominees should be between 8 and 20 years past completion of their doctoral degree. The sponsor encourages nominations of individuals who represent diversity in race, ethnicity, gender, age, disability, and sexual orientation.

Financial data The award is $1,000.

Duration The award is presented annually.

Additional information This award, established in 2004, is sponsored by Division 12 (Society of Clinical Psychology) of the American Psychological Association.

Number awarded 1 each year.

Deadline Nominations must be submitted by October of each year.

[1136]
TRAINEESHIPS IN AIDS PREVENTION STUDIES (TAPS)

University of California at San Francisco
Attn: Center for AIDS Prevention Studies
Mission Hall
550 16th Street, Third Floor
San Francisco, CA 94158-2549
(415) 476-6229   Fax: (415) 476-5348
E-mail: Rochelle.Blanco@ucsf.edu
Web: www.caps.ucsf.edu/training/taps

Summary To provide funding to scientists, especially Asian Americans and members of other minority ethnic groups, who are interested in conducting HIV prevention research at the Center for AIDS Prevention Studies (CAPS) of the University of California at San Francisco (UCSF).

Eligibility This program is open to U.S. citizens, nationals, and permanent residents who have a Ph.D., M.D., or equivalent degree. Applicants must be interested in a program of research training at CAPS in the following areas of special emphasis in AIDS research: epidemiological research, studies of AIDS risk behaviors, substance abuse and HIV, primary prevention interventions, research addressing minority populations, studies of HIV-positive individuals, policy and ethics, international research, and other public health and clinical aspects of AIDS. Recent postdoctorates who have just completed their training as well as those who are already faculty members in academic or clinical departments are eligible. Members of minority ethnic groups are strongly encouraged to apply.

Financial data Stipends depend on years of relevant postdoctoral experience, based on the NIH stipend scale for Institutional Research Training Grants (currently ranging from $43,692 for fellows with no relevant postdoctoral experience to $57,504 for those with 7 or more years of experience). Other benefits include a computer, travel to at least 1 annual professional meeting, health insurance, and other required support. The costs of the M.P.H. degree, if required, are covered.

Duration 2 or 3 years.

Additional information The TAPS program is designed to ensure that at the end of the training each fellow will have: 1) completed the M.P.H. degree or its equivalent; 2) taken advanced courses in research methods, statistics, and other topics relevant to a major field of interest; 3) participated in and led numerous seminars on research topics within CAPS, as well as in the formal teaching programs of the university; 4) designed several research protocols and completed at least 1 significant research project under the direction of a faculty mentor; and 5) made presentations at national or international meetings and submitted several papers for publication.

Number awarded Varies each year.

Deadline November of each year.

[1137]
TRAINING PROGRAM FOR SCIENTISTS CONDUCTING RESEARCH TO REDUCE HIV/STI HEALTH DISPARITIES

University of California at San Francisco
Attn: Center for AIDS Prevention Studies
Mission Hall
550 16th Street, Third Floor
San Francisco, CA 94158-2549
(415) 476-6256   Fax: (415) 476-5348
E-mail: dale.danley@ucsf.edu
Web: caps.ucsf.edu/training/health-disparities-training

Summary To provide funding to scientists, especially Asian Americans and other minorities, interested in obtaining additional training at the University of California at San Francisco (UCSF) Center for AIDS Prevention Studies (CAPS) for HIV prevention research in minority communities.

Eligibility This program is open to scientists in tenure-track positions or investigators in research institutes who have not yet obtained research funding from the U.S. National Institutes of Health (NIH) or equivalent. Applicants must be interested in a program of activity at CAPS to improve their programs of HIV-prevention research targeting vulnerable ethnic minority populations. They must be eligible to serve as principal investigators at their home institutions. Selection is based on commitment to HIV social and behavioral research, prior HIV prevention research with communities and community-based organizations targeting communities with high levels of

health disparities (e.g., communities with a high proportion of disadvantaged or disabled persons, racial and ethnic minority communities), creativity and innovativeness for a pilot research project to serve as a preliminary study for a subsequent larger R01 grant proposal to NIH or other suitable funding agency, past experience conducting research and writing papers, quality of letters of recommendation from colleagues and mentors, and support from the home institution (e.g., time off for research, seed money). A goal of the program is to increase the number of minority group members among principal investigators funded by NIH and other agencies. U.S. citizenship or permanent resident status is required.

Financial data Participants receive 1) a monthly stipend for living expenses and round-trip airfare to San Francisco for each summer; and 2) a grant of $25,000 to conduct preliminary research before the second summer to strengthen their R01 application.

Duration 6 weeks during each of 3 consecutive summers.

Additional information This program is funded by the NIH National Institute of Child Health and Human Development (NICHHD) and National Institute on Drug Abuse (NIDA).

Number awarded Approximately 4 each year.

Deadline January of each year.

[1138]
UCAR VISITING SCIENTIST PROGRAMS

University Corporation for Atmospheric Research
Attn: Visiting Scientist Programs
3090 Center Green Drive
P.O. Box 3000
Boulder, CO 80307-3000
(303) 497-1605   Fax: (303) 497-8668
E-mail: vspapply@ucar.edu
Web: www.vsp.ucar.edu

Summary To provide funding to recent postdoctorates in atmospheric sciences, especially Asian Americans and other minorities, who wish to participate in designated research programs.

Eligibility This program is open to postdoctorates (preferably those who received their Ph.D. within the preceding 3 years) who wish to conduct research with experienced scientists at designated facilities. Applicants must submit a cover letter stating the name of the program, potential host and institution, and where they learned of this opportunity; their curriculum vitae; names and addresses of at least 4 professional references; an abstract of their Ph.D. dissertation; and a description of the research they wish to conduct at the relevant facility. Women and minorities are encouraged to apply. U.S. citizenship is not required, although the research must be conducted at a U.S. institution.

Financial data The salary is $60,000 for the first year and $62,000 for the second year. A moving allowance of $750, an allowance of $5,000 per year for scientific travel, and a $3,000 publication allowance for the term of the award are also provided. Benefits include health and dental insurance, sick and annual leave, paid holidays, participation in a retirement fund, and life insurance.

Duration 2 years.

Additional information Recently, positions were available through 3 programs: 1) the NOAA Climate and Global Change Postdoctoral Fellowship Program (sponsored by the National Oceanic and Atmospheric Administration; 2) the

Postdocs Applying Climate Expertise (PACE) Fellowship Program; and 3) the Jack Eddy Postdoctoral Program in heliophysics (defined as all science common to the field of Sun-Earth connections).

Number awarded Recently, 8 fellowships for the NOAA Climate and Global Change Postdoctoral Fellowship Program, 2 for the PACE Fellowship Program, and 4 for the Jack Eddy Postdoctoral Program were awarded.

Deadline January of each year for the NOAA Climate and Global Change Postdoctoral Fellowship Program and the Jack Eddy Postdoctoral Program; May of each year for the PACE Fellowship Program.

[1139]
VITO MARZULLO INTERNSHIP PROGRAM

Illinois Legislative Staff
Attn: Legislative Research Unit
222 South Chicago, Suite 301
Springfield, IL 62704-1894
(217) 782-6851   Fax: (217) 785-7572
E-mail: lru@ilga.gov
Web: www.ilga.gov/commission/lru/internships.html

Summary To provide recent college graduates, especially Asian Americans and other minorities, with work experience in the Illinois Governor's office.

Eligibility This program is open to residents of Illinois who have completed a bachelor's degree and are interested in working in the Illinois Governor's office or in various agencies under the Governor's jurisdiction. Applicants may have majored in any field, but they must be able to demonstrate a substantial commitment to excellence as evidenced by academic honors, leadership ability, extracurricular activities, and involvement in community or public service. Along with their application, they must submit 1) a 500-word personal statement on the qualities or attributes they will bring to the program, their career goals or plans, how their selection for this program would assist them in achieving those goals, and what they expect to gain from the program; and 2) a 1,000-word essay in which they identify and analyze a public issue that they feel has great impact on state government. A particular goal of the program is to achieve affirmative action through the nomination of qualified minorities, men, women, and persons with disabilities.

Financial data The stipend is $2,611 per month.

Duration 1 year, beginning in August.

Additional information Assignments are in Springfield and, to a limited extent, in Chicago or Washington, D.C.

Number awarded Varies each year; recently, 4 of these interns were appointed.

Deadline February of each year.

[1140]
WARREN CENTER FACULTY FELLOWSHIPS

Harvard University
Charles Warren Center for Studies in American History
Emerson Hall, Fourth Floor
Cambridge, MA 02138
(617) 495-3591   Fax: (617) 496-2111
E-mail: cwc@fas.harvard.edu
Web: warrencenter.fas.harvard.edu

Summary To provide funding to scholars, especially Asian Americans and others who will contribute to diversity, who are interested in conducting research in American history in the Boston area.

Eligibility Historians from any country may apply for this award if they are conducting research on a topic that changes annually; a recent topic was "Crime and Punishment in American History." Applicants must need to conduct their research at Harvard or in the Boston area. They should have already earned a Ph.D. or equivalent degree and may not be degree candidates. Preference is given to those who can accept a full-year fellowship. The program especially welcomes applications from scholars who can contribute, through their research and service, to the diversity and excellence of Harvard's academic community.

Financial data The maximum grant is $57,000.

Duration 1 academic year.

Additional information Fellows are given a private office in the center, as well as photocopying and postage privileges. A recent topic was "Crime and Punishment in American History." Fellows must remain in residence at the center for the duration of the program and participate in a semi-monthly colloquium.

Number awarded Normally, 7 fellows are selected each year.

Deadline December of each year.

[1141]
WARREN G. MAGNUSON EDUCATIONAL SUPPORT PERSONNEL SCHOLARSHIP GRANT

Washington Education Association
32032 Weyerhaeuser Way South
P.O. Box 9100
Federal Way, WA 98063-9100
(253) 765-7056   Toll Free: (800) 622-3393, ext. 7056
E-mail: Janna.Connor@Washingtonea.org
Web: www.washingtonea.org

Summary To provide funding to Educational Support Personnel (ESP) members of the Washington Education Association (WEA), especially Asian Americans and other minorities, who are interested in taking classes to obtain an initial teaching certificate.

Eligibility This program is open to WEA/ESP members who are engaged in course work related to obtaining an initial teaching certificate. Applicants must submit a plan for obtaining an initial certificate, a letter describing their passion to become a teacher, evidence of activities and/or leadership in the association, and 3 to 5 letters of reference. Minority members of the association are especially encouraged to apply; 1 of the scholarships is reserved for them.

Financial data The stipend is $1,500.

Duration These are 1-time grants.

Number awarded 3 each year, including 1 reserved for a minority member.

Deadline June of each year.

[1142]
WAYNE F. PLACEK GRANTS

American Psychological Foundation
750 First Street, N.E.
Washington, DC 20002-4242
(202) 336-5843   Fax: (202) 336-5812
E-mail: foundation@apa.org
Web: www.apa.org/apf/funding/placek.aspx

Summary To provide funding to pre- and postdoctoral scholars, especially Asian Americans and members of other underrepresented groups, who are interested in conducting research that will increase the general public's understanding of homosexuality and alleviate the stress experienced by gay men and lesbians.

Eligibility This program is open to scholars who have a doctoral degree (e.g., Ph.D., Psy.D., M.D.) and to graduate students in all fields of the behavioral and social sciences. Applicants must be interested in conducting empirical studies that address the following topics: prejudice, discrimination, and violence based on sexual orientation, including heterosexuals' attitudes and behaviors toward lesbian, gay, bisexual, and transgender (LGBT) people; family and workplace issues relevant to LGBT people; and subgroups of the LGBT population that have been historically underrepresented in scientific research. Selection is based on relevance to program goals, magnitude of incremental contribution, quality of proposed work, and applicant's demonstrated scholarship and research competence. The sponsor encourages applications from individuals who represent diversity in race, ethnicity, gender, age, disability, and sexual orientation.

Financial data The grant is $15,000.

Duration 1 year.

Additional information This program began in 1995.

Number awarded 1 or 2 each year.

Deadline February of each year.

[1143]
W.E.B. DUBOIS FELLOWSHIP FOR RESEARCH ON RACE AND CRIME

Department of Justice
National Institute of Justice
Attn: W.E.B. DuBois Fellowship Program
810 Seventh Street, N.W.
Washington, DC 20531
Toll Free: (800) 851-3420   Fax: (301) 240-5830
TDD: (301) 240-6310   E-mail: grants@ncjrs.gov
Web: www.nij.gov

Summary To provide funding to junior investigators, especially Asian Americans and other minorities, who are interested in conducting research on "crime, justice, and culture in various societal contexts."

Eligibility This program is open to investigators who have a Ph.D. or other doctoral-level degree (including a legal degree of J.D. or higher). Applicants should be early in their careers and not have been awarded tenure. They must be interested in conducting research that relates to specific areas that change annually but relate to criminal justice policy and practice in the United States. The sponsor strongly encourages applications from women and minorities. Selection is based on understanding of the problem and its importance (10%); quality and technical merit (40%); potential for a

significant scientific or technical advance that will improve criminal/juvenile justice in the United states (20%); capabilities, demonstrated productivity, and experience of the principal investigator and the institution (15%); and dissemination strategy to broader audiences (15%).

Financial data Grants range up to $100,000 for fellows who propose to conduct secondary data analysis or up to $150,000 for fellows who proposed to conduct primary data collection. Funds may be used for salary, fringe benefits, reasonable costs of relocation, travel essential to the project, and office expenses not provided by the sponsor. Indirect costs are limited to 20%.

Duration Up to 24 months; residency at the National Institute of Justice (NIJ) is not required but it is available.

Number awarded Up to 3 each year.

Deadline May of each year.

[1144]
W.E.B. DUBOIS SCHOLARS

Department of Justice
National Institute of Justice
Attn: W.E.B. DuBois Fellowship Program
810 Seventh Street, N.W.
Washington, DC 20531
Toll Free: (800) 851-3420   Fax: (301) 240-5830
TDD: (301) 240-6310   E-mail: grants@ncjrs.gov
Web: www.nij.gov

Summary To provide funding to advanced investigators, especially Asian Americans and other minorities, who are interested in conducting research on "crime, justice, and culture in various societal contexts."

Eligibility This program is open to investigators who received their terminal degree in their field more than 5 years previously. Applicants must be interested in conducting primary research that relates to specific areas that change annually but relate to criminal justice policy and practice in the United States. The sponsor strongly encourages applications from women and minorities. Selection is based on understanding of the problem and its importance (10%); quality and technical merit (40%); potential for a significant scientific or technical advance that will improve criminal/juvenile justice in the United States (20%); capabilities, demonstrated productivity, and experience of the principal investigator and the institution (15%); and dissemination strategy to broader audiences (15%).

Financial data Grants range up to $500,000. Funds may be used for salary, fringe benefits, reasonable costs of relocation, travel essential to the project, and office expenses not provided by the sponsor.

Duration Up to 36 months; residency at the National Institute of Justice (NIJ) is not required but it is available.

Number awarded Up to 4 each year.

Deadline May of each year.

[1145]
WILLIAM J. PERRY FELLOWSHIP IN INTERNATIONAL SECURITY

Stanford University
Center for International Security and Cooperation
Attn: Fellowships Coordinator
Encina Hall, Room C206-10
616 Serra Street
Stanford, CA 94305-6165
(650) 723-9625   Fax: (650) 724-5683
E-mail: perryfellows@stanford.edu
Web: cisac.fsi.stanford.edu/fellowships/perry_fellowship

Summary To provide funding to professionals, especially Asian Americans and other minorities, who are interested in conducting policy-relevant research on international security issues while in residence at Stanford University's Center for International Security and Cooperation.

Eligibility This program is open to early and mid-career professionals from academia, the public and private sectors, national laboratories, and the military, either from the United States or abroad. Applicants must have a record of outstanding work in natural science, engineering, or mathematics and a genuine interest in and dedication to solving international security problems. Their proposed research may involve interlapping issues of nuclear weapons policy and nuclear proliferation, regional tensions, biosecurity, homeland security, and effective global engagement. The sponsor welcomes applications from women, minorities, and citizens of all countries.

Financial data The stipend depends on experience and is determined on a case-by-case basis. Health care and other benefits are also provided.

Duration 9 to 11 months.

Additional information Fellows are expected to produce a publishable manuscript based on their research. They should not plan to spend any time conducting research abroad or in other parts of the country.

Number awarded Varies each year; recently, 3 of these fellows were in residence.

Deadline January of each year.

[1146]
WILLIAM L. FISHER CONGRESSIONAL GEOSCIENCE FELLOWSHIP

American Geosciences Institute
Attn: Government Affairs Program
4220 King Street
Alexandria, VA 22302-1502
(703) 379-2480   Fax: (703) 379-7563
E-mail: govt@agiweb.org
Web: www.americangeosciences.org

Summary To provide members of an American Geosciences Institute (AGI) component society, especially Asian Americans and other minorities, with an opportunity to gain professional experience in the office of a member of Congress or a Congressional committee.

Eligibility This program is open to members of 1 of AGI's 51 member societies who have a master's degree in engineering and at least 3 years of post-degree engineering experience or a Ph.D. Applicants should have a broad geoscience background and excellent written and oral communica-

tions skills. They must be interested in working with Congress. Although prior experience in public policy is not required, a demonstrated interest in applying science to the solution of public problems is desirable. Applications from women and minorities are especially encouraged. U.S. citizenship or permanent resident status is required.

Financial data Fellows receive a stipend of up to $68,000 plus allowances for health insurance, relocation, and travel.

Duration 12 months, beginning in September.

Additional information This program is 1 of more than 20 Congressional Science Fellowships operating in affiliation with the American Association for the Advancement of Science (AAAS), which provides a 2-week orientation on Congressional and executive branch operations.

Number awarded 1 each year.

Deadline January of each year.

[1147]
WRITERS OF COLOR FELLOWSHIPS OF OREGON LITERARY FELLOWSHIPS

Literary Arts, Inc.
Attn: Oregon Book Awards and Fellowships Program
   Coordinator
925 S.W. Washington Street
Portland, OR 97205
(503) 227-2583   Fax: (503) 243-1167
E-mail: susan@literary-arts.org
Web: www.literary-arts.org

Summary To provide funding to Asian American and other writers of color in Oregon interested in working on a literary project.

Eligibility This program is open to writers of color who have been residents of Oregon for at least 1 year and are interested in initiating, developing, or completing a literary project in the areas of poetry, fiction, literary nonfiction, drama, or young readers' literature. Priority is given to writers whose work promotes perspectives from a variety of cultural, ethnic, and racial backgrounds. Writers in the early stages of their careers are especially encouraged to apply. Selection is based primarily on literary merit.

Financial data Grants are at least $2,500.

Duration The grants are presented annually.

Additional information This program began in 2016.

Number awarded 1 each year.

Deadline June of each year.

Indexes

Program Title Index

If you know the name of a particular funding program open to Asian Americans and want to find out where it is covered in the directory, use the Program Title Index. Here, program titles are arranged alphabetically, word by word. To assist you in your search, every program is listed by all its known names or abbreviations. In addition, we've used an alphabetical code (within parentheses) to help you determine if the program is aimed at you: U = Undergraduates;   G = Graduate Students;   P = Professionals/Postdoctorates. Here's how the code works: if a program is followed by (U) 241, the program is described in the Undergraduates chapter, in entry 241. If the same program title is followed by another entry number—for example, (P) 901—the program is also described in the Professionals/Postdoctorates chapter, in entry 901. Remember: the numbers cited here refer to program entry numbers, not to page numbers in the book.

U–Undergraduates   **G–Graduate Students**   **P–Professionals/Postdoctorates**

U–Undergraduates   **G–Graduate Students**   **P–Professionals/Postdoctorates**

U–Undergraduates   **G–Graduate Students**   **P–Professionals/Postdoctorates**

U–Undergraduates   **G–Graduate Students**   **P–Professionals/Postdoctorates**

U–Undergraduates   G–Graduate Students   P–Professionals/Postdoctorates

U–Undergraduates   G–Graduate Students   P–Professionals/Postdoctorates

U–Undergraduates   G–Graduate Students   P–Professionals/Postdoctorates

Mayes EDAC Scholarship. *See* John A. Mayes EDAC Scholarship, entry (G) 748

Mayme Noda Scholarship. *See* NSRCF Scholarships, entry (U) 361

McClellan Scholarship. *See* Surety and Fidelity Industry Scholarship Program, entry (U) 446

McGuigan Dissertation Award. *See* F.J. McGuigan Dissertation Award, entry (G) 676

McGuigan Early Career Investigator Research Prize on Understanding the Human Mind. *See* F.J. McGuigan Early Career Investigator Research Prize on Understanding the Human Mind, entry (P) 1048

McGuireWoods/NLF Internship Program, (U) 297, (G) 803

McJulien Minority Graduate Scholarship. *See* Patrick D. McJulien Minority Graduate Scholarship, entry (G) 870

McKay Scholarship Program. *See* Jim McKay Scholarship Program, entry (G) 745

McKinney Family Fund Scholarship, (U) 298, (G) 804

McLean Award. *See* Franklin C. McLean Award, entry (G) 680

McLendon Minority Postgraduate Scholarship Program. *See* John McLendon Memorial Minority Postgraduate Scholarship Award, entries (G) 750, (P) 1067

McTavish Leadership Scholarship. *See* Michigan Accountancy Foundation Fifth/Graduate Year Scholarship Program, entries (U) 302, (G) 808

Media General Minority Scholarship and Training Program, (U) 299

Medical Library Association/National Library of Medicine Spectrum Scholarships. *See* MLA/NLM Spectrum Scholarships, entry (G) 822

Medical Library Association Scholarship for Minority Students. *See* MLA Scholarship for Minority Students, entry (G) 823

Medical Student Elective in HIV Psychiatry, (G) 805

Medical Student Training in Aging Research Program, (G) 806

Meekins Scholarship. *See* Phyllis G. Meekins Scholarship, entry (U) 391

Mehendale Graduate Student Best Abstract Award. *See* Dr. Harihara Mehendale Graduate Student Best Abstract Award, entry (G) 646

Meier Scholarship. *See* Benton-Meier Scholarships, entry (G) 587

Mel Karmazin Fellowship. *See* IRTS Summer Fellowship Program, entries (U) 227, (G) 726

Mellon Undergraduate Curatorial Fellowship Program, (U) 300

Mental Health and Substance Abuse Fellowship Program, (G) 807

Mercado Memorial Fellowship. *See* IRTS Summer Fellowship Program, entries (U) 227, (G) 726

Merritt Humanitarian Fund Award. *See* LeRoy C. Merritt Humanitarian Fund Award, entry (P) 1078

Michael Baker Scholarship for Diversity in Engineering, (U) 301

Michael Memorial HPC Fellowships. *See* ACM/IEEE-CS George Michael Memorial HPC Fellowships, entry (G) 530

Michael P. Johnson Scholarship. *See* Cuba Wadlington, Jr. and Michael P. Johnson Scholarship, entry (U) 128

Michi Nishiura Weglyn Scholarship. *See* NSRCF Scholarships, entry (U) 361

Michigan Accountancy Foundation Fifth/Graduate Year Scholarship Program, (U) 302, (G) 808

Michigan Auto Law Diversity Scholarship, (G) 809

Michigan Chapter COMTO Scholarships, (U) 303

Michihiko and Bernice Hayashida Scholarship. *See* NSRCF Scholarships, entry (U) 361

Mickey Williams Minority Scholarships. *See* PDEF Mickey Williams Minority Scholarships, entry (U) 381

Midwest Asian American Students Union Public Service Scholarships. *See* CAPAL-MAASU Public Service Scholarships, entries (U) 95, (G) 609

Midwestern Region Korean American Scholarships, (U) 304, (G) 810

Midwives of Color-Watson Midwifery Student Scholarship, (U) 305, (G) 811

Mike M. Masaoka Congressional Fellowship, (G) 812

Mildred Colodny Diversity Scholarship for Graduate Study in Historic Preservation, (G) 813

Millard Fellowships. *See* New York Foundation for the Arts Artists' Fellowships, entry (P) 1097

Miller Johnson West Michigan Diversity Law School Scholarship, (G) 814

Millon Award. *See* Theodore Millon Award in Personality Psychology, entry (P) 1135

Minerva Jean Falcon Hawai'i Scholarship. *See* Ambassador Minerva Jean Falcon Hawai'i Scholarship, entries (U) 34, (G) 540

Mineta Scholarship. *See* FAPAC Distinguished Public Service Scholarship, entry (U) 167

Ming and Josephine Ng Scholarship. *See* Chinese American Citizens Alliance Foundation Scholarships, entry (U) 109

Ming Y. Moy Memorial Scholarship. *See* Southern California Chinese Lawyers Association Scholarships, entry (G) 939

Minh Quang Buddhist Youth Association Scholarship. *See* MQ Buddhist Youth Association Scholarship, entry (U) 321

Minnesota Association for Korean Americans Scholarships, (U) 306

Minnesota Association of Counselors of Color Student of Color Scholarship. *See* MnACC Student of Color Scholarship, entry (U) 316

Minnesota Social Service Association Diversity Scholarship, (U) 307

Minnesota Taiwanese American Community Scholarship Awards, (U) 308

Minorities in Cancer Research Jane Cook Wright Lectureship, (P) 1089

Minorities in Government Finance Scholarship, (U) 309, (G) 815

Minority Faculty Development Scholarship Award in Physical Therapy, (G) 816, (P) 1090

Minority Fellowships in Environmental Law, (G) 817

Minority Medical Student Summer Externship in Addiction Psychiatry, (G) 818

Minority Nurse Faculty Scholars Program. *See* Johnson & Johnson/AACN Minority Nurse Faculty Scholars Program, entry (G) 752

Minority Scholarship Award for Academic Excellence in Physical Therapy, (U) 310

Minority Scholarship in Classics and Classical Archaeology, (U) 311

Minority Serving Institutions Partnership Program Internships. *See* MSIPP Internships, entries (U) 323, (G) 826

Minority Teacher Education Scholarships, (U) 312

Minority Teachers of Illinois Scholarship Program, (U) 313, (G) 819

Minority University Research and Education Project (MUREP) Scholarships. *See* NASA Scholarship and Research Opportunities (SRO) Minority University Research and Education Project (MUREP) Scholarships, entry (U) 331

Minoru Yasui Memorial Scholarship, (G) 820

Miriam Levinson Scholarship. *See* APF Graduate Student Scholarships, entry (G) 563

U–Undergraduates   **G–Graduate Students**   **P–Professionals/Postdoctorates**

U–Undergraduates   **G–Graduate Students**   **P–Professionals/Postdoctorates**

P

PA Foundation Scholarships. *See* PA Student Scholarships, entries (U) 375, (G) 867

PA Student Scholarships, (U) 375, (G) 867

Pabilona Emerging Entrepreneur Scholarship. *See* Lily Pabilona Emerging Entrepreneur Scholarship, entries (U) 276, (G) 785

PACCO Regular College Scholarship Program, (U) 376

PACE Fellowship Program. *See* UCAR Visiting Scientist Programs, entry (P) 1138

Page Education Foundation Grants, (U) 377

Pangarap Scholarship. *See* FLOW Pangarap Scholarship, entry (G) 678

Panyha Foundation Student Scholarship Program, (U) 378

Pao Scholarship. *See* General Vang Pao Scholarship, entries (U) 186, (G) 683

Park G. Bunker Memorial Scholarship. *See* Distinguished Raven FAC Memorial Scholarships, entry (U) 136

Park Scholarships. *See* Chunghi Hong Park Scholarships, entry (U) 114, 261

Parks College Scholarship. *See* Rosa L. Parks College Scholarship, entries (U) 412, (G) 906

Parks High School Scholarship. *See* Rosa L. Parks High School Scholarship, entry (U) 413

Paschke Leadership Scholarship. *See* Michigan Accountancy Foundation Fifth/Graduate Year Scholarship Program, entries (U) 302, (G) 808

Patricia and Gail Ishimoto Memorial Scholarship. *See* High School Senior Scholarships of the Japanese American Citizens League, entry (U) 208

Patricia G. Archbold Predoctoral Scholar Award, (G) 868

Patricia M. Lowrie Diversity Leadership Scholarship, (G) 869, (P) 1104

Patrick D. McJulien Minority Graduate Scholarship, (G) 870

Paul E. Williams Memorial Scholarship. *See* Distinguished Raven FAC Memorial Scholarships, entry (U) 136

Paul Fukami Scholarship. *See* NSRCF Scholarships, entry (U) 361

Paul Hoch Distinguished Service Award, (P) 1105

Paul Pearsall Scholarship. *See* Scott and Paul Pearsall Scholarship, entry (G) 924

Paul Stephen Lim Asian-American Playwriting Awards, (U) 379, (G) 871

Paul Tobenkin Memorial Award, (P) 1106

PCMA Education Foundation Diversity Scholarship, (U) 380

PDEF Mickey Williams Minority Scholarships, (U) 381

Pearsall Scholarship. *See* Scott and Paul Pearsall Scholarship, entry (G) 924

Pearson Early Career Grant, (P) 1107

Pearson Minority Scholarship Award. *See* NASP-ERT Minority Scholarship Program, entry (G) 831

Peggy A. Dzierzawski Leadership Scholarship. *See* Michigan Accountancy Foundation Fifth/Graduate Year Scholarship Program, entries (U) 302, (G) 808

Peggy Peterman Scholarship, (U) 382, (G) 872

Peggy Vatter Memorial Scholarships. *See* Washington Science Teachers Association Science Leadership Scholarships, entry (U) 495

PEN Open Book Award, (P) 1108

Pennsylvania Academy of Nutrition and Dietetics Foundation Diversity Scholarship, (U) 383

Perry Fellowship in International Security. *See* William J. Perry Fellowship in International Security, entry (P) 1145

Perryman Communications Scholarship for Ethnic Minority Students. *See* Leonard M. Perryman Communications Scholarship for Ethnic Minority Students, entry (U) 274

Persina Scholarship. *See* National Press Club Scholarship for Journalism Diversity, entry (U) 334

Peter and Malina James and Dr. Louis P. James Legacy Scholarship. *See* APF Graduate Student Scholarships, entry (G) 563

Peterman Scholarship. *See* Peggy Peterman Scholarship, entries (U) 382, (G) 872

Peters Award. *See* Marie F. Peters Award, entry (P) 1087

Peterson Fellowships for Racial and Ethnic Diversity. *See* Ruth D. Peterson Fellowships for Racial and Ethnic Diversity, entry (G) 911

Peterson-Homer Injury Prevention Grant Award. *See* Lizette Peterson-Homer Injury Prevention Grant Award, entries (G) 788, (P) 1081

PFATS-NFL Charities Minority Scholarships, (U) 384, (G) 873

PGA of America Diversity Scholarship Program, (U) 385

Phi Tau Phi East America Chapter Undergraduate Scholarship Awards, (U) 386

Phi Tau Phi Mid-America Chapter Scholarships, (U) 387, (G) 874

Phi Tau Phi West America Chapter Scholarship Awards, (U) 388, (G) 875

Phil and Douglas Ishio Scholarship. *See* Japanese American Veterans Association Memorial Scholarships, entries (U) 241, (G) 740

Philippine American Chamber of Commerce of Oregon Regular College Scholarship Program. *See* PACCO Regular College Scholarship Program, entry (U) 376

Philippine Nurses Association Hawaii Foundation Scholarship Fund, (U) 389, (G) 876

Philippine Nurses Association of America Scholarship, (G) 877

Philippine Nurses Association of Georgia Annual Scholarship for Graduate Nursing Studies. *See* PNAGA Annual Scholarship for Graduate Nursing Studies, entry (G) 880

Philippine Nurses Association of Georgia Annual Scholarship for Undergraduate Nursing Studies. *See* PNAGA Annual Scholarship for Undergraduate Nursing Studies, entry (U) 392

Philippine Nurses Association of Northern California Graduate Nursing Student Scholarship, (G) 878

Philippine Nurses Association of Northern California Undergraduate Nursing Student Scholarship, (U) 390

Phillips Exeter Academy Dissertation Year Fellowship, (G) 879

Phoenix Chapter NAAAP Scholarships. *See* Asian Corporate & Entrepreneur Leaders Scholarships, entry (U) 57

Phyllis G. Meekins Scholarship, (U) 391

Physician Assistant Foundation Scholarships. *See* PA Student Scholarships, entries (U) 375, (G) 867

Pickering Foreign Affairs Fellowships. *See* Thomas R. Pickering Foreign Affairs Fellowships, entries (U) 464, (G) 959

Placek Grants. *See* Wayne F. Placek Grants, entries (G) 984, (P) 1142

PNAGA Annual Scholarship for Graduate Nursing Studies, (G) 880

PNAGA Annual Scholarship for Undergraduate Nursing Studies, (U) 392

Pollack Scholarship. *See* Roy H. Pollack Scholarship, entry (G) 907

Polly Sparks Early Career Grant for Psychologists Investigating Serious Emotional Disturbance (SED). *See* John and Polly Sparks Early Career Grant for Psychologists Investigating Serious Emotional Disturbance (SED), entry (P) 1066

Porter Physiology Development Awards, (G) 881

U–Undergraduates   **G–Graduate Students**   **P–Professionals/Postdoctorates**

U–Undergraduates   **G–Graduate Students**   **P–Professionals/Postdoctorates**

U–Undergraduates   **G–Graduate Students**   **P–Professionals/Postdoctorates**

U–Undergraduates   **G–Graduate Students**   **P–Professionals/Postdoctorates**

U–Undergraduates   **G–Graduate Students**   **P–Professionals/Postdoctorates**

U–Undergraduates   **G–Graduate Students**   **P–Professionals/Postdoctorates**

Sponsoring Organization Index

The Sponsoring Organization Index makes it easy to identify agencies that offer financial aid to Asian Americans. In this index, the sponsoring organizations are listed alphabetically, word by word. In addition, we've used an alphabetical code (within parentheses) to help you identify the intended recipients of the funding offered by the organizations: U = Undergraduates; G = Graduate Students; P = Professionals/Postdoctorates. For example, if the name of a sponsoring organization is followed by (U) 241, a program sponsored by that organization is described in the Undergraduate chapter, in entry 241. If that sponsoring organization's name is followed by another entry number—for example, (G) 915—the same or a different program sponsored by that organization is described in the Professionals/Postdoctorates chapter, in entry 915. Remember: the numbers cited here refer to program entry numbers, not to page numbers in the book.

A

ABC National Television Sales, (U) 227, (G) 726
Academic Library Association of Ohio, (G) 526
Academy of Criminal Justice Sciences, (P) 1038
Accountancy Board of Ohio, (U) 14
Accounting and Financial Women's Alliance, (U) 272
Act Six, (U) 15
Acxiom Corporation, (U) 16, (G) 531
AfterCollege, Inc., (U) 21
Against the Grain Productions, (U) 22-23, 276, 278, (G) 536, 785
Airport Minority Advisory Council, (U) 33, 71
Alabama Society of Certified Public Accountants, (U) 51
Alfred P. Sloan Foundation, (G) 636, (P) 1036
Allina Health System, (U) 158
Alpha Kappa Delta, (G) 571
American Academy of Child and Adolescent Psychiatry, (G) 744
American Academy of Neurology, (P) 1023
American Academy of Physician Assistants, (U) 375, (G) 867
American Advertising Federation. Louisville, (U) 4
American Anthropological Association, (G) 542
American Art Therapy Association, Inc., (G) 614
American Association for Cancer Research, (P) 1089
American Association for Justice, (G) 902
American Association for Respiratory Care, (U) 243
American Association of Advertising Agencies, (U) 40, 76, 135, 372, (G) 589, 863
American Association of Colleges of Nursing, (G) 752
American Association of Critical-Care Nurses, (U) 80, (G) 593
American Association of Japanese University Women, (U) 36, (G) 544
American Association of Law Libraries, (G) 687, (P) 1050, 1103
American Association of Obstetricians and Gynecologists Foundation, (P) 1011
American Association of Petroleum Geologists Foundation, (G) 727

American Association of Physicists in Medicine, (U) 37
American Association of Railroad Superintendents, (U) 18, (G) 532
American Association of School Personnel Administrators, (U) 273, (G) 782, (P) 1077
American Association of University Women, (U) 10, (G) 524, 926, (P) 1007
American Baptist Churches USA, (G) 575
American Bar Association. Fund for Justice and Education, (G) 545
American Bar Association. Section of Business Law, (G) 925
American Bar Association. Section of Litigation, (G) 760
American Bar Foundation, (U) 317, (G) 643, (P) 1037
American Board of Obstetrics and Gynecology, (P) 1011
American Bus Association, (U) 38
American Cancer Society. New England Division, (U) 32
American Chemical Society. Division of Organic Chemistry, (U) 445, (G) 866
American College of Chest Physicians, (P) 1032
American College of Healthcare Executives, (G) 539
American College of Neuropsychopharmacology, (P) 1065, 1068, 1105
American College of Nurse-Midwives, (U) 305, (G) 612, 811, (P) 1030
American Correctional Association, (U) 291, (G) 800
American Dental Hygienists' Association, (U) 119
American Educational Research Association, (G) 546
American Epilepsy Society, (G) 547, (P) 1008, 1012-1013
American Federation for Aging Research, (G) 806
American Federation of State, County and Municipal Employees, (U) 20
American Folklore Society, (U) 247, (G) 753
American Gastroenterological Association, (P) 1114, 1118, 1121
American Geophysical Union, (G) 693
American Geosciences Institute, (G) 636, (P) 1036, 1124, 1146

U–Undergraduates   **G–Graduate Students**   **P–Professionals/Postdoctorates**

Association for Education in Journalism and Mass Communication, (G) 787

Association for Educational Communications and Technology, (G) 870

Association for Public Policy Analysis and Management, (G) 888

Association for Women Geoscientists, (U) 332

Association for Women Geoscientists. Potomac Chapter, (U) 503, (G) 991

Association of American Medical Colleges, (G) 705

Association of American Veterinary Medical Colleges, (G) 869, 1002, (P) 1104

Association of Asian Indian Women in Ohio, (U) 65

Association of Black Sociologists, (G) 571

Association of Corporate Counsel. Greater Philadelphia Chapter, (G) 527

Association of Corporate Counsel. National Capital Region, (G) 528

Association of Independent Colleges and Universities of Pennsylvania, (U) 301

Association of National Advertisers, (U) 40

Association of Nurses in AIDS Care, (U) 41, (P) 1015

Association of Professional Schools of International Affairs, (G) 888

Association of Research Libraries, (G) 567-569

Association of University Programs in Health Administration, (G) 629

AstraZeneca Pharmaceuticals, L.P., (P) 1032

Atkins North America, Inc., (U) 66-68, (G) 584

AT&T Foundation, (U) 70

AXA Foundation, (U) 363

B

Back Bay Staffing Group, (U) 349

Baptist Communicators Association, (U) 29

Battelle Memorial Institute, (P) 1052

Baxter International, Inc., (P) 1024

Bay Area Lawyers for Individual Freedom, (G) 559

Beveridge & Diamond, P.C., (G) 703

Bill and Melinda Gates Foundation, (U) 183

Billy Rose Foundation, (U) 324, (G) 827, (P) 1091

Black Journalists Association of Seattle, (U) 358

Bloomberg, (U) 227, (G) 726

BlueCross BlueShield of Tennessee, (U) 78

Boehringer Ingelheim Pharmaceuticals, Inc., (G) 866

Booz Allen Hamilton, (G) 893

Bristol-Myers Squibb Company, (U) 375, (G) 867

Broadcast Music Inc., (U) 156

Brookhaven National Laboratory, (P) 1052

Brown and Caldwell, (U) 83, (G) 595, 631

Bryan Cave LLP, (G) 596

Buckfire & Buckfire, P.C., (G) 597

Burton D. Morgan Foundation, (U) 89

C

California Academy of Physician Assistants, (U) 416, (G) 912

California Association for Health, Physical Education, Recreation and Dance, (U) 234, 438, (G) 734

California Library Association, (G) 623

California School Library Association, (U) 271, (G) 780

California Teachers Association, (U) 290, (G) 799, (P) 1088

California Wellness Foundation, (G) 601

Cambodian Health Professionals Association of America, (U) 88

Capstone Corporation, (U) 96

CBS Incorporated, (U) 156

CBS Television Station Sales, (U) 227, (G) 726

CDC Small Business Finance Corporation, (U) 48

Center for Asian American Media, (P) 1029, 1083

Center for Asian Americans United for Self Empowerment, (U) 100

CH2M Hill, (U) 102, (G) 615, 710

Charter Communications, (U) 156

Chen Foundation, (U) 480

Chen-Pai Lee Scholarship Fund, (U) 103

Chicago Community Trust, (G) 645, (P) 1039

Chicago Tribune Foundation, (U) 436

Chinese Acacia Club, (U) 106

Chinese American Association of Minnesota, (U) 107, (G) 619

Chinese American Citizens Alliance, (U) 108, 111

Chinese American Citizens Alliance Foundation, (U) 109

Chinese American Citizens Alliance. Portland Lodge, (U) 180

Chinese American Institute of Engineers and Scientists, (U) 85

Chinese American Librarians Association, (G) 598, 929, (P) 1122

Chinese American Medical Society, (G) 603-604

Chinese American Museum, (U) 111

Chinese American Physicians Society, (G) 620

Chinese Institute of Engineers/USA. Seattle Chapter, (U) 116

Christian Church (Disciples of Christ), (G) 635, 936

Christian Reformed Church, (U) 402, (G) 889

Cincinnati Children's Hospital Medical Center, (U) 501, (G) 990

City University of New York. Bernard M. Baruch College, (G) 835, (P) 1094

Cleveland Foundation, (U) 65, 298, (G) 804, (P) 1016

Coca-Cola Foundation, (U) 118

Colgate-Palmolive Company, (U) 119

College and University Public Relations and Allied Professionals, (U) 121

College Now Greater Cleveland, Inc., (U) 89

Colorado Education Association, (U) 120

Colorado Educational Services and Development Association, (U) 101

Colorado Nurses Foundation, (U) 82, (G) 594, (P) 1026

Colorado Society of Certified Public Accountants, (U) 151, (G) 655

Columbia University. Graduate School of Journalism, (P) 1106

Comcast NBC Universal, (U) 156

Committee on Institutional Cooperation, (U) 442

Communities-Adolescents-Nutrition-Fitness, (U) 91-92, (G) 605

Community Foundation of Greater New Britain, (U) 31

Community Foundation of Sarasota County, (G) 696, 918

Conference of Minority Transportation Officials, (U) 66-68, 98, 102, 175, 211, 223, 228-229, 283-284, 327-328, 344, 354-355, 412-413, 463, 468, 508, 512-513, (G) 584, 611, 675, 761, 790-791, 847, 853, 906, 958, 963, 994, 998

Conference of Minority Transportation Officials. Colorado Chapter, (U) 122

Conference of Minority Transportation Officials. Fort Lauderdale Chapter, (U) 469, (G) 728

Conference of Minority Transportation Officials. Michigan Chapter, (U) 182, 303

Conference on Asian Pacific American Leadership, (U) 93-95, (G) 607-609

Connecticut Administrators of Programs for English Language Learners, (U) 126

Connecticut Asian Pacific American Bar Association, (G) 606

U–Undergraduates   **G–Graduate Students**   **P–Professionals/Postdoctorates**

U–Undergraduates   **G–Graduate Students**   **P–Professionals/Postdoctorates**

U–Undergraduates **G–Graduate Students** **P–Professionals/Postdoctorates**

U–Undergraduates   **G–Graduate Students**   **P–Professionals/Postdoctorates**

U–Undergraduates　　　　**G–Graduate Students**　　　　**P–Professionals/Postdoctorates**

U–Undergraduates   **G–Graduate Students**   **P–Professionals/Postdoctorates**

U–Undergraduates   G–Graduate Students   P–Professionals/Postdoctorates

Residency Index

Some programs listed in this book are set aside for Asian Americans who are residents of a particular state or region. Others are open to applicants wherever they may live. The Residency Index will help you pinpoint programs available in your area as well as programs that have no residency restrictions at all (these are listed under the term "United States"). To use this index, look up the geographic areas that apply to you (always check the listings under "United States"), jot down the entry numbers listed for the recipient level that applies to you (Undergraduates, Graduate Students, or Professionals/Postdoctorates), and use those numbers to find the program descriptions in the directory. To help you in your search, we've provided some "see" and "see also" references in the index entries. Remember: the numbers cited here refer to program entry numbers, not to page numbers in the book.

A

Alaska: **Undergraduates,** 69; **Graduate Students,** 972. *See also* United States

Alexandria, Virginia: **Undergraduates,** 450. *See also* Virginia

American Samoa: **Undergraduates,** 70, 118, 169, 177, 330, 338, 453, 497. *See also* United States territories

Arizona: **Undergraduates,** 43, 45, 48, 57, 471. *See also* United States

Arkansas: **Undergraduates,** 46, 455; **Graduate Students,** 566, 794, 954. *See also* United States

Arlington County, Virginia: **Undergraduates,** 450. *See also* Virginia

Atlanta, Georgia: **Undergraduates,** 130. *See also* Georgia

B

Baltimore, Maryland: **Professionals/Postdoctorates,** 1034. *See also* Maryland

Boston, Massachusetts: **Undergraduates,** 130. *See also* Massachusetts

Burnett County, Wisconsin: **Undergraduates,** 158. *See also* Wisconsin

C

California: **Undergraduates,** 43, 48, 58, 69, 86-87, 91-92, 106, 109, 113, 193, 234, 267, 271, 290, 393, 416, 433, 438, 471; **Graduate Students,** 581, 600, 602, 605, 623, 692, 734, 780, 799, 912; **Professionals/Postdoctorates,** 1088. *See also* United States

California, southern: **Graduate Students,** 626, 890. *See also* California

Campbellsville, Kentucky. *See* Kentucky

Charlotte, North Carolina: **Undergraduates,** 130. *See also* North Carolina

Chicago, Illinois: **Undergraduates,** 130. *See also* Illinois

Clark County, Indiana: **Undergraduates,** 4. *See also* Indiana

Clark County, Washington: **Undergraduates,** 59, 180. *See also* Washington

Cleveland, Ohio: **Undergraduates,** 130. *See also* Ohio

Colorado: **Undergraduates,** 43, 82, 95, 101, 120, 122, 133, 151, 163-164, 249, 471; **Graduate Students,** 594, 609, 655, 763, 794; **Professionals/Postdoctorates,** 1026. *See also* United States

Connecticut: **Undergraduates,** 31, 123, 125-126, 168, 199, 226, 238, 264, 417; **Graduate Students,** 606, 671, 913, 980. *See also* New England states; Northeastern states; United States

D

Dallas, Texas: **Undergraduates,** 130. *See also* Texas

Delaware: **Undergraduates,** 134, 417; **Graduate Students,** 637, 794, 913. *See also* Northeastern states; Southeastern states; United States

Denver, Colorado: **Undergraduates,** 130. *See also* Colorado

Detroit, Michigan: **Undergraduates,** 130, 302; **Graduate Students,** 808. *See also* Michigan

District of Columbia. *See* Washington, D.C.

F

Fairfax County, Virginia: **Undergraduates,** 450. *See also* Virginia

Florida: **Undergraduates,** 43, 117, 312, 471; **Graduate Students,** 677. *See also* Southeastern states; United States

Floyd County, Indiana: **Undergraduates,** 4. *See also* Indiana

Fort Lauderdale, Florida: **Undergraduates,** 130. *See also* Florida

Frederick County, Maryland: **Undergraduates,** 450. *See also* Maryland

G

Georgia: **Undergraduates,** 43, 110, 159, 192, 220-221, 362, 392, 471; **Graduate Students,** 880. *See also* Southeastern states; United States

Tenability Index

Some programs listed in this book can be used only in specific cities, counties, states, or regions. Others may be used anywhere in the United States. The Tenability Index will help you locate funding that is restricted to a specific area as well as funding that has no tenability restrictions (these are listed under the term "United States"). To use this index, look up the geographic areas where you'd like to go (always check the listings under "United States"), jot down the entry numbers listed for the recipient group that represents you (Undergraduates, Graduate Students, Professionals/Postdoctorates), and use those numbers to find the program descriptions in the directory. To help you in your search, we've provided some "see" and "see also" references in the index entries. Remember: the numbers cited here refer to program entry numbers, not to page numbers in the book.

Subject Index

There are hundreds of specific subject fields covered in this directory. Use the Subject Index to identify these topics, as well as the recipient level supported (Undergraduates, Graduate Students, or Professionals/Postdoctorates) by the available funding programs. To help you pinpoint your search, we've included many "see" and "see also" references. Since a large number of programs are not restricted by subject, be sure to check the references listed under the "General programs" heading in the subject index (in addition to the specific terms that directly relate to your interest areas); hundreds of funding opportunities are listed there that can be used to support activities in any subject area   although the programs may be restricted in other ways. Remember: the numbers cited in this index refer to program entry numbers, not to page numbers in the book.

A

A.V. *See* Audiovisual materials and equipment

Academic librarianship. *See* Libraries and librarianship, academic

Accounting: **Undergraduates,** 14, 26, 33, 50-51, 71, 84, 117, 125, 128, 151, 160, 162, 194, 233, 272, 296, 302, 309, 318-320, 322, 339, 351, 357, 369, 401, 411, 421, 426, 441, 446, 489; **Graduate Students,** 538, 655, 733, 808, 815, 824-825, 841, 859, 922, 947. *See also* Finance; General programs

Acquired Immunodeficiency Syndrome. *See* AIDS

Acting. *See* Performing arts

Actuarial sciences: **Undergraduates,** 295, 326, 446. *See also* General programs; Statistics

Addiction. *See* Alcohol use and abuse; Drug use and abuse

Administration. *See* Business administration; Education, administration; Management; Personnel administration; Public administration

Adolescents: **Graduate Students,** 744. *See also* Child development; General programs

Advertising: **Undergraduates,** 4, 40, 76, 121, 135, 226, 263, 367, 372, 404; **Graduate Students,** 589, 777, 863, 898. *See also* Communications; General programs; Marketing; Public relations

Aeronautical engineering. *See* Engineering, aeronautical

Aeronautics: **Graduate Students,** 829. *See also* Aviation; Engineering, aeronautical; General programs; Physical sciences

Aerospace engineering. *See* Engineering, aerospace

Aerospace sciences. *See* Space sciences

Affirmative action: **Undergraduates,** 222. *See also* Equal opportunity; General programs

Aged and aging: **Graduate Students,** 806; **Professionals/ Postdoctorates,** 1092, 1096. *See also* General programs; Social sciences

Agribusiness: **Undergraduates,** 168, 357; **Graduate Students,** 671. *See also* Agriculture and agricultural sciences; Business administration; General programs

Agricultural economics. *See* Economics, agricultural

Agriculture and agricultural sciences: **Undergraduates,** 168, 262; **Graduate Students,** 671, 923; **Professionals/ Postdoctorates,** 1125. *See also* Biological sciences; General programs

Agrimarketing and sales. *See* Agribusiness

AIDS: **Undergraduates,** 41; **Graduate Students,** 805; **Professionals/Postdoctorates,** 1015, 1136-1137. *See also* Disabilities; General programs; Medical sciences

Air conditioning industry. *See* Cooling industry

Alcohol use and abuse: **Graduate Students,** 669, 807, 838; **Professionals/Postdoctorates,** 1132. *See also* Drug use and abuse; General programs; Health and health care

American history. *See* History, American

American studies: **Graduate Students,** 813. *See also* General programs; Humanities

Animal science: **Undergraduates,** 431-432; **Graduate Students,** 932-933; **Professionals/Postdoctorates,** 1129. *See also* General programs; Sciences; names of specific animal sciences

Anthropology: **Undergraduates,** 431-432; **Graduate Students,** 542, 548, 932-933; **Professionals/Postdoctorates,** 1129. *See also* General programs; Social sciences

Applied arts. *See* Arts and crafts

Aquatic sciences. *See* Oceanography

Archaeology: **Undergraduates,** 122, 236, 311, 431-432; **Graduate Students,** 735, 932-933; **Professionals/ Postdoctorates,** 1129. *See also* General programs; History; Social sciences

Architectural engineering. *See* Engineering, architectural

Architecture: **Undergraduates,** 25, 33, 39, 53, 71, 85, 122, 170, 193, 376, 470; **Graduate Students,** 552, 573, 692, 813; **Professionals/Postdoctorates,** 1097. *See also* Fine arts; General programs; Historical preservation

Architecture, naval. *See* Naval architecture

Archives: **Undergraduates,** 155, 275, 294; **Graduate Students,** 565, 569, 662, 754, 784, 801; **Professionals/Postdoctorates,** 1079. *See also* General programs; History; Library and Information services, general; Museum studies

Calendar Index

Since most funding programs have specific deadline dates, some may have already closed by the time you begin to look for money. You can use the Calendar Index to identify which programs are still open. To do that, go to the recipient category (Undergraduates, Graduate Students, or Professionals/Postdoctorates) that interests you, think about when you'll be able to complete your application forms, go to the appropriate months, jot down the entry numbers listed there, and use those numbers to find the program descriptions in the directory. Keep in mind that the numbers cited here refer to program entry numbers, not to page numbers in the book.

Made in the USA
Middletown, DE
16 June 2018